A SOCIAL HISTORY OF HESSE

DAN C. HEINEMEIER

A Social History of Hesse

Roman Times to 1900

Heinemeier Publications • Arlington, Virginia

2002

Copyright © 2002 Dan C. Heinemeier. Printed and bound in the United States of America. All rights reserved. No part of this book may be reproduced or transmitted in any form or by any means, electronic or mechanical, including photocopying, recording, or by an information storage and retrieval system—except by a reviewer who may quote brief passages in a review to be printed in a magazine or newspaper—without permission in writing. Please contact the author.

Library of Congress Number: 2002102746

ISBN 0-9671822-1-2

Publisher's Cataloguing-in-Publication
(Provided by Quality Books, Inc.)

Heinemeier, Dan C.
  A Social History of Hesse : Roman times to 1900. --
1st ed.
  p. cm.
  Includes bibliographical references and index.
  LCCN: 20022102746
  ISBN: 0967182212

  1. Hesse (Germany)--Social conditions. 2. Hesse (Germany)--Social life and customs.   I. Title.

HN458.H4H45 2002   306'.094341
          QBI02-200255

For other titles by the same author, please see the order form at the back of this book.

CONTENTS

Foreword	1
Preface	2
Acknowledgments	3
1. Roman Power and Chatti Persistence: The Germans Come	5
2. From Alamanni to Franks: Transition to the Early Middle Ages	26
3. Christianity Comes to Hesse	43
4. The Carolingians Depart: the Development of Feudalism	56
5. The Development of Life in the Hessian Towns	74
6. Approach of the Modern Era: The Sixteenth Century	94
7. War Clouds Gather: The Early Seventeenth Century	121
8. The Thirty Years War and its Aftermath in Hesse	137
9. The Lesser Hessian Principalities to 1800	164
10. Germany and Hesse in the Eighteenth Century	177
11. The Hessians in the American War of Independence	217
12. A Final Look at the Eighteenth Century: Hessian Towns	251
13. The Napoleonic Era	265
14. Nineteenth Century Hesse: Social and Political History	279
15. Life on the Land in Nineteenth Century Hesse	298
16. Growth and Industrialization: Life in the Hessian Towns	333
17. Hessian Emigration 1800-1900	346
Bibliography	365
Index	368

Figures and Maps

FIGURES — **PAGE**

Figure 1-1 The Upper German *limes* in the third century. — 19
Figure 1-2 The improved *limes* in cross section. — 19
Figure 1-3 *Porta Decumana* — 20
Figure 1-4 Artist's conception of Saalburg Fort. — 20
Figure 1-5 Excavations of a Roman villa and statue (Saalburg). — 20
Figure 3-1 St. Elizabeth's Church in Marburg: chancel. — 53
Figure 3-2 St. Elizabeth's Church: gallery. — 53
Figure 5-1 Lichtenberg Castle. — 89
Figure 5-2 Hall in the residence of the Grand Duke, Darmstadt. — 89
Figure 7-1 Construction techniques in *Fachwerk*. — 127
Figure 7-2 Changing building techniques. — 128
Figure 7-3 "*Mannfigur*" style of framing members. — 128
Figure 9-1 Weilburg on the Lahn with its palace. — 166
Figure 10-1 Rheinfels castle. — 183
Figure 10-2 Castle Katz (Cat) at St. Goarshausen. — 183
Figure 10-3 Another view of *Burg Katz*. — 184
Figure 10-4 Karlsaue in Kassel. — 184
Figures 10-5/10-6 Rear-loading oven (*Hinterladenofen*). — 201
Figure 10-7 The Friedrichsplatz, Kassel. — 202
Figures 11-1/11-2 Hessian forces in camp. — 239
Figure 11-3 Regiment von Donop re-enactors. — 240
Figure 12-1 Wilhelmshöhe, summer residence of the Electors. — 261
Figure 12-2 Herkules monument at Wilhelmshöhe. — 261
Figure 12-3 Marburg: a view of the university and the castle. — 264
Figure 15-1 Hessian bride in traditional dress (Schwalm). — 301
Figure 15-2 Traditional spinning wheel. — 301
Figure 15-3 Sign for a local Raiffeisen rural credit cooperative. — 306
Figure 15-4 Flax-working tools: spinning reel & scutcher. — 306
Figures 15-5/15-6 Hessian *Volkstrachten* (traditional garb). — 324
Figures 15-7/15-8 *Trachten*. — 325
Figures 15-9/15-10 *Trachten*. — 326
Figure 17-1 Marburg from the Lahn River. The castle at top faces south. — 362

Maps

Map 1 Historical heartland of Nassau. — 166
Map 2 Taunus region. — 167
Map 3 St. Goar and St. Goarshausen. — 202
Maps 4/5 Campaign of 1776: Long Island and Trenton. — 227
Map 6 Southern campaigns in the Revolution. — 240
Map 7 Gießen and Bad Nauheim. — 263
Map 8 Layout of the Wilhelmshöhe palace and grounds. — 264
Map 9 Hesse-Darmstadt and Hesse-Kassel pre-1867. — 296
Map 10 Hesse-Nassau in its final, pre-empire form (1867). — 297
Maps 11/12 Marburg and Darmstadt. — 331
Maps 13/14 Kassel and environs. — 332
Map 15 Grand Duchy of Hesse (latter 19th century). — 363
Map 16 Northern Hesse Kassel. — 364

FOREWORD

In recent years we have been hearing this complaint: Books on German history, written in English, are available by the cartload—bulging with records about personalities from every period of German history, leaders whom historians have deemed worthy of their pens; yet there can hardly be found a work in English that feeds the hunger of readers looking for accounts of the people who managed to remain unworthy of historians' consideration—like the peddlers, the schoolteachers, the shopkeepers, the shepherds, the famine victims, the weavers, and the military conscripts.

Overwhelmingly, most of history's "cast of characters" played bit parts in its drama. By the hundreds of thousands they were farmers, tradesmen, and just plain down-home villagers. The strife they endured usually led them toward one straightforward goal—survival. An approach to history that ignores these players effectively divides the readers' world into the "them" and the "us" – the "them" being the lead players (like Bismarck, Frederick the Great, Charlemagne), and the "us" being the millions of nameless players, predictably including many of our own ancestors.

This Social History of Hesse does indeed record the battles fought, the treaties signed, the revolutions fought and squelched, and the heroes whose names are taught by rote to reluctant school children. In addition, however, this book brings the "bit players" out onto the stage. Besides the rulers pronouncing from their thrones, the military leaders advancing into new territories, and the politicians and churchmen vying for power, we learn here about the sick and dying during epidemics, the economic miseries of the middle class, the emptied villages following the Thirty Years War, and the overall class-consciousness that went unquestioned by the populace.

Had we been born in an earlier time, we might have found ourselves in these same circumstances. We should thank Dan Heinemeier for taking us beyond a make-believe world where rulers pronounced, where armies battled, and where the powerful played with laws of inheritance—yet where the make-believe tale tells nothing, for example, of why cattle were moved from fields into stalls, why community bake houses became prevalent, or what events led to "America Fever."

Thanks to this history, we can take a look into how people lived from day to day, how they dressed, what festivities they treasured, and how they must have felt as economic circumstances periodically beat them down. A good social history, which this book certainly is, has the power to give us our comeuppance when we presume to make sense of our forebears' motives and actions without having known what it was like to walk in their shoes.

SHIRLEY RIEMER

PREFACE

In this, my second social history of a German principality, I have attempted once again to meet the need of genealogists and others interested in German social history based on the dearth of English-language material for any of the smaller states. Certainly nothing in terms of a comprehensive history of Hesse has been published in English. The present work represents a start at filling this void for one of the more historically complex German polities. My hope is that it will help enlighten those descended from Hessian roots about their forebears' experiences in the Old Country, and the forces that shaped lives and drove decisions to migrate.

For professional historians and others interested in comparative history from an academic perspective, I can say only that it really has not been my intent to explore new approaches to the material, but simply to synthesize information from available sources. My goal was to provide a glimpse into how common people lived, worked, failed or triumphed in the circumstances they faced in their daily lives. I will mention a few of the sources that have been particularly helpful in this task:

Karl Demandt's comprehensive political history in German provided the backbone upon which I was able to develop the story of Hesse beginning in Roman times. Demandt's approach to Hessian history might be compared to what James Michener has done in his field of historical fiction.

The works of Hans Lerch and Brigitta Vits were invaluable in describing conditions on the land at the village level, while similar insights in English have been gleaned from books by William Wright, Peter Taylor, and John Theibault.

Several works published by the Open Air Museum Hessenpark in Neu Anspach were most helpful in adding local context about the tools and customs of common life; Gerd Grein's scholarship on rural clothing styles (*Trachten*) was most useful.

Bruce Burgoyne's yeoman's work has made available in English many journals of the Hessians who fought for the Crown in the American Revolution. His book is well worth the price for those with particular interest in the Hessian forces.

The multi-faceted history of Hesse is fascinating in its complexity. Hessian lands entered the era of recorded history on the great fault line dividing Roman and German cultures; this crossroads position largely defined their subsequent history. Hesse benefited from the geography in terms of trade, while suffering greatly from it in times of war. Always a resource-poor land, Hesse's hilly and mountainous lands barely provided for her inhabitants. It was this poverty that drove the landgraves to rent out their men as mercenaries in the service of Britain and other governments. By the nineteenth century, it drove large-scale emigration to Eastern Europe, America and beyond.

Hesse nurtured her share of illustrious figures, such as Liebig, the father of German agricultural chemistry, and Raiffeisen, the founder of the rural cooperatives that freed so many from the grip of usury and bankruptcy. Boniface, the patron saint of German Christianity, labored in Hesse's spiritual vineyards as well. For the rest, saints and sinners, paragons and rogues, the reader is cordially invited to turn a few pages and begin their saga.

ACKNOWLEDGMENTS

The three-year labor of love that produced this book of course could not have proceeded without the support and encouragement of family, friends and colleagues in German history, genealogy and heritage. I owe each of them a particular debt of thanks.

Shirley Riemer of the Sacramento German Genealogical Society, who edits one of the premier genealogical and historical periodicals in the country, *Der Blumenbaum*, was a fount of encouragement, good ideas, and useful source materials throughout the course of the project. Her introductory foreword of the book is most appreciated.

La Vern Rippley of St. Olaf' College and Don Heinrich Tolzmann of the University of Cincinnati, both leaders in the field of German-American scholarship, have been most gracious and supportive in reviewing the book and providing periodic advice and assistance. German-American genealogy owes them much for helping bridge the lamentable chasm that so often separates professional historians and academics from the wider set of the population that shares a passion for German studies but mostly lacks credentials considered the *sine qua non* by those in the field.

Gary Grassl, immediate past president of the German-American Heritage Society of Greater Washington, DC, and an outstanding historian in his own right, has been a great friend and enthusiastic supporter of my work. This has extended to speaking opportunities at Society meetings and table space at German Heritage events, helping me get the word out about my books. Thanks also to fellow GAHS members who turned out for these events.

In a related vein, thanks to John Humphrey, director of education for the National Genealogical Society—and an American with ancestral roots in Hesse—for his valued counsel and for extending the opportunity for public speaking based on my research. John has done much to further the outreach and services to German-American genealogists provided by the NGS.

Evelyn Heinemeier provided helpful recommendations toward the cover design. Her artistic sense helped steer me away from much less appealing alternatives.

Several organizations kindly extended permission to use artwork or maps that have added to the book's aesthetic and practical appeal: the Saalburg Museum in Bad Homburg, Germany; German Genealogical Digest; The Open Air Museum Hessenpark in Neu Anspach, Germany; and the use of photographs taken by the author depicting Hesse-Kassel soldier re-enactors of the Regiment von Donop in their regalia.

Last and certainly most, thanks to my wife Meredith, who not only endured but encouraged me in the untold hours in which I was immersed in keyboarding and research rather than other activities on the home front. Her support has been more instrumental than I can express.

Chapter 1

Roman Power and Chatti Persistence: The Germans Come

The ancient history of the lands that later would form Hesse is a story of tumultuous change, raging battles, and the clash of cultures played out time and again over centuries. Like other areas of western and central Europe, the geography of Hesse made it a crossroads of east-west travel: the gateway east for the Romans, the gateway west for the ancient Germans. This feature of the landscape would be both the region's blessing and its curse throughout history.

Our story begins at the dawn of the recorded era, an era in which developments still were captured in written form by only one set of invaders, the Romans. Beyond their sparse and often misleading writings, we have only archeology to help us sketch the outlines of events. In the second and first centuries B.C. much of Hesse was still occupied by Celtic tribes whose culture and civilization had attained a fairly high level, one with which the even more highly developed Romans could relate and effectively bargain. The Celts by this time had created expansive urban centers called *oppida*, with dense settlements that served as magnets for trade and strongholds for powerful chiefs. Theirs was a much more highly developed civilization than the neighboring peoples of German and mixed Celtic culture. Celtic trade goods, weapons, and other manufactured items were much in demand by these neighbors, whose own level of civilization seems to have advanced in proportion to their interaction with Celts. Celtic lands were broadly defined by the extent of the *oppida*, nearly all of which were located south of the river Lippe.

On the northern edge of the Celtic lands were border regions in Hesse such as the Main River valley, the Taunus Mountain range, and the Wetterau. These areas were populated with poor, but heavily Celtic-influenced peoples. They were mostly content to live peacefully and trade with their better-off neighbors. Further to the north and east were regions populated by Germanic peoples originating on the Elbe or in areas bordering the Baltic or the North Sea. These tended to be semi-nomadic folk, with no culture of large-scale trade centers or the kind of artisanship and finished goods that were commonplace among the Celts and Romans. Sometime in or prior to the second century B.C., major upheavals among the Germanic tribes caused them to push south and west into Celtic lands, plundering and destroying *oppida* and driving Celts out of their ancestral lands. This process was largely complete by 50 B.C. Why this occurred is unknown, but it likely relates to similar pressures exerted on these tribes by their own warlike neighbors to the east. It is also very possible that expanding German populations simply required new and better-yielding lands to cultivate. By about the time of the birth of Christ this period culminated in the Germanization of the whole area of modern Germany west to the Rhine and south into modern Bavaria. At these points the marauding invaders ran into the solid bulwark of Roman power.

Also in this period a particularly aggressive and resolute grouping of tribesmen known as the Chatti moved south from their territory above the Lippe and occupied much of the Hesse area, including the region around modern Kassel. From here they continued their movement south along the Fulda, Schwalm, and Lahn rivers, driving the people living in these areas before them. At this time a related tribe, the Mattiaci, were displaced from their ancestral homes along the Eder and Ems rivers. They moved south to settle near modern Wiesbaden and adjacent areas in the Taunus. Like many tribes in this period of shifting allegiances they seem to have become Roman allies, settling on the border of Roman territory and later being incorporated within it. This may have been an effort to avoid absorption by the Chatti, and in this they were successful. As clients of Rome they traded with her merchants and provided many celebrated warriors to her auxiliary army units. For their part, the Chatti remained more at a distance from Roman power and control. Before we discuss the military clashes that were to emerge from the relocation of the Chatti, we should first focus on the culture and society of these ancient warriors.[1]

Our best contemporaneous view of the ancient German tribal culture comes from the Roman historian Tacitus. His *Germany* remains unsurpassed as a chronicle of life among the Germans about the end of the first century A.D. It is flawed, however, by the Roman concept of historical and social commentary, in which it was more important to impart timeless social truths and moral precepts than to strive for complete accuracy in detail. It is also based entirely on second-hand accounts from those who had served or traveled in Germany, for Tacitus had never done so. With all its limitations, however, it remains remarkably useful in broad outline for understanding the Germanic culture as it stood in the late first and early second centuries.

Tacitus describes these fierce tribesmen as an unmixed race, distinct from all others. Their "fierce blue eyes" and red hair were as unusual to the Romans as their huge frames and striking ability to galvanize themselves for physical exertion as in the attack. He also finds that they were less able to bear extended periods of physical effort, especially in warmer weather. On the other hand, the cold and hunger common to their intemperate climate were more easily endured. Their semi-nomadic culture was dominated by war and preparation for war, with a man's worth in society based on perceptions of his prowess in battle. Women were known to support their warriors by positioning themselves near the battle lines, where they could exhort them to fight all the harder in order to protect them and their children from capture by the foe. This also allowed the women to tend to their wounded warrior-mates as they came fresh from the fight.

The weaponry of the Germanic warrior changed remarkably little over the centuries from the time he burst on the scene in western Germany in the first century B.C. until the dawn of medieval times. Swords were seldom seen except among their chiefs, the major weapon being the short spear. Often made of ash, the spear might be tipped with iron or bone, or more frequently, simply featured a carved wooden tip hardened by burning with fire. Spears were used for hurling at the enemy in the charge, with each man carrying more than one. When close order fighting occurred, the German would often rely on picking up one of the previously thrown weapons. In a pinch he might use a rock or branch or any other implement that came to hand. The shield was the only other common piece of equipment through the first few centuries A.D., and this was typically either solid wood or woven wickerwork reinforced with leather and iron binding on the rim. It also featured an iron or wooden boss to strengthen it in the center. In case of need, the shield boss itself could be thrust at an opponent. But these crude rectangular or round German shields were much less effective at stopping sword blows delivered in close combat than the shields of their Roman enemies. Similarly, body armor as used by the Roman legionaries was virtually unknown among the Germans, who often fought naked to the waist to ensure freedom of movement.[2]

German forces were overwhelmingly made up of foot soldiers, and while not unknown, cavalry was mostly confined to the well-born and chieftain classes. Infantry tactics consisted of attacking in dense masses so the men could protect one another as they lost their spears in individual combats. Small units tended to be drawn from extended families and clans, augmented by warriors who sought to follow a particularly strong and successful chief. These typically fought in wedge formations that struck with great force against the lines of their enemies, and the shock of these large-framed warriors in the attack was fearsome even to the better-equipped and -disciplined Roman hosts. Tacitus says it was no shame to give ground only to return to the attack, but the abandonment of one's shield on the field was considered a terrible disgrace. Cowardice was considered the vilest crime of all, with drowning in the swamps being the penalty. Treason and desertion were punished with hanging. The bodies of those slain in battle were carried off by the survivors for honored burial.

It is not surprising that a culture that so valued military prowess would raise its sons from a young age to be prepared for battle. Free-born children were raised alongside those of slaves, "filthy and naked" in Tacitus words, until they reached an age at which training could commence. The ceremonial presentation to a youth of his shield and spear conferred recognition of the tribe that he was no longer a child of the household, but a young man ready to assume his place in society. From this point a man would bear his arms with him to any public or private business he had to undertake through the course of his life. Nobility of some warrior-chiefs was recognized based on the established military prowess of a family line. This status could be conferred on sons. Chiefs who had proven themselves as leaders in battle and in plundering raids against other tribes would attract a following of warriors ready to follow them in exchange for enhanced status and the rewards of plunder. Such a following was known as a *comitatus*, and these groups became important building blocks in German society as well as in military campaigns. A chief would reward his followers with military equipment, food, feasts and other support, as well as settlement on farmlands he controlled.[3]

Tacitus records some less positive aspects of the warrior society as well. Chiefs and their followers were said to be given to bouts of drinking and feasting that left them slothful and useless for other work. They were fond of hunting, and supposedly left the management of the farming to women, old men and the infirm. Men were so addicted to gambling that it was not unknown to wager their own freedom and that of their families on the throw of the dice. Apparently the distinguished warrior-chiefs also obtained gifts of food and cattle from the tribal group as a whole to augment their efforts to keep their followings in existence. This fight hard/play hard mentality is understandable in a social order in which being killed or wounded at any time was likely, if not expected. Feuding among the Germans was endemic, a practice recorded in later times and thus documented by others as well as Tacitus. It was a matter of personal honor to exact revenge from neighboring clans or tribes for any slight or injury to one of their own. Over time, the Germans evolved a system known as *wergeld*, which set fines in the form of payments in cattle, sheep, or (much later) money for killing or wounding of a family member. This was to keep cycles of violence among clans from getting completely out of hand.

How much we accept of Tacitus' comments on the sloth and idle pleasures of the Germanic tribes is open to question. The historian Alfons Dopsch argues forcefully that this is an unrealistic picture of what life must have been like among average Germans. He notes that Tacitus himself says this applied to the bravest and most warlike among the tribesmen, while common freemen must have led a more settled and farm life-based existence. He suggests also that only a strong and capable people could have continued to press and eventually conquer a civilization and army as strong as that of the Roman empire. It seems clear that although these ancient warriors were avid in their pursuit of physically-challenging games, feasts, and boisterous entertainment, they also must have worked hard at wresting a living from the soil. [4]

With regard to agriculture and animal husbandry, the main means of sustenance for the Germans, Tacitus counted their land as productive of grain and rich in flocks and herds. Domesticated animals, in order of importance, included cattle, pigs, horses, and sheep. The remains of chickens are seldom seen in the earliest excavations. Pigs were lean and lanky in this period. Fresh meat must have been an important part of the diet, judging from archeological finds of significant numbers of bones from young animals. Pigs were slaughtered at one and one-half to three years of age, sheep at under two years. Cattle and horses were kept longer given the cycle of their productive lives. Other than red deer, wild game was of much less significance, and even deer meat was not as commonly enjoyed as that of domesticated animals. Deer antlers and hides also were used in making various implements and products. The cattle and other farm animals were undersized and not as handsome as the Roman breeds. The Romans' grasp of selective breeding ensured a better class of animal than their primitive German counterparts could raise. The German's chief measure of wealth was considered to be in the number of cattle he owned.

Tacitus' assertion that the land was overwhelmingly untamed forest and swampland has been disputed by modern authors. Barley was the most prevalent grain crop until the early Middle Ages, with wheat and oats also grown. Rye and millet were not as common. Peas and beans were known, as was flax which was used for making linen. Woad was a natural dye that was cultivated. A few wild plants were exploited, including plums, wild cherries, slow and hazel nuts.

Plows were in two forms, a bow-ard and a crook-ard. The crook style was simply a hooked branch fitted to a long handle and yoked to an ox or cow. The bow-ard was a better implement, with an arrow-shaped head fitted at an angle to the ard. This pushed the earth to one side as it plowed. Both plows were used from 500 B.C. or before, and continued in use for centuries. Even heavy clay soils could be worked with these basic tools. Land was apportioned to the whole people when they occupied a new area, with preferred lands and larger allotments assigned to the noble members of society. The concept of private land ownership seems to have a long history, reaching back well into these ancient times.[5]

Clothing among the ancient Germans was most basic. Tacitus indicates that the basic item of clothing was the cloak, fastened with a clasp or pin. He also notes the use of animal skins thrown together rather carelessly across the frame. Later scholarship suggests men's wear as including a thick shirt and trousers along with a short cloak, the latter able to serve as a blanket or simply wrapped around the body as needed in cold or wet weather. Most typically it was fastened at the right shoulder with a brooch. Pants were long, sometimes even providing covering for the feet, although knee-length pants were not unheard of. Some but probably not all people wore leather shoes. A fairly high standard in manufacturing quality had been reached by the time contact with the Romans was made. Dyeing and patterning of the clothes was an established art as well. The basic items of clothing changed little for hundreds of years.

Women's clothing was very different from that of men. Wool skirts and dresses were common, particularly a one-piece dress that extended from shoulder to feet. By gathering at the waist and shoulder, these sack-like garments could be made more attractive. Some included a fold behind the head to serve as a hood. Linen undergarments and perhaps a neckerchief on the throat completed the known list of clothing items.[6]

Housing in the early centuries after the birth of Christ includes certain common elements that appear to have remained in use over long periods and wide areas. Two housing options are most common: the aisled or long house, and the *Grubenhaus*, a sunken dwelling built over an excavated section of ground. The aisled house was the larger of the two styles, and would have been the option of choice for all who could afford it. It consisted of a rectangular building divided into a central hall area with two aisles or wings on either side. Parallel rows of three or more upright posts divided the building in these sections, with part of the center hall serving as living space for humans and other areas divided into stalls for animals and storage. Some aisled houses were designed to hold only animal stalls. Along the stalls a low rack of wood or wicker work sometimes was built to hold fodder for the cattle. The family quarters was one large room built around the fireplace area, which was the only source of warmth aside from that given off by the animals. A single hole in the roof allowed fireplace smoke to escape, and everything in the home must have accumulated a coat of soot over time. The danger of fire was real, and gave cause for frequent concern to these ancient folk. The size of these structures varied widely, from 25 x 20 feet to 90 x 30 feet. The techniques involved in building the larger structures were advanced enough that a class of special craftsmen must have existed to handle construction of these buildings and other major carpentry projects.

The *Grubenhaus*, by contrast, was a simple structure of timber uprights built over a shallow hole that ran the full length and breadth of the house. Various designs of framing work tied into the uprights and a central beam or joist that they supported. Over the framework a simple wattle and daub or plank wall structure was built. Such huts were often only 10 x 6 feet in size, and were often located near larger structures. They could house pottery-making, weaving operations, baking, or more sophisticated trades in later centuries. Some *Grubenhäuser* were less primitive, with special foundation trenches, earth cladding against the walls, and little porches in front of the doorway to block drafts. Roofs for both long houses and the sunken huts were made of thatch. Of course there were variations from place to place, including a few simple rectangular structures designed like the long house but without the aisled wings. Tacitus also mentions a still more primitive option: the use of dug-out caves over which dung-covered enclosures were laid to ward off cold.

For furniture, the hall houses seem to have included wall benches, beds, and perhaps rugs of animal skin. Wealthier people might have single chairs as well, although these were rare even into the Middle Ages in poorer homes. Most people likely would have simply pulled up a bucket or tub to sit upon while eating or visiting by the fire. Containers of pottery, bronze, wood and iron all were known, although wood certainly would have predominated in the earliest times. Roman imports included bronze buckets, bowls, pans and sieves. Much pottery for local use was made at the level of the settlements themselves, mainly by women.[7]

Tacitus is impressed with the mores of the Germans in some respects, particularly where he seeks to impart lessons to Romans whose morality in such matters had slipped noticeably. Here he points out the strict marriage code of the basically monogamous Germans. Adultery was rare, and when uncovered it was punished in very severe terms for the woman. She was shorn of her hair, stripped naked, and driven with the whip through the community by her husband. "No one in Germany laughs at vice, nor do they call it the fashion to corrupt and to be corrupted," says Tacitus. Husbands sealed marriages with the gift of a dowry to the wife's family. Women seem to have controlled matters of the home, where they engaged in and oversaw the efforts of those working on the farm. The latter might include slaves in wealthier households. Slaves were not so numerous as among the Romans, and their treatment by the Germans seems to have been less severe. A master could kill his slave with impunity, however.

The free male members of a tribal grouping were accorded rights to participate in a primitive form of democracy when the whole people met once or twice a year in a so-called folk moot assembly. Here, perhaps at the time of a great annual feast or celebration, the leaders would call people to a regular meeting place. Decisions on war and peace, the choosing of battle leaders, and the resolution of key legal questions that affected the whole people would be dealt with. Priests would call the proceedings to order, bidding the fully-armed attendees to keep quiet and maintain the peace. Men would indicate assent to what was said by clashing their spears and shields together. An ominous quiet or murmuring would greet comments with which they disagreed. Really important matters would have been decided in advance by a council of leaders and nobles whose recommendations were always ratified at the moot. Still, leaders who were too autocratic or over-reached their power would be deposed and perhaps killed, for the early Germans were very uncomfortable with the concept of a supreme ruler such as Caesar. Tacitus says that the Germans chose "their kings by birth, their generals for merit."[8]

The religious practices of the ancient Germans were focused on a few major gods who brought help in battle and in the productivity of the land. Tiwaz, a sky-god, was the lord of battle who later metamorphosed into Woden or Oden. Worship practices for Tiwaz are unknown, as is the point before about 400 A.D. at which he was supplanted by his successor gods. Human sacrifices are recorded to have occurred in the worship of some of the ancient gods, with death by hanging a recurring theme. Captives from a major battle might be sacrificed along with their captured weapons and other booty, with everything being destroyed or rendered useless before being cast into a sacred pond or bog. At one point the Chatti struggled with a neighboring tribe, the Hermunduri, over a river between them, with both sides vowing to sacrifice captives to their gods if victory came to them. The Hermunduri prevailed, and apparently carried out their vow.

Later in the Roman period the Germans, by now a more settled race, had shifted their loyalties to Wodan or Oden, whose character and abilities are not fully understood. He appears to have had the power to create men, and bestowed runes and poetry on mankind. He was god of war and patron of those slain in battle. He was old, gray-bearded, and a father-figure, rather grim and frightening. Fortune telling seems to have played a major role in the religious rites of the Germans. When life was so caught up with warfare, and the survival of the tribe could depend on the vagaries of a particular battle, it is no surprise that the people would harbor a burning desire to know that their timing was right when a major fight loomed. Priests and certain women who it was believed could foretell the future by reading auguries were accorded an honored place in society. Observing the flights and songs of birds, or the snorts and neighs of sacred white horses were thought to be means of divination. A priesthood existed among the Chatti, and it was priests who were permitted to open the folk moot by demanding order. Priests alone, not tribal chiefs, were permitted to exact punishment, including the taking of lives of criminals and those whose deeds were so shameful as to require the death penalty.

Germans also worshipped local spirits thought to inhabit sacred groves, springs, and forests. The oak was very sacred, as well as some groves of beech, ash and thorn trees. The whisper of wind in the foliage might be thought to be the gods' speech, and the deep recesses of woods with their attendant predators must have seemed a fearsome and mysterious environment to the early Germans. Salt springs were thought to have curative powers, and were much sought after and struggled over by the ancient tribes.[9]

The dedication to the gods of fallen warriors and captive victims brings us to the subject of early German burial rites and customs. By the first century B.C. the Germans had practiced cremation for many centuries. Cremation continued to be the dominant form of burial until the early Middle Ages and the advent of Christian practices. Inhumation graves were increasingly in use in the period after about 300 A.D., however. Cremated remains typically were placed in a pottery urn and buried in a pit, with or without a cairn of stones or a mound of earth to mark the site. Only rarely are the remains of children found, suggesting that less formal arrangements were made to bury dead infants and children. Some personal goods, weapons, tools, vessels for food and drink, and the actual remains of feasts such as pork and lamb joints were buried with some of the dead. The weaponry found in these graves is often damaged so as to render it unfit for use, although the symbolism here is unknown. Graves varied widely in the quality and type of weaponry found in them. Spears alone are most commonly found, followed by shields with spears. Only rarely are swords in evidence, and even more rare and clearly indicative of a chief's grave was the cavalry spur.

Particularly interesting is the 18th century record of an excavated grave of the Chatti era located near Maden in the Fritzlar-Homberg area. Here three urns of bones and ash remains were found. The urns had no tops but instead had been topped off with sand, another common practice. A turf mound had been erected over the site to mark and protect it. Tacitus records that illustrious Germans had their graves marked with such a turf mound. The dead in this case were buried with various stone implements such as spear heads, whetting stones for sharpening, and other pointed stones perhaps used for hatchet heads or tips for thrown weapons. Other stones apparently were used as hammer heads.[10]

The final topic we shall consider in our overview of the living practices and habits of the early Germans is that of trade and the use of money vs. simple barter. Tacitus suggests that contact with Rome caused the Germans to take interest in precious metals in the form of decorative vessels and trinkets, and that otherwise they used cattle and other trade goods as measures of value. Only in border areas were certain types of gold and silver Roman coinage considered valuable for trade. Dopsch disputes this, noting that Roman silver found in hoards suggests that Germans sought it for trade purposes, not mere bullion. Roman luxury goods and even wines were widely known among German tribes in the first century B.C. Germans traded with Rome in basic products such as meat, hides, amber, furs, and captives sold as slaves. In this early period the friendlier border tribes also sold grain to Rome to supply her army in Germany. Trade occurred at major trading posts or large military bases. Todd also believes coin-based trade occurred in interior areas as well as along the borders with Roman lands. By about 200 A.D. bribes, subsidies and diplomatic gifts of coinage were paid to and much sought after by the Germans. Bribes were capable of dissuading them from joining in military campaigns against Rome, as well as spreading political dissension that kept some tribes neutralized as threats over time.[11]

ADVENT AND IMPACT OF THE CHATTI

Tacitus accords the Chatti a rather privileged place in the pantheon of tribes he describes. Clearly this tribe was the primary threat and obstacle to Roman power in western Germany. He notes that Chatti lands begin at the Hercynian forest (the forest covering the southern German mountains, including the Riesengebirge), and that they are found in hilly terrain. Hardy frames, strong limbs, fierce features and vigorous courage are their hallmarks. They are intelligent and wily, and tend to obey those they promote to power in contrast to other tribes. They fight in ranks, seize opportunities, keep their headstrong natures in check, and pace themselves in battle. Their strength lay in their infantry, not horses. They constructed defensive trench works to protect themselves at night. Their generals maintained authority so that the Chatti fought in an organized and disciplined manner. In all these respects they differed from most of the other tribes that faced Rome, and these traits were obviously key to their success. They are noted for having better weapons than other Germans as well.

Tacitus says the Chatti allowed their beards and hair to grow in early adulthood until the time when they had slain a foe in the field. After this they shaved as proof of their fitness and virility. The cowardly and unwarlike go unshorn. Some of the bravest among them wore an iron ring around their necks, the mark of a slave. This they did as a perverse mark of pride in their warrior class. This particular class was without farm or home, and always was assigned the foremost place in battle. While they lived, they were supported in their needs by the other members of the tribe, and only death or the infirmities of old age released them from this lifestyle. So much for the specific descriptions of Tacitus, which again must be proven or rejected as best we can from an understanding of other Roman sources augmented with archeological findings.[12]

As noted earlier, the Chatti pushed south into modern Hesse during the second century B.C. By the time of Rome's initial great assault across the Rhine in the late first century B.C., they had lived for generations along the Rhine River north of the Main, in the Taunus Mountains, and east to their historical capital at Mattium (Metze) southwest of modern Kassel. It appears that originally they bore no ill will toward Rome; in fact, in a major attack of other tribes (Sugambri, Cherusci and Quadi) on Roman Gaul (about 12 B.C.) the Chatti failed to provide promised aid and thereby earned the enmity of their neighbors. In a Chatti-Sugambri struggle which followed, the Romans under Drusus were able to exploit the weaknesses of the Sugambri and deal them a serious blow. Chatti lands also were seized in this attack, in which the Chatti quickly submitted. Drusus ordered them to vacate areas they long had held along the Rhine so he could create a more secure zone in front of Roman territory. He seized a large number of strategic sites in a march against the Germans from the Rhine to the Weser. On his return he was cut off and almost defeated in battle in a narrow defile at Arbalo, but the disciplined behavior of his troops eventually won out against the impetuous attacks of the Germans.

In 10 B.C. the Chatti, now convinced that the Romans intended to dominate the entire region, rebelled over the loss of their old home. Such German tribes were actually entire peoples in microcosm, related in habits and customs but joined mainly by a community of interests that could change as discrete groups decided to affiliate with a more energetic or successful war leader or chief. A people such as the Chatti or

Cherusci probably amounted to no more than 15-20,000 warriors out of a population of perhaps 100,000. Along with neighboring tribes, the Chatti now crossed the Rhine and seized and slaughtered Roman officials, including 20 centurions who were crucified. Drusus defeated the allies in 9 B.C., attacking the Chatti home areas and laying waste to their settlements. Drusus died when his horse threw him as he was returning from this campaign. He was succeeded by Tiberius, who continued the pressure in 7-8 B.C.

Drusus used and improved the ancient road system through Hesse along the Main River for his attacks towards the interior. He built a number of forts and supply depots in support of his efforts along this line of march. At Rödgen, on the east bank of the Wetter River, a fort was built to act as a granary to supply his forces in this area. It was not a particularly strong site because the local inhabitants were basically the mixed Celtic/Germanic tribes who feared the aggression of their German neighbors as much as the Romans did. Shortly after 10 B.C. Rödgen was abandoned, probably due to the aggressive actions of enemy tribes. A large legionary base was established at Mainz prior to 12 B.C., and this was continually strengthened and expanded to become the capital of Roman might on the Upper German frontier. What had been Chatti territory in front of Mainz was incorporated in the Romans' possessions behind their new front lines, as were the areas around modern Wiesbaden and the Taunus mountains. The Taunus now was fortified as well.[13]

A few years of relative calm was followed by a renewed Roman assault in 4 A.D. This campaign saw Tiberius defeating a handful of tribes, including the powerful Cherusci. He imposed a treaty of peace on all except the Chatti. Their refusal caused their lands to be marched through by a Roman army on its way to fight other tribes in Bohemia. The noble families of the Chatti and Cherusci had intermarried by this point, strengthening their affinity as allies in war. The Chatti were only too anxious to join the Cherusci leader Arminius (Hermann) in the successful trap he set for the three legions of the Roman governor Varus in 9 A.D. This famous battle inflicted on Rome one of her worst defeats of all time, and apparently convinced the emperor Augustus to consolidate his lines near the Rhine and leave the area to the east to the German barbarians. Such a defeat had to be avenged, however, and in 15 A.D. Germanicus set out against the Chatti in the Wetterau area of Hesse. Taking advantage of the dry season, he crossed the Ohm River at Amöneburg and fell so quickly upon the Chatti in their home area that effective resistance was impossible. Old people and women unable to defend themselves were either killed or made captive, while the younger population including the warrior classes swam the Eder River to escape. They then sought to harry the Romans' return march, probably attacking near the modern Büraberg at Fritzlar. Roman writings suggest the attack was frustrated by the use of catapult weaponry.

While some Chatti now sued for peace, others went into hiding in the forests. The Chatti capital of Mattium (probably the modern village of Metze southwest of Kassel) was taken by the Romans without opposition, but burned by them anyway. The surrounding area also was laid waste. The Romans now headed back, but on the march they learned of another rebellion by Arminius, and wheeled around through the Chatti lands again to attack. In this march they took the Cherusci by surprise as well, capturing Arminius' wife and son. The Wetterau campaign also witnessed the creation of numerous Roman forts at key points along the march. Forts at Höchst-am-Main, Friedberg, Bad Nauheim, and Wiesbaden (*Aquae Mattiacorum*) were either newly created or reinforced in this period (see map on page 19). Another Roman attack on the Chatti in 16 A.D. was halted by bad weather, although the seizure of some renowned captives is recorded; these included a priest named Libes and the wife and daughter of a Chatti prince named Arpus.

Despite these successes, Germanicus was recalled in 16 A.D., and the Romans never again seriously sought to occupy the areas between the Rhine and the Elbe. The price had proven too high, and the seemingly inexhaustible reservoir of wild German tribesmen offered Rome no realistic prospect of success. The new emperor, Tiberius, decided to settle in to govern that which he could most easily control, and wall off the aggressive Germans in the wilderness beyond. Roman bribes and diplomacy now were used to good effect, creating political fissures that destroyed some tribes more effectively than armies could have done. The Cherusci were ruined in this way within a couple of generations, their warlike reputation and leadership passing to the Chatti.[14]

The Romans' unilateral decision to cede the eastern regions to the Germanic peoples and keep the western part of Germania for themselves was never agreed upon by the tribes, however, least of all by the powerful Chatti. With a social order and hierarchy that largely depended on constant raids into neighboring areas, the Chatti regularly probed the Roman territories for any sign of weakness. In 39 A.D., when the regional Roman commander had marched much of the local army forces to Rome to put down unrest, the Chatti joined other tribes in attacking across the Rhine toward Gaul. The Romans threw them back, and spent the following year improving fortifications at what is now Hofheim, Groß-Gerau and Wiesbaden. By 41 A.D. the frontier was again reinforced beyond the tribes' ability to overrun it. A Roman counter-attack secured ten years of peace. Again in 50 a big Chatti assault was beaten back with heavy losses, and hostages had to be handed over to secure peace with the Romans.

German in-fighting between the Chatti and Cherusci caused the latter to be utterly defeated, and the Chatti assumed the mantle of most powerful enemy tribe of Rome in all of Germania. All the major wars between Germans and Romans from now until the next great migration period in the fourth century were fights with the Chatti. In some cases the Romans called on German allies to outflank the Chatti in concert with a Roman assault. In 58 they exploited a period of fighting between the Chatti and Hermunduri over a salt spring (perhaps in the Werra valley). They sallied out to attack the defeated Chatti, but to no decisive effect. Later the Chatti struck back in league with other tribes, attacking and setting fire to Mainz, but not capturing it outright. Forts at Hofheim and Wiesbaden apparently were even more badly damaged. Again the power of Rome was too great, however, and they were thrown back. The Chatti answered the call of the local Roman leader Julius Civilis when he revolted and threatened Roman control of the frontier in 69. After much slaughter of Roman forces the uprising was crushed, and through 70 A.D. Emperor Vespasian again rebuilt and improved the damaged forts. He even rebuilt the abandoned bridgehead over the Main opposite Mainz. At the same time a large military road was built running through Neuenheim to Heidelberg and points south. This was to promote the security of the exposed fortified positions at Groß-Gerau, Gernsheim, Bürstadt, and Ladenburg.[15]

The Chatti apparently maintained a circle of mutually-supporting fortresses of their own in the Taunus Mountains and other high points across the region. These included commanding sites like the Rabenkopf, only a few miles from Mainz itself. Other forts stretched back to the Wetzlar area and the southern flank of the Westerwald. The threat of these strongholds to the ongoing security of the Roman frontier was recognized by the Emperor Domitian, who undertook a major anti-Chatti campaign again in 83. Five legions and a large number of auxiliary troops were sent into Chatti lands. Although no crushing defeats were inflicted, the Chatti were thrown back and Roman rule was extended further into eastern Hesse. Much of the Taunus and the area north of the Main as far as Friedberg probably was absorbed. Now the Wetterau was seized as well, a fertile area of Upper Hesse roughly encompassing the region around Butzbach, Homburg and Staden centered on the Wetter River. The Romans had known of and coveted this area for over a century. Domitian also instituted the beginning of the line of Roman frontier posts and watchtowers that became known as the *limes*.[16] We will explore the design and importance of this military frontier at a later point.

Domitian's victory was short-lived, however, as the tenacious Chatti soon found another opportunity to strike back. In late 88 the military governor of Upper Germany, Saturninus, rebelled against Rome and invited the Chatti to retake the Wetterau in exchange for joining forces. This they eagerly agreed to do. The Roman installations in the Wetterau apparently were struck hard and severely damaged, and the whole area reverted to Chatti control. When they attempted to cross the Rhine in 89 to reinforce Saturninus, a sudden thaw broke up the river ice and rendered the crossing impossible. This gave loyal Roman forces enough breathing space to strike Saturninus a death blow. The Lower German army defeated him utterly, and then threw the Chatti back once again. This brought about a more extended period of peace on this frontier, and Domitian was even able to reduce troop strength in the area.[17]

The Chatti at this point were at the height of their power as a people. A decade after the Saturninus uprising Tacitus would write in impressive terms of their strength and prowess in war making. For over 100 years they had absorbed the best that Rome could throw at them in modern war and poisonous diplomacy, and unlike many lesser tribes who had simply succumbed, they remained the single great threat to Roman dominance in Upper Germany. The constant military pressure of the Romans had served to increase the bonds of unity that held many disparate kinship groups together as a people. By this time the wandering waves of German tribes had settled down in western and central Europe opposite the Roman frontiers and stretching east as far as modern Poland. They had at last created a Germanic culture that was dominant across all of Germany east of the Rhine and north into Scandinavia. Archeologists have noted a striking similarity in finds across this whole area by about 100 A.D. Clothing, weapons, table ware, burial customs and gifts for the dead all bear this similarity, and help scholars generalize across wide areas based on a relatively small number of finds.

As previously noted, the Chatti power base was centered on the modern village of Metze. But other significant political and religious sites were scattered across a wider area; Gudensberg is one such place that may have hosted significant folk moot meetings and remained a traditionally important center of legal affairs into the High Middle Ages. Here the people would have assembled under their priests and senior chiefs to decide on war or peace, choose their leaders for attacks, and agree upon tribal-wide legal matters. This was also a center of worship of Oden/Wodan. Two families of noble birth with important political power are noted in Roman sources. One was headed by a chief named Gänserich (Gandestrius), the other by chief Erpel (Arpus). Gänserich's power base may have been in Metze and around the Altenburg fortress. Erpel was likely leader in an area closer to the Roman frontier in upper and lower Hesse. Amöneburg is probably the best guess as to the center of his influence.

The Chatti seem to have worshipped Thor (Donar) at Dorla as well as at the Thor oak near Geismar. This tree was the cult object that St. Boniface is renowned for having cut down to demonstrate the power of his Christian God. Tiwaz/Tiu worship is hinted at in the name of the village of Züschen, as it is in Dissen, near Gudensberg. These were apparently the key gods of the Chatti, with all the above-named places forming a sacred area in the heart of their land holdings. This was also a tempting target of Rome's wrath in its periodic sweeps to throw the Chatti back and punish their marauding ways. There were similarly revered sites around other areas of Hesse, usually points of high elevation on mountains. One such point was established at the height of the Kellerwald mountains in a place called the "wilderness garden." This site suggests a place at which sacrifices were made. Certain groves of trees and water springs were also considered sanctified to the gods, and inter-tribal fighting could erupt over ownership of such sites. Priests led the people in worship of the gods. As previously noted, the Romans captured the Chatti priest Libes in one of Germanicus' campaigns.

The free Chatti male may or may not have spent significant time working the fields, but it is certain that women, the young and old, and slaves performed farm work. Men may have helped, or simply worked tending herds, which may have been considered a more manly profession. Smithing, carpentry, wagon making and pottery making likely were done by specialized artisans, but again whether these were designated slaves or freemen is unknown. The earliest German-worked gold jewelry and related objects date from the late first century. Evidence of mining has yet to be found, although they may have worked iron deposits close to the surface. The culture of everyday tools and objects was very simple: utensils were few and poor, dowries limited to essentials, and wool and linen clothing were of plain design. Like the other Germans of their time, men wore a sleeveless coat with narrow-cut pants. Women wore a sleeveless over-dress, pinned at the shoulder with a brooch and sometimes gathered at the waist. Men and women alike wore cloak-like garments held with pins for additional warmth. The brooches and pins were simple, usually of bronze and sometimes decorated with glass beads or rings.

The Chatti were big, brawny warriors by Roman standards who were usually defeated in set-piece battles by modern, better-organized Roman military tactics. Yet their fighting prowess was never doubted, nor Roman victory taken for granted. As noted earlier, by about the '20s A.D., their numerous brushes with Roman forces had taught them that success could only be hoped for by enhancing their order and discipline. They learned to follow unit symbols like the Romans followed the legion standards, to take cues from a single command authority, and to hold men in reserve for release at critical moments in battle. Ultimately, the Chatti were only defeated and absorbed by still more powerful German tribal groupings, the Franks and the Alamanni, in the third century.[18]

Since a significant section of what would become Hesse was occupied by the Romans, it is worth reflecting on their presence and influence on the land and people for the nearly two centuries in which they sought to occupy the *limes*. As we saw earlier, it was in Domitian's day that Rome secured a presence on the right bank of the Rhine encompassing the Main River valley and the Wetterau region on both banks of the Wetter. The barrier begun at this time was the *limes*, at first merely a strip of cleared land that ran the length of the frontier established by the emperor. Wooden observation towers were set up at 500-meter intervals. These were reinforced with a few forts, but the bulk of the frontier troops were stationed to the rear in more extensive and militarily defensible installations. The areas immediately east of the border were so thinly populated with Germans that more extensive defenses on a regular basis were not deemed necessary. Over time more forts were added to the frontier line at points where roads and paths led east into the interior. Within twenty years a line of such forts was built in the Odenwald between the Main and Neckar valleys. The Taunus line was protected with screening forts as well, a notable example being the fort at Saalburg. In 83 it was little more than a line of wooden towers along the frontier screened by some earthworks and a moat.[19]

The philosophy of Roman occupation had changed little since the time of Augustus a century before. Augustan fortifications were made of wood rather than stone, mostly with single or double moats or ditches combined with wood-and-earth ramparts. Outlying structures called *canabae* that contained traders' shops and settlements, the legionnaires' workshops, ovens, etc. were not in evidence yet, except near the major camps such as Mainz. Wiesbaden and Höchst-am-Main had some surrounding settlements from an early point, but the overriding impression is of temporary structures built to identify Roman borders, not defend them. Roman strength was so secure that there was no need for a closed border to discourage incursions. The army was very mobile, and if necessary it could easily project its influence well beyond the borders. This seems to have been the outlook even with the more exposed *limes* established by Domitian. The exposed outposts were merely a tripwire of observation posts to warn of any invasions. It was protected by internal lines which were better protected and manned. One ran along the Main River through Höchst, Frankfurt and Kesselstadt to the mouth of the Kinzig. Another followed the line of the Taunus foothills from the castle opposite Mainz to Hofheim, Hedernheim, Okarben and on to Friedberg.

Troops were stationed along the better roads to allow rapid reinforcement of threatened points and block any enemy advance before it got out of hand. The Saturninus uprising of 88-89 changed this outlook, and it was felt that standing troops needed to be assigned to these posts at the expense of the larger fortress garrisons in the interior. Under Trajan (98-117) and Hadrian (117-38) the whole area was further reinforced with troops, and Hadrian ordered a continuous palisade about three meters high to be built linking the network of observation posts. The number of paved roads connecting the various works also increased greatly in this period. The screening forts were set a half day's march from one another (about 9 miles). The palisade later was improved, being replaced with a wall enclosing the watchtowers and including obstructions (fosse) in front to further obstruct movement of any attacker. Forts where men were massed for defense were placed behind this wall at a distance of a third of a mile or less.

In Hadrian's time, the Saalburg fort was expanded in size (to 242 x 160 yards) with a more permanent composite wall of wood and stone built around it. A larger standing force, a cohort, was then assigned to Saalburg, "Cohort II of the Rhaetii." The cohort had 360 infantry and 120 cavalry from Raetia, a province on the upper Danube. The strengthening of the *limes* at Saalburg and elsewhere seems to have effectively impeded major incursions by the Chatti for some decades, although they apparently turned their attention to raids south and southwest, attacking Raetia in 162. They may even have joined a Marcomannic invasion that reached Italy proper in 170 A.D. Absent constant pressure from the tribes, the *limes* line was left fairly porous even with the addition of its walls through the second century. Another dynamic was the consistent stripping of reserve forces so they could be re-deployed piecemeal to the frontier posts. More and more of the watchtowers and forts were rebuilt in stone to better protect occupied areas, for by now much of the captured lands had been assigned to settler farmers. Local Farm production became more and more important to the economy over time.[20]

The Roman soldiers increasingly built improvements to their far-flung posts to enhance their quality of life even in fairly exposed areas. No Roman post of any size could be considered tolerable without the addition of heated baths, nearby civilian settlements (the *canabae*) and trading areas, temples and chapels, and sometimes even amphitheaters. At Saalburg, by no means a huge installation, the men could take advantage of a sumptuous bath works outside the walls that was heated by constantly-replenished fires under the raised tile and brick floors. It included upwards of 10,000 tiles. There were other floor-heated buildings also, with charcoal used for the fires. Among what was probably a crowded warren of structures inside the walls was a sizable granary for storing provisions that would supply the garrison in a siege. Also on hand were stables, large barracks, a hospital and workshops. Soldiers' families, tradesmen, and farmers lived in the local *canabae* in long, narrow buildings arranged along the streets leading into the fort. These buildings had their own water wells, part of a network of 100 wells discovered in the area. These had been used and filled in once they ran dry over almost two centuries of occupation. Sanctuaries to some unnamed Gaulish deity, to the Persian god Mithras, and to another eastern god, Kybele, were in existence outside the camp walls. There was another chapel within the fort itself. A large graveyard was sited to the south, complete with a crematorium which served the needs of the fort and its settlement. Lamps, vessels and coins were buried with the dead. The *limes* line was located about 200 meters north of the fort.[21]

The *limes* was a remarkable engineering feat, stretching 228 miles through the provinces of Upper Germany held by Rome. Effective for a time, it really only guaranteed a reasonably secure peace for a few generations before the Germans began substantial incursions through the frontier. Serious but transitory Chatti attacks had to be thrown back in 162 and again after 170. By the early third century they were again significantly threatening the frontier. In the Wetterau area that cut across Hesse, the defenses were improved continuously through the second century. Stone replaced wood, and castles were added until dozens of large and small forts dotted the *limes* in this area. The nearly 100 miles of frontier here also held 250 watch towers. Other major castles in the Hessian land area were those at Heidekringen, Wiesbaden, Hofheim, Höchst, Heddernheim, Frankfurt, Kesselstadt, Heldenbergen, Okarben and Friedberg. The fort at Kesselstadt was the largest installation in the area, with a circumference of 1,500 meters and the capacity to house a full legion. In 149 the Odenwald line, now eclipsed in importance by the Wetterau, was moved back closer to the Main River. The town of Nida became the most significant settlement north of the Main in Trajan's day, with both trade and manufacturing defining its economy. Auderia (now Dieburg) was a major administrative center. Felsberg in the Odenwald, called the "sea of rocks," and Marmor were important granite quarries for the province. Granite pillars were quarried here.[22]

More than just strategic territories from a military point of view, the arable land areas incorporated within the *limes* were settled by the Romans with various classes of people who could bring the land under cultivation. The *agri decumates*, or "tenth land" as these areas were called, were only fully brought into cultivation under Trajan and Hadrian. By this point it was essential that local economies support the Roman troops quartered on them. Military installations were located purposely near native settlements to encourage trade and growth. Small tenant farms were set up for impoverished settler-farmers brought in from Gaul. In the depopulated areas of Hesse within the *limes* such importation of settlers had to be undertaken on a broad scale. Settlement of subject peoples was employed, with British tribesmen forcibly moved from Britain to the

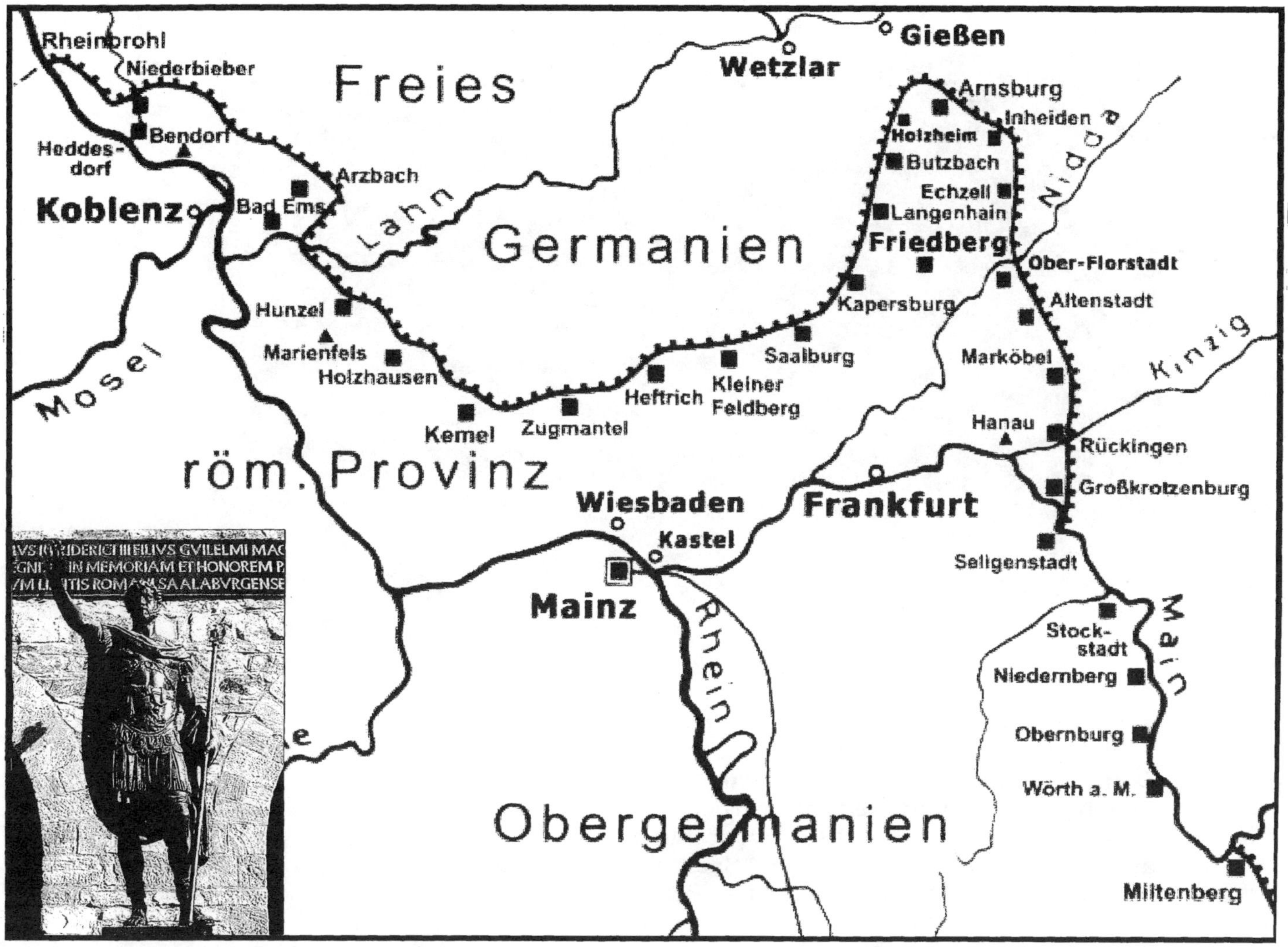

Figure 1-1 The Upper German *limes* in the Rhine/Main River areas at the start of the third century. The network of defensive forts (including Saalburg) is shown. The area west of the *limes* and Main River line is Roman territory. The inset photo shows the statue reconstructed at the main gate at Saalburg. Courtesy, Saalburg Museum. (see ***Figure 1-3***) ***Figure 1-2*** The improved *limes* defense line in cross section (below).

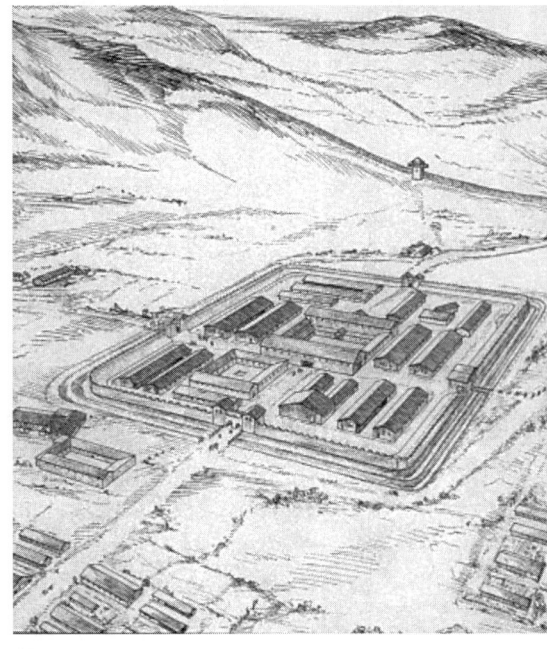

Figures 1-3/1-5 The entrance to the Saalburg Fortress, known as the *Porta Decumana*, is shown here as it would have looked after the improvements carried out under Hadrian. An artist's conception appears at right, courtesy of Saalburg Museum, Bad Homburg, Germany. Below are photos of excavations of a Roman villa and a statue from Saalburg.

Odenwald and Main areas. Over the period of rule of several emperors tens of thousands of subject people from all over the empire were settled in thinly populated areas around the frontiers where they could contribute farm labor and help defend against local threats.

This strategy seems to have paid off handsomely in the Wetterau basin, which by Emperor Domitian's time had become a great grain producer/exporter for the region. Up until the mid-third century, when the German tribes attacked the area in large numbers, the rich local soils supplied foodstuffs to the legions stationed in Mainz, cohorts stationed in the castles around the *limes*, and the large civilian populations in Nida, Mainz, Ladenburg, etc. Two hundred years of largely uninterrupted agricultural production organized along Roman lines was maintained here.[23]

Some areas received an influx of Roman veterans who rented small villas and worked them with local captives and immigrant laborers. The families who worked such farms would be called upon to provide reserves for army service in times of need. At least 111 villas have been documented in the Hessian *agri decumates*, including farms of all sizes from very small to quite large. Some were manors with rich appointments, and even mid-sized farms included residential structures with several outlying farm buildings. The latter were of the *Fachwerk* design so common to Germany in later centuries.

Alfons Dopsch has captured the sweep of the Roman occupation of the *agri decumates* in very effective terms.

> A perfectly methodical system may be traced in the Roman policy of expansion; a preliminary colonization by laying out imperial domains and settling small farmers on them, followed by a military occupation by means of a wider disposition of troops, a continual pushing forward of the *Limes*, an increase in the network of roads, and finally an extension of provincial administration and corporate organization, which completed the internal development. Thus in the second half of the second century the Roman *Limes* was advanced to the right bank of the Main, the territory of the *Limes* being actually on the left bank...In the neighborhood of these [Roman forts], settlements of civilians (*vici*) have been excavated, some of them of considerable size. These were for the most part camp villages (*canabae*), called into being by the material needs of the troops themselves...Beside single farmsteads there were also larger settlements, and the former were by no means uniform in plan or execution. There are *villae rustica* which seem to indicate that their owners belonged to "an upper stratum of the population, comparable at least to our yeoman-farmers"...[24]

The free German peoples too began to adopt Roman-like practices in farming, at first along the areas of the lower Rhine near the Roman frontier, and later spreading further east toward the hinterland through the third and fourth centuries. A differentiated social structure with a noble class and a subservient class evolved as well. This was due to the influence of Roman models and to the influx of new and dominant tribal groupings that exercised rule over existing populations. Contact with Rome brought luxury trade goods and bribes to noble families, and this also served to differentiate members of a leading social class from lesser families. Positive relations with Rome thus tended to make certain families preeminent in society. Settlements with certain larger and more comfortable residences that belonged to these leading members of society are apparent in the archeology of the era, as are social distinctions in some burials. These nobles contributed the political leadership of the evolving tribal confederacies of the second and third centuries. This development also paved the way for the later rigid class structure that evolved in the early Middle Ages.

The late second century was marked by a general enhancement of the quality of German artisanship and craftsmanship in a host of areas. This was due in significant measure to techniques learned or borrowed from Roman models. German ironsmiths, pottery makers, weavers and jewelry makers all excelled in their fields. The pottery wheel came into more widespread use, and goldsmiths and weavers produced wares of sophistication that would have been considered splendid by any comparison. These suggest development of a professional class of artisans in these fields. Carpentry tools were introduced that are close or identical forebears of modern woodworking tools, such as mallets, axes, chisels, rasps, and knives. The burial of these types of tools in certain graves also indicates a higher social class of such professionals than that enjoyed by the average tribesman. Wooden utensils and vessels exhibited a higher quality than in earlier centuries. Roman styles and motifs also caught the imagination of German artists working on metal and glass products of all types.[25]

Despite this ongoing blending of the two cultures, Roman peace and order were not destined to remain in this area of the empire. New Germanic confederacies were in the process of being formed in the late second and early third centuries. The Marcomannic wars fought by the Romans against Germanic tribes southeast of Hesse from 166-80 ended again in German defeat. But this helped usher in a period in which peoples realigned themselves in allegiance to new and larger groupings. The Alamanni people emerged from Suebic tribes that had originated in the Upper Elbe region. They likely also absorbed much of the Hermunduri tribal grouping as well as others when they took over their lands at this time. With a name meaning "all men" or "everybody," the Alamanni were a loose confederation of tribes, but they were destined to become one of the most powerful Germanic groups influencing the affairs of the later Roman empire. Probably as a result of the pressure of incursions by tribes further east, the Alamanni now joined the Chatti in an increasingly determined push to overcome Roman defenses on the *limes*.

The first serious incursion into western Hesse in the third century was a joint push by the Chatti and Alamanni in 213. This was documented along with the first references to Alamanni in Roman records. The *limes* was penetrated on a large scale, and many forts in the Taunus were damaged or destroyed in the same assault. The threat was so serious that Emperor Caracalla himself felt the need to respond at the head of a large Roman army. His counterattack was so stubbornly resisted by the Chatti, however, that he decided to buy his victory through bribes and so earn his triumph in Rome. The *limes* lines again were strengthened and the surrounding roads improved. Damaged forts at Saalburg, Zugmantel and Holzhausen were rehabilitated. Nida (Heddernheim) was reinforced with the last and strongest of its fortifications. The entire *limes* line received more walls and defensive trenches. But the writing was on the wall. Some of the *canabae* began to be abandoned, and villa holders who felt threatened migrated west. The ensuing twenty years were largely peaceful for the Romans as the Alamanni made gains at the expense of the Chatti, pushing north to a point around the Glauberg opposite Roman lines.[26]

By the 230s the Roman urban centers had been given protecting walls to enhance their defenses in anticipation of more incursions, and legions held in strategic reserve for large counter-attacks had long since been re-deployed forward in piecemeal fashion to protect the exposed *agri decumates*. In 233 the next great attack by the Alamanni struck like a hammer against rotting wood. The walled areas were largely safe from the Germans whose siege tactics were never up to snuff. But outlying areas were laid waste, and after this still more *canabae* were abandoned or severely shrunk in size. Damage was suffered over a large area, with most or all Wetterau forts being lost or badly damaged. The Emperor Severus Alexander first fought and then bribed the Germans into submission, and then was killed in Mainz by rebellious troops in 235. The rebels proclaimed Maximinus emperor, and he reestablished order by assaulting the Alamanni in their home areas in spring 236. Their pressure on the frontier was regular, if not constant, for the next twenty years, however. From 254 to about 260 pressure was rather unremitting, and at last the *limes* lines gave way for good. The retreat to the Rhine occurred for the last time.

This collapse and the reentry of the Germans to the area that had become thoroughly Romanized ushered in an interesting and confusing period in the history of this portion of Hesse. Although Roman authority was broken, the victorious Alamanni and Chatti do not appear to have settled down on the land in great numbers at first. Only in the latter third century do recognizably Germanic settlements turn up. Probably the well-to-do Roman settlers lost their estates and positions, but poorer farmers may have remained in place in large numbers. Many probably simply switched masters and stayed on the land willingly or by force. These people left an archeological record of coins and tools, burial customs, house construction and the layout of roads, all with clear connections to earlier Roman models. The Roman domain lands passed to the control of Germanic chiefs who probably ensured that they were cultivated consistent with former practices. This is perhaps unsurprising when one realizes that by this time much of the Roman army was dependent on Germanic allies for its troop strength and even senior commanders and some emperors. These cultures had by now interacted to the extent that Romanization of Germanic culture was extensive. Much continuity was maintained through the change from Roman to German overlordship. In pottery works, masonry building, and even keys and locks, we see evidence of Roman-style production that was maintained in the period after the Romans were expelled from Hessian lands.

This was the time of so-called "frontier societies," neither fully Roman nor German, but drawing on both cultures under the rule of whichever culture was dominant: Romans west of the Rhine, Germans to the east. By this time the Franks had stormed out of their home region in the lower Rhine area and crossed the Rhine in large numbers. Alamannic warriors increasingly served in the Roman armies, and there is evidence of ongoing trade among both peoples in one another's products. For their part, the Chatti seem to have begun to splinter into sub-groups that were re-absorbed in larger tribal groupings, mostly among the Franks rather than the Alamanni. Whether this is because of the latent animosities they felt against their Suebic counterparts in the Alamanni, or some other reason, has remained unclear. Demandt suggests that the historical ties of the Wetterau and Taunus areas to the middle Rhine under Roman influence played a role in the advent of Frankish influence from the north and west; presumably roads, trade and other ties bound these areas together in ways that promoted political union as well. In any case, he feels the Chatti largely remained in place in Hesse after their military and political leadership was spent. Slowly, if at times painfully, they were molded into loyal subjects of the greater Frankish empire. More of this will be discussed in the next chapter. [27]

With this we leave off the story of the earliest period of Hessian history. It was a time in which two major cultures met one another and contested ownership and control of the land. At first dominant and brutally methodical in its methods against the Germanic peoples, Rome at last succumbed to the notion that the Germans' numbers ultimately were unbeatable, even if their armies could be destroyed in detail time and time again. Roman arms and diplomacy then were used to wall off the threat from the east rather than continue to sally forth to meet it in the wild recesses of Germany. For a century and a half Roman ways had significant impact on the people of the Wetterau, Taunus and Main. Throughout this period extensive trade and diplomatic efforts went forth, cultivating an appreciation for Roman goods and bribes, and isolating the Chatti as the only people capable of maintaining spirited opposition. At last a new and even more powerful people, the Alamanni, would arise to take up the fight, and drive the Romans off for good. And always it was the crossroads of paths and rivers leading through Hesse to the interior that made it the focal point of the struggle. This geography, and the cultural and economic forces that swirled around and through it for centuries, would continue to mark the development of Hesse into modern times.

NOTES TO CHAPTER 1

[1] Malcolm Todd, *Everyday Life of the Barbarians, Goths, Franks and Vandals*, Putnam's Sons, NY, 1972, pp. 3,5,10; Malcolm Todd, *The Early Germans*, Blackwell, Cambridge, MA, 1992, pp. 22-29; C.M. Wells, *The German Policy of Augustus*, Clarendon Press, Oxford, 1972; pp. 17-31; Alfons Dopsch, *The Economic and Social Foundations of European Civilization*, Howard Fertig, New York, 1969 reprint, p. 48.
[2] Todd, *Everyday Life*, pp. 97-101; Fergus Millar, *The Roman Empire and its Neighbors*, Delacourt Press, New York, 1967, p. 315; Tacitus, chapters 6, 7.
[3] Tacitus, chapters 13-14, 20; Dopsch, pp. 46-47.
[4] Tacitus, chapters 15, 21-24. Dopsch, pp. 45-46.
[5] Todd, *Everyday Life*, pp. 62-64; Tacitus, chapter 5; Todd, *Early Germans*, pp. 77-79; Dan C. Heinemeier, *A History of Brunswick*, Arlington, VA, 1999, pp. 3-4; Tacitus, chapter 26; Dopsch, p. 39.
[6] Todd, *Everyday Life*, pp. 86-88; Tacitus, chapter 17; Todd, *Early Germans*, p. 137.
[7] Todd, *Everyday Life*, pp. 64-73; Heinemeier, p. 3.
[8] Tacitus, chapter 7; Heinemeier, pp. 2, 5-6, Todd, *Everyday Life*, p. 25.
[9] Todd, *Everyday Life*, pp. 124-26; Tacitus, chapter 9; Todd, *Early Germans*, pp. 104-05, 112, 119; Heinemeier, p. 5.
[10] Johann Hermann Schmincke, and Johannes Österling, *Dissertation über die Graburnen und Steinwaffen der alten Chatten vom Jahre 1714: 250 Jahre Vorgeschichtsforschung in Kurhessen*, issued and edited by Wilhelm Niemeyer, Kommissionsverlag N.G. Elwert, Marburg/Lahn 1964; Todd, *Everyday Life*, pp. 144-47; Tacitus, chapter 27; Todd, *Early Germans*, p. 79; Millar, p. 314.
[11] Todd, *Everyday Life*, pp. 14-15; Tacitus, chapter 5; Dopsch, pp. 359-60; Todd, *Early Germans*, pp. 19, 90-102.
[12] Tacitus, chapters 30-31.
[13] Theodor Mommsen, *The Provinces of the Roman Empire, The European Provinces*, selections from *The History of Rome*, Volume 5, Book 8, University of Chicago Press, 1968, pp. 27-34; Karl E. Demandt, *Geschichte des Landes Hessen*, Bärenreiter-Verlag, Kassel, 1972, pp. 60-62; Wells, pp. 222-30; Herwig Wolfram, *The Roman Empire and its Germanic Peoples*, U. of California Press, Berkeley, 1997, p. 7.
[14] Mommsen, pp. 56-58; Demandt, pp. 62-64; Wells, pp. 244-45.
[15] Demandt, pp. 65-66; Mommsen, pp. 156-57.
[16] Demandt, pp. 67-69; Mommsen, p. 139; Todd, *Early Germans*, p. 52, Millar, pp. 301-302.

[17] Demandt, p. 70; Mommsen, p. 158; Todd, *Early Germans*, p. 53.
[18] Demandt, pp. 70-71, 85-92; Millar, p. 304; Todd, *Early Germans*, p. 125; Todd, *Everyday Life*, p. 105.
[19] Todd, *Early Germans*, pp. 53-54; H. Schönberger, *The Roman Camp Saalburg*, C. Zenner & Co., Bad Homburg, 1949, p. 3.
[20] Wells, pp. 247-48; Demandt, pp. 69-71; Mommsen, pp. 162-69; Todd, *Early Germans*, p 54-55.
[21] Schönberger, pp. 3-16; Demandt, pp. 75-77; Millar, pp. 121-25.
[22] Demandt, pp. 72-78, 82; Millar, p. 303; Peter La Baume, *Romans on the Rhine*, Wilhelm Stolfus Verlag, Bonn, 2nd edition, p. 17..
[23] Peter Janisch, *Die Hessische Landwirtschaft im Wandel der Zeiten*, Freilichtmuseum Hessenpark, Neu-Anspach, 1996, p. 19.
[24] Dopsch, p. 51. Previous section also based on Demandt, p. 80; Dopsch, p. 50; Postan, M.M., *The Agrarian Life of the Middle Ages*, Cambridge Economic History of Europe, Vol. I, Cambridge University Press, 1966, pp. 11-12.
[25] Todd, *Early Germans*, pp. 126-38; Millar, pp. 310-12.
[26] Todd, *Early Germans*, pp. 56, 207; Millar, pp. 316-18; Demandt, p. 82.
[27] Todd, *Early Germans*, pp. 56-58, 147; Millar, pp. 106-07; Demandt, pp. 37, 83-84, 93-94; Dopsch, pp. 54-56, 68-69.

CHAPTER 2

From Alamanni to Franks: Transition to the Early Middle Ages

The collapse of the Chatti as a significant force in Hesse paved the way for the Alamanni people to assume control in the areas that had been Roman territory until 260 A.D. This diverse, loosely organized "tribe in arms" as it has been called was successful in accomplishing by fire and sword what the Chatti had failed to achieve: control of the land up to the right bank of the Rhine. Alamanni would become regular visitors to the left bank as well, marauding into Gaul just as the Franks were doing somewhat further north. Their success had nothing to do with new tactics, since third, fourth and even fifth century Germans had learned little over the centuries they fought with Rome. Attacks were still headlong rushes relying on the shock of the initial assault to break the will of the enemy. Raiding parties and armies in this era were surprisingly small, with several thousand only seen when entire peoples sought to emigrate en masse. Most major attacking forces appear to have included no more than 600-900 warriors. Body armor was still rare, and although the Alamanni had achieved some prominence as horsemen, their cavalry was prone to be less effective than the infantry. When their uncoordinated attacks failed to achieve immediate success, they found it difficult to do anything for an encore, and probably contributed little to determining ultimate success or failure.

Some new weapons were apparently developed by the Alamanni, and later imitated and probably perfected by the Franks. They are recorded as using the *franciska*, a throwing ax that was put to effective use beginning in the fourth century. When hurled just before the lines closed in battle it had real shock value. The javelin modeled on the earlier Roman form was similarly used as a hand-thrown projectile. Those Alamanni who carried swords hung them from their waists or from a shoulder strap. The swords evolved into two-edged, slashing weapons. Alamanni used simple, one-piece bows as well. But the old, reliable spear was always the weapon of choice.

The Alamanni who burst into the *agri decumates* still made no provision for supplies on the march, but depended on foraging on the land they were attacking. This was true throughout the third and fourth centuries. Roman forces could significantly impede them by hoarding food in walled forts or towns, since the Germanic warriors had neither the skill nor the patience for sieges. Alamanni appear to have used forts of their own only rarely, as when they re-fortified an ancient fort at the Glauberg near the *limes* after the Roman retreat. It probably was used as the seat of a chief and continued in existence through the late fifth century. During this time the Alamanni seem to have maintained close trade ties with Roman areas, and the Glauberg has evidence of stone buildings and workshops in this period. Bands of Alamanni, like many other German tribes, also began to serve in units of the Roman army.[1]

Having won the lands west of the *limes*, the Alamanni apparently were slow to assume full control and settle on them. It may be that their approach was geared more toward periodic plunder of their richer neighbors, and the sudden availability of large land areas was beyond their immediate needs or means to absorb. Over time blocks of settlers would move into certain areas under a particular chieftain, taking their name as a group from a local land feature. There was not much of a sense of community. A large tribal grouping, they apparently suffered a shortage of manpower to work the land, resorting in part to the use of captives. Perhaps their warlike nature caused most of the able bodied to spend more time raiding than farming. Their primitive economy has been characterized as "plunder and scarcity," in which periodic hunger was no stranger to the people.

Some of the old Roman villas were likely taken over, but in time the stone buildings were unable to be maintained using Roman techniques. Most scholars hold that the Alamanni avoided the more developed sites and built their familiar wooden structures on the Roman lands, but set apart from earlier structures. Dopsch, however, believes that, "The Germans settled beside, and often in the midst of Romans. They may often have lit their fires on Roman hearths and put their hands to Roman plows." Todd also cites the archeology of the villa of Praunheim at Nida (Heddernheim), where Alamannic owners constructed dry stone walls inside the old villa and must have lived together with Roman provincials. Some restoration along the same lines occurred in a villa at Holheim. Dopsch similarly cites evidence for cohabitation at Stockstadt on the Main River. Although most organized civil settlements of any size were laid low by the Alamanni, there is evidence that at least in individual cases—such as Pforzheim and Ladenburg—Alamannic settlement occurred, perhaps right alongside Roman provincials. These places now assumed a much more Germanic character and were assimilated fully into the Alamannic culture.[2] It is probably safe to assume that for the most part the Alamanni avoided Roman residences and preferred their own style of dwelling, locating them somewhat apart from the existing farmsteads and *canabae*. Regardless of the amount of joint habitation in the settlements, Roman culture continued to exercise considerable influence through trade, military service, and other contacts.

The Alamannic leadership is a virtual unknown in the third and fourth centuries, but all writers allude to its being loose-knit. The traditional German mistrust of strong, centralized rule must have been magnified greatly in a people formed of so many diverse tribes. Although disunited deployment of forces was a recipe for disaster when battling the organized Roman legions, this diverse and difficult to govern mass somehow maintained itself for centuries as a formidable fighting force. Likened to a hydra, it could tolerate defeat of one or many sub-groups while the whole lived on. It does appear, however, that the ongoing battles with Roman armies and others who had trained under them encouraged the Alamanni to accept a greater and greater measure of control from above, particularly in war. This process took centuries to play out, with many defeats in large-scale battles before change was possible. By the late fourth century references are made to kings of the Alamanni. Some seventeen separate kings are mentioned in the period from 357-486, culminating in the appointment of a sole king.[3]

SOCIAL CUSTOMS & CULTURE

Like that of other Germanic tribes in contact with Rome, the Alamannic culture continued to advance after the great migration period of the third and fourth centuries. As they progressed toward a more settled existence the decorative arts developed beyond what previously had been possible. Decorative ware was marked by the use of stamped and rouletted symbols on vessels. Wheel-turned pottery, although not rare, was apparently less important than hand-formed goods made locally in the home. A large quantity of good quality, inexpensive pottery was available from Roman traders.

Major improvements in artistic technique were incorporated in the fourth century. High-quality wooden vessels were made on lathes, with examples of bowls, platters, and flasks having been discovered. In metal working, many smelting hearths and furnaces testify to the Germans' mastery of Roman forms and techniques. Even by the sixth and seventh centuries most production was still attached to widely-dispersed rural communities. Some people probably lived apart from such communities, however, deriving their living from mining and smelting, salt making, herding and hunting.

German-made jewelry, both decorative and functional, also became much more attractive and competitive with that emanating from Roman and other sources. Copper and silver inlay techniques were mastered by this point. Alamannic chiefs and retainers wore ornate jewelry as signs of their power and authority. From the fifth to seventh centuries the majority of brooches worn by both sexes were bow-shaped, with two flat plates affixed to the bow at top and bottom. This was in fact the most popular style throughout western Europe. Styles of clothing and jewelry seem to have diffused rapidly across southern and western Europe despite the primitive nature of life. The next style to catch on with the Alamanni and others was the disc-shaped brooch. A popular motif for brooches was birds of prey, with those worn by the nobility showing ornate features such as the use of garnets. Common folk would have used a circular style brooch with a simple pin crossing it and fastening in a slot. Some had animal heads or other decorative features carved into the metal. Noble women would have had decorative belts or girdles with such features hanging from them. Buckles and the ends of straps or belts sometimes had gold or silver features incorporated in them. Beads or other glass ornamentation, such as balls of crystal, might accompany the precious metal features. Bracelets followed similar themes and were made of comparable materials. By the sixth century intricate weaving was done by both household servants and the women at home who usually managed them. Some farmsteads included sheds or huts devoted to cloth production, recognizable thanks to the modern excavation of clay loom-weights. Everyday leather goods like belts and shoes would mostly have been made by individual households, although larger articles like saddles and harnesses would require more expert craftsmanship.

Grave finds indicate that games of chance were still popular with warrior bands. Modern-style dice, an invention of the Celts passed along by the Romans, have been found in some graves. Beer brewed from barley was apparently the favored alcoholic beverage among the Alamanni, probably spiced with herbs. Mead also was probably enjoyed widely in the Roman period. Six-stringed and eight-stringed lyres were found in Alamannic graves of the eighth century, and variations of these instruments must have been in use much earlier.[4]

Burial rites also changed considerably in the centuries leading up to the medieval period. In the migration period of the third and fourth centuries cremation still held sway, but sometime in the period before 500 A.D. the inhumation of intact bodies seems to have taken over. Frank and Alamanni cemeteries consisted of long rows of graves, often along the sides of a road, called *Reihengräber*. In these the bodies were buried so that heads pointed towards the west. People were buried in their clothes, often with their weapons or other goods used in everyday life. Despite high child mortality, few children's graves are found in these cemeteries.

The Alamanni seem to have worshipped the same limited set of Germanic gods known to their fellow tribes in Germany. In the migration period Thor or Donar seems to have grown in popularity. He was manly, a gifted fighter, and renowned for his bigger-than-life habits of eating, traveling, and solving problems by his wit and cunning. Oak groves and other forest sanctuaries remained favored places of worship.[5]

SETTLEMENT PATTERNS AND TYPES

There was great similarity in the styles of construction and types of settlement used by the Alamanni and other Germans for many centuries. Settlements have been excavated dating from the seventh and eighth centuries that show the same basic features as those common in the fourth century. The oldest forms of layout for villages made up of individual farmsteads are the *Rundling* and *Sackdorf* forms. The *Rundling* consisted of a group of houses built around a central space, while *Sackdörfer* were laid out in a rectangular arrangement on both sides of an essentially dead-end street. Also noted are so-called *Haufendörfer* in which homesteads are laid out in no particular relationship to each other, usually along a street. By studying the size of cemeteries located near villages, it has been determined that the density of most Alamanni settlements was not as great as those typical in other parts of Germany. Hamlets of two and three farmsteads each were scattered far and wide across the land. Three types of settlement can be traced where the Germans settled in former Roman areas: large estates of the well-off; small villages and hamlets of freemen; and groups of lesser freemen laid out around an estate of a member of the privileged class. The latter are attested to by archeological studies of graves in which an obviously well-off man is buried near surrounding graves of his less- wealthy fellows.

Many of the large holdings apparently were assigned to greater and lesser nobles after the period of migration, with little thought given to determining exact boundaries. Later, as the need arose to establish borders more exactly there are indications in Alamannic law that resort was made to dueling between the nobles in question. By this time more than one generation of ownership may have passed, and pressure to the north by the Franks may have made land more scarce and property lines more important. The same pressure probably required the vast majority of freemen to be content with modest holdings in small villages. Smaller holdings, set close together, were marked off with wattle fences, and when so determined these borders were respected by the community. Separate fenced areas for gardens near the residences also are found. Records show farmsteads of over 7,000 square meters, and others of smaller size down to tiny plots of only 100 square meters.[6]

Early on, houses tended to be built in an east-west orientation, built basically in the hall house and *Grubenhaus* styles described in the last chapter. Large buildings were ten to twenty meters in length, with twenty-six meters being the largest encountered. Width was at most about seven meters. Smaller buildings were only four to five meters wide, and at most about twelve meters in length. Most were considerably smaller. All of these were hall house designs. Within the same settlement, there could be considerable differences in construction features. Hall houses needed beams that covered the length and width of the house with supports only on the ends to conserve internal space. An almost standardized width of seven meters is found in one excavated village, corresponding to the limit of the beams' carrying capacity. Roofs were thatched, but the wall construction is difficult to determine. Wattle and daub, planking, or both may have been used. The main building on a wealthy farmstead likely required the skills of master builders that would have formed a recognizable trade in this era. Little or nothing of the earlier Roman techniques seem to have been maintained by their

German successors. However, older Roman structures were incorporated in some Alamanni farm buildings as long as they remained in usable condition.

The *Grubenhäuser* of this era were constructed over rectangular pits from three to five meters long by two to three and one-half meters wide on average. These typically have six support posts, holding cross beams over which the walls and roofs were constructed. The simple joinery of the members suggest construction by the owners rather than specialized carpenters. The rafters may have projected down from the center beam all the way to the ground in an A-frame-type construction that hid the walls from the outside and provided maximum protection from the weather. Walls were wattle and daub. Besides the *Grubenhäuser* there were shed-like structures open on one side (like lean-tos). These were used as workshops for weavers and other specialized trades. Still smaller structures for food storage and similar uses have been found, some with fireplaces for cooking or smoking.

Moving from archeology to written sources, the main house has been described as a one-room structure open to the rafters inside, and with walls nine feet in height. Several doors are discussed. Other structures on the farm are barns, a granary, threshing and storage buildings, pigsties, sheep pens, bath-houses and separate areas for weaving or similar work. The law included specific penalties for arson, with higher penalties for destruction of a barn or granary than for a shed. The basic layout of farms was unchanged from the early centuries A.D.[7]

How were decisions made on the siting of these ancient villages? It appears that primary consideration was given to location near a brook or river on the lower parts of gentle slopes. The earliest settlements seem to have been laid out in rows facing a street, with the more jumbled *Haufendörfer* a manifestation of later village designs surviving into the Middle Ages. Hamlets were concentrations of essentially independent freemen, while villages developed a sense of community based on the use of common fields, woods, water sources, meadowlands, etc.

Average farmsteads had twelve to fifteen individuals, including extended family, servants, etc. Over time the smaller concentrations or individual homesteads gave way to slightly larger village structures of six to twelve farms, on average. Within these settlements, the size of farm holdings could vary widely. An average density of settlement of four or five people per square kilometer across all of the Alamannic areas has been conjectured for the period around the seventh century. This would suggest a total population of some 250,000 persons.[8]

TRADE

Despite the barbarity and violence of the migration period after the fall of the *limes*, not all trade in the latter Roman empire ground to a halt. The Romans maintained trade ties between their possessions in Britain and those along the Rhine. Their traders plied the right bank of the Rhine. A record of 371 A.D. refers to a collection of such tradesmen found at Wiesbaden. Trade with areas now in southern Russia also seems to have crossed through eastern Europe. The Alamanni were active traders too, plying the Romans and neighboring tribes with cattle, slaves, and other basic commodities. Records suggest much trade must have occurred with the Franks and Bavarian tribes on their borders. The old Roman roads through Alamannic territory did not deteriorate for long periods, and the Alamanni must have benefited from their location astride the ancient trade and migration routes. The Thuringian tribes to the east also depended on these routes to gain access to Mainz and the Rhine.[9]

FROM ALAMANNI TO FRANKS: TRANSITION TO EARLY MIDDLE AGES

BATTLES WITH OTHER TRIBES: TRANSITION TO FRANKISH OVERLORDSHIP

Following the fall of the *limes* a period of fighting that has been termed ghastly seems to have set in between the Romans and Germans. The Alamanni from the east and the Franks to the north were constantly challenging Roman control of the Rhine line and Gaul behind it. Internal unrest seems to have weakened Roman resolve periodically, and the Germans made significant inroads in these times. Large groups of Alamanni must have settled with the acquiescence of Rome on the west side of the Rhine after 350, and lived as Roman dependents. Roman troops later invaded their space and manhandled them badly, however, probably to reinforce in the Germans' minds that this was Roman-controlled land and that their independence was limited if they continued living here. Large-scale battles also occurred in the fourth century, and Roman arms still were triumphant in these fights because of better organization and unity of command than the ever-fractious Alamanni could muster. Such a battle at Strasbourg in 357 was a huge and painful defeat for the Alamanni. With two major tribal leaders trying to direct the army and holding only limited sway over their troops, the end was a foregone conclusion. Alamanni also jockeyed for position with other tribes in this era, as when they fought Burgundians over a salt spring in 359.

The Alamanni did seize Mainz in 368, plundering the ancient city. Roman forces again threw them back, however. The emperor ordered bridgeheads across the Main and Rhine to be seized and manned to provide better security, but the Alamanni kept things hot for these occupying forces. A large group of Alamanni from the area around Wiesbaden under a King Macrianus negotiated peace with the Emperor Julian on a barge in the Rhine River near Mainz in 374. Later, a band of Franks under a King Malobaudes attacked the Alamanni and secured a wedge of territory on the lower Lahn River. This turned out to be only an initial incursion, with much more pressure to follow in the ensuing century. Malobaudes' band was in Roman service at this time. They went to war with King Macrianus' Alamanni in a by-now familiar pattern in which Rome used Frankish forces to subdue other German tribes. The Franks defeated Macrianus' war band and killed him about 390. It was also an accepted fact in this confused time that large Alamannic forces often fought as Roman surrogates for pay and influence. Pitting German against German was an effective means of maintaining Roman security in this era. The Frankish victory secured the Lahn area and opened up the Wetterau to them as well. By the mid-400s Roman writers recognized that Frankish power held sway in these areas of Hesse as well as the Nidda River basin. The Frank nobles who ruled these areas were members of a few key families who seem to have maintained residence in the areas around Dornberg, Diez, and Limburg.[10]

This was a time of great and ongoing upheaval for those living in and around Hesse. Mainz was overrun again in 406 by a force of Alamanni and other tribes, and still again in 451 by the latest scourge of Europe, the Huns. Trier changed hands between Roman and German/Hun occupiers four times through 440, falling finally in 475. By this time the Franks had forced the Alamanni back as far south and east as Worms and Aschaffenburg, taking the lower Main as well as the Lahn and Nidda basins. Despite this pressure, the Alamanni probably were at the peak of their power and influence in the latter fifth century, albeit with their center of power shifted to the upper Rhine and north of the Alps.

A last major battle with the Franks was soon to come. By the late fifth century the Alamanni had learned to fight with greater unity of purpose and obey a single command structure, allowing them to be truly formidable opponents to the Romans and Franks. In the pivotal battle of Zülpich in 497, fighting against the great Frankish king Clovis, the Alamanni were only narrowly defeated. In a moment of concern for the outcome, Clovis reputedly promised to accept his wife's Christian God if the battle should end in his favor. It did, and Clovis made good on his vow. The Alamannic power in Hesse was broken for good, and Clovis made the Alamanni a dependent vassal state organized as a duchy. In this form it became a territorial unit of the Frankish empire. Amalgamation was successful, for in future years Alamannia proved a generally loyal and supportive province for the Franks in their battles other tribes.

> As the Franks conceived that each subject "lived his own law," they almost always respected the laws and customs of the peoples they conquered. Military service was exacted of the Thuringians, Alemanni, and Bavarians, but they were ruled by their own tribal dukes and under the Merovingians there was no Frankish count beyond the Rhine. The system helped to reconcile conquered people to Frankish domination...[11]

Thus the Franks never attempted to drive out the subject people of Hesse, who were probably a polyglot collection of descendants of the Chatti, Roman provincials, imported populations from other Roman areas, and Alamannic remnants. Franks did settle more intensively in Hessian lands than before, continuing to take over wider and wider areas through the rule of several Frankish kings through about 550.[12] The local population must have become subservient to these overlords, providing a lesser class of tenant farmers, servants, and levies for Frankish military campaigns. This evolving social differentiation brings us to the subject of how early feudal ties and culture must have grown up within a Germanic culture that valued individual freedom and initiative above other principles.

SOCIAL STATUS AND THE EARLY NOBILITY

When the Roman *limes* were overrun, the Alamanni freemen were still fairly equal in rank even in comparison to their apparent betters among the ancient nobility. For a long time the social order rested heavily on freemen scattered across the local districts on small and independent farmsteads. Slaves also were common, although not in the large numbers that the intensive agriculture systems of the Romans required. Captured Roman provincials or soldiers might have been made slaves, but at no point were slaves so numerous as to become a mainstay of agriculture.

By the fifth and sixth centuries, however, the social structure of the Alamanni was becoming more hierarchical. The old nobility of chiefs and their major retainers in the *comitati*, as well as other families that more recently had distinguished themselves as leaders, formed a special group within the broader society of freemen. These obtained title to large landed estates. The individual social unit was still the farmstead, made up of freemen, servants, and some tenant farmers, but society became increasingly stratified as the decades wore on. More people were slipping into servile status from tenancy into serfdom, in which various goods and services were owed to the landlord in exchange for rights to work the land he controlled. All elements of society became more cemented in their roles and relationships. The larger nobles accrued more and more wealth, the smaller freemen became less and less viable without attaching themselves to the estate of a noble. By the mid-seventh century (under the influence of the eastern Frankish kingdom) it is possible to distinguish three classes based on the *Wergeld* that each commanded in case of death. The hereditary nobility (*primi*), the lesser nobility who also were large landholders (*mediani*), and the larger class of freemen called *minofledi* each was designated with a different value under the Alamannic *Wergeld* system. With the Franks triumphant in Hessian areas, they must have grafted their own hereditary nobility onto the upper ranks of Alamannic society, furthering the process by which the lesser freemen saw their rights and freedoms shrink.

The descent into serfdom and complete legal dependence on a lord was gradual in the early Middle Ages, with the first to fall not surprisingly being the poorest members of society. At first the individual was free to commend himself to any lord he chose, and to change lords if it pleased him. But as land became more fully exploited there obviously was less and less scope for such voluntary change in the immediate area in which a dependent freeman lived.[13]

HESSE IN THE KINGDOM OF THE FRANKS

With Clovis' victory in 496 the Alamannic territories began the process of becoming amalgamated with the Franks. The Franks were just another Germanic tribe, but with some important differences that served them well in establishing the only permanent Germanic successor state to emerge from the Roman age. Unlike others who were largely absorbed within the cultural and political influences of the latter Roman Empire, the Franks maintained an essentially Germanic character with strong connections to the right bank of the Rhine. Once they accepted Christianity under Clovis, they also were positioned to benefit from considerable support from the Gallo-Roman population that remained as the successor to the empire. Although Clovis' conversion was probably only skin-deep, he became a champion of the religious leaders who looked to him to protect them from threats by surrounding heathen tribes. This would help the Franks in their efforts to assimilate large swaths of territory in Gaul that provided a rich and supportive base for further expansion east and south.

The Franks originated in the far north of Germany, expanding south to the lower Rhine and eventually crossing it to attack Roman territory in northern Gaul. Their name means "bold" or "wild," and seems fitting in view of the devastating effect of their military campaigns on any group that stood in their way. At first an "untidy amalgam of insignificant warrior bands from between the Weser and the Rhine" as Todd has called them, they exploited Roman weakness and gobbled up numerous Germanic tribal groups as they built their strength in the third century. Franks eventually served increasingly as Roman army officers and provided large numbers of troops to protect the dying empire. Roman influence probably also helped reign in the inherent disunity that marked the Franks as it did all the Germanic tribes, so that by the time Clovis came to power in the latter fifth century a stronger, centralized leadership structure was achieved. It was from Clovis that the line of Frankish Merovingian kings was to spring. His sons inherited the kingdom in 511, dividing it into four provinces including Austrasia, of which Hesse was a part. Merovingian politics from this point until the early seventh century has been called "a continual succession of murders, cruelty, deceit, treachery, usurpations, accusations of witchcraft, kidnappings of child rulers, war between brothers, and disunity."[14]

Frankish battle tactics were still very basic in this period, with little use of cavalry. Frankish infantry was considered well-trained and fearless, with a larger percentage of men equipped with swords and shields than before. The *franciska*, or throwing ax, was used with great effect, as were short javelins with barbed heads that were used for throwing or thrusting. A standard battle tactic was to hurl the javelins into an enemy line, inevitably piercing many shields and some warriors with the barbed tips. Before there was time to dislodge the javelins, the Franks were upon the enemy, who could either toss away their speared shields or suffer as the Franks stepped on the ends of the protruding javelins, thereby pulling down the guard of the opponent and opening him up for a sword, ax or javelin blow. The throwing ax was the national weapon and trademark symbol of the Franks for centuries, and it was much feared by their enemies. In 507 Clovis defeated the Visigoths largely thanks to the superiority of his ax-men over the spear-carrying Goths. In the seventh century weaponry changed again, with more widespread use of the shorter, single-edged sword called the *sax* or *scramasax*. It was eighteen inches long, and could be used for thrusting or even throwing as the need required.[15]

In society as well as the military, significant changes were afoot by the mid-seventh century. The nobles among the Franks further entrenched themselves in power and privilege to the detriment of the rights of other freemen. More manors belonging to these nobles were established, but it has not been possible to find evidence of manors in every settlement that has been excavated. Cattle raising seems to have been at least as widespread and probably more important economically than agriculture. High protein consumption led to increased body size and mass in the population. By the eighth century grain was assuming a larger role again, an indication of the spread of feudal-style agriculture based on manor systems.

Women died in greater numbers than men from age eighteen to thirty due to the dangers of childbirth; thereafter, men died in higher proportions than women. Marriage and childbirth occurred most commonly between the ages of twenty-five to thirty, during which time women's value in *Wergeld* was three times the norm. Elderly people in the Merovingian period (500-700 A.D.) were endowed after death with richer grave-goods than in earlier centuries, when young men's endowments were far and away the richest. One grave from about 600 A.D. revealed the remains of a noble surrounded by graves of men of lesser means. The chieftain had a *Spangenhelm* helmet of Gothic fabrication which, like his skull, bore scars of battle damage. He was buried with a throwing ax, shield, spear and javelin. Otherwise the grave contained everyday items such as a bucket, glass and pottery vessels, a whetstone and a feather-stuffed cushion. Silk fragments show that trade with the Mediterranean region was known in this period.[16]

Frankish settlement patterns in Hesse in Merovingian times suggest a slow expansion probably determined largely by royal land seizures and grants to nobles by the king of the Austrasian Franks. By 536 the local Alamannic duke was answerable directly to the king in a sometimes difficult chain of authority. More complete incorporation occurred during the rule of Charles Martel (714-41) when he stamped out a final Alamannic rebellion in the year 730. The middle Rhine and Main areas were the first to be settled under direct Frankish control, followed by a push east and north into the Lahn valley and lower Hesse. The Franks seem to have followed the old Roman roads and taken over arable land that had been worked in Roman times. Their power base in lower Hesse was centered in the Fritzlar/Büraburg area; in upper Hesse it was near Amöneburg. Royal assumption of control of these lands added much economic power to the Austrasian crown. The lower Hessian region was not as fully assimilated as upper Hesse, the Wetterau and other former-Roman areas. Only by the late seventh century under Pepin of Herstal (687-714) did lower Hesse join the core Frankish territories. Hessian areas outside strong Frankish control show a history of continuing cremation burials that finally were abolished as Christian practices gained a more solid foothold.

The Franks seem to have moved forward into their Hessian holdings in stages. First, they secured the lands through the occupation and improvement of old fortifications such as those at Büraburg, Kesterburg, Amöneburg, and Glauberg. Büraburg was improved from the period of the mid-sixth to the late seventh centuries, with the creation of barracks, workshops, and other structures to help in withstanding a siege. Over the next fifty years these centralized defensive positions were largely given up in favor of a wider system of smaller, well-distributed forts located a day's march or less from one another. Many were built upon the remains of earlier Roman castles. This system was particularly important for defense against the greatest threat to Frank suzerainty in this era, the Saxons. It also ensured a cooperative local population less given to sedition or revolt. The fortifications were manned by a large-framed soldiery drawn from the nobility. These men often left behind well-appointed graves: long swords, short swords, helmets, two knives and a *franciska* typically were buried with the dead. Wealthy women's graves of this period might include rich jewelry, gold rings, and ornamented items with amber, glass, bronze and silver decorative work.[17]

In the evolution of their occupation of Hesse the Franks provided for administration by organizing the land into a system of local districts called *Gaue*. By the eighth century a *Gau* was established in each of these areas: Lahngau, Wetterau, Maingau, Rheingau and the Hessengau, located in lower (northern) Hesse. A *Gau* would include an administrative center where justice was adjudicated. Often this was centered on more ancient locations where folk meetings had taken place. A *Gau* also could have one or more forts to which people could retreat in times of peril. These points became important later as outposts from which Christian evangelizing could take place among the wider population, and trade centers with local or even regional significance.

Within these *Gau* districts settlement patterns were shaped largely by land forms and related natural conditions. Place names seem to some extent to occur in patterns traceable to the quality of the soil. Early settlements with names ending in -ingen (and later -heim), seem to have been founded on the best soils. Somewhat poorer soil quality is found at places ending in -hausen, -dorf, and -weiler. By the latter Frankish period there is more evidence of planning in settlement layout compared to the Alamannic times when everything was arranged to meet the immediate agricultural needs. It appears that most people still lived in hamlets or tiny village groupings in which each individual farmstead had its own little complex of farm structures, generally of the dug-out *Grubenhäuser* type construction. The preferred architecture for dwellings for those who could manage it was clearly the hall house design.

These settlements would have depended on trade with neighboring communities for some goods and for brides. Communities were located from one to three kilometers apart from one another. Grave goods show a standard trade radius of fifteen to twenty kilometers for rural settlements. Bride seeking by gangs of young men is documented, sometimes with violent results. Presumably the more brutal behaviors on these expeditions would have caused ongoing feuds and/or the need for *Wergeld* payments.[18]

From the sixth century, members of the loyal nobility were recognized by the king of Austrasia with grants of land. Grants often were based on the old Roman system of villas, in which the land remained a crown holding but the grant carried with it the right to collect dues from the inhabitants. Originally the noble landholder was considered the social equal of those on his land grant, having only the right to tax them. The villa was the accepted unit for tax purposes quite early, since the king saw merit in maintaining the old Roman tax structure that had worked for centuries. By the late Merovingian period (latter half of the seventh century) change in the social structure was accelerating in the direction of further entrenchment of a select class of nobles. The wider part of society was becoming ever more dependent on their social betters for protection and land. Over time social status relied more and more on royal favor, which was easily lost if one did not provide sufficient support to the king.

ROYAL MANOR FARMS AND FORESTS

After the accession of Charles the Great to the Frankish throne, state-owned manors proliferated across Hesse. These were used both to increase the crown's tax revenues and provide local bases of support for military forces and operations. A manor farm used specifically for military support was called a *curtis*. The expanded fortifications system became all the more important to protect these manors and ensure their continued viability in ongoing campaigns. A manor at the Glauberg was expanded in this period into a larger production unit called a *fisc*. It encompassed the local villages of Rommelhausen, Himbach, Langenbergheim, Eckhartshausen, Vonhausen, and Effolderbach. Local fortified areas were set at Enzheim, Lindheim, and Düdelsheim. This area was typical in its pattern of densely-cultivated lands radiating outward toward less-developed areas further away from the central *curtis*. Some centralized manors such as those at Eschwege and Amöneburg had compact central holdings but a more widely-distributed structure of dependent villages with military curtises on surrounding hills.

Charles the Great also exerted considerable effort in managing his forest resources. Forests were given as fiefs to retainers or to local church foundations. No wood or other materials could be removed from forests without royal permission. Charles' predecessor, Charles Martel, had given out smaller parcels of woods to his nobles for their service. These wooded areas were largely unpopulated through the early period of the rule of Charles the Great: Odenwald, Spessart, Vogelsberg, Westerwald, and the southern Rothaargebirge. Odenwald remained so even by the year 1000. As his campaigns against the Saxons finally brought security to northern Hesse in the early ninth century, he also ordered a vigorous program of forest clearance to promote settlement and productivity.[19]

FRANK AND SAXON CLASH ON THE HESSIAN FRONTIERS[20]

As difficult to conquer as the Alamanni and other tribes were for the Franks, by far their greatest challenge came from their neighbors and bitter enemies to the north, the Saxons. This people had crushed all opposition to its expansion from the northern recesses of Germany until it crashed in the seventh century against land claimed by the Franks and was held in check. The Saxons then settled down to the business of raiding across the borders, sacking churches, stealing cattle, and seizing war captives as slaves. The Franks periodically struck back, giving as good as they received. When a strong Frankish king arose, the Saxons were pushed back and tribute payments were re-imposed. Charles Martel, who seized power in 714 A.D., was one such strong man. He forced on the Saxons renewed respect for Frankish borders, and his son, Pepin, who became king in 741, conducted more campaigns against the Saxons. Over time his treaties wrung tribute as well as access and protection for Christian missionaries working in Saxony. For the most part, however, these wars only aimed to kill Saxons, take booty, and capture slaves in retaliation for earlier attacks. When Pepin died in 768, the Saxons promptly stopped paying their annual tribute of 300 horses.

Now, however, the Frankish king Charles the Great (Charlemagne) came to power. His single-minded determination would lock the two peoples in mortal combat for over thirty ruinous years. From now on the Saxons would have to reckon with ongoing occupations and establishment of Frankish fortresses in their heartland, as well as a determined effort at missionary work. Charles' goal was not just to defeat, but to unify two sovereign peoples into a new nation that would be the undisputed ruler of early Medieval Europe. Little did he know that this goal would take more than a generation to be realized.

It is important to understand the details of how the Franks outfitted their forces and committed them to battle, since conquered areas of the Frankish Empire such as Hesse would have had to provide troops for all these campaigns. Hessians would have joined Bavarians, Franconians, and others providing men and material for Charles' wars. The instrument of Charles' power was the Frankish host, an army called up each spring by the king's summons of all the free male warriors of Frankland. The eastern or Austrasian Franks, including those in Hesse, were the king's mainstay. From at least the time of Charles Martel the army increasingly relied on cavalry, so that the typical freeman was unable to serve effectively unless he were wealthy enough to maintain a war horse and its associated equipment. Great expense was required to acquire and maintain these horse soldiers. Hans Delbrück has determined that one such man required the following equipment, with comparable costs indicated in cattle, the currency of the day:

Helmet	six cows
Coat of mail	twelve cows
Sword and scabbard	seven cows
Leg greaves	six cows
Lance and shield	two cows
Battle steed	twelve cows

Such costs were obviously out of bounds for the average Frankish freeman, who might possess only a few hides of land. The ability to serve effectively in the army became more and more the province of a small, professional class of soldiery drawn from the wealthy nobility. To promote such service Charles decreed that individual Franks should pool their resources so that several of them could afford to outfit one of their number as a mounted warrior.

This equipage was organized by the counts that ruled the local areas at the king's behest. These officials, again drawn from the noble classes, had to maintain local order, administer laws, and ensure each year that they could lead as large a group of warriors from their districts as possible to attend the king's muster. Even the monasteries endowed with sizable numbers of peasant farmers had to outfit men for the campaigns. Huge financial penalties could be levied on those who failed to serve. The army was well outfitted with equipment, the standard soldier having a spear, shield, a bow with twelve arrows, a spare string, and a scramasax, an ancient Germanic heavy short sword similar in shape to a modern machete. Mail coats and conical helmets were common also. Horsemen carried spears with a crosspiece set behind the spearhead to allow the riders to extract them more easily from opponents they had run through. Horsemen also carried round shields, long swords, and scramasaxes. The Franks were renowned for the excellent design of their swords.[21]

Charles gathered his army in the period from March through May each year, with the timing depending on the duration of the campaign and where it would be fought. Charles also revolutionized the support of armies on the move. He directed that enough supplies and provisions be gathered to sustain his troops on long campaigns, and landowners were ordered to replenish the army along its march. Supplies were hauled in wheeled carts, together with cattle on the hoof. Soldiers had to bring along as much as a three-month's supply of food, as well as their own tools. They also brought with them numerous non-combatants and animals to manage and transport the goods, so that the supply train for the army was much larger than the army itself. This saved the local populace from being looted out of house and home along the line of march, which was the typical means of sustenance of ancient armies. Once enemy territory was reached, however, looting and the seizing of booty was permitted. Army battle tactics were most basic; it seems likely that after an initial charge the cavalry dismounted to fight on foot. Organized training was non-existent. Some infantry were brought along to perform functions not suitable for cavalry, such as storming forts. Unlike most commanders of his time, Charles would split his forces to confuse the enemy and throw them off balance. He was well known for the ability to move his men quickly to any point requiring application of military force.[22]

Charles' immediate goal as he surveyed the Saxon situation in 772 was to conduct a campaign so punitive that the Saxons would surrender to him once and for all. He also clearly wanted to pave the way for effective conversion of Saxony by Christian missionaries. It is an interesting insight into the relatively small number of troops needed to conduct major campaigns that Charles probably brought along only 1,000 or so troops on this expedition. Even against this rather modest force, the Saxons fell back rather than risk a pitched battle. In later campaigns it is likely that Charles rarely massed more than 5,000-6,000 fighting men, with about 10,000 being the absolute limit, for more would have required such a huge support train that the army would have been bogged down.

Charles struck quickly from his base on the middle Rhine, reaching the Saxon border near Fritzlar in Hesse, and driving his forces ever onward into the spiritual and cultural heart of Saxony during that hot summer of 772. Everywhere his men sowed destruction, burning settlements as far as the Weser River. They pressed north towards the pagan religious shrine known as Irminsul, an ancient tree associated with the tree of the universe in Teutonic mythology. After three days' occupation the tree and its surrounding grove were utterly destroyed, the votive treasure distributed among the Franks. This done, Charles felt his campaign had met its goal of chastising the Saxons, and he marched his men back to enjoy the annual winter respite from fighting.[23]

Little did he realize, however, that he had handed the Saxons a cause around which to rally as a people. In 773-74 Charles turned his hand to an expedition in Italy, and the Saxons eagerly seized the opportunity for a counter-attack in revenge. They attacked south across Hesse, and northwest into Frisia. Fritzlar was put to the sword, and its important mission church was burned. Settlements in the Eder river valley and Fritzlar areas were looted and destroyed, and all manner of barbarity perpetrated on the hapless people of Hesse. Many of the Hessians in the area of Büraburg retreated into the fort in the face of the onslaught, leaving their modest homes to be burned by the aggressors. The fort was held, however, according to legend thanks to the bones of the saint Wigbert that had been removed there from Fritzlar to protect them from the Saxons' desecration.[24] For the rest of 774, the king had to content himself with limited efforts to drive the enemy back to Saxony since his main army could not be brought to bear before the onset of winter. Both sides settled down to a winter of anticipation of the next year's carnage.

True to his nature, in 775 Charles issued his annual call to his forces for a renewed attack against the invaders. He stormed Saxon strongholds and caused a large number of Saxons from the surrounding districts to appear before him to sue for peace. The memory of their attack the year before still burned in the king's breast, however, and he refused their entreaties. The Franks defeated the Saxon forces in battle and forced many nobles to submit to baptism. A so-called "Saxon March" was created to protect Hesse from further incursions and promote the forced acceptance of Christianity. The goals of the campaign seemingly reached, the Franks settled down to feasting and celebrating. In the fall Charles returned home to release his forces for the season.

In 778 huge numbers of Saxons again flocked to attack again as far as the Rhine, putting most of its right bank to the sword as far south as Coblenz. Churches and monasteries again were targeted. Fulda had to be evacuated, its monks carrying away the sacred remains of St. Boniface to prevent their destruction. The Austrasian Franks, reinforced by some Alamanni, rallied to strike the invaders as they marched homeward with the spoils of their attacks. This battle took place at Battenfeld, some twenty miles northwest of Marburg. The Saxons were soundly defeated with the loss of their booty. The next year Charles again fell upon Saxony with his army, smashing every Saxon force that faced him. He demanded many captives, most of whom were committed to monasteries for training as future missionaries. Baptisms at sword-point were numerous. For Saxons, refusal of baptism was made grounds for the death penalty, as were cremation of the dead, eating meat during lent, vandalism of churches, burning of witches, observing heathen religious customs, and other similar practices, including that of *Wergeld*.

As the harshness of these measures set in, another revolt flared in 782. The Saxons succeeded in encircling a Frankish army in the Süntel Mountains and virtually annihilating it. Charles' fury knew no bounds. At his order, supporters of the rebellion were delivered up to the Franks. Bound and helpless as cattle led to slaughter, the king ordered 4,500 to be beheaded in one day. Again the king had miscalculated, however. His act of barbarism galvanized Saxony as nothing had done since the destruction of the Irminsul in 772. When he massed his largest army ever to attack Saxony in the campaign season of 783, the combined Saxon host could not wait to strike back at him, catching his army on the march near Detmold. The two armies hacked and slashed at one another for an extended period, with many casualties but no clear winner on either side. Eventually, in a large battle near Osnabrück the tactically outmatched Saxons were soundly defeated after a tough fight. They never again offered large-scale battle. By 785 both sides were worn down with the struggle and the Saxons again sued for peace.

It was in this period that Frankish source records first referenced the *Hessengau* as a unified political and administrative district. Records of 782 in Fritzlar also first record the names of three royal administrators or deputies in the region: Rabano, Swigar, and Agilgaud.[25]

In the watershed year of 793 another desperate insurrection broke out. As usual, attacks occurred on churches and monasteries, for these remained the most vulnerable and visible symbols of foreign domination. The Franks responded by torching everything in their path across the face of Saxony. Charles compelled huge numbers of the rebellious to be deported to areas throughout Frankland from which they could no longer mount resistance. This was decisive, and by 797 Charles at last had achieved much of what he had embarked upon in his 25-year effort at conquest.

Let us turn now to a description of how common people lived and worked in these times. The large class of dependent peasantry was living in serfdom on large or small noble estates. Many of the latter were fairly small-scale. Lands seized in war were incorporated in the royal estates or donated to support monasteries, and in these cases the peasants were conveyed with the land. This obviously increased the numbers of permanently dependent peasants. Slavery continued throughout the period, although Christian-inspired opposition confined it mainly to some war captives and the offspring of current slaves.[26]

The economy during the rule of Charles and his successors was dependent on agriculture; trade in other goods played a minor role. Peasants worked their farms and provided whatever level of service and rent was due to the overlords and the king based on the level of freedom (and thus social standing) they enjoyed. Larger estates were managed by a steward, and individual peasants paid rents set in terms of crops, animals or other products. Over and above these amounts they could retain production for their own use or sale. In addition, they owed a certain number of service days per week or month for road, fort, or bridge building, plowing, reaping or other farm work on the royal domain lands, cutting and hauling wood, etc. A detailed description of the life of a peasant named Bodo has been developed from basic records compiled on an estate during the time of Charles the Great. Bodo's life provides rich details of how peasants eked out their existence in this era, and it is worthwhile dwelling on it in some depth.

Bodo lived on an estate just outside Paris with his wife Ermentrude, sons Wido and Gerbert, and a baby daughter, Hildegard. This particular estate belonged to a monastery, but it was managed much as any other estate owned by a large landholder or the king himself. It was administered by a steward, who organized the work of the peasants who owing services on the estate lands; the steward received their rental payments in produce when these were due. Because the serfs directly attached to the monastic lands were too few to provide all the labor needed, much of the land was subdivided into small plots rented and worked by one or two families. These would include farm land and meadow land for pasturing animals. Wives of the serfs also had to provide service by making a certain amount of cloth or a particular garment each year. The steward would oversee women's work as well, making sure the cloth was of the proper quality and quantity, etc.

Bodo would rise early to head off to work under the watchful eye of the steward, and may have regularly plied the overseer with eggs or other produce as a bribe to secure his favor. His ox would be used in the work, together with his son Wido to apply a goad as needed to the big animal. He would join a work group of other peasants, some with work animals, others equipped only with a hoe, scythe, spade, etc., depending on the task for the day. Metal tools were scarce, with wooden hoes, plows, etc. predominating. (One estate with some 200 cattle had only six metal tools: two scythes, two spades, and two sickles.) This made the work difficult and productivity low. Yields of three bushels for every two planted were common. Hunger in a bad harvest year was always a major threat. Bodo and Wido would plow all day, stopping to eat lunch at midday with their fellow workmen, perhaps singing heartily to cheer themselves in their hard and tedious work.

Ermentrude on the same day is seen as leaving her daughter in care of her nine-year-old second son so she can deliver a hen and five eggs as part of the rent. While at the manor house she stops in to gossip briefly with other women who are busy spinning, sewing and dyeing cloth. Their work was supported by providing them with wool, linen, woad, and any tools needed for the production process. Ermentrude soon hurries home to work in the garden, feed the children, tend poultry and/or weave for her own family's needs. She would also be versed in skills such as sheep-shearing. Bodo would come home to eat supper, and all would retire with the setting sun, for their few candles would not go far given much use. Both Bodo and his wife would need to rise early the next day, too.

Although Christian, Bodo's family believed in and relied on many old beliefs and superstitions. Charms would be chanted to make fields fertile, cure sick animals, or convince spirits to do good or avoid harm. The church tried at least to insert Christian concepts and characters into these rites in place of heathen gods, but otherwise had little effect on stamping out their use. Pain was believed to come from a worm burrowing inside the flesh, and the cure called for placing a knife or other metal against the hurt and call for the worm to come out by reciting, "Come out, worm, with nine little worms, out from the marrow into the bone, from the bone into the flesh, from the flesh into the skin, from the skin into this knife, so be it Lord." The latter phrase was added in deference to church teachings. The local priest would ask the peasant whether he had, "consulted magicians and enchanters, made vows to trees and fountains, drunk any magic philter?" The many who had to confess that they had done so were given suitable penance to do as acts of contrition. The church also made possible the Sundays and saints' days holidays from work which the laboring peasants could look forward to. They used the opportunity for feasting, dancing and singing in the churchyard after service, employing their beloved folk songs that most often derived again from pagan sources and tales. This was done much to the chagrin of the churchmen.[27]

Bodo could count on some time off to attend periodic district meetings, particularly if he had been aggrieved by anyone and needed to seek a formal legal judgment against them. He and his family also might take time to attend occasional market fairs where special items could be had by barter or sale, or the opportunity could be taken to gawk at unusual wares and people. Minstrels singing songs of old, lauding the exploits of heroes and times past would add to the fun, as (most likely) would some fermented beverages. Then it would be time to gather the family and get home for another early bed-time. Although a western Frankish peasant, Bodo can serve aptly as an example of the life and thought existing in Hesse in these times. If anything, the Hessians likely were more confirmed in their paganism and superstition.

Besides the expanding peasantry and the nobility, a third key group made up the social order in the time of Charles the Great: the clergy. The churchmen filled an extremely important role in Frankish society, and in the following chapter we will turn to a focused look at their early history in Hesse.

NOTES TO CHAPTER 2

[1] Malcolm Todd, *Everyday Life of the Barbarians, Goths, Franks and Vandals*, Putnam's Sons, NY, 1972, pp. 105-122; Malcolm Todd, *The Early Germans*, Blackwell, Cambridge, MA, 1992, pp. 42-43, 71; Alfons Dopsch, *The Economic and Social Foundations of European Civilization*, Howard Fertig, New York, 1969 reprint, p. 284.

[2] Dopsch, pp. 113, 134; Herwig Wolfram, *The Roman Empire and its Germanic Peoples*, U. of California Press, Berkeley, 1997, pp. 47-50; M.M. Postan, *The Agrarian Life of the Middle Ages*, Cambridge Economic History of Europe, Vol. I, Cambridge University Press, 1966, p. 32; Todd, *Early Germans*, p. 210; Ian Wood, Editor, *Franks and Alamanni in the Merovingian Period, an Ethnographic Perspective*, Boydell Press, Woodbridge, 1998, p. 74.

[3] Wood, pp. 14-16; Dopsch, pp. 182-86; ; Todd, *Early Germans*, p. 207.

[4] Todd, *Everyday Life*, pp. 74-81, 89-93, 157, 169, 174; Wood, p. 66-68.

[5] Francis Owen, *The Germanic People*, Barnes & Noble, 1993 (first published 1960), p. 179; Wood, pp. 177-79; Todd, *Everyday Life*, pp. 127-34, 151.

[6] Todd, *Everyday Life*, pp. 56-59; Postan, pp. 36-37; Wood, p. 54.

[7] Wood, pp. 33-37, 43-44, 45-51, 55.

[8] Wood, pp. 57-60, 182.

[9] Dopsch, pp. 347-48, 349-52, 389.

[10] Wolfram, pp. 62-66; Todd, *Everyday Life*, p. 77; Karl E. Demandt, *Geschichte des Landes Hessen*, Bärenreiter-Verlag, Kassel, 1972, pp. 99-100.

[11] James W. Thompson, *History of the Middle Ages 300-1500*, Norton & Co., New York, 1931, p. 117-18.

[12] Wood, pp. 10, 16-17, 33; Todd, *Early Germans*, p. 208; Demandt, p. 101.

[13] Postan, 34-35, 39-40; Wood, p. 61; Dopsch, pp. 204, 212-18, 237; Todd, *Everyday Life*, p. 30-32.

[14] Friedrich Heer, *Charlemagne and his World*, Macmillan Publishing Co., New York, 1975, p. 13; previous section also drawn from Wood, pp. 11-13; Todd, *Everyday Life*, p. 22; Dopsch, p. 105; Todd, *Early Germans*, pp. 192-197.

[15] Todd, *Everyday Life*, p. 112.

[16] Todd, *Early Germans*, pp. 199-201; Wood, pp. 62-65, 180-82.

[17] Demandt, pp. 28-29, 31, 102-03, 106-09; Todd, *Early Germans*, p. 208; Dopsch, p. 110.

[18] Wood, pp. 74-77, 147, 182-83; Demandt, p. 116; Dopsch, pp. 315, 326.

[19] Wood, pp. 62, 149-50, 158; Demandt, pp. 110-11, 112-13; Postan, p. 46.

[20] This final section draws heavily on material in Dan C. Heinemeier, *A History of Brunswick*, Heinemeier Publications, Arlington, VA, 1999, pp. 32-42.

[21] Heer, pp. 85-91; Hans Delbrück, *Medieval Warfare*, Vol. III in *History of the Art of War*, Walter J. Renfroe, Jr., translator, University of Nebraska Press, Lincoln and London, 1990, pp. 28-29. This work also provides conclusive comments on the Frankish reliance on cavalry, suggesting that soldiers without horses counted for little in the order of battle. He provides equally useful information on the individual soldier's equipment, p. 30.

[22] Heer, pp. 91-93; Delbrück discusses logistics, training and the lack of tactics on pp. 21-22 and 30.

[23] Heer, pp. 119-26; James Westfall Thompson, *The Middle Ages*, 2nd Edition, Cooper Square Publishers, New York, pp. 249-50; C.W. Previt-Orton, *The Shorter Cambridge Medieval History*, Vol. I, 1952, p. 306; Delbrück talks about likely numbers of troops employed in Charles' campaigns, p. 22.

[24] Wand, Norbert, *Die Büraburg bei Fritzlar*, N.G. Elwert Verlag, Marburg, 1974, pp. 28-29.

[25] Wand, p. 32.

[26] Heer, pp. 41-47; James Westfall Thompson, *Feudal Germany*, University of Chicago Press, 1927, pp. 172-73; Dopsch, p. 126.

[27] Heer, pp. 63-64; Eileen Power, *Medieval People*, Doubleday Anchor Books, Garden City, NY, 1955, pp. 17-21. The Old High German pain charm, the priest's interrogatory, and the church and holiday observances are cited on pp. 27-28.

CHAPTER 3

Christianity Comes to Hesse

A most significant development for any society as the ancient Roman era gave way to the early Middle Ages was the advent of Christianity. This had critical social and political as well as religious consequences for commoners and nobles alike. In the ancient imperial period about the year 312 Christianity finally triumphed during the reign of the emperor Constantine; it rapidly made the transition from a rejected and persecuted sub-sect of Judaism to become the dominant religious form of the empire. Despite the intrinsic Christian emphasis on evangelism, for centuries most Roman citizens considered the faith to be theirs alone. It rarely if ever occurred to church officials to actually proselytize among the ignorant barbarians at the fringes of the empire.

Still, as early as the fourth century there appear to have been Christian communities established in Roman areas east of the Rhine. The faith spread by a phenomenon that Fletcher has called "seepage": the unorganized, but locally effective evangelizing done by Roman traders, laborers, slaves, mercenaries, those who intermarried with the heathen, and a host of other economic and social contacts. The earliest Roman adherents were mostly not of the ruling classes, since the latter would have had much to lose from professing a persecuted religion. Thus, early Christians would have been on a comparable social level to many of the emigrating Germans who entered the empire as slaves and dependent laborers. Peoples like the Franks and Alamanni were only converted on a large scale when groups of them settled within Roman boundaries. Organized communities of believers most often grew up in the larger towns, but rural areas also contained Christians. Evidence of this has been found in excavations in Hesse in the Taunus range, at Saalburg and in Wiesbaden. The important Roman administrative center in Mainz had a sizable Christian community in the mid-fourth century.[1]

What happened next is hinted at by the silence of historical records concerning the fate of Christians at the time of the collapse of Roman authority during the fifth century. Much of the organized practice of the faith seems to have died away as the heathen Franks and Alamanni captured towns such as Trier and Mainz. Christian communities did not die out entirely, but they shrank within the now-circumscribed enclaves of walled towns or other protected areas where the dominant pagan culture could be held somewhat at bay. Gravestones and grave goods are almost our only record of Christian practices in southern and western Hesse in the chaotic fourth, fifth and early sixth centuries. By the first quarter of the sixth century church officials in Gaul sought to reintroduce Christianity and reconnect with remaining pockets of the faithful in some former centers of church organization such as Trier. The evidence of their broader success in bringing a sense of strong, personal faith to the nominally Christian Frankish rulers of these areas is all but impossible to find. More important was the increasing pressure of Frankish kings who sought to impose the outward signs of piety on their noble retainers, many of whom were still being buried in the sixth century with grave goods that would have done any heathen chieftain of the fourth century proud. Even in this period, the re-Christianization effort does not appear to have re-crossed the Rhine.² This period of Frankish stewardship over church matters in eastern Frankland (including Hesse) must have been characterized by a spectrum of observances among the nobility and commoners. The adherents of Christ and Woden probably sought to capture the minds and hearts of their fellow Hessians in an uneasy competition, in which the outward trappings of Christianity mostly predominated in the larger towns and unabashed paganism ruled the hinterlands. By the early seventh century Christian inroads also were being made by nobles who began to erect churches in the communities in which they ruled.³ These noble foundations were likely established for the benefit of the founders, their extended families, and fellow members of the nobility, however. Regular attendance at services by the semi-civilized rural peasants would have been offensive and probably even disruptive of the proceedings.

There are some indications that the seventh century saw increased missionary activity in some of the old Roman areas in the Wetterau and Vogelsberg, bounded in the east at the more dense woodlands of the Odenwald, and extending north to the Lahn valley. This area seems to have been the particular province of the Mainz bishopric (re-established by the mid-sixth century). Christian missionary work in the Lahn area, at Amöneburg, and as far east as Marburg and Gießen historically was undertaken by the much older Trier bishopric. Trier had expanded earlier because its mission work accompanied the military and civilian settlement of the right bank of the Rhine by the Christian Franks. For centuries it was the advent of Frankish military protection that was the necessary precursor to effective missionary work across Hesse. Trier could reach out into the Lahn River area at a time when the heathen Alamanni still effectively controlled the Wetterau.

The old heathen religions were always a force to be reckoned with; sometimes, partial accommodation was seen as superior to frontal attacks on sites that had been sacred to the old gods from time immemorial. Pope Gregory the Great wrote to an English-born abbot in 601 directing him to convert old heathen temples to Christian churches, destroying only graven images and other outward signs of pagan practices. Altars and saintly relics could then be introduced to complete the conversion. In this way churches were erected in the Vogelsberg and Odenwald areas at the site of springs that for centuries had been dedicated to the ancient gods.

The seventh century also saw an interesting phenomenon in the missionary sphere as itinerant Irish- and Scottish-born monks, and later Anglo-Saxons, entered Hesse to spread the Gospel in places like Büraburg and Hersfeld. They also were active in the Wetterau district, at Lich, Wieseck, Rodheim, Schotten, Sternbach, Bauernheim and Hornufa. These old *limes* areas were more easily converted than the places untouched by Roman influence; here religious cults of all kinds had worn away strict allegiance to Woden and Thor since ancient times, softening up the population for introduction of the new Christian cult.⁴

It would only be in the early eighth century that a powerful religious figure would emerge to begin the task of more systematically rooting out pagan beliefs in Hessian lands that had retained unbroken allegiance to the Teutonic gods since before Roman times. That man was known as Boniface, and later, St. Boniface.

Boniface was born about the year 680 in Wessex, England, and baptized with the name Wynfrith. After his monastery training he determined to follow the path of many of his Anglo-Saxon contemporaries and work to convert the heathen cousins of the English still living in northern Germany. He embarked on an evangelizing mission to Frisia in 716. Here he encountered much opposition, apparently due to bad timing: at this point the Frisians were in revolt against their Frankish masters who otherwise would have protected Wynfrith and assisted him in his mission. He next set out for Rome to request the blessing of the pope in undertaking his work in Germany. Pope Gregory II extended this permission, and christened him with the Latin name Boniface. He now returned to Frisia, working there for several years before traveling back to Rome to be appointed bishop by the pope. His travels through Hesse apparently helped convince him that it would be a fruitful area in which to practice his mission work. Hesse would occupy him for years to come.

Boniface embarked in early 721 on mission work in Hesse at the fortified stronghold of Amöneburg, then the seat of power of twin brothers whose commitment to the letter of the Christian laws was rather questionable. Named Dettic and Deorulf, these two chieftains seem to have mixed some pagan sacrifices in with their nominally Christian worship practices. He appears to have reformed the wayward brothers, baptized many new Christians, and drawn many others into stricter adherence to Christian practices. To further buttress his successes he also established a Benedictine monastic community in this place. As a well-settled crossroads of middle Hesse obviously still in need of evangelizing, the Amöneburg area was well suited as a jumping-off point for Boniface's Hessian crusade.

Probably in the spring of 722 Boniface struck out for the fringes of society on the Frankish border where the true adherents of the old faith still lived in great numbers. This was the land of the lower Eder River around the Fritzlar area. Here he found success with mass baptisms, but the vast majority of the population was still stalwart in their heathen ways. This partial success, in which the leadership of the established Frankish Christian church lent no support, seems to have convinced Boniface of the need to return to Rome to obtain better credentials and authority from the pope. In late 722 he arrived in Rome, and was made a full bishop by the pope on November 30. He was empowered to conduct missionary work anywhere east of the Rhine in Germany, and without an established seat such as Mainz or Trier. Returning to Hesse the following year, he made it his business to seek the assistance of the highest authority in the land in the next phase of his mission. Armed with letters of commendation from the pope, he was able to secure support from the king of the Franks, Charles Martel. This in turn opened the door for him to enter royal forts or residences in Hesse and obtain the support of local authorities for his missionary work. Such a place was the fort known as Büraburg, an outpost of Frankish military power securing the border against the Saxon threat. The presence of Charles Martel's men provided him with the military protection necessary to undertake bold moves against the local pagan religious sites and practices.

Now he undertook his most famous action, one that would demonstrate his determination and begin to secure his fame as a missionary: he confronted the local heathens at their most sacred shrine, the so-called Donar (Thor) Oak. This great and ancient tree had stood for many generations as the focal point for local observances of pagan worship. Boniface proved the superiority of his own religion by personally cutting down the oak as its worshippers looked on. Legend has it that he was assisted by a great wind that came up and broke a section from the top of the tree, further demonstrating his triumph over the old gods. In any case, many baptisms and significant inroads for Christianity apparently followed. The wood of the old oak itself was used to build a chapel at Fritzlar in 724, later expanded into a significant monastery in its own right. About 725 a similar foundation followed at Ohrdruf in Thuringia. With the death of the pope in 731 Pope Gregory was appointed in Rome, Boniface headed back to Italy to re-confirm his standing with the new pope. Gregory now raised the missionary to archbishop, with the power to appoint local bishops who could administer the gains he was making for the church. With numerous disciples now attending to the missionary work, Boniface turned his hand to strengthening the administration of his growing diocese and building for the future. At this time his old wooden oratory at Amöneburg was rebuilt and expanded as a stone church dedicated to the archangel Michael, and the Fritzlar chapel was converted to stone as a newly-dedicated church of St. Peter.

This period also was one of great frustration for Boniface, for his local successes had sparked the jealousy and animosity of the Frankish church hierarchy, including Bishop Gerold of Mainz. The Frankish church operated with considerable independence from its nominal masters in Rome, with local churches founded and controlled by the Frankish nobility from whose ranks were drawn bishops and other church officials. However supportive Charles Martel was of Boniface's efforts in the field, he would do nothing to antagonize the state churchmen by favoring the English missionary in his efforts to promote reforms of the church. Boniface must have threatened the power and influence of the local church to a large degree. Not without success, Gerold and his forebears themselves also had worked to evangelize many of the areas in which Boniface now was active. They resented the interloper who clearly held their authority, works and piety in low regard.

The death of Charles Martel in the fall of 741 finally altered the political equation decisively in favor of Boniface. Charles' sons inherited and divided the kingdom between them, with Carlomann taking control in Hesse and the rest of Austrasia. Himself the product of monastic training, the new king determined to support Boniface in reforming the state church and reigning in the independent, noble-sponsored churches across the land. The archbishop now embarked on a crusade to reorganize and recommit the Frankish church to Roman papal authority and to the true tenets of the faith. He created new bishoprics under the control of his chosen followers, installing the Anglo-Saxon Witta as bishop of Büraburg in 742. Büraburg likely included a sizable part of Hesse within its jurisdiction, including the Ittergau, Wetterau, and the upper Lahn River. Boniface's little mission bishoprics were an unusual phenomenon: historically, only much more sizable towns in well-settled and politically solid areas would have been so designated. The Büraburg bishopric was in fact disbanded shortly after 745 when Boniface was appointed to the role he so long had sought: Archbishop of Mainz. Now he could directly administer his far-flung missions from a major, recognized seat of Christian authority.[5]

Boniface acted as a representative of papal authority when he was directed by Pope Zacharias to anoint Carlomann's brother Pepin the sole king of the Franks in 750. This was after Carlomann had decided to retire to a monastery, and Pepin had sought the pope's advice about whether to assume the throne directly from the terminally weak line of Merovingians. With papal support he thus founded the Carolingian line whose most famous descendant would be his son and heir, Charles the Great. Boniface's role in this matter both reflected and reinforced his long-standing political connections to the ruling line that had brought him so much success in Hesse.

In 744 Boniface presided over the creation of perhaps his most lasting legacy to the church: the monastery at Fulda. Legend has it that he sent out a Bavarian disciple, Sturmi, with several companions to search for an appropriate place on the frontier to found a monastic house. Their brave and torturous journey through the wilderness by way of Hersfeld is chronicled by Sturmi's biographer, but in fact it appears that the Fulda location already boasted an expansive dwelling-lodge belonging to the king, as well as surrounding manor lands. Boniface readily endorsed Sturmi's recommendation of the location, and soon secured the royal blessing to erect his planned monastery. Sturmi oversaw and may have participated in the initial construction, and was appointed the first abbot of this Benedictine foundation. The king and many other nobles made additional gifts of land and wealth in the eighth century, so that in short order the monastery became both viable and much renowned. Boniface himself was buried here in 754 after he died a martyr's death at the hands of hostile pagans in Frisia.

In later years Fulda was recognized throughout the Christian world for its bible exegesis, and became the leading educational institution of its kind for much of Germany. Sturmi died an old man in 779, due in large part to the insistence of Charles the Great that he personally go into the field and do mission work among the heathen Saxons. At this point there were some 360 monks in residence at Fulda, and a significant part of their evangelizing was and had been directed at the Franks' Saxon enemies. This irritant doubtless contributed to the Saxons' frequent attacks on churches and monasteries across Hesse. Around 752 Saxon marauders burned over thirty such structures, probably mostly in Hesse.[6]

Ultimately, the works of Boniface may be seen as necessary but not sufficient in winning Hesse for the Christian faith. But subsequent Christian evangelists and Frankish leaders (for religion in this era was truly politics by other means) would build upon the groundwork he laid. Succeeding centuries—and it was the work of centuries—would see an ever-broadening network of Christian foundations and successful outreach to people at all levels. The ancient Germanic gods of the Hessians now would be forever in retreat.

The other towering figure in the Christian history of Hesse in the early Middle Ages was Charles the Great. Unlike his father and grandfather, Charles seems to have faithfully sought to serve the cause of reform and expansion of the faith as a personal mission. He was clearly over-zealous in his cause: he hounded the old abbot Sturmi literally to his death, and required the swordpoint-conversions of thousands of heathen Saxons. But these excesses were merely the imperfect expressions of a personal commitment to the faith that was never doubted by those of his day. His long reign began in 771.

Charles addressed a host of structural problems in the church that he saw as impeding its ability to function and minister to the laity. The rank and file clergy were notoriously lacking in formal education. Illiterate priests could barely conduct mass in the Latin tongue that they themselves understood poorly or not at all. Formal education consisted of being taken into a bishop's extended family as a youth, and the education so obtained could be spotty at best given the busy nature of the bishop's life. Gifted clerics who emerged from such training were seldom sent to parishes, but were used to support the bishop's own administrative apparatus. Many villages had no church or priest to serve their needs. Compounding these problems was the practice of nobles who appointed their own parish priests, mostly to maintain control of parish tithes. Often these appointees were barely-literate peasants who could impart little in the way of Christian values to the laity.

Charles stepped in to enact rules requiring specific courses of study and training in monasteries, including the ancient classics. He recruited teaching scholars from across his realm and beyond to improve the level of instruction. Among his requirements for learning by the clergy were the Lord's Prayer, the Creed, psalms, exorcism, the church calendar, biblical texts, musical liturgy, and the ability to read and understand the gospels. Although sermons had to be done in the local language, Latin was required for other liturgy because it was felt to be a deterrent to heresy that could arise if too much of the service could be understood and interpreted by lay people. Many monasteries had by now allowed their original organizing principles, the Rule of Benedict, to lapse, many monks were living downright dissolute lives. Hunting, war fighting, fornication and debauched revelry were common. Charles sent to Italy for a pure form of the original canons, and imposed them on the cloisters. Friedrich Heer has summed up the Carolingian efforts to promote education in this way:

> This concern for the parish reveals that the direction of the Carolingian renaissance was towards ordinary people, for whom the parish priest was the main contact with Christian life....[B]ishops were reminded that preaching was essential if the Christian people were to understand the gospels, and were commanded, if there was a shortage of parish priests, to send the cathedral clergy out into the countryside to preach....[A] rural clergy capable of preaching intelligently and intelligibly was the ultimate aim of Charlemagne's efforts in education.[7]

Charles reorganized the parish structure by requiring that all priests, even those privately appointed, must be under the authority of their local bishops. He recognized anew the system of parish tithes promoted by his father to support the needs of the local clergy and poor as well as the bishops. He similarly encouraged the creation and repair of churches throughout his realm.

In efforts to improve religious practices generally, he enacted laws detailing what was expected of priests and laity. He specified the determination of holiday schedules, sermon content, and the like. Because the laity was so little touched on a regular basis by effective preaching and teaching, much backsliding and superstition had crept into the faith. Adherents of belief in Thor and Oden simply added a Christian veneer to their belief systems rather than reject the old familiar gods out-of-hand. Other superstitious beliefs are reflected in a capitulary of 742 by Charles' uncle, Carlomann: banned are profane offerings for the dead, fortune telling by casting lots, pagan sayings, sacrifices intended to bring about favorable events, etc. Charles virtually reenacted the capitulary in 789, with more prohibitions reflecting the long-standing nature of these problems. At this time he also banned weather incantations, pagan dancing, and "leaping and singing by women" at religious festivals.[8]

The practice of Christian baptism had evolved by this time from the original adult-oriented ritual tied up with profession of faith that dated to the founders of Christianity, to the more modern process of baptizing infants. In adult baptism, such as that practiced by Boniface in the newly-converted parts of Hesse, it seems from available evidence that the new Christians were required to cite their old gods individually by name and renounce them as part of the baptism process. This process must have seemed part exorcism, part surrender to Christ in His personal vanquishing of Thor and Oden. The liturgy had to be delivered in Latin for it to be valid, so it required a reasonable level of education by the priesthood. For infants, godparents were appointed to undertake the necessary vows on their behalf, although the notion of sponsorship of adults also is known as when a Christian king sponsored and supported the conversion of a heathen counterpart in baptism. Given the concern that too few educated clergymen were available to perform the rites satisfactorily, and that infants obviously could not act on their own volition, the church developed the concept of confirmation, in which a bishop would confirm the faith of the believer later in life.[9]

Taken as a whole, by the latter stages of his reign in the early ninth century, Charles the Great had enacted a significant body of laws aimed at creating a Christian society: a body of faithful citizenry acting on the basis of shared Christian morality. His successors—sons and grandsons—tried with varying degrees of effort and success to maintain and expand this work. Given the crude, impoverished and cruel times in which the average Frank lived, this was a goal that could never completely be realized. But it is a remarkable reflection on the Frankish leadership that the effort was maintained over so long a period.[10]

After Charles the Great, a period of slow but steady deterioration of central authority occurred, and with it the emphasis on creating a Christian society lapsed. The landed nobility exploited the church, seizing or appropriating many of its properties. Bishops exerted increasing influence at local levels at the expense of the Roman See. Latourette, however, is of the view that the seeds of future strength and success for the church somehow had been planted in the Carolingian age. Later, these would grow into a strong and pervasive force in the lives of people in the Middle Ages.

> [A]s a result of what had been achieved between the year 500 and the year 950, in the centuries which immediately followed the latter date, was more nearly molded by the Gospel than it had been before the disintegration of the Roman Empire and the great invasions. This was seen in almost every phase of its life. It was also apparent in individual after individual. Even when the majority fell so far short of Christian ideals that they seemed not to deserve the Christian name, they recognized and honored those rare men and women who unmistakably displayed the fruits of the spirit. These they called saints, cults arose in their honor, their physical relics were venerated, and they were regarded as worthy of emulation by all Christians.[11]

CHRISTIANITY IN THE POST-CAROLINGIAN AGE[12]

After a century of marked decline, after 950 Christianity was again resurgent. In the early Middle Ages St. Benedict had devised a set of rules under which pious men could live and work together as a community devoted to the worship of God free from most secular constraints. His monastic foundations were self-contained communities, supporting themselves through labor in field and workshop, with monks' lives organized round-the-clock to avoid the evils of idleness. The day was to include eight religious services, punctuated by periods of work, eating and rest. Work could be in libraries or fields depending on the skills of the monk. A new brother could join the community after a one-year trial period. All his worldly wealth had to be surrendered to the monastery or the poor. Silence was deemed a good thing, while joking and contact with the outside world were frowned upon. This Benedictine Rule became the standard for monastic foundations across Europe. Generally, it was adhered to best in the early years. Monasteries tended to lose their dynamism and strength of purpose over time. As the foundations amassed wealth by selling their surplus crop production and by donations and endowments from the pious nobility, adherence to the rules of poverty and separation from the secular world fell by the wayside.

Beginning in the tenth century and continuing into the fourteenth, various monastic orders arose to combat the evils into which the broad class of monasteries had fallen. They achieved renown by reinstitution of important elements of the old Benedictine Rule, often embroidering on it new practices that added strength to their orders. The first among these in prominence originated at the monastery of Cluny in 910. It became a center of monastic reform under whose direction many established houses were cleansed and new ones created. The Cluniacs stressed the original Benedictine approach, but devoted much more time to worship. This was accomplished by managing their field holdings through serfs just like their counterparts in the secular nobility. The more progressive popes encouraged the Cluny reformers; local lords also invited them in to clean up the abuses in many long-established houses. Efforts also were made to achieve freedom for monasteries from inappropriate interference and control by the local authorities who too often diverted their wealth to secular purposes. This freed the brothers to spend more time working to promote the faith among the common people in their communities.

This work was sorely needed, since commoners still tended to resent the parish tithes and often were known to uphold many of the heathen beliefs and practices of their forebears, whether through ignorance or indifference about the finer points of the faith. It would take more centuries for anything like a concerted effort to be undertaken to improve the religious understanding of the masses.

Of course, not all church figures were avaricious and corrupt. Some bishops provided well for the moral and even economic climate in their dioceses, championing agricultural reform, literary and artistic pursuits, and otherwise improving the lives of their flocks. They built cathedrals and fortresses to protect the parishioners. Monks cleared land, pioneered new agricultural methods, built churches, and brought religious training to people on the outskirts of civilization. The German emperor Henry II was a committed reformer who pushed the clergy to institute reforms and generously supported them. Henry III sought to promote the Cluny reforms throughout his empire and called for a day of indulgence in which he forgave his enemies and urged his subjects to do likewise. Many monasteries were cleansed, clergy were made to return to celibacy, and other reforms were spawned. Despite these positive influences, the collective weight of immorality and corruption of the church organization weighed it down and over time cost it both credibility and much of its ability to exert positive influence on society. Most organized religious activity seems to have been directed inward to the care and maintenance of the church's structure and the clerics themselves. As the decades passed, even Cluny lost its moral force and compass as its ever-more-worldly adherents fell prey to the temptations of wealth and secular influence.

A new generation of reformers rose to the occasion to try again to improve the church. The Cistercian order, begun in 1098 at Citeaux. The Cistercians reemphasized the Benedictine ideal with revisions providing for strict poverty, unadorned church buildings and plain accouterments of worship, establishment of houses in remote locations, and less time spent in worship so that more could be devoted to individual prayer. All the churches of this order were dedicated to the Virgin Mary. The Cistercians used lay brothers or the monks themselves to accomplish the land clearance and building in waste areas that were their preferred sites on which to build. No serfs or servants were maintained. Finally, more extensive provisions were made for communal management of the monasteries of the order, with the Citeaux headquarters both overseeing and regularly being overseen by its daughter foundations. Some twenty years later a similar order came into being known as the Premonstratensians, who used the

Cistercian Rule but emphasized preaching to the faithful around the world as their major mission.

As with the Cluniacs, the latter orders were called in to cleanse the old and establish new cloisters. Their influence in Hesse was seen in the establishment of Cistercian monasteries at Arnsburg and Haina. The Cistercians were renowned for producing orderly and fertile farmlands from rocky, forested, and marshy areas in remote locations. These manor-like monasteries established extensive outlying estates controlled by the monks at these two central locations. Arnsburg's dependencies were in Amöneburg, Bergen-Enkheim, Frankfurt, Friedberg, Gelnhausen, Gießen, Grünberg, Mainz, Marburg, Wetzlar, and Wickstadt. Haina boasted fifteen rural farms at Altenhaina, Espe, Halgehausen, Ellnrode, Elgershausen, Singlis, Hoflotheim, Ransbach, Gontershausen, Wallersdorf, Hubel, Utphe, Roth, Bergen, and Riederhof near Frankfurt. It had dependent properties in Fritzlar, Niederwildungen, Frankenberg, Treysa, Wetter, Marburg Amöneburg, Alsfeld, Gelnhausen and Frankfurt.

Most impressive was the Cistercian monastery at Eberbach. It had twenty-three manors with more than 300 *Morgen* of land each, for a total holding of over 17,000 *Morgen*. These included Mappe, Erfelden, Flörsheim, Breidenfaß, Hanheim, Weiterstadt, Ginsheim, Mosbach, Draise, Schierstein, Steinheim, Leheim, Neuhof, Weilbach, Gehaborn, Riedhäuser, Haina, Dienheim, Walheim, Frankenfeld, Sandhof, Bensheim, and Birke. Other possessions were scattered across seven separate syndicates including areas as far-flung as Bingen, Mainz, Frankfurt, and Limberg. A renowned manor in Köln was famous for its wine production. The monastery even owned its own boats on the Rhine with which its goods could be transported. The monks in these foundations contributed much knowledge toward improved cultivation of the lands around them. Along with these cloisters created in the thirteenth century, many Cistercian nunneries also were established, but none achieved particular renown. Cistercian cloisters were centers of art and science as well as agricultural innovation. The Augustinians founded numerous monasteries in Hesse in the twelfth and thirteenth centuries, but these apparently also were of little renown.[13]

By the thirteenth century an ominous breach existed between the church and its parishioners. Quite apart from poor adherence to its vows of chastity and other moral lapses, probably the greatest offense in the eyes of the populace was the clergy's avarice. This was evidenced in the tithes demanded of everyone with no visible resulting benefit to meeting any of the spiritual needs of the church. It was seen in the feudal structure of church-controlled manors, which differed little in practice from those of the nobility. Both placed comparable demands on the peasantry for financial and personal contributions to their lords. All this wealth was channeled upward to the church hierarchy or outward to absentee officials, while the task of ministering to the parishes all too often fell to poorly-paid, under-educated and otherwise unqualified local pastors. Religion stressed guilt and punishment, the overriding need to obtain atonement for sin through penance. Sunday masses were well attended but poorly conducted in many cases, with the congregation scarcely paying attention to the proceedings. Many priests were still unfamiliar with the Bible or even with the Latin in which they conducted services. Over time the concept was developed that the church could address the sins of both the living and the dead, and the sale of indulgences to relieve the dead of their burden of sin became widespread after 1300.

This was still a time in which supernatural forces were believed to be at work in the world for good and ill. The devil and his henchmen were held to be responsible for many day-to-day problems, and Christianity offered at least the promise of divine assistance in combating these ancient enemies. Thus the saints and their relics were called upon for help in the fight against the works of demons, and belief in the power of the Virgin Mary grew rapidly after 1200. Saints were seen as helpers to be called upon in time of need as well as objects of superstitious practices and adoration in their own right. The number of holy relics on display at shrines and churches expanded greatly in this period.

The most remarkable and saintly religious figure in medieval Hesse was Elizabeth of Thuringia, later simply called Holy Elizabeth. She was born a princess of Hungary, and married very young the Landgrave of Thuringia. His untimely demise left her feeling completely bereft, and led her to move to Marburg and found a hospital that would serve the needs of the poor and ill. She took the Franciscan vows and worked in the hospital, pledging to do so for life. Here her ministration to the sick and good deeds in service to the poor and elderly gave her a local reputation for saintly works. She particularly ministered to the needs of lepers in her hospital. In the small amount of spare time she found from her labors, she spun cloth for the nuns in Altenberg. It was said that in one day she gave away a quarter of her available wealth of 2000 silver marks to the local poor. Her father confessor was Conrad of Marburg, a controversial figure and ruthless inquisitor who persecuted supposed witches and heretics on authority of the pope. He was equally ruthless in exercising authority over Elizabeth, and apparently did not spare her even the physical punishments of flagellation or striking her in the face when she brooked his admonishments. This was not uncommon in such religious training of the nobility of the day. It seems Conrad also consistently ordered her to rest more from her labors as her regimen was injuring her health, and he demanded that she not give away her family fortune too quickly or easily.

Despite visits to a doctor, Elizabeth's own growing illness began to restrict her ability to continue her labors for the poor. In the end her body simply gave out. She took a turn for the worse and died in the night of 16-17 November 1231. She was only twenty-four at her death. Her reputation created a growing following toward her canonization. In this Conrad led the chorus of support, tirelessly working to promote her cause. Her gravesite became a place of pilgrimage for the poor and others, and tales of 126 separate miracles attributed to her ministrations before and after death began to roll in. Elizabeth's canonization followed on June 1, 1235, an extremely quick step for the church to take so soon after her death. The German Order erected a magnificent church to honor her in Marburg. On May 1, 1236 the bones of the new saint were honored in the church; the landgrave's entire court joined the massive crowds in attending. Church officials of all levels and the emperor Frederick II himself appeared. He set a golden crown on her lifeless head and served personally as a pallbearer. The cult of Elizabeth spread across Christendom, and especially in Thuringia and Hesse. Huge numbers of churches, chapels and hospitals dedicated to her were created in Hesse alone. For a long time Marburg's popularity as a pilgrimage site was exceeded only by a handful of cities including Rome and Jerusalem.[14]

Conrad the confessor would outlive his tortured charge by only a few years. With the sanction of Pope Gregory IX, who was himself combating a wave of apostasy that threatened the whole church, Conrad had become a notorious inquisitor who charged and executed many people as accused witches and heretics. He was quoted as saying, "We would gladly burn one hundred innocents if necessary to destroy the one guilty man among them." His excesses in fact were so great that Archbishops in Mainz and Trier spoke out forcefully against him. Rather suspiciously, he focused his persecutions on two great families who were partisans of the Archbishop of Mainz, those of von

Figures 3-1/3-2 Two views of the St. Elizabeth's Church in Marburg: the great cross in the chancel (lt.) and the carved altar-work and magnificent stained glass in the gallery.

Solms and von Sayn. Eventually he was killed by local nobles who took advantage of his leaving Marburg to travel to western Germany to defend himself against the charges of his foes. His death in the hills along the Lahn (July 1233) effectively ended the organized Inquisition in Germany.[15]

Elizabeth's story illustrates the positive side of the efforts of the church in providing hospitals and invalid homes, ministering to the poor, and opening its doors to the needy. The outlying houses of the Cistercians and other orders similarly offered the weary or wounded traveler the only available succor and replenishment for the journey, in which he could be hounded by wolves, petty bandits or impoverished local nobles turned to brigandage. The church's threatened banning, interdiction and penance represented the only check on the powerful and wealthy in their dealings with the rest of society, and sometimes even the haughtiest and most unscrupulous of despots backed down rather than face religious sanctions. The church formed a political counter-balance to the growing commercial power of the towns, whose interests were often at odds with those of the agricultural sector. Although it failed over time, the church did what it could to combat businessmen who practiced usury and money lending. It naturally supported the agricultural economy in which religious wealth was heavily invested.

Yet the church's wealth and power, which assumed its greatest extent in the twelfth and thirteenth centuries, was both a boon and a curse. It allowed influence over the powerful of the day, in some cases promoting change for the better. But as the list of its properties and extent of its wealth grew, this very prosperity worked against its principles and continually served to corrupt its officials. The individual holdings of the churches, monasteries and bishoprics were often astoundingly large. The Cistercian monks were said to brag that they could undertake a journey to Rome without ever spending the night outside their order's holdings.

In the thirteenth and fourteenth centuries ordinary people spontaneously formed a reaction to the worldliness of the wealthier religious orders and the nobles who corruptly took bishoprics and other church offices for themselves and their retainers. Pious men and women banded together in small groups and founded their own monastic cells based on rules of their own creation. They lived in these mendicant (begging) orders by their own work, or by begging from the faithful, living cheerfully in poverty and doing good works. The established church was mostly opposed to such cloisters, speaking out against them and sometimes conducting inquisitions to stamp them out by violent means. Mainz held some twenty-eight such convents, while Worms had sixteen and Frankfurt fifty-seven. All the other major Hessian towns had similar cloisters, including the Wetterau towns of Friedberg, Gelnhausen and Wetzlar.

Besides these spontaneous foundations, some new mendicant orders arose focused on the spiritual needs of the towns. First among these was the order of St. Francis, which often placed its foundations where they could minister to the city masses. Unlike the smaller mendicant groups not connected to Rome, the Franciscans tended to come from the wealthier classes of the nobility and were able to look to them for financial support. These reform orders again re-instituted the stricter aspects of Benedict's Rule, confining their members to lives of poverty and preaching in their large, unadorned, hall-style town churches. The mendicants quickly achieved great renown, being referred to by one pope as his "army" with which he could oppose the power and self-centeredness of the largely independent bishops. The friars could hear confession in any jurisdiction, and involve themselves in ministering to the real needs of the local parishioners. Many German bishops by contrast remained more men of the sword than of knowledge and grace.

The more pious members of the nobility founded churches, chapels and cloisters in this era, often paying sizable sums to maintain and outfit them with elaborate furnishings and religious and secular artworks. Besides the larger religious foundations in the towns, the fourteenth and fifteenth centuries saw the outfitting in this way of a host of smaller institutions across the land. Smaller churches that benefited from such largesse in the creation of elaborate carved altars include those in Hofgeismar, Wildungen, Netze, Schotten, Orb, Rauschenberg, Wetter, Niederweidbach, and Aufenau.[16]

NOTES TO CHAPTER 3

[1] Richard Fletcher, *The Barbarian Conversion, From Paganism to Christianity*, Henry Holt & Co., New York, 1997, pp. 132-33, 228-29; Malcolm Todd, *Everyday Life of the Barbarians, Goths, Franks and Vandals*, Putnam's Sons, NY, 1972, p. 140; Alfons Dopsch, *The Economic and Social Foundations of European Civilization*, Howard Fertig, New York, 1969 reprint, pp. 241-44.
[2] See the excellent treatment of this very remote period in Fletcher, pp. 132-135.
[3] Ian Wood, Editor, *Franks and Alamanni in the Merovingian Period, an Ethnographic Perspective*, Boydell Press, Woodbridge, 1998, p. 58.
[4] Karl E. Demandt, *Geschichte des Landes Hessen*, Bärenreiter-Verlag, Kassel, 1972, pp. 121-25; Norbert Wand, *Die Büraburg bei Fritzlar*, N.G. Elwert Verlag, Marburg, 1974, p. 34.
[5] Wand, pp. 35-48, 54; Demandt, pp. 119-22, 127; Fletcher, pp. 205-09; Dopsch, p. 278-79; Kenneth S. Latourette, *A History of Christianity*, Harper & Row, New York, 1953, pp. 348, 352-53.
[6] Fletcher, pp. 207, 216; Demandt, p. 120; Latourette, p. 349; Marsha L. Colish, *Medieval Foundations of the Western Intellectual Tradition 400-1400*, Yale University Press, New Haven, CT, 1997, p. 68; James H. Robinson, *Readings in European History*, Ginn and Co., Boston, 1906, pp. 54-56, 62-63; Wand, p. 52.
[7] Heer, Friedrich, *Charlemagne and his World*, Macmillan Publishing Co., New York, 1975, pp. 178-79.
[8] Heer, pp. 172-76; Latourette, pp. 356-57.
[9] Fletcher, pp. 276-78.
[10] Fletcher, pp. 274-75; Heer, p. 180.
[11] Latourette, p. 371.
[12] The following section is drawn heavily from complementary treatment in Dan C. Heinemeier, *A History of Brunswick*, Arlington, VA, 1999, pp. 112-16, as well as Latourette, pp. 334-36, 370, 416-22, 462 and 525.
[13] Demandt, pp. 136-37; George Zarnecki, *The Monastic Achievement*, McGraw-Hill, New York, 1972, p. 69.
[14] Demandt, pp. 177-78; W. Kürschner, *Geschichte der Stadt Marburg*, Elwertsche Verlagsbuchhandlung, Marburg, 1934, pp. 34-42; David H. Farmer, *Oxford Dictionary of Saints*, Oxford University Press, 2nd Edition, 1987, p. 139.
[15] Demandt, pp. 169-177.
[16] Demandt, pp. 138-39.

Chapter 4

The Carolingians Depart: the Development of Feudalism

The ninth, tenth, and eleventh centuries saw the end of the realm built by Charles the Great as his squabbling sons and grandsons tore off pieces of the empire for themselves and then gradually died out, or left heirs too weak to maintain rule. The pattern that now established itself would mark German and Hessian history for centuries: weak central rule coupled with the unchallenged power of local strongmen who aggrandized themselves and their families at the expense of church and state alike. Over this period the manor-based agricultural system that formed the social, governmental and military sinews of the Middle Ages continued to develop. Feudal forms of land tenure were perfected, mostly at the expense of the smaller freeman who sought only to farm his acreage and provide for his family in peace and security.

When we left off with Charles the Great in chapter two, he had completed the subjugation of the Saxons through a series of brutal and bitterly-fought campaigns. In these struggles Hesse had played the role of battlefield, supply house of men and material, and an important connecting path for the march of Charles' armies against the heartland of Saxony. By the early ninth century Charles' physical ability and mental focus were beginning to erode. Many signs and wonders were recorded which contemporaries cited as evidence that with the passing of his rule a fearful period of uncertainty and conflict would occur. His death in 814 brought his less-competent son, Louis the Pious to the throne; Louis' reign would end in the breakup of his father's great empire. Louis appointed his sons as counts and dukes in various areas, only to see them rise against him in revolt as they sought to obtain even greater power. Hesse was now an integral part of Franconia, forming the western portion of this duchy that also stretched across northern Bavaria to the borders of Thuringia. Louis and his eldest son, Lothar I, held the reigns of power directly in this area, which in turn was given in fief to a collection of greater and lesser nobles. This petty nobility provided for local security and administration, including management of the agricultural production of the peasant farms organized in large and small manors across the land. It was this production of course that provided the nobility with its wealth, the king with his dues, and maintenance of the armored warriors who protected the interests of the duchy and the empire in these dangerous times.

> The boundaries of the empire continually called for defense. What an opportunity for young nobles to distinguish themselves...At this time the only important and permanent form of power was the possession of land. The officials around the king were assigned land; the counts transformed their feudal fiefs into hereditary estates. The mass of freemen mattered less and less in political life. The king whittled down his own property in order to reward devotion. Aristocratic families arose which, holding numerous offices and large possessions, became allied among themselves by marriage and thus developed territorial power. These groups pushed themselves in between the king and his officials. Such was the origin of the new tribal duchy, which was rooted in the soil, in local tradition, and in personal attainment.[1]

Louis' sons eventually deposed him, and then went to war with each other over the spoils. A three-way split was effected in 843 at the Treaty of Verdun, in which Lewis, now called "The German," assumed rule in much of what is now Germany. A revised partition of Meersen in 870 moved Lewis' borders even further west and south toward modern France and Italy. Germany then consisted of a collection of tribal-based duchies with no cohesive political ties. Unity, such as it was, depended on the authority of local dukes who alternately coerced and rewarded the landed nobles who formed the backbone of their power and authority. The land was divided into a crazy-quilt pattern of petty fiefdoms owing allegiance to the next higher level of nobility, culminating in counts who themselves were beholden to one of the dukes. Any vassal who became too strong and grasping ran the risk of being deposed by his lord, and having his land reassigned to a seemingly more pliant line of rulers. Any count who failed to effectively coerce such upstarts ran the risk of himself being superseded, especially if he were to die with no clear heir. The dukes took advantage of the weakened state of central authority to force their "protection" on bishops and abbots, and many church lands effectively were appropriated by the secular nobility.[2]

Among the most loyal subjects of the king were the Conradiner family in Hesse. About 836 the Conradiner assumed control of lands along the *Gaue* (administrative districts) in the Rhine/Main and Lahn River areas as well as the Wetterau and Vogelsberg in southern Hesse, taking over from the Rupertiner who seem to have been displaced at this point and moved west into France. This may have been thanks to effective imperial politics played by the Conradiner as they backed Lewis the German in the struggle against his father. These helpful ties to the German ruling house were maintained for generations to come. In 876 Count Berengar of the Conradiner held Hesse, passing it along to an heir, Conrad the Elder, in 897. Conrad was elevated from his role as ruler over an area along the Lahn River, and became extremely influential at court and powerful in his own county. He expanded Hessian holdings south to Speyer and Worms, bringing them back into the Hessian orbit. He also built upon Berengar's earlier efforts to acquire land to the east and northeast adjacent to Thuringia. Here he ran into the holdings of the Saxon Liudolfinger, themselves attempting to push their boundaries south and west. An east Franconian family, the Babenberger, centered on Bamberg, had allied themselves with the Liudolfinger in efforts to control Thuringia. This threatened to be too powerful a coalition for then-emperor Arnulf to control, and he encouraged the loyal Conradiner to block it.

The spark that set off this political powder keg occurred in 897, when Arnulf deposed Poppo von Babenberg as Duke of Thuringia, giving this honor instead to Conrad. Conrad's brother Rudolf received the lucrative bishopric of Wurzburg at the same time, a further provocation to the Babenbergs. Soon local war was declared, an uneven match between the Conradiner and the more powerful league of the Liudolfinger and Babenberger. Conrad's only trump card was his strong ties to the emperor, weakened temporarily when Arnulf died and his six-year-old son Lewis the Child became emperor in 900. Hostilities with the Babenberger became intense in 902-03, as fighting erupted along the Main River. Adalbert von Babenberger's goal was nothing less than to drive his rivals out of this area of Franconia. The Conradiner were in fact driven across the Spessart forest in northern Bavaria, and Conrad's brother Eberhard died in the fighting. Royal forces now came to Conrad's aid, and battles raged as far east as Würzburg, whose church was damaged in the fighting. In February 906 Conrad himself was caught with an outnumbered force and killed in battle at Fritzlar. Later, the combined forces of the emperor and Archbishop Hatto of Mainz inflicted a severe defeat on the Babenberger. Adalbert was captured and executed for treason (906). The Liudolfinger were required to surrender Hersfeld to Hesse as a penalty for their involvement. Despite this positive outcome for the Conradiner, it may be assumed that villages, monasteries and other local holdings suffered mightily at the hands of any invading forces that entered Hesse. An accepted tactic in this era was to strip the land bare of food and fodder to provision one's army, all at the expense of the powerless.

With the advent of more peaceful times the Conradiner turned their hands and attention to developing and consolidating their far-flung holdings. The heirs of Conrad the Elder held districts across Hesse, providing a unified style of rule that had been long absent. His sons and nephews held countships (*Gaue*) along the upper, middle and lower Lahn, the Eder River, Ohm/Lahn, the Niddagau, and in Swabia. Conrad the Younger assumed supremacy in Hesse after his father died. This centralized power structure was key when Lewis the Child died without heir in 911. Archbishop Hatto of Mainz lost no time in engineering Conrad's own ascendancy to the German throne in the same year. Conrad was elected by a majority of the representatives of the German duchies, effectively reinforcing the precedent that the dukes had the right to elect the imperial leadership. The king or emperor now had to rule more through cooperation and discussion than with the iron hand that the great Charles had wielded. Lewis the Child's passing also marked the formal end of the rule of Charles' descendants, the Carolingians. Conrad's Franconia now became crown land without a formal duke in residence, a position it would continue to occupy periodically in centuries to come.

Conrad's rule was brief and terribly wearying, as he tried to crush a succession of rebellious dukes in Saxony, Bavaria and Lotharingia and bring them under more centralized control. He enjoyed the full support of the church, whose officials had supported Hatto's elevation of Conrad as emperor and now looked to Conrad to protect them from the depredations of the local counts and dukes. Unfortunately for them and for Conrad, it was not to be. His influence outside central Germany was weak and continued to wane, and he grew tired and ill with the struggle. On his deathbed in late 918 he sent his brother Eberhard with the symbols of the crown to his archenemy, Henry of Saxony, known as the Fowler. Henry alone was strong enough to attempt to rule the fractured empire, and in facing death Conrad proved himself much more far-seeing than in life. Henry did rule Germany well, forging more unity with the fractious dukes and proving a match for the most dangerous invaders of the realm, the Slavs and Hungarians. He appointed his own brother (another Eberhard) duke in Franconia, but much of the Conradiner holdings and power structure apparently was left in place under the existing lords. Their house would live on to provide a future line of German kings.[3]

When King Henry died in 936 his son Otto I (the Great) was his hand-picked successor (936-73). Otto became another strong and effective ruler, but like Conrad before him much of his attention had to be focused on rebellious dukes and even relatives for years at a time. He earned lasting fame by the defeat of the barbarous Hungarian (Magyar) marauders, who had struck Germany annually with impunity for much of the time since Arnulf's day. Hesse must have suffered greatly from the periodic inroads of these cruel horsemen of the steppe, who attacked Bavaria hardest but also ranged as far west as France from their bases in Hungary. Otto assembled a host drawn from all the duchies and caught the Hungarian by surprise on the Lechfeld on August 10, 955. At first the enemy succeeded in charging around behind the German host, scattering several divisions and seizing the army's baggage train. None other than the Franconians, under their own duke, charged to the rear and set upon the victorious

Hungarians. These were driven back, allowing Otto to continue to march against the main Hungarian force to the front. The enemy host was smashed and scattered, the remnants pursued like game for days afterward and slaughtered like cattle. The annual Hungarian threat to Germany was over.

Otto's rule saw some other significant battles in Franconia and Hesse with rebels such as Eberhard, the brother of Conrad the Younger, who used Otto's family squabbles as an opportunity to try to reclaim family lands along the Diemel River in 937. Otto defeated him at Obermarsburg in northern Hesse. He sued for peace, then rebelled again with a coalition of local nobles in 939. He was killed that year at Andernach near Coblenz by his cousin, Udo, who held the Wetterau and now came into possession of Eberhard's lands. Otto transferred control of Hesse to the Duke of Swabia.

Otto's own son, Liudolf, appointed by him as lord over significant holdings in Hesse, was involved in one of the local rebellions, and had to be suppressed and stripped of much of his land. Otto declared him deposed along with the Archbishop of Mainz and some other rebels in a proclamation at Fritzlar in 953. He besieged them at Mainz in a seesaw battle that favored first one side, then the other. He was forced at one point to raise the siege, shifting to attack his enemies at Regensburg and finally defeating them at Langenzenn near Nuremberg. After besieging Liudolf in Regensburg, his rebellious son finally surrendered, begged forgiveness, and was pardoned with the loss of his major holdings. The archbishop of Mainz also had to forfeit his position in favor of William, another son of Otto. It was at this point in 955 that the Hungarian threat forced the suspension of all hostilities so the duchies could unite against the common enemy at Lechfeld, as described above. Again it should be born in mind that fighting caused major hardship for local peasants and others unable to defend their property from marauding bands of warriors looking for provisions.

After this period of rebellion, the emperor obviously wanted to secure central Hesse against future unrest, and so more direct royal rule was his response. Otto thus carried out the program of his Liudolfinger ancestors who had sought to carve a major role for themselves in Hesse. He transferred the old governing points of Fritzlar, Hersfeld, Amöneburg, Weilburg and surrounding areas to royal control, ensuring their loyalty in any future uprisings. Thus the recent and hard-fought unity forged by the Conradiner went by the boards as Otto appointed his own retainers to rule within each of the counties of the land. Counties were subdivided into smaller fiefs to ensure that no over-powerful nobles were created. In the process, a stronghold of Saxon power and influence was developed that would serve Otto and his successors for years to come. Hereditary and class distinctions were of no importance, as close relations with the crown became the main guarantor of position.[4]

Otto also pioneered the tactic of transferring major land holdings to the church through crown grants that left him in the position to demand income and even mounted warriors from the bishops who received his grants. His alliance with church officials undermined the authority of local dukes by transferring land to the church that otherwise would have fallen to them or their retainers. This concentrated control of the land in the hands of officials who could not marry or pass their wealth along to heirs, and thus was safer than building up secular authorities. By granting whole counties to them, Otto and his successors gave the bishops power bases equivalent to those of local counts for the first time. The emperor also personally appointed bishops, making them directly dependent on the crown, and systematically "replacing untrustworthy lay officials by trusty ecclesiastics," as Previte-Orton has termed it.

Bishops and monasteries had overlords in this era along with everyone else. Usually they owed obeisance to the king or emperor who had appointed or founded them. Even small churches owed obedience to their founders, most often local lords, paying to them a portion of their annual tithe money. It is impossible to over-emphasize the importance to the crown of the income derived from church lands, as well as the well-trained and fully equipped supply of warriors the bishops had to maintain and provide to the crown upon request. Most often, the bishops themselves were expected to join in campaigns and lead their forces. In one such campaign in 981 over 75% of the soldiery was drawn from such ecclesiastical forces (1,492 of 1,990 men). These were apportioned among the greater and lesser institutions such that a major bishopric like Mainz had to send 100 knights, a large abbey like Fulda sixty knights, with lesser vassals beholden for much smaller numbers.

In time the bishops became great princes in their own right, with wealth and power the equal of the counts and dukes. They were secular governing officials as much as religious leaders, expected to efficiently administer the manors under their control, ensure local security on the roads, encourage taxable trade, fortify and promote development of towns, and cultivate local markets. They worked diligently to consolidate their holdings by trading properties further afield for ones closer to home, and were quite successful in this effort up through the early eleventh century. These ecclesiastical princes had reputations that far transcended their local jurisdictions. Unlike the monks, some lesser abbots, and other local religious officials, they were national figures expected to focus mostly on affairs of this world, not the religious concerns of the next. It was they who provided the military muscle that permitted the German kings to act as international power brokers as far away as Italy, and to ward off the depredations in Germany of barbarian invaders from eastern and northern Europe.

Noblemen from every level of the medieval pecking order similarly maintained and provided mounted warriors to the lords above them in the chain of authority, for this was the ticket to influence, increased landed wealth, and power. Ultimately, the kingdom itself benefited by being able to draw on this collective national army in times of emergency. An unfortunate side effect was that so many men-at-arms were available that bishops, kings and nobles alike turned on each other in constant land squabbles that ravaged the duchies.[5]

When Otto the Great died in 973 he was succeeded by his son, Otto II, who ruled from 973-83, and then his grandson, Otto III, whose effective reign was shortened because he was but a child when his father died. He and his regents held power from 983 until his own death in 1002. During these times Franconia was without a duke, being ruled directly as crown land by the Ottonian kings and emperors. This situation continued under their successor, a Bavarian duke, who was elected by his fellows and ruled as Henry II from 1002-24. This period saw the quiet emergence of some trading towns in the Rhineland. Their halting steps at building up merchant activity would only really take off in the century that followed. Still, they traded in the grapes that were cultivated with renewed vigor not seen since Roman times. Merchants of Mainz bought up the grain and cattle produced by Hessian monasteries at Fulda, Hersfeld, and elsewhere, selling these at a profit once they had been transported down the Main and Rhine rivers. The upper Main too provided grain grown for export by Slavic peasants.[6]

The tenth century was a time of great misery for common people, trampled by the feuding of their overlords, and struggling in every season to scratch enough sustenance from the earth. It was a cruel and barbarous age. The Christian faith found a shaky co-existence with a host of minor but discernible pagan customs and superstitious observances left over from the ancient Teutonic gods. Parish priests suffered from a lack of training, and many were married in these times despite papal direction to the contrary. They tended to support the crown in any squabbles with the religious hierarchy, for fear they would one day have divorce thrust upon them and have to turn away their wives and children.

The year 993 saw natural disasters of almost biblical proportions. The Annals of Hildesheim recorded, "From the Nativity of St. John the Baptist [June 24] until November 9 there were drought and intense heat; unnumbered crops did not ripen at the proper season because of the blazing sun. There followed extreme cold and great fall of snow, with outbreak of plague that destroyed far and wide both man and beast." The next year was marked by more bad weather, with a harsh winter lasting until May 995. Cold winds and frost were even experienced as late as July. Drought followed, drying up ponds and scorching the earth. Famine and more illnesses followed. Whole villages were stricken. As the new millennium was at hand, many people firmly believed that the end of the world was near, that the winter solstice of the year 999 would directly precede the biblical apocalypse. The disorder of the times often was attributed to divine retribution for sin. As the new millennium dawned, many people must have faced it with a combination of relief and trepidation.[7]

The eleventh century began with Henry II, who continued to rely heavily on the church for learned officials, counselors, and trusted vassals with estates laden with produce and armed men. He would have liked to reduce all the duchies to the status of Franconia, which had dependent counts but no duke. Huge royal grants of Franconian land were made to the bishops of Würzburg and Bamberg, among others. Henry did not neglect church reforms at the level of the monasteries, however, where ecclesiastics had generally lost the vision of the founders of their houses. Many monks were living in carnal sin, ate like gluttons even on fast days, and generally overindulged in drink and other pleasures in violation of their vows. The Cluny reform movement sought to clean up these abuses and made considerable headway by the late tenth century. Henry gave it active support.[8]

Henry's death in 1024 ushered in a period of rule by Franconian kings of the old Conradiner house, starting with Conrad II. Their reign through Henry IV, who died in 1106, was unremarkable except for its constant infighting, a process that Hans Delbrück has described well: "All the partial sovereignties, each with a certain independent military force, constantly rubbed against one another." This line of kings also expanded the use of the so-called *ministeriales*, a class of non-noble officials independent of church and nobility alike, and thus more pliant and reliable as retainers to the king. Even the major ecclesiastic princes raised up these men who could serve as bodyguards, administrators on manors, or even armed men in case of need. They were cheaper and easier to maintain than nobles who demanded fiefs of land as the price of their service. One especially egregious example of the brutal acts of retainers working for men of the cloth occurred in 1063. On Pentecost eve the vassals of the Bishop of Hildesheim and those of the abbot of Fulda set upon each other with swords and knives in the cathedral at Goslar, and many were wounded or slaughtered. This was an era in which the king was weak, being a boy at his accession in 1057. The bishops and counts alike used the opportunity to steal land and place monasteries and crown lands under their direct control. Conflict over tithe rights among bishops and abbots ground along for years at a time.[9]

Despite their often strong hand on the administration of the state, the German emperors could do nothing to combat certain social conditions that continued to work against the prosperity of many areas of their kingdom. Personal feuding and vendetta-based killings and assaults remained epidemic. The Bishop of Worms in southern Hesse noted in 1025 that his diocesans thought nothing of killing each other in drunken brawls or for no apparent reason whatever, and that thirty-five had died over the course of a year in his parish alone. Murder victims' families felt themselves honor-bound to kill the murderer or a member of his clan, with the result that numerous killings back and forth could occur. Because of these murders (not to mention severe injuries) the bishop remarked that productive capacity of his own manors was suffering terribly. Royal peace ordinances of 1083 and 1085 ruled that the typical penalty of cutting off the hand of the perpetrators of malicious wounding should not be applied if the offender were under twelve years of age. This suggests that knife-play among even young children must have been somewhat common. An ordinance of 1103 held that if one met an enemy on the open road, it was permissible to attempt to kill him, but that once he reached the safety of his home or that of another, he must be left alone. This was expected to improve public safety; the prevention of violence spilling over into the home was seen as real progress. Dannenbauer compares the endemic, society-wide violence of this age to the effect of smallpox in later centuries, depressing population growth and economic progress.[10]

Also in these years Pope Gregory VII decreed the prohibition of secular investiture, i.e., the royal appointment of church officials, igniting the massive War of Investiture (1075-1122). This was a dagger thrust aimed at the throat of imperial rule, for the German kings had divested themselves of most of the crown lands in gifts to supposedly pliant churchmen. As Henry IV struggled with a variety of internal rebellions swirling around this papal decree, more and more control slipped into the hands of local rulers and bishops who declared open season on church and crown lands alike. Any church lands and property unprotected by their own knights were pillaged, many on numerous occasions. Monks fled the country in droves. By 1085, when the truculent pope died, Germany was again under Henry's control, including almost every bishopric in the kingdom. Secular investiture had triumphed, but its days ultimately were numbered by the strong papal stand. A successor would eventually see this policy through to acceptance.

Despite the king's ultimate success, the nobility and some of the higher church officials had made away with the true spoils of the Investiture War. The Mainz bishopric suffered major loss. All the abbeys had been plundered or destroyed, including those at Goseck, St. Gall, Schaffhausen, Prüm, Stablo, Lüttich, St. Trudo, St. Hubert, and Corvey. The monks who remained had again largely strayed from their strict religious orders and become a sordid disgrace to their faith.

The War of Investiture was probably the most destructive force to hit Germany up until the seventeenth century, dividing everyone across lines of class and calling. Franconia, as the home of the royal ruling house, had mostly supported the king, as had the parish priests still concerned about protecting their marriages and other illicit prerogatives from papal interference. The conflict seems to have helped some of the old Hessian ruling families to consolidate and accrue property again after the massive breakup of holdings that had been the policy under the Ottonian kings. With close ties to the kings and emperors from Henry II to Henry IV, as well as Archbishopric of Mainz, the Werner family was one of the more influential beneficiaries of the re-consolidation trend in Hesse. The archbishop in turn absorbed much of the Werner family holdings when their last male scion died childless in 1121. The still-developing towns of the

Rhineland also did their best to support the king in the war, working against the power of the bishops who sought to control their trade.

As for the lower classes, their lands had been overrun and despoiled time and again. They simply wanted peace, a longing reflected in the "truce of God" decreed in 1085 by the bishops of Mainz and Bamberg. Many freemen were forced to pledge themselves to local lords who could provide them a measure of physical protection. In this they gave up personal title to their lands, but maintained the right to work them in greater safety. This contributed to German society becoming more rigidly feudal, a tendency which increased in the twelfth century.

Nobles and church officials everywhere who sought to enhance their security had conducted a massive castle-building program during the war. Outlaw knights did likewise, using them as bases from which to prey on the surrounding peasantry with impunity. Much of the countryside was reduced to waste. The example of Wazo, bishop of Liege (1041-48), who used his own cadre of armored warriors to besiege and reduce one such outlaw group, is indicative of many such efforts that had to be carried out to re-impose order.[11]

By the mid-twelfth century a new force of feudal power and influence entered the field in Hesse: the landgrave of Thuringia. By marriage and inheritance they assumed enhanced control of a broad expanse of Hessian land, and accepted still more in fief from the Archbishop of Mainz. The land included holdings around Marburg, the state court in the ancient seat of Maden, the area around Wetter, and the castle and town of Gudensberg, Fritzlar, the Hersfeld abbey lands, and areas in the Westerwald region including Herborn, Haiger, and Löhnberg among other areas. This ushered in an extended period of conflict between the Thuringians and the archbishopric, which continually sought to uphold its original rights to the lands granted as fiefs in the face of Thuringian efforts to pull free of this authority. The Thuringians maintained a leading role in Hesse from 1122-1247, and battles with Mainz and her allies were almost constant.

The Thuringians were challenged also by the assertion of rights of a number of local Hessian strongmen, including the counts von Ziegenhain who ruled in the areas between upper and lower Hesse. Counties of Waldeck and Wittgenstein appeared on the Westphalian border, and the lower Lahn River area spawned counts von Nassau, von Diez, von Solms, and von Katzenelnbogen. In southwest Hesse efforts to consolidate power by the Hohenstauffen family, later a famous line of German kings, collapsed, and this area sunk into numerous territorial divisions. The Archbishop of Mainz sought allies among these lesser nobles wherever they could be found to help oppose the Thuringian landgrave. In 1165 Emperor Frederick I marched against Mainz, and his close ally Ludwig of Thuringia seized Amöneburg and laid waste to the Rheingau possessions of Mainz.

The Thuringian landgraves pursued a consistent policy of engaging the towns as allies, extending formal recognition to them of "town rights," which brought extensive trading privileges and other benefits conferred by the landgrave. From 1190-1240 many towns accepted these benefits, including: Grünberg, Alsfeld, Homberg on the Ohm, Marburg, Biedenkopf, Frankenberg in upper Hesse; in lower Hesse were Homberg on the Efze, Melsungen, Rotenburg, Witzenhausen, Eschwege, Kassel, Wolfhagen, and Gudensberg.

Battles with the archbishopric of Mainz were frequent through this period, and it became a time of substantial rolling back of the rights and holdings of Mainz in favor of the Thuringians. A turning point of sorts occurred in 1232 when a great battle at

Fritzlar saw the defeat of the forces of the archbishop at the hands of Landgrave Conrad. In the course of the struggle the famous church at Fritzlar was destroyed with most of the town. The archbishop quickly rebuilt it, however, with much stronger defenses that were continually improved over time until Fritzlar became among the strongest fortresses in Hesse. By the late fourteenth century it boasted town walls with thirty defending towers. Conrad, however, was penalized with the ban of the church for his actions, forcing him to join an order of religious knights as atonement.[12]

The wars of the period forced more freemen into servitude on the manors of the nobility, who absorbed their lands and granted them back the rights to work them. The dues owed to the lords in produce and personal services continued to grow as violence on the land forced commoners to take protection at any price. Landless ministeriales joined the ranks of the vassals serving men of rank, who could augment their forces in this way without enfeoffing their lands. Ministeriales enjoyed some of the same benefits as armed vassals without their social status. Most remained administrators, not warriors. This also became an outlet for freemen to find protection without sinking completely into servile status.

This disturbed and violent time also saw the flowering of the ideals of knighthood, and a certain *noblesse oblige* was felt among many of the nobility. In architecture, art and literature major advances occurred which were as outstanding as they were characteristic of this age of the Hohenstaufen kings (thirteenth century). The church of St. Elizabeth in Marburg exhibits the pure, early gothic style of the period. People like Elizabeth stood out in this troubled era, and far from being ridiculed, they were held up as examples of lives well spent. As Demandt has noted, matchless buildings such as the cathedral at Limburg (built 1212-35) and the cloister church at Fritzlar were never again to be created in such small towns in Hesse. Along with churches, the Hohenstaufen period witnessed the creation of scores of great castles such as Gelnhausen and Münzenburg. A renowned sculptor of this time was the Master of Naumburg, who along with his disciples worked extensively in western Hesse. The landgraves of Thuringia were men of letters as well as war; they sponsored some of the best poetry produced in this era.

Hesse's symbols from an ancient period were the lion and the star. These, along with calls to service, the good works of noblewomen, and other themes from this period of knighthood in bloom were reflected in the following place names of castles and villages established by the nobility. Love: Lißberg/Liebesberg; Joy: Windecken/Wonnecken; Beauty: Schönberg; Women: Frauenstein; Light/Sun: Lichtenfels/Sonnenberg; Honor: Ehrenfels; Freedom: Freienfels; Help: Helfenberg & Schützeberg; Pride: Stolzenburg; Strength: Starkenburg. Animal and flower symbology also was common, as in Flowers: Blumenstein, Rosenstein, Lilienstein; Lions: Löwenburg; Eagles: Adlerburg; Falcons: Falkenburg.[13]

In education, Kassel's reputation continued to grow (see chapter five). The number of students studying here rivaled the numbers emanating from the older centers of education in Fulda, Hersfeld and Fritzlar. By the fifteenth century it finally outstripped them all. Taken together, the institutions in these towns were graduating several hundred students in the fourteenth and fifteenth centuries. This was considered a huge number. Fritzlar was particularly renowned for its training of doctors.

The last of the Thuringian landgraves died out on February 16, 1247, throwing Hesse into a succession crisis. Among those who claimed his lands, the Archbishop of Mainz figured prominently, with his allies the counts of Ziegenhain and Babenberg. Arrayed against him were Henry the Noble of Saxony, allied with Sophie, a duchess of

Brabant whose minor son was considered next in line to inherit the landgraviate in Thuringia. Sophie's claims were aided in no small part because she was the daughter of Holy Elizabeth, by now the most revered saint throughout Hesse and beyond. Sophie's forces attacked savagely in 1249. The forces of Mainz meanwhile occupied Wetter and the archbishop created a fortress at Mellnau about 1250 to block Sophie's troops and control passage on the Weinstraße or Wine Road. But the archbishop was fought to a draw by 1254, and was forced to grant fiefs of the Thuringian and Hessian lands to Henry the Noble.

Sophie next allied herself with Duke Albrecht of Brunswick, who attacked and imprisoned the archbishop for a year. Another succession crisis occurred in 1260, with Sophie again opposing the archbishop. She now attacked Wetter causing heavy damage, and the local abbess even appealed to the pope to intercede. In September 1263 a truce at last awarded fiefs from Mainz to her son, the young landgrave, including the county of Hesse, stewardship over some cloisters, other rights of patronage, and the towns of Grünberg and Frankenberg, which were enfeoffed for the first time. He also reclaimed some towns along the Werra River previously held by Henry of Saxony. Wetter was awarded to him in joint tenure. Another conflict with the archbishop brought the landgrave more land in 1270, including Naumburg, Weidelsburg and Heiligenberg in Lower Hesse, and in Upper Hesse, Staufenberg, Gemünden, and the castle Wenigen in Amöneburg. In the next decade the Archbishop Werner tried issuing the ban of the church, political moves at the German court, and outright force, but was defeated by the landgrave's forces at every turn. In a battle at Fritzlar in 1280 the archbishop's troops were utterly crushed, and more of his lands had to be surrendered.

Landgrave Henry I next succeeded in forging an alliance with Archbishop Gerhard of Mainz, the successor to Werner. Gerhard helped him obtain the title of prince of the realm from the German emperor, along with an imperial fief of the town of Eschwege. This raised his line to become the leading house in Hesse. He began in 1275 to improve the castle in Marburg, elevating it to a much more princely state. He also improved the fortress in Kassel, but it could not hold a candle to the princely Marburg.

The Hessian landscape still was dotted with minor countships and ruling houses. There were the counts von Ziegenhain, von Waldeck and von Wittgenstein; in the north were the von Dassel and von Everstein counts, along with the archbishopric of Paderborn, who sought Hessian holdings at the expense of the others; and the von Schönebergs ruled in the Reinhard forest. The landgrave had an onerous struggle ahead to bring these contenders under control, and to weed them out to his own advantage. This was particularly true because of the undying enmity of the Archbishop of Mainz, who almost always sided with the nobles in opposition to the landgraves. The archbishop still held expansive districts around Wetter, Amöneburg, Neustadt, Rosenthal, Battenberg, Jesberg, Fritzlar, Naumburg, and Hofgeismar.

Landgrave Henry's death in 1308 created a three-year power sharing between his sons Johann and Otto. When Johann died in 1311 Otto faced the old struggle over the rights of Mainz to the Hessian fiefs in years-long, generally indecisive conflicts. In 1318 a pact made at Eisenach with Friedrich of Thuringia ended the encroachments of Mainz on Otto's holdings. In 1323 the German king recognized the two princes' rights to their respective lands. The Archbishop of Mainz was resolute, however, trumpeting his claims in Hesse and attacking Otto again in 1324. In 1327 he and his army took Gießen, but Landgrave Henry II, son of Otto (d. 1328), engaged the archbishop's forces at Wetzlar and defeated them. Four weeks later the archbishop was dead. Archbishop Heinrich renewed the conflict in 1344, but was defeated in 1347 at Gudensberg. Heinrich's death in 1353 brought about a more lasting peace. Centuries-old land disputes were resolved consistently in favor of the landgrave. In 1354 his rights to the Reinhard Forest were acknowledged, securing his claim to northern Hesse.

Another calamity, this one of natural causes, stalked the land with the outbreak of the Black Death in Europe in 1348. This terrible time touched off persecutions of Jews, for prejudice against them was never far beneath the surface. After a long period of growth this period brought about a loss of population, with villages going back to wasteland.

The developing Hessian territorial state received a sharp setback in the late fourteenth century, when the Hessian nobles allied with external enemies of the state to attack the landgrave. The landgraves had grown proud and haughty, particularly Hermann II, who assumed power in 1367. This cost them the support of their subjects in the towns and among the nobility (the "Estates," see p. 70). Hermann demanded higher taxes, and remained hardheaded and inflexible. The same year he came to power he burned Wetter to the ground in fighting to try to seize sole control from the Archbishop of Mainz (with whom his line shared the Wetter area). The political unity of Hesse suffered greatly. Duke Otto of Brunswick led the coalition against Hermann, joined by the knightly "Brotherhood of the Star," a collection of Hessian nobles led by Count von Ziegenhain. Tremendous pressure was brought to bear on the landgrave, especially in 1372, when legend holds that he swayed many Kasslers to his side with an impassioned complaint that he could feed all his supporters with a single loaf of bread.

As Hermann besieged his enemies in the castle at Herzberg without success, the Star Brotherhood forced an end to the siege and raided his lands up to the walls of Fritzlar. But the landgrave's imperial politics helped him in extricating himself. On June 9, 1373 he concluded a hereditary compact with the landgrave of Thuringia. This was decisive, raising Hesse to the status of an imperial feudal principality on a par with more important German states. For over two centuries this compact with the Saxon ruling house was renewed. The Star brotherhood collapsed when it suffered a defeat in 1374 at the hands of Hermann's forces near Wetzlar. But this had been just the opening act to more conflicts that followed. Fighting with Mainz again raged periodically from 1376-80, with battles at Kassel, Wetzlar, and elsewhere. Hermann finally achieved "protectorate" status over Mainz territory in Hesse. More on this period is discussed in the next chapter.

Archbishop Adolf of Mainz now collected a huge number of allies and troops from Brunswick, Saxony, Thuringia, local knights, and elsewhere to attack Hesse. They invaded the land in campaigns of 1385 and 1387, subduing it and capturing many towns and castles, including Wanfried, Boyneburg, Sontra, Rotenburg, Melsungen, Gudensberg, Niedenstein, and Falkenstein. They unsuccessfully besieged Kassel. The landgrave was only able to reclaim most of his towns after agreeing to make peace, paying huge reparations, and suffering personal humiliations. After Adolf died in 1390, his successor Conrad was less warlike, making peace with Hermann and giving him back some of his lost towns in feudal tenure. The more quarrelsome Archbishop Johann followed Conrad, renewing war with Hesse in 1400. The landgrave had allies this time among the Brunswick dukes, and he was able to conclude a satisfactory peace in 1405 (See also chapter five and the related history of Kassel).[14]

THE CAROLINGIANS DEPART: DEVELOPMENT OF FEUDALISM

LIFE ON THE LAND: FEUDALISM IN FULLY DEVELOPED FORM

The social and political environment of the ninth and tenth centuries has been described as a world that was "small, harassed, impoverished and overwhelmingly agrarian." Another author has described it as follows:

> [A] protracted period of confusion and struggle: at one time or another every social group, every village, every family had to fight for property, liberty, and physical survival not only against foreign invaders but also against their closest neighbors. It is not surprising that the voices reaching us from that period are full of distress and frustration; the more so, as most of them come from monasteries, churches, royal officers and other beneficiaries of the old order, whose holdings were choice targets for the depredations of the new barbarians, the usurpations of ruthless lords and adventurers, and the uprisings of dissatisfied tenants and serfs.[15]

By 1300 this small, impoverished world, "...had become much larger, both in the space it occupied and in the population it included. Its economy, with a small but important and dynamic urban sector, was considerably more varied, its governments were more effective, and its culture more creative."[16] The story of how these changes came about is the history of the high period of feudalism in Western Europe, and in closing this chapter we will describe how Hesse was caught up in these changes.

By the ninth century the worst of the continent-wide periods of pestilence had ended, and an apparent turn in the weather brought an extended period of warmer conditions that made it possible to raise much more food than the previous centuries typically would allow. The warm trend perhaps peaked by 1200. Population began to rise, such that the small, widely-scattered communities of the early Middle Ages became overcrowded, and it became necessary for many to migrate to new communities or to areas in which ecclesiastical or secular lords were seeking to develop wastelands into productive villages. Malnutrition was chronic among the peasant class from time immemorial, but true famine and outright starvation still were events terrible enough to be chronicled in records from the period. It appears from these sources that higher population did not spell a greater rate of famine, so agricultural production likely rose in this period as well. The pace of trade and communication between isolated communities also probably increased, facilitating the movement of people and food to areas lacking either or both. Records of the late tenth and early eleventh centuries are full of accounts of peasants in the Rhineland and elsewhere taking matters into their own hands and expanding their holdings into forests and other undeveloped areas. The Archbishops of Mainz and other ecclesiastical lords found themselves granting concessions after the fact to permit these encroachments into church-owned forest lands that by law and custom should have been kept inviolate. Secular lords tended to be somewhat less willing to condone such behavior. Clearly the peasants' loss of status as freemen when they accepted servile tenure did not diminish their land hunger.[17]

By this time, the three-field system of crop rotation had long been a staple of most of the cultivated areas of the west, including Hesse. It is uncertain at what point this system came into being, but records of the late eighth century show that it pre-dated that time period. Three-field rotation held that cultivated lands were divided into thirds, so that a given piece of ground should be planted to yield a winter crop of wheat one year, and a spring crop of oats or barley or even beans and peas the next. Then it was allowed a year to lie fallow. The ancient two-crop method of the Romans was a spring crop followed by fallow, and this suited the soil and climate of the Mediterranean. But the better soils and abundant rains of northern Europe made possible the three-field approach. It had many benefits, such as freeing the farmer from dependence on a single crop that might be wiped out in adverse weather conditions. Two-thirds of the land was able to be productive in any year, and the peasant's workload was spread out over more seasons, making him more productive throughout the year. Soil was improved with the alternation of crop types, especially when nitrogen-rich legumes were grown. More fodder for animals and an accumulation of dung for garden fertilizing also could be made available.

The types of crops grown were heavily weighted to produce the grain products that were the staple of this era. By the tenth century the soft wheat known to the Romans was again replacing the rye, millet, barley, and oats that were easier to grow and therefore favored by early medieval man. The new wheat allowed production of white bread that was always in favor with the upper class, and eventually came to be available to commoners. The cheaper and more easily grown barley, millet and rye were never fully displaced from the tables and palates of the peasantry however, who shared the same less-expensive bounty with their farm animals. A popular soft wheat was a huskless form that shared the trait of rye bread of not drying out as fast and keeping better than some white breads. Barley was favored in ancient and early medieval times for its hardiness and ease of cultivation. It fed men, horses and cattle for centuries, and was the primary grain crop up through Carolingian times. It was replaced in the medieval era by rye and later wheat as the preferred food for men, while oats came to be preferred for horse fodder. Barley and some other grains were favored as well for their use in beer brewing, which surpassed the more ancient mead as the alcoholic beverage of choice for the commoner. The innovation of using hops was slower in being discovered and therefore less widespread until later in the Middle Ages.

Grain production increased century by century, due largely to the increase in the area of land worked. Seed yields of four to one were probably usual through much of the Middle Ages, a level so low as to be considered disastrous by today's and even by Roman standards. Still, this yield rate was probably as much as double that of Carolingian times.

In non-grain crops, peas, beans and lentils came first into use, along with the root crops, rapes and turnips. Radishes, carrots and parsnips came somewhat later, along with cabbages and onions. Wild fruit and nut trees were always exploited in the woods wherever they could be found as additions to the normal diet. Organized orchards of pears, apples, and other fruits were mostly an innovation of the later Middle Ages. The reintroduction of the extensive vineyards so common in Roman times was accomplished at least as early as the Carolingian era in the Rhineland, and it continued to expand greatly under the ecclesiastical lords who sought steady and improved supplies for the needs of the church. By the ninth century Worms and Speyer boasted huge vineyards, as did a large and growing area of Franconia.[18]

The plow used to work the fields was the simple wooden scratch plow, little more than a couple of carved branches attached together and hitched to an ox. This was the first recorded implement of its kind, being the standard of Roman times adapted for use in light Mediterranean soil. The heavier and wetter soils of Germany brought about the adoption of the wheeled plow, a much improved form used at least from the fifth century that gave the user better leverage and the draft animals an easier load to pull through denser ground. Later forms included plowshares to make wider cuts and a moldboard to turn the furrow. Another innovation of northern Europe in Carolingian times that spread widely thereafter was the shoulder collar used to harness the horse to plows and carts. This was a great innovation from Roman times, when the neck harness that rode higher on the horse's frame tended to cut off his oxygen supply the harder he pulled against it. The new collar increased the animal's ability to pull by a factor of four.[19]

The other tools used to till fields, gardens, and grape vines were few and simple at first, increasing in sophistication with the passage of time and expanded use of metal either with or to replace implements of wood. Sickles were used to harvest grain, which was cut off about halfway up the stalk leaving stalk ends suitable for forage by farm animals. Later a long scythe came into broader use. Threshing was done with a simple flail that was easily made on the farm and worked better than the older beating stick. Threshing was often done out in the open in the late summer or early autumn, although records of the later Middle Ages indicate some was done indoors in barns even in the winter.

Early in the Middle Ages oxen were almost exclusively used for plowing, since horses were expensive to acquire and maintain and were reserved for transporting men and some goods. By the 1100s this situation had begun to change with improved and more expansive horse breeding, but the common man typically could only afford oxen to plow his fields through much of the medieval period. Pigs were the most commonly kept food animals. They were cheap and easy to maintain, hardy and able to be pastured in woods where they could forage for acorns, beechnuts and other wild fodder. Most animals had to be slaughtered not later than early winter, since fodder was at a premium and never sufficient to last all the animals through the winter. Hens and geese also were commonly kept.[20]

As we have seen, the progress of feudalism from the early Middle Ages was greatly assisted by centuries of warfare and insecurity that forced freemen to commend themselves to lords or church officials for protection. When more than just a perceived need for immediate self-preservation was required to persuade, the strong often were capable of pressuring the weakened freemen to accept tenured servility. In this way the lords amassed rights to a peasant's lands as well as a share of his crops and labor. Single farmers or even whole villages could pledge themselves into such dependency. Over time a lord might demand more and more services and produce from his peasants, even in violation of the original agreement through which the land had passed to him. Ignorant peasants were seldom in a position to obtain legal redress, for by customary law a man's lord was also his judge in legal matters. The landlord could as easily be a church cloister or monastery as a knight, for often the protection of the church was considered preferable to the more capricious nobility who recognized fewer checks on their avarice. A farm here, a village there, the great secular and ecclesiastical officials built up large and usually scattered manor holdings across the face of Hesse.[21]

The process of commending oneself to a lord took two distinct forms. A knight or other member of the nobility would pledge himself and own his life to his lord in return for tenured land, while a peasant seeking protection had to give title to his land to the lord. He then would receive it back in the form of what was almost a rental property. This act bound not just the man, but his heirs as well. They generally could stay on the same parcel of land after his death, but only if they paid their annual dues in produce and service work. Often the parcels of arable land were laid out in long strips across the fields adjoining the village, with each strip a separate peasant holding. In addition, the lord would have lands belonging to himself laid out alongside the others, and often the peasants were expected to provide service by working these lands along with their own.

Another feature of these dependent communities was the concept of "common" areas recognized as available to the farmers of a certain area but not to resident freemen, day laborers, or others who failed to pledge themselves to the local lord. Over the centuries the enfranchised peasants guarded their rights to the common meadows, pastures, or woods against use and encroachment by such outsiders. The commons had real economic and practical value for grazing by farm animals, for firewood, building materials, sheep folding, etc. They also represented a compelling reason to commend oneself to the lord rather than go it alone.

The ecclesiastical lords were less frequently the landlords of whole villages than the secular lords, since so much of their land was acquired through gifts of small and scattered parcels. As noted earlier, much effort was expended towards exchanging these far-flung parcels with other lords to make the holdings more compact and nearer the seat of the district where the bishop or other churchman held sway. The church was instrumental in encouraging immigration of people from over-crowded or dangerous places to areas where marginal land needed to be cleared or drained to make it productive. Often these pioneers received concessions in terms of lower rents and reduced service requirements while the land was being developed and before it became fully productive. This helped the settlement to succeed, encouraged essentially free labor to move where it was needed, and brought more arable land into existence.[22]

The lands belonging to the monarchy itself also were extensive, especially in Hesse. For long periods much of the king's land had been transferred to church control so it could be worked effectively without fear of local nobles who were always seeking to convert it to hereditary fiefs of their own. Later, when the Investiture Conflict and other squabbles with the church called the ownership into question, efforts were made to bring the king's "fisc" back under his direct control. Up through the twelfth century the fisc lands were very extensive across Germany and especially throughout Franconia. These included huge expanses of forest and lakes or streams in which hunting and fishing rights were exclusively held by the king. By the thirteenth century and the post-Investiture period of turmoil, the fisc had gone into steep and irrecoverable decline.

In place of the now-weakened monarchy, the local duke or landgrave asserted control over lands grouped into counties (literally, count-ships). They provided a consolidating force in the face of the efforts of local nobles to absorb ever more of the fisc into their own petty holdings. The landgrave thus functioned increasingly like the monarch of a small but stable state, particularly once his line had acquired the credentials of a prince bestowed by the emperor and the recognition that came with them (see p. 62). The lesser nobles were made to serve the local prince in a feudal relationship, under which they provided a share of the production of their own properties in taxes. As in other German principalities, the prince came to have a vested interest in seeing to it that his nobles did not demand so much of their peasants that productivity was adversely affected. For if it were, the state's own ability to tap their always-finite resources would be reduced. The nobility constantly sought to expand their wealth by squeezing their tenured peasants, while the head of state often enacted rules to regulate what could be demanded. This dynamic tension became a characteristic feature of life in the latter Middle Ages.

The nobles and senior church officials, collectively called the "Estates," came to serve as advisors to the prince and members of his court. They demanded to be consulted on matters of state, especially including finances, for their contributions were critical to the prince when he needed to improve a palace or castle, build up his military strength, and live as lavishly as his peers in other principalities. The prince might coerce or cultivate them depending upon his personality and theirs, and upon the perilous or smooth dictates of statecraft at any given time. They in turn might support him, oppose him rather passively, or even engage in blatant rebellion, depending on where he stood in their good graces or upon his personal strength as a leader. A weakened German monarchy; stronger, land-consolidating princes; and the development of towns and trade that lessened the ability of the estates to control matters locally; all these forces paved the way for Hesse to develop as a more modern state through the latter medieval period.

From the early Middle Ages most Hessian peasants were organized in legal and social terms in manorial holdings of the king, the church or the lesser nobility. These landlords required a huge proportion of the farmer's production and personal labor, leaving him a relatively small portion for his personal needs. Almost every aspect of his life was controlled by the ordinances established by his lord and the officials that represented the lord's authority in the village community. In the north Hessian village of Körle, over which the landgrave himself exercised lordship, the local bailiff who represented the lord was called a *Dorfgrebe*. Although he lived in a fine house in the village, the ordinance spelling out his qualifications made clear that he was no simple local farmer with influence in high places. He had to reside in the village, be a subject of the landgrave of good reputation, learned in reading and writing, and possessed of enough arithmetic skills to perform his function of ensuring that the requisite produce and services owed to the state were faithfully provided. These qualifications were specified in an ordinance of 1739, but the office itself at that point had existed for centuries. It was obviously a position serving the needs of the lord, not the village residents themselves, for none of them would have possessed the required training and the *Dorfgrebe* thus would have been named from the outside.

What and when the farmer planted, when he reaped, where and when he could pasture his few animals, and whether his heirs could remain on the land he worked his whole life long, all were matters dictated in greater or lesser measure by authority outside his control. When he determined to marry, a small tax needed to be paid to the lord to obtain his consent, a practice that was expected and automatic but must have been no less irritating for its ubiquity. On top of the farmer's manorial dues, the church had rights to take tithe money from him to support the local parish. Sometimes rights to the parish tax would have been sold in times past to a secular noble who continued to collect it without any requirement to put it to the use of the church. As local judge, the landlord also profited from fines and penalties he could impose on those who broke local regulations.

Although strong princes increasingly held the power of the lesser nobles in check, the nobles imposed their remaining rights as landlords to the fullest. The local districts were laid out in hides (*Hufen*), parcels of ground amounting to thirty acres, and these were subdivided and assigned to peasants who held them as renters. In hilly areas, along higher elevations, or on marginal ground the number of acres per farmer would be greater to compensate for the reduced productive capacity. Thus, holdings differed considerably from place to place. Until land reforms in the seventeenth century the leasehold seems to have predominated in Hesse, in which parcels were held by lease for a specified period without the farmer gaining inheritable and therefore automatic rights for himself and his heirs to stay on the land. Despite this so-called "bad-hire" (*schlechte Leihe*) land leasing practice, it is likely that a productive farm family would keep the same land over long periods and even generations, since this would have maximized productivity for the lord as well.

Common people wore loose fitting and simply designed clothing of homespun cloth, usually of flax or wool. It was very coarse in texture, and men would also wear tunics belted at the waist. Sometimes they wore hose or trousers. Women were similarly attired in loose-fitting dresses worn long over the body. Fur was confined to the nobility. Most people had only one or at most two outfits of clothing at any time, for cloth was laborious to make and thus quite costly. The same clothes, or more likely none at all, would be worn to bed.

Men would work every day dawn to dusk, except Sunday and some key religious holidays, either on the plots of land they held as vassals or when required on assigned lands belonging to their lords. As the saying goes, women's work, whether in their fields, gardens, or houses, was never done. Their home was likely a wattle and daub hut with a hole cut in the roof that served as chimney for the small fire that warmed them and cooked their food. In warmer weather cooking would be done outside. Everything in the home from food to furnishings to people would have been permeated with soot over time, and animals would have shared the home in inclement weather. Bad teeth, terrible body odor and a generally slovenly appearance set the under class somewhat apart from the nobility and higher church officials that lived at the apex of the social order. The common people were completely unschooled in art or letters and satisfied to be so. This poverty and ignorance created a sense of scorn and repugnance on the part of the upper class that was cordially returned by the peasantry; it was abundantly clear that everyone's living depended ultimately on this scorned laboring class. These conditions persisted over the centuries; a peasant of the year 900 would not have found life greatly changed if he were transported to the year 1100.[23]

The standard living conditions of the early medieval peasant were largely unchanged from those of his ancestors in centuries past, and would have been identical to his counterparts across most of Western Europe. Around the twelfth century, however, his lot seems to have improved somewhat thanks to various social and economic forces. Trade and commerce picked up, creating markets that opened up the inward-focused economic life of the individual manors. Money came into more general use again, making it easier to put aside savings for use in acquiring land or other means of production. The worst of the cycles of civil and private warfare were subsiding as the Crusades drew off much of the war-making population and the local princes did a better job of controlling the lesser nobility. As the monastic orders and others set about clearing wastelands the created opportunities for peasants to obtain better working conditions by emigrating away from their ancestral homes. To keep servile laborers under these changed conditions the overseers sometimes had to find ways to improve their daily lot. Inheritable holdings, the exchanging of service requirements for reasonable monetary payments, and other means of easing the burdens of the peasantry were introduced, and over the following centuries the outright bondage in which their grandfathers had toiled became a thing of the past for many peasants.

The growth of commerce also brought with it efforts to improve the roads in the twelfth and thirteenth centuries. This made travel easier, and promoted the growth of towns that could cater to the needs of travelers for food, shelter and markets. The larger villages thus began to grow into small towns, and the larger towns into cities. We will turn now to a look at these developments and how they affected Hesse.

THE CAROLINGIANS DEPART: DEVELOPMENT OF FEUDALISM

NOTES TO CHAPTER 4

[1] Veit Valentin, *The German People*, Alfred Knopf, New York, 1952, p. 15.

[2] C.W. Previte-Orton, *Shorter Cambridge Medieval History*, Vol. I, Cambridge, 1952, pp. 334-48; James W. Thompson, *Feudal Germany*, University of Chicago Press, 1928, pp. 21-22.

[3] Karl E. Demandt, *Geschichte des Landes Hessen*, Bärenreiter-Verlag, Kassel, 1972, pp. 139-46; Eleanor Duckett, *Death and Life in the Tenth Century*, University of Michigan Press, Ann Arbor, 1968, pp. 12-39; Hans Delbrück, *Medieval Warfare*, History of the Art of War, Vol. III, University of Nebraska Press, Lincoln, 1990, p. 95; Thompson, pp. 24-25.

[4] Duckett, pp. 64-76; Demandt, pp. 147-50; Previte-Orton, p. 432.

[5] Thompson, pp. 28-46; Delbrück, pp. 94-95, 99-100, Previte-Orton, p. 434.

[6] Thompson, p. 47.

[7] Dan C. Heinemeier, *A History of Brunswick*, Heinemeier Publications, Arlington, VA, 1999, pp. 59-60.

[8] Thompson, pp. 49-56.

[9] Valentin, pp. 35-40; Thompson, pp. 128-34; Heinemeier, p. 61; the Delbrück quote is found on p. 95.

[10] Heinemeier, p. 63; Dannenbauer, Heinrich, *Politik und Wirtschaft in der Altdeutschen Kaiserzeit*, Wissenschaftliche Buchgesellschaft, Darmstadt, Special Reprint, 1966, pp. 23-24; Thompson, p. 315.

[11] Heinemeier, p. 63; Thompson, pp. 136-39, 164-66, 217-235, 297-98; Demandt, pp. 160, 165, 167.

[12] Demandt, pp. 169-177.

[13] Demandt, pp. 180-84.

[14] Thompson, pp. 325-32; Demandt, pp. 184-93; the foregoing references to events in Wetter are taken from Karl Wenckebach, *Zur Geschichte der Stadt, des Stiftes und der Kirche zu Wetter*, Selbstverlag der Evangelischen Kirchengemeinde Wetter, 1966, pp. 11-16.

[15] Robert S. Lopez, *The Commercial Revolution of the Middle Ages, 950-1350*, Cambridge University Press, New York, 1976, p. 31. The brief preceding quote is from David Herlihy, "Ecological Conditions and Demographic Change," in Richard L. DeMolen, ed., *One Thousand Years: Western Europe in the Middle Ages*, Houghton Mifflin, Boston, 1974, p. 31.

[16] Herlihy, p. 31.

[17] Herlihy, pp. 13-14, Lopez, pp. 29, 36; Postan, pp. 68-69.

[18] Postan, pp. 137-40, 159-70; Herlihy, 16-17; Lopez, pp. 37-40.

[19] Postan, p. 149-50; Herlihy, p. 17.

[20] Postan, pp. 155-58, 172-78; Lopez, pp. 144-47; Thompson, p. 275.

[21] In German the word for manor is *Hof*, plural *Höfe*. Postan, pp. 264-71, 288.

[22] Postan, pp. 201, 265-71; James W. Thompson, *History of the Middle Ages 300-1500*, Norton & Co., New York, 1931, p. 272.

[23] Kurt Wagner, *Leben auf dem Lande im Wandel des Industrialisierung: Das Dorf war früher auch keine heile Welt*, Insel Verlag, Frankfurt am Main, 1986, pp. 44, 47-48; Duckett, p. 109; Thompson, *History of the Middle Ages*, pp. 268-80; Daniel D. McGarry, *Medieval History and Civilization*, MacMillan Publishing, New York, 1976, pp. 235-50; George C. Selery, and A.C. Krey, *Medieval Foundations of Western Civilization*, Harper Brothers Publishers, New York, 1929, pp. 145-54.

Chapter 5

THE DEVELOPMENT OF LIFE IN THE HESSIAN TOWNS

Our initial look at the history of town life in Hesse begins in the ancient world and culminates in the High Middle Ages with the extension of town rights by feudal authorities and the towns' struggle to continually expand these rights. These efforts were opposed by the same feudal lords, who both granted limited rights and sought to maintain ironclad control over local trade and government. The areas that later spawned Hessian towns in some cases were first settled by people of Roman, Alamannic or Frank backgrounds. These locations had much to do with trade, security and the need to exercise administrative control over nearby land forms or important travel routes. Often an ancient fortified place, improved upon over the centuries by various overlords, became the seed that blossomed into a town. Such a stronghold would slowly expand with the local settlement of traders and farmers who retreated behind the security of its walls when threats arose. In turn they provided it with products to sell and a magnet for itinerant traders and more settlers. In broad outline this is the way that towns grew up in Hesse and throughout Germany, and we will focus on three examples: Darmstadt, Kassel and Marburg.

KASSEL[1]

This ancient capital of lower Hesse was first mentioned in recorded history in 913 with reference to a royal Frankish manor or *castellum* at which King Conrad I spent some time. The Latin term suggests very early settlement at the point when the Franks first annexed the area. It was perhaps used first as a staging area for Frankish troops, and later settled by traders plying the local road or river networks. King Henry II granted the area to his wife Kunigunde, who in 1017 founded a nunnery known as Kaufungen. As later emperor, Henry provided well for his empress' foundation, granting it the manor of Kassel and its inhabitants, local hunting and fishing rights, and much surrounding land and woods. Later the manor reverted to royal control and the cloister retained only the rights to some surrounding villages. The manor lands eventually passed to local Hessian lords including the Werner family; when the male Werners died out in 1122 the surviving female heir brought these lands to her marriage with Ludwig, a future landgrave of Thuringia. This alliance also brought with it a powerful enemy, the archbishopric of Mainz, whose efforts to exert control over much of Hesse brought it into generations of conflict with the Thuringian landgraves and other local strongmen. Mainz erected strongholds of its own in the area to cement its claims.

The first recognizable town government was formed of a group of *ministeriales* in the service of the landgrave of Thuringia. These generally were men of non-noble birth who served the nobility as paid stewards, guards, administrators, and in other roles. By 1189, when Kassel was referred to as a *civitas* or town, a group of these administrators were set up as town elders or *Schöffen*. Kassel was evolving as a more and more important center of trade and local security for the landgraves. Before 1200 they extended town privileges to Kassel, a distinction that usually provided rights to hold markets and fairs, maintain independent local courts and administrative functions, and otherwise operate independent of direct control by the overlord. This freedom provided opportunity and incentives to expand trade and thus benefited the lord through increased taxation, tolls, and other duties.

When the Thuringian ruling line died out in 1247, a major period of insecurity and conflict set in, as the Archbishop of Mainz tried to assert his ownership rights and seize Kassel. A fief of the town and surrounding area was given to the brothers von Wolfenhausen, overriding the prerogatives of the local *Schultheiß*, the primary governing official of the town. As it turned out, The brothers were opposed successfully by local officials loyal to Heinrich, the heir of Thuringia, and local conflict was only ended in 1263 with agreement by Mainz to enfief the area to Heinrich's ally Sophie of Brabant: Sophie held the town in trust for her minor son. It was this line that would form the ancient ruling family of landgraves that forged the state of Hesse as it was known throughout the Middle Ages (see Chapter Four). Henceforth it was independent of both Thuringia and Mainz.

From this time Kassel grew rapidly. Mendicant orders of monks came into the town, including the Carmelites. Modern town walls were erected by the early thirteenth century, including a recognizable town gate and a crenelated tower. A sizable bridge here over the Fulda promoted connections and trade ties from Thuringia to the Rhine. Where the bridge met the right bank of the Fulda a new town quarter grew up known as the *Neustadt*. It included its own market square later known as the Wood Market, and a church dedicated to Mary Magdalene. Neustadt was a planned extension with well-laid-out streets fanning out from the square. This contrasted with the unplanned, helter-skelter aspect of the original town. By 1300 the wife of the landgrave had erected a hospital in town dedicated to Holy Elizabeth, and near it the Annaberg Cloister was constructed. Around the same time the Carmelites finally obtained permission from Mainz to build a house for their order as well.

In 1342 a great flood of the Fulda River engulfed the town, even sweeping over the altar of the Mary Magdalene church. The Fulda Bridge was so weakened by this flood on top of many years of heavy use that a rebuilding program had to be undertaken. Landgrave Heinrich raised tolls on use of the bridge in 1346 to collect the needed repair funds. The tax-related documentation gives some insight into the trade products of the day that crossed its span: fruit, coal, woad-ashes, hops, wool, peas, cork, beer by the cart load, herring and butter by the ton, baskets of figs, copper, tin, soap, alum, wax and oil sold by weight, and both local and Moroccan leather taxed by the piece. The outbreak of plague in Germany in 1348 cost many lives in Kassel as well. It was said that wolves at this time roamed surrounding areas in large packs, attacking the unwary.

By now Kassel consisted of three separately administered precincts with their own market squares, churches, town halls and seals. Neustadt, *Altstadt* (old town), and Freedom (founded in 1328) were their names. Only in 1378 did these areas come together to form a common town administration, probably in the face of great pressures exerted by Landgrave Hermann.

In 1336 the landgrave received permission from the emperor to hold three annual market days in Kassel: the first Sunday in Lent, St. James Sunday (around July 25), and St. Martin's Day (November 11). Another existing market day was held on the Sunday after Easter. All merchants that traveled through Kassel were required to make their wares available for sale for at least three days. Trade competition was fierce, and market rights attained by nearby Münden in 1246 soon began to adversely affect trade in Kassel. In 1316 then-Landgrave Otto enacted a retaliatory trade ordinance against

Münden, but apparently without effect. Another enactment with significantly greater effects on Kassel's economic prospects was a prohibition on leaving one's property to the church or any of its tax-free entities. This was to restrict a common practice that was depriving the state of tax revenue and causing more and more peasants to fall into dependence on ecclesiastical lords.

As we saw in Chapter 4, a defining figure of the late fourteenth century was Landgrave Hermann the Learned, a stubborn, autocratic and controlling figure whose nickname was probably applied more with derision than respect by his unfortunate subjects. He seemed to spawn enemies on all sides, and imposed heavy taxation on his towns to pay for the military forces he needed to defend himself. Commerce suffered, and the landgrave increased taxes further on imported food, cloth and metal products. This sparked a years-long rebellion among the merchant citizens of Kassel and other Hessian towns, who allied themselves in a compact of January 1, 1377 to oppose the landgrave's import tax. The dissatisfied local nobility also formed an anti-landgrave alliance and joined with the towns. The townsmen seized the landgrave's castle in Kassel in 1378. This appears to have been the last straw, and the landgrave counter-attacked to restore his authority shortly thereafter. By 1380 the rebels were thoroughly cowed. In June the town elders, *Bürgermeister*, and other upper class citizens swore their undying loyalty to the landgrave with hands outstretched to the heavens. But the next few years saw the landgrave take back much of Kassel's rights to self-administration. He suspended the monopoly rights of the existing guilds, giving outsiders the chance to settle and sell their wares in the town. Judicial decisions were made subject to the landgrave's approval as well. Many of the wealthier merchant families who previously had opposed Landgrave Hermann felt compelled to leave town in this period.

Another rebellion broke out in 1384 (see again Chapter Four) when these disenfranchised citizens allied themselves with the rulers of Thuringia, Brunswick and the Archbishop of Mainz to try to topple the landgrave. From three sides these forces converged to besiege Kassel and lay waste to the surrounding lands. Twice the town was stormed, and over 200 stones weighing one hundred pounds apiece were heaved over the walls. Over five hundred flaming arrows were shot in as well. But in this crisis the citizenry stood by their landgrave, beating off the siege. Similar attacks ensued over the next few years. But all were driven off in failure, and Hermann punished the traitors severely. Many were beheaded, drawn and quartered and their goods and property forfeited. Similar extreme measures were taken in other Hessian towns.

This time the landgrave also chose to reward those who had stood by him. The punishing ordinances of 1380 were set aside, guild rights were restored, and the town elders again were permitted to choose their own officials to administer the local markets. But as a residence of the reigning ruler, many of the rights enjoyed by other towns were never restored in Kassel, for the landgrave wanted to control matters in his capital through his own picked officials. Another cycle of terrible violence broke out in 1400, with more attacks by Mainz. Kassel again was besieged and stormed through the orchard behind its castle. Twelve local villages were put to fire and sword at this time. Herman the Learned continued his troubled rule for decades, only dying in 1413. He left an eleven-year-old successor, his son Ludwig.

Ludwig was to prove as accommodating as his father was irascible, his first official act being to restore and expand many of Kassel's town rights. These included giving the citizenry the rights to local pastureland and reducing or eliminating taxes on many local properties. The town guilds received new rights at this time as well. Ludwig reigned for many years, and he often issued proclamations that further expanded town rights. These were announced by a bell ringer who called the citizens to assemble on the steps of the Altstadt town hall. Good news and bad was delivered here over the centuries until well into the 1800s. Under Ludwig's father's rule a weighing house had been built on this square (1404), and four years later the foundation was laid on the same site for the town hall. The cellar of this building was expansive and served as a public tavern accessible through a pointed-arch doorway. Here everyone sat together, even the landgrave, who periodically joined his subjects in good times and bad. It was also during Ludwig's rule (1421) that a cloth- or merchant-house was built next to St. Martin's Church in Altstadt.

Ludwig's forces struck Mainz such a blow in 1427 that its influence in the land was greatly reduced. Hesse at last had found a worthy ruler whose sovereignty was much more secure. The nobility became increasingly loyal to the state, and stopped supporting the ambitions of Mainz. Perhaps the most important land acquisition by Ludwig I was that of the counties of Nidda and Ziegenhain in 1450. The latter had long divided upper and lower Hesse, its counts exercising great influence in opposition to the Hessian landgraves. At this point the towns of Ziegenhain, Treysa, Rauschenberg, Gemünden and Staufenberg came into the landgrave's hands.[2]

Despite the restoration of many economic and governmental privileges and freedoms to the towns, this was an era in which laws were established to regulate various behaviors that must have caused many problems. Strong penalties were enacted for gambling with dice, as well as wandering around town at night without a light. Patronizing taverns after ringing of the nine o'clock closing bell was proscribed, as was the misuse of weapons in hunting or other activities. Too much ostentation in dress and celebration also were regulated. Betrothals and weddings were banned unless parents gave their consent. The number of guests one could invite to wedding and baptism feasts was limited, with severe fines for those attending without invitations. Eventually a public facility was built in which larger-scale entertainments could be held, the so-called Wedding House, built at public expense in 1421. This stood until 1909 near the Fulda on the market square, after which it was torn down to make way for a new bridge. It was here that the annual birthday celebration was held for the landgrave, including the distribution of food and gifts to the poor.

Education for the sons of Kassel was provided for with the landgrave inviting in a Dutch religious order, the *Kogelherren*, who were renowned for their course of teaching. Their house was dedicated to more than devotional learning, with trades, book writing, and private studies of all kinds offered. The graduates became sought after in service to various German princes in need of strong skills in business and administration. By 1528 four had become chancellors in other states.

A most interesting feature of life in Kassel was the availability of the public baths. Townsmen and local farmers alike patronized the baths for personal hygiene and camaraderie alike. Men and women both used the baths, and enjoyed food and drink while bathing. The baths were open regular hours on specific days, with the servants advertising their availability by hanging out basins in public view. The baths were a service of the state, which collected admission fees and ensured the continued maintenance of this key public service. Ludwig is recorded as having visited the baths personally some sixteen times in one year in Kassel and elsewhere across his lands. He often invited his noble guests who attended his tournaments to come with him to bathe.

This brings us to a description of life at the landgrave's court. The state tax register of 1431 provides some insight on the lifestyle of the prince and his courtiers. A court band included two pipers, a trumpeter and a trombone player. This compared favorably to the size of such ensembles in other princes' courts. There was a court architect/builder, Ludwig Guldener, a stone mason, and a painter, the priest Johann von Waldau, who painted the Spangenberg castle chapel in 1464. Court servants included a master gunner and gunsmith, a physician, a barber/surgeon, jesters, and numerous members of the nobility serving as councilors. Paid servants performed numerous household and military duties. All these were clothed and fed at court and provided the landgrave with companionship as he hunted, feasted, carried out feuds with his enemies or went on pilgrimage. The state marksmen, although small in number, served as a kind of bodyguard for the landgrave. Twice annually he hosted outside guests in large-scale medieval tournaments.

Food and drink at court included local Hessian wines, and meat from the state manor farms, especially mutton. Wild game came from the rangers in the state forests. During religious fasts meat gave way to fish (usually herring or cod) and eggs, as well as grain dishes. Most food and clothing for commoners and the court alike were produced locally.

Landgrave Ludwig the Peaceable also had a keen interest in alchemy, searching for the means to turn base metals into gold. His interest mirrored that of other small German princes who were poor in resources. One account of his death in 1458 after 45 years of rule suggests that he inhaled some noxious fumes during alchemy experiments and never fully recovered.

Ludwig's son and namesake, Ludwig II had to share his inheritance with a brother, William, who was given upper Hesse as his own landgraviate. Ludwig II apparently had more in common with his warlike grandfather, Hermann, than with his peace-loving father. Kassel was in open dissent at the time of his accession to power, with the town council pitted against various elements of the citizenry in the guilds and other citizens. As Ludwig returned to Kassel with his forces in 1464 after engaging in a feud he found a large group of the citizenry in open revolt under a ringleader named Amelung. He wound up seating a new ruling council to end the strife. He also undertook to remodel the ancient castle, adding a large half-timbered section (*Fachwerk*) to a wing facing the town. Three years later this section was blown up in an accidental gunpowder explosion and had to be rebuilt.

In 1472 Ludwig's son William the Elder came to power. At this point the town included 843 households, about 4,500 souls in all. It was not a particularly prosperous town, with its main income consisting of tolls from local traffic on the Fulda and the roads, as well as some fees derived from mill works. Some rental income from local lands was available, as was tax revenue from local butchers, tavern owners, bakers, weavers, leather workers, and brewers, the latter taxed by the batch. Weavers rented space in the merchant house on the town square, bathers paid for use of the baths, and even the local bordello was taxed. Weighing fees were charged for the scales in the markets, tapping fees were charged in the wine cellars, and there was income from fines and penalties assessed on such law breakers as bakers who sold goods that did not meet prescribed weights.

The town treasury in turn bore the expenses of a variety of its servants and employees. Soldiers had to be paid, employees had to be clothed in various ways, and even the boots of the *Bürgermeister* had to be paid for by the town. The landgrave had to be paid his dues in various ways and at various times, such as New Years, when gifts were due to him and his officials and family members.

William the Elder reverted to his own grandfather's mild ways of dealing with the towns, and was even able to quell a nascent rebellion in 1490 by personally interceding with the rebels. Among his most appreciated reforms (1489) was to free his citizens from the ancient prerogatives of the court to interfere in marriage rights and dictate marriages of townspeople to members of the landgrave's court. William later became sole ruler in Hesse and succeeded in imposing a much-enjoyed and unusual peace across the land, freeing its travelers from most of the depredations of highwaymen and other criminals. For this he was remembered in poetry and song long after his reign. This also brought tremendous economic advantage to his realm by encouraging many merchants to come there to do business. This was especially true of the Kassel market fairs. He minted the first Hessian *Taler* in 1502 with the image of Holy Elizabeth on it. This was apparently made of the Peruvian silver now flooding Europe after the discoveries of Spain in the New World. Wage rates had been very low in Hesse due to the appreciation in currency values through most of the fifteenth century.

More legislation was needed against ostentatious entertaining, public drunkenness, and lavish clothing styles that frittered away the money of those who sought to ape the conventions of the wealthiest of society. Common citizens were ordered to wear clothes made of cheap and ordinary English cloth. Restrictions were laid down on the wearing of ornate embroidered clothing, the amount of wine to be served at weddings and other feasts, and the taking of spirits made of the dregs of wine casks and originally used for medicinal purposes. Its price was set at a maximum of two *Heller*. Prices for beer and wine in taverns were pegged at no more than ten *Weißpfennige*. These renewed rules suggest the failure earlier ordinances to address most of the same practices.

MARBURG[3]

The town of Marburg is a good example of a fortified place giving shelter to people over many centuries and eventually evolving into a city. It is one of a handful of places in upper Hesse where natural features provided the opportunity to protect truly large numbers of people and their animals from danger of attack. In ancient times the layout was improved with a simple narrow entrance and a trench and wall structure, probably including thorn hedges and perhaps a blockhouse. When the stone walls were added remains a mystery, although they pre-dated the first reference to Marburg in written records in 1130. Marburg's Achilles heel was water. No convenient local source existed until a five-kilometer canal was dug to bring in supplies from the Marbach.

Beyond protection of the local lords and their wealth, possessions, and underlings, the fort also afforded a sphere of control over important roads heading west from Amöneburg to three crossing points of the Lahn River. Like many other small towns in this early period, Marburg also served the needs of itinerant traders for overnight shelter. About twenty-eight kilometers is the limit such a merchant could travel comfortably in a day, and Marburg is located twenty-eight kilometers from Frankenberg and twenty-six from Gießen. This also created fierce competition among the towns for the goods and income of local markets.

Beyond the early merchant families who located here, most of the common population drifted in from surrounding villages, many of which were abandoned to waste. The wealthier merchant families formed the *Schöffen*, an organized ruling caste for the town. When this agglomeration of merchant and peasant immigrants achieved town status also is not known. The Marburg *Pfennig* coin is known to have existed from an early time, probably from at least 1140, although documentation of the minting operation dates from 1194. This was a period of great hardship, as in 1195 the town was burned to the ground by the forces of Mainz, then feuding with the landgraves in Thuringia. This may have been the impetus for the creation of more substantial town walls. An official appointed by the landgrave called the *Schultheiß*, an office translatable as mayor or magistrate at the village level. This official originally presided over the Schöffen. By 1284 a *Bürgermeister* was in this role and the less prestigious *Schultheiß* had been relegated to the role of petty judge.

When Sophie of Brabant brought her young son who aspired to be landgrave of Hesse to Marburg in 1248 she established the town as the residence of the Hessian ruling line. She stayed in Marburg until her death in 1275, making it the political epicenter of the state. From here she directed the efforts of her forces against Mainz in her efforts to establish the boy's right to rule. Almost immediately she presided over forays to destroy the neighboring fortresses of Weißenstein, Blankenstein, and Hollende, from each of which the troops of the archbishop had to be expelled. She also directed the creation of the Frauenberg castle to protect her interests along the approach to Mainz-controlled Amöneburg. At this time a number of families settled in the town were appointed to the castle garrison, and some upper Hessians acquired hereditary titles: the Riedesels of Eisenbach became hereditary marshals. Other castle guard families were Von Dernbach, Von Dörnberg, Von Eringshausen, Engel, Imhof, Hobeherr, Von Holzhausen, Von Kalsmunt, Von Milchling, Von Nordeck, Rode, Von Scheuernschloß, Weißberger, and Von Weitershausen.

Marburg joined the Rhenish league of towns that formed in 1254-56 for common protection against the Archbishop of Mainz. After Sophie's death, her son Landgrave Henry I lost no time in remodeling the castle to make it a more fitting seat of rule. He also moved his official residence to Kassel in 1277, the better to combat the efforts of Mainz to absorb this area. Although he moved back to Marburg prior to his death, the precedent was established and Kassel generally was the designated capital of Hesse from this point forward.

Growth during Sophie's life had been rapid, and by 1260 a "new town" or *Neustadt* section was being referred to; it would later be brought within the town walls along with a later section called "*Renthof*". Still later reference is made to sections called Zahlbach, Weidenhausen, Grün, Bulchenstein and Leckerberg, the latter being the section in which the poorest lived. Fires largely destroyed the town in 1261 and 1319, probably due to a combination of overcrowded conditions, straw roofs and timber houses, and of course the shortage of available water. By the early fourteenth century there was a settlement of Jewish traders in Marburg who established a "Jewish school" or synagogue.

The *Schöffen* families in this period included the following: Zollner, Raustein, von Fronhausen, Imhof, von Steinhaus, von Graben, Schinebein, Zahn, Engel, Süßkirch, Wurstbendel, Brüning, and von Gladbach. Sometimes fathers and sons, brothers, and/or cousins served concurrently. The citizens not represented by guilds or the *Schöffen* naturally formed a strong opposition to the ruling caste. This led to the opening up of the ruling body in the early fourteenth century to permit representatives of various town precincts to join: six from the Altstadt, four from Weidenhausen, and two from the Neustadt. But unlike the original *Schöffen,* who continued to be appointed for life terms, the new members had to serve one-year terms.

Various feudal taxes and tithes were owed to an array of lords who held landlord rights to local lands. Marburg's treasury had to compensate those who held such authority over publicly used lands. The town constitution indicated that these charges amounted to 300 silver marks, including fifty to the Stefan Monastery in Mainz for use of the Ebsdorf lands and fifty more to Agnes of Nuremberg. All payments were directed to be made in a reliable currency, Köln *Pfennige*. In Marburg two forms of dues typically had to be paid to the landlords: taxes and the *Bede*. Taxes were extraordinary payments, e.g., war or bride taxes, paid to provide a dowry for a princess. The *Bede* included regular payments in winter and summer to the landlords for rights to live on and use the land. Along with this the city levied the so-called *Geschoß* tax for its own budget needs. This was a form of property and building tax levied on the basis of income. The "fire-shilling" was a hearth tax levied on every hearth.

The thirteenth and early fourteenth centuries were times of great building and remodeling in Marburg. The Elizabeth Church was completed in 1283 except for the towers that were added later. The castle was again expanded with a section known as the new castle. The Franciscans built an expensive cloister building around 1277. The Dominicans also settled here near the *Lahntor* entrance to town, beginning to build their church in 1291. New walls, towers and doors consumed huge sums in these times, as did the improvement of streets. At the end of the century a new church building was under construction as well. This was a three-story, Gothic-style hall church with four arches. Its famous church tower was only added in 1447-73. At the beginning of the fourteenth century the old Rathaus was built. This and other construction kept the local stone masons very busy, along with many sculptors, painters and other artists. Marburg was then an influential cultural center of the first order.

In the time of Ludwig the Peaceable the state was coming into its own as an acknowledged force on the German political landscape, largely safe from the centuries-long quest of Mainz to absorb large sections of its lands. Marburg now sat comfortably astride the route from Frankfurt to Kassel, an important trade road. Landgrave Ludwig even resided here for a time. His death in 1458 brought about difficulties as his two sons squabbled over rights to the landgraviate. This was resolved by dividing the lands of upper and lower Hesse, although the death within three years of one of the brothers resulted in reunification. More lands came to the state with the Katzenelnbogen inheritance of 1479, and Marburg benefited from the general prosperity. The town landscape was not greatly altered, but the castle itself was improved significantly. The desire for more room and sumptuousness as well as the advent of firearms entailed a major building program. The landgrave's quarters on the south front was expanded with new stories in a stone and half-timbered construction. This brought it to approximately the same height as the chapel and knight's room. The women's quarters were moved to the corner tower where they could be accorded more space. Cisterns and a deep well were installed for water. Under the floor a heating system was installed, while other rooms received Dutch tile ovens and fireplaces, with the first iron stove appearing in 1498.

The architect of the reconstruction also had to improve the castle defenses. The frontal works had to be pushed further forward and firing positions erected in which flanking fire could be delivered against an attacker. The walls were made four meters thick to guard against cannon fire and loopholes were made for shooting down upon attackers before they reached the outer walls on the north and west sides. All this was prudent given the array of conflicts the Hessians rulers were party to: from 1350-1478 almost twenty major and minor conflicts broke out. Villages surrounding towns like

Marburg were always the object of pillage and destruction, stealing of animals, etc. Some local villages never recovered from the destruction.

All citizens had the duty of helping defend the town in emergencies. For small, day-to-day requirements the town had about fifteen armored troops with crossbows. For larger contingencies all able-bodied men were expected to arm themselves and turn out to defend the town. The *Bürgermeister* and *Schöffen* were to act as officers to lead the troops. They mustered the troops on the town square with their weapons and tents. Shields and tents had to be marked with the town arms. Dominicans and Franciscans turned out to act as chaplains for the soldiery. The main weapon up to 1511 was the crossbow. After this the town maintained musketeers, and an arsenal of small cannon was procured. The general populace also was required to turn out to perform manual labor as needed to improve the town's defenses. This occurred in 1375, when moats and palisades had to be built to secure areas of the town built in front of its walls, and in 1498 when the Weidenhäuser Bridge had to be rebuilt.

The Marburgers were quick to avenge themselves when attacked. In May 1327 Mainz forces from Amöneburg marched in and stole cattle and took citizens of Marburg prisoner. The Marburgers struck back, losing many men before the gates of the strong fortress at Amöneburg. In the war with the Star League of Hessian nobles (see Chapter Four) the town was attacked but not taken in 1373. In 1381 Mainz forces from Mellnau fell on Marburg in a surprise assault in which townsmen again were seized and others driven behind the town walls. The Landgrave Hermann attacked and besieged Mellnau and bottled it up long enough that water ran out, but a relief force arrived in time to save the town and kill so many Marburgers that the phrase "Go to Mellnau" came to mean the same as dying. From 1404-11 Marburg attacked Amöneburg almost annually, never conquering it but always destroying the surrounding villages, farms and fields. In 1410 and 1411 Count John of Nassau struck Marburg with similar blows, but the town and its castle were so strong that it never was taken by enemy force during the Middle Ages.

The financial situation of the town was in crisis during the period of rule of Landgrave Hermann the Learned and his incessant conflicts with neighboring powers. He had to pay back 4,000 guilders to the town after the Star League war, money that the town had had difficulty in borrowing to provide to him. It had been forced by the landgrave to impose taxes on sales and purchases of goods such as food and other daily necessities (metals, wax, leather, clothing, cloth, etc.). Internal and external trade were crippled to a large degree, just as in other towns across the land. After a year of these taxes Marburg was able to repeal them, but only on payment of 3,000 more guilders to the landgrave. This repeal just saved the *Schöffen* from disaster at the hands of the common citizenry who had opposed the taxes. The landgrave's finances still were in disastrous shape. He had to pawn the towns of Marburg, Gießen and Grünberg to Frankfurt Jews, and in Marburg this gave them rights to impose excise taxes. He later reclaimed ownership from the Jews but did not at the same time relive the town of its responsibility to continue paying them the excise taxes! The extensive holdings of church foundations were tax-free. Also untaxed were the castle guards and their families, state administrators, the town *Schöffen*, and some other local bureaucrats. This too became grounds for ongoing conflicts between and among guild members, town council, religious and secular officials in Marburg. If taxes were waived, still the wages of the town officials were low, including those of the *Schöffen*. This probably reflected the perception that it was an honor and a privilege to serve the town in such a leadership capacity.

As in Kassel, the opposition of the *Schöffen* to the tax policies of the landgrave caused him to side with their enemies in the guilds and others in the community who sought inclusion in a more democratic government. In 1390 a new constitution was promulgated. The old council elected by the *Schöffen* was overthrown, and guilds and other townsmen were permitted to choose their own representatives to enter into discussions about matters such as taxes and budgets. The most important officers in town were doubled in number to allow the non-*Schöffen* citizenry to appoint some of these as well. More squabbles broke out in 1410 and 1414, followed in 1446 by an even greater revolt pitting the ruling families against the guilds. The curfew bells were rung, town doors were locked down, and general upheaval resulted. The landgrave's influence on the appointment of officials in the town was very strong in the fourteenth and early fifteenth centuries; rights of self-administration suffered significantly. The constitution of Landgrave Hermann II of 1390 basically remained in place with only minor alteration until 1834.

In 1396 Jewish financiers lost their remaining investments when the German King Wenzel waived their rights to continue to collect such debts in Marburg and other German towns. Many of them lost huge sums of money. In 1350 when the Black Plague broke out Jews also had been accused of bringing it on by poisoning wells. This rumor seems to have spread as a result of the statement of a Jewish physician who had been tortured and broken on the rack, who confessed to poisoning wells at the orders of the chief rabbi of Toledo, Spain. Terrible anti-Semitic pogroms were kicked off in which whole Jewish communities were driven out or their members killed by fire and the sword. Such reactions were especially strong in the Rhineland. The Jewish community in Frankfurt was destroyed in spring 1349, and the 3000-strong Jewish community of Mainz, among the largest and most prosperous in Germany, soon met the same fate. Through 1351 over two hundred such communities were attacked.[4] In Marburg and across Hesse Jews likewise were robbed and killed, their synagogues put to the torch. The Jewish School in Marburg apparently was among the casualties.

After the disastrous financial period under Hermann the Learned, his son Ludwig worked to promote Marburg's financial health. Within a few decades the town was able to resume a robust program of church building. The Hessian state now could exercise its influence fully on the road network that connected east and west Germany, imposing lucrative tolls. For Marburg the most important of these was the road through Marburg from Frankfurt to Kassel, as well as a shorter route running through Hesse by Marburg. Ludwig also began to reside more often in Marburg.

The time of Henry II brought another economic decline. The town had to pay out so much for its troops that took part in the various conflicts that it was impossible to pay its own creditors properly. His son William III likewise forced the town to endure his pawning to other creditors of the town and its income. In the final decades of the fifteenth and the early sixteenth centuries, the economic situation was again on the upswing. As in Kassel, repeated regulations against conspicuous consumption at weddings, baptisms, and funerals had to be issued. An expensive new town hall was begun in 1512, a further sign of good times. Also as at Kassel, patrons were prohibited from being in taverns after the stroke of the "wine bell" at 9:00 p.m. Yelling, mischief making, and throwing things out of windows into the alleys were prohibited after dark. Ordinances were enacted against drunkenness and working on Sundays and holidays.

Marburg early became the key judicial center of Hesse, with three courts. The Town Court met in a public gathering three or four times a year to hear complaints over common trade matters up to a value of five shillings. This court met at the fountain in the market square. The Upper Court served under the authority of the landgrave and his officials, meeting once or twice a year in the town hall to hear cases in which over five shillings were at issue. A third court was the state or criminal court, controlling life and death decisions in judgements against criminals. It met at a place that later became the spot at which executions by fire took place. Those held in jail were treated roughly as a matter of course. Penalties could include death by decapitation or hanging for crimes such as murder. The chopping off of hands was prescribed for endangering the town by bearing arms against the authorities. Lesser offenses such as pilfering gardens or fields could bring a trip to the stocks in the market square (with the pilfered crops hung around one's neck). There also was a pillory near the Weidenhäuser Bridge. A quarrelsome wife might be sentenced to a dunking in the river suspended in a basket. The public announcement of a sentence of death would be accompanied by an ancient tradition in which a stick was broken in half and thrown at the feet of the condemned. The town wall along Burggasse Street was marked with a carving of an ax and a severed hand as a warning to criminals.

Records from 1464 indicate a town executioner was in residence. He and his wife received use of a free house in Weidenhausen, an annual wage amounting to seven ells of cloth, probably something under 16 feet of yardage. The executioner also had the right to attend any wedding party with his wife and enjoy free food and drink at the host's expense. This was so resented by young couples that at last it was repealed, and the executioner instead received rights to claim any fallen animals within the town's jurisdiction. He also had to act as dogcatcher, and annually dispatched about 60 dogs in this way.

During periods of conflict between the ruling party and the other citizenry in Marburg, one penalty that often was meted out was to require that a lawbreaker be banished from the town for a full year. This could accompany fines paid to the landgrave and the *Schöffen* and donating a large measure of wine to the town. Unfortunate citizens who had contracted communicable diseases that could endanger the community might also be put outside the town to die of exposure.

The plague wiped out hundreds at a time, so fluctuation of the population was great. Most of the original inhabitants emigrating from nearby villages were subjects of the landgrave, but efforts were made to bar serfs who were trying to escape their lords. Every new resident had to pledge to the *Bürgermeister* that he would be loyal, pay taxes and support the defense of the town. He had to immediately assume control of a house or an apartment. The plague probably helped make a large amount of housing stock available.

A major role was played by the town guilds economically, politically, culturally and in religion. Their monopoly control over their trades and the goods they produced aimed to guarantee every member a secure existence on an equal footing with that of his fellow guildsmen. At first, legitimate birth and personal honor were the only needed qualifications; later, specific requirements to serve as apprentices, yeomen, and to travel outside their place of training to work were added. A masterwork had to be produced to show skills, and an entrance fee paid to the guild. At last the ranks were closed and only a certain number of members permitted to join. The town constitution laid out the rights of the largest of the town guilds, the wool weavers; it specified that cloth makers were not permitted to work as tailors, for the right to cut cloth was reserved for the prominent local merchant families. Most of them lived in the Weidenhausen area of town. They and the tanners were to take the water they needed for their trades from the defensive moat that was built on this side of town.

Other prominent Marburg guilds included: bakers, linen weavers, painters, grocers, shoemakers, butchers, tailors, smiths, hat makers, and at times vintners. Some lesser trades joined from time to time in a common guild called the community guild ("*Gemeinren*"): potters, fishermen, copper smiths and tinkers, soap boilers, stone roofers, masons, carpenters, saddlers, and goldsmiths. The guilds were permitted to exercise their monopoly rights within a 1.5 German mile radius (about six English miles) of the town. They established prices and set limits on individual production rates. Guild rules were enforced by the town council as well as the landgrave's officials, guarantying the well- being and economic security of guild members for centuries. This is shown in the grand buildings and records of astounding feasts sponsored by the guilds.

Most hand craftsmen in the town led a very poor and difficult existence. Only a few were able to raise themselves above the low average of the rest. The linen and wool weavers belonged to the industrial proletariat. Without also growing some food locally, real hunger would have ensued for their families. This accounts for the efforts of the council and the landgrave to regulate prices at the weekly and annual markets and fairs to keep the poor from being priced out of the market. Crop and meat prices were most difficult to regulate, since plant and animal diseases impacted supply and imported and exported foods were subject to such price fluctuation.

In the Middle Ages street paving was unknown in the towns, being an innovation mostly undertaken in the eighteenth century. To navigate the filth of the streets in rainy times one had to have wooden shoes or stilts. Everyone had his pig or cow, with paid town herders pasturing some 600 pigs and 300 cows in this period. Much of the manure wound up in the streets in front of the houses. The council had to constantly warn the citizenry against dumping dead cats and dogs or farm animals on manure piles. Packs of stray dogs served to keep some of this carrion off the streets, but once they grew too numerous and began to stray into the churches the town executioner had to be called in. During drought conditions the filth gathered in the streets and rotted, raising a terrible stink. Then, the next big rain would wash the mess from the high to the lower points of the town, where it would collect until the authorities got around to having it removed from the traffic areas. With no street lighting, people had to provide lights outside their own buildings or none was available at all.

Unsanitary conditions brought repeated outbreaks of disease, especially plague. Every couple of years it would break out. In 1483 up to 2,500 citizens were killed, about half the population. The plague came frequently, especially in the Thirty Years War. In 1611 alone Marburg lost 1,100 inhabitants to it. Public baths were available and used even by poor people. Poor hygiene here spread other diseases. Many families, not just the higher classes in town, had bathing rooms in their homes and took daily baths since lavatory sinks were still unknown. Actual doctors were unknown, and when plague broke out the sufferers were banished from the town to try to arrest the course of the disease. At one point the sisters of St. Francis operated a local nunnery that served as a hospital.

Marburg was no closed town in this period. Religious pilgrims traveled here to visit the Elizabeth Church, or on their way to various other holy places. Holy men of a variety of religious orders visited the cloisters and order houses in the town. Besides the House of the German Order there were three cloisters in Marburg, plus houses of the Franciscan and Beguine sisters (also a nursing order). There were manors of religious houses outside the area with monks or laymen in residence whose task was to collect tolls and land rents locally and send them to their motherhouses. Quarters for visiting monks and abbots also were maintained. The manor of the Cistercians of the Arnsburg Cloister was founded 1230, that of the Kaldern Cloister about 1365. Several other foundations existed in the town. The nobility of Marburg also had regular contact with their relations outside the town. Travel to other towns was common. Journeymen and wandering apprentices arrived to serve in the guilds.

Major festive occasions for the populace were the tournaments that occurred periodically. In the High Middle Ages the knights no longer jousted against one another in full armor, but competed by lancing targets called "Turk's heads" as a show of their dexterity. In 1466 Henry III invited the nobility from all around to enjoy a Shrove Tuesday tournament celebration. So many came that the town had to make special provisions for their 400 horses.

People rose early in these times, and evening meals in the winter were taken by 4:00 p.m., while it was still light outside. The mid-day meal was taken at 10:00-11:00 a.m. On fast days when the Catholic prohibition on meat eating was in force, fish consumption must have been huge. Salt-water fish were a major article of foreign commerce. In a tariff document of 1425 these types were referenced: Rhine fish, salmon, sturgeon, skinned fish and dried cod. Big feasts were hosted by the town officials at which two or three *Ohm* of wine were consumed (80-120 gallons).

The costumes of the upper classes were grand, taking their cue from those at court. Furriers were kept busy trimming garments. Cloth from England and France was available, but was only salable in the toll-free markets and on May 1. Common people's dress, described in the tailor's guild regulations of 1495, consisted of long smocks.

Education was well regulated like other aspects of life in the town. A school ordinance of 1453 made school mandatory for all children of every class, and suggests that the schools had been in existence since long before this issuance. Children had to bring quantities of cherry stones with them to school; whether these were for doing their counting or for the teacher to use in extracting the oil is not known. At Advent every pupil had to bring along two lights with which to study in the morning and evening hours. Before Christmas and Easter vacations every pupil had to pay two mite coins to the teacher. Students had to go to church daily and sing for mass and vespers services, as well as on Sunday and holidays. The teacher had to see that children came to church in their choir robes, acted with proper manners, did not call out or jostle each other, and did not make loud cries or fool around on their way home. He also had to be sure they kept their books clean. Subjects must have included writing, arithmetic, singing, the beginnings of Latin studies and religion. In a later school ordinance of 1460 the teacher was prohibited from allowing women to enter his school, sitting room or bedroom so as to protect students from improper thoughts and rumors. Finally, he was prohibited from striking students on the head.

We conclude our review of Marburg with the following balance sheet of 1499/1500:

Income
Summer *Bede* and beer tax	695 pounds
Old wine tax	201 pounds
Various other taxes, fees, fines and the Winter *Bede*	862 pounds

Expenses
To the Landgrave as hereditary rents	300 pounds
Other hereditary rents	891 pounds
Distributions to the monastery of St. Stefan, Mainz	175 pounds

Distributions to the town-administered foundations	303 Pounds
Building administration	357 pounds
Watchmen's wages	69 pounds
Keepers of gates, tolls and paths	46 pounds
Community distributions	338 pounds

    72 leather fire buckets bought in Frankfurt (25 Florins)
    Oven tiles for the Town Hall oven
    Provisions for the Council for all occasions
    Executioner's wages for killing 47 stray dogs
    Messenger's wages

Soldier's wages	269 pounds
Gifts of Wine provided to various officials	38 pounds

    Dominican Father Superior (provincial)
    Council of Wetter
    Countess Elizabeth of Nassau
    Councilman's wife when lying in
    State Commander
    Three grandees from Amöneburg
    Landgrave Wilhelm II for the funeral of his first wife
    The Council of Wetzlar
    The town *Schöffen* for various feasts and banquets they hosted

In total, income was 2,854 pounds, expenses 2,647 pounds, for a surplus of 207 pounds.

DARMSTADT[5]

Beginning in Roman times, the opening up of the Odenwald as a frontier defense against the Germanic tribes resulted in the building of numerous roads that were critical to the eventual development of the Darmstadt area. The chain of Roman forts known as the *limes* built in this area were connected to supply depots along the Rhine by these roads. Most important among these was the old mountain or high road that ran along the western fringe of the Odenwald and connected the Rhine and Main rivers by 100 AD. The Wine Road also ran through Darmstadt, connecting it to Eberstadt to the southwest. The other major east-west connecting road from the Rhine ran through Darmstadt on its way to Dieburg or *Auderia*, a larger Roman settlement. The nearest Roman settlements were at Bessungen and Eberstadt.

Bessungen, later a suburb of Darmstadt, included an Alamannic settlement, as did nearby Arheilgen. The nearby Darm Stream may have encouraged Alamannic settlement as it provided convenient water access for their livestock. The Franks entered the area after they defeated the Alamanni in 496, and evidence of Frankish settlement has been found in Darmstadt proper. Some coexistence with the Alamanni seems to have occurred, although the Franks took over the more fertile areas leaving the Alamanni to their animal herding in the less productive Odenwald.

About 1000 a royal forest was established in this area known as the *Dreieich Forst* or Three-Oak Forest. It was a protected area, with both forest and wildlife resources reserved by the ban of the king for royal use only. Darmstadt and Arheilgen were two rangers' posts established for royal officials who looked after the forest and produced game or other products from it as needed by the king, particularly when his travels or hunting interests brought him to the area. Even in the nineteenth century Darmstadt had to provide an annual produce tithe to the Lords von Isenburg in return for use of the forest. This so-called "wild oats" tithe required them to hand over 42 *Malter* (of eight bushels each) of oats, two white geese, and two capons. Although it may be traced in written records back to 1452, this tithe likely was instituted long before.

Hunting in the *Bannforst* without permission originally could result in the loss of one's right hand, and any game taken was forfeited to the nearest forest ranger. Other penalties included monetary fines, or the replacement of any game taken with equivalent domestic stock, e.g., an ox for a stag, a billy goat for a male buck, and a goat for a doe. By 1338 there were thirty-six gamekeepers in the *Dreieich* like the one at Darmstadt. Their so-called "*Sattelhoffe*" or saddle manors included living areas, horse and hound stalls, bakehouses and barns, all to be kept in readiness to host a hunting party of the crown. The ranger also had to provide enough straw to maintain the animals of the visiting entourage, and in return he was to be provided an ample, eight-days' supply of food and drink at royal expense. It was difficult to maintain agricultural holdings in this area in the face of the constant encroachment of the wild forest. Over time the ranger's position was converted to a similar role in service to the local lord who held portions of the forest in fief from the crown. The Darmstadt manor was upgraded by the building of a fort and later a more extensive castle known as the Wasserburg. Darmstadt was first mentioned in written sources in the latter half of the eleventh century when the visit of count Sigeboto von Darmundestat was recorded when he came to go hunting.

Emperor Henry II awarded this area as a fief to the bishop of Würzburg, apparently to appease his wounded ego after the emperor had created a competing bishopric in Bamberg and likewise given it land in southern Hesse. Würzburg in turn enfiefed the area to the Katzenelnbogen counts of the lower Lahn River in exchange for their feudal military support. Other knights who held rights over time to the locally derived taxes, tithes and land use payments included the lords von Falkenstein, von Isenburg-Büdingen, von Münzenberg, and von Frankenstein. This division sought to prevent the creation of an over-powerful independent realm ruled by the counts von Katzenelnbogen alone. But by 1300 they had become the greatest power in the area. The key manor at Gehaborn, finally purchased by the city of Darmstadt in the nineteenth century, originally was a Cistercian manor that brought the local area into contact with this economically powerful religious house. The Cistercians were a very industrious order renowned for turning waste into productive land. From their local base at Eberbach in the Rhineland they created a number of manors from Hessian wasteland or donated lands such as that at Gehaborn that had been given by a knight who took monk's vows in 1170. Cistercian commercial activity had positive effects on local trade and administration.

Over time, less and less of the feudal relationship with the Würzburg bishopric was recognized in any practical sense. By the sixteenth century no vestiges of this tie remained. Darmstadt was only the most important part of an organized grouping of fortified areas that promoted the power of the Katzenelnbogen counts through the fourteenth century. Related acquisitions included Auerberg, Zwingenberg, Dornberg (near Groß-Gerau), Rüsselsheim, Lichtenberg and Reinheim. Significant improvements to the castle in Darmstadt to make it a more worthy residence for the counts were undertaken around 1360. Truly opulent appointments were added by Philip the Elder von Katzenelnbogen when he wed Anna of Württemberg here in 1422. At that time

Figures 5-1/5-2 An aerial view of the ancient Lichtenberg Castle, seat of the landgraves of Darmstadt, and a point of refuge for many refugees in the Thirty Years War. Its commanding presence in the local area may be easily seen. Below, a view of one of the many halls in the residence of the Grand Duke, Darmstadt.

many nobles and their families from near and far were in attendance. This marriage bound two of the most powerful noble houses in Germany.

The partition of the town in four subparts (*Letzen*) likely dates from the fourteenth century. These were at first defensive precincts charged with protecting their individual areas of the town, and each had two masters charged with maintaining the integrity of their part of the town walls. The section known as *Plan* was located around the market square south of the castle; south of this was the *Bessung* precinct. East of the Darm was the *Arheilger* precinct in the north and the *Hundstall Letze* to the south. The precinct also served as administrative districts for assessment of the taxes and *Bede* owed to the local lords. The community comprised about 1,000 people at the end of this period. A circle of prominent families assumed the predominant role in governing the town for long periods; among them the names Gans, Montedil, and Walrabe loom large.

Of course Darmstadt was more than an administrative center for the counts by this time. The gamekeeper's lodge had evolved into a farming settlement with its earliest farmsteads growing up along the old road to Frankfurt and around the east side of the Darm Stream that fed the moat around the Wasserburg. This was probably the area along the modern Alexanderstraße. Fences or hedges were added in time to protect the villagers from predation by robbers who preyed on the land. The land was poor, the dangers of the nearby forest many, but the farmers guarded the fields of their exposed settlement to keep them safe from robbery. Loss of life was not uncommon, but the settlement grew.

The entire arable was divided according to the three-field system and enclosed in hedges and fences to protect the crops. Every farmer was required to maintain the boundary and repair it wherever animals breached it. In the sixteenth century it was among the duties of the two *Bürgermeister* of Darmstadt to oversee and punish those who were dilatory about maintaining fences around the fields. Every year the farmers would ceremoniously patrol the perimeters to make sure the fences were in good condition and the boundary markers remained undisturbed by neighboring villages. In early times this border patrol was a popular annual festival, with the whole community turning out for it. With the advent of Christianity images of saints and similar relics were carried along as the party inspected the frontiers, and prayers were raised to bless the land for the coming year. Over time a specific boundary inspector was appointed to lead the procession, marked by his wearing a special glove and pointing out the features that marked the boundary. In Darmstadt local youths were permitted on that day to drink wine at the community's expense as a reward for memorizing the border signs. They also might be better reminded with a box on the ear if necessary to improve their mental retention of the signs. Any alteration of the boundary was considered a crime. Gruesome penalties awaited those who disturbed the boundaries in ancient times; one penalty called for the lawbreaker to be buried up to his neck while a youth who had never plowed the land before drove a plow with four unbroken foals over the man to decapitate him. This was to appease the wrath of the deity that had been angered by the criminal and provide a sacrifice for good crops.

Woods, pastures and water were held and administered in common by the community. All the farmers who owned homes and land in the community met to collectively decide about rights to use the land's resources. They were referred to as those who "had their own smoke" in a home fireplace. Their meeting (*Märkerding*) was held in the open air, by custom under an ancient linden tree. Over time, local lords took over the rights to administer the land use. The old land constitution gave the lords von Katzenelnbogen such rights over Darmstadt's farmers. They annually chose officials who allotted wood quotas, arrested lawbreakers, assigned lands to individual farmers, and oversaw the work of the gamekeepers. Based on other towns' examples, it seems probable that the commander of Wasserburg castle originally assumed substantial authority for managing the affairs of Darmstadt. By the mid-fourteenth century at the latest, authority for the town administration passed over to the *Schultheiß* and the *Schöffen*. This marked the town's true emergence as an independent political entity.

In 1362 the *Schultheiß* (mayor) and the 14 *Schöffen* (magistrates) were named as follows: *Schultheiß* Adolf Flecke. *Schöffen* Conrad Rehnbrechte, his brother Sifrid Rehnbrechte, Heile Betzil, Henne Gans, Heintze Leist, Thielle Beckir, Gerhart Montedil, Renne Beckir, Contze Walrabe, Contze Ratgebe, Heintze von Dorenburg (Dornberg), Contzel Dytzen Sohn, Alhelm Wylant, and Herbort Wechtir. The *Schultheiß* was charged with looking out for the rights of the lord. As early as the mid-fifteenth century not all the local farmers were permitted to join in the *Märkerding*, rather only fourteen magistrates of the wealthier class and fourteen farmers picked by the local district court. The latter were supposed to uphold the interests of the common farmers. This was a compromise imposed by Philip the Elder von Katzenelnbogen in 1457 to end infighting that had pitted the old ruling families against the disenfranchised members of the town community. Philip's death in 1479 caused the old rulers to reassert their power. Population growth eventually ended the practice of free use of the forest resources for the local farmers, who then had their usage rights restricted such that the larger landholders received proportionately more access and benefit.

Since pastures were seldom privately owned, there was a shortage of good land to produce winter fodder. This kept the numbers of domestic animals rather low. Even in the first decade of the seventeenth century there were no more than 280 cows and about 450 pigs in Darmstadt. In the sixteenth century, Darmstadters owned their own bulls and boars; in many similar cases these were held in common among numerous villages. The forest pasturing of pigs was originally permitted to the farmers for free, but later required a payment to the lord. Over time the pigs of many surrounding areas were brought to the Darmstadt woods to feed, and this became a lucrative source of income for the local lord.

On July 23, 1330 the emperor Ludwig the Bavarian granted the Katzenelnbogen lords the right to hold a weekly market and an annual fair in Darmstadt, as well as to create a town wall and moat structure to protect it. Darmstadt must have warranted such consideration due to its location on trade routes, proximity to some very desirable hunting grounds in the surrounding forests, and the fact that it was now the administrative center of this part of the county. Since the tithes to the lords were paid in a variety of agricultural goods as well as money, a convenient mid-point location was needed to which the surrounding farmers in the Odenwald could bring their produce to hand it over to the counts' authorities. The town walls were a natural step in protecting the town's produce barns or granaries, stalls for farm animals, storage rooms for wool, wine and hides, and the all-important annual market fair. The town held weekly market days on Tuesdays and an annual trade fair lasting from two days before until two days after the feast of the Virgin Mary's birth (September 6-10). Both markets were administered according to the market and trade rules of Frankfurt. Count William I and his consort Countess Else brought about the creation of a number of vineyards around Darmstadt. The population followed their example, and vineyards grew up that even in the seventeenth century still decorated the town.

In this way the Darmstadt farming village slowly grew into a town. By 1380 a church was under construction. The Wasserburg had to be improved further over time as a castle worthy of its lordly owners. The farmers of the entire area had to turn out to help build these structures, as well as the local roads and town walls. Only at the beginning of the fifteenth century were tax receipts sufficient to permit construction of a more modern defensive structure with castle keeps, moats and walls and an all-encompassing outer works. Darmstadt never acquired another wall system; the original one was destroyed in the aftermath of war in the sixteenth century on orders of Emperor Charles V.

Darmstadt was the regional capital but only served as residence of the count on occasion, as when he visited a tournament in nearby Aschaffenburg in 1452. Rheinfels Castle on the Rhine remained the Katzenelnbogens' official residence. Darmstadt was required to send all taxes, produce and other duties to the court at Rheinfels. The monks at Gehaborn likewise had to haul their goods as far as Stockstadt, where these were loaded on a Rhine boat and transported up to Rheinfels. About the mid-fifteenth century more changes were made to the castle residence in Darmstadt. The three-story palace was outfitted with a new kitchen, council chamber, bathroom, wine cellar, dining and entertaining rooms, servants quarters in the first floor, and princely lounges, guest rooms and living areas in the second floor. A separate chancery, gate houses, watchtower, and a 52-horse stable all were added. Only in the fifteenth century did Darmstadt rise to the level of a reasonably important administrative seat.

It appears that the feudal rights to serve as guards of the castle represented a privileged office among liegemen to the counts, and various families of the local nobility held this position, some for fairly long periods of time. Here are some of the families and time periods involved: von Frankenstein (1292-1560); von Bellersheim (1370-1445); von Arheilgen (1373); von Dirmstein (1399); von Grebenroth (1394-1477); von Stockheim (1407-45); von Rödelheim (1408-1515); von Dornberg and von Rodenstein (both 1419); Homberg (1424-80); von Bürresheim (1410); von Waldeck; von Steinach (1483); von Waschenbach (1417); von Rohrbach (1440); and the final family mentioned, the von Reifenbergs of the Taunus Mountains (1472-1515).

Evidence suggests that in this period already about a dozen manor houses of the nobility existed, concentrated mostly in the lower town and around the market square. Based on the locations of the dwellings of the town fathers of the fifteenth century, the areas around the market square and city church probably had assumed a predominantly town-like quality by this time. By about the mid-fifteenth century the city church attained the size and appearance that it still had in the nineteenth century, excepting the somewhat later addition of the belfry spire. The Katzenelnbogen court carried out all construction efforts for the church, chapels and castle. Before it could assume more autonomy the town had to begin to provide funds for its own architectural improvements. A Darmstadt town hall called the *Spielhaus* was first recorded in 1397. It was called the *Spielhaus* because it housed the town meeting room in which feasts were held. For New Years many in the town were wined and dined at the cost of the town treasury. It supposedly stood on the north side of the town square in front of the castle. By the mid-sixteenth century this old town hall was too small and was replaced with a new *Fachwerk* (half-timbered) building on the south side of the square where the current *Rathaus* now stands. The city had to pay property taxes or *Bede* based on individual properties. This was administered and collected by the *Landschreiber* or count's clerk. In the early fifteenth century the precinct of Arheilgen itself paid 300 guilders, Bessungen ninety, and Wixhausen 100.

The heart of the economic life of the town was in the weekly markets and the annual fairs. In ordinances of 1450 and 1456 bread and meat sales by non-resident bakers were specifically regulated. None of the finer handwork trades were resident in the town. Only bakers, butchers, smiths, brick makers, carpenters and cobblers were found there. Saddlers and rope-makers were in nearby Groß-Gerau, probably because it was the local crossroads of the mountain and lowland roads and better situated for their businesses. Darmstadt remained little more than an overgrown farm village with regard to commerce with the wider world. The annual fair in town had only local importance. Only in the sixteenth century is it recorded that Jews settled in the town to carry on trade, although the counts von Katzenelnbogen were well disposed towards them.

Even the count's authorities in this time were rarely on site in Darmstadt. The clerk to the petty sessions, who was the top official in charge of accounts, lived there periodically at most. The local bailiff lived in the castle at Auerbach. Only the administrator of the Darmstadt district lived in the town. The general population grew rapidly, however, and even as early as 1451 records show the development of a suburb in front of the town.

Until the end of the sixteenth century the most important political office in town was the *Schultheiß*. He supposedly represented not only the interests of the count, but that of the community as well. In the Katzenelnbogen period these officials also had opportunities to rise to positions of influence at court. Over time it became clear that the *Schultheiß* increasingly settled differences between the community and the count to the benefit of the latter. For this reason the town-appointed *Bürgermeister* overtook the older office in importance. By the sixteenth century the four sections of the town (Arheil, Hundstall, Bessungen, and Plan) each had a town councilor on the ruling council. The council organized itself somewhat independently from the count, choosing the two *Bürgermeister* from its own ranks. Still, the authority of the council remained greatly circumscribed by that of the many appointed officials of the count. During the century the counts acted to further circumscribe the council's authority by insisting on a council seat for their appointed *Schultheiß*. Some town citizens objected strenuously to this.

When the last of the counts von Katzenelnbogen died in 1479, they left their domain to the Hessian landgraves whose preferred seats were at Kassel and Marburg. In 1521 the young Hessian Landgrave Philip came into office, and this resulted in better and more prosperous times for Darmstadt.

NOTES TO CHAPTER 5

[1] This section is based on Karl Heidelbach, *Kassel, ein Jahrtausend hessischer Geschichte*, Bärenreiter Verlag, Kassel, 1957, pp. 27-66.
[2] W. Kürschner, *Geschichte der Stadt Marburg*, Elwertsche Verlagsbuchhandlung, Marburg, 1934, pp. 55-56.
[3] Marburg history section is based on Kürschner, pp. 24-86.
[4] Robert S. Gottfried, *The Black Death*, The Free Press, New York, 1983, pp. 52, 73-74.
[5] Based on Friedrich Battenberg, *Darmstadts Geschichte*, Eduard Roether Verlag, Darmstadt, 1980, pp. 12-46; and Adolf Müller, *Aus Darmstadts Vergangenheit*, Selbstverlag der Stadt Darmstadt, 1930, pp. 14-34.

CHAPTER 6

Approach of the Modern Era: The Sixteenth Century

Early sixteenth century Germany was perhaps the most dynamic area in Europe, with a fast-growing population, strong economy and widespread prosperity. Socially, Germans were a roiling mass of contradictions. Rather uncouth in manner, they were thought of as jovial in outlook. They were capable of great religious conviction, but also given to carnal pursuits, with out-of-wedlock sex common among the young. The tortures inflicted on convicted criminals of the time were truly ghastly, but there also was a great streak of generosity and mercy in the national character. As in modern times, Germans were considered hard working, disciplined and determined, yet drunkenness was universal. People were healthier than in neighboring lands, with public bathing houses commonly used by men and women. At the same time, resort to prostitution was widespread, and was considered a serious but unsurprising sin. Rulers openly licensed and taxed houses of prostitution. Only outbreaks of syphilis in the 1490s acted to reign it in, having a similar effect on attendance at bathhouses.

The twin revolutions under way in these times were the spiritual/political reforms of the Protestant Reformation and the fundamental economic restructuring brought about by capitalistic trading and production. This chapter will explore both trends in depth as they relate to Hesse.

Even as Germany flourished economically, it remained mired in political chaos. Central authority was non-existent, and across the land dozens of small principalities, most much smaller than Hesse, exercised dominion over their scattered holdings. The Holy Roman Empire which purported to stand above all these petty states and dominions was weak and little able to exercise much actual control outside the immediate sphere of influence of the emperor. Typically, he ruled best in Austria, southern Germany, and neighboring areas. One measure of the influence and importance of Hesse within the Empire was the level of tax it paid as a member state. The dukes of Austria and Burgundy each paid 900 florins annually. A second group consisting of the "electors" (empowered to cast votes in the choice of new emperors) came next, along with the states of Bavaria, Württemberg, Lorraine, and the landgrave of Hesse. These each had an annual assessment of 600 florins. Thus Hesse was by no means insignificant within the constellation of imperial members.

Also a considerable force within the empire were the great ecclesiastical princes, some of whom were pious and efficient administrators, others worldly and corrupt. Upwards of 20% of German lands were in the hands of these bishops and archbishops whose military retainers, large land holdings, and craven pursuits of food, wealth and women little distinguished them from their secular fellows. If anything, these lords were much less appreciated than their counterparts in the secular nobility. Their role as leaders in the church hierarchy sometimes contrasted sharply with their rather blatant disregard of many of its teachings. They served as a blight on Catholicism that helped encourage Protestant reform efforts.

There was incessant fighting among nobles, petty princes and ecclesiastical rulers, much robbery in towns and on the highways, and periodic peasant revolts everywhere; "a universal reign of force" as Will Durant has characterized it. Much of the violence stemmed from the loss of power, influence, and economic success among many of the lesser nobility, who felt pressed on all sides. Their once monopolistic hold on military force broken by the advent of firearms, they felt increasingly marginalized in a society in which their old, comfortable place was being lost. Worse, the stagnant income from their small land holdings failed to keep pace with the prevailing price inflation, and a number were reduced to dire economic straits. This drove many of them to outright brigandage, preying on merchants and other travelers plying the roads around the knights' strongholds. Elton has described these old nobles as "...a sterile and declining class, capable of dangerous nihilism and generally feared." The petty lords Götz von Berlichingen and Franz von Sickingen are typical of this breed across Germany, and their depredations in Hesse and opposition to its landgrave will be discussed later. Many of these nobles held the title of imperial knight, bestowed by the German emperor. They acknowledged no local ruler but answered only to the emperor. A group of them along the Rhine organized for common action in 1522 to try to regain a measure of their lost influence.[1]

The institution of the church in Germany was under siege, yet personal piety was a strong and widespread aspect of the national character. Family prayer was led by the head of the household, often from a prayer book if he were literate or an illustrated religious tract if he were not. The Virgin was venerated and depicted in the arts as much as Christ himself. Reciting of the rosary was frequent among folk who knew how to do so. Despite this orthodoxy, however, Germans chafed under a church structure that more and more seemed corrupted by worldliness and run by flawed officials. As noted above, the bishops too often were mostly grasping and unrepentant sinners who barely hid their transgressions behind a veil of religious practice. The lower clergy in Germany existed in huge numbers, and while some were pious many others were about as ignorant and superstitious as the flocks they sought to serve. Most had children by their common-law wives. The German church structure that was set up to extract payments of all kinds from peasantry and nobility alike was further overlaid with the papal hierarchy of the Church in Rome. It too had innumerable endowments and funding requirements that it laid on its relatively prosperous German adherents to the north. A truly massive amount of money and gifts of all kinds flowed annually into Rome's church coffers from across the Alps. Thus Luther's reforms were more than a spiritual challenge to Catholicism. They were a dagger pointed at its financial jugular.

> All in all the picture is one of a people too vigorous and prosperous to tolerate any longer the manacles of feudalism or the exactions of Rome. A proud sense of German nationality survived all political fragmentation, and checked supernational emperors as well as supernatural popes; the Reformation would defeat the Holy Roman Empire as well as the papacy. In the 1,500-year war between Teuton and Roman victory was once more, as in the fifth century, inclining toward Germany.[2]

The towns and cities of Germany were at a high level of development and prosperity in the fifty years after 1480. It was here that wealthy merchant families lived and traded, and in their ranks was incubated a new class of entrepreneurs that would perfect capitalist practices and generate huge fortunes for themselves in the course of the century. Germany's geographical position now made it the crossroads of European trade. Not until the nineteenth century would it again enjoy so favorable a trading role. Its road system was rough and primitive, but in better condition than it would be in the

A SOCIAL HISTORY OF HESSE

century after 1600, and it was an important and often more affordable alternative to the heavily taxed and tolled river trade routes.

Capitalism at this point was a strong threat to the urban guilds. It also used the guilds as production sources, sometimes providing capital, tools or raw materials for the artisans' use. The products were then resold for profit on a large scale. Mining particularly lent itself to capitalist control, since once surface deposits of ore ran out deep shaft mining could only be undertaken with the infusion of large amounts of money. This was beyond the means of smaller co-ops or even many of the territorial princes who were too adept at spending to generate and retain much seed capital. A third manifestation of capitalism was in the "putting out" system that began in earnest in this era. Large numbers of home-based workers might be paid modest sums to spin, weave, or otherwise work raw wool that was provided to them by financiers who thus bypassed the guild system altogether. The state generally took its cut of the proceeds of enterprises within its borders, mostly licensing mining rights to producers in exchange for regular payments. It also undertook mercantilist practices to mold the economy in ways that benefited local needs. [3]

> Everybody's customary needs were to be satisfied...The preservation of the peculiar class distinctions was a definite objective of the economic and social policies of the German territorial state. To find the "just price" that the producer and the laborer could demand and the consumer could afford was the main concern. Beyond this, disturbing influences from abroad had to be kept out. The export of wool was prohibited in order to keep the price of wool and indigenous cloth low, while the import of foreign cloth was hindered. The sale of victuals was strictly supervised, and middlemen were excluded in order to keep food prices cheap and stable. Similar emphasis was placed on the stabilization of wages. The output and wages of artisans were exactly prescribed; craft guilds were often dissolved so as to make price-fixing impossible. Where a shortage of day workers occurred, people who were idle were forced to work. [4]

EVENTS IN HESSE

To begin our look at the eventful sixteenth century in Hesse proper, it is worthwhile recapping in brief the history of the three major ruling lines that were dominant there from the twelfth century onward. The earliest of these lines, that of the Thuringian landgraves, succeeded in 1122 in establishing and maintaining a toehold in Hesse despite the historical opposition of the important archbishops of Mainz. Shrewd marriages had brought them the inheritance of two powerful families of the Hessian nobility: the Gisos and the Werners. By 1150 their territories included the Maden district with the castle and town of Gudensberg, the Kassel area, Marburg and its environs, Fritzlar, Wetter, the Hersfeld abbey holdings, and the Hasungen and Breitenau cloisters' lands. Some lands further west in the Westerwald region included Herborn, Haiger, Löhnberg on the Lahn and other local holdings.

Still, a host of smaller nobles' lands thwarted the Thuringians' efforts to amass large, contiguous holdings in upper and lower Hesse. The pressure of Mainz also kept Hesse sufficiently separate from the main Thuringian landgraviate that it was never incorporated outright. The line of almost a dozen Thuringian landgraves that ruled from 1122-1247 included Ludwig IV, husband of Holy Elizabeth and father of Sophie of

Brabant. It was Sophie's determination to see her son, Henry I, became landgrave in Hesse that resulted in the founding of the original line of Hessian landgraves.

The landgraves who followed Henry I from 1308-1509 were involved several times in partitions of the land into separate regimes in upper and lower Hesse. This followed the desire of fathers to provide for two sons upon their deaths. The truculent and domineering Hermann II ruled a united Hesse from 1367-1413, but his land was under almost constant attack, usually at the instigation of Mainz. His son, the peace-loving Ludwig I, succeeded in 1450 in bringing a major prize into his family's hands: the Ziegenhain lands that had long severed upper and lower Hesse. After his death Ludwig's sons, Ludwig II and Henry III, ruled lower and upper Hesse respectively, but not without extended periods of fratricidal civil war. Henry's extremely adept political move of marrying into the Katzenelnbogen family brought the Hessian house much wealth and eventually vast new land holdings, especially in southern Hesse around the local capital of Darmstadt.

The Katzenelnbogen counts rivaled the Hessian house in political influence, and exceeded them in wealth. Their lucrative holdings on the Rhine River provided regular income in traffic tolls. Count Johann IV, who ruled from 1402-1444, established a presence in the Odenwald, the *Dreieich* (Three Oak) forest lands, and the counties Schaumburg and Hadamar. The family's far-flung holdings were administered in the west from the Rheinfels castle on the Rhine, and in the east from Darmstadt, as we have seen in the last chapter. This fabulously rich inheritance truly was the making of the Hessian landgraves in later political and religious developments during the Reformation.[5]

The state administrative apparatus of Hesse developed along with the land acquisitions in the Middle Ages. From the thirteenth century district officials were established to pursue the military and political aims of the landgraves, as well as the economic needs of administering taxes and tithes. Two major regional administrations, divided into the Lahn and Werra River areas, oversaw these district offices, each with a *Landvogt* (bailiff) in charge. The bailiffs and another office, that of the county judge, maintained major influence and responsibility over the districts up until the time of Landgrave Ludwig I. They in turn were managed by the highest officials in the landgrave's court, the lord high steward or marshal of the court. Centralized control grew ever stronger through the fourteenth and fifteenth centuries.

Ludwig I again reorganized the districts to add treasurers responsible for financial matters. These managed a group of district servants who served to enforce the treasurer's authority. Local gendarmeries also provided police functions, especially that of safely escorting merchants to the markets in Frankfurt and elsewhere. Ludwig also had much success in rationalizing and centralizing the economic affairs of the land under his authority. He used the guild rights letters of Kassel as his model throughout his realm. He also presided over a huge increase in the mining and working of copper ore in the Richelsdorf Mountains; by 1460 at least thirteen smelting works were in operation.[6]

PHILIP THE MAGNANIMOUS

The sixteenth century saw the first truly great landgrave of Hesse stride onto the scene: Philip, to whom history would attach the moniker "Magnanimous." His father, the Landgrave William I (1493-1509) was a masterful player of imperial politics, and used his connections to increase his landholdings. In the process he made enemies that would challenge Hessian rights to the inheritance of the Katzenelnbogen lands. The resulting conflicts lasted for decades. Until Philip's birth in 1504, it looked as though the line would die out altogether. William's death in 1509 due in large part to the ravages of syphilis left his son too young to assume the seat of power. Only the almost super-human efforts of his mother to protect Philip and promote his rights to succession ultimately ensured his ascent to power. Anna held the regency for her son with an uneasy but unyielding grasp.[7]

Arrayed against Anna and Philip were the local nobility in the so-called estates, the ever-present opposition of the Mainz archbishopric, imperial knights, and other forces who would be only too happy to carve out pieces of Hesse for themselves. The nobles in Hesse's provinces along the Rhine were in the final throes of what has been called a "crisis of feudalism," in which their way of life was being eroded on many fronts. Much of their difficulty stemmed from policies and action by the landgraves, who saw little merit in maintaining a proud and obstreperous class of rowdy malcontents who challenged central authority. This nobility resented the taxes imposed by their prince, as well as efforts to limit feuds and maintain order on the roads in opposition to the marauding knights. The knights also had sided against Landgrave William II in a war in 1504 in which they wound up being beaten and humiliated; they nursed this grudge until William's death when the chance came to take revenge on his minor son and heir.

The regency period, in which Anna acted on behalf of her son, lasted from 1509-18. The estates, consisting of representatives of nobles, townsmen, and churchmen, traditionally met in a diet called and mostly dominated by the landgrave. Now, the nobles called themselves to the diet, and used it to organize opposition to young Philip. They blocked efforts to raise taxes, issue coinage, engage in declared war, or take other steps generally reserved to the state. This opposition was led by Ludwig von Boyneburg, whose lands on the eastern border with Saxony provided easy access to neighboring enemies who were glad to meddle in Hesse while its landgrave was still a child. The nobles grew so strong that they even were able to separate the boy from his mother from 1510-14. Anna and Philip later were able to flee together for two years to escape their enemies. In the meantime, in 1512 Franz von Sickingen and other robber knights attacked and plundered the unprotected towns of Darmstadt, Gross Umstadt, and even Mainz, among others. Smaller towns and villages around Darmstadt were reduced to ashes or forced to pay ransom that brought severe financial hardship all around. Gross Bieberau was among the towns in this category.[8] Anna's entreaties to the emperor and to loyal knights at last succeeded in winning a place for Philip again in Hesse, and precipitating a new crisis in 1517. The emperor recognized Philip's majority in 1518, paving the way for his unchallenged rule. But this was too late to head off an attack by Sickingen, who struck the mounted troops of the landgrave as they attempted to re-impose order on the roads. Philip had to endure a humiliating defeat with terms dictated by von Sickingen.

Philip's own revenge was not long in coming, however. The league of Rhenish knights organized in 1522 under von Sickingen's leadership determined to attack an ally of Philip's, the Archbishop of Trier. The so-called Knight's War proved unsuccessful for the Rhenish knights. Sickingen had to abandon his siege of Trier, which was too ably defended, and retreat to his own castle at Landshut. Philip's forces joined with those of Trier and other rulers of the Palatinate to attack him on his home turf. The siege of Landshut prevailed, von Sickingen soon died of wounds received, and Philip at last was able to crush the knights' power for good. The victorious allies went about pulling down the knights' home castles and reducing them to impotence. Not surprisingly, Philip's cordial hatred of the lesser nobility and staunch support for the peasantry against them stemmed from these tumultuous years. Philip added land to his own holdings in this period as well, with Lipperode, Brake, and Varenholz acquired from Hildesheim, the castles Rodenburg, Hagenburg and Arnburg in the county of Schaumburg, and in 1521 Hoya and Diepholz with the districts of Drakenburg, Nieburg, and Lauenau. Clearly his power was in the ascendancy.[9]

Philip now took steps to exclude many of the nobility from his diet, ejecting them in 1518 and rounding out the membership from the more loyal ranks of the townsmen. With taxes and revenue being the major preoccupation of these meetings, Philip was satisfied to surround himself with the wealthy merchants who could help him. Where his brother princes typically relied heavily on the local nobility to whom they were often connected by family and traditional ties, Philip made his official appointments almost the exclusive domain of the patrician merchant class in his realm. The most senior offices were filled from among a close-knit group of about twenty-five families drawn heavily from Kassel, Marburg and Homberg on the Elfze.

The Hessian chancellery managed the lower officials across the realm, including the *Oberamtmänner* (upper district officials), the *Statthaltern* (governors), and *Landvögte* (state bailiffs). The major local administrative units were still the *Ämter*, or districts, led by an *Amtmann* with both political and military responsibilities. The landgrave's officials had to affix seals to any contracts or other documents affecting property ownership, credit extension, and other legal matters in which the state wished to oversee the peasants' agreements to protect them from being exploited. More powerful at the local level were the *Rentmeister* or *Kellner* who managed financial affairs. County registers known as *Salbücher* were kept in which duties and privileges were set down so that lords—secular and religious—were prevented from arbitrarily altering them to the peasants' disadvantage.[10]

The Reformation brought many changes to Philip's policies on both religion and the socio-economic management of his state. It provided a major financial windfall by paving the way for seizure of the rich assets of the Catholic Church in Hesse. It also made him an important actor on the stage of German politics as he began to play a key role as defender of the new faith. A chance meeting with the Lutheran theologian Melanchthon in 1524 is credited with winning Philip to the Lutheran side, but probably as important were a host of middle- and upper-level Hessian officials who were inclined to favor the new faith. As early as 1521 local clergymen, monks, and leaders in some of the towns, particularly Kassel, also were important in the spread of Lutheranism in Hesse. In October 1526 Philip decreed the thorough introduction of Protestantism throughout his lands, and by 1527 he had appointed so-called visitors (later superintendents) to replace the Catholic hierarchy in appointing pastors, creating or reforming schools, and closing monasteries. They also played a key role in setting up common chests for poor relief. The closure of church institutions and seizure of related assets was a tremendous financial boost in establishing the state on a more modern footing. Philip also now more fully controlled local law and administration where church officials formerly had exerted major influence.[11]

Over time upwards of fifty cloisters and other religious foundations were closed, their inhabitants forced to move on and find work and sustenance elsewhere. This was a difficult process, carried out over the most strenuous objections of those who were displaced. Major foundations of the Cistercians, Benedictines, and the German Order in Haina, Marburg, Lippoldsberg, Kaufungen and Helmarshausen were closed, along with a host of smaller properties. In some cases decades would elapse before the process could be completed. Some 60% of the resulting wealth went to fund good works of various kinds, including the foundation of a university at Marburg in July 1527. It opened with eleven teachers and eighty-eight students. The other 40% of the assets went into the landgrave's coffers for use in state building. Many of the church properties were re-designated as state hospitals, including Merxhausen and Haina in 1533, Hofheim in 1535 and Gronau in 1542. These institutions cared for the helpless poor, chronically ill, blind, epileptics, and insane persons. Despite the positive aspects of the freeing up of this wealth, an unfortunate side effect resulted: opportunities for single women to express piety and devote themselves fully to a spiritual life became very limited. With the closure of the nunneries, their accepted role in the church was limited to that of being devoted wives and daughters.[12]

Other effects of the Reformation across the land were of course equally fundamental. As noted earlier, there was tremendous pent-up frustration with the clergy and church officials who so often lived lives in violation of the church's teachings and extracted payment from the masses like parasites. Popular animosity was so strong that the church-imposed Inquisition that had swept Spain was simply blocked from most of Germany for decades. People in all walks of life enthusiastically embraced Protestantism's promise of reforms, and in later years were more steadfast than their rulers in refusing to compromise these ideals. The peasants sought simple changes that met their immediate needs: They demanded preaching of the "pure gospel," unencumbered by non-biblical interpretation, which they felt was essential to salvation. They wanted appointment of pastors by the community itself, and the right to enjoy doctrinal authority, again based directly on the Bible. They also expected their religious leaders to reside in the villages they served, and wanted churches to provide weddings, burials, etc. that would be free or less expensive. People wanted their pastors to provide consolation in a life of toil and pain, and rejected theological demands that interfered with their lives. Ministers who failed to meet these needs were often ignored or resisted.

Sunday services now included occasional communion and weekly preaching, with preaching now assuming a more important role. Communion was taken once or twice a year on dates tied to the harvest cycle, especially at Easter. Seating was arranged according to social standing, and the singing of hymns had to be done by rote since most parishioners could not read. Even during the church services there could be much talking and napping. Sundays included rest and recreation in the morning after church; this might include gathering in taverns, visiting distant relatives, or attending the occasional fair. Dancing, gambling, and drinking also were popular pursuits. When weekday services were held, only the old and the infirm would tend to come. The printing press made possible the wide circulation of religious tracts that clergy would read to the faithful.[13] Durant has captured the spirit of these times in this way:

> The new ministers were generally men of good morals, learned in Scripture, [and]...devoted to the tasks of their pastorates...."Divine service" retained much of the Catholic ritual—altar, cross, candles, vestments, and parts of the Mass in German; but a larger role was given to the sermon, and there were no prayers to the Virgin or the saints. Religious paintings and statues were discarded. Church architecture was transformed to bring the worshipers within easier hearing of the preacher....The most pleasant innovation was the active participation of the congregation in the music of the ceremony....Luther became overnight a poet, and wrote didactic, polemical, and inspirational hymns of a

rough and masculine power typical of his character. Not only did the worshipers sing these and other Protestant hymns; they were called together during the week to rehearse them; and many families sang them in the home. A worried Jesuit reckoned that "the hymns of Luther killed [converted] more souls than his sermons.[14]

This quote apparently was not fully applicable to Hesse, however. Despite the admonitions of Luther and his clerical leadership that congregations should engage regularly in collective singing, several generations went by without his direction being broadly adopted. Unlike the more musical populations of Thuringia and Saxony, who sang out happily and lustily in services, Hessians had no tradition of singing in church. An old adage from the early Middle Ages held that *Hassia non catat*: "Hesse doesn't sing." In many parishes, pastor after pastor worked without effect. In some cases, only trained men's choirs could be induced to sing, since a strict interpretation of Paul's dictate in Corinthians that women should be silent in church was literally held as gospel. Even in 1628 women were not singing in parish worship in many villages, including the following ones in upper Hesse: Wetter, Lohra, Hassenhausen, Wittelsberg, Ebsdorf, Kirchhain, Cappel, Rauschenberg, Langenstein, Schönstadt, and Betziesdorf. In Niederasphe only one brave woman was known to sing. A pastor who served a church near Gießen remarked that the women in his services behaved as if their mouths had grown closed. Of course, only the larger parish congregations could afford an organ to accompany their services, which also may have impeded the progress of congregational hymn singing. It appears that only the broader expansion in upper Hesse of parish schools in which youngsters could learn and appreciate religious music finally made collective singing widespread.[15]

The initial Protestant advance continued unabated through 1530, with Philip finding religious allies among the leaders of Prussia, Saxony, Mecklenburg, Württemberg, and some of Brunswick. Soon East Friesland, Silesia, Schleswig, and Holstein followed suit. Most of the south stayed in the Catholic fold, as did the territories of the Archbishop of Mainz. Despite these successes, however, neither the Pope in Rome nor the German emperor were willing to tolerate indefinitely the expansion of a faith so at odds with their interests. Their threatening political moves caused numerous Protestant princes to form an alliance at a meeting they held in Schmalkald in March 1531. Philip immediately became a powerful leadership presence in the Schmalkaldic League, not least because he brought strong military resources in men and material to the alliance. His large arsenal of cannon was well known throughout Germany. Over time the league voted to amass an initial force of 12,000 troops to defend their cause. Events on the world stage kept the emperor from dealing directly with the Protestant challenge for some years, but by the latter 1530s it was becoming clear that this was a fight that would be deferred, not avoided. Incidents such as occurred in 1538, when Philip joined forces with other Protestants to oust the militant Catholic Duke Henry of Brunswick, only served to add tinder to a potentially explosive situation.[16]

In 1539 Philip took an unfortunate step that sullied his reputation, set back the Protestant cause, and ultimately damaged fundamentally his legacy of strong statecraft and unified territory. He had grown tired of his wife and fallen in love with another, petitioning Luther to permit him to maintain two wives. If rebuffed, he threatened to return Hesse to the Catholic side. Luther agonized over the decision, but in the end politics prevailed; he granted Philip the dispensation, but insisted it remain secret.

Philip reached an accommodation with his first wife, married his new love, and soon began producing more heirs. But the Catholics had a field day, particularly since bigamy was prohibited on pain of death under imperial law. Now Philip had to deal with the emperor as a supplicant seeking to avoid a death sentence. The emperor was only too happy to keep the controversy alive to maintain leverage over this Protestant foe. In 1540 the matter was at best temporarily resolved when Philip received a conditional waiver of prosecution. Why Philip allowed himself to be so crippled politically by taking such a foolish step remains a mystery. He was a man "in whom political ambitions and religious conviction mingled so inextricably that it is anybody's guess what really drove him on..."[17] Clearly his passions were capable of ruling his head to an extraordinary degree. His later efforts to provide in his will for suitable inheritances for his numerous sons by both wives would reduce Hesse to a level of political weakness it had not seen for generations.[18]

In 1546 the emperor at last felt he had a free enough hand politically and militarily to devote himself to destroying the Protestant threat once and for all. Philip and his allies, particularly John of Saxony, raised 57,000 men to oppose an expected invasion. Had they acted quickly and decisively, these Protestant troops could have attacked before the imperial forces had been brought together and perhaps even captured the emperor. In the end, they were divided about how decisively to act. The emperor created a rift in their ranks by promising Maurice of Saxony a major share of his cousin John's lands if he would mobilize and seize them. The resulting attack forced John to take his army home, and the imperial side triumphed, capturing all the Protestant leaders. Despite promises to the contrary, after Philip surrendered he was ignominiously thrown into jail under a fifteen-year sentence. His eldest son William took up the reigns of power in Hesse, and spent the next several years trying to obtain his father's release.

But despite these gains, Emperor Charles was frustrated in his expectations that the Protestant tide would be rolled back. Although Philip weakly offered to return to Catholicism if he were released, Charles ultimately refused. The only result was that the common people of Hesse were enflamed and even more steadfast than before to maintain their Lutheran faith. The same response met efforts to turn people in other lands. Charles was simply unprepared for grass roots rejection of his plans. Soon he was tied up with world events again, and unable to resolutely oppose Protestant actions. In March 1552 Maurice of Saxony even rejoined the Protestant fold, which regrouped and forced Charles to sign a new agreement in which his gains in the Schmalkaldic war were given up. Philip was released from prison at this time as well. At the Diet of Augsburg in 1555 the final decision was reached that each prince should be able to dictate the religion of his subjects, and that those who would not conform should emigrate to the lands of another prince of the desired religious persuasion. The price of peace was the maintenance of a patchwork quilt of little principalities without political or even religious unity. For centuries they would remain weak players on the European scene.[19]

Philip returned from his hard years of captivity a much-weakened and dispirited man. Although he would rule Hesse for another fifteen years, much of the old spark had gone from him. His mighty arsenal of cannon had been trucked off by the Catholics as war reparations, and his treasury forced to pay 600,000 florins in fines. Magnificent castles he had painstakingly improved in the 1530s and 1540s, including those at Kassel, Gießen and Rüsselsheim, were pulled down. Only the castle at Ziegenhain was left to him. The emperor had further punished Philip by awarding much of the

Katzenelnbogen inheritance to rival claimants in Nassau. Only in 1557 was Philip able to reclaim the lost lands through a separate treaty with Nassau. His once-commanding position in the affairs of Germany was lost.[20]

LIFE ON THE LAND: THE RURAL AREAS

Through wars and calamities, good times and bad, the vast majority of Hessians continued to work hard to eke out a perilous existence on the land. Wolves, boars, and other predators and pests were a constant problem. Flood, fire and drought were regular and frequent occurrences. Diseases struck with equal frequency, felling livestock as well as humans. Hunger was never far away. Forty percent of the children died in infancy, another twenty percent before reaching maturity. A son might be taken for the army, and marauding mercenaries would steal crops and animals or simply destroy villages. Duties and tithes of all kinds still had to be paid to the lords who lived off the peasants. In Durant's words, civilization was "a parasite on the man with the hoe." Hesse was too mountainous to contain enough good farmland to fully feed itself with regularity. Forests covered over 50% of the land area, and soils were generally poor. The climate could spawn killer freezes in early spring or late fall, and sometimes even in the summer. All the grain crops required fairly temperate conditions to survive and yield reasonable returns. Yields of between 1:3 and 1:5 the amount sown were average in this period. In good years, this would meet the needs of a family and provide a small surplus. Crop failures were all too common, with fourteen seasons from 1515-59 in which they were recorded, an average of about one every three years. Especially bad were back-to-back periods of shortage, as occurred in 1524-25, 1529-31, 1537-43, and 1550-52. [21]

The village community remained the cornerstone of society, but it too was being prodded to adapt to social and economic forces beyond its control. Among the most important of these forces was population growth. After a severe fall-off during the previous century and a half, by about 1450 population began to recover in Hesse. By 1500 this growth spurt was very much in evidence, putting pressure on the land and rural society. People responded in a number of ways. Wasteland areas that were vacant and uncultivated for generations were brought under cultivation, and forests or other wild areas were rolled back to create more arable lands. Without informing the authorities, the land might be burned off to clear it, with the ashes providing temporary fertilizer for marginal soils. Sometimes the authorities themselves encouraged land clearance by waiving taxes and other duties on the land. If it turned out to be too marginal, it might be abandoned again once the taxes fell due. Keeping track of what was under cultivation for tax purposes became a major preoccupation of the state and led to the development of more and more accurate records through the century.

There also was increased pressure to subdivide existing arable plots, in some cases making them less viable to support the number of people living on them. Some peasants were forced to migrate to the towns to seek their livelihood. Because forest, scrub and other undeveloped land was of great value to the towns and villages in pasturing animals, providing firewood, and generating other useful materials, complaints were raised loudly to the authorities about the encroachment on traditional village common areas. Similarly, state regulations attempting to slow or halt the dividing of land into non-viable parcels date from this period. The land reclamation continued, particularly in the period 1530-70, even opening up areas considered today too marginal to permit farming. The overall population increase through the century may have been as much as 100%, with towns showing larger increases than villages.[22]

The sixteenth century provides the earliest recorded evidence of differentiated peasant classes in the villages. The better-off peasants increasingly were pitted against their poorer fellows in competition for use of land areas belonging to the community as a whole. A fully enfranchised farmer was a "neighbor" in the community in ways that a later-arriving peasant could not lay claim to; he had guaranteed use of the local woods, common meadows and pastures, rights to pasture a set number of animals, a voice and a vote in meetings where decisions were made about when and what to plant, etc. Much of the social friction of this era stemmed from poorer farmers trying to amass enough wealth to move up the social ladder and achieve rights comparable to the larger landholders in the village community.

The upper class peasantry was known by various names, most commonly as *Hüfner*, since they held one or more *Hufen* or hides of land. A hide was considered workable by an average peasant family, and sufficient to ensure enough yields to support them. This hide in northern Hesse consisted of 30 acres according to Kassel measures, or just under twenty American acres. Other names for these fully-enfranchised farmers included *Ackermänner* (fieldsmen), *Vollbauer* (literally, full-farmer), and *Meier* (originally, stewards). These farmers typically owned a barn and other outbuildings in addition to their houses. The *Hüfner* possessed full rights to take part in the common life of the village community, and in the state records created at this time these rights were laid out in some detail. These rights also brought with them responsibilities to pay various land and use taxes to the local landlord, in many cases the landgrave himself. Thus, the state took an active interest in the productivity and viability of its peasantry.

Alongside the *Hüfner* a second class of farmer arose known as the *Köter*, or cottage farmers. Originally these were landless underclass peasants who migrated to the villages and worked as laborers for the better-off farmers. These might have been allowed to erect a shack or cottage on their employer's lands, but would own no rights as an enfranchised neighbor in the community. These social and economic distinctions were recorded in the land records of the state. Over time these peasants would often acquire rights to a garden plot or slightly more land so they could begin to supplement their meager wages by growing some crops. In good years they might even save some money and expand their holdings until they could sustain themselves on the land. Now, they were in a position to challenge the *Hüfner* for expanded rights to a share in the community common areas. Again, this would require their assuming responsibility for taxes and similar duties paid to the landlord, the church, the common chest, etc. As time passed there would be fewer and fewer overt differences between the two classes, until only the size of their land holdings distinguished them. Social status continued to derive from the amount of land held, however, since larger farmers could pasture more animals on common lands, obtain more from the forests, and otherwise draw more resources from community-held property.

Not surprisingly, as population continued to rise and more landless peasants sought a place in the communities, a third class of peasant evolved: the *Beisaßen*, probably analogous to the English term "squatter." These peasants again had to work for wages, and lived on the margins of the community on less productive lands or in shacks permitted them by their employers. They went unrecorded on the state books, but they had a significant effect on local society, often being resented for the pressure they placed on local resources. Of course, these social distinctions were not ironclad, since a lower class *Köter* was virtually indistinguishable from the *Beisaßen*, as was an upper class *Köter* from the *Hüfner*. At each stage of this social continuum the lower level peasants would be trying to better themselves, while their better-off fellows resisted this advance since it brought more pressure on local resources. Conflicts over land issues roiled over the centuries, with the authorities often petitioned to step in and resolve differences.

A further social differentiation came from whether or not one owned draft animals. The *Hüfner* were always better positioned to do so, since it took rights to an extensive part of the village common areas to maintain horses and cattle. Draft animals allowed those who owned them to provide the services they owed the local lords using the animals instead of working by hand. Such service would include plowing, hauling firewood, crops or dung for fertilizer. Aside from its more obvious advantages, this teamster service also was a class-distinguishing factor in the villages. Hand services included reaping, sowing, and binding up the lord's crops. Those who served traditionally had to be fed lunch, perhaps be given something to drink, and allowed grazing rights for their draft animals. When these reciprocal benefits were withheld, the workers would lodge complaints to the landgrave's authorities. Service hours were set by custom, usually from six to eleven in the morning and one to six in the afternoons. The landgrave's own fields and manors had to be serviced like those of other landlords, with local officials carrying the titles *Kellner, Amtmann,* or *Schultheiß* overseeing the work. Often these officials would squeeze additional work for their own benefit out of the peasants.

Taxes that were owed varied with the size of the land holding. A *Hüfner* might owe ten shillings for his farm, an enfranchised *Köter* only eight. Those with draft animals also might pay more than those without. When the *Hüfner* lands were divided up, this created challenges for the authorities, who might have to partition the tax burden several ways among the new owners. In some areas the *Beisaßen* were taxed as well, at levels much lower than their landowning counterparts. Rents in money or in produce were payable annually on September 29, St. Michael's Day. Beyond rents, other taxes were due to the lords, such as the state head tax known as the *Bede*.[23]

The other means for underclass peasants to make ends meet was the taking up of trades. Blacksmithing, carpentry, weaving, tailoring, butchering, baking, and brewing are all trades that lent themselves to such side occupations. Spinning and weaving were particularly common because the materials, including flax, were easily obtained and all members of the family could take part. Textile work was an occupation of last resort for peasants across Germany, and untold thousands found the means of scraping by over the centuries by pursuing it. These peasants also found ready employment in the new capitalist-based economy in which entrepreneurs practiced "putting out," or supplying the raw materials and paying wages to home-based peasants to do the work. All the trades competed to a greater or lesser extent with local town-based guilds, which complained widely about this violation of their exclusive production rights. Given the poverty that characterized so much of the Hessian landscape, it appears the landgraves were mostly content to look the other way. Flax weaving was an important local pastime in the production of cheap cloth for peasant use. It was usually dyed blue when used for women's dresses, the so-called local *Trachten*.[24]

The remaining forests were under such pressure over the course of the sixteenth century that numerous edicts were issued to restrict their use, as well as impose taxes on woods use by the local peasantry. Oak for building could only be harvested legally by consulting district officials who themselves had to seek advice from two carpenters. By the time the ordinance of 1593 was issued efforts were under way to hold down the number of new peasant homes being constructed. Forest pasture rights too had to be constrained to prevent over-harvesting by goats and other animals. Depending on the class of farmer, only eight, six or four pigs per household could be turned loose in the woods. Unlicensed woods clearance was outlawed in 1532. This was bitterly resented by the farmers. Forest use taxes were imposed on villages that could not demonstrate a 300-year recorded history of unbroken use. Half fees were assessed where over 200 years' unbroken use could be proven. In 1541 the following were representative of the amounts of use taxes charged: *Vollbauer* and *Köter* with two horses, one florin; *Köter* (with one horse), one-half florin; other *Köter*, one-quarter florin. The landgrave's extensive sheep holding also generated much complaining from peasants who felt their local pasturage and forests were being over-grazed by these sheep (1514). A pronouncement of 1539 on the same subject made it clear that this was an ongoing grievance.[25]

The basic agricultural organization in Hesse continued to be the three-field economy, in which land would be exposed to summer crops, winter crops, and fallow periods in regular rotation. Hesse suffered from having much more marginal agricultural land than highly fertile arable, and its population never was able to generate the kind of comfortable surpluses on a regular basis that made for secure existence. Too many mountains and uncultivable forest regions crisscrossed the land, their soils all but useless for farming. Because of this, much local variation existed in the three-field approach, with fallow periods often minimized or replaced altogether with the growing of legumes and other vegetables, or more commonly, rape and flax. Rye, wheat, barley and oats were the most common grain crops. Oats was more widely grown in Hesse than in more fertile regions, and here people rather than draft animals ate the oats. Hops also was grown frequently for use in beer production. Good years would allow some grain to be stored by the peasantry to tide them over a succeeding bad year, and crop failures would result in price ceilings and export restrictions being imposed by the landgraves. Sometimes they would even have to buy grain abroad to bail out their beleaguered populace. A period of wetter, colder weather prevailed in this century, depressing the yield of the winter crops, in particular.[26]

From the fifteenth century, grain mills in Hesse were increasingly the province of the landgrave himself, who owned almost all of them. Some were worked by millers who held life-long leases and paid him a concession fee. New ones could only be built with state permission.

Livestock were raised widely in Hesse, and in many of the mountainous regions the small, sturdy Hessian cattle were preferred to the horse for use in plowing. In teams, they had a better time of it in the rocky soils, and they ate less grain than the horse. When they grew old, they were also more useful since they could be sold for meat. The larger, meatier animals driven through Hesse from Central and Eastern Europe were preferred by all who could afford them for meat. Cheese and butter from cattle, or among the poor, from goats, was also an important food source in these times. Thanks to the availability of forest grazing, pig raising was widely and profitably pursued. They were driven into the woods a week or more prior to the fall slaughter to add pounds, especially in much-sought-after fatty meat, to their frames. Pork prices went up as a result of the forest use restrictions imposed by the state.

Beyond a doubt sheep raising was the most important aspect of animal husbandry in Hesse. The terrain favored sheep folding as much as it failed to provide effectively for agriculture. Hesse's central location and trading opportunities allowed it to serve as an important supplier to the wool industry in nearby countries. Raw wool, weaving and other ancillary activity of the wool trade was the mainstay of the Hessian economy. Mutton was also a rather important food source, but only when herds had to be thinned out in the fall. The huge herds of the landgraves grazed across most state lands, encroaching on the rights of local villages who often shared these same common pastures and woodlands. Shepherds themselves thus provided a critical service to the state and village herds alike, but their compensation and rank in the social order never reflected this. Shepherding was seen for centuries as a low-class and dishonorable profession across Germany, and shepherds barely made a living.[27]

The shepherds and other specialized herdsmen (for the village pigs, cows, horses, geese, etc.) worked under the authority of the local village headman, called the *Grebe* or *Dorfsteher*. As an appointee of the landgrave or the local landlord, the *Grebe* was charged with upholding public order and security in the community, and counseling the lord on local matters. He was to be of good reputation, typically drawn from among the wealthier farmers in the community, and needed basic skills in letters and math. In some cases the lesser (cottage) farmers were represented by their own *Kötergrebe*. The sixteenth century saw the state reaching more and more into local affairs through ordinances. The *Hüfner* and cottage farmers, despite their class differences, tended more and more to cooperate to counter negative pressures from above. They also had to work together to manage the communal affairs of village life, guarding their rights as part of the community against encroachments by the non-enfranchised under class. Together they managed the maintenance of local paths and roads, working by hand or with spans of horses depending on their means. Villagers of both classes helped each other in times of hardship as a matter of duty to the community.

The herdsmen and watchmen who protected crops and flocks from wild animals and other threats were among those in the under-classes. Their pay was low, but they also were forgiven some of the taxes imposed on their better-off fellows, such as the hearth or chicken tax. They had to swear to respect land use regulations, and to be vigilant for outbreaks of pestilence in their herds. Even within the herdsmen there was a social order, with horse and cowherds outranking pig and geese herders. The growing ranks of the *Beisaßen* and lower class *Köter* farmers were unable to own animals since they held no rights to have them fed by pasturing them with the village common herds. Squabbles over land use rights could escalate to the local legal authorities, as happened in Harle (Felsberg District) when lower class farmers brought a successful suit against a *Hüfner* farmer because though they paid their share in taxes to the local lord they were denied commensurate pasturing rights. In most cases such issues were resolved within the community itself by polling the adult male inhabitants from the enfranchised farmsteads. Other matters, such as woods use, admission of new settlers into the community, etc., also were resolved in this way. In villages with expansive common areas newcomers might be welcomed periodically to help share in the local tax burden.[28]

The state authorities were concerned about the tendency for population growth to force the splintering of farms from *Hüfner* farmsteads into *Köter*- and even smaller-sized plots. The larger farms paid more taxes and were more easily administered. Regulations were issued in Kassel in 1535 (and promulgated across Hesse in 1545) requiring so-called "closed" inheritance. In this approach one primary male heir inherited the whole farm, perhaps with the proviso that some money be given to other heirs to allow them to set off on their own and establish themselves elsewhere. The major heir then had to provide for the elderly parents through their lives. W.J. Wright has noted that these types of inheritance practices were particularly common in the areas around Kassel, Wolfhagen, Eschwege, Kirchain, Biedenkopf, Frankenberg and the districts of Schmalkalden, Gelnhausen, and Hanau. At the same time, the state was concerned not to promote a larger under-class of landless workers. So the policy could not be enforced too strictly, and there seems to have been wide variation in how closely it was followed even within fairly small geographical areas. Splitting of farms among numerous surviving sons remained common enough throughout Hesse. Ironically, Landgrave Philip himself found it impossible to devolve his lands on a single heir, providing for numerous sons from his two wives in a manner that split the landgraviate asunder.

Hard times also forced farmers to mortgage their farms to get by, sometimes taking out loans against parts of their property that they would later lose for failure to repay. Too little cash was available to the farmers by other means. So much of this was going on in the second half of the sixteenth century that state regulations required the sanction of the authorities before loans could be taken out. This allowed some oversight to prevent loans on ridiculously unfair terms from being foisted on the peasantry. Jewish moneylenders also formed a key part of the system of local credit extension, again with the state authorities overseeing the practice to ensure that interest rates of about 5% remained the norm. Jews also had to swear that they had not bribed authorities for the privilege of money lending. Trafficking in stolen goods or pawning them could be punished with death.[29]

Despite efforts to hold down their numbers by state action, the population growth among the under classes continued unabated. Once all the accessible marginal lands were brought under cultivation, population continued to outstrip agricultural productivity. Prices for agricultural products slowly rose over the century, making it more expensive to pay rents and dues calculated in grain rather than money. The full *Hüfner* farmers could keep pace and benefit from the price rises, while everyone else suffered proportionate to their lot in life. Most incomes fell perceptibly over the period, and loud complaints were raised to the authorities as a result. A 1585 survey of northern Hesse villages spanning five separate areas suggest that from 65-94% of the inhabitants were of the *Köter* class, presumably with substantial variation from (mostly) very poor to (occasional) middling wealth. In any case, the wealthier *Hüfner* were very much in the minority everywhere. In the Fritzlar area the under class population amounted to over 70% of the total, not fully accounting for the landless and homeless who went uncounted. Late in the century pestilence again stalked the land, slowing the rate of population growth.[30]

Life in the local village communities of these times may be sketched by considering some basic human needs: food, clothing, and shelter; beyond them, we will look at social relations, recreation, and morality. Food costs were the single largest expense for families in this period. As the population expanded, raw or cooked vegetables and especially grains were consumed in greater quantities and less meat was consumed. Hessians probably ate more oats and rye products in soups and gruels than their counterparts in other parts of Europe. Fernand Braudel's description of the prevailing European diet as, "insipid and always monotonous, whether they were fermented or not: gruels, sops and bread..." is most descriptive. He also notes that "chronic scarcities" were the lot in life of the overwhelming number of the population. A thick and filling rye bread was widely used in town and country to feed servants at relatively low cost. Some cabbage, carrots, lettuce, potatoes, lima beans, and strawberries were used to supplement grain diets in this era.

Meat was a diminishing part of the diet, probably 14% of the caloric intake or less. Beef and pork were the most important meats, and with the rise in prices and scarcity of good meats more fat and mixed products like sausage were consumed. Chickens and pigs raised at home were the major source of meat for the common man. Service in taverns and other places where meals were eaten outside the home was often provided on a so-called "trencher" made of a large piece of stale bread served on a slab of wood or metal. This dish-like piece of bread served to hold the food and soak up the drippings. Sometimes the uneaten trenchers were given to the poor after use. People ate from a common pot or bowl, mostly with their fingers. Spoons were also available from an early period, but individual forks were only beginning to appear in the sixteenth century. The boring diet of grain-based gruels made salt most popular, with huge amounts consumed per capita. Beer and wine were taken at all meals, even in the morning. Getting drunk was a major preoccupation, despite the hard-working nature of most agricultural workers. The main meal was eaten about 11:00 a.m., with a lighter supper eaten about 7:00 p.m.[31]

As in modern times, people dressed as well as their means allowed. Farmers had simple peasant garb of homespun cloth, and would most likely have only one or at most two changes of clothes. Common workers wore a short shirt, a cap or hat made of felt, and pants that either hung over the shoes or were tucked into them. The somewhat better off might add a vest or a coat trimmed or lined with fur. The upper classes competed among themselves in their finery. Many had silk shirts and trimmed their hats with feathers, pearls or gold. Men were clean-shaven, but had long hair. Fancy rings were popular as signs of wealth, and bright colors were favored. Men were typically more resplendent than women on special occasions, although the women liked to flaunt gold embroidery and golden crowns. Fashions were always changing.[32]

Farmhouses in the sixteenth century were typically constructed of the same wattle and daub materials and techniques that had been used for centuries. Larger houses had courtyards for storage of farm implements and penning of animals. Houses sometimes included elaborate carvings or inscriptions meaningful to their owners. Fire was an ever-present threat to these wooden homes. In the towns, houses could be more elaborate, particularly for the well off, and were perhaps the most comfortable in Europe. Houses had wide staircases, windows of colored glass, walls hung with tapestries, and even carpeted floors.[33]

Furnishings in the village houses of this period were extremely basic. Probably simple oak benches that could be brought out for eating were the norm. Tables themselves might be capable of being set up and taken down as needed. Few peasants would own chairs, and upturned barrels or other sturdy items would double as seating. There was no interior lighting besides that afforded by the hearth, so after dark it was unlikely that people stayed up to busy themselves in work or conversation. A farm bride would often bring a bride's chest to her new home filled with personal items of clothing and household goods collected over years. In wealthier homes furniture was large and heavy, since it was produced by carpenters who may or may not have had particular skill in furniture making. Benches and chairs now had cushioned seats, however. Canopied beds were also common. Storage would be handled in massive carved chests. Decorative items might include musical instruments, flowers, books, and the family silver plate arranged for show on shelves. Walls and furniture alike were painted in this era. Imperfections in furniture could be hidden with cloth and plaster prior to painting. In this century joiners who worked on smaller and finer pieces of furniture were branching off from the carpenters to form their own trade. Some became cabinetmakers specializing in marquetry or other veneer treatments. Later in the century waxing and varnishing became more widespread in place of the cruder painted finishes. In inns and taverns people sat on benches along narrow tables, with their backs to the hearth for warmth whenever possible.[34]

Recreation in the sixteenth century typically occurred at fairs and festivals, many sponsored by the church, such as All Saints, Christmas, and Easter. May Day celebrations and harvest feasts marked the spring and fall. Given any excuse, a considerable amount of drinking was the norm. Towns and villages celebrated the so-called *Kirmes*, a kind of annual founders' day sometimes celebrated on the feast day of the patron saint of the local church. A throwback to pagan times, it was a day for riotous behavior, games, feasting, dancing and drinking. Local village or town citizens attended, as did outsiders who knew what fun was to be had at the *Kirmes*. Perhaps to control this kind of behavior the state authorities had to be contacted to obtain permission for other village celebrations or even productions by wandering musicians.

The upper classes also had their hunts or the occasional jousting tournaments, which were slowly but surely on the wane. Marriage feasts were always as sumptuous as the participants' families could afford, and also a time for loud partying. Solemnity in the ceremony and relative luxury in the provision of food and drink characterized these celebrations, whether the participants were rich or poor. As described earlier, sumptuary laws by the landgrave were enacted to set limits on the ostentation and waste attendant to the more opulent weddings. Still cruder entertainments such as bull- and bear-baiting, cockfighting, and gambling were known, and outdoor dancing was very popular, especially since Luther tended to encourage it as a harmless pastime.[35]

Finding a mate was a socially involved and obviously momentous task for both parties. It would never do for a man of the *Hüfner* class to consider a mere *Köter* girl for marriage, no matter how friendly their families might be. Engagement once announced and formally witnessed had tremendous force and effect, about as strong as marriage itself. Families in this time were often large, for mortality was high. Eight to ten children per couple were normal, with fifteen not uncommon. Bastards resulting from pre-marital affairs were also common, often taken in later by the father when he married. Children would most often be named for their godparents, who would in turn assume a key role for their spiritual upbringing as well as providing for them in times of calamity. The illegitimate might have groups of godparents taking responsibility for them in the absence of the strong, two-parent tie so necessary in the village setting. This also was the time when family names began to come into common use.

The man of the family held the legal and traditional authority in matters of the home, and it was through him that the enfranchised family had input on the affairs of the village community. The land-holding men of the village community would meet at the village common, often under a traditional Linden or other community tree, to decide local matters within their purview. Only these men would appear in any state or local records, other family members' identities being unimportant by comparison. Wives on the other hand exercised great traditional authority on matters of the home and family, a role broadly if informally recognized by the community. Children of both sexes worked on the farm and in the fields from an early age. Tending animals was a commonly assigned task for youngsters.[36]

The weak position of women in law and local authority compared to men seems to have made them prone to prosecution as the century wore on in cases of infanticide, illegitimacy and especially alleged witchcraft. Although the pressure of Protestant ferment and general lack of interest in Germany had held off the worst of the Catholic Inquisition, superstitious fears about witchcraft throughout Europe set in here as well. The worst excesses occurred from 1580-1660, in which 40-50,000 victims were killed throughout Germany, including many in Hesse. Local communities often accused their own, particularly older, physically unappealing, quarrelsome or otherwise socially outcast single women. Trials took place in secular and religious courts, and conviction rates were high, particularly since torture-based confessions were considered normal and acceptable. About half the accused were eventually executed. Old midwives were common targets, since people often blamed them for the deaths of newborns. Herb-based potions and remedies concocted by old hags would one day be considered a tremendous service, and the next become the basis for allegations of devil-worship when the intended positive effects failed to materialize.[37]

Beyond witch trials, other aspects of crime and punishment were likewise crude and brutal in this century. Life was unsafe on the land and even in towns at night. Highwaymen forced people to travel in groups for protection. Petty crime was practiced in epidemic proportions, and legal penalties of the most draconian type were relied upon in the absence of police protection to deter crime. Robbery was punishable by death, petty theft by cutting off the ears. Other capital crimes included: murder, treason, heresy, witchcraft, sacrilege, forgery, counterfeiting, smuggling, arson, perjury, adultery, rape, homosexuality, bestiality, falsifying weights and measures, adulterating food, damaging property, escape from prison.[38] Death could be levied by hanging or beheading in the towns, although heretics and those who killed their husbands might be burned. Drawing and quartering was practiced for the particularly egregious murderer. Common people turned out in crowds and were enthusiastic witnesses to the executions. Afterwards, the bodies might be left hanging to rot as a warning to other perpetrators. Blasphemers could have their tongues torn out, those returning illegally from banishment might be blinded by gouging. Torturing with hot tongs, scourging, cutting off or racking the limbs, burning the soles of the feet, blinding one or both eyes, and an array of other tortures were available to extract confessions and speed the process. The most minor offenses could be punished by use of the ducking stool, stocks, pillory, or simple imprisonment.

There were state regulations on dress, jewelry, furniture, meals, and celebrations. Efforts were made to stamp out drunkenness by requiring innkeepers to warn their customers against too much drinking and even swearing, which went hand in hand with public drunkenness (1543). State officials were ordered to eat and stay at taverns and inns to check on the innkeepers, and fines could be levied on those who failed to comply. Philip banned the most intoxicating beverages in 1524, particularly *Brandwein* (brandy), originally intended for medicinal purposes only. This edict obviously had little effect since it had to be re-issued in 1556. In 1562 Sunday dances were banned to uphold public order.

Life in the villages was more inward-focused and somewhat more secure because of community regulation of behavior. But violent outbreaks among members of the community were common. Thiebault writes that, "Assaulters grabbed any object to use as a weapon. Knives, stones, beer mugs, axes, rakes, whips, pitchforks, and hoes were all mentioned as weapons used in fights in *Amt* Sontra." Violence rarely led to outright murder or manslaughter, however. Fines for violent fighting were imposed, tailored to the severity of the harm done. Most violence was spontaneous and unplanned, with alcohol playing a role in many cases. Slanderous insults could be fined as well, since they struck at the honorable reputation of the slandered, a major blow to their standing in the community. Examples would be calling a man a "rogue" or suggesting a wife was a "loose woman." [39]

Personal morality across society was seen to be at a low ebb by contemporaries of this period (1520s to 1540s). Tradesmen cheated on weights and measures for goods and adulterated foodstuffs and other materials they sold. The rise of capitalism placed a premium on maximizing profits, and concern for one's fellow man assumed a much less prominent place in society. Self-interest reigned supreme. Private trade dealings based on personal contact and trust were de-emphasized, while impersonal long-distance trade practiced by entrepreneur capitalists was on the rise. Because of these tendencies, the landgraves felt compelled to issue regulations to punish the use of unfair weights and measures, efforts to corner markets to the detriment of the common man, and unfair money lending practices. Increasing numbers of people were reduced to pauperism, with the evicted homeless, the unemployed, and other unfortunates begging or stealing to try to make ends meet. Under the influence of Martin Luther's teachings begging was outlawed (1524); in its place, Luther prescribed public charity for the truly needy and demanded that others be made to work. He quoted St. Paul in saying, "...whoever will not work shall not eat."

State regulations read like a litany of the perceived ills in society. In 1524, begging and alcoholism were attacked, along with over-sumptuous celebrations of marriage, baptism, etc. In 1526 a ban on idleness, blasphemy and fornication (by those who thus "shamed maidens"), was decreed. Training orphan children in productive trades was also mandated. People who separated from their spouses were urged to reunite. A 1538 rule criticized the poor who used public aid to buy liquor, waste time, and wallow in useless pursuits. By 1543, drunkenness again was the target, and innkeepers were ordered to address this issue as we have seen above. The same edict ordered people to attend church services on pain of fines. In 1562, the issue was banning Sunday dancing, which was accused of leading to too much drinking. Looking just to the clergy to enforce morality was problematical, since even some Protestant churchmen continued in the old practices of too much imbibing and other public sinfulness. As in other places across Germany, public baths fell out of favor because of the combination of the rise of venereal disease and the church's fulminating against the evils of both sexes bathing together. Despite the host of legal pronouncements, none of these problems proved very susceptible to state-ordered solutions.[40]

The state of public morality in general and the feeling of the lower classes that they were being cheated and preyed upon by lords and tradesmen alike served to foment a spirit of rebellion that was expanding fast in the early sixteenth century. Initially, Luther's teachings helped to spawn this rebelliousness when they challenged the authority of one pillar of feudal land holding, the Catholic Church. The new religion seemed to offer many the prospect of a more egalitarian society based on Christ's teachings, freeing them of the old church practices that supported the exploiters at every turn. The goal was a new society based on the sharing of property and respect for the poor. In southern Germany alone some 30,000 peasants took to arms in 1524 to demand enhanced rights. They refused to pay their feudal duties and tithes to the church. This was the beginning of the so-called Peasant's War of 1524-25. Initially successful, the rebels were emboldened by their ability to seize sizable towns like Würzburg and Frankfurt and to chase away the archbishop of Mainz, forcing his deputy to pay a large ransom. Franconia and Württemberg were almost totally won over to the peasants' cause. Monasteries everywhere were seized and sacked.

Initially, the response of the ruling powers was muted. Secular and religious lords and princes feigned cooperation and compromise, until they could organize to respond with force. Luther soon distanced himself from the rebels, even arguing for a strict and brutal crackdown in an effort to save his movement from being crushed out in the backlash he saw as inevitable. It was soon in coming, and Landgrave Philip of Hesse was in its van. His forces joined those of Saxony and Brunswick in crushing a peasant force of 8,000 men. Some 5,000 were massacred as the farmers were no match for trained soldiery. In a few weeks the lords in Southern Germany regained the upper hand as well. Retribution was brutal, even gory. Upwards of 130,000 peasants were killed, their leaders in many cases made to suffer incredible torments. Many others were lamed, blinded, or otherwise left to wander aimlessly with no land or trade to support them. New feudal agreements even revoked rights of those who were left to labor on the land.

In Hesse, the situation never got so far out of hand. Philip mobilized his forces, but also portrayed himself as a defender of his people against the unfair requirements imposed by the lesser nobility. There was some irony in this, for he was the largest landholder in Hesse, with huge numbers of peasants working on his own fields. But in April 1525 he swore before his own troops to uphold the interests of his people by reigning in the abuse they suffered at the hands of corrupt state officials and opposing any efforts by their overlords to increase unduly their traditional rents and duties. As it related to the lesser nobility, this promise was readily kept, since as we have seen there was never any love lost between Philip and his nobles. Philip seems to have used this opportunity to eliminate any vestiges of serfdom that remained in the land: compulsory dues and services were permitted, but no petty lord could own persons outright like cattle.

Probably the biggest challenge Philip faced was in the towns. The under classes and others disenfranchised from involvement in town governments, including some of the guilds, had joined in the general insurrection. Towns in the area of Hersfeld and Fulda, in which the Archbishop of Mainz had long disputed Hessian authority, were the first to be cowed into submission. Philip thus used the crisis to bring these areas under his complete control. With a strong hand he similarly snuffed out local rebellions in Gießen, Marburg, Wetter, Treysa, Rotenburg, Vacha and other towns. In some cases the local peasantry was simply forbidden to bear arms in the future on account of their rebellion.[41]

If the peasants' revolt in Hesse did little more than confirm existing relationships and duties vis-à-vis their lords, the same cannot be said of the wave of economic change that was sweeping the land under the new capitalist forms of production and trade. Philip pursued a form of mercantilism in which state policies did everything possible to align the productive capacity of the land with the needs of the developing state. The more modern, state-controlled approach to forest management is a good example of this policy. Wood for building and burning in Philip's foundries and glassworks was too valuable to allow free exploitation by the peasantry. Much better records of local affairs were being kept by this time, allowing policies to be formed on the basis of what was really happening at the level of the village. This was promoted by the Reformation Order of 1526 and the Hide Edict of 1535, which established requirements for registering farmers by name and setting forth their individual dues. (The 1535 edict also set September 29 as the annual day on which rental dues were payable.) Unfortunately, Philip's regime suffered from the corruption of many of his local officials, who exploited the peasants under their charge for their own profit. Illegal sales of livestock, wood, exported grain, and other materials apparently occurred.

The Reformation Edict of 1534 was perhaps the fundamental expression of Philip's mercantilism. It tried to stabilize prices and promote supplies of key commodities (grain, meat and wool) for the benefit of his subjects. It addressed unfair and unregulated trading practices, and fixed the maximum levels of interest that could be charged on loans. Five percent was set for monetary loans, and interest paid in kind (grain) was likewise regularized and limited. These measures favored the debtor over the creditor, and represented a rollback in current rates. The 1534 regulation established the role of "market master" to regulate markets and promote honest and fair dealing, with two such officials appointed in each of the towns. All buying and selling was to occur in supervised markets and at established prices. No underground economy was to be tolerated, in which unregulated buying or selling of grain or livestock outside the market towns took place. Restrictions were placed on foreign buyers who might try to undercut these measures by surreptitious buying. They were allowed to buy only after products had first been offered for sale to local Hessian customers. Weights and measures were standardized, and towns were required to have bread scales. Cloth measures were standardized on the Kassel *ell*. The market regulation and efforts to confine markets to the towns had the effect of breathing some new life into the guilds, which were always pressed by competition from the local village producers.[42]

The social policies promoted by Martin Luther and his leading disciples also seem to have been formative in Philip's development of state doctrine. In the decade after 1524 Philip wholeheartedly embraced Luther's concept of prohibiting begging but providing extensively for the truly needy poor out of community and state resources. Those who were only periodically needy, such as elderly or sick people who lived in their own homes, would be given temporary help, while those who were too sick to work or support themselves in any way would be assigned to a state hospitals. Territorial hospitals for the elderly (those over 60) and ill peasantry of all ages were set up regionally, in Hofheim, Merxhausen, Haina, and Gronau. Here they were ministered to by pastors who counseled, prayed with them and preached to them regularly. Healthier inmates were expected to weave baskets, care for trees or even cut wood. They also probably worked at herding or other less physically demanding pursuits on the state farms that supported the hospitals.

The at-home poor might receive payments in money or grain to tide them over and keep them from slipping into more abject poverty. Local secular officials appointed by the landgrave were assigned to work integrally with the local pastor to distribute this aid. Loans also could be made, in addition to outright gifts. In hard times, the landgrave sold grain at low prices to the needy from his own extensive stores, thus helping stabilize prices at levels stipulated in his edicts. Such sales are documented to have occurred over fifteen times from 1515-65. When necessary, the landgrave also prohibited exports of Hessian grain and livestock to help maintain local supplies.[43]

Despite these fervent efforts, the price inflation that was afflicting all of Europe was by no means curtailed in Hesse. As a resource-poor but centrally located smaller state, Hesse had to live or die by its trade and was subject therefore to the price swings of the larger markets. Elton has termed this an age, "naturally constructed for entrepreneurial success, and equally naturally entrepreneurs responded..." The wealthier merchants sought successfully to buy up the production of entire regions of weavers, metal workers, and many other guilds who could provide them with semi-finished goods at favorable prices. Often they supplied the raw materials, and their market purchasing power was so strong that they could virtually compel involvement by most of their suppliers. Local entrepreneurs arose within Hesse to perform this role on a small scale. A subset of wool weavers working in Marburg for example doubled their individual net worth from the 1520s to the 1560s. They created specialization within the trade and used the "putting out" system to accomplish the early stages of working of the wool by hiring local workers. They prospered well beyond the experience of some of their fellows on the land, who were increasingly impoverished through much of the same period.[44]

To end our overview of the sixteenth century, we will review the history of various trades in Hesse. Foremost among these in overall economic importance to the state was wool weaving and related fields. The weavers represented a key source of employment in the towns and an important profession to which other trades sold their goods and services. Philip initially set out to regulate the trade in wool in ways that would benefit the weavers. Many of his officials were involved in the trade as well, and their sometimes-shady dealings undercut the landgrave's policy efforts. The middlemen wool dealers who bought the raw wool and sold it to the weavers had to be licensed by the state, and were required to sell good wool to the local weavers at a regulated profit margin. The wool sales were held from Pentecost through June 29, after which time sales to foreign merchants were permitted. The nobility who controlled wool were likewise required to abide by this law. Guild member weavers also were protected from rural competitors who might undercut them in the market. Peasants were required to wear, and tailors to provide to them, only Hessian-produced woolen goods. Townsmen of the upper classes were permitted a suit of clothes made of "London cloth." A fine of five florins was levied on those who flouted the rules. Foreign competition was never completely blocked, however, as in 1529 when the weavers at Kassel lodged a complaint about inferior foreign goods being sold locally by merchant entrepreneurs.

By 1545 the reality of the marketplace again had to be accepted with a policy change that permitted foreign buyers to purchase locally grown wool from the producers, provided they obtained licenses from the state. Districts officials were now permitted to buy wool from the producers in their own jurisdictions, in an obvious bow to what had been occurring illegally. Finally, the local nobility was excused from following the rules laid down for other producers, recognizing the difficulty of enforcing the landgrave's edicts as it related to the local nobles. The same edict permitted foreign sales of raw wool despite the impact on local weavers; the state by now taxed foreign sales heavily, and it needed the money. Succeeding decades saw the sale abroad of raw Hessian wool increased in importance in the economy of this otherwise resource-poor land.

As early as 1546 Kassel weavers were petitioning Philip on account of the inflationary effects of foreign buying on wool prices. They could not compete with the economic muscle of the foreign capitalists, who had access to capital that local weavers could never match. The weaver's numbers were also too great to permit them all to make a decent living, with 120 masters in Kassel alone. Like many peasants on the land, the weavers' lack of access to capital on easy terms caused many of them to fall into debt. Competition also continued with rural weaving that was done on a "putting out" basis. Another blow came with the advent of a stylish new wool, "Moorish" cloth, or "devil's black," as it was called locally. It was blacker and shinier than any the local trade could produce, and thus more sought after. All these problems saw wool weavers in Hesse lose ground steadily in the course of the century.[45]

Bakers too occupied a critical place in a society so dominated by grain-based diets. Like many tradesmen of this era they often sought to wring out higher profits by cutting back on the content of their goods and adulterating them with inferior grains. A 1534 ordinance attempted to regulate the baking trade in various ways, ordering local officials to head off infighting between guild and private bakers to preserve social order. Weights for goods were set based on the current price of grain to allow some variation to protect bakers' incomes. In Marburg the inflation in grain prices created continuing difficulties over many years. From the 1520s to the 1560s the bakers sought to effectively double the price of their loaves by holding prices steady but cutting back their size by half. They also used inferior grain in their products, causing much unrest in the streets and warnings from the authorities. They sought unsuccessfully to have village bakers prohibited from selling in town. Lots of indictments were brought against the guild bakers for their shoddy and anti-competitive practices, until in 1540 the state abolished the guild outright in Marburg. By 1549 the guild was back in business, however, and it succeeded in gaining a higher legal profit per loaf. After this, disturbances seem to have ended.[46]

Butchers, like bakers, had a difficult history in this period. The 1534 edict also dealt with regulation of the butchering trade and the sale of its products. Supervisors were set up to watch over the trade, and ensure set prices were charged for various meats such as tongues, entrails, and veal. Butchers had to sell less expensive cuts alongside the higher-priced goods in their establishments. Specified weights and measures also had to be followed. From the mid-1520s indictments were continually being raised against the trade for overcharging, withholding meats from the poor in favor of those who could pay more for them, and slaughtering calves that were too small. In 1539, the landgrave abolished the guild in Marburg as he had done with the bakers. Still, from 1529 to 1569 the price of meat doubled. The poor were priced out of the market. Meat prices followed those for grain, which were shooting up quickly through the century. State prohibitions on exporting livestock were enacted periodically to address local shortages of meat. Foreign purchasers had to obtain special permission to buy Hessian animals and were taxed one *Heller* per head. Imports of livestock were encouraged, since huge herds from Poland, Hungary and the Balkans were annually driven through Hesse on their way to western markets. Here again, state officials were involved at the local level in livestock trading that profited them in violation of the landgrave's orders.[47]

Millers were very prosperous men in rural areas because like bakers they occupied a critical niche in the village economy. They enjoyed rather high social standing in most of the villages, as did the innkeepers and tavern owners who provided the only available places for travelers to stay and everyone to find solace and camaraderie in song and drink. The tavern owners generally brewed their own beer in competition with the town guilds.[48]

The state itself was most instrumental in the development of several basic industries, including mining, glass making and salt production. All were important sources of revenue for the landgrave. Iron mining started out in Hesse in the Vogelsberg region where small groups of freemen mined surface deposits and worked the metal into products themselves. As elsewhere in Europe, however, these easily-mined deposits wore out soon and by the fifteenth century it increasingly required the massive capital and organizing skills of capitalist entrepreneurs to mine successfully. Late in the century the Hessian state was soliciting investors to take out mining contracts, including financiers in Frankfurt and Hessian towns. Mines near Haina and

Frankenberg were active in this era. New technology allowed more metal to be worked faster and at higher quality through the use of water-driven bellows and hammers. Costs of production also increased beyond the capacity of smaller investors to afford. The Dodenhausen foundry near Haina had an annual capacity of thirty huge heating stoves in the years 1556-73. Pipes also were commonly produced in this region. Decorated stoves from the region were shipped far and wide throughout Germany, Scandinavia, and the Netherlands. Mines in the Werra region provided employment opportunities beyond agriculture, including transportation and hauling.

New metal works were continually opened by Philip during his reign, including: Renssdorf (1530), Lanbach (1550), Stahlberg/Hirzenhain (1555), and Ysenberg/Hitzkirchen (1557). Much of the production was for the lucrative export trade. Contracts let out on facilities in Lippoldsberg and Heisebeck proved unsuccessful by 1584, causing Philip to concentrate on improving those near Haina. Of course, Philip's most renowned products from his iron industry were the cannon that formed one of the premier artillery arsenals in Europe at this time. The guns were made at Kassel, Marburg, Fulda, Neustadt, Haina and Homberg. Production was maintained at a fast and furious pace in the 1550s to replace the guns seized by the emperor after the disastrous Schmalkaldic War. The mining in the Haina/Frankenberg area may even have allowed it to escape the more difficult economic times experienced during the course of the century by agriculture-dependent regions.

Beyond iron, there were silver mines in Hesse as well, with thirty facilities producing silver and its by-product, copper, by the 1560s. Mining operators were forgiven customary taxes on some of their wood use, which was considerable, as well as beer and wine they produced themselves. In return the landgrave received ten percent of the mines' output.[49]

A rather more pitiful picture is that presented by the salt mine workers in this era. The state owned these lucrative facilities outright and direct, and every effort was made to ensure the workers remained productive and pliant. In Sooden near Allendorf Philip prohibited the workers from practicing any trade (even farming) except salt working. They were to be kept dependent on the mining trade, and their holidays were set by law at only eight days a year. They were prohibited the use of even beer and wine except on a very limited basis at weddings and the like. As in iron mining, salt working also provided employment for huge numbers of local teamsters to haul the output to market.[50]

Glass making was a key component of the landgrave's income derived from foreign trade. By the sixteenth century Hessian glass was controlled by a single consortium of producers. This federation or guild actually was regionally based beyond the borders of Hesse proper; when the political muscle-flexing of the Archbishop of Mainz became a problem, the headquarters of the guild was simply relocated to Grossalmerode in Hesse. This was a coup for Philip. Its location on the southern end of the Kaufungen Forest was indicative of the presence of a large group of producers in this area, mirroring another area of concentration in the Rheinhard forest. Forest locations were key because the trade chewed up huge amounts of lumber to feed an insatiable appetite for firewood. Beech, pine and oak were felled in huge numbers and fed into the glass ovens to produce temperatures of 1,000 to 2,000 degrees. The landgrave ensured adequate timber supplies, protected the glass works from foreign competition, regulated quality and quantity of production, and organized boycotts of competitors. Drinking glasses and sheet glass for windowpanes were the main products, shipped by water to the northern European ports. Three reasons have been noted for the decline of the industry by the end of the century: The fear of completely devastating the forests, the effects of increased taxes Philip began charging to pay off his war debts, and his death in 1567, eliminating the great patron of the industry.[51]

EFFECTS OF THE SIXTEENTH CENTURY

This tumultuous period was the hammer that reformed the social, economic and administrative aspects of life in Hesse and forced its development along the lines of the modern nation state. The landgrave moved into the role of patron and protector of the common man, both because of his traditional opposition to the petty nobility and his undoubted commitment to the ideals espoused by Martin Luther. Lutheranism gave Philip a stage on which he could play an international role in statecraft, and secured the assets of the local Catholic Church for his treasury. It gave him the religious rationale for exercising political power over the ecclesiastical lords that had long blocked his ancestors' influence over much of their lands. But it also led him into the disastrous Schmalkaldic War and forced him to spend heavily on troops and material needed to protect the new faith. It was a violent time in the towns, in rural areas, and especially on the highways.

Philip took an active role in efforts to stabilize prices and ensure fair trade for his citizens, using mercantilist techniques to promote his state building. Always poor in resources, Hesse was materially better off for its foreign trade, capitalizing on its location astride major trade routes. Yet this too was a double-edged sword, for the price inflation and the distortion of markets that came with the great capitalist tide then sweeping Europe was very disruptive of people's lives. The most important and broad-based profession in the land, that of the wool weavers, was severely disrupted. The community-based trade of the market town guilds, where customers and suppliers knew each other by name and felt the need to trade fairly with one another, was another casualty of the impersonal market dealings of entrepreneurs not located in the communities where they did business. People felt increasingly exploited by merchants, tradesmen and the lords whom controlled their lands. The Peasant's War and the embrace of Lutheranism were two responses born of frustration and a desire to change the status quo.

The ability of markets to provide more goods and services, including food, played a role in the population increases that were the other defining feature of the age. Pressure on the land and on the cost of food drove up the number of landless poor reduced to poverty. Forests and marginal wasteland everywhere shrank as they were burned and hoed into fields. Population growth swelled the ranks of the towns and villages alike, creating opportunities for entrepreneurs to tap inexpensive labor pools through putting-out of various tasks. The landless also flocked to any trades they could undertake to make extra money, competing directly with the guild structure for customers. The competition for resources at the village level made everyone more conscious of his class and protective of his rights to the village common areas in opposition to the efforts of his fellows who likewise were scrambling to better their own lot. Philip recognized the dire straits in which many were living by enacting extensive measures to provide for the truly needy out of a statewide system of community chests and hospitals.

On balance, the Hesse of 1599 was more crowded, more expensive, more class-conscious, and less community-oriented than it had been in 1500. The state tried all the means known to the age to blunt or stave of the worst of these trends for its citizenry, not only on the basis of religious conviction but because it recognized its own dependence on the productivity and well being of the laboring classes. Yet in the end the forces unleashed in the sixteenth century were too great for any state, let alone one a small as Hesse, to attempt to control. The next century would see even more powerful forces unleashed, equally uncontrollable and much more destructive.

NOTES TO CHAPTER 6

[1] G.R. Elton, *Reformation Europe 1517-1559*, Harper and Row, New York, 1963, pp. 23-26, 27-28; Will Durant, *The Story of Civilization*, Vol. VI, *The Reformation*, Simon and Schuster, New York, 1957, pp. 293, 299, 302-303; Hajo Holborn, *A History of Modern Germany*, Alfred Knopf, New York, 1959, pp. 38-39, 116.
[2] Durant, pp. 305, 328-29, 332.
[3] Holborn, pp. 67-68, 71; Durant, 294, 296.
[4] Holborn, p. 35.
[5] Karl E. Demandt, *Geschichte des Landes Hessen*, Bärenreiter-Verlag, Kassel, 1972, pp. 207-15. See also the relevant town histories of the previous chapter.
[6] Demandt, pp. 199-201.
[7] Demandt, pp. 220-22.
[8] *1200 Jahre Groß-Bieberau: Beiträge zu seiner Geschichte*, Magistrat der Stadt Groß-Bieberau, 1987, pp. 34-35.
[9] William J. Wright, *Capitalism, the State, and the Lutheran Reformation: Sixteenth-Century Hesse*, Ohio University Press, Athens, 1988, pp. 49, 59-61; Demandt, pp. 222-23, 229; Durant, p. 299.
[10] Wright, pp. 50-51, 55, 61; Demandt, p. 230.
[11] Demandt, pp. 224-225, Wright, pp. 62-63, 65-67.
[12] Demandt, pp. 225-27; Thomas Brady, et. al., editor, *Handbook of European History 1400-1600: Late Middle Ages, Renaissance and Reformation*, Vol. I, E.J. Brill, Leiden, Netherlands, 1994, pp. 254-55.
[13] Brady, Vol. II, pp. 172, 590-91, 595; Durant, p. 332; Joseph Lortz, *Die Reformation in Deutschland*, Vols. I & II, Herder & Co., Freiburg, 1940, pp. 103, 108, 111-13.
[14] Durant, p. 447.
[15] Karl Wenckebach, *Zur Geschichte der Stadt, des Stiftes und der Kirche zu Wetter*, Selbstverlag der Evangelischen Kirchengemeinde Wetter, 1966, pp. 151-53.
[16] Durant, pp. 438-45; Holborn, pp. 216, 220.
[17] Elton, p. 154.
[18] Holborn 223; Durant 449.
[19] Elton, pp. 249, 355, 263-66; Holborn, p. 227; Durant, pp. 453-56.
[20] Demandt, pp. 233-36.
[21] Durant, pp. 751-52; Wright, pp. 76-77, and endnote, p. 91; Brady, Vol. I, p. 81.
[22] Wright, p. 87; Brigitta Vits, *Die Wirtschafts- und Sozialstruktur ländlicher Siedlungen in Nordhessen vom 16. Bis zum 19. Jahrhundert*, Selbstverlag der Marburger Geographischen Gesellschaft, Marburg, 1993, pp. 6, 11, 104. It should be noted that the Vits book refers specifically to three areas in northern Hesse located around Wolfhagen, Fritzlar/Gudensberg, and south of Homberg (Efze).
[23] Vits, pp. 22-34; Wright, pp. 82-83.
[24] Wright, pp. 88-89.
[25] Wright, pp. 77, 79-80; Vits, pp. 25, 105-06.
[26] Wright, pp. 75-78.
[27] Wright, pp. 78-80; John Thiebault, *German Villages in Crisis: Rural Life in Hesse-Kassel and the Thirty Years' War, 1580-1720*, Humanities Press, Atlantic Highlands, NJ, 1995, p. 132.

[28] Vits, pp. 35-43.
[29] Vits, pp. 63-71; Wright, pp. 83-84.
[30] Vits, pp. 106-08, 146; Wright, p. 85.
[31] Fernand Braudel, *The Structures of Everyday Life: Civilization and Capitalism 15th – 18th Centuries*, Vol. I, Harper & Row, New York, 1981, pp. 106, 112, 120, 123, 136, 205, 208-09; Durant, p. 769; Wright, pp. 222-224.
[32] Durant, pp. 304-05.
[33] Durant, p. 303; Thiebault, p. 47.
[34] Braudel, pp. 303-04, 310; Durant, p. 303.
[35] Durant, pp. 303, 305, 769; Thiebault, pp. 35, 60-61.
[36] Thiebault, pp. 48, 53-54, 77-79, 83-84, 87, 121; Durant, p. 303.
[37] Brady, Vol. I, p. 98, Vol. II, pp. 367, 614-23. See also the tragic story of the accused witch, "Tempel Annecke" in Dan C. Heinemeier, *A History of Brunswick, Life in a German Duchy from Roman Times through 1900.* While outside Hesse proper, this provides an overview of the causes and means by which witchcraft trials were carried out against innocent, mostly single and elderly women.
[38] Durant, p. 758.
[39] Durant, pp. 757-59; Wright, pp. 169-71; Thiebault, pp. 125-27.
[40] Durant, p. 763; Wright, pp. 161-80, Braudel, p. 329.
[41] Demandt, pp. 223-24; Durant, pp. 382-92; Wright, pp. 61-62, 82-83; *Groß-Bieberau*, p. 35; Holborn, p. 173.
[42] Wright, pp. 137-40, 220.
[43] Vits. pp. 103-04; Wright, pp. 147-49, 187-205.
[44] Braudel, pp. 316-18; Elton, p. 321; Wright, pp. 218-23.
[45] Vits, p. 92; Wright, pp. 149-57.
[46] Wright, pp. 144-46; Braudel, p. 139.
[47] Wright, pp. 146-49; Braudel, p. 192.
[48] Thiebault, pp. 114-15.
[49] Wright, pp. 122-24, 226; Thiebault, p. 115; Braudel, Vol. II, pp. 321-23.
[50] Wright, pp. 172-73; Thiebault, p. 115.
[51] Wright, pp. 124-25.

Chapter 7

War Clouds Gather: The Early Seventeenth Century

In the seventeenth century the vast majority of the population continued to live off the land. A "crisis of subsistence" that many times turned into outright starvation prevailed throughout much of the century. Most people in this time never knew when adverse weather conditions would ruin their crops, drive up the prices of their staple cereals, and bring starvation upon them. Weather patterns in fact seemed to be getting worse in the course of the century, crop failures occurring with frightening regularity in 1625, 1630, 1649, 1660, 1661, and worst of all during the 1690s. These patterns also brought the worst periods of extended cold for centuries, the rule of Louis XIV of France being known as the "Little Ice Age" (1648-1715). Hessian and other German peasants dressed mostly in coarse cloth that offered poor protection from the cold. The grimmest times came when hunger and disease struck together, leading to sizable drops in population. Conditions deteriorated in much of Germany as the Thirty Years War raged over the land (1618-48), the armies of all sides stealing crops, animals, and the meager possessions of even impoverished villagers they encountered along the way.[1]

Cereals continued to form the overwhelming share of the diet in this period. Barley, oats and especially rye were used to make bread, coarse soup, gruel and related products that were the staples upon which most people lived. The yields of wheat were so low, perhaps five or less to one, that it only caught on as a staple crop later in the century. It was rare that all the crops taken together brought abundance, and scarcity was chronic. The average yield in Germany for all grains even as late as 1700 was about 4.2:1.[2]

In contrast to cereals, the eating of meat fell compared to earlier periods in the Middle Ages, when 100kg (over 220 lb.) per person was the average annual consumption. By 1800 it had dropped to only forty-four lb. The exception was the period just after the Thirty Years War when for a number of years German livestock production exceeded the growth in human population. Salt was another staple much in demand to preserve meat and add flavor to the "insipid farinaceous gruels" described by Braudel, which were still the predominant foodstuffs. German population in the sixteenth century averaged about twenty-eight persons per square kilometer, compared to thirty-four in France, and forty in Holland. The more populated, less productive areas such as Hesse suffered unemployment and land shortages that made them fertile grounds for the recruiters for mercenary armies that ranged across Europe at this time. Armies were still small; the achievement of Wallenstein of maintaining 100,000 men under arms through much of the Thirty Years War was an administrative feat unheard of elsewhere.[3]

The German economy in general suffered downturns in a variety of areas as the new century dawned, the 1620s in particular being a time of economic depression, with high food prices and blighted trade. Mercantilism was all the rage among the German rulers: its proponents held that prosperity resulted from amassing more bullion than other lands by selling more to them than one bought in return. Stockpiling precious metals was the goal, and no one took note of the negative effect on trade as everyone pursued variations on this policy. It seems that trade with the wealthy trading towns of

Italy slowed in this era, bank collapses reduced available credit, and transportation became less reliable and more risky. The debasing of coinage also became rife in these times. Embraced across Germany as a means to make precious metals go farther, the minting of coins with less gold and silver content promoted inflation and increased market uncertainty. By 1619 the exchange rate between the north German *Taler* and southern German guilder (*Gulden)* was in constant flux. In Hesse Kassel these trends can be seen in the shrinking value of the *Taler*. A *Taler's*-worth of goods in 1606 (1=32 *Albus*) cost one *Taler*, sixteen *Albus* by 1618. By late 1620 it cost over two *Taler*, and one year later, eight *Taler*. Values fell 100% or more again through 1622, to sixteen to twenty *Taler* by the end of the year.[4]

Despite these pressures and the strain on the trade-dependent Hessian economy, the life of small farmers across the land remained largely unchanged in the period prior to the war. Based on a study of villages in northeastern Hesse centered around the Werra River, one author has determined that rural productivity was outwardly unhindered, even increasing against inflation through 1610. Population likewise was expanding at a healthy rate, suggesting no looming shortage of laborers for the fields or soldiers for the military. The landgrave in Kassel must have had every expectation that his coffers would continue to be blessed for years to come with steady or increasing amounts of taxes, tithes and other duties from his peasantry.[5]

Once the war broke out, peasants learned to become quite mobile, flocking to the towns for protection in times of famine and danger, and flowing back onto unoccupied farmlands as these again became available and relatively safe. The towns harbored a shifting mix of under class laborers, journeymen, apprentices of the guild masters, and others for whom periodic unemployment meant financial disaster. Together with skilled artisans in lesser guilds who were shut out of the government of the towns, all these elements often created unrest or outright revolt, periodically threatening the social order.

The towns in this era primarily relied upon the produce of their local farmlands for sustenance, their citizens owning and working much rural land with their own shepherds, gamekeepers, agricultural workers, vine dressers, etc. Orchards and gardens could be found both within and outside the town walls, the fields being located somewhat further away. Pigs and other domesticated animals still wandered the streets.[6]

The general harshness of the times also was reflected in ignorance and prejudice against things that were new or strange. It was a time of extreme narrow-mindedness, reflected in the development of a rigidly orthodox Lutheranism that rivaled Catholicism in its strict adherence to doctrine. It was dominated by the secular authority of the landgraves, dukes and princes to which it long since had flocked for protection from its ecclesiastical enemies. Now the Lutheran clergy were at odds with another Protestant faith, Calvinism, which they found more threatening than orthodox Catholicism. (The Calvinism of Landgrave Moritz will be discussed later in this chapter.) Religious and social intolerance and superstition were coupled with broad fear of supposed works of the devil. This brought efforts to root out witchcraft to a fever pitch. Fear of witchcraft transcended every class and religion, and by 1600 the church was condoning and encouraging witch hunters who could whip whole communities into hysteria. Local eccentrics and social outcasts became the victims of the hunters' torture-induced confessions. This led inexorably to execution, with death by burning usually seen as the only known means to stamp out the demonic evil. By 1700 the worst of these attacks thankfully had died out.[7]

WAR CLOUDS GATHER: EARLY SEVENTEENTH CENTURY

Religious intolerance, greed, and the outright indifference of the rulers of the German principalities—as well as their Danish, Swedish and French counterparts—also fueled the crisis that brought about one of the truly cataclysmic wars of German history. The Thirty Years War became in many ways the defining feature of the century.

Before we recount the history of the war in its Hessian context in chapter eight, we will review the course of events that caused the cousins who ruled in Kassel and Darmstadt to become such bitter enemies, and look at the lives of their subjects on the eve of the war. As we have seen, Philip the Magnanimous split the landgraviate among his sons in such a way as to cause permanent division of an already small principality. When the heirs who ruled in Kassel and Darmstadt themselves died in the 1590s, their sons' poisonous attitudes only served to harden already awkward relationships. Moritz of Kassel (landgrave from 1592) was brilliant, a multi-talented and well educated prince of his day. Unfortunately, his gifts did not include diplomatic and military savvy, and this would cost him and his land dearly in the politically-charged climate in which he ruled. Ludwig V. of Darmstadt, less intellectually gifted but much more capable at political scheming, combined a cordial dislike of his cousin with jealousy and greed for land and power.

The succession issue in nearby Hesse Marburg presented the cousins with a conflict that eventually became grounds for war. In 1604 Landgrave Ludwig of Hesse Marburg (upper Hesse) died childless. His will divided his lands among his nephews. Kassel was to have the northern half, dominated by Marburg, while Ludwig of Darmstadt was to receive the southern, less well endowed half, centered on Gießen. Ludwig immediately asserted that he should have received more. In 1605 he took up his case with the emperor, with whom he had forged a close alliance. The issue was clouded further because one condition of the will stated that the Marburg lands had to be allowed to remain Lutheran by whoever ruled them. Moritz, however, was a committed Calvinist, and in 1605 he began to force conversion on his new subjects. This provided Ludwig with further cause for imperial review of the terms of the will. An almost 50-year conflict over these lands now ensued, with imperial power, the Thirty Years War, and constantly shifting alliances all influencing the outcome. [8]

As in other matters of state, Landgrave Moritz of Kassel was convinced of his own genius and infallibility when he decided to embrace the Calvinist reform faith. In many ways this was to have disastrous consequences for his family, his land and its people. His second wife was the countess Juliane of Nassau Dillenburg, who stemmed from a family of Calvinists. Moritz embraced her faith with passion, even composing an extensive set of new articles for the faith known as the *Verbesserungpunkte* or Reform Points. Their purpose was to revise Lutheran practice and teaching to conform to Moritz' adopted views. The landgrave was convinced that Luther's reforms were halfway measures. A general synod of clergy endorsed the reform program at his urging, and he set about imposing it throughout the Kassel lands. The reforms called for a strict ban on any graven images in church buildings or religious services, revised treatment of communion, and emphasis on readings from the Bible and Psalter. To show the error of Lutheran ways in believing that the Host indeed became the body and blood of Christ during the service (transubstantiation), he ordered the use of the hardest bread available to drum into his subjects' heads that it could not be the transformed flesh of Christ.

These and other seemingly minor differences were magnified in the popular mind. Calvinism appeared to be trying to discredit Lutheranism and violate the settlement of Augsburg; this was the treaty that had headed off Catholic-Protestant warfare in the sixteenth century and still remained the cornerstone of social and political order. As noted above, it also became a cause celebre for Moritz' cousin in Darmstadt as he sought to obtain more of the Marburg inheritance. The synods of Kassel and St. Goar seem to have adopted the new faith without serious opposition, while the Synod of Eschwege and many of the local nobility across Hesse objected strongly and demanded to be able to remain Lutheran. The Marburg synod was another difficult case. Unrest required the military to be called in to require submission to the new order. The requirement to dispose of religious art in the churches was greatly resented by the citizens of Marburg, who complained to the landgrave that their bare churches looked like Turkish mosques.

Most clerics in the upper Hessian synod of Marburg refused to implement the reform points and had to be dismissed from office by the superintendent. This brought great hardship on these dispossessed men who suddenly were deprived of their vocations. Many fell into poverty. Among the parishes whose pastors suffered dismissal were: Oberrosphe, Amöneburg, Bromskirchen, Vöhl, Niederasphe, Langenstein, Sterzhausen, Ebsdorf, Battenberg, Wetter, Elnhausen, Bottendorf, Willersdorf, Röddenau, Wolkersdorf, Grüsen, Winnen, Viermünden, Frankenberg, Dodenau, Bracht, Bürgeln, Treis, Cappel, Battenfeld, Gemünden/Wohra, Rosenthal, Lohra, Dautphe, and Bauerbach. The lucky ones were able to find employment in Darmstadt lands or other Lutheran territories.

Locally, many individual congregations objected as well. Many of their pastors were dismissed by the landgrave in an effort to bring them to heel. In some cases, reform pastors reverted to Lutheranism based on the demands of their people, and had to be replaced yet again. Some people in border areas went to worship weekly in Thuringia or Hesse-Darmstadt rather than accept the new faith. Over time, however, more and more people accepted the landgrave's imposed faith. By 1650, Calvinism had completely replaced the old faith in Moritz' realm and itself seemed quite orthodox. [9]

LIFE ON THE LAND ON THE EVE OF WAR

A modern observer of life on the land in Hesse in the seventeenth century would have discerned little or no difference from a similar look during the century before. Farming methods, relationships and duties owed to the lords of the land were unchanged. Social relationships, and village life as a whole remained rooted in comfortable and familiar patterns that transcended centuries. Peasants everywhere were slow to embrace change in an environment where mistakes could reduce crop yields and throw people into dire straits. Most people were "powerless, ignorant and indifferent" to the events outside their immediate circle of life, as Wedgwood has written.

Yet even these simple people were emboldened from time to time to try to better their lot by resisting the efforts of their social betters to extract payments and services from them. It was common for villages to address grievances to the landgrave, seeking redress in various ways through the sacking of supposedly corrupt officials or the reduction of tithes and taxes due to economic hardship. Passive resistance to authority was not uncommon, such as by working more slowly than normal or failing to turn out for service duties. Boundary markers might be subtly changed so as to reduce the size of more heavily taxed parcels in favor of others. Sometimes resistance brought about fines by the authorities, such as in Amt Sontra in 1622 where penalties followed refusal to deliver logs to the local salt works. In 1621 the village of Dens was similarly fined, "because they were called to mow at Cornberg and took five days of beautiful weather to do what they should have accomplished in just five hours." These anecdotes show the very real difficulty of a fairly unorganized bureaucracy trying to impose the will of the seventeenth century prince on his people.[10]

Another activity that in no way diminished from the previous century was the Germans' love of food and drink. The French had a proverb that, "oxen stop drinking when they no longer thirst, Germans only begin then." Germans themselves laughed about the tendency, their own proverb maintaining that, "we pour money away through our stomachs." Even among the Germans, Hesse was recognized as a hard-drinking land. The landgrave started a temperance society to try to counteract public drunkenness. Its first president later drank himself to death. Wine, not beer was the drink of choice for all classes up until the Thirty Years War. The Hersfeld town cellar dispensed 194 *Fuder* of wine in 1604, the *Fuder* being an ancient measure equivalent in the public mind to a large cart-load. The total appears to have amounted to tens of thousands of gallons. Every village had to have its wine shop or tavern.

A major change came about in the course of the war. By mid-century, beer and brandy had taken over as the drinks of choice for all classes. Beer brewing and selling in the 17th and 18th centuries was a lucrative business. In many areas the religious establishment took up the trade, as did the landgrave's own court. In 1669 the court in Kassel used 644 *Fuder* of beer per year. By 1673, Hersfeld's wine sales had fallen to only ten or eleven *Fuder* per year, a 95% drop. The move away from wine in no way eliminated the Hessian tendency to drink too much, however, particularly among those who adopted brandy as their preferred means of intoxication.

Only in the largest villages along the highways were there actual inns. In Niederaule there was a state-owned public house that for eighteen years was let out as a *Meier*-style rental establishment based on an initial payment of 100 *Taler* plus annual rent. The community as a whole assumed ownership and operated it. A community barkeep held the job for three years at a time, charging a 20% commission on each drink for his wages. Local villages were required to patronize this state establishment to buy beer for their marriage feasts, holidays, and ceremonies.[11]

No doubt drinking played a role in the continuing trend toward violent behavior across the land. Sibling conflict often led to blows, and fines had to be imposed on such actions in order to maintain social order. In *Amt* Sontra in 1610 one Valentin Kaufman was fined for trying to strike his sister and hitting his father instead. In the same year and district there were seventeen other fights recorded that did not involve relatives. Domestic violence may have been perpetrated by adolescents in some cases. In Königswald in 1607 a man named Blum Sontag was evidently very unpopular. Various rounds of violence were committed against him by members of his village community. Only the court rulings of the state courts seem to have been able to provide him any relief. He was verbally insulted and beaten "blue and bloody" along with his wife, both of whom were left lying in the street. This time the fines set were so high that no further sign of attacks is recorded.

More than crimes of violence drew such penalties from the government in these times, however. Harboring a prostitute or a known promiscuous woman was a punishable offense, as was premarital sex resulting in pregnancy. Husbands could be held liable and fined if their wives gave birth too soon after marriage.[12]

As in ancient times, probably the most feared collective threat to the community as a whole was the outbreak of fire. Houses in towns were narrow and built close to one another, their roofs most often of flammable straw. The loss of a house, particularly one burdened with a mortgage, could reduce a family to inescapable poverty. Outbreaks were so bad in this century that the landgrave issued regulations directing blacksmiths to have on hand ladders, shoemakers leather buckets, and rope makers poles for fighting fire. Each farmer was to maintain water and two buckets at the ready, while laborers had to have only the buckets. A fire in Herborn in 1626 destroyed 100 houses in the southeastern part of town. Some 300-400 people were left homeless, and were given such shelter and assistance as the other townspeople could provide. The landgrave granted a special wood allotment for rebuilding.[13]

Building techniques and designs changed over time. Time-honored methods had to be altered because of the increasingly acute shortage of suitable building wood. The larger, straighter oak trees so much in demand for housing timbers were no longer available in the required numbers. Where earlier methods called for beams running from the ground to the roof, now two-story construction had to be done in smaller stages with beams only one floor in height. A framing technique known as *Mannfigur* or man-figure was developed to tie the structural elements together, and this characteristically Hessian development then was used for centuries. It consisted of two long beams attached to a center beam like legs, a horizontal piece above these forming the stylized arms. This was capped with two smaller members that attached the vertical beam to the header above in a triangular design that formed the stylized head of the man-figure. This joining technique lent strength and was attractive as well, typically being left open to the eye on the prominent sides of buildings.

Trees for housing construction were often felled in the fall so they could be worked into finished forms during the winter or spring while they were still fresh. The *Fachwerk* framing structure then would be built in the spring. Straw for the roofs was often a difficult material to obtain, since it was in great demand for many common uses on the farm. The wall area between the framing was filled in with community help, probably like the barn raisings common for generations here in America. The spaces were first filled with at least three hardwood stakes, generally of oak. Between and through these was woven a wide basket-work of softwood branches like hazelnut wood, birch, willow, or the remnants of the earlier oak work. The basket weave then was plastered with a mix of clay (loam), sand, chopped straw, and water. The clay came from local pits. The mix was made in a shallow hole dug into the ground and then worked to the correct consistency with bare feet. The exact recipe varied by area, with more sand needed where the clay was particularly rich and liable to crack in drying.

A wall made in this way needed from two to six weeks to dry properly, depending on humidity. So the work had to be done after the end of the frost season, about mid-May, and before the expected start of the fall rainy season in mid-September. After drying customary local artwork would be applied; in some areas decoration would be applied to the surface of the plaster while it was still wet.

Room layouts in Hessian homes also differed by region. Common styles in nearby principalities influenced the Hessian border areas. In south Hesse the three-zone form with enclosed animal stalls was common. In the west, a two-zone living/storage house was more usual, drawing on Rhenish influences. In eastern Hesse the Thuringian influence led to three zone homes as in the south, while in northern Hesse the lower German hall house was common as in Waldeck, Wolfhagen and Hofgeismar. Boundaries between the various styles were never exact. Originally the trend was to build in the "*Ernhaus*" style common across Germany, the *Ern* being the room with the fireplace. This room was open to the roof to allow smoke to escape before the use of chimneys became common. Later a second room, the *Stube*, was built with a lower

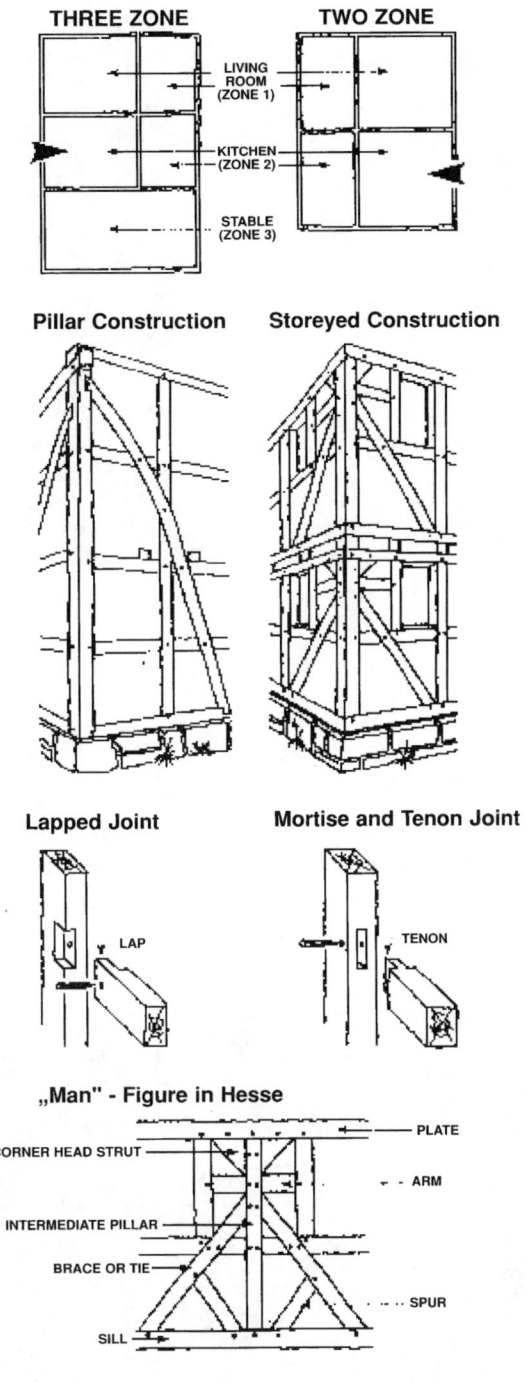

Figure 7-1 Construction techniques in the production of *Fachwerk* (half-timbered) buildings. Courtesy, Open Air Museum Hessenpark, Neu-Anspach, Germany.

Figure 7-2 A view of the change in building technique brought about by the landgrave in his efforts to save the larger oak trees. Individual framing timbers were to run the height of a single story only (rt.) in contrast to the earlier practice of members that ran from the ground to the roof line. *Figure 7-3* (below) shows the classic "*Mannfigur*" style of framing members in the second story of the center building, described in Chapter 7.

ceiling that kept it mostly smoke free. This became a universal living area, used for work, sleeping, and relaxing. Sometimes even young or small animals needing protection from the elements would shelter here with the family. The hearth room was used for cooking, keeping warm in winter, for smoking foods, and its smoke helped in driving out mice and other pests.[14]

The hall houses of the north had their roofs pitched steeply, and extending all the way down past the walls nearly to the ground. The openings under the low part of the roof (where it extended beyond the walls) were fitted out as animal stalls. The living area or *Diele* included a hearth at the rear, and here most of the cooking and living took place.

The hall house was different from the *Ernhaus* which otherwise was the predominant form. The door of the house brought one first into the *Ern* room, in the middle portion of the house. From here another door led to the adjoining room. On the other side of the house was a stall for the larger farm animals. The second story rooms were laid out in the same floor plan and used as storage areas.

Barns would be located either parallel or at a right angle to the living areas of the house. In very productive areas like the Wetterau, the barn would be used to store winter supplies of food and fodder. Wagons and tools would be kept there as well. In autumn and winter the barn floor would be used for threshing. Less productive regions would have single, stand-alone houses (*Einhäuser*) that enclosed living areas, stalls and barn under one roof. These were seen in the villages of the *Mittelgebirge*. By the post-Thirty Years War period these were found in the Hessian Odenwald as well. This could have come about because growing incomes permitted larger houses but the shortage of building wood dictated compact designs. These houses typically had the stalls located next to the hearth room, with a connecting door between. This made it easier to care for the animals without going out into inclement weather in winter, and also allowed the heat from the animals to help ward off cold on one side of the house.[15]

The early seventeenth century was a period of slow but marked change in the linen industry throughout Germany, and this was especially important for Hesse where the industry was so key to the economy. More and more economic troubles were driving old-style textile operations out of business in favor of large-scale "putting out" operations that paid rural workers a pittance for their unskilled labor. War only accelerated the pace of these changes.

Whether for their own use, for sale in the local markets, or working for piece work wages, yarn spinning and linen weaving continued to be winter work of the Hessian rural masses in the seventeenth and eighteenth centuries. Most often the work of women, in many places men labored at the trade as well. Where land lacked productive capacity and heavy taxes and tithes further eroded earnings, people mostly looked to the textile trade for supplemental income. Generally it was a critical adjunct to their traditional farming. Often the whole family engaged in the spinning and weaving at home, from preparing the flax to finishing the cloth. Even 12-year-olds knew how to spin.

This yarn was a rough, hard, middle-fine to very crude product only suitable for coarse cloth. Before sale it had to be soaked, boiled and then plunged in cold water. It was then dried on a pole hung behind the stove. The resulting yarn commonly was called Hessian yarn by salesmen in the trade. It made its way to Elberfeld, Bielefeld, the north German Hansa cities, Leipzig, Frankfurt, and Breslau.

Everyday Hessian clothes included linen pants and a blue shirt for the men, as well as blue linen aprons for the women. Shirts for the whole family were made only of home-spun cloth. A rural proverb held that self-spun and -sewn clothing was best for the farm family ("*Selbst gesponnen, selbst gemacht, ist die beste Bauerntracht.*") A bride's chest full of clean white linen was an object of pride and evidence of prosperity for a farm wife. No adequately appointed woman's trousseau failed to include a reel and a spinning wheel with a flax distaff. These were symbolic of her future productive efforts. The tools of the linen trade differed somewhat by region. At base, though, they all produced for sale the basic yarn or linen goods that were died or woven in a variety of colors and styles based on the local village customs. All were sold as "Hessian goods."

The best raw linen in the region was produced in the villages of the Reinhard Forest, the districts of Fritzlar, Homberg, Rotenburg, the mountainous area of the Witzenhausen district, and especially in the area of Herzfeld in villages a couple of hour's distance to the right and left of the mountains. The best and thickest Hessian linen was recognized as coming from the villages in the areas from Almershausen to Raboldshausen, Mengshausen, Niederaule, and Goßmannsrode, and the Rohrbacher villages Ober- and Niederthalhausen, Gerterode, and Biedebach, as well as Eschenstruth.

This all-important production was something the Hessian state sought earnestly to cultivate and protect. Specific regulations on all facets of the trade were issued, and every effort was made to head off fraudulent goods that might spoil the name of Hessian products in the external marketplace.[16] Despite his best efforts, the landgrave could not stave off the impact of growing foreign competition and capitalistic organization on a massive scale; these were slowly squeezing the Hessian textile industry at every level.

An interesting aspect of Hessian history in this period is the treatment of Jews. Basic separation from those of the Christian faith was maintained through the seventeenth century, and Jews seldom appear in official records. Sometimes they were the victims of insults, but probably not much different from the insults other villagers hurled against each other as we noted above. On rare occasions Jews were singled out for attack. In Abterode, several Jews complained of efforts to drive them from the village and forbid their use of maids on Saturdays. Abterode is the only village where Jews appear regularly in the householder lists. Elsewhere they generally were forbidden to hold land, forcing them to work mainly as middlemen, petty lenders, or in other jobs not tied to the land. Jews mostly made few claims on the community. They sometimes paid protection money but few people would stand up for them against ill treatment by their neighbors. Jewish interests were not even considered when community complaints to the landgrave were raised.[17]

The peasant-lord relationships on the land were among the least changeable features of rural life in Hesse as the centuries wore on. The *Meier* contract whereby the farmer struck an agreement with his overlord to manage farm acreage for a set period of years was still commonly in force. The contract required the farmer to maintain the three-field system of cultivation and keep using specific plots of land as they had traditionally been cultivated. Pasture was to remain pasture, arable was to remain arable, etc. When the agreement expired, the farm had to be handed back to the lord with all the tools, animals, etc. that it had when the farmer took it on. Should anything be missing, it had to be paid for at full replacement value. Rents were due annually on St. Michael's Day, paid in money and/or marketable produce of specified kinds. A 1688 contract called for the annual payment of 100 florins, 26 *Albus*, plus sixty measures of rye, thirty-two of barley, thirty of oats, and five of wheat. Most such farmers acquitted themselves well, fulfilled the terms of their agreements, and were permitted and even encouraged to renew. Others could bid against the *Meier*, however, in an effort to take over the land by paying a higher rental fee. Over time, an increasing number of these contract arrangements were converted to inheritable and life-long holdings. Stability in holdings was seen as a plus by the landlords as it promoted more secure revenues from the land.

The landgrave owned so much land that he often hired on his local officials to act as *Meier* and manage his farms. A typical official in this role would be the district mayor, or *Amtschultheiß*. Alternatively, private farmers or even a village community might contract for the management role. In 1687 the village of Niederaule bid against the local mayor for continued management of the landgrave's local manor. They won by outbidding him by 100 florins plus twenty measures each of rye and oats. His officials were unsure about whether to trust the community to follow through with the agreement, but the landgrave personally directed that they should be given the chance. The old mayor must have given the villagers trouble in the hand-over, since he had to be directed by the landgrave to be more cooperative. A similar arrangement was struck by the Oberlengsfeld community, who bid 950 *Taler* plus a 50-*Taler* origination fee for management rights to the manor at Ehrenthal. In both cases the land was likely divided up among the farmers immediately after the deal was done.[18]

Such land deals would not have altered the farmers' continuing responsibility to provide manual labor and services of various kinds as needed. An interesting example was the need to turn out to help with the landgrave's organized hunts. All able men had to help with the periodic wolf hunts in these times. As soon as snow had fallen each year, the hunt would be announced. Some 250 beaters were needed, and the men had to fabricate beating sticks and snaring nets at home and bring them along. These were always unpopular activities, and sometimes a quantity of firewood was promised to those who turned out as an incentive to participate.[19]

Another form of peasant holding in Hesse was the *Leibgut*, or life-hold farm. This form predominated in the area around Hersfeld, and permitted life-long landholding with the capability of extending the holding through inheritance to a child or other relation. The property could not be sold; other children would have to content themselves with a portion of the deceased's movable property. If a land holder died without heir, the farm reverted to the lord for re-renting to another life holder based on bids. A high origination fee also had to be paid, usually sixty to 150 *Taler* or more. These arrangements were established via a letter signed by both parties and surrendered to the lord when the agreement came to an end. They were also very commonly used by religious institutions who owned manor farms.[20]

At the other end of the economic spectrum were people too poor to aspire to a *Meier* or *Leibgut* farm. The landgrave's concern for their welfare also was reflected in regulations dating from this era. Wages for community herders were supposed to be set at a level that would preclude their need to beg for subsistence. The truly poor of all occupations were permitted to allow their goats—poor men's cows as they were called—to wander freely in common areas and even in the landgrave's own forests. However, this was destructive of new growth and thus only the truly needy and those who required goat's milk for medicinal purposes were allowed to do it. To offset this type of damage, people were required to plant new trees in the local forests at certain milestones in their lives. Farmers had to plant three trees a year in local woods, foreign settlers just entering the territory five trees. Prospective bridegrooms also were to plant four trees as a condition of permission to marry.[21]

Under the various forms of landholding agreements with the lords the duties and burdens of the farmers remained largely unchanged from the original forms discussed in chapter four. Land rents and taxes could have originated from one of three sources. First, rent payments to the lord for usage rights to the land. Secondly, a set annual domicile tax had to be paid. In Hersfeld and many other areas of Hesse this was the so-called "hearth holder" or "hearth hen" tax assessed on each house. Finally, in times of crop failure, war or other severe need, the farmer was often forced to take out a mortgage on his property. This mortgage was almost always re-salable with the debtor having the right to buy it back. In most cases, however, he was unable to fully pay off the mortgage and this became just another duty owed on the property.

Ground rents still were owed to the landgrave, a lesser noble, or in rarer cases a religious order or foundation. These were mainly payable in produce, or less often in cash payments. The produce had to be market quality, containing no weeds or grass. The rents that went to the lesser lords often were insufficient to support their lifestyles, and many sank into debt and poverty, particularly during and after the war. It became impossible for farmers to deliver up the rents in years of crop failure and famine. In such years the landgrave sometimes provided seed for planting or grain for making bread out of his own store houses. The farmers were required to either pay for the produce or increase their rents to cover it the following year.

Compulsory services also were a holdover from the early feudal period. These included manual labor in cutting grass or harvesting produce, making hay, threshing, plowing, planting, etc. The lord required a few regular servants, day wage laborers and transport animals on his land. His peasants also were expected to provide building services on his lands: forest and hunting services, dams and trenches kept in good repair, etc. Tree felling, helping with the hunt, working on roads and bridges, hauling goods to support military campaigns, and a host of similar activities, all had to be done for free by his dependent landholders. The construction of many princely buildings in Kassel, the Marburg castle, and other forts were all dependent on the service of the populace by hand and with their transport animals. These services remained a heavy and much resented yoke on the farmers.

The church's rights to large amounts of tithes in the Middle Ages also continued, mostly delivered in the form of produce through the seventeenth century. These differed from the land rent, collected on the whole farm. The tithe was based on specific acreage, and unlike the land rents that were always fixed, tithes could be increased over time with the value of the land. In Hesse the landgrave was the greatest holder of tithe rights. Whole districts were tithe-free in Hesse, while others had a heavy tithe to pay. The individual tithable acres lay scattered among the arable fields. They were accounted for each year in a written document provided to the district authorities by the local village *Grebe*. In the seventeenth century tithes in produce required the payer to advise the tithe collector twenty-four hours in advance of harvest so he could come and collect the lord's share. If he simply failed to show up the harvest could proceed.

These tithes hindered the farmers in their harvesting efforts, since they usually had to be collected before the farmers were allowed to take their own produce home. This sometimes caused spoilage in bad weather. They complained loud and long about the inability to afford both tithes and ground rents together. Sometimes they would allow the tithe lands to simply lie fallow rather than incur the tithe on them. The authorities also accused the farmers of moving boundary markers or otherwise seeking to limit the extent of tithable lands. Some ordinary fruits grown on the fallow lands during the three-field rotation remained tithe-free, including lentils, peas, cabbage, beets, and vetches. [22]

WAR CLOUDS GATHER: EARLY SEVENTEENTH CENTURY

Like landholding rights, the rights to operate grain mills had to be granted by a lord, and in Hesse this was the landgrave. As noted in the last chapter, mill owners were prosperous men in the sixteenth century, although mill rights were generally extended only for the life of the miller. By the mid-seventeenth century inheritable milling rights became the norm. During the Thirty Years War almost all mills had to be abandoned. The few remaining in operation were enough to handle the needs of the reduced population. Much later than most other agricultural properties many of the old the mills were brought back into operation. In Hesse mill regulations protected the landgrave's right to control the building and operation of mills. State authorities had to approve any intent to modify the mill works. To protect the operation of the mills across the country farmers were required to use the mills in their own districts, even if there were closer or more convenient ones in neighboring districts.

Mills had another interesting responsibility under the ordinances: each had to provide the food for one or two of the landgrave's hunting dogs. They had to provide a set amount of rye or oats and obtain a certification from the hunting scribe to show they had paid their dues. Landgrave Friedrich set an annual monetary amount of two *Taler* per dog from the millers, but after severe complaints they were allowed to go back to payments in grain. [23]

The government of the state in the seventeenth century had not yet assumed the national character of modern nation-states. The landgrave's own estates formed the basis for much of the revenue, and he spent it as he saw fit on state or personal expenditures as the need arose. Similarly, he considered his administrators personal servants and employed them as such, quite apart from their role as public officials. These included not only high officials such as the *Rentmeister* and *Amtmann*, but even low-level servants such as wine stewards, gardeners, donkey drivers, etc. He maintained just two servants in the district of Germerode, and up to sixty-four in the Kassel district. C.V. Wedgwood put the role and commitment of such officials succinctly: "The routine of government was ill-organized; politicians worked with inadequate help; honesty, efficiency and loyalty were comparatively rare, and the average statesman seems to have worked on the assumption that a perpetual leakage of funds and information was inevitable."

Many officials had poor relationships with the people whose lives they were charged with administering. This is hardly surprising given their role in extracting tithes and duties from the locals, and the fact that many officials used local service requirements to benefit themselves by making farmers work on their own lands. Often the community would direct written complaints about his officials to the landgrave himself. The *Amtschultheiß* of the Sontra district was criticized in such a letter in 1621, which alleged to Moritz that his official had demanded excessive payments under the militia maintenance tax just to line his own pockets. [24]

A final focus of our look at Hessian history before we review the Thirty Years War itself is the development of mercenary military forces in Hesse-Kassel. The landgraves began selling the services of their mercenary troops as early as the sixteenth century to try to overcome lack of revenue and the unfortunate terms of Philip the Magnanimous' will. William IV of Kassel maintained a foreign policy that was basically defensive. Moritz, his son, was addicted to costly show, impoverishing his court. He made a first attempt at revolutionizing the military in his domains. He believed a disciplined, well-trained militia could be created based on trained peasants who served part-time (1601). His plan was a radical departure: the armed forces of the day were by now the sole domain of trained professional soldiery who understood tactics and timing in engagements. The landgrave sought to avoid various problems by his plan: the crushing expense of standing forces, disloyalty of commanders, and unrest and mutiny among the rank-and-file. Looting and banditry of dismissed units was a frequent cause of strife in Hesse Kassel. On the other hand, he thought peasants would be motivated to fight for their faith and families. He sought bi-weekly training at the village level with occasional three- or four-day day centralized training sessions to teach tactics. Food and equipment could be managed by the troops themselves. This interesting experiment failed, however, to eliminate the need for professional troops. In practice, the outbreak of the Thirty Years War meant that two armies, professional and militia, now had to be maintained.

THIRTY YEARS WAR

The Hessian experience in the war that stood for centuries in the popular mind as Germany's most horrific and destructive was among the most horrible of any of the German lands. Hesse Kassel and Hesse Darmstadt were on opposite sides during the years of the conflict. In the last few years they engaged in what amounted to civil war. In the end, they also experienced very different outcomes as a result of the Treaty of Westphalia; Kassel achieved much better terms in the peace.

The Holy Roman Empire was fraught with tension in the early decades of the seventeenth century. Many expected a spark at any moment that would set off war between Protestant and Catholic princes over control of the empire and influence in its disparate lands. Yet none could have predicted the course of events that would be set in motion by a short-lived and obviously doomed effort by the Protestant Elector of the Rhineland Palatinate to assume the crown of Protestant Bohemia under the very nose of its current sovereign, his Imperial Majesty Ferdinand Habsburg of Austria. This abortive attempt by Friedrich, the "Winter King," to seize Bohemia by popular acclaim seems in hindsight a ridiculous catalyst for general war. In fact, some scholars look at the Thirty Years War as four separate wars fought over religion and great power politics over the course of a generation. According to this schema the Bohemian war (1618-25) was followed by a Danish war (1625-29), a Swedish war (1630-35), and finally a Franco-Swedish war (1635-48). The common denominator was misery for most of the German population, depending on what areas of the empire were being tramped through by the armies at any given time.[25]

Warfare in this period was in transition from the tactics and equipment of the Middle Ages to more modern forms. This was the last era in which privately-recruited and -led armies held sway in Europe; hereafter, nation states alone would have the wherewithal to raise and support effective armed might. Military forces were considered too expensive and difficult to maintain except in wartime, and kings would draw on the talents and resources of private princes or mercenary generals with the ability to recruit and organize armies when war broke out. The officers and men might be drawn from anywhere across the continent. They could be expected to fight against the interests of any power opposing the ruler who paid them, even the states of their birth. Scots and Germans were prized throughout Europe as soldiers, as were the Swiss and northern Italians. Well-trained troops in this period all were mercenaries who spent their lives learning and practicing war as a trade. When captured in battle, these professionals very often simply joined the side of the victors and continued their lives in the familiar pattern. As in later years and among state armies, officers always were drawn from the ranks of the nobility and landholding classes, though they might be impoverished nobility in search of their fortunes.

Cavalry was important in this period, being armed generally with muskets and sabers or lances. Infantry fought with pikes up to eighteen feet in length, arrayed in squares called hedges. Inexperienced men who could hold the weapon would sometimes be used to help fill these squares. Infantry also were equipped with muskets in separate formations from the pikemen. The pikes were used to cover the musketeers in defense, the muskets being the primary weapon used in attack. Uniforms were largely unheard of, with well-appointed men in the ranks simply wearing a knapsack and heavy leather coat against the elements and the blows of the enemy. Siege warfare with all its implements and tactics was an important and much-studied science in this century.

Easily the most problematical aspect of large-scale warfare in the sixteenth century was the pay and provisioning of the troops. Unfortunately, the chronic inability of the princes to pay or even feed their troops over the long haul meant that the soldiers had to be quartered and fed by the helpless populace in the lands through which they marched. Marauding bands of mercenaries fanned out on all sides of the armies to plunder town and village alike, and animals, women and anything else of value to the men were seized without compunction. Stealing, raping and wanton destruction by their men were accepted facts of life for leaders seeking to keep armies together; these soon became typical pursuits for those trying to eke out a living without the promised support of their generals. In between the bloody but infrequent battles they did what they could to relieve the boredom, fear and frustration of lives filled with mostly squalor and disease. Entertainment and diversions, such as there were, were obtained most often at the expense of society at large. Simply quartering an army in the borders of an enemy land was a standard and effective tactic for bringing one's foes to heel.[26]

After the quick collapse of King Friedrich's Bohemian dreams at the hands of an imperial army in the battle of White Mountain, Protestant Europe might have settled down peacefully and accepted his chastising by the emperor. Unfortunately, it was not to be. In the next chapter we turn to a detailed look at the thirty years of horror that descended on the hapless people of Hesse.

NOTES TO CHAPTER 7

[1] D.H. Pennington, *Seventeenth Century Europe*, Longman, London, 1976, pp. 25-28, 50-5.; Fernand Braudel, *Structure of Everyday Life, Civilization and Capitalism 15th-18th Centuries*, Harper & Row, 1981, pp. 49-51. I relied heavily on the Pennington and Braudel works for most of this overview of the seventeenth century.
[2] Braudel, pp. 110-136, 192-96; Pennington, p. 52.
[3] Braudel, pp. 192-96, 52, 60-61.
[4] Pennington, pp. 73-76; Brigitta Vits, *Die Wirtschafts- und Sozialstruktur ländlicher Siedlungen in Nordhessen vom 16. Bis zum 19. Jahrhundert*, Selbstverlag der Marburger Geographischen Gesellschaft, Marburg, 1993, p. 71; C.V. Wedgwood, *The Thirty Years War*, Penguin Books, London, 1957, pp. 47, 150.
[5] John Theibault, *German Villages in Crisis: Rural Life in Hesse-Kassel and the Thirty Years' War, 1580-1720*, Humanities Press, Atlantic Highlands, NJ, 1995, pp. 105-10.
[6] Braudel, p. 487; Pennington, 76-89, 98, 300.
[7] Pennington, pp. 114, 125-28.
[8] Karl E. Demandt, *Geschichte des Landes Hessen*, Bärenreiter-Verlag, Kassel, 1972, pp. 244-45.

[9] Demandt, p. 247; Wedgwood, pp. 42-43; Theibault, pp. 36-37; Karl Wenckebach, *Zur Geschichte der Stadt, des Stiftes und der Kirche zu Wetter*, Selbstverlag der Evangelischen Kirchengemeinde Wetter, 1966, pp. 132-40.
[10] Wedgwood, p. 14; Theibault, pp. 58-60.
[11] Wedgwood, p. 46; Hans Lerch, *Hessische Agrargeschichte des 17. Und 18. Jahrhunderts*, Hans Ott-Verlag, Hersfeld, 1926, pp. 126-27, 131-32.
[12] Theibault, pp. 86-89, 126.
[13] Bettina Schümmer, *Mit Seiner Hülf von Oben, Religiöses Leben auf dem Lande*, Freilichtmuseum Hessenpark, Neu-Anspach, 1999, p. 11; Vits, p. 38.
[14] Bernd Blumenthal, *Aus Holz und Lehm Gebaut...eine kurze Einführung in das ländliche Haus in Hessen*, Freilichtmuseum Hessenpark, Neu-Anspach, 1995, pp. 7-20.
[15] Blumenthal, pp. 20-25.
[16] Pennington, pp. 56-57; Lerch, pp. 134-37.
[17] Theibault, pp. 64-65, and endnote p. 70.
[18] Pennington, p. 87; Lerch, pp. 14-17.
[19] Lerch, pp. 107-08.
[20] Lerch, pp. 18-20.
[21] Vits, p. 38; Lerch, pp. 98, 110.
[22] Lerch, pp. 30-37, 58-68.
[23] Lerch, pp. 25-28.
[24] Wedgewood, pp. 13-14; Theibault, pp. 20-21, 27.
[25] William L. Langer, ed., *Encyclopedia of World History*, Houghton Mifflin, Boston, 1968, pp. 431-32.
[26] Pennington, pp. 236-42; Wedgewood, pp. 80-81.

Chapter 8

The Thirty Years War and its Aftermath in Hesse

The opening moves of the great war came and went, leaving Hesse untouched. There was an immediate wave of invaders that had to be repelled, however: the recruiters who were scouring Germany for mercenary troops to support the imperial Catholic cause. They would happily press Protestant Hessians into service against their own land if given the opportunity. Hessian officials halted recruitment efforts and sent any money they seized to Kassel. Some areas were also fortified against the potential for future attack in this period.

Based on a favorable legal judgment of the imperial high court, the counts of Waldeck, who long were feudal underlings of the landgraves in Kassel, now sought to become independent. Moritz resisted them by invading and occupying their lands despite ominous warnings of retribution from Catholic forces mobilized within easy march of Hesse. He also allowed a Protestant force to cross his lands on the way to the Palatinate in November 1621. This force, under the so-called "Mad Halberstadter" Christian of Brunswick, seized the opportunity to lay waste to some lands in upper Hesse claimed by Ludwig of Darmstadt. The same year saw Spanish-led forces seize and burn the magnificent church and other religious buildings in Lorsch. Christian was soon chased out of Hesse by Catholic forces under Tilly, but returned in May 1622 by way of Fulda, where he captured and plundered Alsfeld. On May 22 Darmstadt was seized by Palatine troops allied with Christian, and Landgrave Ludwig was taken hostage along with his son. After a late night escape attempt on foot, the landgrave was recaptured and ordered to hand over the fortress of Rüsselsheim. His refusal seems to have slowed down the Protestants and kept them from linking up with Christian, who then lost a battle to Tilly at Höchst. In June Tilly freed the landgrave from Protestant forces, chased them out of Hesse, and quartered his troops in the Hessian Wetterau area.

Despite Moritz's protestations of neutrality, once Tilly's imperial forces had stripped the Wetterau bare they showed no compunction about invading lower Hesse. Tilly invoked Moritz's many obvious affronts to the emperor's authority when he marched into Hesse-Kassel in April 1623. By now relations between Moritz and his nobility were at a new low; his obvious bias toward the Protestant cause had been a dangerous game in their eyes. By promising these nobles that they would be protected if they supported his advance, Tilly gained entry for his forces unopposed. Moritz's private militia too dropped away without a fight; his military weakness was painfully apparent. Hersfeld and the Werra region fell first, followed by the rest of lower Hesse outside Kassel.

About this time the emperor also issued a determination that Ludwig of Darmstadt was the rightful heir to the Marburg inheritance, and that Moritz should not only surrender his share but pay his cousin a sizable indemnity for use of the lands illegally since 1605. By October Moritz felt compelled to flee his lands to seek help in northern Germany, dropping all pretext of neutrality and making his land the implacable enemy of the imperial cause. In March 1624 a Catholic army seized the Marburg lands and handed them over to Ludwig's control. After twenty years of

Calvinism, the people now were forced to convert back to the Lutheran faith. As we saw in the last chapter, Calvinist clergy suffered what their Lutheran brethren had experienced in 1605-06, being thrown out of work and often descending with their families into poverty and hardship.

Tilly sought to use the existing local officials and their noble overseers to organize the flow of money and supplies from the locals to his troops. At first, this was hardly more resented by the farmers than the regular tithes and duties that the landgrave and other local lords extracted from them anyway. Complaints in this early period were surprisingly few, although the troops did get out of hand at times and demanded more than the villagers could produce. The Bavarian cavalry roughed up the landgrave's steward in Sontra, forcing him to open up the state warehouse so they could steal grain. They also stole most of the landgrave's coal, but no other valuables. [1]

The longer any occupation went on, the more desperate the soldiers became for food and fuel, and the more violent and demanding their tactics became to extract resources from the local population. In time, villagers began to flee to the nearest town that could offer them some protection. They shared information with neighboring villages about troop movements, and stood ready to flee on short notice. Unattended homes, fields and animals suffered the worst damage, but the rising tide of violence left no choice. The peasants now were expected to provide payments to both the occupiers and the landgrave, who still required income to run state activities. Not surprisingly, the occupiers mostly won out. In 1624 in Abterode the "contribution" or military tax was assessed on ninety-two households at a flat percentage based on the value of their holdings. The ten wealthiest villagers thus paid 40% of the total, the twelve poorest paying together only 1%. The local miller and innkeeper figured among the wealthiest, as were others with side occupations.

Despite graphic descriptions of violence and turmoil suffered at the hands of the soldiery, petitions to the landgrave to excuse the farmers from their duties often fell on deaf ears due to his own urgent need for resources. Partly this was because there was a long tradition of such petitions in peacetime as well as war, whenever fire, hail, famine or plague might be used to justify reduced payments. Some efforts were made during the war to send out officials to verify the communities' claims.

The spring of 1625 was cold, and the summer even more bitter. It snowed in June, and crop failure was common. Soon plague stalked the land, mostly brought on by the squalid conditions of soldiers living or marching through Germany. In the fall another imperial force under Wallenstein crossed through Hesse in the Werra area. Tilly's troops spent a miserable winter there scratching out the best existence they could on the backs of the increasingly impoverished people. Both plague and dysentery ran riot in this area. By 1626 even Tilly wrote to the landgrave about the "distress and poverty of the completely worn down lands." [2]

The year 1626 was a turning point for Hesse-Kassel in several ways. Tilly's dealings with the local nobility and other members of the Hessian estates resulted in their call for Moritz' ouster as landgrave. His treasury was now bankrupt, his administration of the land all but destroyed, and his refusal to heed his nobles' call to make peace with the emperor on any terms cost him the last vestiges of their support. By 1626 only Kassel and Ziegenhain were under his direct control. His efforts to reorganize a defense with the support of the towns also collapsed. Tilly's forces acted to ensure that his cousin Ludwig received the promised indemnity for use of the Marburg lands by handing over various Kassel-owned properties to him: Rheinfels, the lower county of Katzenelnbogen, Groß-Umstadt, Schmalkalden and others.

Despite Tilly's promises of protection for cooperative nobles and their lands, he lost control of his forces on the ground. An example is the village of Rittmarshausen, controlled by the von Boyneburg family. The lord's administrator ordered the peasantry to leave their valuables in their homes rather than carry them off into hiding. This was based on a protective agreement he had signed with Tilly's administration. When the troops looted the village anyway, the peasants wrote a letter of complaint to the landgrave concerning the matter (April 15, 1626). Villagers everywhere were now being killed gratuitously, and it became dangerous to move abroad even in daylight hours. The soldiers tortured and killed to extort food or valuables from people, or just for sport. The nobility now fled the area as well, and more villagers abandoned the land for town. In Grandenborn, another Boyneburg holding, the farmers wrote to the landgrave to ask him to take over their lands because the Boyneburgs had fled, leaving them without advice or support in dealing with the occupation forces. Plague and dysentery continued to increase the misery.

Christian of Halberstadt re-entered Hesse in 1626 to try to force Tilly to move, but without success. Moritz actually shunned him this time for fear of reprisal. Another widespread harvest failure due to bad weather led to food shortages later in the year. Along the Rhine, there was terrible famine by winter. Diseased people and animals marching with the armies spread illness everywhere. Moritz lived to see the end of his bitter enemy in Darmstadt, Ludwig V., who also died in mid-1626. He was succeeded by his son George, a milder, less grasping prince who was devoted to improving the lives of his subjects in educational and religious pursuits. He had read the Bible cover-to-cover seven times by his eighteenth birthday. He was to prove a better statesman than a general. [3]

In March 1627 the pressure for abdication became so great that Moritz agreed, handing over the landgraviate to his son, William V. His second son, Hermann, was likewise provided for by giving him the so-called *Rotenburger Quart*, made up of the districts of Sontra, Eschwege and Wanfried. The *Quart* was set up as a dependency of Kassel, however, so Hermann and his successors were dominated by the Kassel landgraves. Moritz left his land a million *Taler* in debt, much of which stemmed from his spendthrift ways prior to the war. William tried to be cautious and neutral at first, given the terrible shape of his lands and administration. He was a capable and devoted ruler. He bought some time for the land to begin to heal, and even enacted currency reform to address the debased coinage that caused inflation to run rampant. He had full-value gold and silver coins minted. He worked hard to regain the respect and trust of the nobles and towns, succeeding more with the latter.

By 1628 the emperor felt strong enough in his dominance of Germany to announce the intent to issue an Edict of Restitution. This would restore to the Catholic church many of the lands and properties seized by Protestant rulers after the Augsburg Peace. This announcement broke over the Protestant princes like a thunderclap. It was aimed at their jugulars, for like the Hessian landgraves, many of them held large amounts of former church property. William V. would have to surrender huge expanses of land. Worse yet, when it was issued on March 6, 1629 the edict denied existence to Calvinists, prohibited Protestants from even purchasing church lands, and made the emperor sovereign in all land disputes. The Protestant protests were loud, but without a military option, they availed nothing. The edict had one unintended consequence, however: it all but forced the Protestants into the arms of any power that could rise to oppose the emperor.

By the summer of 1630, imperial defeat of Denmark and its Protestant allies ended war in Germany for a brief time. This was the high water mark for the emperor's power and influence during the war. After four crop failures since 1625, Germans everywhere were literally dying for peace. Those who survived the famine often had to face death by plague that terrible summer. The people of Wetter, in the Marburg inheritance lands, suffered a horrible fire in their town in May, in which most of the houses were destroyed. The town still possessed enough vibrancy to rebuild promptly, however. [4] Germany now had to face invasion by the King of Sweden, Gustav Adolph, the self-styled protector of the Protestant cause whose real aim was to seize a large portion of German lands for himself. He was an able commander, with one of the best trained and most experienced armies in Europe. He scooped up the support of the Protestant princes who looked for any help in the face of the Edict of Restitution. William of Hesse signed a compact with him and other Protestant princes in Leipzig in February 1631.

William now created a small but potent mercenary force with borrowed funds. His regiments were named after the colors of their standards: red, green, white, and blue-and-white. The white regiment was predominantly made up of Hessian officers and men. With Swedish support he was able to fend off Tilly and retake Hersfeld on August 24 and Fritzlar on September 9. In October he had to stand by and watch as the more powerful army of Tilly crossed again through Hesse. By this time the affected villagers knew simply to flee at the approach of any troops. Those in the Werra headed off as far away as Bremen, Holstein, Brunswick or the Palatinate, although Kassel was a most common destination for security. Village requests for remission of rents and tithes were so numerous that William's court could no longer even answer them.

Frankfurt fell to the Swedes on November 27, 1631. William now marched to join Gustav Adolf in the siege of Mainz, which fell to them on December 23. After this his troops successfully seized the Taunus forts at Reifenberg, Falkenstein, Kronberg, and Königstein. Gustav Adolf's relations with Landgrave George of Hesse-Darmstadt were a bitter pill for William to swallow, for George was the son-in-law of the powerful Elector of Saxony, and so was treated with some deference despite his close alliance with the emperor. George signed an alliance with Sweden on November 29, but remained politically mostly in tune with the emperor. The Swedish king was relentless in belittling George for his clear imperial sympathies, treating him as an untrustworthy lackey in open conversation. [5] George's wife the landgravine was quoted in 1632 in a statement that shows their frustration and powerlessness at this turn of events.

> It is hard to hand over the best and most valuable places in our land to a foreign king on so new a friendship, to sacrifice thereby all our undefended country, to make enemies of the neighbors with whom we have lived at peace for countless years, to bring down the Emperor's heavy hand and displeasure upon us, to give help to others but utterly to destroy ourselves.[6]

Landgrave William contented himself with leading his army in a successful campaign in Westphalia, although he suffered defeat in battle at Volkmarsen in June 1632. Worse, however, was the news from the battle of Lützen on November 16, in which the king of Sweden was killed and the Protestant cause again temporarily thrown into disarray. The Swedes remained committed to the war, however, and William remained their truest ally. In the battle of Oldendorf on June 28, 1633 he succeeded with their help in completing the conquest of Westphalia.

In 1634 the Swedes again suffered a huge defeat at the hands of the imperial armies at Nördlingen (September 6). In retreat they occupied the Hesse-Darmstadt lands. The depredations of these troops were often horrific beyond words. In Groß-Bieberau in the eastern part of Hesse-Darmstadt the retreating Swedes arrived immediately after the battle. Close on their heels were their imperial pursuers. Each new party of troops seized whatever they could from the townspeople, and when nothing was left to give, everyone had to flee to the landgrave's castle at Lichtenberg to escape the reprisals. There they had to lie out in the streets exposed to the cold and rain, some with a tub or cask in which to shelter. Disease claimed many that winter, by which time the landgraviate was virtually in ruins. The troops robbed and murdered their way across the countryside, bringing plague in their wake. Outside the fortified towns the death toll was massive. The towns were offered little respite, however, as the inhabitants of eighty villages learned when they crowded into Nidda only to suffer an outbreak of plague in 1635. About 1,800 died, including about 500 of the town's normal population of 1,000. Gießen suffered 1,500 such deaths, including 283 of the town's regular population of 540. The same year saw 2,500 people die of pestilence in Darmstadt. Of sixty-nine pastors in the county, forty-six died that year of the plague.

The parish register of Groß-Bieberau recorded similar events in 1635. "God sent down on us pestilence in the midst of war," the pastor wrote. Great holes were dug for graves into which plague victims were cast in groups of eight, ten or fifteen. Everyone assumed that no one would survive the outbreak. It was called the year of the great death, with eighty-nine people dying in January and February, ten times more than normal. Pastor Huber wrote that his wife and seven daughters of his ten children were among the dead. On March 17 he died as well. A pastor in nearby Reinheim wrote of the fate of the local Jews. "Although they don't belong to the parish itself, I still will record so that it is not forgotten in this time of great death that over sixty of them have succumbed; of these, thirty-six were killed by the sword, beaten to death, forced to drink horrible substances (the so-called "Swedish draught"), or in other ways."

The imperial General Gallas fell upon Groß-Bieberau, although as the parish record noted Hesse-Darmstadt was allied with the emperor. All the local food and even what produce was to be had in the fields was stripped bare; what they could not use the soldiers sold in the local markets. Food prices skyrocketed. With harvest failure and drought in the next two growing seasons, starvation and poverty were experienced for the next three years. People were so hungry that they fell upon the carrion of dead animals and ate it. Dogs and cats were slaughtered and sold as food. Regular bread would be impossible to obtain for three to six months at a time, so people made bread out of acorns, bran, flax, grapevines, turnip and fruit parings, and other materials. By now the inhabitants had shrunk to such a small number that people wondered whether their descendants would even believe it. Much arable had gone back to forest land for lack of use, with only the pastor and one neighbor having plowed fields since the previous year. Conditions were similar throughout the Odenwald.

Despite these terrible losses, the resurgence of Catholic arms in the field and the successful push to drive out the Swedish army finally saw Landgrave George's star begin to ascend once again. The opposite occurred for William of Kassel, whose Calvinism made him persona non grata to the emperor. Mainz fell to the imperial armies in December 1635. The once-proud town was described by a traveling English ambassador in pathetic terms: Poor people were lying prostrate on dunghills…scarcely able to crawl forth to receive alms. The town was "miserably battered," the travelers having to eat and sleep on a barge in the river from which they threw scraps to beggars on shore. The resulting scramble saw many fall into the river, probably to drown. The observer also noted that, "Things were worst along the Rhine."[7]

William of Kassel suffered major reverses in Westphalia in 1636, losing many towns that he had long controlled. On October 21 he concluded a treaty with France which gained him subsidies to put 10,000 men in the field. As an enemy of the Holy Roman Empire, his lands were subject to capture by imperial troops, which followed in 1637. The local diet of the estates wrote to him during this time, perhaps the worst year of the war so far. The revenge of the imperialists had been terrible indeed.

> They have cut down almost everything that has come under their hand and power. They have cut the tongues, noses and ears from people; gouged out their eyes; driven nails in their heads and feet; poured molten pewter, wax, oil and all manner of filth in their bodies through ears, noses and mouths; killed people with all types of painful instruments; tied them together in open fields and shot them through with muskets or dragged them to death behind horses...Like wild animals they fall among the children, cut them with the sword, impale them and cook them in ovens. [8]

Beyond these horrors, the soldiers also burned down eighteen towns, forty-eight nobles' seats, and 300 villages. In Grandenborn the parish pastor wrote that, "Melchoir the sow-herd stayed outside during the plundering, he is said to be buried near Eschwege." This was the first appearance of the feared Croatians, renowned for their brutality and debauchery. They burned Eschwege and the surrounding villages. Six villagers were killed in Grandenborn, including the village head who was beaten to death. After this any foreign-speaking troops in the Werra region were referred to with dread as "Croatians." People were buried quickly, in whatever clothes they died in, without coffins. The dreaded plague again ravaged the area.

Wetter, north of Marburg, suffered the loss of 248 inhabitants in the plagues of 1635-36. Worse yet was the invasion by a force of Swedish and Kassel troops who considered Wetter as Darmstadt territory and therefore fair game. They destroyed much property and fell about the people, indiscriminately wounding and killing them. A child's ditty in the area exhorted the little ones to go to bed by saying, "To bed, child, to bed! Tomorrow comes the Swede!" (*Bet', Kindche bet! Morgen Kommt der Schwed!*").

In June 1636 a Swedish force appeared demanding a huge amount of fodder and provisions. Every house had to be canvassed to surrender needed food to make the payment, on pain of having troops quartered in the town. Every house sank into hard times as a result, and even when the payment was made, 300 troops still broke into Wetter. They stole most of the town's cows and horses and shot at or impaled townsfolk, even chopping at them with axes. They broke into the church, stole the poor alms, damaged the organ, smashed into the pastor's house and beat and stabbed him, molesting a number of wives and young girls (aged ten to seventy) who had sought shelter there. Next they turned on the local hospital, striking with their axes at the lame and blind all around. They forced a blind man to carry a bag of booty for them, and when he failed in the attempt they struck him in the head with an ax and ran him through with a sword. A pregnant woman was roughed up in search of valuables. They dug up the church graveyard in search of jewelry on the corpses. After six days of this maltreatment, many townsfolk fled to the surrounding woods. Even here, however, they were liable to be set upon by prowling marauders. Such atrocities caused the parish pastor to cease making entries in the parish register in 1637. It seems that soldiers had begun using church books to identify the wealthier members of the parishes so they could extort valuables from them.[9]

Landgrave William and his family had to relocate to his possessions in East Friesland, where he died in poverty in October 1637. His wife Amalia Elizabeth now took responsibility to rule in her son's stead until he reached his majority. The state could not have been placed in better hands, for she was determined and gifted, a Calvinist to the last, and committed to handing over a secure and expanded landgraviate to her son. She soon negotiated a brief respite for her land from further attack, dealing with the emperor and the landgrave in Hesse-Darmstadt. After the pretense of being willing to come to terms with the emperor, in August 1639 Amalia Elizabeth concluded a treaty of support with France and Sweden on favorable terms. By now the last phase of the war was under way, in which France and Spain were the major players on opposite sides.

In February 1639 the landgravine called for a survey to determine the status of her plundered lands. The districts south of Kassel were described in terms of total devastation. People had lost the means of making a living, with overgrown fields that were full of mice and ravaged by cold frosts. There was talk about whether further exploitation of these lands by the state was possible, or even moral. Rambach, as an example, was found to contain: a handful of married people; two impoverished widows living at home, one with several children; six homeless widows with children; seven old men, some raging with disease; one wagon that might in an emergency handle half a load; one plow; one ox; two cows; and no sheep, pigs, or horses. The Croatians had killed many men, leaving their widows behind. One man had not only been killed but his body had been thrown into the fire of his burning home.[10]

In the Felsberg district (*Amt*) there were only 300 hectares of land in productive use. Only 338 married people lived in the district at this point; the population in 1592 had included 697 homesteads with families, a decrease of over 48%. Villages were impacted to varying degrees, with those along major roads the worst hit. Geismar, Haddamar and Cappel were almost wiped out. Some experienced little or no loss of housing stock, but huge losses in farm animals. The Felsberg district as a whole experienced population loss of an estimated 37%, while estimates for the Schwalm area were 35-50%. Each of the villages in the region had been at least temporarily abandoned, but none reverted to total waste. Still, some individual plots of farmland remained unoccupied until the eighteenth century. Wehren was burned so thoroughly that it no longer resembled a village. Much of its farmland remained workable, but the last eight families in the village could not manage to do so. Some inhabitants in the villages were living in simple huts erected over holes dug into the ground. In Darmstadt territory, Groß-Bieberau's mayor recorded in 1638 that only six out of seventy-five heads of household remained from the pre-war population (apparently not counting himself, the pastor, and a grave-digger). He spoke with almost incredible optimism about the fact that at least the harvest was good that year and the six farmers were healthy and able to rebuild. Indeed, by the next year the pastor reported that everyone had acquired farm animals to work the land, apparently borrowing money from local Jews to buy the animals.[11]

In mid-1640 the landgravine moved with her retinue back to Kassel. These remained difficult times, and Kassel was a magnet for the frightened and dispossessed in the villages and smaller towns. The pastor in Reichensachsen recorded a general flight to Kassel in May 1640. During the flight many horses and other animals died of hunger. Flight was necessary even in face of troops supposedly allied with Hesse because they threatened the village. Huge mice, big as cats, were recorded in the village fields, consuming all the crops. Everyone was near starvation, with even the richest reduced to begging. The pastor said he had not seen meat for over a year. No one had more than a few handfuls of grain. He wrote that the conditions he described had to be seen to be believed.

In January 1642 the Hesse-Kassel army with its Franco-Swedish allies defeated an imperial force near Krefeld, improving the landgravine's position tremendously. She also inherited her father's lands in Hanau when he died without male heirs, merging these with Hesse. She later was able to negotiate with the emperor and the Swedes to obtain control over the county of Schaumburg after its count died in 1640. Her efforts to wrest control of upper Hesse (Marburg), Katzenelnbogen, and Schmalkalden from Darmstadt were equally unrelenting. In 1644 she repudiated the agreement forced upon her husband that had awarded these lands to Darmstadt in 1627. In May 1645 much of upper Hesse was won back with the help of her allies. In November the Hessian forces conquered Butzbach and the town of Marburg; its fortress only surrendered in January 1646. The 74-year-old fortress commander paid for the surrender with his head when he returned to Darmstadt. George of Darmstadt appointed a new commander of his forces the same year. Now the terrible final act of the war, the so-called Hessian civil war, began in earnest. [12]

The Kassel forces next took the castles at Rauschenberg, Wolkersdorf and Blankenstein, while the Darmstadt army retook Butzbach. Darmstadt next lost Kleeberg and Gleiberg, but recaptured Kirchhain, Rauschenberg and Blankenstein in August 1646. Kirchhain changed hands yet again, but Darmstadt then retook Wolkersdorf. Schmalkalden fell to Kassel, and the Darmstadt forces' ability to resist began to weaken after an imperial force under Melander ceased its participation in the campaign. Alsfeld was seized by the Kasselers in October, and a month later they fell upon the Darmstadt forces in a surprise attack at Frankenberg. The resulting victory forced Landgrave George to sign an armistice with Amalia Elizabeth that lasted through April 1647. The fighting and fortunes of the two sides swung back and forth in the following year, ultimately to the misfortune of George of Darmstadt. His capital seized by the Swedes in the spring of 1647, he was forced to take his family to the fortress at Gießen. But still he refused Swedish calls to make peace with Kassel. By July the Kassel forces were in possession of many more of his properties, notably Katzenelnbogen, St. Goar, and the powerful Rheinfels on the Rhine that had been seized from Kassel decades before. Yet another armistice was concluded between the landgraviates.

In fall 1647 a powerful imperial army broke into lower Hesse through the Werra area, driving the Swedes before it and seizing almost the whole land. Amalia Elizabeth remained immovable and safe in her fortress at Kassel, refusing all entreaties to make peace with George and the emperor. By year's end the imperialists even retook the town of Marburg, albeit not the fortress. Fire from the fortress drove them out of the town again in late December. At the same time a Franco-Swedish force attacked George's lands, seizing the fortress at Otzberg and forcing Darmstadt to pay a massive indemnity to avoid destruction. On June 14, 1648 the Kassel army defeated an imperial force of twice its strength in a renowned fight that became the last battle of the great war (Grevenboich).

Landgravine Amalia Elizabeth really shined at the peace table after the war. Although most of her hopes for land in Westphalia were dashed, she obtained both Hersfeld and Schaumburg on the Weser. On April 14, 1648 the so-called treaty of peace and unity was signed with George of Darmstadt. Kassel regained its predominant position in the old Marburg lands. George lost a quarter of the lands he had been given in the imperial court order of 1627, including Katzenelnbogen and Rheinfels, Schmalkalden, and a share of Groß-Umstadt. Upper Hessian lands that went to Kassel again were supposed to be given a choice, but in practice mostly reverted to Calvinism. Darmstadt was left with the districts of Königsberg, Blankenstein, Biedenkopf, Battenberg, and Hatzfeld, as well as half of Itter. George also was forced to give up some land to the Palatinate and other neighbor states, including Otzberg, the Kaub District, and a share of Groß-Umstadt, a quarter-share of Butzbach, and the district of Habitzheim.

Less positive for Kassel was the continuing conflict over inheritance with the landgraves of Hesse-Rotenburg, heirs to the so-called Rotenburg *Quart*. On August 2, 1648 this years-long conflict was settled as follows: the Rotenburg landgraves received Katzenelnbogen with Rheinfels, St. Goar, St. Goarshausen with the Castle Katz, and the districts of Reichenberg and Hohenstein, with Bad Schwalmbach. But Kassel retained the rights to garrison the castles at Rheinfels and Burg Katz, which left it the dominant military power in the area.

An incident of 1649 demonstrates that even in the face of general rejoicing in peacetime terrible hardship could strike a community without warning. The small town of Wetter, newly returned to Kassel's administration, was experiencing its best harvest in years. At 10:00 in the morning on the Saturday before Easter the whole town was out in the fields bringing in the crops. A careless baker by the name of Peter touched off a fire in the town, which spread quickly due to high winds. As the helpless harvesters watched, all but four of their 400 houses went up in flames; by late afternoon the town was a smoldering ruin. For many, this was the last straw. They left for good to seek their fortunes elsewhere.[13]

By way of further understanding the effects of the war on the two Hessian states, the wartime experiences of three of the more important Hessian towns will be considered. The capitals of Darmstadt and Kassel, and the much-fought-over upper Hessian seat at Marburg will be considered in turn.

MARBURG[14]

As the focal point of conflict between the two Hessian ruling houses, Marburg became the goal of competing armies several times during the war. Her strong fortress, however, was often her saving grace, as it was much easier to take the town itself than the castle commanding the heights behind it. The early years of the war saw most of the contending armies operating outside upper Hesse and away from Marburg. In 1623 the Catholic General Tilly quartered a small force of cavalry in the town, forcing its Lower Hessian (Kassel) defenders back into the castle proper. In March 1624 a larger force forced them to surrender, and Ludwig of Darmstadt gained control of the prize he had long strived to obtain. The overwhelming majority of the population seems to have preferred life under Darmstadt rule, and probably much rejoicing was made. More difficult was the economic situation in these times, in which debased coinage and wartime plundering did much to drive inflation and cripple trade. Those on fixed salaries, preachers, teachers, and administrators were hurt the most. The institutions of higher learning, like the university in Marburg, also suffered as parents were unable to pay tuition. Bakers and butchers found their coinage unacceptable to their suppliers in the villages, and could not buy grain and animals.

With the return of resurgent Lutheranism in 1624 people who for almost twenty years had defied the authorities and traveled five hours to Homberg on the Ohm for communion services now could worship at home churches. The converse was true for Calvinist believers; they traveled as far as Hohensolms for their services.

In 1625 Landgrave Ludwig was able to relocate his university from Gießen back to Marburg; it had been reopened in Gießen two years after Moritz took over Marburg and forced the Lutheran faculty to leave. Now the Calvinist professors had to give place to Lutherans again. Moritz established a competing institution at Kassel for the duration of the war. Unfortunately the student population continued to drop, from 108 in 1620 to thirty-six in 1625 when Darmstadt retook control. About 200 students and many professors came with the relocation from Gießen. The university was as plagued with the destruction of marauding soldiers as the rest of the town, and scholarly pursuits often were interrupted during the war. Plague stalked the town in 1633, with 400 people dying, and the university population largely relocated temporarily to Gießen and Grünberg.

By 1635 Marburg had long since become a haven for farmers and others seeking security from the warfare across the land, including Jews. The refugees would come with their animals and the few goods they could carry. The town officials complained bitterly that many tramps and beggars came as well, costing the citizenry already scarce food and money to support them. The regular population shrank due to disease, malnutrition, and emigration to safer locales.

In 1636 Marburg escaped plundering at the hands of Swedish forces, but only by paying a huge sum as part of a 100,000-*Taler* indemnity demanded of upper Hesse as a whole. The Swedes also took hostages with them from the town leadership in an effort to maintain leverage over the town in future demands for money.

The years 1637-39 also passed fairly quietly, with good local harvests helping the town recover some of its wealth. However, the Swedes, Kassel forces, and even imperial troops demanded periodic and heavy contributions to avoid attack or the dreaded quartering of troops in the town. In 1639-40 such contributions to the invading French forces amounted to 315 *Taler* per week; this was later raised to 630. Other allied forces quartered in the area from 1643-45, again demanding assistance. In the latter year farm animals from the town were hauled off to Kirchhain and presumably sold. In one week in May the impoverished town was called upon to provide Protestant forces with 80,000 pounds of bread, a huge amount to produce. Demands were made for significant sums of money as well. In this period the university was heavily impacted by the constant inroads of marauding mercenary troops.

The armies brought with them a huge retinue of wives and children and other hangers on; what the soldiers left behind was often stolen by these ever-present vagrants. They were notorious carriers of disease. Not every appearance of soldiers brought disaster, however, since often these would seek to sell Marburgers animals or other products looted elsewhere. Bargains were sometimes to be had, and the money looted from the towns might flow back to them in part through market purchases. It seems that in this way the town soon was able to replace its pilfered animals after their having been hauled off and sold in Kirchhain.

Up until 1645 the war in fact went much easier on Marburg than it had on surrounding towns like Amöneburg, Kirchhain, or Rauschenberg. In 1645, however, the landgravine in Kassel ordered her troops to take Marburg back from the Darmstadters, and in November the battle began. The garrison commander, the 70-year-old Willich, at first put up a spirited defense. The cannons of the Kassel forces were dug in and trained on the weakest part of the town walls, and eventually a 125-foot breach was blown open. The townspeople were exhausted after the two-week bombardment, and they overruled their civil and military leaders and sued for peace. The Kassel troops marched into town virtually unopposed, the Darmstadt garrison retreating into the castle. The people were enraged in the months ahead with the announcement that a Calvinist preacher was to relocate to the town, under the guise of being a chaplain for the troops.

After bringing in hundreds of musketeers as reinforcements, the Kassel troops were at last ready to storm the fort in January. But over the previous weeks the quartering of the troops had greatly damaged the town. The wood of abandoned houses was torn out to provide firewood, and even this rather mild occupation clearly cost the townsmen many resources. After an eight-day bombardment the garrison was running low on food, water and firewood, and was forced to surrender. It marched off to Gießen, where the unfortunate Willich and a sergeant major were tried and executed for treason.

The court in Kassel now demanded the townsmen swear fealty to their new lord. Much time was spent in wrangling over this because the town still felt bound to George of Darmstadt and most unsupportive of the Kassel lordship. The alternative of further occupation by the troops eventually turned them around, however, and they swore the oath in February. The rest of the year was more peaceful, with only the periodic calls for provisions and ransom money coming from various forces marching through the land.

In fall 1647 the imperial armies reappeared upon George's request to retake his regional capital. After much loss of life they took the town, which had been significantly strengthened by the Kassel garrison with the impressed help of the townspeople. The castle also had been repaired and made less vulnerable to assault. The attackers eventually took the town after numerous bloody assaults. The defenders retreated intact into the castle, and both sides settled in for what would likely be a long siege. But a single stroke of luck cost the imperial forces the town. The Protestant commander in the castle learned where the imperial commander liked to dine in the town. He trained numerous guns on the place at the appointed hour, and opened a murderous fire. The unsuspecting general was badly wounded when a soldier standing in the room was struck with a cannon ball that smashed his skull, a piece of which hit the commander in the face. He was too wounded to continue the battle, and pulled his forces out of town December 23. Before leaving, they blew up parts of the town walls and the towers that dominated the town gates. They also plundered the town thoroughly over the next few days before departing, causing great destruction. Many people were wounded or killed, both Darmstadt loyalists and those supporting the Kassel defenders.

As difficult as the years 1646-48 were for the entire population, it is noteworthy that somehow Marburg still provided alms for a large number of beggars who found their way into town: men and women, sick, crippled, or well, most ruined by the war, some whose homes had been burned or their possessions plundered. Often they were Protestants dispossessed by their Catholic overlords, such as the many teachers and preachers from Bohemia or Austrian lands. Some men begged in groups of up to five. Widows of pastors begged singly or in couples on the streets. Also interesting is the history of public morality in this period, in which citizens might have been expected to sink to new lows. Instead, the townsmen upheld laws against cursing and insults, and sexual practices remained reasonably chaste by modern standards. In many years no illegitimate children were born at all, such as the period 1638-43. In the last terrible years of the war, 1647-48, at most three per year were recorded. Promiscuous persons were liable to be ejected from the town. Wine and later beer and brandy consumption remained very high, however. Men and women fell into public drunkenness, and the government set 9:00 p.m. as the time for the "wine bell," after which no further sales of alcohol could be made.

By 1648, Marburg's population was only 3,000 people, about half its 1618 total. The numbers in the resident guilds reflected the changes in the economy that the war had brought about. The wool weavers had dropped to nineteen from a pre-war total of sixty-six. Linen weavers numbered eighteen from their earlier total of thirty-four. Hat makers were down to six from fifteen, and cabinet makers numbered seven from among a pre-war total of twenty-six. Small shopkeepers and grocers, however, had experienced growth. They numbered seventy-five, an increase from the seventy that had worked in the town before the war. Bakers who sold underweight or adulterated bread products could be immediately arrested and fined thirty *Taler*, the approximate cost of three cows. When caught, their whole stock of baked goods would be seized and fed to the poor in hospital or poor house. With the signing of the final peace treaty between Kassel and Darmstadt the university had to be surrendered to the landgravine of Kassel, and Landgrave George reestablished his state school in Gießen once again. The last five remaining professors drove off by coach to the new foundation as Calvinist teachers were recruited to replace them.

Other effects of the war included the huge drop in wild game animals in the forests because of extensive human predation. At the same time wolves increased greatly in number due to the suspension of the organized hunts. On a cold winter night in 1648 wolves entered through a town door that had been left in disrepair since an attack by imperial troops. The wolves proceeded to attack some of the town dogs. Human predators worked their will in this era too, with all manner of thievery being practiced. The income from the forests plummeted even as complaints of wood stealing by nearby villages rose. Garden thievery also was most common, often by tramps or the wives of the many groups of mercenaries traveling through the area. Public brawls often broke out between students and soldiers or guild apprentices. A few duels also took place. Few suicides occurred, probably because of the belief that this was such a terrible sin in the eyes of the church. Capital offenses also were few until the last years of the war, and it was mostly non-citizens who were punished with death. In 1648 a Marburger was executed for murdering his shrewish wife in the heat of argument. He was taken to the market square and torn with red-hot tongs, then led off to be broken on the wheel.

A convicted witch was likewise burned to death in 1648. Torture-induced confessions remained the rule in such court cases. In 1629 a six-year-old girl was accused of sorcery and suffered through the full legal proceedings. Fortunately, at last she was remanded to her mother with direction that she be given a Christian upbringing. In her place, her grandmother was accused and arrested. In 1631 a 15-year-old boy was tried and executed. The last years of the war saw an upswing in arrests for witchcraft, and many public burnings were performed on accused people from around the area. Only after the war were women in Marburg itself commonly accused and convicted.

KASSEL[15]

The defining feature of life in Kassel was the landgrave's court, which lent an air of cosmopolitanism, luxury and great importance to the town, particularly in the early war years under Moritz. He was a free-wheeling spender when it came to maintaining the finer pursuits of a distinguished life at court. As noted earlier, he ran up phenomenal and crushing debts that his son and successor would have to contend with throughout his rule. Even in the worst years of the war Moritz maintained his court orchestra, a small but expensive luxury; the musicians accompanied him on his journeys and played regularly at the courts he visited. Moritz actually composed a substantive body of church music, including two four-voice music books for choir. He reformed Calvinist church music in Hesse just as he had church services. It fell to his son to disband the orchestra in the interest of economy, along with the alchemists, artists, scholars, and other court hangers-on of all descriptions.

In the course of the war the view from the fourteen towers that formed the fortress at Kassel often consisted of burning villages, ruined fields, and other signs of destruction that drove people from the surrounding lands into Kassel for protection. After leaving Kassel for a safer locale, Moritz could not trust the nobility or the town officials, particularly the town council and *Bürgermeister*, to carry through on his policies of opposition to the empire. Instead, they blocked efforts at rearmament and constantly urged accommodation on him to try to avoid further invasions by Tilly or his counterparts. Tilly marched up to the gates of the town and made known his intention to treat it the same as Münden, recently burned to the ground with huge loss of life, if it opposed him. In spring 1626 the local village of Heiligenrode went up in flames, and refugees continued to stream into the town. Although the fortress still opposed him, Tilly quartered as many troops as he could in the houses of the surrounding town. Every house and building in Kassel was completely overrun with soldiers and refugees at this point. Soon plague broke out among the crowded and under-fed masses.

Feverish efforts were made to strengthen the castle's walls even as constant skirmishes were under way with the besiegers. Destruction and arson reigned all around the town. Tilly only gave up the struggle when the landgrave promised to avoid any discussions of alliance with foreign powers opposed to the emperor; the Catholic forces then left to do battle with an approaching Danish force.

Moritz' abdication in 1627 in favor of his son William V. forced the young man to confront over two million *Taler* of debt that threatened to ruin the land. He created a commission of officials including the *Bürgermeister* of Kassel to help him whittle away at the massive sum. Continual occupations by Tilly's troops caused widespread destruction and sapped the wealth of the land. His court and administration had to adopt the most stringent measures to economize at every turn. The luxuries of his father's day were a thing of the past. William had to enact a special ordinance to address the needs of the impoverished citizens and refugees in Kassel.

With the conclusion of a treaty of cooperation with the Swedes under Gustav Adolf, Kassel had to provide provisions for allied troops and serve as a collecting point for Protestant forces. The allied troops often were as difficult to accommodate as the occupation troops of the enemy. The able-bodied male citizenry were trained to report with their arms and armor to various collecting points when the alarm bells sounded the approach of the enemy.

After Gustav Adolf's death, the situation again worsened. A "freebooter corps" collected itself before the town walls in 1634, but was held off. At this time many efforts were made to further fortify the town against attack. The imperial General Götz marched through the area with his terrible corps of plundering Croats, laying waste all around but failing in several nighttime assaults to break into the town. He finally marched away to Westphalia. Every summer from 1635 on Hesse suffered terrible outbreaks of plague, and when William was declared an enemy of the empire in 1637 the region surrounding Kassel became a scene of total destruction as Catholic armies marched through to exact revenge. Eighteen towns, forty-seven castles and over 100 villages went up in flames. Refugees poured into Kassel again and again seeking shelter, only to be met with plague to increase their burdens. In a few months over 1,400 died. The landgrave sent 1,000 measures of grain to the embattled town, and then the news came of his death in East Friesland.

It was only in 1640 that his wife and successor Amalia Elizabeth could reenter Kassel and see to his proper burial in St. Martin's Church. Enemy troops continued to appear, exacting terrible revenge on the local populace and spreading destruction with their every move. Somehow Hesse-Kassel dragged itself through the final years of the war, and by 1649 better days were clearly at hand. That year saw the new landgrave, young William VI, marry Hedwig Sophie, the sister of the Great Elector of Brandenburg. The couple's return to Kassel was met with a glorious celebration within the walls of the brilliantly decorated town that now basked in glory comparable to its pre-war days once again.

DARMSTADT[16]

Darmstadt's role as its seat of power caused the landgrave to issue various pronouncements to ensure its economic and political strength. A wood market was created there in 1614 to promote availability of firewood and spare the local forests. The villages of the Dreieich Forest and those of the Lichtenberg district had to haul wood for sale in the towns.

Regular market days were ordered to be held in Darmstadt on Tuesdays and Saturdays, and the inhabitants of the districts of Lichtenberg, Kelsterbach, Rüsselsheim, Dornberg, Zwingenberg, and Pfungstadt were required to do all their buying and selling of goods in the capital. This was a hardship for those whose produce could have been sold closer to home with less spoilage. Prices offered in Darmstadt also were lower than those available in major nearby markets like Mainz or Frankfurt. A two-florin measure of rye in 1600 cost about the same twenty years later. Water transport to the larger towns also was much easier than taking the rough roads to Darmstadt. Finally, local currency in Darmstadt was much less convertible and sought after than that available on major markets. Ludwig V also sought to encourage various businesses to relocate to the capital, as did the book publisher Balthasar Hofmann from Frankfurt. Within five years (1611) his business was so bad he had to seek government support. Guilds with apprenticeship requirements were established in Hesse-Darmstadt for the first time in 1596, suspended due to complaints about existing artisans being forced to join, and then reestablished in just the town of Darmstadt after 1600.

Ludwig encouraged the rebuilding and improvement of the town hall in 1601 on the site of the older structure. In order to provide funds to retire the resultant debt, as well as promote further building improvements on the market square, he granted the Darmstadt town council a wine sales monopoly in 1609. The town thus had the sole rights to buy foreign wine for resale to the citizenry and local tavern keepers. Other sources of income for the town included a small annual head tax on under-class residents (*Beisaßen*) without citizenship rights; this fee permitted them to live in town and follow a trade. Farm hands and servants of both sexes working the fields around the town were exempt, for the economy was still tied closely to the land. A fee was assessed on new settlers in the town, many of whom were skilled handworkers. Consumption tax was charged on beer and wine. Tolls were also charged for use of the local roads maintained by the town. A tax on Jews was also levied, allowing them to live anywhere in the town. No Jewish "ghetto" colony was maintained as in some other towns. Overall, at the outset of the war Darmstadt was basically a prosperous and growing community.

In 1618-19 the first march-through of troops from Bohemia cost Darmstadt some contributions to the upkeep of the troops, but these were relatively modest at this point. Only in late 1620 with the appearance of a cavalry force did terrified villagers in surrounding areas begin to flock to Darmstadt. The village of Auerbach tried to bar their entrance, and the soldiers killed or wounded many and plundered the place.

By May 1622 the war had caused inflation in food prices, doubling costs over the previous year. At this time the forces of the Protestant general Mansfeld seized the town and kidnapped Ludwig and his son. He was freed some weeks later by Tilly, but his return home revealed the terrible wastage of his lands by Mansfeld's troops. The manors of Rheinfelden, Kranichstein, Sensfeld and Gehaborn, which together had supplied most of the needs of the landgraves' courts since George I, were severely damaged. The stores in the castle had lost huge amounts of wheat, oats and rye. Ten *Fuder* of wine had been stolen and the casks in the wine cellar smashed. The townspeople had lost their animals, which had been driven right out of their stalls by the soldiers. Many terrible acts were perpetrated on the local villagers, with a number killed and wounded and others beaten bloody. In Griesheim a woman was tortured so severely with burning torches that she died. Torture was widely employed to obtain money from victims.

After this, the town sank again for a time into almost a peacetime posture and routine. The population seems to have increased through 1623 to 420 households. This compares to 239 in the town in 1567. In 1624 the first small shops were set up in Darmstadt, including an apothecary, a tinker, a knife and sword maker, and a leather worker. The government directed the town council in 1626 to provide more poor assistance. The burden of care for refugees became more acute with time. Meat and bread price controls were imposed by order of the town council. Records of 1625 complain about the unruly and godless behavior of young men apparently acting impertinently and being disruptive of the social order with their uproarious behavior. Still, it was recorded that the council voted in early 1626 to buy a dozen tablecloths and candle sticks in Frankfurt for Easter celebrations, suggesting a basically normal period of life.

The landgrave died in July 1626, his son George II assuming power. In December the town reported a total of 251 citizens who were fully taxable, indicating the number of heads of household of sufficient means to tax. The new landgrave issued a directive in 1627 that Jews should leave his lands. The town fathers were by no means opposed to this, probably because the economic crisis brought on by the war made this an easy means of eliminating competition from Jewish businesses. Periodic social strife and prevarication against Jews had occurred in the town. George later had to relent when his ally the emperor proclaimed that the Jews were under his protection. A new proclamation issued in February 1629 returned rights to the Jews, albeit more limited than had been the case under George's father. As in Marburg, the war seems to have caused an upsurge in market cheating, with bakers fined in 1628 for selling underweight, adulterated loaves of bread. Death sentences for capital offenses were carried out on the open market square by the executioner who lived in Groß-Gerau. The Darmstadt town hall served as courthouse and prison for the condemned.

The cleaning of the town's streets in these days was quite a task. The swelling immigrant population and periodic danger of disease made this a necessary undertaking. Annual regulations were issued demanding more regular cleaning of the alleys and side streets by residents. Some new building suggests that economic recovery followed even the worst periods of wartime damage. In 1626 a chancellery building was erected by the landgrave on the southwest corner of the palace. The Altstadt ("old town") also enjoyed a construction phase. The main city church was graced with a new tower in this period, and in April 1629 the landgrave also brought about creation of a new pedagogical school (prep school) in Darmstadt. Students were to be admitted without regard to class distinctions, so that they could prepare for university. Much work was done to strengthen the town walls and other defenses.

Outside the town walls, the farming citizenry complained loudly about the depredations of wildlife on their crops. The landgrave wanted wildlife protected for his periodic hunting pleasure, and hedges planted around the woods to protect the arable lands obviously did not entirely do the trick. They also hindered the use of the woods by the locals, who periodically exercised rights to take wood and pasture their pigs and other animals in the local forests. This was a classic complaint between rulers and their underlings for centuries, causing much hard feelings on both sides.

From 1630 with the entry of the Swedes, Darmstadt saw no more peace during the war. The town could not be defended given the state of its fortifications, so George moved his court to Gießen. In 1631 the estates voted in the diet to grant George more money for defense. Little more could be done than to try to provide sufficient military forces to occupy and hold a collection of fortresses across the land. Darmstadt paid to avoid occupation by the Swedes, but had to contribute more to their upkeep as they camped in the surrounding areas. The Swedish queen paid a visit in June 1632, and for a time life again returned to normal, with modest economic recovery. The following winter, however, the black plague ravaged the land terribly. With the Swedish defeat in 1634 at Nördlingen imperial armies again returned with General Gallas, exacting provisions and mistreating the land and its people. (See also the Groß-Bieberau description above.) On December 28 an enemy army under the Duke of Weimar appeared and demanded 80,000 pounds of bread.

The landgrave remained concerned with educational standards in his struggling land even in these times. His ordinance of 1634 directed the Christian religious upbringing of all children in the land in so-called "church community schools," without regard to wealth or position. Unfortunately this laudable goal mostly failed among the children of the poorest farmers, who needed every pair of hands to help in the fields. These children only attended school in the colder seasons when farm work was less pressing. From the youngest ages onward children were to be taught to read using the Lutheran catechism. Each school was to be arranged in three classes based on the abilities and ages of the students, according to the teachings of the Lutheran theologian Melancthon. The school teachers' efforts were to be monitored by the parish pastors, who were directed to appear weekly to drill students in spelling, reading, writing and their memorization of the catechism. Some 86% of the rural school masters were schooled in theology in the period 1620-53. Qualified teachers became very scarce in the war period, and many unqualified substitutes were employed. [17]

In January 1635 the French and Swedes arrived; they seized the town except for the castle and quartered thirty men in every house. Later 1,500 horses were quartered in town. The beasts suffered from hunger as did the people in the terrible winter weather. Ten to twenty people per day were dying of hunger or disease. Within a few days the Weimar troops made their presence known again through the burning of local villages. Only eight or nine houses remained in Arheilgen after it was burned, while Griesheim lost 114 buildings. Erzhausen, Eschollbrüken, Nieder-Ramstadt, and Schneppenhausen were torched too, while Darmstadt was able to combat the instances of fire breaking out through arson.

The lack of wood and food was terrible for the citizenry. Occupation forces tore down mills almost to the works themselves to obtain firewood. Wine casks, window trim, and everything else that could be laid hold of was used. Plague continued to rage. At this point the corpses of dead animals were seldom even hauled from town on account of the lack of security when out and about in the open. In surrounding areas many unburied bodies were lying about, as it was unsafe to go out and bury them. Hungry dogs tore at the bodies. Reports filtered in of cannibalism by Swedish troops in Büttelborn. People were glad to be able even to buy back their own provisions from the occupation troops when they could.

When the enemy was chased away in February 1635 by imperial forces, even these allied troops used the opportunity to plunder the town, steal horses, and mistreat the inhabitants to extract tribute from them. The death toll of the local domestic animals was so huge that meat became unavailable. The head ranger of Hertinghausen wrote that the French had left 500 dead animals in front of the town gates. He feared that the smell of the rotting flesh when warm weather returned would surely cause the town to be vacated. Only one gate was left unblocked. By this time some 600 residents had died in town of the current outbreak of plague. Some houses had up to ten or more sick, and the last doctor in town died at this time. Another 1,600 deaths due to disease occurred that winter. Some fell upon the rotting animal corpses to find any nourishment available. In March forty or fifty dead were being buried each day.

In 1638 the town council wrote that only 100 taxable citizens remained. In early 1639 an imperial army came from Mainz; the town fathers ordered the gates closed to them and the residents to prepare for battle. The soldiers found nothing left to destroy in the surrounding area. A similar invasion of Bavarian troops in the summer resulted in yet more horrors for what remained of the local population.

The early 1640s saw the government attempt to reestablish quarterly market fairs. March 17, June 24, September 29 and November 30 were the designated saints' days. The day before each fair was declared a market day for animal sales. Little came of these efforts due to the general insecurity on the land. Times were too tough even to undertake the full prosecution of witches and those accused of black magic; an accused girl from Bischofsheim was simply remanded to the care of a nurse in the local hospital. Refugees with and without means flocked to town. Houses were bought in these times by immigrants from Bessungen, Eberstadt, Nieder-Ramstadt, Pfungstadt and Wixhausen.

An awful time of civil war now set in, beginning in 1645. General Geyso undertook to break the landgrave's will so that he would surrender to Kassel all the upper Hessian (Marburg) lands. George ordered Darmstadt to give shelter to some imperial cavalry in April; this was done only with great reluctance. Every soldier was to be given a measure of beer and two pounds of bread daily. In June, the French were back to occupy the town. A huge indemnity of food and money was assessed, which the town struggled hard to provide. In April 1646 the landgrave acknowledged the poverty of his subjects by reducing their feudal dues by half. It was tough in these times to protect the crops from groups of marauding troops, who often chased the village watchmen back into the protection of the outer works of the town.

In April 1647 the French returned, demanding ransom of 11,000 *Taler* to keep the town from being burned. The town was broke, and even pleas to the local nobility to help raise money fell on deaf ears. Only 800 *Taler* was collected, a sum which the French commander refused with disgust even to accept. He seized the town and now demanded 40,000 *Taler!* The most extreme efforts resulted in 20,000 *Taler* being collected, enough to purchase the departure of all but a small detachment of French forces. These continued to plague the town and steal all manner of provisions through the end of the year. A peace treaty was signed with Kassel in April 1648. The French at last were induced to leave late in the year once their ally, Amalia Elizabeth, wrote to tell them she had reached an agreement with Landgrave George. Upon leaving, these troops still were able to extort 4,500 *Taler* from the hapless locals.

THE WAR ENDS, RECOVERY BEGINS: HESSE KASSEL

Amalia Elizabeth remained landgravine of Kassel until 1650, when she made way for her son William VI. He too was a remarkably able ruler who worked effectively for the recovery of his lands after the war. His untimely death in 1663 saw his own wife take the reigns of power until their son Karl was old enough to rule (1677). He in turn was replaced by his son, who ruled as William VIII. Hesse-Kassel also maintained a strong military that helped ensure the landgravine remained a player on the European scene.

The war had brought many lasting changes to the political landscape. The Treaty of Westphalia assigned the rulers almost full authority over their subjects' lives. Religious practices, social policies, and authority to conduct foreign affairs independent of other influences all belonged now to the princes. Hesse had lost upwards of half her population, and religious refugee immigrants from Switzerland, Savoy and France were settled in some areas to help make up the shortfall. Cloth, mining, most guilds, and trading centers in major towns were all in a state of collapse. Frankfurt was almost alone among German trading cities to emerge from the war with a strong and growing market position. Many nobles had become impoverished and were less able to stand up to their princes after the war. They tended to seek favor at court to attain positions in the state administration or the military officer corps. The experience of the local nobility in the Werra area suggests what occurred in Hesse. Their property debt had grown enormously during the war and the agricultural price collapse of the postwar years severely reduced their income.

William VI undertook to return his ruined land to productivity after the great war. His officials developed a more modern, centralized administration centered on Kassel and Marburg. He tried to resettle mustered-out troops and enacted strong penalties against highway robbery, murder, and game poaching. He worked to bring stability to the erratic swings in prices and wages of his time. The Hessians now began a regular, coach-based postal service between Frankfurt and Bremen by way of Kassel. Connections to the imperial postal service routes made possible wide-ranging access across much of western Europe. In the 1660s a letter could be sent from Kassel to Marburg for two *Albus*, about the cost of a pound and a half of the best steak. Citizens could purchase tickets to ride on the mail wagons as well. This provided a bumpy and unpleasant journey on what were basically old farm carts with a simple cloth cover mounted over the back. Passengers were accommodated by hard seats hanging from leather straps on the sides of the wagons.

In 1657 William produced a new church agenda to build on the ordinance of 1573 and promote recovery after the ravages of the war years. It sought in particular to promote teachings that would bring the Lutheran and Calvinist elements of the land together in one strong church. The war had tightened the bonds between the villages and their parish churches; the latter had remained the one institution that generally did not desert them during the worst of the war years. Churches now were rebuilt everywhere, often with money from the wealthier farmers who were encouraged to buy personal pews as a means of raising the needed cash.[18]

Continued strife with the nobility was a notable trend in this early postwar period. In October 1655 a compact was concluded to define the relationship of the landgrave with the landed gentry. In place of the ancient feudal requirement to provide troops in times of war, they now agreed to pay an annual tax to support the Hessian military. At the time of the peace, only three companies of Hessian troops from the White Regiment remained, primarily in use for fortress duty. The landgrave also recreated a fifteen-company state militia.

Landgrave Karl (1670-1730) saw his task as promoting security for the empire against the power and tyranny of the French under Louis XIV. With his counterparts in Nassau and Waldeck he was the soul of the anti-French political and military bloc. From 1672 the landgrave continually increased the size of his army. By 1674 they included eleven companies of infantry and three of horse; two years later the companies numbered twenty-three: eighteen of foot and five of cavalry. In 1677 he sold use of 1,600 of his soldiers to Denmark in its war with Sweden and Prussia for 32,000 *Taler*. Thus began a long tradition of the sale and use of Hessian troops as mercenaries. The subsidy was plowed back into the military to continue to improve its equipment and training. Unfortunately, the initial sale of his troops had a terrible ending: half were wiped out in the war due to disease or battlefield deaths; their field flags hang even today in a church in Stockholm.

The so-called contribution tax assessed across the land was continued after the Thirty Years War, converted to a monthly assessment in the form of a sort of consumption tax. But even increased tax rates never sufficed to maintain the large force the landgrave wished to wield. Recruiters were kept busy scouring Hessian lands for loafers, unemployed servants and others considered fair game. Foreign recruiters were barred from Hesse-Kassel.

In 1683 the White Regiment was divided to form a Life Guards Regiment. At this time the army included fifteen companies of cavalry and thirty-one of foot. In addition, a separate force of militia-based internal security troops numbered twenty companies of infantry and two of horse. These served police functions as well as defending the state fortresses. These large forces continually forced the landgrave to sell their services on the open market in order to pay for their upkeep. He rented them to Venice, Holland (1688) and England (1694). The 11,000-man army grew too large to equip and administer effectively.

The army also came into its own in terms of reputation when it performed a critical role in combating French attacks on Coblenz and Frankfurt, and re-taking Mainz and Bonn (1688-89). Even more important in the campaign was their successful defense of the castle Rheinfels, which had been markedly strengthened by Hesse since 1672. It became one of the strongest points on the left bank of the Rhine. Three times the French sought to seize the fortress from 1684-92, as it was the only German-controlled point on the left bank. Probably the middle Rhine and Mosel river areas remained out of French hands thanks solely to this strong defense.

Karl created a new military commissary to oversee the army and all its needs, from financing to recruitment to producing war material. Moneys were centrally administered and kept out of the hands of individual officers. Villages now had to pay their contributions in cash, not produce, which generated many complaints. In any case, the contribution was based on the old "cadaster" records that dated from the 1680s, with no adjustments for growth in the villages. The martial discipline exemplified by the military became a much-prized trait within Hessian society, particularly among state officials and other members of the upper class.[19]

AGRICULTURAL RECOVERY EFFORTS IN HESSE KASSEL[20]

The Thirty Years War has been aptly termed, "Morally subversive, economically destructive, socially degrading, confused in its causes, devious in course, futile in its result...the outstanding example in European history of meaningless conflict." [21] Hesse-Kassel lost 40-50% of her pre-war population, and her village-based economy was left in a state of collapse. Disease and famine left many areas so depopulated that available lands could not be cultivated effectively. Children had died more frequently than adults, and a high percentage of houses were headed by widows after the war. In a major break with traditional methods, these women now had to be counted as family heads in order to make any sense of the status of the villages. The general lack of farm animals also impeded recovery efforts. Pigs, poultry, cattle and horses all had been seized during the war, leaving the villagers with little or no animal stock with which to work. Often their draft animals were stolen only to be ransomed back from the soldiers, who used this tactic often to extort money from the owners.

Villagers returned only slowly to the largely empty villages. While it does not appear that any villages were wiped out entirely during the war, many areas took a long time to bring most of their pre-war arable lands back into cultivation. Even in 1662 a chief bailiff reported that many farms were still lying waste in the districts of Hersfeld, Niederaula, and the Cloister Creuzburg. The first stage in recovery was to make the village fit for habitation again, after which efforts turned to promoting the means of production. The landgrave had records on the productive capacity of the villages from before the war, and these were used to gauge the need and guide assistance from the state. The better-off farmers in the villages took the lead in promoting recovery. Farm laborers were in such demand at first that they could earn high wages without work contracts, simply picking up and leaving if they grew disenchanted. At first, small farmers found agricultural wage labor more lucrative than farming their own lands. Many apparently now refused to take on the old *Leibgut* contracts with their higher fees; the landgrave thus had to make land grants in the more favorable form of inheritable fiefs.

Although land went begging and everyone struggled to rebuild, they typically did not welcome the settlement of outsiders in their communities. Resettled soldiers were vociferously opposed because of their role in the war, and their initial exemption from the tax rolls particularly irritated the villagers. The landgrave felt the need to prohibit opposition to the soldiers' resettlement, since this was considered necessary to reduce brigandage and reintegrate these men into the economy. But resettlement was not very successful: these people were too used to fending for themselves at others' expense and few took to sedentary work like farming. Highway robbery remained a constant danger, and for years merchants had to travel in large groups to protect themselves.

The landgrave found his revenues undercut by some bumper harvests in the immediate postwar years. So much grain was made available that prices collapsed. Thuringian grain also flooded in, and by the 1650s rye was selling at a 60% discount from the prices of 1618. The state attempted to restrict the import of foreign grain, but prices remained high. As the century wore on, more and more farmers began to plant beets, vetches and other fodder crops useful in providing winter feed for animals.

Population growth in the 1660s and '70s was very high, as in the rest of Germany. By the late 1670s, equilibrium in population and production had again begun to stabilize prices and wages at more reasonable levels. Houses were commonly built with two stories to accommodate the growing population, with the unheated upper rooms serving mostly as combination storage and sleeping areas. Land was again at a premium in many areas by the end of the century. State administrators also became more adept at enforcing the landgrave's will through the use of his police forces. Young men now could be identified by name, age and marital status and funneled into the military conscription system as needed.

With the increased population the number of lower-class farmers who sought full rights to the communal lands and privileges in the villages also grew, exerting much of the same pressures seen in the previous century. Not everyone could be accommodated, but many raised themselves in the social order in this period. Their success varied greatly by village, depending on the amount of the more preferred lands available to be redistributed. The better *Hufen* land often had to be divided up where previous owners were gone or unable to fully work their lands. Average farm sizes declined, and this reduced class differences as well, helping the *Köter* and *Beisaßen* classes to progress in landholding if not always in social status. On the other hand, many small farmers had to take on side jobs such as blacksmithing to round out their incomes. About one third of the Werra region had reached its pre-war population again by 1681.

In the Fritzlar area the farmers used the postwar confusion to their advantage by purposely mixing up land boundaries so that old patterns of rents and tithes could not be maintained. The state policies sought as best they could to reestablish the old, familiar landholding patterns and regulate the rebuilding process. The state first emphasized reclaiming all the arable land left fallow by the war. The local populace sought remission of their rents due to the war devastation and the need for money to rebuild their homes. The need here was great, as indicated in a 1648 survey of homes destroyed in one district:

Number of Homes per Village (vs. number left after war) - Gudensberg District [22]

Village	#	(left)	Village	#	(left)
Besse	71	(61)	Lohne	63	(25)
Grifte	29	(16)	Balhorn	87	(33)
Obervorschütz	88	(16)	Sand	67	(23)
Geismar	46	(2)	Maden	34	(21)
Obermöllrich	40	(9)	Gleichen	33	(14)
Wichdorf	22	(6)	Kirchberg	66	(13)
Wehren	20	(9)	Cappel	16	(4)
Werkel	43	(20)	Metze	40	(9)
Haddamar	53	(2)			

The result was that the landgrave agreed to reduce duties on average by about a third in the immediate postwar period. Steps were also taken to restore the damaged and game-depleted forests; an act of 1664 forbade the pasturing of domestic animals in the woods. In 1682 a similar act prohibited reclamation of forest waste land for arable. By the 1690s this regulation was being violated often by under class farmers in areas where all available farmland had been brought back under the plow. The landgrave sought to enforce requirements to set off forest lands by trenching and hedge planting. Forest use regulations brought back into focus the ancient status of enfranchised versus non-enfranchised farmers, since not everyone could be given rights to use the community pastures, and the woods for pig pasturing, firewood, etc. These trends were very much location-specific, however; when crop prices declined in the 1660s the demand for land eased in some areas as well.

In 1680 a program of surveying and recording land ownership in the individual villages was undertaken. A new ordinance concerning the village headmen (*Grebe*) was issued to codify the farmers' relationships to their overlords and set out rights and responsibilities in land management.

As on the land, recovery in the towns proceeded apace. Marburg's university reopened under Calvinist authority only in 1653, since in the early postwar years the citizenry was seen as too poor to send students and mostly engaged in occupations that would benefit little from reopening the school. The first years after reopening were most difficult because the university remained poorly endowed compared to the pre-war period. Marburg's fortress was further improved, including the digging of a new spring some 350 feet deep (1670-75). In 1689 Marburg purchased freedom from military service requirements for her sons by paying a 600-*Taler* annual indemnity to the landgrave. Kassel had a similar arrangement. In case of foreign invasion, however, the arrangement was declared void. This agreement reflected Landgrave Karl's belief that his citizens in the major towns were worth more to him as taxpayers than as soldiers. Despite its ability to make such payments and investments, Marburg's war-derived debt remained huge, amounting to seven times its pre-war levels. Interest on the debt continued to be paid well into the nineteenth century.

A new habit that was becoming more and more widespread in this period was tobacco smoking. In 1661 the Marburg town council complained about smokers enjoying their habit even in the local infirmary. They directing that the foul practice should be pursued only outside the house and away from those who would be bothered by it.[23]

Kassel's return to normalcy coincided with numerous natural disasters and unusual events that caused an upswing in belief in the power of the supernatural: Landgrave William VI met an untimely end in 1663; the current in the Fulda dropped off that year; a great comet was seen in 1664; and the end of the world was widely prophesied for 1666. Fortunately, superstition did not bring a wide return to the witch hunts that had plagued previous generations. The last witch execution was held in 1655. By 1671 an accused sorcerer from Fürstenwald was simply committed to the public pillory and fined; only his magic books were committed to the fire.

Other crimes continued to be punished in the most gruesome ways, however. Those who stole from churches were executed with the sword, while blasphemers had their tongues pierced and were conducted around the country as a warning to others. In 1660 a cow-herd who had committed sodomy was burned along with a cow. In 1674, a woman convicted of killing a child was enclosed in a sack and thrown to drown in the icy waters of the Fulda. By contrast, a local nobleman was given a slap on the wrist when he got drunk with several chums and then robbed some Jewish merchants traveling on the highway. The light sentence was because the justices took into account the fact that his victims were merely Jews. The battle of the authorities against brandy-induced drunkenness remained a visible but failed campaign in this era. As in Marburg, anti-smoking campaigns were similarly ineffectual.

Kassel benefited economically from its role as capital, with the court buying local goods and services and attracting many visitors who did the same. The town welcomed many displaced French Calvinists after the French king expelled them in his Edict of Nante. Wig makers, barbers, dance masters, teachers of languages, tailors, and embroiderers of silk flocked here from France in the 1660s and '70s.[24]

A DIFFERENT PATH TO RECOVERY: HESSE-DARMSTADT

Hesse-Darmstadt was never as richly appointed with lands as its wealthier counterpart to the north in Kassel. Although its 1,300 square kilometers of land and 20,000 souls were kept unified from its inception in 1567 through 1609, at this point provision had to be made for younger sons of the landgrave who were ineligible to inherit the whole. Collateral lines were established in Butzbach (1609), Braubach (1643), and Homburg (1622), but by 1651 only the Homburg inheritance remained independent. It would continue to be ruled by a separate house until 1866. The final resolution of the Marburg inheritance conflict with Hesse-Kassel left the Darmstadt line with only a quarter of the land in question.

The town of Darmstadt revised the practices by which its surrounding farmland was worked as early as 1649. During the war the three-field system was allowed to lapse, and only the close-in fields which could be worked and watched over in safety were regularly in cultivation. Many surrounding villages had been burned to the ground, their refugee farmers flocking to safety in Darmstadt. The huge number of empty farms and unused acres of fields were reapportioned by contracts with new or existing farmers so as to get the land back in production as soon as possible. The old organization of the fields had to be thrown out in this process. In Groß-Bieberau in the Odenwald, the local pastor and *Schultheiß* had to take up lodgings together in Obernhausen, near Lichtenberg, because their village was uninhabitable after the war. However, the little town had an advantage in rebuilding and earning money for the community coffers: the nearby forest was full of oak trees that were much sought after for erecting new buildings, fashioning wheels and wagons, and other products after the war.

Policy changes were taken by George II in the period just after the war to help promote economic recovery. In 1648-49 he reestablished market days in Darmstadt. The weekly Saturday market was rescheduled, and during the regime of Ludwig VI the old market prohibitions were reenacted requiring specific districts to market their goods in the capital. War contributions for departing enemy troops continued in this early period, and nothing further could be collected to help pay for the landgrave's own forces. By 1652, however, much complaint was being raised over the monthly contribution of forty-one guilders that the town had to provide for the domestic military. Even small towns and villages had to pay a share of the "contributions." George reduced or waived the fees ordinarily paid by new citizens seeking to settle and remain in the town. In one case, a goldsmith was allowed to pay his entry fee with a fine silver flask, which was much needed by the town to replace its pilfered silver sets. People from Switzerland, the Austrian Alps and Walloons were all settled in town and elsewhere in the landgraviate. From the 1648 list of tax-paying households it can be determined that 171 families and thirty-one widows claimed citizenship. The comparable figures three years later were 221 and twenty-six, a level at which the population stabilized for some time.[25]

By the 1650s Hesse-Darmstadt consisted of the following territories: the upper county of Katzenelnbogen, with the districts of Darmstadt, Lichtenberg, Auerbach-Zwingenberg, Reinheim, Dornberg and Rüsselsheim and other areas including Bickenbach, half of Jugenheim and Kelsterbach as well as the bailiwick of Kürnbach. The lower county of Katzenelnbogen included Braubach and Katzenelnbogen districts; the estates of Eppstein and Itter; and the districts of Battenberg, Biedenkopf, Blankenstein, and Konigsberg. In upper Hesse the districts included Gießen, Staufenberg, Allendorf on the Lumbda, Burggemünden, Grünberg, Alsfeld, Romrod, Homberg on the Ohm, Grebenau, Ulrichstein, Schotten, Stornfels, and Lißberg. Bingenheim, Kirtorf, Rosbach and Butzbach were held, along with the county of Nidda. In total this consisted of 268 square English miles, and provided an annual income of about 250,000 florins. Its 1629 population of 104,000 sank by almost 50% through 1648. The population in 1669 was about 95,000. With the death of George II in 1661 Ludwig VI ascended the throne. Ludwig administered his lands from the twin administrative capitals in Darmstadt (upper County) and Gießen (upper Hesse). During his world travels undertaken prior to coming to power, Ludwig went to Holland and fell in love with Dutch glockenspiels. He purchased and had one installed in Darmstadt in 1671, ordering that all clocks and chimes throughout the town should be set to correspond with the time kept by his glockenspiel.

Ludwig VI turned his hand to policies aimed at the betterment of his lands until his death in 1678, and many reforms were promulgated in education and religious life. A new instruction was issued for school masters in small towns and villages, directing that children ages five to twelve should be sent to school. Special emphasis was placed on stamping out unruliness, but teachers were to treat their students like loving fathers, and not reprimand them by tearing out their hair, hitting with the fist, or beating about the head. Instead, they were told to use the rod as appropriate. For the first time it was directed that students who learned their reading and writing thoroughly should also be taught basic numbers.

Like his father had done in Darmstadt, Ludwig abolished taxes on immigrants to encourage re-population of his lands. A countervailing force came with renewed outbreak of plague, starting in 1665 in Frankfurt. The following summer it moved into Darmstadt, prompting the authorities to ban begging and the sale of clothing, to bar the doors to all non-residents except those who could demonstrate they had come from plague-free locations. Passes were issued to those traveling outside the town. The measures worked, sparing Darmstadt the large-scale deaths experienced at this time in Zwingenberg. Judging from the records of Groß-Bieberau, orders were given across much of the land to dig graves in anticipation of many deaths. Only by the following spring were trade and markets returning to normal.

Another major conflict at this time was the apportioning of the local dues owed to the landgrave between Darmstadt and its outlying villages. Both sides swore their share was too high and could not be supported. By 1677 the landgrave was being invited by the town government to review the many beautiful and well-recovered outlying villages who should be considered most capable of shouldering a larger share of his duties.[26]

Ludwig died in 1678. His son and successor was Ludwig VII, who ruled just eighteen weeks before dying. The second wife of Ludwig VI, Elizabeth Dorothea of Saxe-Gotha, then ruled until the next son attained his majority. It was during her ten-year regency that Darmstadt began acquiring renown as a center of music and theater. She promulgated new regulations in 1679 against begging, gypsies, and punishments for blasphemy, swearing, whoring, and infidelity. She also presided over the issuance of anti-luxury regulations meant to tone down the wasteful spending of the wealthy on costly clothing, hair styling, "colorful high shoes," and other manifestations of foreign fashion (1684). In 1687 she turned her hand to admonishing the Darmstadt town leaders about the bad discipline among young men in the town, with constant fist fights breaking out between soldiers, regular citizens and apprentices. She also assailed the selling of spirits past curfew, and the smoking of tobacco that was seen as a fire hazard. Freewheeling drinking and carrying on was well practiced in the countryside as well as in the big towns; in 1672 the Groß-Bieberau town accounts reflected payments to provide "May wine" each year for the young men of the town. [27]

For decades after the Thirty Years War the landgraves found themselves embroiled in squabbles with their distant relations in Hesse-Homburg, who tried to deny the ultimate lordship of the Darmstadt house over their possessions. Only in 1664 was the conflict partially resolved, although in 1669 Landgrave Ludwig VI had to mortgage the Braubach and Lißberg districts, the parish of Katzenelnbogen, and Philippseck castle to Hesse-Homburg. Darmstadt later wound up paying significant sums to repatriate some of the Homburg properties, including Braubach and Katzenelnbogen (1673), Bingenheim (1681) and Lißberg (1700). During the same period the landgraves felt compelled to mortgage various large properties to wealthy persons to make ends meet. These included the Eppstein and Itter estates. The conflicts with Homburg were personal as well as legal, and the Homburg line's decision to turn Calvinist and establish closer ties with Hesse-Kassel only soured relations further. Darmstadt sometimes turned to military means to protect its status as overlord, invading Homburg lands in 1699, 1739, and 1747. Only with imperial arbitration was the conflict finally resolved in 1768, largely in Homburg's favor.

Religious life was governed by the landgraves' adherence to orthodox Lutheranism. The spiritual center of the faith in the landgraviate remained Gießen, whose university had played a leading role among the Lutheran institutions in the time leading up to the Thirty Years War. Late in the century Landgrave Ernst Ludwig welcomed Waldensian and Huguenot Protestant refugees into his lands.

The foreign policy position of Hesse-Darmstadt remained precarious for a number of years after the war, as did internal security. The onslaught of the French in 1673 hit the land hard as it was beginning to recover from the great war; in that year the French seized the rich Wetterau farmlands and the lower Main River. They next fell upon the area around the Auerbach castle, storming and destroying it. The garrison of Darmstadt was strengthened in 1680-81 with the addition of forty new musketeers quartered in the town. Far from making them feel more secure, the locals detested the garrison soldiery, who cost them money to support and now numbered 130 heads. The soldiers were said to make the streets less secure at night and were even accused of robbing local fields of produce.

The young Landgrave Ernst Ludwig came to power at age twenty-one when his mother stepped down in 1688. Just a year later, the French attacked and captured the fortresses at Rüsselsheim and Dornberg. Rüsselsheim later was blown to bits under the "scorched earth" policy of the French armies. Much of the landgrave's little army was then in Greece in the pay of a foreign power. In 1691 and again in 1693 the French forced Darmstadt to pay huge ransoms to avoid being burned, and in the latter year they also seized, plundered and burned Zwingenberg. By this time the glockenspiel had been taken down and shipped off to Frankfurt for safekeeping, and the landgrave's court moved to Gießen where the defenses were better. Both the court and the glockenspiel returned after the peace in 1698 amid general jubilation.

The landgrave did his best to pull together a more credible army in this crisis period, in 1691 establishing the infantry regiment Schrautenbach and in 1697 the Crown Prince cavalry and Karl Wilhelm infantry regiments. As early as 1672 Ludwig VI had possessed a sizable armed force that he made available to the German emperor in a military alliance of 1677. (Their absence in Greece at a critical moment has been noted above.) In 1704 Ernst Ludwig again sold three regiments to Brunswick-Lüneburg for subsidies. These troops supported imperial forces against the French in 1705-06 during the War of the Spanish Succession.

The close historical affiliation of the Darmstadt house to the emperor had a negative consequence late in the century, as four of the five sons of Landgrave Ludwig VI turned Catholic (1693-1704) in the interest of pursuing their fortunes in other courts of Europe. These sons brought honor on their house through noteworthy military and administrative service for courts in Italy, Spain, Russia, England and Austria.

The economic position of Hesse-Darmstadt remained so precarious after decades of war that little real progress against the damage and destruction could be made during the balance of the seventeenth century. Mercantilist economic policies were inadequate to the task, and the state debts grew year by year. By the time Elizabeth Dorothea assumed power in Ernst Ludwig's stead (1678) the debt was two million guilders. At his death in 1739 he and his mother before him had racked up another two million, largely due to massive building programs for a theater, opera house, elaborate hunting lodges, and a new palace at Darmstadt. In the period up to 1687 a guilder was worth about thirty *Albus*, and an *Albus* about eight *Pfennige*. A pig herder could buy a pair of shoes for a guilder and fifteen *Albus*. A bull cost about seven to nine guilders and an ox hide, four. A quart of wine cost six *Albus*, while an errand runner between Groß-Bieberau (in the Odenwald area) and Darmstadt was paid about ten *Albus*. The values of each of these items were recorded in the village ledger books of Groß-Bieberau.[28]

The vast majority of the peoples of Hesse-Kassel and Hesse-Darmstadt of course cared much more about shoes and bulls, wine and ox-hides, than about the state of theater in the towns. They must have looked forward with hope bordering on desperation for a longer period of peace and prosperity than most of the miserable seventeenth century had shown them.

NOTES TO CHAPTER 8

[1] Karl E. Demandt, *Geschichte des Landes Hessen*, Bärenreiter-Verlag, Kassel, 1972, pp. 250-52; John Theibault, *German Villages in Crisis: Rural Life in Hesse-Kassel and the Thirty Years' War, 1580-1720*, Humanities Press, Atlantic Highlands, NJ, 1995, pp. 135-43; C.V. Wedgwood, *The Thirty Years War*, Penguin Books, London, 1957, pp. 137-38; Manfred Knodt, *Die Regenten von Hessen-Darmstadt*, Verlag H.L. Schlapp, Darmstadt, 1976, p. 19; Karl Wenckebach, *Zur Geschichte der Stadt, des Stiftes und der Kirche zu Wetter*, Selbstverlag der Evangelischen Kirchengemeinde Wetter, 1966, p. 141.
[2] Theibault, pp. 118, 143-49; Demandt, pp. 251-52; Wedgwood p. 183.
[3] Wedgwood, pp. 185, 192; Theibault, pp. 149-50; Demandt, pp. 252-53; Knodt, pp. 22-24.

[4] Theibault, pp. 150-51; Wedgwood, pp. 213-16; Demandt, pp. 253-54; Hajo Holborn, *A History of Modern Germany, 1648-1840*, Alfred Knopf, New York, 1959, pp. 336-38; Wenckebach, pp. 154-55.

[5] Wedgwood, pp. 226, 260, 270, 278; Demandt, pp. 254-55; Theibault, pp. 151-52.

[6] Wedgwood, p. 293.

[7] Wedgwood, p. 365; Demandt, pp. 256-57; *1200 Jahre Groß-Bieberau: Beiträge zu seiner Geschichte*, Magistrat der Stadt Groß-Bieberau, 1987, pp. 35-37, 50-56, 272.

[8] As reprinted in German in Demandt, p. 257.

[9] Wenckebach, pp. 154-57.

[10] Theibault, pp. 154-56; Wedgwood, pp. 376, 381; Demandt, p. 258; Wenckebach, p. 154.

[11] Brigitta Vits, *Die Wirtschafts- und Sozialstruktur ländlicher Siedlungen in Nordhessen vom 16. Bis zum 19. Jahrhundert*, Selbstverlag der Marburger Geographischen Gesellschaft, Marburg, 1993, pp. 109-11; *1200 Jahre Groß-Bieberau*, pp. 238, 272.

[12] Demandt, pp. 258-59; Theibault, pp. 157-58.

[13] Demandt, pp. 260-62; Wenckebach, pp. 157-58.

[14] This section was taken from W. Kürschner, *Geschichte der Stadt Marburg*, Elwertsche Verlagsbuchhandlung, Marburg, 1934, pp. 131-66.

[15] This section is taken from Karl Heidelbach, *Kassel, ein Jahrtausend hessischer Geschichte*, Bärenreiter Verlag, Kassel, 1957, pp. 105-18.

[16] For this section the sources are Adolf Müller, *Aus Darmstadts Vergangenheit*, Selbstverlag der Stadt Darmstadt, 1930, pp. 48-75; and Friedrich Battenberg, *Darmstadts Geschichte*, Eduard Roether Verlag, Darmstadt, 1980, pp. 129-83.

[17] *1200 Jahre Groß-Bieberau*, pp. 144-47.

[18] Demandt, pp. 263-65; Holborn, pp. 5, 22-38; Theibault, p. 197; Kürschner, p. 170.

[19] Demandt, pp. 265-70; Peter K. Taylor, *Indentured to Liberty: Peasant Life and the Hessian Military State, 1688-1815*, Cornell University Press, New York, 1994, pp. 31-54; Hans Lerch, *Hessische Agrargeschichte des 17. Und 18. Jahrhunderts*, Hans Ott-Verlag, Hersfeld, 1926, pp. 78-81.

[20] This section was derived from the following sources: Theibault, pp. 160-74, 193-206, 216-17; Vits, pp. 45, 52, 76-78, 92, 97, 111-19, 141; D.H. Pennington, *Seventeenth Century Europe*, Longman Group Ltd., London, 1976, p. 238; Wedgwood, p. 444; Lerch, p. 21; Bernd Blumenthal, *Aus Holz und Lehm Gebaut...eine kurze Einführung in das ländliche Haus in Hessen*, Freilichtmuseum Hessenpark, Neu-Anspach, 1995, p. 20.

[21] Wedgwood, p. 460.

[22] Vits, p. 110.

[23] Kürschner, pp. 166-74; Wedgwood, p. 448.

[24] Heidelbach, pp. 120-23.

[25] Battenberg, pp. 177-84; *1200 Jahre Groß-Bieberau*, pp. 125, 196.

[26] Battenberg, pp. 197-203; *1200 Jahre Groß-Bieberau*, pp. 148, 194.

[27] Demandt, pp. 299-302; Knodt, p. 26; Battenberg, p. 211; *1200 Jahre Groß-Bieberau*, pp. 197-98.

[28] Demandt, pp. 305-06; *1200 Jahre Groß-Bieberau*, p. 192; Battenberg, pp. 211-16.

CHAPTER 9

THE LESSER HESSIAN PRINCIPALITIES TO 1800[1]

Hesse presents one of the most complicated histories of any of the German principalities. Because its landgraves were unable and unwilling to maintain primogeniture as an inheritance practice within their ruling families, numerous sons (if not daughters, too) again and again were provided for by dividing small lands into smaller and smaller splinters. This chapter provides a summary review of the early history of the Nassau counties, Hesse-Hanau, and the principality of Waldeck.

HESSE-NASSAU

The counts of Nassau had their genesis in Count Dudo von Laurenburg, first mentioned in written records in 1117. Dudo was related to Archbishop Adalbert I of Mainz, whose home territory was in Saarbrücken. The Lauenburgs began calling themselves counts of Nassau around 1160, based on their stronghold of the same name. They probably acquired this territory after the demise of the Werner line of counts who had held it as vassals of the Weilburg monastery. This inheritance from the Werners may account for the broad extent of the Nassau possessions in the Dillenburg, Breidenbach, Lahn and Eder areas. These expansive holdings also were secured thanks to the Nassau counts' strong relationship with the Staufen line of German kings, including the Emperor Frederick I. The counts Henry I and Rupert III were particularly supportive of the emperor in his Italian campaigns, supplying men and resources. They received in return the fief of the royal manor at Wiesbaden. Later, the counts seem to have attempted to play ends against the middle politically; they swung back and forth between alliance with the emperor and with the powerful religious houses of Köln and Mainz, who opposed his interests.

Nassau's early rise in influence received its first check when it was partitioned between the brother counts Walram II and Otto I in December 1255. The split was made along the Lahn, with Otto receiving the northern and Walram the southern lands. The north included Siegen and Dillenburg, the south Weilburg and Idstein. Nassau itself was to be held in perpetuity in common. The partition served to strengthen centrifugal tendencies by increasing the influence of local lords in the counties of Diez and Katzenelnbogen, the Runkel-Westerburg lords, and especially the archbishop of Trier. All these did their best to acquire lands at Nassau's expense and hinder her expansion.

The major lines that arose over time within this partitioned realm included The Nassau-Weilburg counts (Walramians), that broke into a half dozen sub-units over time. The original line then split again in 1355 into the Idstein line of Wiesbaden and Idstein, and the Weilburg line centered on Saarbrücken. The latter in turn divided itself periodically through the seventeenth and eighteenth centuries into sub-lines in Saarbrücken, Ottweilen and Usingen.

Alongside the Walramian line was the Nassau-Dillenburg line of counts, known as the "Ottonian" line. This line was based around the towns of Dillenburg, Siegen, Diez, Hadamar and Beilstein. Various partitions and re-combinations of these lands were made over the centuries due to inheritance and land deals of various kinds.

THE NASSAU-WEILBURG-SAARBRÜCKEN COUNTS

The Walramian or Weilburg counts were politically active outside their Hessian and Saarbrücken holdings, supplying a German king, Adolf, (from 1292-98); an archbishop of Trier, a bishop of Utrecht, four archbishops of Mainz (through 1475), and many senior officials serving religious rulers. The most important single area held by the Walramians was its imperial fief of Wiesbaden, stretching from the Taunus mountains to the Main and Rhine rivers. By comparison, the Weilburg and Idstein holdings were less populated and fruitful. All three of these areas remained isolated from one another with no connecting lands controlled directly by the Walramians. Count Adolf became king in 1292 through the political maneuvering of his overlord, the Archbishop of Köln, to whom he remained indebted during his brief reign. Six years later he was deposed through the politics of another archbishop in Mainz. By 1355 a further partition divided Weilburg/Saarbrücken from Wiesbaden/Idstein.

In 1372 the death of one of the counts left his wife as regent for their minor son, and this was to cost the county Weilburg/Saarbrücken dearly in power and influence; their underlings, the counts of Solms, now asserted themselves to become independent of the Nassau overlordship. Trier also used the opportunity to repatriate many properties that had been mortgaged to the Walramians. Worse, however, were the efforts of the dead count's brother, Rupert VI, who was able to seize on this weakness to mortgage away Weilnau, Usingen and Wehen from his brother's widow. Later, the Weilburg counts made good these losses by obtaining richer lands in Lorraine and other areas in the Pfalz (Palatinate).

The Wiesbaden-Idstein counts fared badly over time with their small inheritance. Count Johann II supported his brother's cause against the Archbishopric of Mainz, lost in the conflict, and had to mortgage Wiesbaden to his son-in-law, Count Otto of Solms, to pay his war debts. Other lands were lost to the landgrave of Hesse.

The Reformation only proceeded in the Saarbrücken lands after 1574 when they returned through inheritance to the Weilburg main line under Philip IV. Philip's father previously had invited Lutheran clerics into his Weilburg lands in 1526, issued a new church ordinance in 1533, and sponsored the first state-wide church visitation in 1536. He allied himself with Landgrave Philip of Hesse and joined the Schmalkaldic League in 1540, fighting on the Protestant side in the Schmalkaldic War of 1545-47. In 1546 the southern part of his lands, especially Wiesbaden, suffered terribly when they were occupied by imperial forces. When the war was lost, Philip ingratiated himself again with the emperor by paying a huge fine. In 1576 Philip IV brought forth a new church agenda into the Saarbrücken lands. The same was promulgated in 1609 for the Idstein-Wiesbaden lands. With the Reformation came a new school administration throughout the land, especially in rural areas, but the Thirty Years War caused the collapse of this notable reform.

The Hessian political connection made it possible to exchange some lands to the benefit of both powers: the Hessian district of Burgschwalbach and 25% rights to Löhnberg were swapped in 1536 for some Nassau rights to Wetzlar. From 1605-09 Count Ludwig II had to combat efforts by the archbishops of Mainz and Trier to assert rights to Wiesbaden-Idstein and Nassau itself. With the help of the League of Counts of the Wetterau, the archbishops were stopped, but even in 1609 it was feared that Wiesbaden would be invaded by Mainz. Ludwig II was able to implement a common administration throughout the oft-divided Walramic lands.

Figure 9-1 shows the town of Weilburg on the Lahn with its palace. This was the residence of the dukes of Nassau-Weilburg until 1816. The palace dates from the sixteenth century, and was enlarged in 1721. **Map 1** below shows the historical heartland of Nassau, including the towns of Nassau, Limburg, Weilburg and Braunfels.

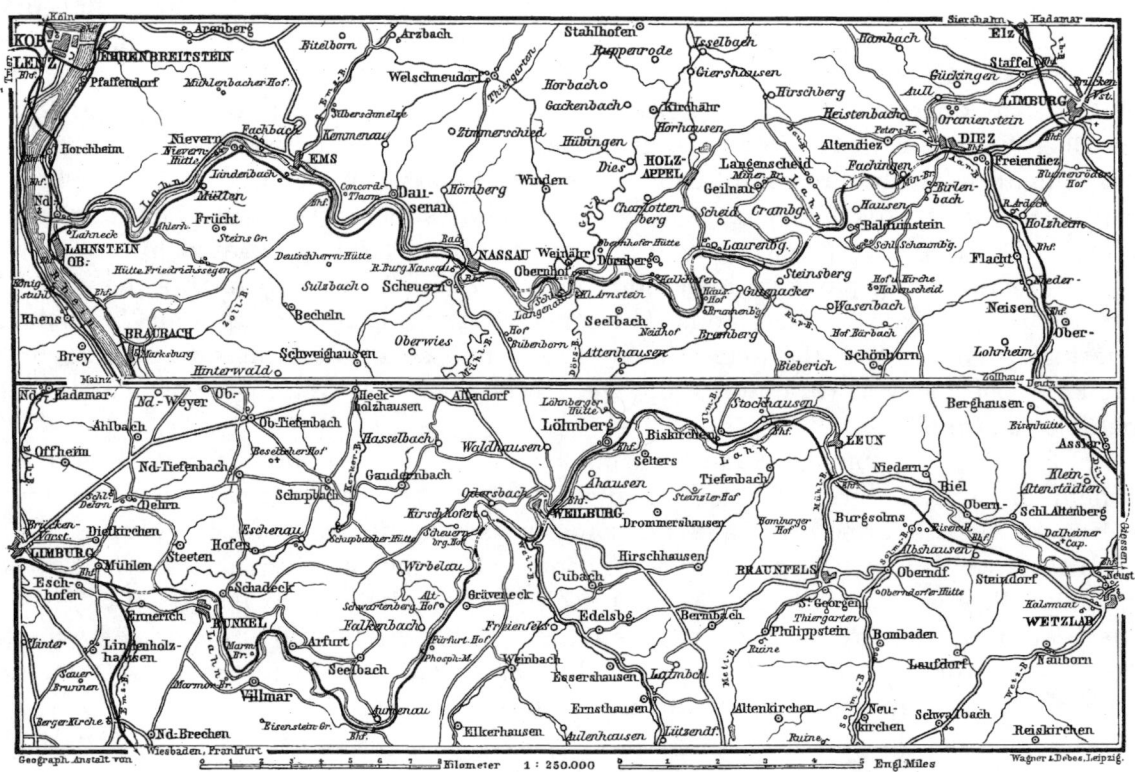

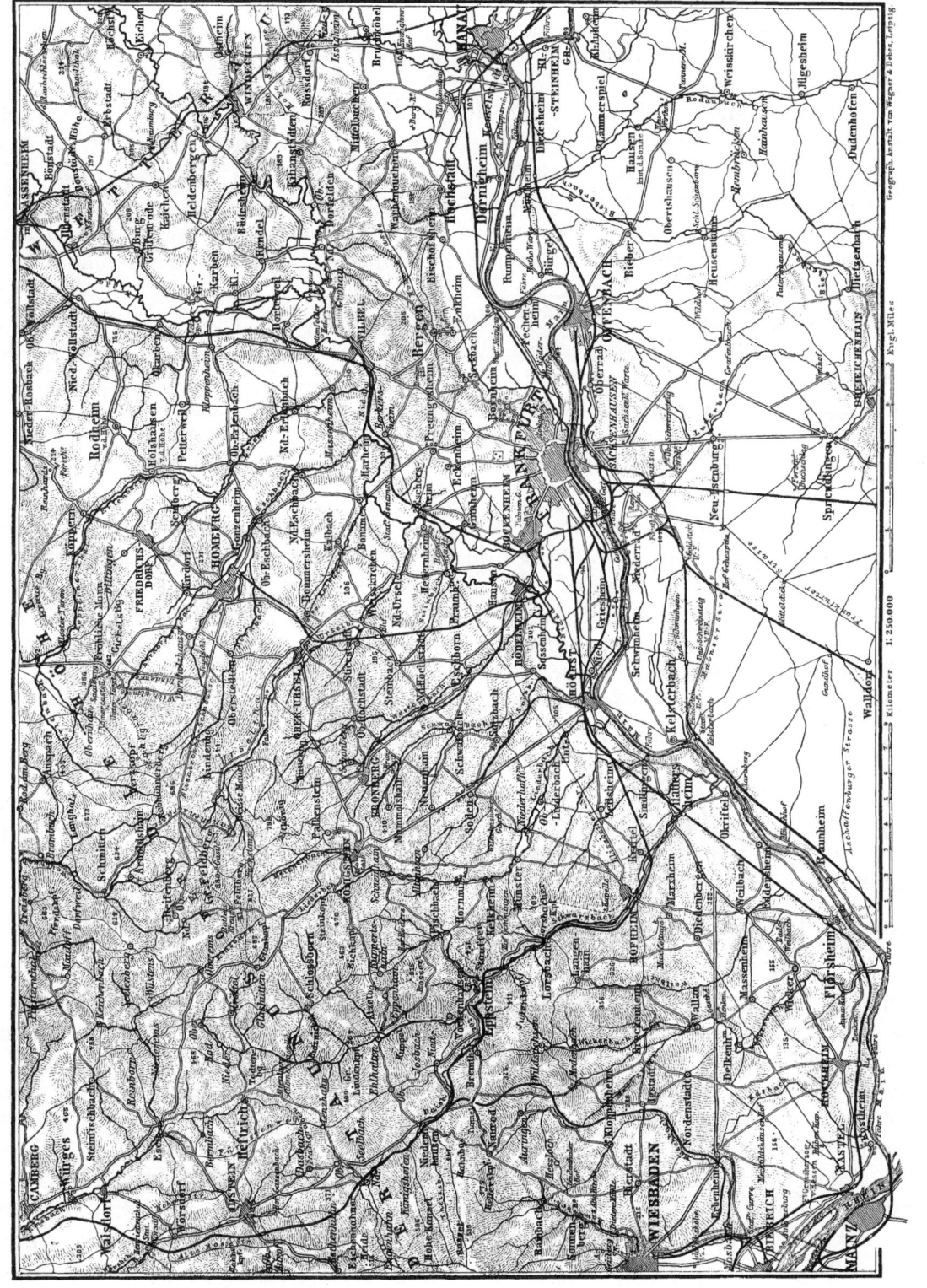

Map 2 Shows the Taunus region, historically contested by Germans and Romans, and in more modern times the focus of contention between the Hessian states.

In the northern Taunus area of the county, especially in the Weil valley, an iron industry had been in existence since ancient times. In the fifteenth century there were over a dozen iron works in the forests, regulated by the mining ordinance of 1495. After further development in the following century, the operations were laid low by the Thirty Years War. Later in the seventeenth century most of the foundry and casting works were rebuilt.

In 1629 another partition cut the county into three parts that completely obliterated their already marginal political and military influence through the rest of the Thirty Years War. The little principalities all but disappeared as independent political entities during the war. The constant invasions of troops, with their plundering, forced contributions and extortion of money and goods to avoid having towns and villages set afire, all brought down misery on the inhabitants. Especially gruesome were the depredations of the imperial commander von Görzenich. Even in this era of wholesale destruction his actions in the Nassau and Wetterau regions were so brutal that he incurred the wrath of his own emperor, who sentenced him to death. The counts had tried to remain neutral, but were driven into the arms of the Swedes to seek shelter from these depredations. This in turn caused them to be declared dispossessed of their lands by the emperor. Mainz now took Wiesbaden, the counts of Schwarzenberg gained Idstein, the princes von Lobkowitz occupied Weilburg, and the Duke of Lorraine stole Saarbrücken.

The peace of Westphalia returned these possessions to the counts of Nassau, after years of exile in Metz and Straßburg under the embarrassing charity and protection of the French emperor. Recovery was extremely difficult after the war. Economic stimulus was expected from the Huguenots and Walloons who were induced to settle in the county, especially in and around Usingen. In the period 1718-35 some helpful administrative reforms came about through a crafty countess, Charlotte Amalia, who ruled for her minor son. District seats were established in Usingen, Idstein, Wiesbaden, Wehen, Ottweiler, Burgschwalbach, and Saarbrücken. In 1730 a school and confirmation ordinance was issued that made school attendance for children mandatory in the winter months.

Nassau-Weilburg fared even worse that the other Walramic line. Except for a school ordinance of 1737 that similarly made school attendance mandatory, local administration was weak and unsuccessful. The county did succeed in adding some land to its holdings: parts of the Hesse-Darmstadt district of Hüttenberg and some villages in the Rhineland were obtained by exchange.

Even in the eighteenth century the continuous warfare kept the people of the Walram lands from prospering economically. Many took any opportunity to emigrate that presented itself. The Emperor Joseph II invited immigrants to Galicia, and many came from Nassau-Weilburg and -Usingen at this time. Evidence of the misery of their lives is suggested by the criticism and jibes of other Galicians, who derided them for their small stature and often ugly appearance; their children by contrast were considered beautiful.

The wars also produced huge bands of highway robbers who preyed on anything that moved and were difficult to combat because of the weakness of local authority in the tiny Nassau lands. The robbers frequented the forests of the Middle Rhine and the other rivers, Main, Lahn, Mosel, and Nahe. In 1781 a Wetterau band was said to have eight-seven known members. Most of these outlaw groups, who regularly committed murder, arson and thievery, were smaller. These plunderers plagued Hesse even as late as 1812-14, striking both banks of the Main, in the Odenwald and Spessart areas, the Vogelsberg and the Wetterau.

By 1797 the last of the Nassau-Saarbrücken line of counts died out. The Nassau-Usingen counts now inherited the land, and later would form the basis of a new, expanded Duchy of Nassau.

THE NASSAU-DILLENBURG COUNTIES

The 1255 partitions created the Ottonian line of counts centered on Dillenburg and Siegen, two areas with significant iron deposits and ironworks. After Otto's death, his sons divided the lands three ways in 1303, with their holdings centered on Dillenburg, Siegen and Hadamar. They were marginalized politically and economically by this action. The Hadamar line expanded its holdings in Driedorf and its rights within Hadamar. In 1367 the death of the last of this line capable of ruling threw its ownership into question. It was split between the Dillenburg heirs and another Nassau count, Ruprecht. Ruprecht's share eventually fell to a count of Katzenelnbogen (1403).

The Siegen-Dillenburger counts succeeded in expanding their holdings by shrewd dealings with the counts von Wittgenstein, taking over much of the Wittgenstein lands in fief in the early 1340s. In 1343 the line generated a Beilstein branch that remained independent for over 200 years. About 1350 a terrible war took place between Count Otto of Dillenburg and local nobles who sought to gain enhanced independence from the Nassau house. The count was killed in battle, and it was only with great difficulty that the feud with the local lords von Wildenburg, von Elkershausen, and von Walderdorf could be brought to a conclusion in 1352. The nobles successfully racked up some territorial gains in the war.

With the reign of Count Johann I the family fortunes took a brief turn for the better. He won back the Hadamar lands, and in negotiation with Landgrave Hermann of Hesse (1377-78) he was able to scale back somewhat the huge debt in war reparations that he owed Hermann after backing the losing side in an uprising of nobles against Hesse (The "Star Revolt"). The debt amounted to hundreds of thousands of guilder. He married off one of his sons to the heiress of the county of Diez, which came back to the Dillenburger line in 1386. But feuds with Hesse and Katzenelnbogen clouded the final years of Johann's rule. In 1398 he was compelled to mortgage his largest Hessian holding, the town of Herborn with twenty of its local villages, to Landgrave Hermann. He lost Greifenstein to the counts von Solms in 1395, and half of the Hadamar holdings to Count Johann of Katzenelnbogen. In 1410 a league of his enemies opposed Johann of Dillenburg because of his political support of the Mainz archbishopric; as a result of the ensuing conflict Nassau's control of the manor of Limburg was lost. In 1420 the Nassau-Dillenburg line lost Diez again when Johann's son died without having produced a male heir. Diez eventually came to Hesse by way of its inheritance of Katzenelnbogen (1479).

The Siegen-based iron industry was critically important to the economy of the county, and the counts applied great effort to maintain their authority over this area. Between 1417 and 1463 the number of foundries here increased to forty from twenty-five. In this period the Siegen works were renowned for gun casting and casting huge ovens. The ovens were noteworthy for decorative plates cast with scenes from the Bible, the ancient world, or ornamental heraldry and similar decorations. The iron region of Dillenburg was not as important or extensive, with only ten foundries by about 1460.

Count Johann IV (died 1475) had more than fifty foundries in operation at the height of his rule.

Conflict with Hesse over disputed lands heated up in this period. The great feud with Nassau over rights to the fabulous Katzenelnbogen inheritance beginning in 1479 was to drag on for many years. The Hessians also took away Nassau's interest in Wittgenstein in 1493. In 1507 a judgment of the imperial supreme court granted Nassau rights to half of Katzenelnbogen, but it was not possible to lay claim to them and dislodge the Hessians without military intervention beyond the capacity of Nassau. The matter later was caught up in the greater Schmalkald feud between the crown and the Protestant princes, although Count William embraced the Reformation and implemented it in Nassau from 1526-38. William also managed a 200,000-florin program of strengthening the defenses around Dillenburg against Hessian attack.

The defeat of Philip of Hesse in the Schmalkald War briefly strengthened Nassau's Katzenelnbogen claims, but in the peace of 1555 a compromise was reached to buy Nassau off with land concessions. Nassau reclaimed Hessian interests in Diez and Hadamar, and set aside her dependent relationship to Hesse in her Herborn and Driedorf holdings. All Hessian claims to lands north of the Lahn thus were subordinated to Nassau. Hesse paid Nassau an indemnity of 450,000 florins for any other disputed land rights that remained in question. This agreement shows in stark terms the weakness of Nassau vis-à-vis her larger neighbor; the entire agreement provided cash and property worth about 600,000 florins, while the value of all disputed properties including those granted by the imperial court judgment was nearly 6,000,000 florins. Count William in the meantime had committed upwards of 200,000 florins in legal fees to the fifty advocates he had hired to press his case at the imperial court. Much of the rest of the settlement he squandered on lavish court displays and expensive travels.

The ascension of Johann VI to the countship in Nassau-Dillenburg (1559) saw its greatest prince assume power. A gifted administrator, deeply religious and committed to the good of his land, Johann would need all his gifts to steer his small land into better times. After the dissolution of the Beilstein line in 1561, Dillenburg now controlled Beilstein, Diez, Weilstein and Hadamar. Yet even a high consumption tax imposed in 1566 brought only 16,382 florins from these holdings into the count's coffers. The land was basically quite impoverished. Johann set about instituting reform programs in the judicial system, mining practices, religious life, agriculture and forestry, pubic health, and other areas. His decision to make his land Calvinist under the influence of Holland and the Palatinate was to have far-reaching consequences. Johann's leadership in the league of Wetterau princes also helped him encourage Calvinist proselytizing in nearby Sayn, Wittgenstein, Wied, Solms-Braunfels, Büdingen, Hanau, and even Hesse-Kassel. Herborn formed a local spiritual center of the new faith. It became noted throughout Germany as a Bible-printing center as well.

Johann also increased school attendance, building on the Latin schools created by his father in Siegen, Diez, Dillenburg, Hadamar and Herborn. He now built similar institutions in Haiger, Kirberg, Driedorf, Freudenberg, Ferndorf, Burbach, Nassau and Wehrheim. He also built public schools (or "German schools") and girls' schools in Diez, Herborn, Haiger, and Dillenburg. These laudable efforts were mostly swept away in the Thirty Years War.

Upon his death in 1606 Johann VII of Nassau-Siegen partitioned his little land among his five sons. They formed an alliance among themselves in 1607, and it was twice renewed over the next thirty years. But the Siegen inheritance was greatly marginalized politically by this step. One of the heirs, Count Johann VIII of Siegen, even decided to return to Catholicism in 1612.

The lands of Nassau-Dillenburg contained about 7,638 households at the time of the Siegen partition, or about 38,000 people in total. It was 620,000 florins in debt. The households were apportioned among the various land areas as follows (those with percentage figures indicate partial ownership by the Dillenburg counts, with other owners possessing rights to the remaining portion):

Dillenburg	2,313	Löhnberg	76.5	(75%)
Siegen	1,974	Kirberg	89	(50%)
Diez	1,105	Camberg	164.5	(50%)
Nassau	615	Altweilnau	76.5	(50%)
Hadamar	583	Wehrheim	123.5	(50%)
Beilstein	518	TOTAL	7,638	

In the Thirty Years War the Nassau lands suffered badly, particularly in the mid-1630s. Count Ludwig Heinrich of Nassau-Dillenburg served as an officer with Swedish forces, and sought with their help to conquer the neighboring Catholic holdings of Trier, Siegen, and Nassau-Hadamar. The battles swayed back and forth over the land, and Ludwig Heinrich proved an able leader in besieging strongholds such as Braunfels (1635). The imperial forces struck back hard, despoiling his lands in revenge. This caused the count to re-think his strategy; he dropped allegiance to the Swedes and sought imperial help in maintaining his war gains in Trier, Hadamar, and Siegen. He became just as able a commander for the emperor as he had been for the Swedes, conquering Amöneburg and Hanau.

In the Nassau Siegen lands the war went badly, with Count Johann VIII first prevailing in attempting to convert his people to Catholicism with the emperor's assistance, and later having to surrender part of the inheritance (1632) to his brother, Johann Moritz, who returned it to Protestantism. In 1636 Johann VIII was able to reclaim the land, but failed in his Catholicization efforts. After the war, the two brothers were directed by the emperor to split the inheritance into separate Catholic and Protestant areas under their individual lines. The northwest part of the Siegen lands (Freudenburg to Hilchenbach) thus became Calvinist, the southwest part Catholic. Siegen itself remained a common possession of both lines, and each faith was designated a main church to serve its needs in the town.

By 1705 the Siegen lands were again the scene of conflict as the cousins William Hyacinth and Adolf battled for control. Adolf called on Prussia to back his claim, while William played imperial politics in Vienna. His religious repression of the Protestant population combined with huge demands for taxes actually caused a popular rebellion in 1706. The emperor finally had to declare him dispossessed, and he was retired off with an annual indemnity of 4,000 *Taler*. When Adolf's son died heirless in 1734, the Siegen lands again reverted to a Catholic branch of the family, but only for a year before this line too died out. The last remaining heir of the wider family turned out to be William IV of Nassau-Diez. With his impending death without male heirs the landgraves of Hesse-Kassel and Hesse-Darmstadt signed a compact in 1745 to jointly pursue claim to the Dillenburg lands. They renewed the agreement in 1764, but never succeeded in dispossessing Nassau heirs to the Diez countship. In 1783 an inheritance pact was concluded between the Walram and Oranien (Dutch) branches of the Nassau families to reunify much of the old Nassau lands under one line.

William IV proved a good ruler who allowed much local freedom in religious practices among his mixed population of Catholic and Protestant subjects. Local seats in Siegen and Diez were established to administer the county. Lesser districts were managed from these towns as well as Dillenburg and Hadamar. During the Seven Years War the ancient castle residence of the counts in Dillenburg was completely destroyed in fighting between Hannoverian and French troops, wiping out a long tradition of rule of the Dillenburg lands from this capital. Such terrible times were experienced in 1771-72, that new policies on land use and inheritance by farmers were enacted by the government in 1776. Inheritance was required to flow to the first-born son, instead of the general practice of dividing land up into uneconomic parcels to provide all heirs with some land (partible inheritance). This was rather thoroughly implemented in the Siegen lands, less so elsewhere. Many tiny, often-divided plots were consolidated into more economically-viable farms by government order in 1784. By 1820 the consolidation had been implemented in 120 communities, mostly in the Westerwald area.

The Siegen lands had very different land structures than those elsewhere in the Nassau-Dillenburg lands. Here the iron industry was so extensive that its structure had a heavy impact on land use practices. Intensive use was made of many hills and slopes of the local mountains to produce charcoal, as well as wood, farmland and pasture land. By 1785 there were eleven iron and six steel works with tall oven foundries. There were eighteen iron and thirteen steel hammer works for further refining the metal. The development of the forest economy in the Dillenburg lands also progressed in this era. A school for forest rangers produced many influential leaders and managers of forest economies in Prussia, Hesse and elsewhere.

FÜRSTENTUM WALDECK TO 1800

Waldeck is not strictly speaking part of the Hessian state, but their histories were closely linked from the Middle Ages because of Waldeck's location along the much-disputed border region between Hesse and Westphalia. Borders and land holdings changed often over the centuries, so that Hessian landgraves sometimes held title to areas in Waldeck, and vice versa.

The conflict over land in the Waldeck area was inevitable in the High Middle Ages since there were few natural borders between the lands of the major players in the region. Besides the Hessian and Waldeck counts, the bishoprics of Paderborn, Köln, and Mainz contested one another's ownership of the lands in this border region. Many lesser nobles also struggled for bits and pieces of the area. Up through the sixteenth century the saying "The Westphalians are coming!" was heard often, summing up the ongoing sense of dread of the northern Hessians. The much-fought-over line of contention was more or less traced by the towns of Wetter, Frankenberg, Wolfhagen, and Trendelburg.

An ancient line of counts who strove to carve out a realm for themselves here were the von Schwalenbergs. Astute marriage agreements led to the counts' acquisition in the mid-twelfth century of the Itter and Wildungen areas and their dependent villages. By 1180 this line became known as the Waldeck counts after a stronghold of that name. This was territory owned by the Mainz bishopric from whom the Waldeckers held their lands in fief. It gave them sufficient independence from the Archbishop of Köln that the counts were able to break free of his jurisdiction, but at the cost of generations-long conflict with the Köln diocese that lasted into the seventeenth century.

About 1260 the ownership of Wildungen came into dispute, with the Hessian landgrave seizing it for himself in opposition to the claims of Mainz. With Waldeck's help, Mainz drove the Hessians out again and regained the area, which in turn came back to Waldeck as a fief from Mainz.

In 1228/29 a major partition of Waldeck lands among a family of counts was undertaken. At this time separate counties of Waldeck and Schwalenberg were created; only the former is meaningful in this history. The Waldeck count lived so long that he saw his sons die before him (1223-71), and his grandson, Otto I, became the heir. Otto was also the son-in-law of the Hessian landgrave. Waldeck and Hesse found some common ground in their opposition to the political aims of the bishoprics of Paderborn and Köln. Conflicts with the local religious powers brought rich properties to Waldeck via mortgages, including the castle Lichtenfels and the towns of Sachsenberg and Fürstenberg. In the thirteenth and fourteenth centuries the properties of Korbach, Külte, Freinenhagen and Usseln were acquired, as well as feudal rights to the free county of Grönebach and mortgage rights to Düdinghausen. The castle and town of Züschen followed suit, at which point Waldeck's historic high point of land acquisition was reached. Count Henry IV (1305-44) signed an inheritance compact in 1344 that ensured the principle of primogeniture would be upheld and a single count would be maintained as ruler of the land. This was a major step in protecting a principality that remained small by the standards of its enemies.

Soon enough the competitors in the area would succeed in dismantling some of the gains of the previous century. Köln had designs on the west and north of Waldeck, while Hesse sought gains in the east and south. In 1359 the manor of Itter became available when its lord was assassinated by his nephews about 1357. Hesse, Mainz and Waldeck all stepped in to claim a share of this prize. Waldeck's gain was only temporary, however. Its terrible financial condition forced Count Henry VI (1370-97) to mortgage properties to local nobles. Later it became very difficult to repatriate them. These included Itter, Züschen, Düdinghausen, and Lichtenfels. In 1424 Hesse obtained half the county of Waldeck via a mortgage from Count Henry VII. This was repatriated in December 1427.

From 1538-98 three separate Waldeck lines of counts existed, based in Eisenberg, Wildungen and Landau. By this time Hesse was playing a leading role in Waldeck compared to the influence of its other neighbors. This led to Waldeck's early adoption of the Reformation, with Count Philip III issuing an ordinance on reform in 1525. The secular takeover of Catholic properties began in 1526 with the Arolsen Cloister, and continued for decades thereafter. Korbach maintained the old faith until 1543, and did not fully implement the reforms until 1556.

Waldeck also followed Hesse into the Schmalkald War, and suffered by being part of the losing side. Count Wolrad had to pay a large fine to appease the emperor after the Augsburg Diet of 1548. Imperial pressure seems to have brought about Waldeck's loss of the Düdinghausen property to the lords von Büren in 1548/49. In 1588 Mainz also reclaimed the mortgaged properties of Naumburg and Itter that Waldeck had only wrested from the control of local nobility with Hessian help in 1542 and 1544. Itter then was handed over to Hesse-Marburg in fief.

By 1598 the Wildungen and Landau lines died out, but the Eisenberg heirs promptly created a new Wildungen line that remained separate from Eisenberg until 1697. Waldeck now was trying its best to escape the constricting Hessian influence, a difficult move since at this point it was represented in the Hessian diet and had even accepted the jurisdiction of Hessian courts over its citizens. Count Christian tried to use his influence at the imperial court in 1613-19 to return his lands to imperial fiefs, thereby rejecting Hessian overlordship. Landgrave Moritz of Hesse Kassel objected violently, invading and occupying Waldeck lands in 1621. Imperial rulings went against Hesse, however, and the advent of Tilly's troops enforced the emperor's view. The Peace of Westphalia (1648) saw nominal Hessian control restored, but its direct political influence was much reduced.

The Thirty Years War was said to have cost Waldeck "eighteen tons of gold and half its population." As in Nassau, this small and impoverished land scarcely provided enough resources to provide for the wider members of the ruling family, so in many cases they went abroad to seek their fortunes among the larger European powers. Many became great military leaders and achieved renown on battlefields all over the world. The greatest was Count Georg Friedrich (1664-92). Anton Ulrich (1706-28) had to broker a major controversy within Waldeck between the Pietists and the orthodox believers. In 1711 he resolved the problem by expelling the Pietists.

The capital of jurisprudence in Waldeck was at Korbach, where the state court held forth. From the sixteenth century regional capitals of administration were maintained in Rhoden-Eilhausen, Mengeringhausen, Landau, Wetterburg, Korbach, Sachsenberg, Waldeck, Lichtenfels, Züschen, and Wildungen. The sixteenth century also saw the development of a fairly extensive iron industry. In the Wildungen area alone some twenty-three copper mines were in operation. But the Thirty Years War so badly destroyed the forges, mines and foundries that these only began to recover in the eighteenth century. State finances were always in arrears. Prince Friedrich (1763-1812) was forced to borrow a million *Taler* from Hesse-Kassel at the end of the century. His efforts to raise funds by selling Bad Pyrmont to either Hannover or Hesse fell through. The population of Waldeck in 1780 was just 37,019 people. They formed 6,954 families living in 6,004 houses, an average of five per family.

HESSE-HANAU

The original Hanau counts were the lords von Dorfelden. By 1191 they had begun to use the name derived from the castle they held at Hanau. The castle was built in the mid-twelfth century at the point where the Kinzig entered the Main River. The counts expanded their little realm from their core holdings in the eastern Wetterau. They obtained the von Münzenberg holdings when this line died out in 1255, thereby greatly expanding their lands in the Wetterau and the Dreieich area south of the lower Main. Count Reinhard I obtained the imperial title of bailiff of the Wetterau (1273), in which he exercised considerable authority in the name of the Habsburg King Rudolf. His line continued to exercise this role through the following century. By the end of the thirteenth century the counts had obtained a large portion of the holdings of the lords von Steckelberg, now organized into the Schwarzenfels district.

A powerful enemy of the Hanau line was the imperial city of Frankfurt, over which the counts sought to obtain various forms of influence. Over Frankfurt's objections, in 1320 the German Emperor Ludwig granted Count Ulrich II a mortgage over the neighboring Bornheimerberg province. In 1349 the very capable Ulrich III used his influence at court to win the position of imperial *Schultheiß*, or mayor, of Frankfurt. With this award came a mortgage over the Frankfurt city forest, as well as various feudal grants and privileges in the town. A town patrician named Siegfried Paradies later succeeded in outmaneuvering Ulrich and neutralizing his influence in Frankfurt, apparently because Ulrich's favored position at court had begun to erode.

In 1377 the Hanau lands were increased again through inheritance of rights to the district of Altenhaßlau, as well as the northern half of the Brandenstein district; Hanau had held the southern half since 1316. A crisis period ensued when Ulrich V. proved incapable of rule, and fell into conflict with his brothers. The Archbishop of Mainz was appointed interim caretaker (1403), taking over the towns of Hanau and Babenhausen and refusing to relinquish them to the counts again until his death in 1419. Count Reinhard II then took matters into his own hands and seized Hanau with the help of its citizenry. The immediate threat from Mainz was ended, but the struggle would continue for many generations with this most powerful adversary. The conflict often served to frustrate the counts' ability to increase their land holdings. Once in a while the Hanauers would emerge triumphant, as when Mainz was lamed by its conflict with Hesse in 1427. The following year the Archbishop granted Hanau a mortgage over the town of Orb and its dependent villages.

Count Reinhard II (1411-51) succeeded in restoring the influence of Hanau at the imperial court. The Hanau line was raised in status to the ranks of the imperial counts in 1427, and granted freedom for its lands from the judicial authority of any foreign power (1434). Hanau now was able to work with the Palatinate to share an imperial mortgage over the town of Gelnhausen. Partial rights to other properties came as well: the Bracht district, Wertheim, Klingenberg, Brückenau, Schildeck, and others. A quarter-title to Dreieichenhain also came to the county.

In 1458 the county was divided between a minor son of the ruling count and his uncle, Philip the Elder. The boy's line retained the territory north of the Main with Hanau as its capital, thereafter called Hanau-Münzenberg. The uncle took the southern lands with Babenhausen as the seat, later called Hanau-Lichtenberg after some inherited lands obtained in Alsace. The Münzenberg line also expanded their holdings, buying more rights to Ortenberg and taking over Homburg v. d. Höhe (1487). These lands were acquired by Hesse in 1504 and 1539.

Marriage and other close personal ties brought Hanau-Münzenberg into close alliance with the Nassau counts in Dillenburg. This led to the advent of the Calvinist Reformed faith in the Hanau lands over the decade ending in 1540. The reformed faith was only fully implemented through the Hanau lands near the end of the century. At this time a number of religious refugees from the Netherlands settled in Hanau, and the count granted them rights to found an important new section of the town called the *Neustadt*. In 1607 he created a system of reformed schools whose development was hindered in the Thirty Years War but was at last completed in 1665.

During the Thirty Years War Hanau was one of the strongest and best-defended fortresses in Germany. It was besieged in 1630 by Catholic imperial forces and compelled to open its gates, but the next year the Swedes re-conquered it for the count. After the defeat at Nördlingen in 1634 Count Philip Moritz fled to France for safety, leaving the Swedish General Ramsey to hold the city. This he did in the face of all imperial army attacks. In June 1636 the forces of Landgrave William of Hesse-Kassel chased away the besiegers, and Ramsey marched out to occupy the whole Main River area with the Wetterau and Vogelsberg. A particularly notorious plundering of Schotten ensued on July 22. In February 1638 imperial forces under the Nassau-Dillenburg Count Ludwig Heinrich conquered Hanau and captured Ramsey. He died in prison at Dillenburg of wounds received in this battle.

The Hanau-Münzenberg line died out during the war with the passing of Count Johann Ernest. The ownership rights were disputed by various powers, but Hanau-Lichtenberg was able to reclaim the lands thanks to support by Hesse-Kassel. This support came with strings attached, however; Count Friedrich Kasimir had to surrender the districts of Naumburg and Schwarzenfels to Hesse and sign an inheritance treaty on August 5, 1643 that gave Hesse-Kassel rights to inherit the land in case of the death of any count who had failed to produce a male heir.

Friedrich Kasimir was an eccentric ruler also remembered for his decision to found a colony in South America called Hanau-India under the auspices of the Dutch West Indies Company. His plan foundered based on the count's lack of money, settlers and political influence. In 1661 he founded the oldest faience factory in Hesse, and the second-oldest newspaper, the "Hanau Mercury." In 1670 he succeeded in convincing the Imperial Privy Council to sanction by treaty the re-imposition of the Lutheran faith in his lands.

The count's death in 1685 brought about another partition of the Hanau lands. The subsequent death of one heir led to their reunification in 1712 under Count Johann Reinhard (1712-36). He would prove to be the last count of Hanau. Landgrave Karl of Hesse-Kassel lost little time in gaining the count's signature on a renewal of the inheritance treaty of 1643 (1718). The emperor recognized the inheritance treaty as well. Days before the death of Johann Reinhard, Landgrave Friedrich I of Hesse-Kassel invaded Babenhausen to assert his rights to the area. In the end, Hanau's territory was partitioned among three rival claimants: Kassel, Darmstadt and Mainz. Kassel obtained Gelnhausen by buying out the rights held in it by the Palatinate. Mainz and Darmstadt compromised in splitting up areas that Kassel was unable to claim outright. The Babenhausen area was divided roughly 60/40 between Kassel and Darmstadt.

At the time of the 1736 inheritance by Hesse-Kassel, Hanau-Münzenberg consisted of twelve districts with eighty-five sub-jurisdictions: Büchertal, Bornheimerberg, Windecken, Rodheim, Dorheim, Altenhaßlau, Bieber, Lohrhaupten, Schlüchtern, Babenhausen, and Ortenberg. There were other jurisdictions held in common with Electoral Mainz, including Solms, Isenburg, and Stolberg-Gedern. In 1754 this area comprised the five sizable towns of Hanau, Windecken, Babenhausen, Steinau and Schlüchtern, plus nine market towns and seventy-one villages. Of the 48,000 inhabitants, 11,500 were in Hanau alone. By 1796 the population had increased to 56,000, and nine years later to 72,000.

NOTES TO CHAPTER 9

[1] This chapter is taken almost exclusively from Karl E. Demandt, *Geschichte des Landes Hessen*, Bärenreiter-Verlag, Kassel, 1972, pp. 288-99, 367-435, 521-33.

Chapter 10

Germany and Hesse in the Eighteenth Century

The eighteenth century in many ways represented the perpetuation of social and political trends that had characterized German life in the previous century. Some 300 separate political entities still ruled in Germany, frustrating the efforts of the "Holy Roman" German emperor in Vienna to exercise fully his imperial authority. Most Germans were still land-bound peasants who toiled to provide for themselves as well as the host of noble, ecclesiastical, state and/or town-based lords who compelled them to provide the dizzying array of taxes, tithes, special fees and personal services that held the social order in place. By the early eighteenth century commerce was well on the road to recovery after the disaster of the Thirty Years War. Frankfurt and Hamburg now rivaled Paris and other major capitals in merchant activity.[1]

It would take Germany the better part of a century to recover the population she lost in the Thirty Years War, but by the 1730s she once again approached a population of twenty million from a post-war low of perhaps thirteen million. This was very different from the experience of other European nations whose rates of growth were much less rapid over this period. Fertility rates were high in Germany, and overall these tended to overcome even high levels of infant mortality, epidemic disease, and death rates that matched or exceeded births in many areas. Significant levels of immigration helped account for the population rise in some regions, where Swiss, French, Dutch and Scandinavian immigrants flooded in to escape persecution or economic adversity at home. French Huguenots were particularly numerous, many arriving in Hesse at the invitation of the landgraves. On the whole, Protestant areas seem to have gained more than Catholic ones from this relocation tide.

Other reasons which may help account for the increase in population include a lessening of the duration and severity of warfare in the eighteenth century compared to the seventeenth; this in turn allowed more food to be grown without disruption. The climate seems to have become somewhat warmer and drier, and better cereals and grains, particularly wheat, were able to be grown across broader areas than before. The population rise increased demand for foodstuffs, stimulating agriculture and the introduction of improved methods of husbandry. The diet was still heavily cereal based; increased meat consumption would have to await the improved animal husbandry practices of the nineteenth century.

Population growth and price increases for foodstuffs brought about tremendous expansion in arable land from 1750 onwards. By 1800 land being tilled reached its historical high point. This also created the conditions for overpopulation on the land and a ready pool of workers to meet the later needs for an industrialized, urban-based work force. After the mid-point in the century the dreaded plague all but died out as the black rat disappeared from much of Germany and western Europe. Still, diseases such as typhoid, dysentery, typhus and syphilis remained common.[2]

On the upper end of the social spectrum, the nobility was heavily represented in the towns where they aped the customs of their still wealthier social betters in assuming all manner of French affectations. Many of these families became impoverished after a few generations, their members seeking to keep up appearances as they scrambled for positions at court, in the military, or government. This served to tie them to the princes who could extend these positions as perquisites. The lower orders of the moneyed classes, such as smaller tradesmen and artisans, remained more German than French in their customs, outlooks, and values. The general trend in the smaller German states, especially after 1770, was toward improvement in the social, political and economic conditions of the rising middle classes.

Although the universities were considered excellent by European standards, the sorry state of the rest of German school instruction was an unfortunate feature. Some schools passed from religious to state control, with instruction in German rather than Latin. Unqualified, poorly paid teachers were common, and brutal treatment of students for even minor infractions was considered appropriate and normal. Teacher shortages became acute later in the century as inflation completely overtook the perpetually-inadequate salaries that were offered. Teaching was considered a low-class profession, and teachers often were forced to go shamefaced from house to house like beggars to collect meals and back wages.[3]

Class differences were closely watched and strictly maintained across the social spectrum.

> Class distinctions, however, were emphasized in most of the German states, as part of the technique of social control. Nobles, clergy, army officers, professional men, merchants and peasants constituted separate classes; and within every category there were grades each of which stiffened itself with scorn of the next beneath. Marriage outside one's class was almost unthinkable, but some merchants and financiers bought nobility. The nobles held a monopoly of the higher posts in the army and the government, and many of them earned their privileges by bravery or competence; but many were parasites, composed of uniforms, competing for social precedence at the court...[4]

As population increase swelled demand for the produce of the land, food prices inevitably began to rise. Wages seem to have kept pace, or at least prices were fairly stable until about 1750. From then until the end of the century wages remained flat or sank even as prices spiraled sharply upward. Rye prices rose 80% from 1740-1800, while wages seem to have risen only about 10% in the same period. From 1780-1810 grain prices apparently doubled again. The price of arable land also skyrocketed even as the glut of unskilled manual labor depressed earnings.

Cattle plagues were a substantial problem throughout much of the century, particularly in war years such as 1711-14 and 1744-45; this further exacerbated the high cost of food. As much as 50-90 percent of the stock perished in these plagues. Livestock was not yet selectively bred to improve their physical strength and other attributes. Animals were typically too small to pull plows well or manage other heavy loads required of them. Agriculture similarly suffered from lack of innovation through most of the century due to the inadequacies of the three-field system and the almost universal practice of holding productive land such as pastures and forests in common. The shortage of animals reduced the amount of dung available for fertilizer, another barrier to productivity.

Serious crop failure dogged the German agricultural scene in the mid-eighteenth century. Reforms in agricultural techniques were slow in coming and productivity failed to keep pace with population growth. A particularly bad period from 1770-72 led to the widespread introduction of potato farming, providing a cheap source of vital calories and one which could not be so easily destroyed by marauding armies bent on inflicting damage on the land. Germany faced such times in the war years 1756-63 and 1778-79. Still, it took many years to change the cultural patterns that initially led many Germans to look down on the potato. In 1781 it was recorded that servants in the Elbe region would change masters rather than be forced to eat their *Kartoffeln*.[5]

The economy that emerged in Germany after the Thirty Years War was much less integrated in world markets, and has been described as the "back yard" of the emerging Atlantic trading world. Without colonies or a strong maritime tradition Germany was forced to rely on her own internal devices and markets for economic development. Consequently, the eighteenth century failed to bring about a recovery of the economic strength that Germans had known in earlier centuries through the Hansa and the major trading houses of the Middle Ages. German economic prospects were even more agrarian-based than in centuries past. The rest of the world forged ahead on many fronts, and Germany found itself flooded with cheap, attractive and stylish foreign wares such as Dutch and English cloth and French luxury goods. Some of the German princes created protected markets to try to help locally-produced goods compete with these imports, but for the most part these efforts were destined to fail. The local markets were just too small to make them viable. To a great extent the practice of German princes of selling their troops as mercenaries to the great powers stemmed from the lack of other options for generating wealth. This practice has been likened to the slave trade maintained by the major maritime powers.[6]

Production of goods in this pre-industrial period still was mostly guild-based, small-shop manufacturing. An exception was the high-volume trade in military goods for such commodities as wool cloth, metals, ammunition, weaponry, etc. Guilds continued to exercise influence until after 1750, but their social standing was much reduced compared to previous centuries. The master and his handful of apprentice artisans toiled up to sixteen hours a day in squalid, poorly-lit and -ventilated workshops. A Frankfurt clothing ordinance of 1731 placed the guildsmen only one step above the lowest social class.

Textile production was already entering the precursor period to the industrial revolution, with continued "putting out" of spinning and weaving among peasants. The working poor labored like drudges for very modest returns in an effort to supplement their incomes. Women and children were used extensively in this production. More and more centralized, factory-style production was developing out of this old *Verlagssystem*. Much use was still made of barter, particularly among artisans such as cutlers, miners and weavers of wool and other cloth.[7]

The landlords generally had used the chaos following the Thirty Years War to gain even more control over the productive lives of the peasantry. They increased peasant duties and thus impeded agricultural progress by drying up available capital. Lords periodically asserted rights to common areas claimed by villages, embroiling themselves and their peasants in litigation in the local courts. Peasants were most assertive in pushing their rights to these areas since this was historically their due in return for continual assessments of taxes and tithes. They paid for everything, from parish upkeep to bridal dowries for the daughters of their lords and poor relief.

By the eighteenth century, however, the princes had won out over their local nobility in the struggle for state power; for the most part, the power and influence of the nobility over their princes had been swept away in the Thirty Years War. The princes became the active leaders in economy and government, and the age of "Absolutism" stretched from 1660-1789. Still, the ruler's word was rarely absolute in all matters of state, such as imposing new taxation. In many cases the agreement of the noble and town estates was necessary before new taxes could be levied.

Many of the smaller German principalities were blessed with rulers who sought earnestly to build up the wealth and prosperity of their lands and people, recognizing this as both an inherent good and a means of securing their own prosperity. This gave rise to the term "enlightened despotism." Princes became the champions of the peasantry—as had been true of numerous landgraves of Hesse in past centuries—because better-off peasants could best afford the myriad duties demanded by the state. Hannover took an early step (1753) by requiring that peasant service duties be converted to established monetary payments to free them from manual work away from their farms. This became one of the economic and political experiments to watch among scholars, statesmen, and large landholders exploring the need for thorough reforms in agriculture. It likely influenced matters in Hesse because the rulers of most German principalities kept a sharp eye on the policies of other states to learn of their intended and unintended effects. Reforms perceived to be positive in one state often would be copied immediately by its neighbors.

Such an innovation was pioneered in Prussia: rural credit extension. The coming of price inflation and the conversion of service requirements to monetary payments created a huge shortage of capital on the land. Frederick the Great created a rural credit bank in 1770 along the lines of one his father had implemented in East Prussia in 1729-30. Little was done with comparable reforms in most of Germany for another generation.

The ultimate measure of a state's strength was the ability to impose its will, and for this reason the many smaller German rulers such as the landgraves developed standing armies and increasingly elaborate and centralized state administrations. Larger armies and bureaucracies demanded increased tax levies to keep them in being. Military levies were largely based on mercenary troops, since extensive recruitment from among a state's own citizens would tend to weaken the available pool of workers in directly-productive, tax-generating fields (as Hesse would find in its mercenary trade of 1776-83). Sending one's forces off to fight for pay in foreign wars also allowed them to be supported at someone else's expense, a tried and true tactic popular for centuries. Recruitment was heavily concentrated in areas with little scope for effective farming, as well as in some of the smaller, generally over-populated states. Much recruiting was done among the dregs of society, individuals who were thought to be better pawned off on a cash-paying neighbor than left to wander the open roads or narrow alleys of their own homeland. Many states developed specialized military training academies through the mid-seventeenth century. Troops were employed in peacetime to crush minor local rebellions and keep order like policemen.[8]

The bureaucrats who came to assume more and more control over affairs in the German states often were the product of state universities that trained both clerics and administrators for state service. Training in the management of effective bureaucracy was an increasingly popular feature of higher education in the eighteenth century, with the Prussian administrative machine generally accepted as the best and most efficient in Europe. Hesse Kassel's landgraves in particular recruited numerous Prussian officials to manage their affairs of state. The life of such a minister could be extremely gratifying, with tremendous power and influence available to those in the good graces of the prince. Conversely, a minister who fell from favor could be disgraced, exiled or imprisoned by a capricious master.

In addition to the high regard for Prussian administrative forms, Frederick the Great forged a very positive reputation that among northern Germans who took particular pride in finding at last a counterweight to the long-term dominance of the imperial court in Vienna. Goethe himself summed up this regard by saying, "We were no partisans of Prussia, but partisans of Fritz," during the Seven Years War.[9]

Religious life in Germany in this period was as dominated by the state as other aspects of individual existence. The princes were particularly influential in Protestant lands, where they served as de facto heads of their churches. Religion was too dynamic a consideration, too fraught with the potential for heresy and civil unrest to be left to individual conscience. The influence of secular scholarship on Bible studies, as well as prevailing trends in scientific and philosophical thought, served to weaken the hold of religion on national life among the upper classes. An important role of the clergyman now was to keep the lid on practices that might disrupt the social order. He also had to operate more like a petty bureaucrat, assuming a role in census taking, appointing and monitoring village officials, school administration, etc. In return, the princes worked to repair the damage of the wars of the seventeenth century by strengthening religious training centers, improving the lives of the clergy as they could, rebuilding rectories, etc. Visitations were popularly carried out to assess the observance of the approved religious forms, including the beliefs and attitudes of individual congregations. Church attendance remained a matter of the law, and absence from services for even fairly brief periods was a punishable offense. Clergy appeared to many as mere underlings of the state, a role which hardly suited them to promoting strong individual relationships with the Almighty.[10]

Through it all the German family remained the bedrock institution in the society, more influential by far than the state or its educational system. The average German husband and father was fully in control of his home, disciplining his wife and children as needed to enforce his will. Women provided a softer influence in the home for their children, and outside the home environment men tended to socialize with each other without their women. Germans maintained a higher standard of morality than the French, and most were scandalized by stories of loose morals at the French court. Some German courts increasingly exhibited the same tendencies as their role models in Paris, however, as the century wore on. They developed more drinking, gambling, and philandering among the sexes. Germans also maintained their ancient appetite for good food and plenty of it. A day-long bout of good eating was considered an enviable way to spend one's time. German homes were as warm and charming as any on the continent, with their half-timbered facades and much-admired ceramic tile stoves. The presence of music graced all but the poorest homes; small-scale singing societies, playing of musical instruments at home, and musical instruction in school were all very widespread.[11]

With the foregoing as background on the broad state of affairs in Germany, we turn now to a more specific look at Hesse and the extent to which it fit the broader trends.

SEVEN YEARS WAR, SHEEP AND SOLDIER SUBSIDIES: HESSE-KASSEL

The eighteenth century opened with Hesse-Kassel heavily involved in providing mercenary troops to various European powers in exchange for subsidies. Alliance with Prussia also created problems with the emperor in Vienna, who opposed Prussian influence and ruled that the key Rhenish castle at Rheinfels should be controlled by the militarily weak Hesse-Rotenburg instead of Kassel. For years Landgrave Karl refused to surrender the castle, and when at last he was forced to do so, he retained control of nearby Reichenberg in easy striking distance of the fortress. In 1700 he also obtained control of two districts along the Weser River, Uchte and Freudenberg. In 1719 he added the Brandenstein district to his holdings via a mortgage granted by Hanau. Karl and his successors maintained a broad policy of opposition to France, which worked doggedly over decades to impose its hegemony in much of western Germany.

The subsidy income allowed a powerful Hessian army to be supported over time, providing Kassel the means to play a more substantial role in European politics than its relative size and wealth might otherwise have dictated. Hessians served in every war on the continent in this era. Upon Karl's death in 1730 the army consisted of six cavalry regiments, twelve regiments of infantry, plus assorted specialized companies including artillery.

Hessian opposition to France also paved the way for it to offer a home to Protestant refugees forced to choose between Catholicism or flight. Beginning in 1685, this provided a large influx of skilled and educated people capable of adding to the wealth of the country, making up for some of the losses of the Thirty Years War. By 1704 the population numbered more than 175,000. In the decades around this time some thirty settlements of French Huguenots were created. The resultant upswing in trade caused the creation of banking and finance institutions, and promoted commerce.

The mercantilist practices of the age were well represented in Kassel, and the guilds were politically and economically disadvantaged in new regulations of 1693 and 1730. Many of their ancient rights and prerogatives were set aside. Karl also tried to promote trade by improving the road system in his centrally-located realm. Postal service was established by 1700 from Leipzig to Holland via Kassel, and in 1704 service was established from Kassel to Nuremberg. From 1710-29 he presided over the building of a canal linking the Weser and Rhine rivers, and although his death stopped it from being completed it nonetheless afforded better water-born trade connections to the north centered on the Huguenot-run harbor at Karlshafen.

Karl's artistic interests resulted in the improvement of his residence town with many baroque features. He caused a major Huguenot settlement to be built adjoining the old section of Kassel, known as the New Town. He built a great palace and parks complex known as the Karlsaue, with a renowned *Orangerie* and marble baths. In 1710 a palace of the crown prince was built. Most impressive of all was the grand development of the Herkules building on the adjacent heights of the Habichtswald forest, with adjoining park land and fountains. In 1709 he built the Carolinum College as an institution of higher learning.

Karl's son Frederick I ascended in 1720 to the Swedish throne through a fortunate marriage into the Swedish ruling line. He thus gave his Hessian possessions over to be ruled by his brother William upon their father's death in 1730. When the county of Hanau was acquired by Kassel in 1736 this also was given over to William's rule. Landgrave William VIII succeeded in obtaining the emperor's consent to re-occupy Rheinfels. Later he was able to prevail in the strife with his cousin's line of Hesse-Rotenburg which had opposed Kassel's possessions in the Katzenelnbogen lands since the Treaty of Westphalia in 1648. Now Kassel ruled again in the line of Rhine castles in the Katzenelnbogen lands, including the strongholds of Rheinfels, Katz, Reichenberg, and Hohenstein. St. Goar and St. Goarshausen and all other defensible points in the county returned to the landgrave's control. Kassel now exercised predominant military control over a significant part of the Rhine.[12]

Figure 10-1 Views of portions of the ancient and fabulously wealthy Katzenelnbogen inheritance that came to Hesse in 1470. Rheinfels castle (top) commanded surrounding areas on the left bank of the Rhine. It was a Hessian stronghold for centuries and long a bone of contention between the related ruling lines in Kassel and the Rothenburg *Quart*. The French blew up the castle in 1797 after seizing it without a fight. **Figure 10-2** (below) shows the Castle Katz (Cat) at St. Goarshausen, erected by the Katzenelnbogen counts in 1393. *Burg Katz* too was blown up by the French (1804).

Figure 10-3 is another view of *Burg Katz*. ***Figure 10-4*** provides a view at the Karlsaue in Kassel. This was the favorite promenade of the townspeople by the late nineteenth century. Originally laid out in 1709, it was later redeveloped in the English garden style, and featured many trees. Boats could be hired for enjoyment on the *Aue Teich*.

William undertook many internal administrative reform in Hesse as well. In 1736 he created a general tax reform commission to improve the so-called cadaster land records that recorded the holdings and tax duties at the village level. The commission set about a thorough overhaul of these records, including the addition of local maps. These records were further expanded upon during his son's rule, documenting population, farm animals, taxable income and property, draft-eligible males, as well as traditional feudal services and payments.

William's greatest personal challenge came with the decision of his son, the crown prince Frederick, to convert to Catholicism in disregard of the generations-long heritage of the Hessian ruling house. William was shocked and outraged, and he set in motion a host of measures to protect the realm from any steps Frederick might try to take in the future to return Hesse to Catholicism. He forced the prince to sign an accord in 1754 by which he forswore any future effort at imposing his faith on the state. He obtained formal assurances from other Protestant states to guarantee that this agreement was upheld. Similar assurances were obtained from the local estates of influential townsmen and nobles who worked with the landgraves in ruling the land. Frederick's prerogatives to address Hessian social and religious policy were formally curtailed.

The worst blow of all came as William set up an enclave in Hanau in which Frederick's wife could live in protection and independence with her eldest son and Frederick's heir; this ensured an eventual return to rule by a landgrave of the Reformed faith. Frederick and his consort had long been estranged by his frequent absences from court to serve in various campaigns, as well as his rather notorious reputation for womanizing while away from home. His Catholic conversion became the last straw.

In 1755 William signed a renewed agreement with Britain to rent the use of 12,000 Hessian troops in exchange for subsidies during the Seven Years War (1756-63). This brought him into conflict with the Franco-Austrian alliance whose troops chased him out of Hesse. By 1757 the treacherous surrender of the British Duke of Cumberland at Hastenbeck left Hesse isolated and helpless. Much of the Hessian army had to be disbanded, and Kassel surrendered to the victorious allies. Kassel stood true to her traditional ally, Prussia, throughout the war. The crown prince served with the Prussian army, commanding garrisons at Magdeburg and Wesel. The French forced the Hessian territories to provide ruinously high levels of financial support to their troops in the field. From 1758-59 Kassel changed hands several times between the French and English combatants, suffering terribly in the fighting. Once again her central location along lines of march cost Hesse dearly during the war as troops plundered the land thoroughly. The worst years were 1759-62, in which numerous battles occurred in upper Hesse.

In mid-war the government changed hands when William died and Frederick II assumed the seat of power. The actions of his father to ensure the reformed tradition had severely foreclosed Frederick's ability to act unilaterally in internal administration and external imperial politics alike. The depredations of the French kept Frederick out of his land until the peace was concluded in 1763. He brought with him three senior Prussian officers who served as his key advisors. Civil servants throughout the government were well paid by European standards, and most came from noble families with a tradition of government service. Many of these families intermarried over generations, reinforcing their ties as a ruling caste and cementing together relationships among families in the three administrative centers of Kassel, Rinteln and Marburg. Many were joined in social camaraderie in Masonic lodges that were founded beginning in 1743 with one at Marburg. The Kassel lodge grew to over 200 members.

Only with great difficulty did the land begin to recover from the wartime devastation. Five years of bountiful harvests helped the process along, but thereafter multiple years of crop failure ground the people down. With too little arable land, some of the worst climate conditions in Germany in terms of excessive rainfall, and 90% of the population dependent on farming, Hesse-Kassel always struggled to feed itself. Roads were difficult to maintain, and much traffic went around Hesse despite its central location. One of Frederick's Prussian-born officials lamented the lack of industry, stating that, "...all Hesse is a village. The towns and cities are merely villages enclosed with walls."[13]

The reforms undertaken by the government were basically conservative so as not to create problems for any particular group within society. As indicated earlier, the estates represented in the Hessian diet were active partners with Frederick and his government in promoting reform. They did not dominate him in these efforts, however, for his financial position was based on his personal ownership of most Hessian lands. He was landlord over two-thirds of the arable land and more than 80% of the population of 275,000. His trade in soldiers generated funds that accrued to his personal coffers, not those of the state. He also loaned money freely to influential members of the estates, tying them closely to him. These loans and appointed positions in government were key to the 100 or so old Hessian noble families who had lost much in the Seven Years War and found it increasingly difficult to squeeze enough out of their peasants to keep their lifestyles intact. About a third had already emigrated lock, stock and barrel to other states to seek brighter fortunes.

Frederick set about rebuilding his war-ravaged land according to the principles of the Enlightenment, a broadly-defined set of humanistic and liberal ideals for government. He addressed welfare, economic, and jurisprudential reforms, constraining the use of torture in legal practice and limiting fines and corporal punishment. He also insisted that punishment should be made public as a deterrent to crime. Free representation for peasants was instituted. The legal process itself was so replete with loopholes that numerous tactics could delay justice for years. The system was streamlined and lawyers were fined for undertaking purposeful delays. Their high fees were curtailed and they were required to pass proficiency exams for the first time. Hesse was somewhat under siege in the post-war period as many hopeless people had turned to crime. Use was made of the soldiery as constabulary forces and night watches and locked gates were ordered for all towns. The efforts to restrain torture and corporal punishment met with years-long opposition and required Frederick to act diligently and persistently to prevail. A common torture he eventually abolished was the *Drehhäuschen*, which were boxes mounted on turntables in which offenders could be placed and spun to punish lesser crimes. Frederick reserved the right to exact corporal punishment on deserters and other offenders in his military forces.

Working in partnership with the estates and his own bureaucracy, who seem to have been equally sincere in their desire to promote societal welfare, he passed many reform measures. Among these was passage of a national fire insurance fund in 1767. By 1768 the fund had four million *Taler* and was so successful it was copied by Hesse Darmstadt.

In 1761 the landgrave set up Kassel's expectant mothers' hospital and foundlings' orphanage; in 1772 a similar institution was opened to care for the indigent sick. The childbirth hospital sought to address the rise in illegitimate births that wartime had brought on, as well as a deplorable increase in infanticide. Parental authority seems to have eroded in the years 1763-87, often due to government policy that systematically altered patterns of inheritance, landholding and marriage to push children of the family farm at earlier ages and without adequate means. Hessian soldiers also had to seek the permission of their officers to marry, and this was not readily given. Rather than abstain, the soldiers not surprisingly maintained relationships with women near their garrisons that produced illegitimate offspring in growing numbers.

Unwed mothers could come in and not worry about public condemnation or the fines and penalties often associated with this offense against public morality. At the orphanage, parents could drop off infants through an anonymous turnstile that opened into the director's heated office, ringing a bell to alert the staff. The foundlings either went to paid foster families or stayed at the orphanage where they were taught trades. The hospital was also used as a training facility for midwives.

Frederick worked to promote expanded educational opportunities at all levels. At first he focused on the needs of the nobility because his father's broad-ranging edict prohibited Frederick from involving himself in the Calvinist religious system that ran basic education in Hesse. He tried to prop up the sagging fortunes of the universities in Marburg and Kassel by requiring more Hessian students to study at home rather than going abroad. He provided student stipend, bought new equipment, and hired more professors.

Reforms of all kinds drew heavily on the Prussian model, as well as other policies and practices Frederick encountered on his travels abroad. An ongoing tension existed among Hessian officialdom between the ideals of looking out for the economically challenged while still expecting budgets to remain balanced and public institutions to become self-supporting.

Hesse had very little of value to export. The raw wool trade, centered mainly in the Hersfeld and Eschwege areas, generated some income abroad. A small amount of iron production for export was done in Schmalkalden. The guilds in the towns were left impoverished by the war, and most members lived very marginal existences. Many were driven to begging. On the land, livestock losses to the marauding soldiers during the war amounted to two-thirds of all stock. A number of villages had been abandoned during the war. Conditions in town and country alike were so difficult that Hessian migration to others parts of the empire was common. The government immediately implemented a temporary tax moratorium to relieve the population of at least the most obvious financial strain. Proceeds from Frederick's soldier trade during and after the war was responsible for providing the cash needed to provide aid to the towns. Road improvements were implemented by hiring paid laborers at state expense. Forest protection was instituted by requiring the use of community bake ovens to cut down on wood use.

An Agrarian Society was set up to increase understanding and implementation of new farming techniques. It provided a forum for debate of related social conditions, such as the often crushing burden of feudal service duties owed to lords and local communities. In some cases up to half a farmer's time could be eaten up with performing these services. Taxes, tithes and service requirements varied greatly even over short distances within the country, creating much resentment among those heaviest burdened. The local nobility depended so greatly on the existing system for its livelihood that change came at a very slow pace. Still, hunting and forest labor services were curtailed on Frederick's own lands by his order, and peasants still required to participate were to be compensated with wages. Hauling service requirements could now be commuted on payment of a reasonable fee, the proceeds of which were used to pay for hauling. Other types of services also could be commuted beginning in 1776 on payment of similar fees.

Poor relief reform was another effort Frederick undertook in this period, providing bread, livestock, and seeds and encouraging the public at large to pitch in with private alms. Food prices were closely watched so the state could regulate any unreasonable price spikes. Minimum wage rates were promulgated for laborers, and minimum and maximum price levels were set up to ensure small farmers received decent compensation in boom years just as consumers were protected somewhat in years of crop failure.

Frederick tried to improve the environment for trade and commerce by instituting larger trade fairs and holding them more often, beginning with one in Kassel in March 1763. Merchants were given subsidies and waivers from import taxes to encourage their participation. Still, few merchants outside Hesse bothered to show up. Frederick recognized the need to address trade problems on various fronts, as he did in 1763 when he withdrew debased coinage from circulation and avoided issuing new money. Export taxes were abolished and the interest rate for loans was frozen at 5%. He founded many local factories, creating them at the rate of one a month on average from 1764-65. Textiles, tobacco, porcelain, plate glass, silk, and tapestries were all items of output from these concerns. A trading company at the Huguenot settlement of Karlshafen on the Weser was established to hawk these wares outside Hesse. By 1774 it was selling up to 800,000 *Taler* a year in reasonably-priced Hessian linen. Although free trade was an ideal that Frederick probably would have embraced, the protectionist practices of all his neighbors made this an impossible goal.

After a decade of hard work, the landgraviate had begun to turn the corner, and Frederick himself had been rehabilitated in the eyes of his subjects at all levels. The fear that he would impose Catholicism was seen to be misplaced, and his selfless work to restore the fortunes of his realm was clear for all to see. Henceforth Frederick ruled with more than the grudging acceptance of his subjects.

Now, however, the disastrous years of crop failure in 1770-71 struck across Germany and within Hesse. Here again, Frederick's conservative fiscal policy and well-stocked coffers would eventually prove sufficient to the task. In the beginning, however, the people across Hesse found themselves in very dire straits. Grain prices in Kassel doubled, tripled and then sextupled from 1770-72. The local bakeries were set upon by crowds of townsmen who went days at a time without food. Starvation was reported across the country and emigration again picked up. The government banned sales of grain abroad, froze prices and again waived tax payments for the suffering. Government grain stores were released in aid. Some 230,000 *Taler* in grain was purchased on foreign markets for shipment to Hesse. Relief included providing peasants with seed grain, allowing them to farm on Sundays and reducing their mandatory service requirements.

In the face of the crisis, Frederick's agrarian reforms moved ahead on many fronts. Uncultivated plots of land were identified and their owners given notice to use them, rent them out, or lose rights to them. Newlyweds were required to plant four fruit trees on unused lands. Efforts were made to replace the less-efficient three-field system with crop rotation, although lack of fertilizer and tradition-bound opposition had to be overcome. The increased use of stall feeding was necessary to generate manure to be stockpiled for fertilizer; this in turn required broader planting of clover for animal feed. Animal holders in towns protested the need to buy fodder for the first time to implement stall feeding. From 1773 to 1781 livestock production increased over 50% to more than

810,000 head. Other measures included the reduction of the number of church holidays on which peasants were forbidden to work. About two dozen work days were thus saved. This was patterned on a similar law that was in force in Hesse-Darmstadt. The peasantry were resistant to this change as well. More popular was the introduction of the potato. Famine makes for a greatly increased willingness to innovate, and potatoes clearly were capable of promoting caloric intake in hard times.

Frederick established a policy of intercepting migrants as they traveled through Hesse for promised lands in Prussian and other areas. He granted them identical concessions in Hesse, settling them in sixteen settlements with the goal of replacing some of the population losses his lands had suffered. These efforts were not blessed with much success, however. The newcomers lacked skills and ambition, and the lands they received were not very fertile. Most were sent away again by 1779.

In 1775 the landgrave introduced hereditary leases to all the peasants on his expansive land holdings. This was in contrast to the shorter lease terms that were gaining popularity elsewhere. This increased peasants' incentives to make their land as productive as possible. The nobility over time began to follow suit. Less successful was an effort to eliminate feudal tithes by payment of a fixed fee to the lord. The landowners' opposition squelched this reform effort. Taken together, the government's reform programs had the beneficial effect of increasing productivity on the land by 1777.

In broader areas of reform, Frederick's Italian travels inspired him to create a Hessian academy for the antiquities in 1777, after which he passed a law for the protection of Hessian monuments and other ancient artifacts (1780). In 1767 he began to have the old Kassel town fortifications torn down to provide room for further architectural development. From 1769-79 he had a renowned modern museum built and filled with interesting objects; it was named the Fridericianum. An opera house was developed in the palace of prince Maximilian in 1765. His work in developing Kassel reflected Frederick's love of French culture, art and architecture, which set the predominant tone for all his renovations. A less positive development was his decision in 1771 to establish a state lottery. It was an instant success, but complaints were soon raised that people were taking off from work for a day at a time to attend the drawings. Net profits of 12% explain the popularity of the lottery in the mind of the prince.

A final important reform program under Frederick was the variety of efforts he undertook in the middle years of his reign to alleviate poverty and care for the indigent. Public assistance was extended along with encouragement to the better-off citizenry to do more in contributing alms to the needy poor. Poverty had dropped off in the post-war years of economic reform, but it spiked up again when the famine years struck. Private giving to charities in the same period had greatly tapered off. The orphan's home in Kassel was overwhelmed with the number of children coming to it via the laying-in hospital and child drop-off system. Most children in the crowded and unsanitary conditions of the two institutions never made it to maturity.

At last the landgrave decided in 1773 to enact a poor tax in larger towns that was geared to the ability to pay of individual citizens. The proceeds were to go to local poor relief as well as hospitals for the poor and similar institutions. About this time free health care was given to the indigent victims of epidemic diseases. Medical training and the right to practice health care was addressed by regulation, requiring recognized providers to pass test and enjoining barbers and other laymen to cease ministering to patients. Another means to free up money for relief was seen to be restrictions on sumptuous displays in entertainment and other forms of conspicuous consumption. Expensive clothing of various types was again prohibited. Chocolate and coffee consumption was tightened down upon because these were seen to lead to laziness and lack of ambition. Coffee was considered a health risk because it made men jittery and induced miscarriage and bleeding in women. Imported goods of various kinds were attacked, particularly non-Hessian clothing purchases, foreign beer, and tobacco. Hessian-brewed beer was touted as the ultimate promoter of good health. Peasants were ordered to wear good Hessian wool and linen instead of calico and cotton that were becoming fashionable.

The government confronted a variety of other problems in its war on poverty. Textile workers who processed flax into piecework were receiving wages that kept them in poverty and the buyers were warned to increase the rates or risk punishment. Much attention was paid to policies that protected farmers from losing their land, tools or animals in hard times. Debt moratoriums for set periods were extended, along with prohibitions on tax collectors' seizing livestock or other assets from those who could not pay. Reimbursements were given for losses due to hail, fire or other natural disasters, including livestock deaths.

Upwards of 33% of farmers were reduced to working plots of under five acres at a time when the government found that it took twelve to eighteen acres to feed a family. A revised land edict in 1773 strictly prohibited dividing lands in inheritance, directing that a single heir should obtain the lion share of the inheritance, including all the land. Protests from the farmers were loud and constant because of the hardships this brought to non-inheriting children. Begging and indigence grew out of the rule as well because the dispossessed had no recourse. This became another spur to emigration. On the plus side from the point of view of the government, many more young men joined the army as a means of earning their bread.[14]

By 1784 it became apparent that much of the mercantilist government policy that created and favored local factory enterprises was a failure. Some factory owners were so deeply in debt and hounded by their creditors that they committed suicide. But state subsidies and protective tariffs were continued where the government perceived a vested interest in keeping an enterprise going, even when there was no business case to be made for continuing in the face of outside competition. A 50% tariff on coffee was maintained because the government wanted the revenue despite the negative impact this had on the trade fair in Kassel; few foreign merchants were bothering to visit. The porcelain factory operated at less than half of capacity notwithstanding its penetration of the American market as a result of the contacts it made during the Revolutionary War. It had to dump its unsold products on the local market at liquidation prices. A hot chocolate factory received government support and a complete ban on competing imports in an effort to redirect local consumption. In Eschwege 57% of the textile guild masters were out of work.

Agricultural policy in this era was ripe for change as the government finally began to acknowledge that farming was and would remain the dominant trade in Hesse. Efforts were made in 1782 to finally enforce at the local level the existing prohibitions on many feudal services. These had been honored in the breach for years. Service requirements to support hunts and provide forest service were widely abused, causing interruptions in peasants' efforts to work their lands and bring in harvests. These abuses were creating hundreds of cases of litigation in which peasants were suing to alleviate this burden. The first halting steps were taken to allow peasants to buy themselves out from feudal obligations altogether, but only in the following century would a thorough reform program emerge. After a long hiatus during the war service of the army in America, peace allowed the government to reinstate the *Kontribution* tax paid by everyone to support the army (1784). These were years of crop failure again, however, and desperate times drove many honest men to become robbers on the highways. Debt relief had to be implemented to stave off wholesale bankruptcy by the people. The tax went on, however. Population growth in this period consumed the fruits of any effort to improve agricultural output. Land was at a huge premium.

With such pressures, poor relief also was naturally the focus of renewed debate. The poor rolls continued to grow in the 1780s. Kassel's poor rolls included 4-5% of the population, and although larger German towns had double digit numbers, the poor remained a significant problem for such a poor state. Groups of beggars going door to door in the capital was a bothersome sight. The supposed solution was to pare back the rolls to only the truly indigent and handicapped, and put others to work in the poor house. By 1785 almost a quarter of Kassel's poor were consigned to the workhouse. The lying-in hospital and orphans' home were in a state of crisis due to overcrowding. Hesse was experiencing the same trend common across Europe at this time: an explosion of illegitimate births.[15] One- and two-year-olds were being stuffed at night into the turnstile meant only for newborns. The laying-in hospital was being visited multiple times by shameless girls who continued to bear illegitimate babies. The turnstile approach had to be given up, first at night and then altogether.[16]

HESSE-HANAU

Frederick's son and heir went about his own efforts to improve the financial and architectural life in little Hesse-Hanau, appointing Meyer Amschel Rothschild his court *Faktor* in 1769 and providing him with the proceeds of troops subsidies that amounted to over 465,000 pounds sterling. Rothschild's masterful financial dealings gave the landgrave a tremendous return over many years. Rothschild's sons and heirs similarly benefited by building a financial empire in Frankfurt and London. The advent and publication of the first magazine of local Hessian history occurred in Hanau (1778-85). Similar publications later appeared in Kassel and Marburg based on the Hanau model.

William succeeded Frederick into the government in Kassel in 1785 as one of the wealthiest princes of his time. He quickly canceled the state lottery that was seen as sapping the wealth of too many of the Hessian poor with its empty promises of instant wealth. Like his father he too circumscribed what remained of torture in the legal system, abolished the mandatory and highly unpopular church penance payment, and curtailed the mortgaging of various districts of the realm that had been undertaken in 1773. He even enacted a law (1785) to protect his subjects from air-borne fire hazards coming from hot air balloons flying over his land. The new landgrave also called a halt to excessive display and overly-sumptuous life at court, and like his grandfather and other previous landgraves he made clear his abhorrence of French fashion and culture, dismissing Frenchmen from his court. French comedies and ballets were quickly deemed unfashionable. He enriched the architectural beauty of Kassel by building the famous Wilhelmshöhe, an English-style castle opened in 1798.

William IX turned his hand to numerous efforts to improve the Hessian economy. Road building, factory creation, and improving the lives of the peasantry by abolishing various forms of enforced labor on state farms all were undertaken.

Externally, William also hewed to the traditional political line of his forebears by maintaining the closest of relations with Prussia. He overreached in 1787 in an attempt to seize by force the Lippe portion of the Schaumburg inheritance when the reigning count died. His own Prussian allies forced him to give way in this effort, which clearly violated the law of the empire. He also used further English subsidies obtained by renting his troops to further pad his treasury. A dedicated opponent of the French Revolution, he was among the foremost participants in the Austro-Prussian invasion that tried rather half-heartedly to nip the revolution in the bud. He also led his forces in ejecting French forces from Frankfurt in 1792. The French were handed the magnificent Rheinfels castle by a foolish Hessian commander who gave up without a fight in 1794, much to William's mortification. The French blew it to smithereens before abandoning it in 1796.[17]

RURAL LIFE IN HESSE-KASSEL

Life on the land in the eighteenth century was fraught with challenges. As indicated above, natural disasters, social change, and economic dislocations came in waves through the century. In contrast to the widespread practice of the seventeenth century of landlords letting out their land for specific contract periods, during the eighteenth century land use practices evolved to the point that almost all peasant holdings became inheritable. As we have seen, the Landgrave Frederick was leading the charge here with his revised policy of 1775. Barring misuse of the land, inability to work it, or some other extraordinary circumstance, the peasant family could rely on holding a given parcel of farmland for generations. They could not be dispossessed so long as the designated dues and obligations were paid to those who controlled the land. The peasant holder could also mortgage or sub-lease parts of the land with the landlord's permission. This type of landholding arrangement provided both the personal incentive and the legal responsibility to make the land as productive as possible.

Predominant but by no means exclusive was the *Anerbensystem*, the practice of endowing a single offspring with almost the entire family inheritance of house and land. Other children typically were provided for with a sum of money intended to give them a start elsewhere in life. In practice, the *Anerbensystem* inheritance required that the farm be inventoried and a value assessed on every item, animal and implement. The parents were permitted to choose which child would be favored with the bulk of the inheritance, male or female. Title usually passed upon the marriage of the favored child. A wife marrying an inheriting son became a 50% owner with him in the family holdings. The woman's dowry became at the same time the shared property of her husband. To compensate other inheritors, the assessed value of the family property was heavily discounted below actual value and the resulting sum became the basis for paying the others their share. This often was called the "brothers and sisters tax" (*Geschwistertaxe*). Payments were usually due upon the marriage of those siblings or at the time when the parents passed away. Younger children often stayed on the farm until they became adults at about age eighteen, or in some cases as late as thirty.

The alternative was known as *Realteilung*, in which multiple heirs were given parts of the arable land, and sometimes even shared ownership in the family home. *Realteilung* often gave limited precedence to the eldest child, who would receive the house and outbuildings. Other children each would receive an equal portion of the available farmlands. *Realteilung* was predominant in the following areas: many villages around Kassel; the districts of Schmalkalden, Gelnhausen, Hanau, Biedenkopf, Wolfhagen and Frankenberg; in some villages in the districts of Eschwege and Kirchhain; in Nassau; and Hessian areas of the Rhineland. Over time some government action had to be taken to prevent partitioning of lands into plots too small to support anyone adequately. In Nassau some parents even tried to partition their farmhouses for multi-family dwelling. Areas in which R*ealteilung* was practiced for any length of time came to have large numbers of economically marginalized smallholders. Burdensome debts were incurred to pay off siblings.

The state took an increasingly active interest in inheritance practices because the landgrave was by far the largest landholder. His tax revenue was dependent on the peasantry under his personal control, since the lands and peasants of the lesser nobility were exempt from taxation by the state according to centuries-old law and practice. Prosperous farmers were solid taxpayers, but economically weak farmers made poor contributors to the state's coffers as they struggled to eke out a living on tiny, oft-divided sub-plots. The state sought to protect its tax base by ensuring that inheritances were kept together in plots large enough to sustain a family and generate surpluses. A so-called hide edict (*Hufenedikt*) was promulgated in 1773 to preclude the endowment of more than a single heir to the family property and limit payments to siblings. This was intended to avoid laming inheritors with small plots and too much debt. The Kassel authorities long had held that anything less than a full *Hufe* farm (over eighteen acres) was too little to guarantee a living to an average family. Their efforts to force compliance with a winner-take-all approach must be understood in that light.

The practical effect of this law was to inflict hardship on the disinherited. It aggrieved many parents who were unable to provide for children destined to face poverty upon reaching maturity. Loud and long complaints were heard across the land about the effect of this policy. Disinherited people often were unable to afford to marry and raise families. Older children who knew they were destined to be cut out of inheritance became unwilling to contribute to the upkeep of the family farm. Even local officials picked up the refrain in reports to the capital. Impoverished citizens were creating problems and cost burdens for many local areas as poor relief rolls rose. The government relented and repealed the edict in 1786, allowing partitions in two to four pieces with official consent.[18]

Pressure for multiple-heir inheritances increased in the eighteenth century as population grew; growth was sufficient by the 1730s to have made up for all the losses of the Thirty Years War; after the mid-century mark it continued at an even faster pace. War and epidemic disease, two primary agents that previously had kept growth in check, were mostly absent in this period. A good case in point was the village of Körle in the Fulda valley, about twenty kilometers south of Kassel. It grew 76% in population from 1776-1834, numbering 532 inhabitants by the latter date.

At the century's end the majority of Hesse-Kassel farms were so small that their owners had to take up another trade to make ends meet. In many villages weavers, potters, nail makers, turners, etc. numbered among the farming population. It was in this time period that basalt quarrying in the Westerwald area developed as a second source of farmers' income on a wide scale. The stone was easily removed and transported on the roads. On the high Westerwald plateaus the quarrymen-farmers created cooperatives. These were worked intensively when the major farm chores were done each season, and paving stones and column-shaped road edgings were cut and shipped to other parts of Germany for sale. Towns snapped up these paving materials, giving farmers a source of side income when agricultural downturns occurred.[19]

The pursuit of a trade as well as farming had a major impact on the social structure of the rural class system that prevailed in Hesse in this era. The 1745 cadaster records from the village of Grandenborn, northeast of Sontra, provides an interesting view of a typical village hierarchy in a 350-person mixed community of farmers, laborers and farming tradesmen. The wealthiest strata was that of landowners who made their living by farming alone. They held on average 64.6 *Acker* of land, about forty acres, and constituted 17% of the population. The next group were also endowed with land, but they supplemented their incomes with a trade. They were 27% of the population, and averaged about thirty acres in landholding. Third in line were still smaller farmers practicing a trade, 19% of the population with just under twenty-five acres apiece. The last two categories constituted the poorest villagers: those with houses but just under five acres of land, who were 25% of the population; and the so-called *Beisitzer*, who owned no house but worked as laborers and took lodgings with others in the village. This group formed 12% of the population, or forty-two souls, and averaged only three acres of land. Grandenborn was in microcosm a representation of many Hessian villages in which the majority of people depended on trade in non-agricultural goods and services to supplement their incomes. [20] "Enfranchised" farmers, or those who held rights to common lands such as pastures and meadows by virtue of their landholding in the village, had enormous economic and social advantage over the *Beisitzer* and others not so endowed. Speaking of upper Hesse in the mid-eighteenth century, Peter Taylor has described this phenomenon.

> ...[E]nfranchised villagers dominated the disenfranchised because the latter could make ends met only through their ties of dependence on the better-off. The system of authority and domination in village corporations rested on three legs. (1) As part of the system of tributary *Herrschaft*, the village corporation and its officials acquired the power to use sanctions against other villagers...(2) The capacity of enfranchised villagers to act in common thwarted undesirables from taking up residence in villages and protected common resources from the village poor. (3) Finally, control over common resources gave the dominant group in any village a way of selecting who might serve as an independent household in the village and under what conditions...Less fortunate villagers continually faced the choice between dependence on these clients of nobles or varied forms of ruin.[21]

Taxes, tithes and compulsory services owed to lords continued to play a huge a role in the common person's life in this period. Taxes and services were assessed against villages as a whole, and apportioned among the villagers according to their ability to pay. In Körle, whose overlord was the landgrave himself, we find a typical example of the types and amount of burdens imposed. The landgrave's arable land in the Melsungen district (which administered Körle) amounted to 253 *Acker* (over 156 acres) of farmland, fifty-one *Acker* (31.5 acres) of meadow, and over eighteen acres of garden land; these holdings formed the basis for compulsory labor services assessed on the local farmers. But by the latter eighteenth century these lands had long since been given over to local people in rental agreements. This meant that the district owed monetary payments in lieu of services to the lord. The district tab was 244 *Taler* and two *Albus*, divvied up as annual debts owed by individual villages and their farmers. Körle's share was forty-nine *Taler*, twenty-eight *Albus*. Every homeowner in the village had to pay just over twenty-two *Albus*; the rest was apportioned to the villagers in proportion to the amount of acreage they held.

The enfranchised villagers also had to haul wood from local woods for use by the court at Kassel. Since the only feasible way to do this was to ship the logs on the river, the villagers had to pay annually for the transportation. This came to more than fifty-two *Taler* per year. Another thirty *Taler* were payable annually to cover transport costs for hauling "his lordship's produce" from areas south of Kassel to the capital. Fifty more *Taler* had to be paid for hauling building materials. Eight cords of wood had to be cut and hauled to the landgrave's local rent collector in Melsungen, and more in the form of firewood for the landgrave's use when he was visiting. Other hauling had to be done when requested by the state administration. Körle's location on the main postal road between Kassel and Nuremberg meant that the local farmers for generations had sold their hauling services to a variety of customers as a side occupation. Hauling services were thus a logical imposition to place on them. Beyond these services and payments, individuals could be called upon to help with other hauling in connection with repairs to local mills and public buildings, assistance to overlords in local hunts, providing forest maintenance services, and even carrying mail locally. In wartime, an artillery horse had to be provided by Körle, the cost of which was shared among five farmers.

These duties and services were obviously a huge burden, especially in lean years, for the population of Körle. By extension, hundreds of other villages provided additional volumes of free labor, produce and money. In bad times the landgrave and other lords were supposed to waive some of these burdens, but this largely was a matter for their own consciences dictated no doubt by the press of their own needs. The communal need to provide services made for endless wrangling and arguments among the local farmers who had to decide how to apportion the burden among themselves as a community. Men would do the harder physical work, and women lighter work on specially-designated women's work days. Two women's work days were considered equal to one man's day. Better-off farmers with horses would undertake heavy hauling and other farm tasks, while the underclass farmers had to serve in manual labor and messenger work.

The peasants rarely but increasingly resisted these burdens in the late eighteenth and early nineteenth centuries, with the result that police and even military forces had to be used to enforce compliance. Arrest or corporal punishment could be levied, or sometimes the complaining farmers' horses would be impounded as punishment, only to be released on payment of fines.[22]

In one case, collective opposition seems to have forced some rethinking by the authorities. In 1737 a tithe ordinance was issued aimed at requiring the tithe on a class of crops previously exempt, those grown as side production on the fallow ground held back from grain production every third year. These were typically peas, beans, cabbage, etc., and were a traditional source of extra calories for the farmers. In the 1740s a series of court cases were brought against the tithe lords seeking to have the rule reversed. At last the landgrave relented and withdrew the state ordinance on which the tithe claim was based. But by 1754 this new tithe was re-imposed.

Grain and produce tithes had to be stored in barns out of the elements, and for many reasons were an inconvenience to the collecting lords as well as to their peasantry. Many of these barns fell into disrepair over time, and keeping them up was a significant task. For these reasons the practice arose beginning in the mid-eighteenth century of selling the tithing rights back to the peasantry themselves. This was called *Vermalterung*, and allowed tithes to be eliminated based on payment of a set sum of money or crops each year. Lesser tithes could be bought out for three- or six-year periods. In 1766 the Hersfeld district's total cost for its *Vermalterungen* amounted to over 1,842 *Taler*.[23]

Despite such substantial amounts imposed on the communities they controlled, in many cases the income proved insufficient to maintain the lords' lifestyles. Many had to mortgage or sell their lands to the landgrave or to other secular or ecclesiastical lords, as the widow Anna Margarethe von Buchenau had to do in 1702 when she needed to outfit her son for military service and her daughter for life at court. She mortgaged the tithe rights to various of her properties to four separate mortgagors, including the landgrave. He soon bought up the debt from the other three. By 1722 this allowed him to acquire rights to the Schildschlag district, formerly Buchenau lands.

A most difficult time for the peasantry came in the fall after harvest when most of their taxes and tithes fell due. Often they had to hand over so much of their produce that it was all but impossible to live through the winter on the remainder. One local official reported that his peasants barely had the wherewithal to last until the feast of St. Peter (February 22). From 1786-88 the tiny hamlet of Solms had to hand over almost two-thirds of its rye and 80% of its oats. Officials often wrote to their higher ups asking that taxes be remitted until later in the winter when villagers could at least sell their produce for decent prices to obtain their tax money. Too often they all were forced to sell at the same time when the market was glutted and prices were too low to turn much profit. Such reports seem to have been as common in the 1730s as the 1780s.[24]

Hesse was blessed with poor land but a central location, and the landgrave jealously guarded his right to impose tolls on those who used the roads. The condition of the roads had much to do with their attractiveness to merchants who had various routes to choose from in traveling to markets in Frankfurt and elsewhere. Sometimes roads were so bad that driving had to be done on the sides of the road, often damaging farm fields. Roadwork was another aspect of personal service periodically demanded of local farmers. Twice a year in spring and fall the state road inspector would survey the roads and record any damage to be repaired. The communities would have to turn out masses of men with their own shovels, picks, axes, etc. to make the needed repairs. The surfaces were smoothed with heavy blows in the absence of rolling machines that only came much later. Fines could be levied on those who sent the infirm, children, or others incapable of doing the hard work. Lesser lords had to organize road repairs in areas under their control using their own peasant levies.

Exemptions from standard services were made for various classes of people, whose numbers increased in the course of the eighteenth century. State officials were mostly exempt, although if they held property on which service duties were assessed they had to see that the peasants living on those lands provided what was required. Shepherds, village heads (*Dorfgreben*), and judicial officials were exempt. Widows had the requirement reduced by half. The exemptions were only from normal services, not those imposed in times of disaster or emergency.[25]

When a farmer obtained a farm by taking on a letter contract (*Meierbrief*) from the landlord, the practice from ancient times was for him to host a celebratory banquet for his new lord with food and wine. This *Weinkauf* became the recognized means of sealing the deal and making it fully legal. Over time the *Weinkauf* feast went out of style, and was commuted into a standard monetary payment to the lord. This payment then became the act that rendered the contract legal. A similar payment of 5% of the land value had to be paid to the lord if the farmer wanted to sell or lease rights to the land to another person. Sometimes transfer of the ownership to the heirs of a deceased peasant also required a payment, known as *Lehngeld*. The payment due could be a much as 10% if the lord was one of the lesser nobility.

Taxation of the peasantry in Hesse-Kassel was in major part levied under the so-called *Kontribution*. Originally a periodic tax to support the defense of the Landgraviate, later a monthly tax to support the standing army. Tax reform took place in the eighteenth century, as indicated earlier. It was based on actual values of land and other assets determined at the local level by the "cadaster" records. These surveys were much more accurate than the records previously relied upon for tax assessments, (the old *Salbücher*). The properties and peasants of the nobility were exempt from the *Kontribution* because from time immemorial they had been required to help provide for the common defense by making available men, peasant services and other means of support whenever wars occurred. Although this support had become meaningless in the modern era of professional armies, the tax exemption remained. Those required to pay the tax along with their typical land rents were hard pressed financially.

The cadaster records allowed the state an unparalleled view into the inner workings and resources of the villages, permitting them to be administered much more directly and efficiently (from the landgrave's perspective). The village headman and other senior members of the community became recognized officials of the state administration to a degree never before experienced. Their responsibilities at the local and district levels increased apace.[26]

Not only income and land holding generated tax fees for the lord, but so did other major milestones in life, such as marriage. The *Zuchthaussteuer* tax was introduced in the eighteenth century as yet another income source for the state. Every newly married couple had to pay four *Gutegroschen* in taxes. Later this was made a progressive tax based on the couple's position in one of eight social classes. Not surprisingly, many who lived near the borders began going to nearby jurisdictions to marry in order to escape the tax. This led in 1731 to the tax being removed from marriages and instead imposed on public dances, festivals and annual church founding celebrations (*Kirmesen*).

What was life on the farm like in these times? Unquestionably it was largely driven by hard work, for with soils of indifferent quality and weather that tended to be raw, Hesse was no agricultural paradise. The Wetterau with its richer soils may have been something of an exception. Rye and oats were overwhelmingly the crops of choice in this era. Wheat and barley were grown only in the areas with richer soils, such as the Landeck district. The poor, stony soils mostly demanded the brute force of the ox to plow; use of plow-horses had diminished greatly by the eighteenth century. The three-field system of winter crop/spring crop/fallow annual rotation was in full force, with regulations set in place to govern communal land use. The fallow could not be broken up in the spring before May 1 (*Walpurgis*); and in fall it could not be plowed over until St. Michael's Day (September 29). In between times it was to be left to grazing by the huge numbers of sheep that roamed the lands.

Yields were from three to (at best) four times the amount of seed sown, an extraordinarily low yield for this era. As noted earlier, the state championed any reform measures it could identify to help boost yields. An obvious requirement was to increase the number of cattle and other farm animals whose dung could be gathered for use as fertilizer on the fields. But to make this effective fodder had to be made available in amounts sufficient to permit stall housing and feeding. Otherwise the animals had to be pastured on the harvested fields and meadows where their droppings would be lost for purposes of intensive fertilizing.

In a land as poor as Hesse it is perhaps not surprising that some would resort to crop stealing, which became a considerable problem. Despite severe penalties being enacted for these miscreants, the problem persisted. Night watches had to be posted in the fields at harvest time to protect them. In the Hersfeld area all manner of crops were pilfered night and day. The perpetrators were described as "day-thieves and farm hands," and a watch was placed on all four of the town gates to try to catch them in the act. Combined with immediate and severe penalties for those caught coming into town with stolen goods, this seems to have helped to a degree.[27]

Life depended to a considerable extent on access to the forests for firewood, building materials, and pasture for pigs and other foragers. All these aspects of forest use were strictly controlled by the lords who held rights to the forests, especially the landgraves and many lesser nobles who were particularly concerned with care of the woods because of their love of the hunt. More than half the land was still covered by forests in which oaks and beeches predominated. The common pine tree was much more in retreat at this time. But the use of forests for grazing, charcoal production, and other purposes was creating barren stretches in many areas.

Tension between the forest owners and local peasants and townsmen was a constant phenomenon because local needs always exceeded the lords' willingness to grant access and use. The preservation of existing woods and wild game to ensure viable stocks of prey for the hunts also created much wrangling. The game animals often emerged from the woods into nearby fields to eat crops, yet killing them was forbidden under poaching laws. Farmers had to hire watchmen to guard the fields day and night, and still much was lost to the animals. The periodic hunts were grand spectacles of butchery. It was common for 500 head of deer to be dispatched and sent around to local communities. Here the game was required to be sold to the locals. To add to the unpopularity of hunts, they also generated compulsory service by local farmers, as noted earlier. A major hunt in 1721 in the Landeck District required that 440 horses be provided by the district population for use by the hunting party, plus another eighty provided by other districts. Periodic efforts were made by the landgraves to reduce the nobles' use of compulsory service in support of the hunts because it was eating into the time when peasants needed to be working in their fields and providing mandatory service in more important tasks. Such a regulation was issued in 1763.

Over the years the landgraves began to fear for the health of their forests because oak trees were in obvious decline. By the 1730s new building could only be undertaken with the express approval of the state exchequer. Lower stories of houses were to be built of stone or other materials to spare the scarce oak, and spaces between the beams were directed to be increased. Penalties of up to 100 guilders were levied on those who sold wood outside Hesse. In 1740 a man in Widdershausen (Werra District) had to pay a five *Taler* fine for sending a cord of wood to his widowed sister near Eisenach when the woman was in dire need. In 1790 joiners were directed to stop using so many unnecessary horizontal spars that consumed the scarce oak.[28]

A combination school house and prayer room built in 1721 in the Westerwald area (between Koblenz and Siegen, formerly part of Nassau) illustrates the competing demands of forest preservation and community buildings. Decorative gothic elements were added to its façade by about 1730; shortly thereafter this type of building and wooden decoration were banned in the interest of saving wood. It is typical of the kind of structures that appeared in the center of many small villages, serving as multi-purpose meeting houses for secular and religious needs. Communal bakeries were central to village social life. Individual bake ovens on every farm property were outlawed over time to promote wood conservation. In Nassau the community bakery was the first public building created in many villages. As noted earlier, these might double as sites for other public purposes. Schools, teachers' quarters, poor houses, and other uses have been recorded. Fire stations might be sited in bakeries too, or have their own separate buildings. In Nassau, compulsory fire brigades existed as early as the seventeenth century. The old stations were called *Bollesje*, and traditionally beggars and other indigents could be locked up there as punishment.[29]

Population increases in the eighteenth century brought about changes in the structure and layout of many villages. Villages laid out in long, ribbon-like strings of structures were becoming filled in and turning into compact settlements as dwellings were built around a central square. Streets between the houses were narrow and jumbled with little thought given to future needs. Custom often dictated that a linden tree would grace the town square; superstition from time immemorial held that these trees warded off witches, storms, lightning and other evils. It was on the square that wells, communal bakeries, chapels, schools and other public buildings might also be found. This was the heart of village society, where people young and old met to converse, decide matters concerning agricultural activity, hold court about local disputes, or witness the performances of wandering players. Here a town crier made announcements that concerned the whole community.

Village trades included forges for fabricating wagon wheels and other implements. Such forges had grinding stones mounted on wooden frames for bending metal tires. Stone blocks were used to mount the tires on the wagon wheels. Heavier-duty metal working could be performed by water-driven hammers, such as one authorized by the landgrave for construction in 1773 in Battenberg on the Eder. The founding owners were a bureaucrat administrator of ironworks named Döpp, a lawyer named Klingelhöfer, and a Captain Stapp of the town militia of Battenberg.[30]

Sheep holding and the production of wool remained of critical importance to the Hessian economy. Sheep were the most widely cultivated type of farm animal at this time. The landgraves held the rights to sheep folding on any land not otherwise being cultivated. Many villages had long since been granted rights to maintain flocks, but creation of a new sheep fold could only be done with the express permission of the state exchequer. Sheep holders had to pay annually for the right to maintain their flocks, including tax money, mutton, and pasture fees. Even butter, cheese and sour sheep's milk had to be provided in specified amounts to the landgrave or other granting lord. The lowly shepherd performed a critical function for the state economy, but his profession was looked down upon by society. Shepherds would accompany their flocks around the pastures, some with huts on wheels or wagons that allowed them to carry along a bed, a bench and perhaps a small stove.

Every year before the feast of St. Peter (February 22) a survey was made of the number of sheep being held so a basis for taxing the herds could be established. No animal could be sold prior to this annual accounting. A certain number of lambs and sheep were taken by the landgrave's shepherds each spring for his own flocks. After a summer of being fattened on the landgrave's pastures sheep would be slaughtered in the fall to provide the court with mutton. In 1735 the landgrave's share in such sheep amounted to 1,700 head which were brought from around the landgraviate and pastured near Kassel. Well over 200,000 sheep were being held across Hesse by the second half of the century when sheep holding reached its greatest extent. Communities often were at odds over access to the same pastures. By the close of the century a noticeable fall-off was under way.

Hans Lerch has described the wool trade as a gold mine for the Hessian poor living in marginal areas along hills and mountains. Spinning took place in homes and the resulting sales of thread brought much-needed cash to many a family. Wool was easier than flax to work into yarn. Carding was done to loosen the fibers and make it easier to spin. Spinning twisted the fibers together to form a knot-free thread, and the foot-powered wheel left both hands free to feed the fibers. Hessian wool goods were shipped regionally down the Rhine and sold internationally via the markets in Köln (Cologne) and Aachen. Master wool weavers employed thousands in Frankenberg, Hersfeld, and other areas of upper and lower Hesse.[31]

In addition to wool, flax weaving also was an extremely common means pursued by lower income folk to earn additional wages. The whole family got into the act of harvesting, processing and spinning the flax. Even twelve-year-olds could master the spinning wheel and while away evening hours in productive effort. In winter the family could spend every waking hour processing flax from four or five in the morning until dark. Hired hands and servant girls would be given an allotted amount of thread that they would have to produce in addition to their daily chores, which presumably were lighter in the winter when so much of the farm work was no longer possible. Spinning groups of young men and women would gather across the land to socialize as they worked on the wool or the flax. Singing and other music, dancing, telling tall tales, or reading aloud were means of entertainment at these get-togethers.

A rural linen weaver's guild was recognized by the landgrave and granted guild rights alongside the town guilds. Based in Hersfeld, it embraced the districts of Petersberg, Johannisberg, the Dechanei area with Tann and Rohrbach, Niederaula, and Obergeis. The original monopoly rights of the guild to buy and sell linen thread were set aside in 1745 so that anyone could trade in the thread across Hesse-Kassel. This created competitive pressure from foreign merchants and Jews that eroded profits greatly. Still, in 1774 the rural guild had 600 masters and the linen makers gave the wool weavers a real run for their money during the eighteenth century. As with wool, the linen trade reached its greatest extent in the latter half of the century. Market ships would ply the Fulda, picking up and transporting the linen produced in villages like Körle that lined the river routes. America became an important export market after the Hessians developed ties there during the American Revolution. The Leipzig and Frankfurt fairs snapped up the Hessian product, which was both expensive and high in quality. Increasing volumes were shipped to Bielefeld and other Westphalian towns from which it was transshipped abroad via major German and Dutch ports, especially Bremen. English and Spanish colonies in the new world were major customers.[32]

Beer and brandy were the drinks of choice in the eighteenth century, and many people grew their own hops and made their own home-brew. In rural areas the landgrave bestowed exclusive brewing rights on the larger settlements in exchange for taxes and fees. These concessions were agreed upon for set terms of three, six or nine years, and had to be renewed when they expired or upon the death of the reigning landgrave. A forty-gallon keg of beer cost about ten *Kopfstück*, or forty *Albus*. Unlike beer, the brandy trade was commonly seen as a problem by the authorities, leading to drunkenness with all its adverse consequences. A recess of 1791 sought to constrict consumption at a time when every village had one or two dram shops selling brandy. They were apparently much more common than beer shops.[33]

Farmhouse furniture in this era was made by carpenters, and was mostly of very basic design. Tables were outfitted with benches rather than chairs, although a single flat chair with ornamental backrest was common. A decorative plate shelf often graced the kitchen/entrance area. Chests were the most common and prized possessions of the farm wife, originally containing her trousseau and storage for her clothing. Other common elements were a bed and cradle brought to the marriage by the bride. Late in the century the classic German wardrobe or *Schrank* was introduced in northern Hesse based on rural adaptation of styles becoming increasingly common in towns.

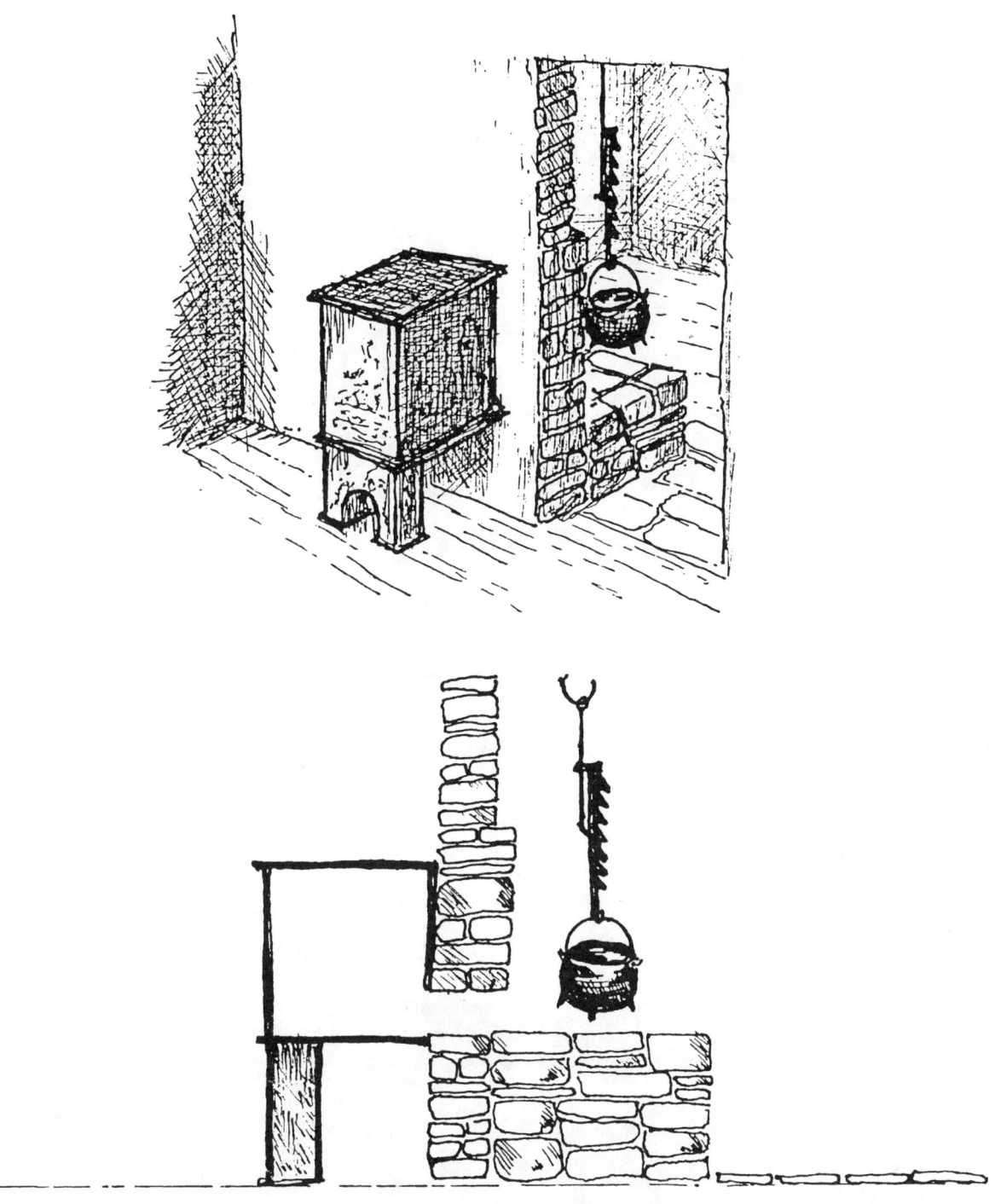

Figures 10-5/10-6 Shows the rear-loading oven (*Hinterladenofen*) used for heating, as discussed in this chapter. The oven was loaded with wood from the kitchen side working through the opening in the raised hearth. The smoke escaped back through the same hole into the kitchen, sparing the sitting room or *Stube* from smoke. Courtesy, Open Air Museum Hessenpark, Neu-Anspach, Germany.

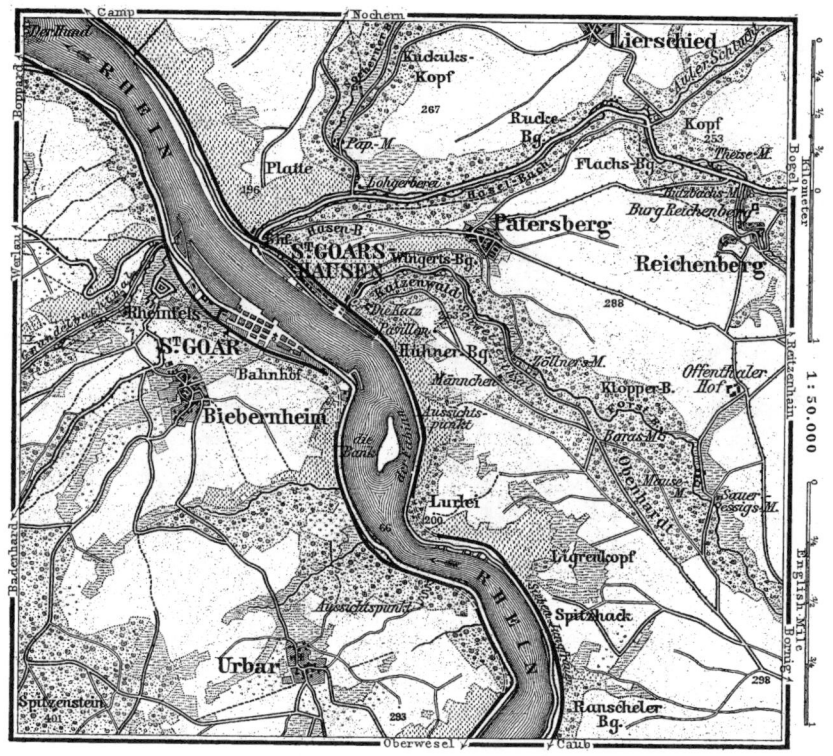

Map 3 St. Goar and St. Goarshausen, with the famous Katz and Rheinfels castles.

Figure 10-7 The Friedrichsplatz, on which Landgrave Friedrich II of Hesse-Kassel reviewed and drilled his troops.

House designs and layouts included a two-zoned style common across central Hesse. Houses were of half-timbered construction, with thatched roofs. A building regulation in force for three centuries beginning in 1541 required the building of foundations to preserve the all-important oak wood from being damaged by rot. Stone and later brick were used for this purpose. Cellars were usually dug out for use as storage for foodstuffs such as potatoes. Roofs in the larger towns were required to be made of fire-proof or fire-retardant material beginning as early as the fourteenth century. This meant tiles or slate when the roof could support them, or if not, large shingles made of a combination of straw and mud. The same prohibition was extended to rural areas in the eighteenth century at a time when more concerted efforts to combat fire were being made. Some barns and houses had external walls covered with the combination thatch-and-daub shingling. Often this would be a north wall or other area needing extra protection against heavy rains.

The kitchen area in many homes had a hearth without a chimney, capped with a hood of sorts to direct the smoke upwards. This allowed meat to be smoked over the kitchen fire. Much later a stove would often be added in an adjacent living area with access to the fire box from the kitchen side. There were of course no indoor bathroom facilities, and in smaller, scattered villages even out houses were rarely available. In such places the people would use the fields in temperate weather, and animal stalls during the cold winter months.[34]

THE HESSE-KASSEL MILITARY: RECRUITMENT AND OTHER SOCIAL IMPACTS

The cadaster system of records keeping did more than establish an accurate basis for tax collection. It involved a larger group of local officials in administering state needs in taxation and military recruitment. Locally-based judicial officials oversaw oath-taking by the citizenry concerning their wealth and taxability. The *Greben* and other village headmen testified about the assets of their villages and verified the truth of villagers' statements. Although corruption was not unknown, it became more difficult to skirt one's responsibilities than before. Changes in land ownership now had to be recorded officially with the authorities or they would not stand in court. This included inheritances within families. Land holding was recorded according to type, such as woods, meadows, garden and arable land, and average productivity in good years and bad. These more scientific valuations ended some of the wrangling over tax fairness issues of previous centuries. By the time the records surveys were being completed across Hesse in the 1770s and 1780s the landgrave was extracting more wealth from the land than his predecessors had ever hoped to do.

Local records of the population were developed to include lists of male children subject to future conscription for army service. Wealthy farmers who were able to contribute most to the tax coffers were granted the right to exempt a male heir from the draft. Also, the subjects of the lesser nobles were exempt by customary law. The original targets of recruitment were loafers, vagabonds, and others lacking the means to be upstanding citizens. This was aimed at making productive use of members of society not tied to the land, people who were in a position to threaten the social order through crime or burdening the relief rolls. But over time it had to be admitted officially that the target group had to be expanded because too few of these "dregs" of society were available and able to serve. Next, farm servants without a demonstrated contractual relationship to a productive landholder were targeted. Only those proven to be key to a householder's productive capacity were exempted. Manual laborers and apprentices were snatched up in large numbers. A new ordinance in 1762 made clear that more resort was to be made to recruiting from peasant families at all levels, and God's name was even invoked in calling on young men to subject themselves to the authority of their lawful prince. Families with multiple sons now found the younger boys increasingly subject to service. Exemptions also existed for those with at least thirty *Acker* (over eighteen acres) of land; over 250 *Taler* in personal net worth; factory workers, artisans, clergy, state bureaucrats, students, and those working for the nobility. Some larger towns were also exempt.

The *Hufenedikt* of 1773 became another means to the goal of unlocking manpower reserves for use in the army. Single-heir inheritance practices ensured that a wider group of dispossessed young men became available. The cadaster-based assessments also were manipulated to reduce the portions of wealth that had to be provided to the disinherited. This did hold down the amount of debt that inheritors had to take on to buy out their brothers and sisters, but it also reduced the financial options for potential new recruits to the army. This was not coincidental, and it had unintended adverse consequences in the form of lowered land values for all and downward social mobility for the disinherited.[35]

The administrative process of recruitment started with lists of potential draftees drawn up by various local authorities such as *Greben* and village councilmen (*Schöffen*). Whether or not one's children made the list thus had something to do with local politics and social standing in the villages. Registration was required beginning at age seven. The 1762 ordinance eliminated some of this unfairness by assigning regiments the recruitment rights to geographical areas (cantons) including in theory all families within those boundaries. Civil officials still were given oversight responsibility to determine eligibility of individual recruits. Parish pastors also now had to provide information from the church rolls on correct age, marital status, etc. These measures curtailed the arbitrariness of local officials in drawing up the lists.

Recruits swore an oath of loyalty and obedience to the landgrave rather than the state, for his trade in mercenary soldiers was a personal, not a state, activity. The men were given a small recruitment bonus immediately as a means of sealing the deal. As in Britain, "taking the king's coin" meant an irrevocable commitment to his service. By 1782 one in thirteen Hessians were channeled into the landgrave's service. In many areas every other household counted a soldier among its members.

The draft was always enormously unpopular, and draft-eligible men went to great lengths to escape. Desertion or failure to appear at the annual spring musters were severely punished. Young men had to appear beginning at age sixteen so regimental recruiters could begin to get to know their future recruits. Property confiscation was common, but probably not overly effective since most draftees had little in the way of personal resources. Captured deserters were beaten, but often general pardons had to be given to try to induce them to return. Treaties with neighboring states were made for the reciprocal return of their deserters. An internal passport system indicating draft status was devised for those traveling on the land. Peasants were rewarded with cash or a portion of the confiscated wealth of any deserters they betrayed to authorities. Many men simply absconded and found contract work with landed farmers outside Hesse. Ironically, the better-off peasants closely tied to the land were the most likely to appear at the musters, violating the intent of the draft policy. Some relatives tried to provide a means of escape for their boys through legal loopholes. Married men working land with a team of oxen were exempt, so some fathers helped draft-eligible younger sons to marry early and settled them on small parcels of land with a plow team. In the 1780s officials were noting that in many cases the acreage did not justify the use of a team to plow it.

Despite its unpopularity, the draft does not appear to have brought about any serious organized protests. The upper classes might have opposed the extent to which the landgraves used the draft and huge tax revenues needed to support the army (*Kontribution*) for their own purposes. It was accepted that the state should have a large army, which in any case offered substantial opportunities for military careers for the sons of the nobility. Even commoners could hope to rise by merit to the officer ranks. The military was the career choice of last resort for the poor as well, whose ranks swelled the military rolls during the lean summer months before the harvests. There was also a widespread sense of the need to defend the homeland based on the frequent incursions of French and other Catholic troops who ravaged the land wherever they marched.

The large number of young men fleeing Hesse with their families constrained agricultural productivity, as did the huge number of men pulled away from the farms for service in the American Revolution. More of this is discussed in Chapter Eleven. Draftees also left behind wives and children who began to burden relief rolls when they could not make ends meet. More female farm servants were hired by wealthy farmers to replace the unavailable males. The *Kontribution* had to be reduced by half in 1776 to relieve the financial pressure of the myriad state- and private-based payments that peasants had to make. This resulted in the forgiveness of 1.3 million *Taler* by 1783. For the first time the so-called militia soldiers had to be used for regular army service abroad, and the resultant loss of agricultural workers was ruinous for many families. Some 9.5 million *Taler* in military salaries were paid to the soldiers and their families, plus plunder or wages earned while working as prisoners of the Americans. Much of this money was sent home to augment the income of families left behind.[36]

For the many reasons cited above the *Hufenedikt* was reformed completely in 1786 by Landgrave William IX. In 1789 the landgrave also reduced the legal term of enlistment to a maximum of twelve years, effective in 1794. He required that the regular army, subject to service abroad, to draw its recruits from the non-productive elements of the population as had been the case in the early years of his father's rule. Recruitment was now mandatory for all citizens, but the recruits still needed in agriculture were used for militia duty near their homes, where they could go on frequent leave to help with the seasonal chores. Service was now unavoidable, but perhaps less threatening for many.[37]

THE STATUS AND POSITION OF JEWS IN GERMANY AND HESSE

The number of Jews in Germany dropped during the turbulent times of the Thirty Years War. Prior to that time they had prospered under imperial protection in exchange for the economic support they provided the emperors. They were typically denied the right to own and farm land, so were forced to make their living in commerce and money lending. This brought sufficient prosperity to attract the envy and enmity of their non-Jewish neighbors. Their debtors and competitors sometimes incited riots and violence against them, particularly in difficult economic times or war. They often were used as scapegoats and were blamed for spreading disease in epidemics. Their fate was determined in most cases by the views and policies of the local prince who ruled the lands in which they lived. When they were seen to promote trade and prosperity, chances were good they could find a place and prosper. When sufficient opposition to them came from the estates or other influential elements in society, they could suffer banishment or other punishments.

In towns such as Frankfurt and Hamburg Jews lived in separate quarters of the city, but were reasonably well integrated in the life of the community. In limited numbers they also were increasingly called on by their sovereigns to provide services as court Jews or *Hoffaktor*, where they essentially served as ministers of finance. Often enough the debts owed them went unpaid by their princes, particularly when a prince was succeeded by an ungrateful successor. But the interest alone seems to have brought them good compensation in many of their transactions. William IX employed the Rothschilds in this way, as we have noted above.

In Hesse Jews were allowed to live on the land by a decree of 1730, practicing their money lending, small-scale trading, and some trades. They lived in autonomous communities under elected leaders who saw to their religious and educational needs, levying local taxes as needed to pay off the prince or other lord who ensured their right to live in peace. Often they were not enumerated in official records. The village of Abterode is a notable exception, where over 30% of the households were Jewish in the 1750s. They claimed little in terms of social rights from the community, and were largely ignored in return. Their trading and money lending provided rural credit and brought products to the villages where they lived, selling livestock for instance in post-war periods after losses of domestic animals had been heavy. In the village of Niederaula Jews were required like their neighbors to provide local manual labor services to the landgrave; they held two of the twenty-two little houses on which these services were based. Like their Christian counterparts, they had to help harvest vegetables, and help keep the district headquarters building clean and in good repair.

Disastrous times for the 7,300 Hesse-Kassel Jews came with the hungry years of the early 1770s. Commoners and officials alike complained to Frederick that Jews were taking unfair advantage of the peasantry, competing unfairly with Christian traders, and violating the traditional economic boundaries between town and country on which guilds and other productive activity depended. Jewish reluctance to take up farming, an occupation so often denied to them that they were uncomfortable working at it, seems to have been their downfall in terms of public perception. It was often difficult or impossible for them to legally acquire land, as well. In August 1773 Frederick agreed revoke the act that had allowed their settlement on the land. Many had to leave the land and flocked to the cities in impoverished conditions.

By 1785 this decision was revisited by Frederick's son. Noble landowners were complaining that the loss of their Jewish underlings deprived them of labor services, and even peasants found they lacked access to the rural credit that only Jews were providing. In limited numbers the Jews were invited back into rural areas.[38]

As in Kassel lands, the Jews living in Hesse-Darmstadt lived separate and apart from their neighbors. In Groß-Bieberau a record of 1738 mentions the payment of a four-florin tax by a Jew named Jacob, a *Beisaß* who held no rights in the village community. The tax was paid to the community itself by all persons of the *Beisaßen* class, but non-Jews paid only three florins. This tax seems to have compensated the community for use of its water resources and pasture. Two other Jewish heads of families appear in local tax records for Groß-Bieberau through the century. In the case of one Löw Levy the tax amount had to be reduced by half because of the extreme poverty in which he lived. In 1801 he was listed as having died in poverty. The reduced tax apparently had to be implements for other local Jews as well. The minor trading undertaken by this tiny group does not appear to have allowed them to prosper in the village over time. Their small numbers also afforded them little mutual support in times of crisis. At the end of the century some new emigrants to the area caused their numbers to grow slightly, however.[39]

The situation of the Jews in Groß-Bieberau is probably indicative of a larger number of similarly impoverished Jews who lived at the fringes of their communities and failed to live up to the stereotype of the wealthy Jewish merchants who often were accused of prospering in trade even when their Christian customers suffered through hard times.

HESSE-DARMSTADT: THE STRUGGLE FOR SURVIVAL, THE QUEST FOR PROSPERITY

The landgraves in Darmstadt had a much more difficult time in bringing prosperous times to their citizenry than their cousins in Kassel. The landgraviate ended the seventeenth century in difficult straits, and a tax reform effort in 1719 did little to improve things. Mercantilist practices had limited positive effects in such a small and isolated state. The depredations of French troops had even worse effects here than in Hesse-Kassel, and the government's debts continued to mount. The landgraves' debts doubled from 1678 to 1739, when they stood at four million guilders. Much of the debt was traceable to the fantastic building sponsored by Landgrave Ernst Ludwig (d. 1739), which graced Darmstadt with a rebuilt castle and theater/opera house. He also spent huge sums on hunting, including the building of new hunting lodges and palaces, earning the reputation of the greatest hunter among the landgraves of Darmstadt. He also spent lavishly on alchemy in a fruitless effort to reverse his bad fortune by manufacturing gold. In 1737 the total state income was just 345,000 florins, some 120,000 less than the annual expenditures. Interest on the debt alone was 185,000 annually. The landgrave turned to Jewish financiers in Frankfurt to float the loans needed to run his impoverished land.

In this period Ernst Ludwig seems to have granted permission for a huge number of windmills to be built despite his budget problems. Mercantilist economic ideas were behind this, but the results were disappointing. A fantastic new design for a mill was implemented in Groß-Rohrheim in 1720, but it apparently had technical flaws and by 1721 the miller was described as impoverished, an unusual situation for someone in a generally well-paying occupation. Huguenot refugees settled in Offenbach and created mills whose output was aimed at the major market in Frankfurt.[40]

Ernst Ludwig issued a revised school ordinance "for the German schools in the upper principality" in 1733. It ordered that regular school hours be kept in summer and winter in every school where a regular school master was employed. This was to include three hour's instruction in the morning and in the afternoon. Even during the harvest times instruction was not to cease entirely, with at least two hour's instruction per day for older children who were helping with the harvest work. Fines were imposed for teachers dismissing school for non-approved holiday periods. This was a particular hardship for masters in this era when their pay was typically so low that side jobs had to be undertaken to help make ends meet. The law pointed out the concern it was attempting to address that parent who depended on their children to do farm chores were keeping them out of school and thereby raising poor Christians and bad subjects whose ignorance and behavior problems later would become a concern for the state. The ordinance stated that:

> 1. Some parents were holding their children back from going to school until age eight or nine. 2. Such children were undisciplined and exhibited behavior problems once they entered school. 3. In some places (particularly in the Vogelsberg area) children were being sent to school for only about four months during the winter, and in between times they were so forgetful of the lessons they had learned that nothing was coming of their instruction.[41]

Schools remained under the control and administration of the church through its parishes. The new ordinance regulated the course of instruction, oversight duties of the pastors, financing methods, and duties of the teachers. The oldest church official in each diocese, known as the Metropolitan, became the recognized school inspector for the diocese schools. Despite these measures Groß-Bieberau's school instruction remained in dire straits in this era. The teacher had 100-150 pupils to deal with in three separate levels of instruction. With so little time for individual help, many children left school after eight years without a solid command of the alphabet. Not until the next century were standards set for teachers' training to be sure basic competency was attained. The effort to force students to come more regularly to school and spend more hours per day in instruction does not appear to be effectively carried out in this century.[42]

Perhaps evidence of the landgrave's difficult financial situation are two agricultural ordinances of 1743 and 1761 aimed at protecting the landgrave's income from tithes of local produce in Groß-Bieberau. State authorities were directed to enter the fields to inspect them, and to administer oaths to trustworthy local people to assist with gathering the tithes. Bringing in the harvest was prohibited until after the tithe was collected. State officials had to be advised and approval obtained for use of part of the crops as fodder for animals. Removing crops from the fields at night or taking wagons into the fields to haul away some of the produce was forbidden. Steps were outlined to keep domesticated animals from foraging in the fields as well. Among the produce cited in tithe records of 1755 was potatoes, a crop that the Groß-Bieberau farmers apparently adopted early and without the reticence encountered elsewhere in Germany.

The landgrave also renewed Groß-Bieberau's rights to hold regular market days, as had been done since the Middle Ages. Even as late as 1770 the village was suffering from the after-effects of the Thirty Years War, with much arable land still lying in waste, overgrown with weeds and forests of firs having encroached for generations on previously productive land. Property values were very low. Recovery as seen in most of Hesse-Kassel appears to have eluded many of the Darmstadt lands even as late as this period.[43]

Landgrave Ludwig VIII (1739-68) followed in his father's footsteps when it came to hunting pursuits. He had a huge stag, the largest in Hesse, captured near Battenberg and brought to Darmstadt to grace his private wildlife park where it was considered a great wonder to see. Ludwig's hunting companions found him a gregarious and cheerful sort. He practiced English-style hunting, with a hundred or so hunters on horseback led by packs of hunting dogs who ran the stags into a state of collapse. At this point the hunt master, the landgrave himself, gave the harried prey the final death shot. The primary hunting areas in Hesse-Darmstadt were in upper Hesse and in the so-called hinterland around Biedenkopf and Battenberg. The hunting castle at Kranichstein was his favorite haunt. The hunts visited terrible destruction on the local areas where they took place; hunters added insult to injury by demanding local peasants support them with services and produce. Local clergymen preached against the burden on the populace, and after Ludwig's time the hunts fell largely out of favor.

Ludwig VIII's international politics favored the Austrian court of the Empress Maria Theresa. He provided military support to Austria in the War of the Austrian Succession and the wars she fought with Prussia over Silesia; in return, he received a commission as field marshal in 1741. The empress also interceded with his debtors in Vienna and elsewhere to save the landgrave from financial ruin.

Most notable during Ludwig's rule was the acquisition of the county Hanau-Lichtenberg on the left bank of the Rhine. This occurred through his marriage to Charlotte, the only daughter of Count John Reinhard of Hanau. On the count's death in 1736 Darmstadt received Lichtenberg as Kassel took Hanau-Münzenberg. The Babenhausen area remained in dispute between the two until 1771when it came to Darmstadt. The Lichtenberg inheritance brought ten districts in Alsace under French sovereignty to Darmstadt: Brumath, Buchsweiler, Hatten, Wörth, Staab, Offendorf, Ingweiler, Pfaffenhofen, Westhofen, and Wolfisheim. The districts of Lichtenau and Willstätt on the right side of the Rhine also were part of these lands, as was Lemberg. The Hanau possessions were given over to the crown price's rule in 1741 when he turned twenty-two. He assumed power in his new residence town of Buchsweiler, and later Pirmasens. In the same year he married his consort, Caroline, Countess of Nassau-Zweibrücken.

Ludwig VIII tried mightily to turn the state's financial situation around, but it proved impossible. The estates, consisting of three religious authorities, twenty or thirty representatives of the nobility, and twenty-three of the towns, were likewise unable to provide enough funds to relieve the crushing debt load. Even the status of the land itself presented a great challenge. He died in 1768 at age 78 while appearing in an opera in the capital.

On assuming power Landgrave Ludwig IX found himself serving as both a German prince with a seat in the imperial Reichstag and also a vassal of the French court by virtue of his Alsace land holdings. Ludwig spent his whole reign in Pirmasens, living a Spartan existence in this garrison town where he occupied his time in drilling his troops on the Prussian model. Despite his pressing financial difficulties, he refused on principle the entreaties of Britain to rent his troops as mercenaries, dismissing this as "selling people for blood money." Not all his troops served as volunteers, however, and a wall was built around Pirmasens to discourage desertion. Unlike his father, Ludwig IX was a partisan of Prussia, and he spent years at court in Berlin and Prenzlau, as well as serving Frederick the Great as a field commander.

Ludwig's wife lived in Darmstadt during the period of her husband's rule as landgrave, earning the popular nickname of the "Great Landgravine." She worked with the prime minister Friedrich Karl von Moser who labored hard in the capital to set things right. She undertook a detailed and thorough approach to cutting expenses at court and in the military to hold down costs. She also somehow found the means to promote Darmstadt as a center for arts and letters, attracting the musician Gluck and the poet and author Goethe during her reign. She died in 1774. Her daughters carried this love of the arts with them when they married into some of the major courts of Germany, including Prussia, Saxe-Weimar, and Hesse-Homburg. Moser meanwhile saved the state from its crushing debt through restructuring agreements with creditors in 1772 and 1779. This led to the ability to pay off most of the debt by 1814. After peaking in 1766, emigration to foreign lands began to recede as people felt more hopeful about making a go of it in Hesse.

In 1777 the landgrave promoted school reforms. He suppressed use of torture in the judicial system, and only three death sentences were carried out during his reign, for convicted thieves and highway robbers. As a Lutheran prince, the landgrave nevertheless allowed reformed Christians to settle in Darmstadt and permitted them to hold services in a little-used chapel. He was less tolerant with his Catholic subjects, energetically prohibiting their request of the right to hold services. Only in the reign of his son were these prohibitions lifted (1790).

Stall feeding of livestock was encouraged in Darmstadt as in Kassel lands, with the result that increasing amounts of usable dung were generated for fertilizing the fields. Together with the widespread introduction of potatoes, reform measures began to bring better times to even the most impoverished areas such as the Odenwald and Vogelsberg.

In 1790 the next landgrave came to power, Ludwig X. He found himself confronted with an already small land that was further divided into ten geographically separate areas. Among these were the county Hanau-Lichtenberg (districts in Baden, Alsace and Dreieich), the upper and part of the lower county of Katzenelnbogen, and the Eppstein district, which shared some jurisdictions with Kassel and Württemberg. About 290,000 people lived across these scattered holdings, administered in three major districts: upper and lower Katzenelnbogen, upper Hesse, and Hanau-Lichtenberg. Lesser districts were created for administration within these larger areas, with twelve in Katzenelnbogen, twenty-four in upper Hesse, and twelve in Lichtenberg.

Ludwig IX's efforts to remain neutral had prevented Darmstadt from effectively cultivating an ally in either of the two most powerful German courts: Prussia and Austria. The French Revolution of 1789 was a further blow as Hanau-Lichtenberg's feudal tithes, services and levies on his properties on the left bank of the Rhine were lost to the new landgrave. French troops swept the 5,000-strong Darmstadt army aside as they occupied Mainz, Frankfurt, and the Wetterau in 1792. Ludwig X joined forces with Kassel and Prussia in ejecting the French again in 1793. He later had to withdraw his troops for lack of money to support them until English and Austrian subsidies could be arranged under which he sold his forces into the service of the greater powers.

In 1795 an armistice was reached with the French, but they returned to the field in mid-1796, retaking the Wetterau with its local capital Friedberg. Darmstadt also fell, and Ludwig moved his court to Gießen. When Austrian relief forces arrived in the fall, the French troops were forced back again, but not before engaging in horrible atrocities against the civilian population. The latter armed themselves to fight back, falling upon small groups of the French whom they attacked mercilessly. The French struck back in response with raids in retribution. The people in Spessart, Odenwald, the Rhön, and Vogelsberg were heavily engaged in these horrific actions. In early September the Nidda district was plundered terribly and Lißberg was burned out. Only thereafter were the French driven back to the Rhine. Landgrave Ludwig felt forced in 1797 to try to make peace with the French without the support of the emperor, who refused to push for reparations concerning the loss of Ludwig's Lichtenberg properties. Worse, the dividing line between French and Austrian forces was established right across the middle of Darmstadt's Nidda district. Only in 1798 was Ludwig able to execute a separate neutrality agreement with the French. His relationship with Napoleon and its results for his land will be treated in a separate chapter.[44]

GERMANY AND HESSE IN THE EIGHTEENTH CENTURY

HESSE-DARMSTADT AND CLOTHING TRENDS: *TRACHTEN*

The folk dress (*Trachten*) of Hesse-Darmstadt is renowned and well documented, with over twenty-five separate and discernible styles in the nineteenth century. Among these the Odenwald area of Hesse presents some of the most colorful, historically the *Trachten* areas encompassed the following districts: the upper county of Katzenelnbogen with its seat at Darmstadt; Arheilgen; and the districts of Pfungstadt, Dornberg, Kelsterbach, Rüsselsheim, Lichtenberg, Zwingenberg, Jägersburg, Seeheim and Tannenberg. The orientation of this area to Lutheran and Reformed religious teachings had significant influence on clothing practices. Also key to style decisions were issues of class, occupation, age and sex. These *Trachten* evolved over centuries based on such influences.

As noted earlier, even in the Middle Ages government ordinances were issued to regulate clothing styles and curtail ostentation. These sought to limit the use of clothing items and regulate more sumptuous styles according to social class. Protecting class distinctions was always a paramount concern. In the early sixteenth century farmers were permitted to wear broad shirts and smocks with long pants and a large hat. Gray tended to be the color of everyday dress, with blue the color of choice for celebrations of various kinds. Colorful clothes were mostly the province of the wealthy.

By the Renaissance the clothing style differences between the wealthy and the commoners were typically maintained on a class basis across national boundaries. Wealthy Frenchmen, Germans, or Englishmen wore common styles, and the farmers in all these lands also would have been at home with basic dress styles of their counterparts abroad. The wealthy derived their taste in clothing based on what was popular at court among their rulers, and the major urban centers did much to set the tone. By the eighteenth century there was a body of laws on clothing practices that was most influential in setting the style in rural areas. Landgrave Ludwig IX ruled in 1770 that all classes should make use of material produced in Hesse-Darmstadt for their clothing. The clothing ordinance of Elizabeth Dorothea that largely banned ostentatious displays (see previous chapter) also had been renewed and expanded in 1750. Opposition on the land to prohibitions of the wearing of certain colors caused the landgrave to relax the rules somewhat to allow blue and green colors to be worn where these could be produced in inexpensive cloth affordable for commoners.

In 1776 another ordinance was issued patterned on rules issued in neighboring states such as Kassel. This again circumscribed luxury goods imported from abroad that sapped the state of its stocks of currency, ordering everyone to use locally produced goods. In these mercantilistic times, no state could stand alone and permit imports if its own exported goods were being proscribed by its neighbors. The text of the law directed its provisions at "townsmen, farmers and Jews" alike. Jews were further directed to follow the styles of the towns or villages in which they lived. Some allowance was made for workers whose traditional work clothes were long established in tradition. Butchers' traditional red apron and pants were one example.[45]

We turn now to a more detailed look at typical Odenwald clothing styles by the time of the eighteenth century. Men's coats, called *Mutzen*, originally evolved from styles worn at court. They were made of linen or mixed-weave cloth reinforced inside with a stiffened ticking material and wee without collars but had pockets on both sides. Originally green, this color had to be given up based on the ordinance of Landgrave Ludwig VIII. By the end of the century blue was the color of choice.[46]

211

Through much of Hesse a linen smock was the garment of choice for workers' daily wear. In the Odenwald area it was a traditional garment for teamsters and others who did hauling work, useful for keeping the road dust off their clothing. Linen leggings also were used for this purpose. The smock was usually blue and white in color. A work apron was common among other trades, such as the butchers noted above. In the Odenwald this was most common in the north and in the area known as Ried. Illustrations exist of farmers in Langen and Dietzenbach wearing white work aprons stretching down to cover two-thirds of the lower body. White aprons were the occupational and status symbols of the millers in Bachgau and the potters in Roßdorf, east of Darmstadt.

Pants early on were knickers or knee pants, derived originally from the styles at court in the baroque period. These were worn tight without suspenders or belt to hold them up. Later styles were laced up in the back. A possible decorative feature was a flap secured with two buttons, plus a third button in the middle as decoration. This also might have stitched decorations on it. Stockings were worn from the knees down, and were often of blue and white design as a decorative feature. After the French Revolution long pants began to eclipse the old knickers and long stockings were no longer used.

Hats were of two basic types: three-cornered hats and fur caps. The better off wore the three-cornered hat as a sign of status rather than practical need. By the second half of the century it had found its way into typical farmers' garb across Germany. These hats were always made of stiffened black felt, with brims varying from about nine and one-half to sixteen centimeters. Sometimes the brims were worn turned up high on the three sides.[47]

Women's clothing, like men's, evolved from very old forms. The sleeved shirt was basic, being made from anywhere from three to four and one-half ells (81 to 121 inches) of linen cloth. The neck opening of the shirt was cut in a half-circle or square form in front, and this area was often painstakingly decorated with stitching work as it would show beneath the cut-away portion of the bodice. If the shirt opened in front the slit would be nineteen to thirty-three inches in length, decorated at the top or bottom with red stitch work, sometimes giving the year the shirt was made. It was held together with a small tie of two white bands, or later with buttons of porcelain or glass. The sleeves were cut at right angles, and could be long or short. In the Odenwald the long sleeves ended about halfway down the lower arm and cuffed. Under the shoulders a square plait was added to protect against splitting. A less-costly, combination-style shirt evolved for use in festivals and other dressy occasions with fine linen on top where it showed behind the bodice and coarser linen on the bottom where it was hidden from view.

The skirt evolved when the bodice and skirt were made separate clothing items in the sixteenth century. Sunday and festival skirts were made at home of wool or other heavy cloth. The daily work skirt was of lighter linen. The color of choice was dark blue, or later black. Up until age ten girls might wear lighter colored skirts as well. A woman's skirt would require up to two and one-half meters or more of cloth. The better-off the woman, the more cloth would be used. Some of the skirts were pleated three-quarters of the way around, with 100-170 pleats. The area under the apron would not be pleated. Poor women would use lower-quality cloth in the front part that was hidden by the apron.

The favored rural style was to appear broad in the pelvic area, and this was accomplished by wearing several skirts layered one on top of the other. The thinner a woman was, the more skirts would be layered on. Skirts were closed with hooks and eyes, often in combination with laces and ties. Once the apron was tied on, the pressure on the stomach area also was often most uncomfortable and led to an illness called "*Röckwäih.*" The apron was an obligatory feature; no woman would be seen without one. The size and length of the apron was determined by the size of the skirt. It was usually a hand's breadth shorter than the skirt. Aprons were made of many materials. The older versions were of a single color.

Stockings for men and women were made of cotton for summer use and wool in winter. Stockings were held up with simple woven garters, about the width of a thumb.[48]

Women's caps or bonnets were worn from early times as it was considered unseemly for women to display their hair down and uncovered. Young girls were the exception. From the time of marriage the bonnet became obligatory, referred to as "coming under the bonnet." Two forms evolved, one of French the other of Franconian extraction. There were two sub-forms popular in the eighteenth century as well: a two-part design made of square pieces of cloth with one rounded corner sewn together at the top. This created a simple open cap that could be tied under the chin. A more elaborate form had three pieces sewn together and reinforced to form a more box-like look on the head. The French style led to adoption of a more bonnet-type head covering that swept over wide areas of Germany in the course of the eighteenth century. It came to dominate head wear in the Odenwald, Spessart, Taunus, Westerwald, Rheinhessen, Hunsrück, Pfalz and Saarland. This so-called *Karnette* style had front flaps that framed the face and a rounded area in the back of the head to cover the hair that was tied in a bun.[49]

EMIGRATION TRENDS IN HESSE: THE EIGHTEENTH CENTURY [50]

Overpopulation in much of Hesse in the course of the eighteenth century led to the decision by many Hessians to emigrate to various foreign locales. As noted earlier, hereditary practices had so often splintered farms that they could no longer support the families that worked them. Many "economic refugees" headed east to Russia and southeastern Europe or overseas to America during the century.

Hesse was only one source of such emigration An estimated 200,000 German farmers emigrated to Russia and America in 1756-66 alone. One hundred people from the little Hesse-Darmstadt town of Fränkisch-Crumbach and its environs responded favorably to an invitation from the Russian Empress Catherine to emigrate to her lands in 1766. The Sartisson family in Lindenfels answered this call in April 1766, settling in Ukraine. Later they moved with other Germans to the Black Sea area where they lived for generations until their expulsion to Siberia by Stalin. The Russian Crown even maintained an emigration office in Büdingen in the eighteenth century. It collected groups of 60-100 emigrants, gave them travel money, and sent them to Lübeck where they caught ships for St. Petersberg. Here they obtained wagons for the trip to Sartova in the Volga lands, traveling by way of Novgorod, Moscow, and Pensa. Most Volga German settlements were founded in the years 1763-69. Other migrants took a similar route, but were settled in the Belorussian Colony northeast of Kiev. Surprisingly, 75% of the German inhabitants migrating to the Volga region were of Hessian extraction in these times.

Other Hessians became part of the emigration wave of so-called *Donauschwaben* who settled in Austrian-controlled areas retaken from the Turks in the seventeenth and eighteenth centuries. Most of these left Swabian lands centered around Stuttgart, but

Hessians also joined them in migrating to the Batschka, Baranja, and Banat, then in Hungary (later Yugoslavia). Emigration to Hungary is documented as early as 1723 in Groß-Bieberau (Hesse-Darmstadt), when a Johann Konrad Stork left with his family, handing his house over to his brother. More families were making the same trek as late as 1780-85 from Groß-Bieberau and nearby Fränkisch-Crumbach. Three groups totaling fifty-seven people from the latter place headed off to Hungary in 1784-85 alone.

America too was a recognized destination for Hessian emigrants in the eighteenth century and before. Some Nassau Hessians had set out for William Penn's colony after they were recruited in Frankfurt by Daniel Pastorius. They arrived in America in 1683 to found Germantown, Pennsylvania. Other groups followed their example, and a steady stream of letters home began to acquaint Hessians with the opportunities and pitfalls of life in the New World. From 1719-33 a group of Anabaptists from the County Wittgenstein and the Isenburg area of the Wetterau also left for America with the goal of finding religious freedom. Others, simple laborers, small shopkeepers, and the like, succumbed to what even then was being called "America Fever." They saw emigration as their means to escape the feudal burdens under which they labored. A large group set out from Hesse-Darmstadt and Nassau-Dillenburg by way of England in 1709, settling along the middle Hudson River in New York. In 1741 another wave, this time the so-called Herrenhuter, came from the county Büdingen to Pennsylvania, where they helped establish Bethlehem. Around 1750 other Hessians left for new lives in Massachusetts.

Local governments in Hesse were unsupportive of emigration and erected various road blocks to hinder it. They saw population loss in terms of reduced tax revenue, army recruitment, and productivity. Undocumented and therefore illegal emigration was made punishable by fines in Hesse-Kassel. A general prohibition was laid down in 1765, singling out workers, professionals and miners as occupation groups required to remain at home. Other Hessian territories followed suit. Emigrants did not lose their inheritance rights at home, however, as an exchange of correspondence in the 1780s indicates. It describes the efforts of Johann Adam Germann of Gumpen, who emigrated to Northampton County Pennsylvania in 1764, to obtain the inheritance due him after his father's death in 1775. After exchanging many letters with his mother, who finally died in 1797, Germann received his share of the inheritance, valued at 354 guilders.

A formal emigration request dated April 18, 1766 has survived, indicating the desire of one Nicholas Rahmgen of Breuberg to emigrate to Russia with his wife and five children. After selling his property and paying his debts under the watchful eye of the local *Schultheiß* of Kirchbrombach, Rahmgen was reported to have 661 florins to his name. Another family of the name of Weyrich from Wallbach sold its home for 100 florins, paid outstanding debts of ninety-nine florins and eleven *Kreutzer*, leaving them a net travel kitty of just forty-nine *Kreutzer*. The sales contract on the house had an interesting clause allowing Weyrich to return anytime within ten years with rights to repatriate his house by repaying the 100-florin sales price to the new buyer.

Hessians without the means to travel abroad sometimes sold themselves as indentured servants to sea captains who in turn sold them into service to farmers in the New World. Others made the trip free courtesy of the landgrave, who sold their services to the English Crown in the American Revolution. Many Hessian soldiers chose to remain in America after the war. More on their story is told in the next chapter.

NOTES TO CHAPTER 10

[1] Will and Ariel Durant, *The Story of Civilization, Vol. IX, The Age of Voltaire*, Simon and Schuster, New York, 1965, pp. 397-98.

[2] William Doyle, *Short Oxford History of the Modern World, The Old European Order 1660-1800*, Oxford Press, 1978, pp. 6-7; Hajo Holborn, *History of Modern Germany 1648-1840*, Alfred Knopf, New York, 1964, p. 23; Fernand Braudel, *Structures of Everyday Life*, Vol. I, Harper & Row, New York, 1981, pp. 91-92, 105, 196-97; Wilhelm Treue, "*Wirtschaft, Gesellschaft und Technik*" in *Deutschland vom 16. bis zum 18. Jahrhundert*, in Gebhardt, *Handbuch der deutschen Geschichte*, Vol. 12, Deutscher Taschenbuch Verlag, 1974, p. 134.

[3] Holborn, pp. 37-39, 291; Eda Sagarra, *A Social History of Germany 1648-1914*, Holmes & Meier Publishers, New York, 1977, pp. 94-97; Durant IX, p. 400.

[4] Will and Ariel Durant, *The Story of Civilization, Vol. X, Rousseau and Revolution*, Simon and Schuster, New York, 1967, p. 503.

[5] Doyle, pp. 8-14, 21, 23, 105-06, 115-17; Braudel, p. 170; Treue, pp. 134, 135-37, 144; Sagarra, p. 152-54.

[6] Holborn, pp. 27-28, 40.

[7] Doyle, pp. 31, 40-42, 136-37; Holborn, p. 35; Braudel, p. 447; Sagarra, p. 69.

[8] Doyle, pp. 221-22, 240-53; Holborn, pp. 21, 32; Treue, pp. 134, 142, 144.

[9] Holborn, pp. 278-79; Doyle, pp. 254, 262.

[10] Doyle, pp. 156, 238; Holborn, pp. 128-29; Sagarra, pp. 119-20; Durant IX, p. 402.

[11] Durant IX, pp. 403, 407; and X, p. 504. Section one of this chapter was adapted from a comparable section in my book *A History of Brunswick*, published in 1999.

[12] Karl E. Demandt, *Geschichte des Landes Hessen*, Bärenreiter-Verlag, Kassel, 1972, pp. 270-75.

[13] Charles W. Ingrao, *The Hessian Mercenary State, Ideas, institutions and reform under Frederick II, 1760-1785*, Cambridge University Press, 1987, p. 56.

[14] Ingrao, pp. 9-121, Peter K. Taylor, *Indentured to Liberty: Peasant Life and the Hessian Military State, 1688-1815*, Cornell University Press, New York, 1994, pp.176-79; 197-98.

[15] Paris in this era was overrun with illegitimate foundlings who were unable to be cared for by their impoverished parents. Of 30,000 births a year, up to 8,000 were abandoned to the poor house! A delivery man carried three at a time in a padded box on his back. Often one would be dead when he opened his pack to pick up the next. As soon as he unloaded his burden at the house he would turn round and head back for another load. Braudel, Vol. I, p. 491.

[16] Ingrao, pp. 97-98, 188-210.

[17] Demandt, pp. 277-87; Veit Valentin, *The German People*, Alfred Knopf, New York, 1952, p. 278.

[18] Hans Lerch, *Hessische Agrargeschichte des 17. Und 18. Jahrhunderts*, Hans Ott-Verlag, Hersfeld, 1926, pp. 23, 85-93; Taylor, pp. 91-92, 96.

[19] Eugen Ernst, *Die Hessische Landwirtschaft im Wandel der Zeiten*, Freilichtmuseum Hessenpark, 1996, pp. 49, 53-55; Kurt Wagner, *Leben auf dem Lande im Wandel der Industrialisierung*, Insel Verlag, Frankfurt am Main, 1986, pp. 54-55; John Theibault, *German Villages in Crisis: Rural Life in Hesse-Kassel and the Thirty Years' War, 1580-1720*, Humanities Press, Atlantic Highlands, NJ, 1995, p. 209; *Guide to Region Lahn-Dill-Ohm*, Open Air Museum Hessenpark, Neu-Anspach, 1989, pp. 15-16.

[20] Theibault, pp. 210-13.

[21] Taylor, pp. 129, 139.

[22] Wagner, pp. 45, 51-53.

[23] Lerch, pp. 63-67.

[24] Lerch, pp. 35-37, 84.

[25] Lerch, pp. 48-50, 57-58; *Guide to Region Lahn-Dill-Ohm*, pp. 16-17.
[26] Lerch, pp. 72-75, 79-83; Theibault, p. 196.
[27] Lerch, pp. 94-102.
[28] Lerch, pp. 103-114, *Guide to Region Lahn-Dill-Ohm*, pp. 19, 93.
[29] *Guide to Region Lahn-Dill-Ohm*, pp. 12, 40-42, 54, 56.
[30] *Guide to Region Lahn-Dill-Ohm*, pp. 30, 61.
[31] Lerch, pp. 117-124; *Guide to Region Lahn-Dill-Ohm*, pp. 35, 85.
[32] Lerch, pp. 135-47; Wagner, pp. 46, 59-60.
[33] Lerch, pp. 127-33.
[34] *Guide to Region Lahn-Dill-Ohm*, pp. 21, 28, 36, 90, 96; Guide to the Open Air Museum Hessenpark, Neu-Anspach, 1998, p. 41.
[35] Taylor, pp. 57-61, 64-74.
[36] Taylor, 65, 78-85, 89-90, 103, 179-80; Ingrao, pp. 130-35, 147.
[37] Taylor, p. 109.
[38] Theibault, pp. 64-65; Lerch, p. 51; Ingrao, pp. 93-94, 203-05; Taylor, p. 62; Sagarra, pp. 156-59; Durant, Vol. 10, p. 634.
[39] *1200 Jahre Groß-Bieberau: Beiträge zu seiner Geschichte*, Magistrat der Stadt Groß-Bieberau, 1987, pp. 273-75.
[40] Ernst, pp. 21-23.
[41] *1200 Jahre Groß-Bieberau*, pp. 148-49.
[42] *1200 Jahre Groß-Bieberau*, pp. 150-52.
[43] *1200 Jahre Groß-Bieberau*, pp.32, 240-41.
[44] Demandt, pp. 306-314; Manfred Knodt, *Die Regenten von Hessen-Darmstadt*, Verlag H.L. Schlapp, Darmstadt, 1976, pp.33-77.
[45] Gerd J. Grein, *Odenwälder Trachten*, Collection of Popular Folklore of Hesse, Museum in the Old Rathaus, Otzberg-Lengfeld, 1980, pp. 4-9.
[46] Grein, p. 29.
[47] Grein, pp. 31-34.
[48] Grein, pp. 35-36, 38-39, 42-44.
[49] Grein, pp. 47-49.
[50] Sources used in this section include: Peter Assion, *Von Hessen in die Neue Welt*, Insel Verlag, Frankfurt am main, 1987, pp. 11-16; *1200 Jahre Groß-Bieberau*, pp. 70-71; Valentin, p. 294; Ella Gieg, *Auswanderungen aus dem Odenwaldkreis*, Lutzelbach, 1992, pp. 17, 23-24, 26-27, 35, 38, 45-49, 51; *Guide to Region Lahn-Dill-Ohm*, p. 78; Ernst, p. 51.

Chapter 11

The Hessians in the American War of Independence

Although a thorough treatment of the subject is well beyond the scope of this work, at least an outline of the early phase of the American Revolution is helpful in setting the stage for the advent of Hessian troops. The Hessians arrived with the main body of British forces in mid-1776.

The growing agitation of the American colonists over efforts by the British crown to impose various forms of taxation is well documented even in middle and high school textbooks. In 1768 the first British troops were sent to Boston with specific orders to enforce the Crown's authority, rather than simply protect the inhabitants from external threats. In March 1770 it was some of these troops who engaged in the now infamous "Boston Massacre," the reaction to which was so violent that the troops had to be moved to safer quarters nearer the harbor. The "Boston Tea Party" in December 1773 caused the British to move troops back into quarters in town among numerous unwilling "hosts." They then closed Boston harbor in June 1774, crippling the local economy and making Bostonians into martyrs in the eyes of their countrymen. Aid and food poured overland into the town.

In April 1775 British efforts to seize weapons and gunpowder stored in Concord were met by armed resistance and the battles of Lexington and Concord touched off a true shooting war. In June, the Continental Congress appointed George Washington to head the American military forces. From now until the following March the British remained in control of Boston proper, but the surrounding landscape was held by thousands of armed rebels. The battle of Bunker Hill flared on June 15, 1775, and even by British accounts this was a Pyrrhic victory for the Crown. A stalemated siege ensued through the following winter, until Washington made the British position untenable by occupying Dorchester Heights with cannon on March 4, 1776. The British evacuated the town by sea March 17. July 4 saw the issuance of the formal declaration of independence from British rule, by which time military operations had shifted south to New York.[1]

The British king was determined to crush the rebels. He sought to reinforce his army in America to a total troop strength of over 50,000. But the war was unpopular among his subjects and recruitment lagged. England thus turned to a familiar source of manpower: the petty German states. Existing, retainer-like arrangements made it relatively easy to tap this source, albeit for a hefty price. As early as August 1775, after reports on Bunker Hill in German papers, Landgrave William of Hesse-Hanau, the heir to the Landgraviate of Hesse-Kassel, wrote to George III offering to sell him troops. Later in 1775 the Crown sent Col. William Faucitt to the continent to conclude agreements for soldiers. On January 15, 1776 an agreement was signed with Hesse-Kassel. It contained the most lucrative terms Kassel had ever obtained from Britain, with £50,000 more than she had received previously for a comparable number of troops. Her forces included some of the best-equipped and most experienced fighting men of the day. Many of these professional soldiers were used to being hired out regularly to fight in far-flung battle fronts across the continent of Europe. The Kassel contingent numbered over 16,000 by the end of the war, that of neighboring Waldeck almost 800. Hesse-

A SOCIAL HISTORY OF HESSE

Hanau provided 2,257 men under its agreement of February 5, 1776. (English efforts to procure troops from Hesse-Darmstadt failed in the face of opposition by its landgrave, Ludwig IX.) The troops' German and English leaders harbored no doubts about the fighting prowess of the rebels they were to face; to a man, they believed they would make short work of their opponents in any contest. Few events of the opening months of the war would serve to alter their impression.[2]

THE HESSIAN FORCES: PREPARATION AND TRANSPORTATION

Somewhat under-manned by then-current standards, the Hessian infantry regiments had 633 men on paper: twenty-one officers, 585 non-commissioned officers and men, twenty-two musicians and five non-combatant officers. Grenadier battalions had sixteen officers, one non-combatant officer, twenty musicians, and 464 non-commissioned officers and men. The *Jäger* companies, made up of rangers and hunters skilled in riflery and irregular combat tactics in woods and other difficult terrain, included: four officers, twelve non-commissioned officers, one non-combatant officer, three musicians and 105 men. The *Jägers* were an elite corps, paid well in excess of their counterparts in the infantry regiments. They were the only all-volunteer troops in the army. Artillery companies consisted of 129 men, five officers, fourteen non-commissioned officers, one non-combatant officer, and three musicians. Grenadier battalions had four companies, while the infantry regiments had five. However, in practice the regiments only contained one battalion each, so the designations were all but interchangeable.

The Hessian army in 1776 had an effective strength of 12,054 men, including engineers, supply train men, servants, etc. There were fifteen regiments of infantry, four grenadier battalions, two *Jäger* companies, and two artillery companies, organized into two divisions and four brigades. An excellent medical unit also was dispatched.[3]

For a land with roughly 340,000 people, the 12,000-man Hessian army—augmented in the next few years with another 4,000 replacements and reinforcements—represented a huge force. The French statesman Mirabeau said of Prussia that it was not so much a state that maintained an army, but an army that maintained a state. At this time the ratio of Prussian soldiers to households was about one to fourteen, while in Hesse-Kassel it was more like one to four! Unlike the practice in prior rounds of mercenary service, in this case many more of the Hessian militiamen had to be impressed into service. These reserve units typically were used only at home for garrison and police-like duties. At this time, however, four of the five garrison regiments too had to be pressed into service. Thus the second division of Hessian troops was mostly inexperienced plowboys and other first-time conscripts.[4]

In order to arrive in America by mid-summer, Hessian troops had to be mustered in time to start their great journey in early spring. Private Johannes Reuber of the Rall Regiment of Grenadiers in fact received his orders to report to Immenhausen for duty with his company on January 1, 1776. Each company was formed with three others into a battalion, and each battalion in turn was quartered in a small town; Reuber's unit was assigned quarters in Grebenstein. Here equipment was issued and twice daily drills were ordered to bring the men into top fighting form. Often the men drilled in deep snow through that cold winter, their noses and ears freezing. This regimen was maintained through February. By mid-month the men learned they were to form part of the first great division of Hessian troops to march toward the sea for transportation to America. The first units of this division, under the command of General Leopold von

Heister, began their march on February 20, 1776. Reuber's battalion stayed at Grebenstein until ordered to move out on March 3. Reuber's diary described what followed. "...we received live ammunition, sixty rounds per man, flints, kettles, flasks, axes and broadaxes, hoes and shovels, knapsacks and linen bread sacks, and everything needed for war. We looked around in bewilderment and then each one saw that this was serious...In the evening the order came to march to Kassel the next morning, to be mustered before Landgrave Friedrich." In Kassel they were greeted by large and cheering crowds. 5

One historian has captured the challenge that this massive mobilization presented to the Hessian military and civilian leadership, and the wrenching change in lifestyle it brought to the rank-and-file soldiers as they prepared to leave home for America.

> Three kinds of battalions were leaving for America: field regiments, garrison regiments and grenadier battalions. Field regiments were composed of professional servicemen enrolled for twenty-four years, mainly native Hessians although recruiting of sturdy foreigners was recommended. But maintaining large force in peacetime was a heavy burden on the treasury of a small state like Hessen, and also deprived agriculture of necessary labor. Therefore thirty of the ninety privates in each company were on furlough (*beurlaubt*) at a single time. These men were either pursuing trades as craftsmen, or helping in the fields on family farms or as hired laborers. The same men were not always on furlough, but there was a constant coming and going, from military duty to civilian occupation and back again. Since the regiments were stationed in the cantons from which they were recruited, nearly all the soldiers except foreign mercenaries were close to their family homes.6

Like Reuber's diary, the Platte Grenadier battalion journal describes the experiences of its men, whose commissioned and non-commissioned officers tended to be experienced but whose privates were mostly first-time recruits. Quartered in Wolfhagen, these men were trained in barns and houses until the coldest weather broke and they could train outdoors. Their first live-fire training occurred March 19. Those deemed unfit to soldier were dismissed and replaced with more useable men. The Platte unit was part of the second Hessian division, made up of garrison units who previously would not have served as front-line soldiers. Although instructed not to do so, the officers conducting training of the new battalions apparently had the men beaten if they failed to absorb the drill fast enough. The second division only left quarters early in May to march for the transports. British transport capacity for both divisions was limited, so the men had to be marched out in stages. At least one first division unit, the Leib Regiment, was ordered out too soon in February and had to be sent back to barracks for almost two weeks before again heading out for Bremen. Left behind on garrison duty were the draft-ineligible men who now formed the domestic militia: property owners, only sons, and similar men whose importance to the social and economic well being of the state made them ineligible to be shipped out.

According to Lieutenant Johann Heinrich von Bardeleben, the Regiment von Donop left its quarters in Homberg to the cheers and well-wishes of townsmen and the wailing and crying of the parents, sweethearts, wives and children left behind. He described, "Inconsolable mothers, weeping wives, and whining children in great numbers [who] followed the regiment and made with this sad scene the most heartrending impression." A Hessian officer recorded his view that the officers and men accepted without complaint their assignment with the British, and heard no assertions from others that it was wrong for them to serve in this way. On February 14, 1776 Chaplain Cöster of the von Donop Regiment had recorded that he married one Adam Schuchard, sergeant, with Anna Martha Jacob from Homberg. A later note indicated that this man cut his own throat in hospital at New York in 1782.[7]

Reuber's unit wound up making several forced marches in mid-March to catch up with the rest of the first division. On March 31 he described coming upon a wide area that had been flooded when the Weser overflowed its banks. Men and equipment had to be moved by wagon through this area, some twenty miles from Bremen. After reaching their next village quarters a day of rest was called so that equipment could be put back in order. (The second Hessian division experienced much the same flooded conditions in mid-May.) On April 4 the men resumed march, being transported in farmers' wagons to the Bremen bridge. From here they formed into column and resumed their march on foot. On April 7 the transport ships at last came into view. When marching through the territories of foreign powers, as often had to be done on this trip, foreign troops were assigned to escort the Hessians along their march to head off desertion and protect the property of the local inhabitants. Because of the forceful and often involuntary recruiting methods desertion was a constant problem, both in transit and once the troops reached their destination in the New World. In anticipation of this, in the 1760s and 1770s Kassel had signed agreements with many of the neighboring states by which all agreed to prohibit desertions and make every effort to return deserters to the states from whose armies they had escaped.[8]

The food provided on the march was of uneven quality and quantity. The officers were of course the best provided for, often staying in the homes of the town leaders and enjoying the choicest provisions and entertainment the house could provide. However, even the officers' accommodations varied greatly from place to place, as Lt. Bardeleben of the first division found in Driftsethe on March 18: "My host was an old man, whose only room seemed, by all indications, to be furnished comfortably. Pigs, geese, chickens, dogs, and cats were his companions and all slept together in this room...at night it became a smoky room, perhaps out of custom or necessity, even during my stay...Even though I opened the windows and doors, it was all in vain...I acquired lots of fleas when I crawled in bed...I killed herds of them but their numbers were unending."[9]

The rank and file often experienced even less pleasant quarters, sometimes lacking even straw on which to sleep. The Platte Grenadiers' journal of May 1776 noted that, "The quarters and rations were terrible and many individuals complained that they were not provided with the least bit."[10] By contrast, another unit once received pancakes from the locals for their evening meal. Sometimes the local farmers who had to provide sustenance for the men were most generous and accommodating. They seem to have taken pity on these troops that were seen by all as bought and sold by their prince. On average, quarters seem to have been better in the Hannover lands than in those controlled by Brunswick. The officers in charge of the march were expected to spend up to two *Groschen* per day per man for rations, but sometimes they failed to deliver either through negligence or efforts to save on expenses. This forage money was considered a boon to the officers, who could pocket substantial sums if they were careful in spending it on the march.

As difficult at times as the journey was for the Kassel troops, they were fortunate in being able to travel directly from their own prince's domains through the English-controlled lands of Hannover and on to the ports. This was not the case for the smaller treaty states. Hesse-Hanau was ruled by the son of Frederick II of Kassel, and there was bad blood between them. Hence the Hanau troops had to take a more round-about path through the lands of numerous other petty states, sometimes passing easily but at other times hindered in their march. The first units in 1776 made it through all right in their shipment down the Rhine. A later unit made up of *Jägers* and other infantry in March 1777 did not fare so well. The archbishop of Mainz stopped them in his territory and took eight men away, arguing they were his subjects. In Holland, several deserters jumped ship and got away with the help of local farmers.[11]

Upon arrival at the ports, the men were mustered in for inspection and sworn in as servants of the English crown. They were ordered into small boats and transported to the waiting English ships. The mood was somber, for they did not look forward to leaving the familiar feel of solid earth for the ever-swaying ships. The playing of the musicians could not dispel the foreboding. Quarters aboard were Spartan but not terrible for the officers, who might have windowed cabins, beds, chairs, a stove and a table. Storage was at such a premium that near one such cabin were found stored some smelly hams, weapons, a drum, a pastor's wig, and many other items. The lesser ranks stayed below decks, and each man was issued a mattress, a colored and white blanket, and a small cushion or pillow. From March 23 to April 7 the first division of Hessians under von Heister sat in their ships awaiting favorable sailing weather. When good weather arrived, over forty miles were covered in seven hours, sailing from the Weser out into the North Sea. Cannons were sounded in celebration as the fleet made its way. Much music was played by the regimental *hautboists* (oboists) as well. Fish were bought from Dutch sailors who hove alongside the ships, and the sea became rougher so that wives and officers became seasick. Those below decks noticed less of the movement of the waves, so most were less affected.[12]

Food on board consisted of the following: four pounds of bread for every six men, with a pound and a half consisting of salted biscuits. The latter were so hard that they had to be broken up by pounding or soaked in water to make them edible. On different days of the week each group of six also would receive: peas with four pounds of pork; oats gruel with butter and cheese; four pounds of beef, three of flour, half a pound of raisins, and half a pound of beef fat, made into puddings served to the groups of six in numbered sacks. These menus would be rotated to provide a bit of variety through her week. Food was served in numbered bowls matching the berthing spaces, one bowl per six men. The portions would be divided by one man, who pointed to each portion in turn as another man (whose back was turned) called out the names of each of the six berth mates to apportion the helpings. These were too small to provide enough food to fully satisfy. The quality of the food seems to have varied based on the ship in question. As the trip progressed, some of the meat was old and rancid by the time it was served, and the biscuits might come with maggots, which one man said they ate like a relish to augment their rations. The water often was bad, with long strands of muck growing in it. Dark in color, it smelled so bad that one had to hold his nose to drink it. But it was always in demand.

Most appreciated were the four measures of small beer and can of rum distributed daily. Given the alternately bland and salty diet the older men in particular always thirsted for more to drink, some trading their bread for brandy. Surreptitiously, other men engaged in trade of their rum rations to the sailors, although this was against the rules, and made friends with them in this way. In contrast to the poor rations of the men, officers received heartier, German-style meals prepared by cooks. They ate seated together at table.

An interesting trick of the sea-going trade was use of the "wind sack." While the men were turned out on deck a long sack held open to the wind with a barrel hoop was attached to the mast. The other end of the sack, also open, was let down into the ship and fresh air was thus directed down below decks. Vinegar was sprayed on the berths below to help clean them. In this way the air below was made as fresh as that on deck. Some men of the second division, being shipped in June, found their quarters much hotter and more foul than those of the earlier group. The ships were overcrowded, some men lacking proper berths. The Platte Grenadiers had poor rations of coarse rye bread and smelly water. Each man was given a pound and a half of snuff in lieu of smoking tobacco, which was prohibited aboard the ships. Some of the berths were so overcrowded that six men had to squeeze into a berth meant for four. They slept "spoon style," having to roll over as a group to change from their left to right sides and back again. The vermin aboard ship, particularly lice, became a plague on everyone thanks to the close quarters.

Up to six men per company were allowed to bring along their wives, with about twenty women on average in each battalion. Some hasty marriages occurred prior to leaving so the women could come along. Three couples were assigned to the six-person berths to "prevent any disorder." Later waves of recruits violated the rules and began to bring more women than was allowed by the regulations, and efforts to crack down had to be made. The women were mostly rough and hardy types, no shrinking violets these, to be able to put up with life on the transports and later as camp followers.[13]

Chaplain Cöster of the von Donop Regiment recorded a birth by the wife of one of the men in his regiment on March 23, 1776 aboard the ship *Jenny* in the Atlantic. Hamilton Carl Henrich Hämer, legitimate son of the musketeer Johannes Hämer, was born to Maria Elisabeth Hämer, nee Lohr, at 3:00 am. He was baptized the next day "while the sea was rather calm." His first name was that of the ship's captain, used despite the man's objection. Later, Cöster would record that the mother and child died in the autumn of 1777.

On May 7 and again May 16-17 the first division's transport fleet encountered rough seas, and many men again were seasick. Everyone was tossed about in their quarters, and even the officers found themselves tumbling around with chairs, tables and all manner of items not securely tied down. Another, more terrible storm struck from May 25-29. Wave after wave crashed on the ships, surrounding them on all sides, and Bardeleben said the water was two or three feet deep on deck. It even crashed into the officers' quarters, flooding everything. The ship seemed to "lie at the bottom of the deepest pit," according to the lieutenant. The ships of the fleet became hopelessly separated in the storms, with only a handful in contact with each other. A number of incidents of ramming, as well as near misses, occurred throughout the voyage.

By late July the food was rotten, the beer all but gone, and huge numbers in the first division were suffering from vermin-born itch and swollen legs. Many soldiers and sailors were diagnosed with scurvy by this time, and a number of them died. The dead were sown up in sacks, weighted with stones or sand, and lowered into the sea. Rats were a plague as well, eating uniforms, cartridges, tents and what remained of the provisions which they got at by gnawing through barrels. A duel between two officers occurred over the treatment of a dog owned by one of them; one captain was badly wounded by pistol fire and died the following day. The other duelist was arrested.[14]

When the ships finally arrived in American waters in mid-August, some of the soldiers had been aboard for five months. On-board diversions included lectures, and practice at learning better English from the ships' crews. Rain actually was of benefit at times as a source of clean water, making everyone feel much better. Great relief accompanied the landing and entrance into camp on Staten Island on August 15. Here they joined thousands of British soldiers previously disembarked from hundreds of British transports and warships that had arrived off New York from June 25 to July 12. The Germans now were given sauerkraut to cook and sassafras tea to ward off the effects of scurvy. The camp was a pleasant change from shipboard life, although fresh food remained mostly unavailable. A few ducks were obtained by hunting. Officers also were taught to cut the rank insignia and fancy gold and silver decorations from their uniforms to avoid becoming the special target of rebel snipers. Coincidentally, the rest of the Hessian first division also arrived August 15, although it had left twelve days after their first division comrades.

The Hessian troops' arrival in America brought them many new experiences. The generally high living standards of even common people impressed many, and over time the Hessians got to know the Americans with whom they boarded and from whom they bought the necessities of life. This was particularly true during the long periods of enforced inaction during the winter. Over the years many marriages to American girls resulted from this fraternization. The wealth of the land was impressive, with its expansive acres of arable that did not exist in cramped little Hesse. One officer requested permission to marry a local girl because he knew no girl of comparable wealth in Hesse who would ever contemplate marrying him. The wide use of beautiful mahogany furniture in the colonies impressed some as well, as did the unusual sight of tobacco crops in the fields. The Hessian troops also came to appreciate the local female population, which compared very favorably to the women at home, particularly given the relative wealth of many of the Americans. Attractive hairstyles, clean clothes and good looks were all commented upon.

Indians and their ways also were fascinating to the Hessians. Controlling their more savage tendencies to conform to European mores was a challenge in itself, such as instructing them on when it was permissible to scalp an enemy. Part of the guidelines held that any deserting German *Jägers* could be scalped if caught. Even the landgrave was so fascinated with the Indians that he asked General von Knyphausen to round up some Indian weaponry he could add to his collection.

The sight of blacks, called Moors by the Germans, also was a matter of interest. Black boys were much sought after as drummers for the regiments. Some of these young men returned to Kassel with their regiments after the war, and by the 1790s records existed of their baptisms, marriages and the baptisms of children they had by Hessian wives. Among the many baptisms was one in which the Landgrave William IX served as godfather.

Not the least of the surprises for the well-trained Hessian troops was the odd but obviously effective tactics of the American forces. These were described by the quartermaster of the von Minnigerode Grenadiers. Unlike the set-piece attacks in long lines in use throughout Europe, the raw American recruits posted themselves singly in trees or bushes and fired off rounds that were well-aimed at distances up to three times the range of the Hessians' guns. Upon firing, they ran off so fast that they could not be caught. This was a marked contrast to Hessian practice; their regulations put plenty of stock in being able to perform the firing drill flawlessly and fire volleys in unison on command. Exact marksmanship was not considered important outside the *Jäger* units.[15]

THE CAMPAIGN OF 1776

Washington felt the need to do all within his power to protect New York from occupation by the enemy. He recognized that control of the excellent harbor and unimpeded access to the surrounding river routes offered the British the opportunity of cutting the colonies in two. He decided to occupy the heights around Brooklyn with his little army, and wait here for the first large-scale assault by the British. His counterpart, Sir William Howe, was only too happy to accommodate him. Howe obviously expected to crush the rebellion in its infancy with a single, overwhelming assault that would bag the whole rebel army.

The Hessians were issued new cartridges because the ones they had brought from home were mostly ruined. Ensign Rüffer of the von Mirbach Regiment noted that, "the younger recruits waste powder." On August 21 Hessian grenadiers were loaded on boats for transport to Long Island. A bombardment by the warships drove off the light American defense of the shoreline, and 8,000 of the Germans landed without opposition. After the intervention of a huge rainstorm, another 15,000 men landed August 22, and Flatbush was occupied by Col. von Donop's men. Minor skirmishes followed each day, but the Hessians found the opposition offered little real resistance. An artillery duel ended quickly as the Hessian guns emerged victorious. More regiments came ashore August 25, "with muskets sloped and in column of march, preserving the well-considered pomp of German discipline."[16]

Assigning command at Flatbush to Lt. General von Heister, General Cornwallis moved with much of his force to British headquarters at Flatlands village. Washington continued to reinforce the American positions until he had about 7,000 men under arms. These were spread across Brooklyn Heights, their right secured by a bay, their left largely open, with only a handful of sentinels assigned to sound the alarm in case the British attacked here. A well-trained tactician, Howe quickly sized up the situation and moved his forces by night on August 26 to exploit the wide-open American left.

Von Heister was assigned to stand fast with his troops in the British center and occupy the Americans in that area by bombardments and threatened advances. As the British fell upon the American rear he finally set his Hessian forces in motion to the beat of the regimental bands. Far from an inflexible mass of troops advancing in column as if on parade, the Hessians first sent forward their *Jägers* and some picked grenadiers who advanced in broken order to skirmish with the American front ranks, also firing off three-pounder artillery and some smaller guns. When the regiments themselves attacked, it was with the bayonet, a tactic that consistently overawed the Americans, who fell back. It was here the Hessians earned a reputation for giving no quarter in the close-order fighting. The American lines broke, and Lord Stirling, an American commander, surrendered his sword to von Heister. Many rebel troops were killed or captured in the ensuing pursuit.[17] The battle of Brooklyn Heights only reinforced Hessian perceptions that the rebels were a ragtag bunch of amateur soldiers: badly led, ill-disciplined and easily driven off.

Howe was in no hurry to follow up his victory by a frontal assault on the remaining American troops, who had fallen back to fortify a narrow front before Brooklyn. Here their flanks were better protected by water and marshland. In short order, Washington realized the peril of his position. In an amazing feat of arms, on the night of August 29 he pulled off a retreat of his entire command across the narrow bay to New York, right under the noses of the English army and navy. Howe's landing of Hessian and British troops north of New York on Manhattan Island on September 15 at last forced Washington's retreat out of the city and up to the northern part of the island at Harlem Heights. Here the demoralized Americans stood their ground, and on September 16 they stopped the British advance. They fought upwards of 5,000 British and Hessian regulars to a draw before being called to retreat to their original lines. Both sides now could see that the one-sided contests of the first weeks of the war were not inevitable. The rebels could stand up to seasoned troops when well led and effectively positioned on the field. Ensign Rüffer of the von Mirbach regiment noted that the losses in this action were seventy killed and 150 wounded. On the American side about thirty were killed, another 100 wounded and missing.[18]

Now a campaign of British landings by water along the New York coast ensued, each undertaken to outflank Washington. The Americans became more effective over time at contesting these landings, but inevitably the force of numbers and Howe's maneuvering around the flanks of their positions forced the American forces back time and again. The Hessians did not particularly like these sea-born assaults. They expected at any moment to be fired upon while crowded in the boats like cattle, and they would take to singing hymns to comfort themselves.

In a gesture apparently aimed at maintaining at least some defense of the area around New York City, Washington left behind about 2,800 men at Ft. Washington on the northern part of Manhattan Island. A sharp fight at White Plains (October 28), in which the regiments Lossberg, Knyphausen, and Rall joined British forces in driving the rebels back through very difficult terrain, generated almost eighty casualties among the Hessian units. Howe now turned his attention to reducing Ft. Washington, far in his rear.

Ft. Washington was built to take advantage of terrain along the heights along the Hudson River, incorporating it in its defenses. Although some historians are dismissive of the fort's defenses and rightly question the waste of leaving 2,800 men behind to certain defeat, the Hessian troops who had to assault the place were impressed with its fortifications. Along with about 5,000 British regulars, some 3,000 Hessians and Waldeckers were assigned the task. Von Knyphausen requested and was given the distinction of carrying out the main assault with his Hessians, many of whom were the less-experienced garrison troops of the second division. The order was given to attack November 16: Col. Rall commanded one column, which attacked from the north as the Hessian General Schmidt made a demonstration further east. Rall's force encountered rocky terrain and trees previously felled by the defenders to slow any advance. One soldier wrote that the abatis formed of interlaced trees looked impossible to surmount, but it was done despite the loss of "many good Germans." The men had to pull themselves up under a murderous fire from above, giving one another a hand up as each new elevation was reached. Cannon fire and bullets rained down on them, and casualties were heavy. After two hours, the defenders' guns began to foul from constant use and could not be loaded properly. The Americans fell back into the fort, as did other defenders facing British assault teams. The end was inevitable, and Knyphausen soon was receiving the surrendered sword of the fort's commander.

A Waldeck soldier wrote of his dead and wounded comrades lying beside and on top of one another, "battered and shattered," imploring their fellows to end their pain one way or another. A Hessian *Jäger* shot through the head was mourned by his brother, standing beside him. Another *Jäger* had both eyes shot out, but lived. The passion generated by this fight was too hot to subside as soon as the shooting was done, and some of the American prisoners received blows from the grenadiers who had conquered them at such great cost. The Americans had to walk between the lines of two

German regiments which had been drawn up in review. One man acted a bit too haughty even in defeat, and found himself grabbed by the ears by a big grenadier who sneered, "Wait a bit, and I'll show you Kassel!", whereupon the American found himself boxed about the head by two others and kicked in the pants, landing several yards back among the ranks. The last comment on the incident was, "The poor guy never knew what hit him, nor why he had been hit."[19]

The Hessian and Waldeck losses were fifty-eight killed and 272 wounded. The badly injured with a chance of being saved by medical attention had to be taken back to the Hessian medical corps set up at Harlem. The journey was accomplished in bouncing wagons that greatly increased the suffering of the wounded. The Waldeckers were most impressed with the sympathetic treatment they received at the hands of the Hessian doctors. By mid-November it was getting very cold, especially at night, and camp conditions were harsh at best. Fog and rain soaked the troops, whose boots began to rot on their feet.

Pastor Cöster of the von Donop Regiment continued his duties in this period as well. On November 20 he married the musketeer Johannes (Adam) Sustmann and Maria Elisabeth Wiederhold, daughter of the deceased resident Reinhard Wiederhold, born in Udenborn, District of Borken. This was done at Camp Blumenthal on New York island. Due to insufficient funds the groom was unable to pay the usual eight *Taler* married fee, but his company commander Col. von Gose promised it would be paid later. [20]

Washington had left the field at White Plains and pulled his men back to Peekskill, where they crossed the Hudson and most made their way south to New Jersey. The British pursued him doggedly throughout November. Washington arrived in Newark November 22 with only 3,000 exhausted and beaten men. His pursuers kept up the pressure, driving him to Trenton and then across the river into Pennsylvania. During this part of the campaign, which stretched into December, the Hessians had difficult duty marching through snowy New Jersey and making camp without adequate shelter. At this point Howe recognized the need to get his men into winter quarters. According to European custom, operations now should cease until the spring. He ordered the occupation of a string of towns across a wide arc of territory in New York, Rhode Island, and New Jersey, the latter including posts at Pennington, New Brunswick, Trenton and Bordentown. American snipers and raiding parties kept the British forces from enjoying a completely peaceful season, but no one doubted that these pin pricks were more desperate than dangerous.

In New Jersey Col. von Donop commanded the southernmost military district from his headquarters in Bordentown, including the exposed post in Trenton. Here Col. Rall took over command December 14 in recognition of his heroism in the recent battles in New York. His brigade numbered 1,400 men, comprised of the Knyphausen, Lossberg and Rall regiments, fifty Hessian *Jägers*, and a few mounted British dragoons. Although urged to better fortify the town by both von Donop and some of his own subordinate officers, Rall agreed with the contrary advice of the British General Grant that New Jersey could be held with a corporal's guard. "Let them come! Why defenses? We will go at them with the bayonet." Rall's command reflected his high standing with the senior British officers based on his battlefield heroism. Many of his Hessian counterparts had real doubts about his ability to command more than his own regiment.[21]

Christmas Day 1776 dawned gray and rainy in Trenton. The outlying Hessian pickets were drenched and miserable, and sluggish in their duties after celebrating the holiday in as fine a fashion as their circumstances would permit. Rall himself had been

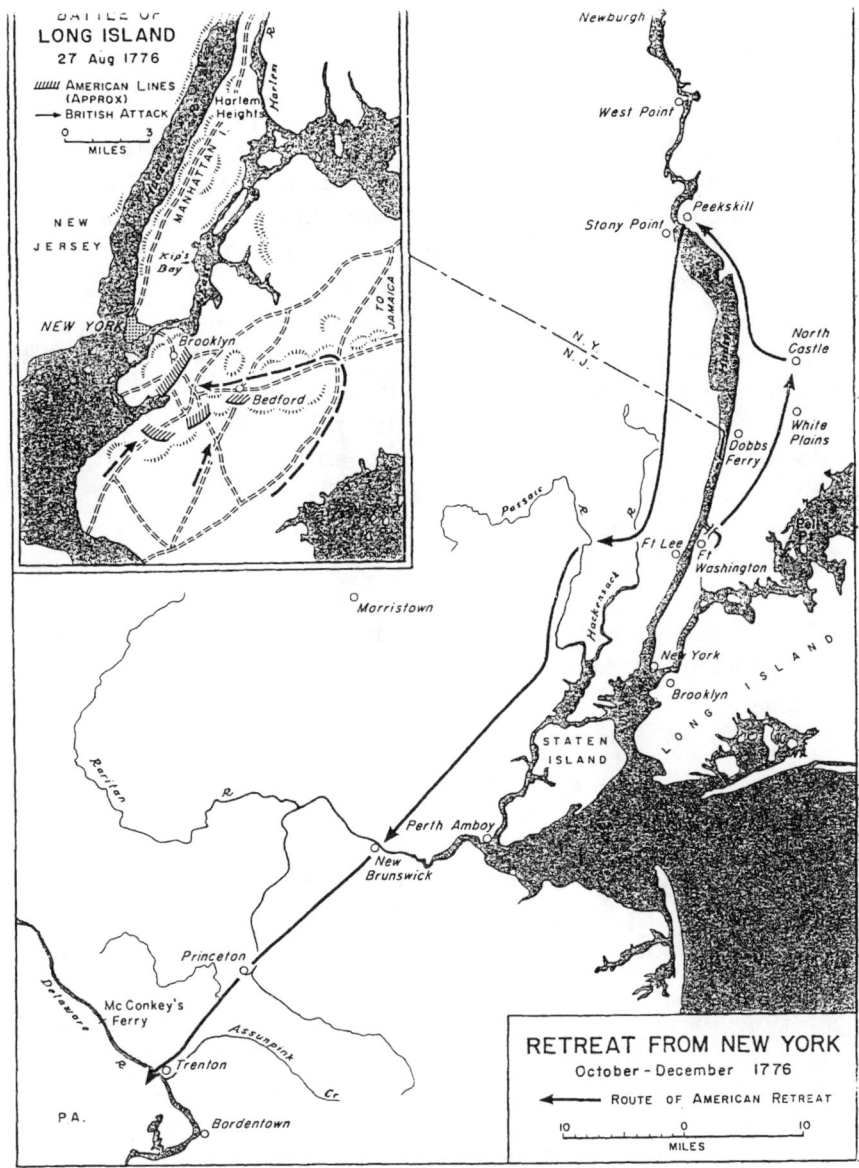

Maps 4 and 5 Show the progression of the campaign of 1776. In the battle of Long Island, Hessian forces moved forward as indicated in the center arrow (pointing towards Bedford). The path to the battle of Trenton, among the most important actions of the war in which Americans faced Hessians, is shown in the lower map. Taken from *The War of the American Revolution*, Coakley and Conn.

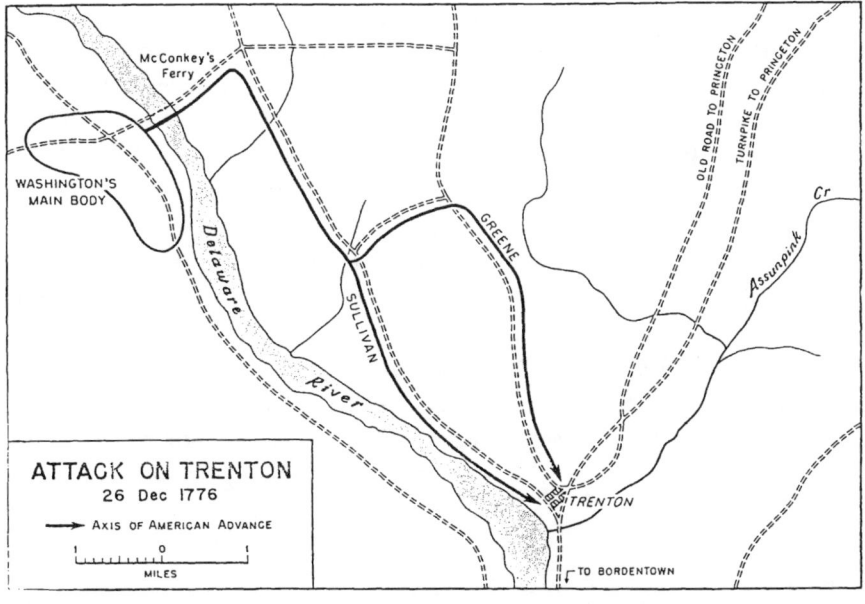

wined and dined in the home of a wealthy loyalist the night before, and retired to his bed late in expectation of sleeping in the next morning. Judging from several accounts of Hessian officers engaged in the battle, Rall was something of a martinet who kept the men marching around the town in procession to the music of oboists. Other than perhaps his own, he appears not to have been well loved by the regiments under his command at Trenton. Most accounts of the battle are highly critical of his organization of the town's defenses before the fight and his orders during the battle. But the alarm was raised in time for the Germans to muster for battle despite the previous night's revelry. The rain that morning kept Americans and Hessians alike from being able to use their flintlocks with full effect; much resort had to be made to the bayonet and the available cannon. The Americans seized Rall's artillery and turned it on the defenders. Cannon were used with telling effect in the close quarters of the town. Ward describes the battle:

> From the beginning to the end, the little town was the scene of a hurly-burly of 4,000 fighting men moving here and there by regiments, by companies, and in smaller groups. Single men fired on their enemies in the streets, from inside the houses, from behind houses and fences. The usual chaos of street fighting was made worse by the fog of gunpowder smoke that hung over the town and by the hail, snow, and sleet that continued to beat upon the fighters. It was a grand mêlée...The roar of the fieldpieces, the yells of both sides in their bayonet charges, the vociferous words of command or of encouragement of the officers, the indescribable tumult filled the little town with a howling pandemonium of sound, even when the musketry fire slackened.[22]

After ordering his men out of town to regroup, Rall initially called for a bayonet charge, but by this time the town was full of American troops and the assault was futile. Men were falling all around as he ordered another retreat. Just then, he was struck by two bullets and fell from his horse. Surrender was the only course. Rall was mortally wounded and pale from blood loss, but he was cogent enough to surrender his sword to Washington and ask that his men be well treated and their possessions left to them. He was left behind in the town and two days later would die of his wounds.[23]

This small victory was truly transformational in its effect on American hopes. Although the dilatory efforts of a few American commanders who failed to arrive for the battle allowed about a third of Rall's command to escape, 948 prisoners fell into American hands, along with a large amount of stores, forty horses, and 1,000 muskets. The Hessian losses were twenty-two killed and over ninety wounded, twenty-eight of whom were so badly hurt that they were left behind in the town when the Americans marched their captives away. In Kassel and throughout Germany the news fell like a thunderclap, and exaggerated reports held that of 8,000 men engaged only 800 had escaped capture. The landgrave was furious, arguing that lax security had brought down this fate on his forces and demanding an investigation to determine fault. He told Knyphausen that he expected a string of victories to bury the memory of this stain on his good name and that of the Kassel troops. General von Heister also apparently took the brunt of the landgrave's criticism when he was recalled to Kassel in early 1777. An old soldier even when he set out for America, he died after just two months at home. Knyphausen took over command of the Hessian forces.

Even on-site Hessian accounts mostly seemed to exaggerate greatly the numbers of the enemy faced in the battle. Most heaped blame on Rall for his poor defense of the town. The return march to captivity behind the American lines was cold and fraught with danger. Shipment of the captives across the Delaware was imperiled with strong winds and ice floes that threatened to smash the boats. Some of the Hessians decided to take their chances wading ashore in water up to their chests rather than risk being swept away. In Newtown, Pennsylvania they filled churches, prisons and other buildings, then were marched as spoils of war through Philadelphia on December 30. Even in defeat their attractive uniforms made quite a good impression on the locals, in sharp contrast to the ragged looks of their American escorts. From here the officers were marched south to Baltimore and on to Dumfries, Virginia, arriving January 24, 1777. The trip south had been arduous because of bad weather and roads. Although they were not badly treated, the officers felt that they were always on display as the local inhabitants turned out in droves to see the dreaded Hessians. Lt. Piel of the Lossberg Regiment had his first taste of bread made of Indian corn on the trip; he clearly did not care for it. Once in Dumfries, the prisoners gave their word not to try to escape, and so were allowed to go about the town freely. [24]

The non-commissioned officers and lesser ranks met with some hostility from the crowds in Philadelphia, particularly from older women who called for them to be hanged because of their role in the war. Their escort took pains to protect them, however, and Washington interceded with a published broadside that argued that these were involuntary draftees who should not be considered enemies. After that the treatment improved, and reasonably good daily rations of bread and meat were provided. On January 8 the men were marched to the barracks prison in Lancaster, arriving on the 12th. This was to be their home for much of 1777. On balance, the Hessians came to be liked much better by their captors than their English counterparts, perhaps because the Germans submitted more willingly to the Americans' authority. Some prisoners' wives and children came along as well, having been captured as "camp followers" along with their men. They received half rations compared to the soldiers. More food was provided when the prisoners were marched to a new location to fortify them on the march, including extra rum or whiskey for the men. [25]

Late in January over 800 more Hessian and Waldeck prisoners arrived, and conditions became so crowded that seventeen men were packed into each room in the barracks. Preachers were assigned to minister to their needs, and a regular roll call was organized. Sometime during the month the prisoners were accused of holding goods stolen from colonists, but a search turned up nothing. A survey was taken of the prisoners' peacetime occupations and skills, and thirty-nine professions were identified. Two linen weavers, two tile makers, a distiller, a silversmith, forty-nine tailors and thirty-eight shoemakers were among those identified.

The Americans hit upon the idea of using the men's skills for the war effort, even paying them a small stipend for wages. Uniforms and shoes began to be turned out by the Germans, and over time 95% of the shoes supplied for the American army came from Lancaster. Soon townspeople and businessmen from around the area began to seek low-wage Hessian laborers for their businesses. Inns, lawyers' offices, butchers, carpenters, gunsmiths, carpenters and many other tradesmen readily hired them on. Some Hessians even were hired out to an iron mill operator who used them to cut a channel through limestone twelve by fifteen feet deep and 250 feet long to redirect water flow to power his millworks! In September twelve Hessians were sent to work in the iron works in Cornwall, Pennsylvania. The works had had trouble up until this time delivering acceptable-quality cannon to the American forces. Eight of the Hessians were artillerymen, and in short order the quality of the guns had improved enormously.

As summer arrived, farm labor was much in demand, and again Hessians agreed to serve. They received a small daily food allowance in addition to their modest wages, although often they ate free at the tables of their employers. Farmers had to agree to keep a close watch and prevent escapes on pain of a $200 fine. Such escapes were rare, however. On June 4, 1777 British prisoners celebrating their King's birthday got riotous in their celebrations, disarmed their guards, and even had to be fired on to calm them down. The Hessians refused to take part in the riot; the English were much chagrined over this, but the Americans were so pleased that even better treatment was forthcoming.[26]

Sometimes security was quite lax among the American captors, and with Hessians wandering all about the town trying to alleviate the boredom of captivity some problems were bound to occur. Some Lancastrians complained of being insulted in the streets by the prisoners, and allegations were made of Hessians stealing wine from a local cellar and of drunkenness in the home of one George Huffnagle. The local preacher of the German Reformed church castigated the prisoners in one sermon about having, "sold your souls for naught!"[27]

In late August the British army under Howe landed at the head of the Elk River, and the threat to Lancaster was sufficient that it was ordered that many of the prisoners be moved inland to safer places. Those working on far-flung farms were unable to be rounded up fast enough. At this time 345 Hessians were marched to Lebanon and another 365 were taken to Carlisle and its environs. The officers in Dumfries and hundreds of the remaining enlisted men in Lancaster were marched to Winchester, Virginia. Here their good behavior on the march was rewarded with permission to be quartered in local houses, while the misbehaving British had to go into prison quarters. Private Reuber of Rall's Regiment noted in his diary the positive relations between Hessians and Americans at this point.

> We Hessians were allowed to go ten to fifteen miles and even farther and no citizen stopped us as an enemy, but as friends of America, because the inhabitants of the land believed that the Hessian prisoners of war would not return to the English army, but would rather remain in America. Many did this...and some of the Rall Regiment married. The other Hessian and English prisoners were still in Pennsylvania...During the spring the farmers again came forward from the countryside and took Hessian soldiers to work on the land...This continued until into the summer of 1778.[28]

In late September the Hessian officers and 300 of the men were sent on to Staunton, which was so poor that the officers petitioned Congress to be sent to Fredericksburg instead. In December their request was granted. By now they had earned such trust that they were permitted to take their time and even choose their own routes to the new location, some even using the opportunity to stop to visit friends in Dumfries.[29]

THE CAMPAIGN OF 1777

While hundreds of Hessians adjusted to life in captivity, the bulk of the German forces remained in winter cantonment in 1777 with their English comrades. The Delaware line of winter quarters in New Jersey was given up by von Donop after the Trenton debacle, and Washington reoccupied Trenton in hopes of moving north and driving the British out of Jersey. But General Cornwallis with 8,000 troops, including many Hessians, was bearing down on Washington's 5,000-man force, much of which consisted of untried militia. After another end-run of British lines at night and a pitched battle south of Princeton in which he mauled a smaller British force, the American commander realized his men were completely spent and even he had to go into winter quarters. This they did at Morristown.

Howe thus ended the 1776 campaign with only two small encampments in New Jersey, at New Brunswick and Amboy. Most of the Hessian forces were cantoned in and around New York. The Hessians and British riled the populace by looting of some of the areas around which they were quartered. In return, the Americans made sure that no foraging party or bivouac was secure outside the main British lines, and many men were killed, wounded or captured in skirmishing up and down the whole British-held line. Despite American propaganda and extremist press reports, the Hessians were not the most prolific looters in the war. Rebels and loyalists alike preyed heavily on one another's property, and the British troops also took plenty of opportunities to seize valuables when these were available.

There was quite a lot of sickness among the Hessian troops at this time, some of whom had a relapse of scurvy due to the bad weather, hazardous duty, and poor rations. Quarters were often crowded, which also spread illnesses. In the spring, reinforcements from Hesse-Kassel and other principalities also arrived by transport to replenish some of Howe's losses. As good as the Hessian captive's uniforms looked to the Americans in Philadelphia, there was a major problem with their durability on campaign. The landgrave had made sure that all his men were outfitted in Hessian-made, not English uniforms, giving a tidy chunk of business to local cloth makers. The goods turned out to be so inferior that by the end of the 1776 campaign Heister was requesting new ones regardless of the color. Even in 1780 after the siege of Charleston the inferior uniforms were deteriorating so that the men looked like a bunch of tramps.[30]

Little or no campaigning occurred before Washington deployed his troops in New Jersey at the end of May. Howe tried various maneuvers to bring him to battle, on June 26 marching his force of 18,000 men to try to cut off Washington and force a fight. In this hot summer march the Hessian troops suffered in their heavy uniforms; many were felled by sunstroke. After a minor engagement, it became clear that Washington again had gotten away. The first anniversary of Independence Day was celebrated July 4 with fireworks displays everywhere except British-held New York. A Hessian regimental band captured at Trenton was even invited to play at the celebration in Philadelphia.

Howe next decided to make use of his most potent strategic capability: control of the seas and the ability to move troops anywhere along the seaboard. He embarked his forces July 8, but left them baking in the ships for two weeks before moving out on July 23. The Platte Grenadier regimental diary recorded that, "Today [August 3] makes one year since we first landed in America and a year and one-half since we marched out of Hesse; nine months have been spent on water and nine months on land." Unbelievably, Howe now dallied at sea for many weeks, losing horses by the score to starvation and disease. Alternate calms and storms stopped or battered the 260-vessel fleet, making things miserable for the men. Lightning smashed into one ship, destroying the main mast and killing two horses. Heat, hunger, and lack of fresh water plagued man and beast alike.

At last the fleet made its way up the Chesapeake Bay and landed the troops August 25 at Head of Elk, Maryland. A few days were required before the men and surviving horses could recover enough to permit a move. As they marched north towards Pennsylvania without maps or exact directions, no local inhabitants could be found to guide them. One of the two divisions on the march was led by von Knyphausen. Lt. Rüffer of the Mirbach Regiment recorded that there were no women anywhere about because they had been told that the Hessians would abuse them if they were caught.[31]

Forage parties brought back hundreds of cattle and sheep, and given the lack of fresh meat on the long sea voyage, the latter were consumed rapidly by the Hessians. Some sharp skirmishes ensued with parties of rebel troops, the *Jägers* as usual giving good service against the foe. By September 10 Howe's two great divisions confronted Washington's army at Chad's Ford in the battle ground that would become known as Brandywine, after the local creek of the same name. While Knyphausen's divisions fired cannon rounds at the main body of American forces, Howe directed Cornwallis to conduct a twelve-mile end-run of the American right. As at Long Island, the Americans at first were fooled into believing that Knyphausen's forces included the entire British army. Howe moved deliberately and cautiously, giving the Americans just enough time to react and shift forces to the right to meet him. The British forces, including Hessian *Jägers* and grenadiers, launched their attack in column down a mile-long hill. Like a parade drill they walked unhurriedly ahead until the *Jägers* on the left absorbed a thunderous volley from a nearby orchard. They rushed to the orchard fence, and fired a volley in return. The Americans had quickly occupied a smaller, facing hill known as Battle Hill. The British rushed forward to confront them, and hand-to-hand fighting ensued. The bayonet as usual proved too much for them and the first American line collapsed and fled. Another group arrived in the nick of time to reinforce the first, but it too was driven back in ninety minutes of close-quarter fighting.

Eventually the entire American line had to be withdrawn, but they did so in good order, periodically contesting the enemy advance. When Knyphausen heard the guns of Cornwallis' men, his cue to advance, his men threw themselves furiously at the American positions holding Chadd's Ford. They too fell back and joined the general retreat; nightfall ended the pursuit. Eventual losses were about 570 killed and wounded on the British side, and perhaps 1,000 on the American side. To the Hessians' doubtless satisfaction, among the captured cannon were several that had been taken from Rall at Trenton.[32]

Chaplain Cöster performed another marriage in camp near Dilworth on September 15, 1777. The *Jäger* Conrad Sacket was joined with Carolina Wetzler of Sebbeterode. The major in charge of Sackert's company promised to collect the marriage fee subsequent to the service. Six days later the new bride was chased out of camp for being a prostitute.

After resting his men, Howe marched his two divisions forward again on September 16. Some sharp skirmishing with groups of American troops apparently afforded the Hessian *Jägers* some good opportunities to show off their sharpshooting skills, as well as their ability to attack using fences, trees and other cover to their advantage. No large-scale actions developed, perhaps because of the intervention of a torrential cloudburst that soaked everyone's powder and shot. The "Battle of the Clouds" as it was called was described by Major Baurmeister of the Hessian forces as the worst he had ever seen. "It came down so hard that in a few minutes we were drenched and sank in mud up to our calves." The Americans lost 400,000 cartridges, and the mud stopped any chance of a bayonet assault by the British. The Americans fell back again. The British went into camp to wait out the rain and spent some miserable days in this place a few miles west of Paoli. Their next march would be unopposed, taking them all the way to Philadelphia, which fell on September 26. The bulk of their forces, about 9,000 men, camped at Germantown. Several thousand more were detailed away to escort supplies from Head of Elk and others were ordered to seize a fort in Billingsport, New Jersey. This gave Washington the chance to concentrate his more numerous army on those at Germantown.[33]

Howe had so far dismissed the notion of an American attack at Germantown that he failed to require his men to dig in and form effective defensive works. The American assault on October 4 was planned in four separate columns, a complicated series of maneuvers that were too difficult for the largely green troops to bring off. The columns failed to arrive at the battle simultaneously, and although they drove back the defenders and nearly took their camp, they eventually were defeated in detail. Three Hessian battalions plus 300 *Jägers* took part in this battle; the *Jägers* distinguished themselves by foiling the advance of one of the four enemy columns. The brunt of the fighting seems to have been born by British regulars, but the Minnigerode and von Donop grenadier regiments were ordered to reinforce them and helped halt the American advance, participating at some length in the pursuit that followed.

Howe next turned to reducing the American forts and river barriers on the Delaware that were blocking his water-born supply line into Philadelphia. On October 21 Col. von Donop volunteered to undertake an assault on the Americans in Ft. Mercer at Red Bank, New Jersey. He was an experienced but also a most ambitious officer, anxious to make a name and reputation for himself quickly in the campaign. He was given three Hessian grenadier battalions, a British regiment, four *Jäger* companies and assorted cannons with which to do the job. Although he apparently complained that his 2,000-man force needed more artillery not to mention scaling ladders if they were to succeed, he seems to have failed to insist on these before heading out. His pride and rivalry with Cornwallis may have played a role here as well, since he did not wish to appear hesitant to undertake a job the English might be called upon to do instead. Another problem was faulty intelligence. Three weeks old, the story was that the fort was incomplete and could be easily taken. The brigade set off from Philadelphia for the attack.[34]

On arrival, von Donop took three hours to reconnoiter the area, but seems to have missed seeing the American gunboats on the river that later would play havoc with the assault forces. Worse, he could see that the works were not only complete but very well constructed. To retreat even in the face of this new intelligence would be personally humiliating, however. An officer was sent forth with a drummer to demand surrender in the name of the British king, warning that no quarter would be given. Hearing this from the German troops tended to enrage the defenders, and they sent the messenger away with the news that they too would give no quarter. The battle was on.

Von Donop opened the assault with a bombardment and attacked the fort in two columns, one against the northern side, the other against its main redoubt. He personally led the latter group. At first both assaults seemed to go well. The northern attack carried the Hessians over an abandoned section of the fort, but stalled against a wall recently erected to shorten the area that had to be defended. Here the assault bogged down completely. The group with von Donop got over the barriers of the outworks with few losses, but like the first group found themselves stuck without scaling ladders in the space between a defensive ditch and the fortress walls. It was at this point that the American commander ordered his men to open fire, aiming at the wide belts on the Hessians' uniforms. Solid walls of shot rained down on the now-hapless attackers, and the dead and dying piled up like cordwood. If accurate, the report of von Donop's offhand remark before the battle that he would take the fort or die in the attempt proved fateful. He was found mortally wounded among the 371 killed, wounded and captured, a huge proportion of losses for the attacking force. Over 100 men fell from the Mirbach Regiment alone. The Americans lost less than forty men. The captured wounded, von Donop included, were extremely well treated by the Americans, according to the diary of Lt. Rüffer of the Mirbach Regiment, even allowing some Hessian doctors to journey to the fort to treat the colonel. Von Donop died the same day, however.

The return march of the survivors took them back inside their works in Philadelphia on the night of October 23. One man described this period of occupation as most miserable; food was bad and in short supply, and the inhabitants made no secret of their hatred of the Hessians. Looting or mistreatment of the locals was prohibited, and the record reflects that the Hessians had to be more on guard against the local farmers than the enemy troops. Within weeks, Howe took Ft. Mercer by maneuver without firing a shot. The Americans decided it could not be held, and blew it up along with their now-trapped naval forces on the Delaware. The irony of this easy victory must have been great for the survivors of the von Donop assault. In any case, this battle may have marked a turning point in the war for the Hessians. Their heavy losses could only be made up with inferior-quality replacements, and the mass of Hessian units were no longer viewed as invincible or elite. Enthusiasm waned for a war that at first seemed eminently winnable, but now increasingly had to be viewed as a quagmire for the British forces.[35]

For the most part, Philadelphia favorably impressed the Hessians. In a report back to his professor in Göttingen Captain Johann Hinrichs of the *Jägers* spoke of the practical layout along the streets. "A wide stone pavement in front of the houses makes walking very easy, and I must admit that it is better than in Göttingen. Here the gutters do not adjoin the sidewalk, so that the pedestrian is not forced to leave it during the rain to avoid becoming twice as wet as he would walking in the middle of the street. Each householder gets two poles in the summer, on which to fix canvass, so that one may walk in the shade."[36]

The balance of 1777 was taken up with skirmishing without strategic advantage gained by either side. The best news of the war for the Americans came when it was learned that Gen. Burgoyne had surrendered his entire command at Saratoga, New York.[37] Among the German troops lost were the Hesse-Hanau infantry and artillery forces. In the theater commanded by Howe, the British took up winter quarters in relative comfort in Philadelphia, which they fortified with a string of a dozen forts. Some men, including the hard-hit Mirbach Regiment, were shipped back to New York City for the season. The Americans by contrast suffered hardship and deprivation at its worst in their mean winter quarters at Valley Forge.

THE CAMPAIGN OF 1778

Little action of consequence occurred in the period from late 1777 to the spring of 1778, somewhat to Washington's chagrin, as he was spoiling for a fight. His army had been swelled with spring enlistees. What he could not know was that London had directed the new British commander, Gen. Henry Clinton, to abandon Philadelphia, concentrate his forces in New York, and wait for more temperate fall weather to begin a new campaign in the southern colonies. Clinton was a popular choice among the

German troops: he had served with German forces on the continent during the Seven Years War, knew their language, and enjoyed good relations with them. This period of pause made most of 1778 somewhat anti-climactic, except for Washington's efforts to harass the British move to New York. Hessian forces from this point forward were increasingly used for garrison duty in New York and other larger towns, freeing up British forces to undertake more of the free-flowing campaigning forced on them by the American style of warfare. The Hessian *Jägers* were a major exception, however. They continued to provide invaluable service as skirmishers and sharpshooters throughout the campaign. The Regiment von Bose, which marched with Cornwallis, was the other exception.[38]

On February 28, 1778 Chaplain Cöster of the von Donop Regiment heard the expressions of penance of Musketeer Johannes Schneider of Felsberg. This took place in camp at Philadelphia. Schneider confided that he had committed an act of fornication with Elisabeth Assesmann of Felsberg, but was sorry for this and promised to marry the "unfortunate" girl on his return home. Since he then took communion, the chaplain decided to waive the usual penance fee. Also in early 1778 arrangements at last were made to exchange the Hessian officers captured at Trenton along with British officers for a like number of captured Americans. In February and early March the Hessians imprisoned in Virginia set out for Lancaster, Pennsylvania. From here it was planned they would go on to Philadelphia to be exchanged. Although held up for a few weeks at Hanover, they arrived in Lancaster at last on April 10, and took the opportunity to visit with the rank and file Hessian troops still held there. About this time the barracks were hit with an epidemic of "camp fever," or typhus, which threatened to spread through the town. By April 20, the officers were back in Philadelphia and met with the remnants of the regiments that had escaped capture at Trenton. By mid-May their parole pledges were given back to them and they resumed their service.

Like their officers, many enlisted men were exchanged at this time. Some 400 men arrived in mid-July from captivity in Pennsylvania. This allowed the Lossberg and Knyphausen regiments to be re-formed at effective strength. Dozens more arrived over the next few months, including non-commissioned officers and drummers. Private Reuber of the old Rall Regiment noted that Hessians were gathered for exchange in August in Winchester, Virginia, and that those who did not return had to be paid for by their farmer employers. Some men returned but then deserted to rejoin the farmers and sweethearts they had found during their work on the local farms. These 300 Virginia-based prisoners took longer to get repatriated, only arriving in Lancaster in September after Philadelphia had been abandoned to the rebels. They finally were delivered to British hands on October 28. Reuber notes his "joy and pleasure" at escaping slavery even though his party had to travel an extra 500 miles compared to the Hessians that had been held in Pennsylvania. Reuber rejoined the remaining elements of the old Rall Regiment, now renamed the Trümbach Grenadier Regiment and commanded by Col. Köhler.[39]

It was well that these seasoned troops became available, since further efforts by the British Col. Faucitt to buy new recruits among the German princes were proving difficult. The countryside had long since been swept clean of the more desirable men, and the remaining recruits were of a lesser quality, more liable to be unsavory types and prone to desert. The perception was that the war had gone badly for Britain, and even the landgrave in Kassel was in no mood to be of further support. He was at last induced to allow some voluntary recruitment of *Jägers* and others among his subjects, and by February 1778 about 250 of his men joined another 660 from Hanau and Anspach who headed for the coast to be transported.[40]

Gen. Clinton's task in mid-June was to evacuate his 10,000 men, plus 3,000 loyalist non-combatants and a huge wagon train of baggage and booty from Philadelphia, without being set upon and defeated in detail by the large and increasingly seasoned American army. On June 16 the line of fortifications that protected the city were stripped of their artillery. Much baggage was put on ships along with the possessions and families of the loyalists, and the Anspach and Bayreuth regiments that Clinton feared would desert on a long march. These departed by sea. The rest of Clinton's troops prepared to march in two great divisions north through New Jersey to New York. The last of the units left the town June 18. The Americans avoided direct attacks, but they spoiled all the wells they could find on the British line of march, felling trees on the roads and otherwise obstructing their progress.

The days on the march were terribly hot, and the Hessians suffered perhaps most of all from their especially heavy uniforms and packs that weighed almost 100 pounds apiece. Sunstroke felled large numbers, and many had to be loaded on officers' horses to keep them from falling into enemy hands. Swarms of mosquitoes assaulted the men as well, and many faces were swollen beyond recognition. Water was hard to come by, and many of the Hessian troops apparently deserted to the Americans. The army was also slowed by 1,500 wagons and carts carrying all manner of items stripped out of Philadelphia. There were frequent sharp attacks on the rear guard by American troops. It was here that the always-busy *Jägers* once again proved their worth in beating off the attacks. As Clinton's ponderous train of troops and wagons under von Knyphausen slipped off to the north, he prepared for a more general and large-scale battle by reinforcing the rear guard under Cornwallis. At Monmouth it was attacked by a large American force (June 28), but the British succeeded in pushing back the Americans, due largely to lackluster leadership by their senior officer, Gen. Charles Lee. When Washington arrived on the scene, however, the Americans held their ground and traded blows with the British until the heat stopped the fighting late in the afternoon. The Hessian corps embarked at Sandy Hook with the rest of the British army, arriving in New York July 5. Losses on the march had included 136 British and 440 Hessian deserters.[41]

The only other action that year for the Hessian troops came in the south. The Trümbach and Wissenbach regiments boarded ship November 9, and after being provisioned a storm struck with such intensity that anchors were torn loose and many Hessians became very seasick. Some ships were driven aground, and everyone feared being sunk. It was only on November 27 that a fair wind permitted the transports and warships to head south. The men traded rum for bread with the sailors, although this was against the rules. Private Reuber recorded the great pleasure the officers and men took from a church service held on board December 5. Another huge storm struck with a whirlwind on December 13, and the quick-thinking captain had to puncture the main sail with a harpoon, causing it to shred in the storm and free the ship from the grip of the wind. The flotilla arrived at Savannah, GA on December 23. The little army included about 3,500 men. The British and Hessian troops stormed the town successfully late in the month, and the Americans evacuated Georgia. The Hessian troops now settled in to garrison duty. At about this same time, the Waldeck Regiment was shipped to the British West Indies in preparation for a 1779 assault on Pensacola.[42]

THE CAMPAIGNS OF 1779-80

As in the year before, little militarily relevant activity occurred on either side through the first half of the year. But Chaplain Cöster continued in his duties of officiating at various services. On January 17 he married the 24-year-old Fusilier Friedrich Busch of Schermbach in Bückeburg to Wilhelmina Catherina nee Ohm, the widow of a fellow fusilier. As a non-Hessian, the groom was relieved of the usual marriage fee. The pastor at first refused to perform the marriage because the required twelve-month mourning period had not passed, designed to ensure the bride was not pregnant with any of her dead husband's offspring. He was induced to waive the requirement because she had just given birth two weeks after the death of her husband.

In late May Clinton sent a force out to capture the American fort at Stony Point, New York. The Americans under Lafayette promptly recaptured the post, but soon abandoned it again. A similar attack on the little British outpost at Paulus Hook resulted in its capture, but thanks to the efforts of a small group of Hessian troops who holed themselves up in a blockhouse, the Americans soon decided to leave without even destroying the guns and war material on hand. Also in May, Clinton sent a small fleet with troops including Hessians south to Virginia, seizing and burning Norfolk, Portsmouth and Suffolk.

In late September a disaster at sea occurred when two Hessian regiments, Lossberg and Knyphausen, were in the process of being transported to Canada. A terrible storm struck, smashing masts and scattering the fleet. One transport with Hessian troops of the Lossberg Regiment was sunk, while two others with Knyphausen grenadiers were captured by American privateers and taken into enemy ports. The men were all made prisoners.

Around this time on September 7 Chaplain Cöster recorded a rather poignant entry in the von Donop regimental church book. An illegitimate girl was born in New York to Cornelia, daughter of Mr. Bayeix, a citizen of New York. She was "a pleasant young girl, whose fate touched me," said Cöster, because she asserted that the father was a Hessian lieutenant in another regiment who had promised marriage and so induced her to have relations with him. "Nothing new in America, unfortunately," said Cöster. In this case, however, the father was discharged in 1783, married Cornelia, and moved to Canada. In October, Captain Ewald of the *Jägers* complained in his journal of the bad effects of the highly changeable weather on the health of the men. "Since the burning southern wind [in the daytime] and the cold spells are coming again [at night], putrid fever increases among the units who have been in the south. The men die like flies, and the hospitals are filled."[43]

In the southern colonies, a combined French and American force landed at Savannah and attempted to take it, first by siege and then by storm, October 9. The Hessian garrison troops gave good service with the English forces, beating off the attack. The siege was given up.

Near the end of the year Clinton determined to follow up on the successful Savannah attack by using Georgia as a springboard to reclaim the southern colonies. He embarked with 8,500 men in New York December 26, leaving von Knyphausen in command of the city. Five regiments of Hessians were among those in the transports. Once again, this time off the coast of Hatteras, heavy storms hit and badly damaged and dispersed the fleet. Most of the cavalry horses on the ships were killed, and four of the ninety transports were sunk. One was captured and several went missing. The transport *Anna* was blown out into the Atlantic, lost its masts, and was forced to float helplessly for eleven weeks. With food for only four weeks, the 250 men (and some wives) aboard, including thirty Anspach and Hessian *Jägers* and Hessian artillerymen, suffered terribly. They survived in part by eating the dogs aboard, then ground up the bones and boiled them with shavings from the salt-beef barrels. At last the ship ran aground in Cornwall in February and its starving passengers escaped. In August 1780 the men were shipped back to New York, arriving there in October.

These men would have been sorely needed, for the typical recruits after 1776 were foreigners, including "adventurers, misfits, and failures of all sorts...Deserters, bankrupts, ne'er-do-wells—such reinforcements must have caused anxiety even to hardened veterans like Knyphausen and Lossberg."[44] Poor people tended to sign themselves up in winter when they needed food, clothing and warm quarters. In the latter years the recruits tended to be rebellious and downright threatening to their officers if they did not receive as much pay as they had been given to expect by the recruiters. Once in America, they were responsible for a large increase in violence and thefts.[45]

The rest of the fleet eventually limped into port at Tybee Island off Savannah. Here in the deep south there were oysters, wild horses, alligators, snakes, opossums, cardinals, and other exotic game of all kinds that the arriving Hessians could never have dreamed of, as well as cotton, indigo and many other products. In contrast to widely-available rice, the few locally-grown potatoes at first were sought after by the Germans as more familiar fare. But Private Reuber recorded that these were so inferior to the European variety that, "they stuck in our throats." A much more difficult aspect of life in the southern colonies was the epidemic outbreaks of fevers and tropical diseases against which the northern European constitution offered little resistance. Diseases of all kinds felled more Hessians than war wounds during the conflict. The Germans also were personally disturbed over the treatment of slaves by their slave holders in the deep south. Many were disfigured and worked until they broke down, with inadequate food and mere rags for clothing. The Hessian officers considered the black slaves to be humans as worthy as the whites, and lamented that they often were treated worse than dumb animals. In several cases they interceded with the local masters to improve the slaves' treatment or head off abuse.

Reinforced to an effective strength of 10,000, the southern army under Clinton undertook the siege of Charleston in April 1780. After a classic siege by land and sea in which the Hessian and English troops braved broiling heat, bad water, the lack of tools and much hard work digging trenches, the city was bombarded and induced to surrender (May 12). The garrison numbered some 5,000 men, a surrender of American forces not equaled until the US Civil War. The booty from this wealthy trading town was great, and the practice was to distribute it among the conquering troops. The total came to some £300,000. The Prince Charles Regiment captured a ship laden with goods that brought each man a bounty, from £2,000 for the colonel to £7 for each private. The siege had cost the Hessian troops seventy-three men killed and wounded.[46]

Also in April 1780 Chaplain Cöster recorded another illegitimate birth in New York, the product of a liaison between a Hessian artillery lieutenant and Barbara Rheider, daughter of an Anabaptist. The woman already had another child by the same man. Cöster adds the following poignant remarks. "NB – She calls herself Mrs. Dietzel, because she says, her marriage was made in Heaven. A soldier of the Leib Company of the von Donop Regiment named Andreas Zülch was the sponsor on 20 April 1780 at New York. Therefore another pair of wretched boys and girls more in the world!

Figures 11-1/11-2 Hessian forces in camp, showing their weapons and tents. Members of the Regiment von Donop Revolutionary War re-enactors.

Figure 11-3 Regiment von Donop re-enactors standing at attention in camp. ***Map 6*** shows the progress of the southern campaigns in the latter phases of the Revolution, from *The War of the American Revolution*, Coakley and Conn.

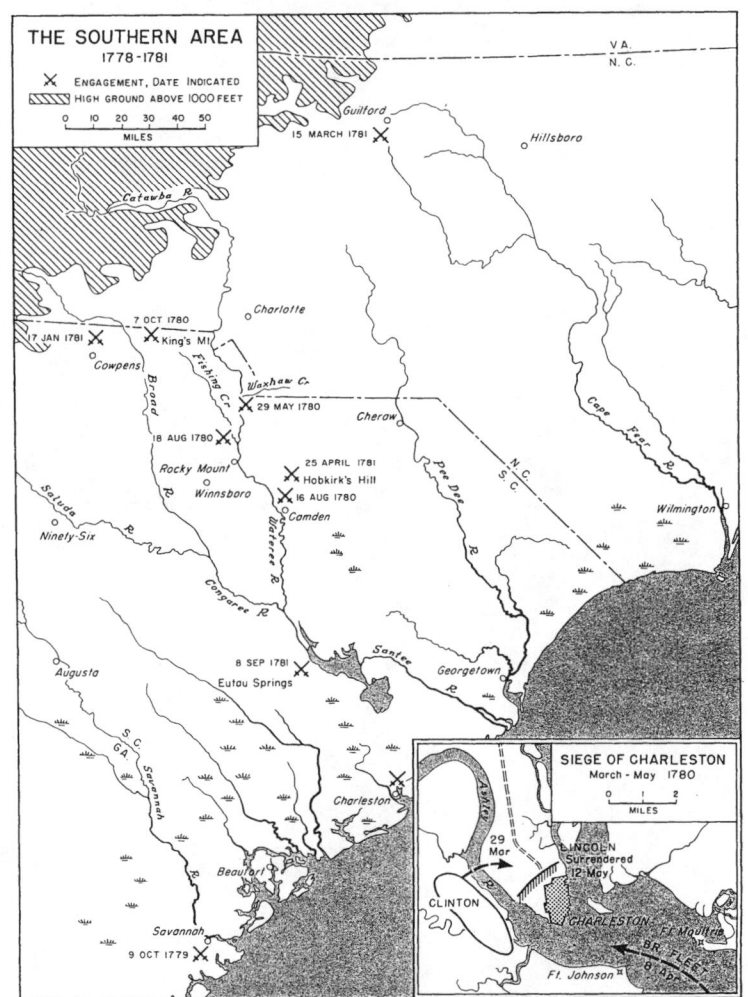

Therefore, take care and do not be fooled by a man who promises to marry you! NB – Father and child died at New York in 1781."

By this time the Hessians' letters home showed a definite turn against their English employers. Complaints were legion that the British were arrogant and careless as soldiers. The officers were seen as dandies, too focused on maintaining their toilette, complete with powdered wigs and perfume. They seem to have developed an increasing appreciation for the cruder, more manly approach to war of their American opponents. Still, the German military mentality could never grasp why these very well-endowed commoners could stoop to revolting against their just king, who if anything had been too lenient with them. "[The Hessians] were motivated primarily by a concept of 'honor' which involved both doing their duty on the battlefield and fulfilling the trust granted them by their sovereign when he commissioned them. It seemed to the Hessians, however, that American society was moved by the bourgeois principle of individual self interest..."[47]

In May 1780, Cornwallis was left with a smaller force to complete the conquest of South Carolina. This force included the Hessian Ditfurth, Huyn, and Trümbach regiments. The rest of Clinton's forces were shipped back to New York. Here von Knyphausen could report to his commander on a relatively uneventful season. In March he had sent out forays of men who sacked the finer homes in the areas around the Hudson through which they marched.

After demolishing the untested and poorly-led American army in the southern colonies at Camden in August 1780, Cornwallis determined to follow up British success in Georgia and South Carolina by moving on North Carolina and from there, Virginia. In the fall he marched on Charlotte, but lost a third of his command October 7 when 1,000 American frontiersmen surrounded and annihilated a like number of loyalist militia operating independently from Cornwallis at King's Mountain. Cornwallis gave up his advance, and fell back to South Carolina to await reinforcements. Among the troops arriving at Charleston from New York in November were the Hessian and Anspach *Jägers* that had been blown off course the previous year and shipwrecked in Britain. The balance of the year was spent by the two sides in resting, supplying and obtaining reinforcements.

On October 30 Pastor Cöster heard penance from another man among his regimental flock. Artillery Sergeant Johann Henrich Brethauer of Klein Almerode said that he had made an American girl pregnant, one Polly Tiezen of New York. The child lived, and he said if given permission he would marry the girl, but in any case would always support the mother and child.[48]

THE CAMPAIGN OF 1781

As the new year arrived the Waldeck Regiment in Pensacola found itself under increasing pressure from Spanish forces, by now also at war with Britain. From early March until May the siege continued with increasing ferocity, until the garrison surrendered May 10. The surrender terms held that the Waldeckers and British were to be transported to New York and released, on condition that they not take up arms again against Spain or her allies. Fortunately for the British, Spain's allies at that time did not include the Americans. The released captives arrived in New York in mid-June.

Cornwallis began 1781 with a new infusion of Hessian and British troops sent by Clinton. Among these were the Hessian von Bose Regiment and 600 *Jägers* under the command of Gen. Leslie. Leslie was ordered to Camden to hold it against any enemy attack. In the battle of Cowpens in January the Americans destroyed the legion of the dreaded British cavalry commander Tarleton, much to the shock of the British and Hessians. No Hessians fought in that battle. Cornwallis now marched his men north and east into western North Carolina to try to avenge the loss. The two sides clashed at Guilford Court House on March 15. The American force actually outnumbered Cornwallis by two to one, but his men were all battle-tested veterans compared to the untried militia that formed much of the American force. The Hessian forces formed the right wing of the British advance, taking the brunt of a volley of musket fire and losing dozens of men as they marched in column on the American positions. Their own volley was followed with a bayonet charge, and the American left wing fell back into some woods. The Hessians followed, and hand-to-hand fighting ensued. As the rest of the battle raged on, the Hessians remained largely separated from the main British forces. The firing ignited the brush, burning many of the wounded.

On the British left, the *Jäger* companies were actively engaged. With their British counterparts, they drove through two lines of American defenders, only to come upon a third line of the more experienced troops of the continental line. Charging with the bayonet they took the full force of an American volley, and their lines broke and fell back in the face of an American bayonet charge. The hand-to-hand fighting was intense, and soon it looked as though the Americans would break through and win the day. Now Cornwallis resorted to a ruthless but ultimately decisive tactic: he ordered the artillery to pour deadly grapeshot into the thickest part of the fight, downing many of his own men as well as the Americans. But this stopped the American drive and allowed the British to re-group.

All this time the von Bose Regiment continued the fight in the woods separated from their comrades. As the Americans began to withdraw from the field Tarleton's horsemen charged the riflemen in the woods, disengaging them from von Bose and ending the last of the fighting. The British casualties amounted to over 500 killed and wounded, the American loss about 260. Although technically he won the battle, Cornwallis now had no way to sustain his troops and was forced to march them towards the sea to seek provisions. His hungry men first had to do what they could to round up and provide for the hundreds of wounded on the field, much of the time in a pouring rain. The Anglo-German forces had not eaten for two days at this point, and food was still in such short supply that four ounces each of flour and lean beef was all that could be allotted to each man. They then began an arduous trek of hundreds of miles that took its own toll on the victors. Often the army would stop in order to bury those who had died of their wounds. These included many British officers and two from the von Bose Regiment. They reached Wilmington at last on April 7.

Sgt. Koch of the von Bose Regiment recorded his impressions of the march. "The lightly wounded men were taken in wagons and on horses. No enemy followed us. We marched eighteen miles each day. At evening the royal militia brought us cattle and some flour. The cattle were slaughtered and the meat was cooked or roasted and the flour was made into cakes and cooked on a board in the fire. From the hides of the slaughtered cattle, each soldier cut a strip and tied it to his feet. On April 5 we went to Williamsburg in Virginia, a seaport [sic – he clearly means Wilmington]…We camped there for fourteen days. We received a double ration of rum each day…and our full provision of meat and ship's bread. Each soldier received two pairs of shoes, three shirts, and a pair of long trousers. Because our Hessian weapons had become useless, the von Bose Regiment received…new English weapons at the same time." The landgrave was as pleased as the British with the fighting done by the von Bose

Regiment in this campaign. He wrote to von Knyphausen to ask him to express his satisfaction to the men of the regiment.[49]

Still seeking an effective strategic move that would bring a decisive victory, Cornwallis decided to take his 1,400 remaining men back into the wilderness and invade Virginia from the south. As the Americans went about conquering every fortified British outpost in the Carolinas except Charleston, Cornwallis marched north to begin what would become the last major campaign of the war, culminating with the siege at Yorktown. His forces sparred with those of Lafayette in the early summer, and a more general engagement at Portsmouth resulted in a bloody nose for Lafayette.

Hessian forces in New York were engaged in skirmishing and foraging from time to time, but nothing on the scale of the operations then taking place in the south. General Clinton often fretted about a possible American offensive in coordination with the French fleet, which periodically menaced various parts of the Atlantic seaboard. The Hesse-Kassel *Jäger* Corps journal records that German recruits arrived in New York August 11, but that they were terribly sick after a 93-day voyage. The journal also reports on spy operations conducted by the *Jägers*' Lt. Col. von Wurmb, who had been granted permission to manage spies. He advised General Clinton in mid-August that the American army was in fact headed south to rendezvous with the French and take up operations in Virginia. He based this on such evidence as the report that the American mistress of a French officer had been sent to meet him in Trenton where he was expected to arrive with the French forces, and that food and forage was ordered to be placed in readiness for the march of Washington's troops through the same area. Clinton seemed perpetually undecided about whether and to what extent to reinforce Cornwallis in the face of threats to his command. In an effort to comply with Clinton's direction to remain in contact with New York and protect his ability to be supplied by sea, Cornwallis decided to seize and fortify Yorktown with his command of about 6,000 men. These included the Hessian Bose and Hereditary Prince Regiments, plus sixty-eight *Jägers* and two regiments from Anspach.[50]

Washington and his French allies bore down on Cornwallis' position with about 15,000 men in total. A preliminary naval action resulted in the English fleet giving up the Chesapeake to the French, thus cutting off Cornwallis from aid by sea. Expecting aid from just this quarter, as Clinton recently had promised, Cornwallis gave up the outer works his men had constructed in order to better concentrate his force and resist the coming assault. The allies' entrenching work in preparation for the siege began in early October, and heavy siege guns were brought up from the James River. The allies' cannon did deadly work beginning October 9. They continued the bombardment largely unabated until the surrender. A French attack on some of the von Bose men in an exposed position was attempted when it was noticed that they were rotated off duty at a specific time in the early evening. The attack was beaten off by the relief unit.

The bombardment was ferocious. Sgt. Koch noted that one round hit the tent of Major Scheer, destroying it but without hurting anyone. The same happened to Koch's tent and several others, blowing to smithereens numerous knapsacks belonging to his company. More heavily bombed were the British camps. Over time the English cannon and magazines were destroyed, and supplies of powder ran dangerously low. Notorious for their lack of fortitude, many of the Anspach troops in particular began to desert. Cornwallis tried at one point to shift his forces across the river to Gloucester, held by his subordinate, Tarleton, but a freak storm blew up and scattered his boats as this plan was under way. Cornwallis tried some gallant and marginally successful forays to capture groups of the besiegers and spike their guns, but with no real effect on the siege. Meanwhile the bombardment continued, one of the last shots killing the surgeon of the Hereditary Prince Regiment and a drummer boy from the von Bose. By October 17 the game was up, and Cornwallis agreed to unconditional terms of surrender. The British and Hessian regiments marched out October 19 as if on parade between the French and American ranks, piling their weapons in a field west of town. About 8,000 soldiers and sailors of all ranks surrendered. The German regiments gave up eighteen standards and eight artillery batteries. It was said that the German officers bore their disgrace with more military bearing than their English counterparts, some of whom behaved like "whipped schoolboys." Still, Sgt. Koch's journal expresses bitterness at having to surrender to rebel forces, suggesting that without the French the Americans never could have triumphed.

The casualties on the British side in the siege had been only 156 killed and 326 wounded. The same day as the surrender Clinton had embarked 7,000 troops to come to the rescue. By the time they arrived off the coast Cornwallis' men long since had headed for imprisonment in Maryland and Virginia, his principal officers paroled and allowed to go to New York.[51]

Interestingly enough, there were Germans and probably even Hessians on both sides of this fight. The French Royal-Deux-Ponts Regiment included troops from Zweibrücken, and volunteers from Hesse-Darmstadt (recruited in Darmstadt lands within French territory) also were in service with the French in America. They served with the tacit support of their prince, Landgrave Ludwig IX. The Royal Hesse-Darmstadt Regiment was quartered in Brest in fall 1781 preparing for transport to America when news of the Yorktown victory reached France.[52]

Many of the remaining Hessian prisoners of war were likewise on the move in 1781. In March, those at Winchester, VA were marched back to Lancaster, the barracks having been ordered to prepare for 1,200 men. Major Baurmeister, adjutant general of the Hesse-Kassel troops, waited with great anticipation at Philadelphia on April 29 during a mass repatriation of prisoners. Despite the fact that 309 English troops arrived April 12, no Hessians were coming in. He wondered whether the blandishments of local women and the resultant marriages were to blame, an obvious fulfillment of "the intentions of the Americans." He also offered the opinion that men induced to desert to the American side were running away as soon as they were issued equipment, but rather than heading for New York it seems clear that many were simply disappearing into the surrounding farm lands they had come to know so well. The men captured with Cornwallis seem to have been moved initially to Frederick, Maryland. When Congress ordered another move of prisoners from Winchester to Frederick, the Prince Frederick and von Bose men were sent to Lancaster and were quartered in the local poor house. In October, most of the remaining von Knyphausen Regiment's prisoners (taken in 1776 at Trenton) had returned to New York.

The winter of 1781-82 was a lean one for the prisoners, officers often having to buy provisions for the men out of their own funds. Clothing was also in great demand. Death through disease and loss due to desertion continually reduced the ranks. In May some back pay was provided that helped everyone afford more of the necessities. Apparently many men fell into the familiar pattern of hiring themselves out on local farms. On September 1 the farm hands were all ordered to report back to Frederick, at which point it became clear that many had married and settled on their farms. For eighty Spanish dollars they could buy their freedom, or contract as "redemptioners" to work for someone willing to advance the money until the debt could be paid.

After peace was declared in 1783, Major Baurmeister was permitted to travel the country from Philadelphia to Lancaster to try to locate some of his lost sheep. He wrote that summer of finding, "162 Brunswickers and thirteen Hesse-Hanauers, most of them married and settled on their own land. Thirty-nine of the Brunswickers showed a desire to return, but none of the Hesse-Hanauers."

The Savannah garrison troops of the Regiment von Knoblauch returned to New York in August, 1782. The Hessian troops left in Charleston had a long, mostly dull garrison duty from 1780 until the city was evacuated in October 1782. Many deserted, particularly near the time when the evacuation was to occur, at which point from four to ten men a day were leaving. A bounty was paid to black dragoons who rode out and dispatched with the sword any deserters they could find. A stormy passage finally brought these southern garrison troops back to New York in December and January. They went into winter cantonment and suffered greatly in their inadequately-protected quarters. Also in December, a transport fleet returned to Europe taking with it all the invalids and other assorted members of the army bureaucracy and logistics train. This reduced the cost and the number of people who had to be sustained at government expense, saving on food and wood. Despite rumors of peace, the Hessians continued to drill and train through the winter months. At last, in April 1783, peace was concluded.[53]

The ensuing months were much taken up with efforts to exchange prisoners and re-form the broken units into something approaching normal strength. The Hesse-Hanau prisoners, as we saw earlier in the abortive effort made by Major Baurmeister, were apparently most difficult to re-collect. Captain von Eschwege wrote many reports from New York to his sovereign in Hanau over the months, documenting by individual name the successes and failures he had in pulling the troops together. On May 23 he wrote:

> Since 13 May I lie on the ship and during this time more of the men of the regiment have returned. I hope at least that still other men who are scattered about in the countryside will return. It will surely be difficult for those who have indentured themselves to farmers for a fixed number of years to get away. However, I hear that Congress has sent an order to the farmers that all such men are to be released. It may possibly be another fourteen days before I leave from here, and during that time I hope that more will return.
>
> Of Your Highness' Leib company, I have sixteen privates here. I have reports of five or six who will surely return, if it is possible, since they have indentured themselves. However, the others have told their comrades, who have returned, that they have no desire to return to Germany and that they wish to seek their fortune in America. Among this number, the most definite are: Musketeers Köhler, Ort, Wald, and Stein, who have told their comrades they wish to remain in this country. Concerning Rüffer, Wiskemann, Traut, and Maul, and several others, I still have the hope that if they can get away from their farmers, they will return to the company.

On July 31 he wrote from England, after his sea voyage from New York:

> Since my last report to Your Highness, dated 3 June, six more men of the 1st Battalion have returned to duty. Four of them arrived at the last moment prior to the ship sailing and therefore could not be provided with weapons. A

Grenadier Schlingellof deserted from the ship at New York on 5 June 1783 and went inland again.

As Major Baurmeister discovered, the great majority of the Hanauers who failed to return from captivity were not held back by their indentures, but rather had long since made the decision to make a life for themselves in the new American nation. Why it was necessary for von Eschwege to write to his prince with the names of specific privates who had deserted is not known; however, it may relate to the fact that such men were subject to confiscation of their goods and property by the state. Eschwege's detailed account handed off by the landgrave to his officials would give them the ability to investigate and seize property where possible. As great as the desertion problem appears to be in modern eyes, in percentage terms it was actually as good or better than that experienced by the armies that fought in Europe in the eighteenth century.

The death rate of Hessians in the American war was high. One in four died, and only ten percent of these died of battle wounds. Disease, particularly in the fever-plagued southern colonies, accounted for the loss of many men.

BACK TO HESSE: THE RETURN VOYAGES AND RECEPTION AT HOME

No sea voyage of the time was entirely without its challenges, and the return trips of the Hessian troops were no exception. Private Reuber of the D'Angelelli Regiment (formerly Rall) recorded that his unit shipped out with the rest of the first Hessian Division in mid-August. The fleet was becalmed for several weeks, and when his transport did pull out it soon struck something so hard that the Hessian troops thought it would founder. The captain went below and found nothing amiss, however, so they went on. For several days afterward the Hessians below complained of a terrible sloshing sound and of cargo floating and bumping below the deck while they were trying to sleep. The English sailors made fun of their concerns for three days, until the ship began to slow down and handle sluggishly. It was then discovered that a major leak had produced seven feet of water below the decks. The rest of the fleet was signaled to wait until the pumps had drawn down the water, and for the balance of the trip the Hessians had to take turns at the pumps, sixteen at a time. A careless sailor on pilot duty caused the ship to lose the rest of the fleet one night, sailing right past it. This created considerable fear throughout the trip, for a single ship on the Atlantic was always at risk. As it turns out, the ship arrived four days ahead of its fleet on October 8. The dilatory captain was hauled off the boat and prosecuted, his first mate taking over command as they sailed on to Germany.

Those who sailed with the second Hessian division left New York in November, and arrived in England at the end of December. Quartermaster Zinn of the von Donop Regiment recorded that his unit filled three ships: almost 200 people in each of two transports, and 159 in the third. This included many wives and children of the soldiers. Another author, perhaps of the Landgrave Regiment, which also shipped out in November, recorded that on November 16 his ship rolled heavily from side to side, the waves pounding against it. He wrote, "It is a pitiful situation when men have women with them in dangerous situations. When the weight of the water burst into the ship, a scream arose each time, for fear the ship would sink." The next night the ship rolled so badly that those who slept in beds situated lengthwise in the ship were caused to roll over, first on one side and then the other. Those whose beds were crosswise, however, were constantly either standing on their feet or their heads. Later, a sail split apart in the wind, and a piece of wood flung about by the storm broke the jaw of a two-year-old child.[54]

The first division of Hessian troops was sent directly home, arriving in Hesse in October and November, and were received in review by the landgrave. A number of Hessian battalions, including the Platte Grenadiers, remained in English service and were quartered in England for some months in early 1784. Their behavior was so exemplary that a news article appeared in April in the local paper lamenting their upcoming departure and praising their sobriety, orderliness, piety in church services, and general civility. It even held the Hessians up as models for the English soldiery to emulate. Glad to be going home, many of the troops had enjoyed their service in England so much that they lamented leaving that land for good. When back in Germany, the Platte journal noted that, "It must be conceded by everyone, that we arrived here completely changed."

On arrival in Bremen April 29, the troops were served coarse, dark German bread for the first time since 1776. They now were unused to it, and many made complaining faces. Some desertions began to occur at this point as well. Traveling down the Weser none of the enlisted men were allowed to disembark from the barges in Prussian territory because recruiting officers were out in force to try to encourage desertion to the Prussian service. Some of the non-Hessian-born soldiers were discharged at Rinteln May 12, and were given two weeks' pay. On May 22 the men left the barges behind for the five-hour march into Kassel and their final parade review. The Platte journal ends abruptly as follows: "24 May – The grenadier battalion disbanded and ceased to exist, and so this journal ends."

Some of the *Jäger* units had already reached Kassel by May 17. Native Hessian soldiers received leave, non-Hessians the chance to be discharged. Most of the *Jägers* were reassigned as support units among existing regiments that were to be kept in service, while those who wished to go back to their jobs as hunters and rangers were placed on half pay until they found jobs. Dismissed men were given two weeks' pay and allowed to keep the shirts, socks and other items of personal clothing issued with their uniforms. The rest had to be returned. Much of the clothing they had used was in very poor condition, in any case. Many seem to have found it difficult to return to civilian life. The Hessian guilds prevented many from simply assuming a trade as they may have wished. Many became little more than impoverished beggars, particularly the invalids.

On November 4, 1784, deserters from the Kassel forces were given two additional years to report back from service in America without penalty. After that, their properties were subject to confiscation, and family members turned out. As a practical matter, however, most of the confiscated estates of deserters amounted to less than ten *Taler* each. These seizures were donated to the military hospital established at Karlshafen. An official record put the number of discharged men at 914, the missing and deserted at 2,949. It is impossible to determine with any certainty how many of the 8,029 Hessians that had been taken prisoner reported back to duty. Thousands certainly remained behind in America and became productive citizens.[55]

THE RESULTS FOR HESSE OF ITS SOLDIERS' SERVICE IN AMERICA

Although the huge army was unaffordable and had to be reduced greatly after its return home, Hessian veterans of the American war had become among the most gifted and battle-worthy soldiers on the continent. In the 1792 campaign against France, they gave very exemplary service. Many of the officers became sought-after leaders in the armies of other states, often achieving the most senior ranks in their adopted armies. One military innovation adopted by the Hessians was born of their American service: units made up of skirmishers that would go out ahead of their regiments prior to the attack to disrupt and engage any light infantry screening the enemy's lines of battle. They were masterful at seeking out individual cover and using it to shelter behind as they harassed the enemy with relative impunity. They combined these innovation with their existing close order tactics rather than favoring one over the other. A major recognition of this strength in the knowledge of military science may be seen in the decision of Prussia to base her own military reforms on the Hessian military regulations of 1802.[56]

The landgrave's subsidies during the war had wiped out a substantial portion of Hessian debts, but the income was always treated as his personal funds rather than moneys controlled by the state. His profit after expenses seems to have amounted to over 12.6 million *Taler*. As noted below, much of this fortune was simply spent as he pleased, for sumptuous entertainment at court, the creation of grandiose buildings, and other pleasures. In the decades to come, as the mercenary trade was ever more roundly condemned, the subject of subsidy money often was raised when pressing financial needs were discussed. People wondered aloud about what had happened to so much money and why nothing remained to pay for current needs. Of the estimated twenty-one million *Taler* taken in, almost nineteen million could not be properly accounted for. This "blood money" remained an issue throughout much of the nineteenth century, with poisonous results on Hessian politics.

The economic benefit to Hesse of this trade has always been a subject of debate. The loss of productive farming manpower undoubtedly retarded agricultural productivity for a time. But many other trades benefited greatly from the landgrave's mercantilist approach to spreading the wealth. Architects and builders and their workmen were able to build libraries, museums, a hospital, guardhouses, a porcelain factory and a new town hall, as well as refurbishing the Kassel city defenses. A magnificent new palace and grounds was created by the landgrave's son and heir, who used subsidy money to create Wilhelmshöhe to rival the grandeur of the courts of greater powers. He also was able to loan much of the money out to princes and bankers across Europe, amassing a fantastic fortune that made Hesse-Kassel financially secure to a degree unknown in the other Hessian provinces and smaller principalities across Germany.

Metal workers and miners were exempted from the draft and kept busy turning out the raw materials for the war machine. Wool weavers, tailors and others in the textile business did extremely well in this period, producing and selling to the government every stitch of clothing for the troops as well as plying their trades to support the huge number of courtiers, musicians, opera singers, dancers, theater players, and officials drawn in to support the sumptuous life at court created by Landgrave Frederick.

The people on the land gained much less than those in towns. Yet one important feature of the soldier trade did cause large amounts of capital to flow back to rural areas: the wages of the troops that they mailed home in support of their families. This amounted to 591,721 *Taler* by one estimate. The landgrave also waived some tax and contribution payments during the period when English subsidies were being paid to him. He also founded sixteen new farming villages of ten families each, using subsidy money to provide each with thirty acres, and loans of 300 *Taler* for a building and 100

Taler for animals. He waived taxes and military service requirements for three years for the settlers. The landgrave also took the advice of his councilors and established a rural agricultural fund to extend help to farmers, and introduced or expanded potato cultivation, a major innovation. He created an annual market fair in Kassel to improve domestic trade. He even fixed prices to protect consumers. Far from being more impoverished, from 1773-81 the number of sheep being held in Hesse-Kassel rose from 258,000 to 472,000.[57]

Only in 1831 was a pension system established for the remaining veterans with citizenship in Kassel lands. This occurred when some of the remaining funds from the subsidy era came under the jurisdiction of the diet. By this time, and increasingly through the ensuing two decades, America became a most popular destination for emigrants from Hesse-Kassel.[58]

NOTES TO CHAPTER 11

[1] Craig L. Symonds, *A Battlefield Atlas of the American Revolution*, Nautical & Aviation Publishing Company, Baltimore, 1986, pp. 5-19.
[2] Christopher Ward, *The War of the Revolution*, Macmillan Company, New York, 1952, pp. 208-09; Bruce E. Burgoyne, *Enemy Views, The American Revolutionary War as Recorded by the Hessian Participants*, Heritage Books, Bowie, MD, 1996, pp. xiv-xv; Max Von Eelking, *The German Allied Troops in the American War of Independence, 1776-1783*, Heritage Books, Bowie, MD, 1987 (facsimile reprint of 1893 publication by Munsells' Sons, Albany, translated by J. G. Rosengarten), pp. 16-19; Rodney Atwood, *The Hessians, Mercenaries from Hessen-Kassel in the American Revolution*, Cambridge University Press, 1980, p. 24. For those interested in more information on the Hessian soldiers, The excellent Burgoyne book may be obtained from Heritage Books, 1540 Pointer Ridge Place #E, Bowie, MD 20716 [www.heritagebooks.com].
[3] Von Eelking, pp. 22-23; Burgoyne, p. xv; Atwood, footnote, p. 27.
[4] *Hessen und die Amerikanische Revolution 1776*, Hessian State Archives, Marburg, 1976, p. 6. This book accompanied an exhibit of the same name presented in connection with the 200th anniversary of the Hessian service in the war.
[5] Burgoyne, p. 2; von Eelking, p. 23.
[6] Atwood, pp. 39-40.
[7] Burgoyne, pp. 4-5, 562; von Eelking, p. 15; Atwood, p. 37; Atwood, pp. 40, 44.
[8] Burgoyne, p. 7; *Hessen und die Amerikanische Revolution*, p. 19.
[9] Burgoyne, p. 13.
[10] Burgoyne, p. 9.
[11] Edward Lowell, *The Hessians and the other German Auxiliaries of Great Britain in the Revolutionary War*, 1884, reissued by Kennikat Press, Port Washington, NY, 1965, p. 47.
[12] Burgoyne, pp. 20-22; Eelking, p. 17.
[13] Burgoyne, pp. 24-29; Lowell, p. 56; Atwood pp. 52, 238.
[14] Burgoyne, pp. 31-46, 565; Atwood, p. 54.
[15] *Hessen und die Amerikanische Revolution*, pp. 33-36; Lowell, p. 82; Atwood, p. 66.
[16] Burgoyne, pp. 66-68; Ward, pp. 209-214. The quote comes from p. 211.
[17] Ward, pp. 222-26; Atwood, p. 68.
[18] Ward, pp. 250-52; Burgoyne, pp. 78-79; Symonds, p. 27.
[19] Burgoyne, pp. 92-97; Ward, pp. 271-74, Atwood, pp. 70-71, 77.
[20] Burgoyne, pp. 95-98, 562.
[21] Ward, pp. 288-96; Burgoyne, p. 118; von Eelking, p. 54, 59-60. Illustrations for this chapter include photos of members of the Hessian Infantry-Regiment von Donop, the largest German living-history unit involved in Revolutionary War reenacting. They

preserve the traditions and culture of Hesse-Kassel, portraying a typical soldier's life through encampments, battle simulations and military drills. Contact: Joseph Malit, 94 Jacoby Street, Maplewood, NJ 07040 [www.netaxs.com/~gothic/VonDonop.html]

[22] Ward, p. 301.
[23] Eelking, pp. 66-71.
[24] Ward, pp. 304-05; Eelking, pp. 78-81; Burgoyne, pp. 128-29; Lowell, pp. 97, 115.
[25] Rollin C. Steinmetz, *Royalists, Pacifists and Prisoners*, Lancaster County Historical Society, 1976, pp. 61-63; Burgoyne, pp. 131-32.
[26] Samuel M. Sener, *The Lancaster Barracks, Where the British and Hessian Prisoners were Detained During the Revolution*, Harrisburg Publishing Co. (PA), 1895, pp. 5-6, 19; Steinmetz, pp. 64-65; Kipping, Ernst, *The Hessian View of America 1776-1783*, Philip Freneau Press, Monmouth Beach, NJ, 1971, p. 24.
[27] Steinmetz, pp. 70, 75.
[28] Burgoyne, p. 135.
[29] Von Eelking, p. 81-85; Sener, p. 6.
[30] Burgoyne, pp. 139-40, 149; Ward, pp. 306-18; Atwood, p. 217.
[31] Ward, pp. 325-36; Burgoyne, pp. 163, 171; Kipping, p. 31.
[32] Ward, pp. 341-53; Symonds, pp. 52-53.
[33] Ward, pp. 356-61; Symonds, pp. 54-55; Burgoyne, p. 563.
[34] Ward, pp. 362-74; Burgoyne, p. 183; von Eelking, pp. 114-17.
[35] Ward pp. 373-83; von Eelking, pp. 117-20; Burgoyne, pp. 227-32; Atwood, pp. 124-29.
[36] Kipping, p. 17.
[37] A useful overview of the arrival and deployment of German forces (mostly Brunswickers and Hanauers) in Canada and their participation in the Burgoyne campaign may be found in *A History of Brunswick*, Dan C. Heinemeier, Arlington, VA, 1999.
[38] George F. Scheer and Hugh F. Rankin, *Rebels & Redcoats*, De Capo Press (reprint of 1957 edition by World Publishing Company), New York, p. 325; von Eelking, p. 155; Atwood, p. 130.
[39] Steinmetz, p. 68; Burgoyne, pp. 250-52, 572.
[40] Von Eelking, pp. 153-54;
[41] Ward, p. 570-85; Burgoyne, p. 262-64; Scheer and Rankin, p. 326-28; Symonds, p. 65.
[42] Burgoyne, pp. 280-84; Ward, pp. 679-81; Scheer and Rankin, pp. 392-94.
[43] Kipping, p. 19.
[44] Atwood, pp. 211-12.
[45] Ward, p. 696; von Eelking, pp. 176-78; Lowell, pp. 243-44, Burgoyne, pp. 563, 568; Atwood, 211-12.
[46] Ward, pp. 695-701; Burgoyne, pp. 320-23; von Eelking, pp. 179-84; *Hessen und die Amerikanische Revolution*, p. 44; Atwood, 166-68.
[47] Atwood, pp. 162, 154.
[48] Von Eelking, p. 190; Burgoyne, pp. 403, 568, 572; Ward, pp. 737-50; Symonds, p. 89.
[49] Burgoyne, pp. 448-51, 438-41; von Eelking, p. 201; Lowell, pp. 253-54; Ward, pp. 753, 788-97.
[50] Burgoyne, p. 459; Ward, p. 878.
[51] Ward, pp. 886-96, Burgoyne, pp. 460-67; Scheer and Rankin, 494.
[52] *Hessen und die Amerikanische Revolution*, p. 42.
[53] Steinmetz, pp. 67, 69, 80; von Eelking, pp. 214-17, 233-34; Burgoyne, pp. 487-90.
[54] Burgoyne, pp. 510-18.
[55] Burgoyne, pp. 552-61; von Eelking, pp. 259-60; *Hessen und die Amerikanische Revolution*, pp. 47-48, Atwood, footnote 31, p. 190.
[56] Atwood, pp. 83, 247.
[57] Atwood, pp. 227-33, 250-51.
[58] *Hessen und die Amerikanische Revolution*, pp. 49-51.

Chapter 12

A Final Look at the Eighteenth Century: Hessian Towns

Life on the land clearly differed markedly from that in the towns, although striking parallels continued through the course of the century. The towns retained many aspects of rural life. In this chapter we will continue the story of three of the prominent Hessian towns: Marburg, Kassel and Darmstadt.

MARBURG[1]

Despite its proud past, Marburg's fortunes continued to slide in the eighteenth century. Devastated physically and economically by the Thirty Years War, Marburg was still struggling to recover her pre-1618 living standard by the time the Seven Years War broke out in 1756. The citizenry in many cases were living on the point of starvation on a regular basis, eking out an existence on plain bread or dried potatoes. The guilds were still influential but much weaker in comparison to the strength they had enjoyed in earlier times. They contented themselves with blocking the aspirations of both competing merchants and new members applying for admission to their ranks. The latter could only hope to be accepted by marrying the widow or daughter of a current guildsman. Many journeymen left their professions to soldier in the army or beg on the roadways in desperate efforts to get by. The landgrave tried to promote economic progress by sanctioning the creation of town fairs and markets; six trade fairs and four livestock markets were held in the town.

By 1724 Landgrave Karl had established numerous postal routes that crossed through Marburg including the main route from Kassel to Frankfurt. Both coach and rider services plied these routes on a regular basis during the week. The roads were so bad that in wet weather coaches had to be pulled by large numbers of horses, up to fourteen at a time. Even at this rate, only six passengers at most and a small amount of baggage could be hauled. In addition to the regular coach prices bribes were expected by the drivers without compunction. A Hessian saying held that, "He who bribes well, rides well." One was also expected to pay a two-*Groschen* per mile fee for "drink money."

In 1726 the landgrave directed mandatory school attendance for children. The local school was required by the Treaty of Westphalia in 1648 to be maintained as a Lutheran institution, but the state religion was now that of the Reformed faith, so the landgrave refused to pay for its upkeep as the state was doing for the Calvinist schools. Marburg had to raise money locally to provide its own support.

A fire ordinance of 1678 remained in force through the century. Among its many provisions were requirements for carpenters, roofers and chimney sweeps to rush with ladders and axes to any fire that broke out. The town watchmen and constabularies were to report immediately as well to eliminate any threat of looting. Everyone was to come to fight the fire, and guildmasters and other craftsmen were to turn out with their journeymen, bringing buckets to form bucket brigades. Fines were imposed on those who failed to heed the call. Straw roofs were banned in town by the same regulations. Smoking was strictly prohibited in barns and stalls and near the straw upon which many still slept in inns and homes. The town continued to suffer from the age-old problem of the lack of accessible water supplies.

The old university in Marburg had switched from Reformed to Lutheran control and back again in the Thirty Years War. This disruption had a negative impact on the student population. The student body doubled in the period after 1723 when the landgrave appointed a famous Pietist philosopher, Christian Wolff, as professor. In 1727 the university celebrated its 200th anniversary with a raucous banquet in the large town hall. Five hundred students made merry at this feast. It was thought that peace could be enforced by requiring everyone to check swords and daggers with the fencing master. Still, the windows, glasses, tables and benches wound up being smashed in a thousand pieces by the inebriated crowd.

A freemason's lodge was opened in Marburg in 1743, called the "Lodge of the Three Lions." The Duke of Braunschweig who had heroically led the forces of Hesse and other allies against the French in the Seven Years War joined the lodge after the war, boosting its popularity and membership. It was closed down by Landgrave William IX in 1794 in response to an anti-Masonic imperial decree issued at Regensburg.

The Seven Years War was the defining and disastrous feature of life in Marburg during the century. It perpetuated and deepened the pattern of economic distress that had plagued the town since 1618. Marburg changed hands in battles between the combatants some fifteen times, its protecting castle seven times. The advent of modern artillery by now had greatly reduced the military value of its fortifications. Occupying armies in this era needed to control the major roads upon which they depended for supplies and communications. Marburg's position on the great north-south highway linking Kassel and Frankfurt to points south made it a natural and essential target for any occupying force.

The town was seized by a 25,000-man French army in mid-summer 1757, its town hall converted into a combination horse stable and magazine for supplies. Troops were quartered in the town, bringing difficult times for the inhabitants. The French demanded high payments in money and goods to support their army, including huge amounts of meat and vegetables. Upwards of 16,000 *Taler* in payments were made through the end of the year. Furniture and bedding was also demanded of the townsmen. Packed into close quarters in the summer heat the French began to suffer from dysentery that spread through their ranks like wildfire. Over 1,000 perished from the pest, crowded as they were into a makeshift quarantine hospital. The delivery of beds for this institution was also laid on the backs of the citizenry. Each guild was allotted a share in the requirement; the bakers as an example had to provide thirty beds.

When winter arrived the French were ordered to sleep three infantry, two cavalry or one commander of the watch per bed. The town was ordered to provide 2,000 cords of firewood for use by the occupation troops. Also in 1757 Marburgers were directed to turn out en masse to work on improving the local fortifications to defend against an expected Prussian attack. Day and night, seven days a week, 400 men toiled on the works.

The following year saw Prussian and allied forces under the Duke of Brunswick drive the French out of Hesse, but not before the enemy demanded 850,000 *Taler* in indemnities. Marburg's share was 50,000 *Taler*, but only a total of 20,800 could be raised so the French took several of the town officials hostage when they retreated. Marburg now was occupied by Hessian grenadiers serving with the allied forces. They did not stay long before a 30,000-man French force returned to reoccupy the city in mid-July. At this time a somewhat more positive image of the French emerges in a local story that has been passed down. A shoemaker in nearby Weidenhausen had a pair of shoes stolen from him by a passing French soldier. He complained to the man's commander, who had him pick the offender out of a lineup of his troops. A quick trial was held after which the soldier was convicted and ordered to be hanged from a nearby tree. Even eighty years later people avoided passing the tree at night out of fear that the dead soldier still wandered the place.

Despite this evidence of bounds set on looting, the sanctioned seizure of rations and other goods went on uninterrupted. Marburg had to surrender to the French 19,000 rations of bread, nearly 15,000 rations of meat, 5,000 allotments of oats, as well as assorted amounts of hay, straw, beds, and linen. A difficult summer and fall passed slowly for the hard-pressed citizens. Local places that failed to provide the demanded rations and goods were threatened with being burned out. Farmers fled with their animals to the woods, and sometimes clashed with French raiding parties with deadly results. When caught, these resisters were hanged and their houses destroyed. The shortage of fodder was so great that St. Jacob Hospital had to sell off its three cows.

In 1759 a French occupying force camped on a hill near Weidenhausen burned down fruit trees, hedges, garden gates and other obstructions so their herds of livestock could graze freely. The Marburg population was feeling the pinch of shortages of grain because local farmers were too afraid of confiscation of their draft animals to bring grain into town for sale. As far south as the Wetterau everyone was so tapped out from the French exactions that almost no one could scrape together adequate food supplies. This served to slow the advance of allied relief forces who could find no food or forage along the highways through Hesse. So it went, year after grinding year, until peace was declared in late 1762. The French departed Marburg December 19. Hessian forces reentered the town in time for Christmas.

After the war it was recognized that neither the town walls nor its castle afforded real protection any more from invading forces. To spare Marburg from attacks and sieges in future wars the town walls and outlying fortifications were pulled down in 1776 by order of Landgrave Frederick II. This ended the role as an important military stronghold that Marburg had played since the early Middle Ages. The war also had a terrible impact on local streets and roads that had been marched upon repeatedly by French cavalry. There was no money for re-paving, however, so a new tax was imposed on food animals brought into town for sale. Half the money thus raised went into the paving fund, the other half used for different needs identified by the town government. The paving fund was never adequate to do the job, however.

In 1788 Wilhelm von Humboldt wrote of his travels and time spent in Marburg, which he referred to as the ugliest and least commodious town imaginable. The houses were old and unattractive, the streets dirty and so steep as to be difficult to travel. He stayed in the Crown Hotel, later known as the Hotel Ritter, and attended balls in the evening populated with ugly women—in Humboldt's estimation. He did like the beautiful views of the countryside available from the vantage point of the castle. A meeting with six of the local professors moved him to write further deprecating remarks in his journal about their assorted failings. He noted that the university students were a somewhat better lot than those he found elsewhere, for they at least removed their hats in class. But he complained that they also brought their big dogs along with them to school, talked and laughed during the lectures, and made all kinds of inappropriate jokes. He complained that the university was in poor shape because the landgrave refused to invest in it; this was not entirely true, since from 1774-94 William IX had worked successfully to double the number of students and professors to 300 and thirty-three, respectively.

At the point when the Seven Years War broke out Marburg numbered only about 5,100 people compared to over 6,000 that had lived there in 1618. The war had thrown everyone into poverty and debt. In 1776 a quarter of the town's budget was paid out in interest every year on war-related debts. The five annual fairs and six livestock sales did little to boost local wealth. A report to the landgrave of 1774 by the lower *Bürgermeister* complained bitterly of the continuing poverty of the guilds throughout the town. Trade was severely reduced and the reporter predicted the financial ruin of the whole town. Half the population maintained small farms and kept livestock as a means of getting by. In 1778 the town still had four small cattle herds, two herds of swine, and a little flock of sheep. Marburg obviously was a good example of the Hessian towns of the period, described (as we saw in Chapter 10) by the Prussian-born minister Bopp—then in service with the Hessian landgrave—as merely villages enclosed with walls.

New forms of production in early factory-style concerns began to loosen the grip of the guilds on productive life. The introduction of the Huguenots to Hesse had similar effects. New members could more easily find places in the guild memberships. But competition brought about a general fall in prices that worked to the disadvantage of the producers. Hordes of tradesmen and merchants flocked to Marburg from 1774-1800. Their numbers increased to the following extent in this period: cabinet makers grew from fifteen to twenty-six; the tanners from thirty-two to fifty-eight; the bakers from ninety-four to 119; and the shoemakers from 121 to 169. The butchers by contrast fell in numbers, from seventy-eight to sixty-nine, as did the small shopkeepers, from 103 to just ninety-three. Another important trade was that of hauling and transportation services, with thirty-two names in the business in 1776.

A particularly large increase also occurred in the pottery-making industry. From 1750-85 the number of manufactories increased from five to twenty-five, their assorted works employing fourteen journeymen and thirteen apprentices. This coincided with a new process of coating the pottery ware, including bowls, pots, beer steins, plates, coffee cups, and other items. Much of the production was exported to Westphalia and other German areas adjacent to Hesse, shipping the goods down the Rhine and Weser rivers. Annual revenue was reckoned at over 20,000 *Taler*. After 1800 new markets included Darmstadt, the Pfalz area, Thuringia, and the northern German ports of Bremen and Hamburg.

Another renowned local industry was beer brewing. It collapsed in the difficult economic times as a cheaper, poorer-quality product became common. In order to promote recovery a government ordinance was issued in 1791 to regulate quality and processing. Wine was but little drunk by the common man at this point, but the bad state of the beer industry had led to a huge increase in the consumption of brandy. In 1776 the 5,000 Marburgers were purchasing the output of twenty-seven little brandy-making operations, amounting to some 227 kegs per year. Much additional brandy was imported from outside the town. The resultant increase in drunkenness did much to sap the productivity of the under classes.

The town administration consisted of a *Bürgermeister* and council, made up of *Schöffen* and *Vieren*. The *Schöffen* were partly learned and partly unschooled men. The highest-paid official was the town scribe who made seventy-one *Taler* a year. The *Bürgermeister* was paid a salary of fifty-five *Taler*. The town income in 1776 came to a total of 4,099 *Taler*, derived as follows: Wine shop sales 521; Beer sales 653; real property tax 143; citizen's tax (*Bürgerschilling*) 369; road tax 105; signage tax 146;

livestock tax 731; mortgage on city properties 272; immigrants- and citizen's fees 141; income from the town forest 135; inheritance tax 84; town road tolls 50; interest on loaned funds 46; capital repayments 51; other income 32; retained earnings of previous years 620. Of this total, 876 *Taler* had to be paid out in interest on debts. By 1782 the town's regular income had shrunk to 3,335 *Taler* and some of its properties had to be sold to raise money. Among these were the three wine shops that previously had been mortgaged.

The church in this period was beset by the rationalist thinking of the age that had all but reduced church life to the province of the ignorant and superstitious. Most people who fancied themselves learned stopped attending, but the broader group of the lower classes clung to their faith and came to church as often as ever. When the landgrave forbade the celebration of matins at three festival days in orders of 1772 and 1776 many people went to the competing Lutheran services from midnight to one o'clock, or carried their prayer and song books to the nearby Ketzerbach and sang the forbidden songs out in the open air. For centuries May 1 was celebrated as founders' day at the church dedicated to St. Elizabeth, for this was the anniversary day when her bones were interred in the church. Celebration of this saint's day was a holdover from Catholicism and survived through the Reformation period, but it was ended by decree of the landgrave in 1772. In 1766 a Lutheran orphans' home was founded. The small Catholic community in town finally obtained a place to worship in 1788 when the chapel at St. Elizabeth's hospital was made available for them.

The locally-worn traditional garb known as *Tracht* was discussed at length in Chapter 10, but a few more comments relative to Marburg will be offered here. The traditional dresses were retained in local style as mourning clothes after they were no longer considered fashionable for other purposes. In this era the formerly uniform styles and tastes were divided into separately-influenced practices based on religion. The Catholic styles were the most colorful, with bright tones of red, green, yellow, blue and lilac. The Lutherans also adopted more colors than the traditional dark *Trachten*; the latter were mostly black and white with small touches of red and blue. By the end of the eighteenth century forms of the traditional garb had evolved in Marburg that in the ensuing decades spread to the rural hinterland. Features including clock stockings, ever-higher waists, ever-smaller caps, and cut-away shoes.

KASSEL[2]

In 1723 Kassel had almost 12,300 inhabitants, including 773 government officials and 1,413 artisans. The *Bürgermeister* and council (*Rat*) presided over justice and administration in the local government. Still, the heavy hands of the landgraves and their picked officials often entered into matters of day-to-day government in ways unknown outside the capital. Town income was not large, and consisted mainly of the proceeds from the public wine shop, fees for weighing goods at the markets, application fees from new citizens permitted to settle in town, sales of produce grown on town-owned lands, and the proceeds of rented or mortgaged buildings. There were twenty-four significant guilds in this era.

An unpleasant feature of life in town stemmed from the standing order to bar the gates at established times, giving one the feeling of living in a military fortress. Passage in and out of the town was barred not only at night but on Sundays during the times of the weekly services (which people were expected to attend). Also burdensome was the array of petty taxes and fees that were collected regularly, including a beverage tax, excise taxes, business licenses, and a progressive "wig tax" assessed on various classes in town based on their level of income. In 1723 the government imposed a tax to support new street lighting using lanterns, although this does not appear to have been accomplished on a broad basis. The *Neustadt* (New Town) section did erect over 100 lanterns fired with rape seed oil, which must have helped lighting considerably in that section.

In 1730 the first regular newspaper in town was published by the court publisher. This "Kassel Police and Commercial Newspaper" includes references to some of the major inns that provided rooms for travelers in this era. They had colorful names such as the "Ox Head" and "The Carp and Thirsty Stag." At this point the Lutheran community was permitted to hold its services openly in an established location, and by 1738 a new Lutheran church building had been erected. In 1732 a group of 240 Salzburg refugees from religious intolerance in Catholic Austria also were settled in the town.

William VIII, who became landgrave in 1730, was a great patron of the arts. He saw to the creation on Five Windows Street of a renowned museum called the Picture Gallery. This housed his collection of works by well known masters such as Rembrandt, Rubens and Dürer. The best of these works were stolen by the French under Napoleon and carted off to Paris. Most but not all were repatriated after his fall in 1815. Many of the works in the collection still carry the seal of the Napoleon Museum dating from this period. Unfortunately, Napoleon gave away many of the works as gifts or otherwise dispersed them beyond recovery by the Hessians. The many Flemish, Dutch, and German works that remain have served to accord continuing recognition of the Kassel museum as housing one of the finest collections of its kind in the world.

William VIII also graced Kassel with the Rococo palace known as Wilhelmsthal, recognized throughout Germany as one of the grandest residences of any of the German princes. It featured a marvelous fountain called the grotto as well as beautifully laid-out parks. One of the final battles of the Seven Years War was fought in June 1762 in the park and around the castle, in which the French defenders had taken shelter. The Duke of Brunswick led allied forces against them, killing 1,500 and taking 3,000 prisoners.

In the war Kassel itself fell four times to the French, and was twice besieged by the allied forces. As in Marburg, authorities and citizens alike were required to provide huge sums of money and food to support the French occupiers; in one case the massive sum of 100,000 *Taler* was levied. When it was not immediately forthcoming, dozens of the local officials and leading townsmen were arrested and held hostage. Some 300 wagon loads of booty were stripped from the town and sent west to Frankfurt and on to Düsseldorf. The sieges cost the town much of its attractive gardens and buildings around the town walls. People were driven into the cellars to escape the bombardments. The second siege was especially difficult, with many brought to the brink of starvation.

Landgrave Frederick II succeeded his father in 1760, but the war kept him from his capital until 1763. Building on the efforts of his father and grandfather before him, Frederick was responsible for the development of Kassel as a worthy residence for a prince of stature. As discussed in Chapter 10, he worked hard to improve the city culturally and architecturally. As in Marburg, the old town walls were torn down as it was recognized that they no longer served the purpose of protecting the town. This promoted the connections between the old part of town and the *Neustadt*. Streets paths were altered to make travel through town an easier experience. The old, alley-like ending for street names, *-Gasse*, now was replaced with the more regal-sounding *-Straße*, or street, and awkward- or boorish-sounding names were replaced with ones more fitting for a residence town. The names of the apostles were used to replace some of the older street names. The town gate names were similarly spruced up by renaming them after the major highways that led into them.

Re-paving also was undertaken on a wide scale in this period. Stone sidewalks were built for the convenience of pedestrians, and street drainage and cleaning was improved. Animals were no longer to be fed or kept on public streets. In 1775 the driving of herds of cows, pigs and sheep on public streets was also prohibited. Too many farmers still lived and pursued their livelihoods in and around the town for this regulation to stick, however. Frederick had to relent and rescind it in the face of widespread protests. To keep the streets somewhat clean of manure, community barns and stalls were set up on several of the major roads leading into town.

Frederick took Paris as his model in various reform efforts undertaken to change the complexion of life in his capital. Rows of ugly, old-style houses were pulled down to make way for more modern buildings, especially in the inner city and near the landgrave's palace. New housing sections sprang up outside the town gates, significantly extending the inhabited area. The new building program was so extensive that trained builders were in short supply. As early as 1766 the local building trades guild had to open its doors to new builders without restriction. Carpenters, roofers, masons and other members of the trades came from far and wide to work in Kassel.

Flower sellers plied their trade on the streets, as did armies of shoe shiners and taxi coaches, all for the comfort of visitors to the town. Coffee shops and eateries were encouraged to open across Kassel for the same purpose. Shoemakers and tailors were directed to make up inventories of their goods in advance for sale to shoppers. The large squares around the town also were beautified. By 1780 the Kassel police commission was asserting that Paris had nothing over their town in cleanliness.

French was the language at court and among the learned members of society in Frederick's reign. A French publishing house and a French book store were created under the landgrave's direction. His goal was for Kassel to assume the role of a crossroads between French and German culture. Much French literature was imported into the country, and projects were kicked off to translate important German works into French. Although the theater was freeing itself from French influence elsewhere in Germany, in Kassel the style was all French.

The landgrave's cultural and architectural dreams could only be fulfilled at great financial cost to Hesse, and he was fortunate to have the large soldier subsidies provided by Britain in the American Revolution. He also started up a state lottery that generated no little wealth for his personal use. An Italian lottery director at one point embezzled some 70,000 *Taler*. As noted in Chapter 10, Frederick's son ended the lottery when he assumed the throne.

More positive foundations by Frederick included the 400-bed hospital built just outside the town gates to serve the poor and indigent; he also founded the orphans' and foundlings' homes referred to in the earlier chapter. He sought to improve the town's economy by sanctioning merchant fairs and livestock markets. A merchant exchange was created in 1771 for similar purposes, but it never caught on and was closed. Similar failures occurred in various manufacturing ventures during his reign, including a soap works, viticulture operations, and a variety of factory works in which foreigners were induced to settle and work in Hesse. The state-sponsored porcelain works bumped along year by year without turning a profit.

Frederick's death in 1785 marked something of the end of an epoch, for his son William IX entered power with a single-minded determination to cut costs, end frivolous aspects of life at court, and be rid of the influences of the hated the French. The costly state menagerie of animals was quickly sold off, local opera and ballet curtailed, and the court orchestra dispersed. For all its grandeur, Kassel was already being described as lacking in liveliness and stimulation. The grand streets and parks were scarcely traveled by the locals. The renowned figures who taught or otherwise held forth in Frederick's reign emigrated one by one to greener pastures. William's practicality also led to the creation of six new free schools for the education of poor children that previously would have been unable to afford schooling.

William seems to have been almost as enamored as his father with the idea of improving his residence with the marks of grandeur befitting a prince of his stature. The Wilhelmshöhe Palace (built 1786-1801) is evidence of his taste and designs for the capital. The beautiful handwork that went into the decoration of the building was most impressive. Not surprisingly given his Francophobia, his tastes reflected English rather than French artistic and architectural styles.

DARMSTADT[3]

By the standards of his day, Landgrave Ernst Ludwig (reigned 1678-1739) was a tolerant prince in matters of religion. Over the opposition of the Darmstadt council he enacted an ordinance in 1691 granting enhanced rights to the small Jewish community in Darmstadt (as well as other areas in which at least ten male Jewish adults were resident). This allowed them to worship openly on the Jewish Sabbath and other holidays. No regular synagogue existed at this time for the Darmstadt Jews, who lived grouped together in the *Altstadt* on *Ochsengasse* Street. Only in 1735 was a formal synagogue opened in the house of a Jewish widow. In 1710 the town council opposed the admission to town of Jewish peddlers, arguing that they were having an adverse impact on the ability of their Christian competitors to make a living. At this point there were some thirty Jewish heads of households living in Darmstadt. In protecting the Jews the landgrave was also quick to uphold the time-honored tradition of imposing special taxes on them. Their community had to pay 5,000 guilders a year for the maintenance of state hunting dogs and cavalry, among other taxes.

The secular and church authorities were not just prejudiced against Jews, but others practicing beliefs that differed from the state-sanctioned Lutheranism. Local church authorities squelched the suggestion that the Latin school should be opened up to orphan children of the Catholic and Jewish faiths. They did not wish to see these groups become too upwardly mobile. The orphan's home was barred to illegitimate children and those born to criminals who had been given the death penalty. The Protestant authorities were less successful in opposing the landgrave when he gave permission to Catholics to worship in town. His concern apparently was based on the religious persuasion of a Spanish actor in his service, as well as the state postmaster general, who also was a Catholic. The latter established services in the post office from 1727 until his death.

The landgrave began planning for a new opera house beginning in 1709, using the talents of a French architect he was able to borrow from the service of the Elector of Hannover. Louis Remy de la Fosse commissioned more than forty cabinet makers, twenty carpenters, nine painters, four sculptors, and assorted masons, smiths and other workers to labor on the project. He complained bitterly that it was terribly hard work because of the argumentative nature of the workmen. Despite this, the opera house opened at last in 1711. Landgrave Karl of Hesse-Kassel and his crown prince were in attendance at the opening, a sign that the ancient enmity between the two Hessian ruling houses at last was on the wane. The architect was only too happy to escape back to Hannover, as he complained that he was seldom paid properly for his efforts in Darmstadt. He was to return for some future projects, however, including a major renovation of the palace. He died while working on this project in the fall of 1726.

Ernst Ludwig's rabid attachment to hunting also placed him at loggerheads with the town authorities. He had the local forest enclosed with hedges to protect and imprison the game animals within, and this brought protests from townsmen accustomed to use of the woods for pig mast (pasturing) and other purposes. A half dozen hunting lodges were erected within a short distance of Darmstadt at substantial cost so that Ernst Ludwig and his son—who was equally smitten with the pleasures of the hunt—could enjoy them. Great impositions were made on the locals to provide hauling and bush-beating services in support of the hunts, which also caused wide and loud complaints. Worst of all was the terrible damage caused by the mounted huntsmen who rode through crops and fields with impunity. A diary entry of a visitor to town in 1730 noted the proliferation of wild game, such that they often wandered up to the town walls and local farmers had great difficulty in protecting crops from their foraging.

Population numbers rose from about 1,900 in 1700 to over 3,000 by 1721. Most of this increase came through immigration. Many master builders and others in the building trades were attracted by the court building projects. This era also was marked by renewed efforts by the landgrave to require members of the town guilds to prove themselves worthy by demonstrating competency in their trades. In several cases workmanship was so poor and costs so high that the landgrave threatened to import more masters into town to enhance competition. The largest guilds were those of the shoemakers and tailors, who often were called upon to meet the resurgent demands of the army in times of crisis; in peacetime, their numbers were excessive based on normal demand. The butchers, bakers, locksmiths, blacksmiths, saddlers, hat makers and building trades guilds also had many more members than necessary to meet the normal needs of the population.

Average people were barred from enjoying the productions of the town opera house and court orchestra; these were restricted for the pleasure of the landgrave and the highest caste of courtiers and town fathers. Church music, including bell ringing, organ playing, and choral productions were open to wider audiences, however.

The poor economic situation of the landgraviate was reflected in a variety of ways in life in the capital. The landgrave's appetite for sumptuous hunts, his major building programs, plus the typical costs of maintaining opera companies, orchestra productions, and other trappings of princely life ran up huge debts that tax income could never accommodate. Economically hard-pressed citizens often chose to emigrate to Hungary or other places, as we saw in the previous chapter. A local school master was complaining by the late 1720s that so many of the locals had emigrated or sunk into poverty that his income from school taxes was shrinking fast. Emigrants' reasons for leaving included too many compulsory services, the huge, destructive hunts, and predation of their fields by game animals protected by the landgrave. The landgrave also debased the national coinage in an effort to make it stretch, causing inflation and economic hardship. When he died in 1739 he left behind a debt of four million guilders.

The new landgrave, Ludwig VIII, was as avid a hunter as his father but even less capable at financial management. The financial affairs of state continued to drift during his reign. His efforts to remain neutral in the War of the Austrian Succession failed to prevent French forces from marching into his lands in mid-1743, seizing Darmstadt and occupying nearby Arheilgen, Griesheim, Eberstadt, Bessungen, and surrounding areas. The usual requirements for quartering troops at local expense and providing food, money and provender were laid on the populace. Over the following two years the lands round about were often plundered of grain, vegetables, beets, and other food. Even four *Morgen* (about eighty acres) of land planted in the newly-introduced potato crop were ravaged by French foragers. Fortunately, the following years were quieter on the Darmstadt front.

After this war the locals were bedeviled continually by the landgrave's hunts. Large areas were trodden down to the point of having harvests ruined. Many crops suffered predation from wild animals. It is recorded that poorer farmers in the latter 1740s were driven to hunger and forced to sell off what little crops they had over time to purchase basic needs. Many took the opportunity to emigrate to Prussian lands newly opened up along the Oder River; others sank into poverty and even drunkenness. The landgrave preferred to live at his nearby hunting lodge, Castle Kranichstein, in these times.

Darmstadt itself saw relatively few major building projects undertaken within the town limits. The large-scale building took place at the string of hunting lodges and castles frequented by the landgrave. One major exception was the orphan's home, built from 1747-50 near the Bessung Gate. This was largely thanks to the continued insistence of the state preacher, Johann K. Lichtenberg. The two-story building had sleeping, eating and school rooms, but also workplaces for teaching the trades of weaving and spinning.

A new market ordinance of 1765 reflected the thinking of the authorities about the need to promote trade. The surrounding districts were directed to conduct their trade in the town markets at prescribed times, and a long-dormant market held on Tuesdays was ordered revived. Bakers and fruit sellers from Ober-Ramstadt and Traisa were directed to bring their white flour, barley and millet for sale, those from Nieder-Ramstadt were also to bring rolls. The fish trade was addressed by ordering the fishermen from Biebesheim, Stockstadt and Erfelden to sell their fish in town year round. By contrast, those in Trebur, Rüsselsheim, and Ginsheim were only allowed to sell their catch from October to March. Jews were prohibited from fish selling. People from Georgenhausen and Groß-Zimmern could sell fowl until ten o'clock under specific conditions. During market times the local peddlers and hawkers were prohibited from selling on the streets. Specific quantities of meal could be sold at the town scales by the millers of Ober- and Nieder-Ramstadt, Modau, Beerbach, Eberstadt, Pfungstadt, and Stockstadt. In the same year a regulation for street lighting was issued, providing for oil lamps to light the streets in the darkest months from September to April.

Regulations governing hygiene and street cleaning also were issued in these times. Butchers were ordered to do their work in the town slaughter house to keep the mess out of private shops and streets. The home fire ordinance of 1767 sought to reduce fire risks by requiring tile roofs, solidly-built ovens and regular cleaning out of private ovens on at least a quarterly basis. A sillier and more controversial law of 1766 sought to stamp out coffee drinking in rural areas as unhealthy, and townsmen who drank the stuff were enjoined to do so only in moderation. Any members of the lower social classes, such as day wage laborers, hand workers, journeymen, and washing and ironing women caught wasting too much time in coffee drinking were to be severely warned against this practice by the police.

Figures 12-1/12-2 Wilhelmshöhe was the summer residence of the electors of Hesse, built from 1787-94 and surrounded by park land and fountains. [See map following endnotes.] The 33-foot-high Herkules monument on the grounds tops a 98-foot obelisk. The Octagon building on which it was built was designed to resemble a ruin (1714).

Upon Ludwig's death his son and successor Ludwig IX entered office with a cordial indifference to hunting but a compulsive interest in all things military. Darmstadt now was ruled by a landgrave determined to pare costs and reduce debt. His wife Caroline, however, was a gracious patron of the arts who brought a renewed spirit to the capital. She was active in rejuvenating park land and formal gardens. In the same period the landgrave's building of barracks served the useful purpose of relieving local people from having to put up with the quartering of soldiers in their private homes. He also ordered the end of the use of instruments of torture in the judicial system. In 1771 he decreed freedom of religious worship to all members of the Reformed (Calvinist) religious faith in the town. Catholics were not provided with similar rights. The landgrave's mercy did not extend to deserters from his beloved army, however. When the alarm was raised three cannon shots signaled the immediate need to close the town gates and bar access to bridges. Desertion could be punished by the cutting off of fingers.

In 1774 a census of sorts was conducted in Darmstadt. This revealed that there were 1,490 households in the town, including 865 with married couples. The homes included 2,356 adults and 2,025 children. Servants up to thirty years of age numbered 378 males and 441females. The forty-three Jewish households had ninety-eight sons and daughters, plus four male and thirty female servants. Including military men and their families the total population was about 6,600 people. These numbers are perhaps less than completely trustworthy, however, as a similar count in 1777 found over 9,000 living in Darmstadt. The town included about 574 buildings in these times. Animals kept in town included eighty-five horses, 940 cattle, 672 sheep and 594 pigs.

Beginning in this period an intensive effort was put forth to end the ancient but wasteful practices of the three-field economy that left a third of the available arable land to lie fallow each year. The Rural Land Commission encouraged the broad use of fertilizer in the fields around Darmstadt, accompanied by efforts to grow fodder for stall feeding of animals whose waste could then be used on the fields. Pastures and meadows previously given up because they regularly fell prey to forest animals now were successfully re-cultivated. By 1791 a report indicated that the field areas around Darmstadt and Bessungen were being successfully cultivated without fallow periods. Local potato production rose appreciably in the same period, with positive effects on diets of people and livestock alike.

The death of Ludwig IX in 1790 brought his son, Ludwig X, to the throne. Among his first acts was to grant freedom of worship to Catholics in Darmstadt. This was the first time Catholic worship had occurred openly in the town since the death in 1727 of the Catholic postmaster, Brand. The next few years also saw the lifting of prohibitions of land ownership by Jews. In 1796 the first Jew was accorded full citizenship rights.

Previous negative impressions about the trade in soldiers for subsidies as practiced by the landgrave's cousins in Kassel subsided in the period after 1789 when French revolutionary forces were becoming a serious threat. Some lucrative subsidy deals were struck with England for the use of Darmstadt troops that otherwise would have been cost-prohibitive to maintain at home. Subsidy moneys were put to use in creating fortifications and otherwise improving the state's defenses.

The 1790s also witnessed the first hints of the future period of rapid industrialization. The politically strong but ultimately non-competitive guilds still were able in most cases to pressure town fathers to turn down requests to build factories where these might disadvantage the guilds. An application to build a carpet factory was approved because it was believed this would create local employment opportunities.

Snuff and soap factories were turned down on the basis that the resulting odors and other obnoxious health effects would be an ongoing problem. An application to erect a local mechanical works was not approved because the noise of the steam engine was expected to disturb nearby residents. In 1797 a planned cloth factory was refused the right to open on the basis that it would compete with local guild production.

NOTES TO CHAPTER 12

[1] W. Kürschner, *Geschichte der Stadt Marburg*, Elwertsche Verlagsbuchhandlung, Marburg, 1934, pp. 169-92.
[2] Karl Heidelbach, *Kassel, ein Jahrtausend hessischer Geschichte*, Bärenreiter Verlag, Kassel, 1957, pp.125, 150-211.
[3] Adolf Müller, *Aus Darmstadts Vergangenheit*, Selbstverlag der Stadt Darmstadt, 1930, pp. 95-145; Friedrich Battenberg, D*armstadts Geschichte*, Eduard Roether Verlag, Darmstadt, 1980, pp. 218-88.

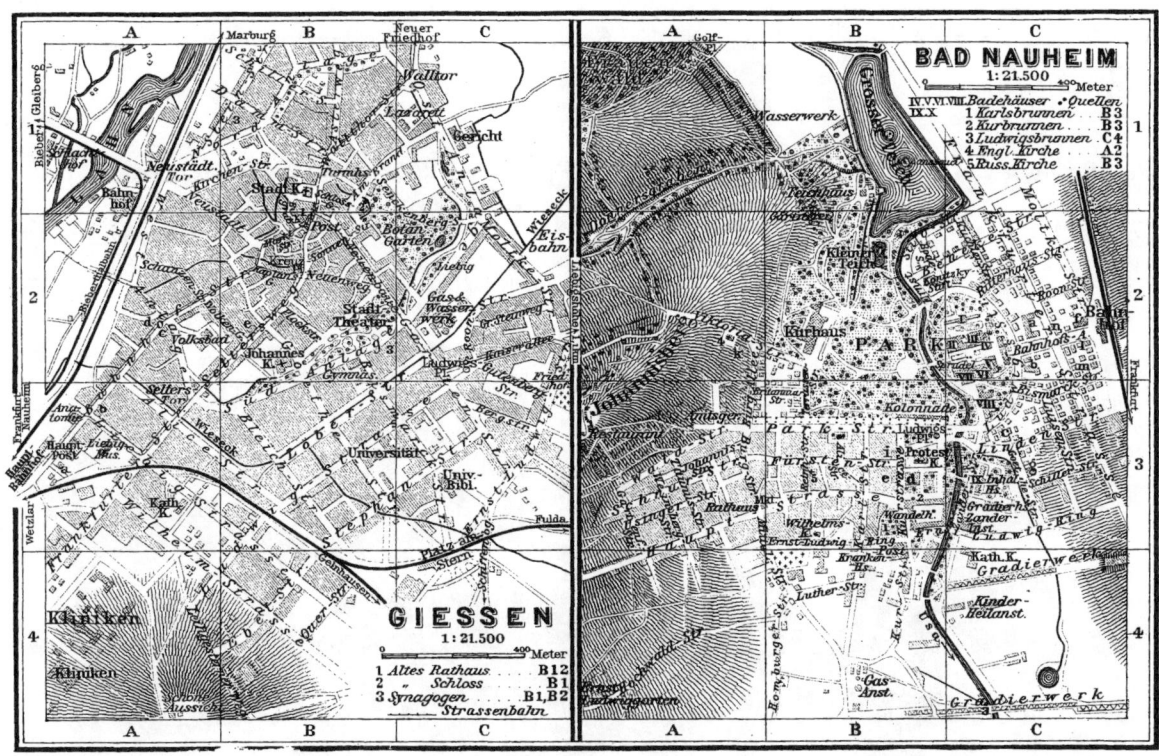

Map 7 The old town of Gießen, so much a part of Hesse-Darmstadt history. Bad Nauheim came to the Grand Duchy in 1867 via an exchange of lands with Kassel. It was long renowned for its spring waters, said to have curative properties.

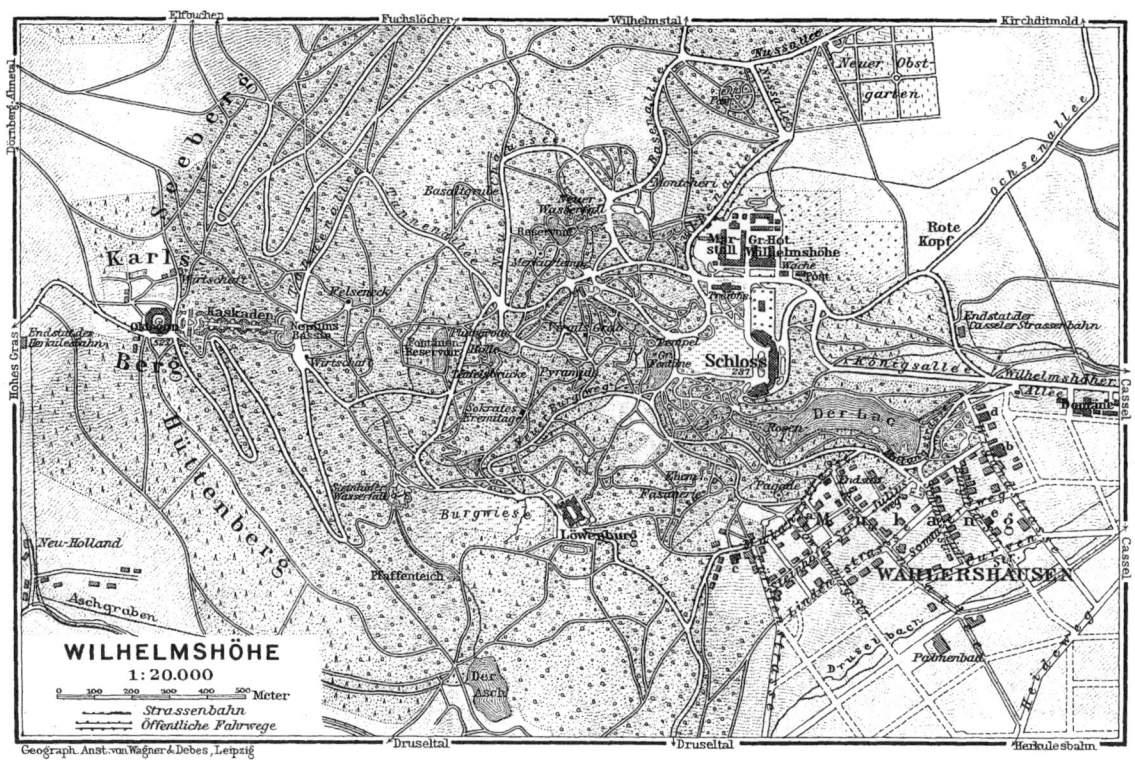

Map 8 Layout of the Wilhelmshöhe palace and grounds. [See also *Figures* on p. 261].

Figure 12-3 Marburg: a view of the university and the castle on the heights above.

CHAPTER 13

THE NAPOLEONIC ERA

The French revolution of 1789 ushered in massive upheaval and unrest in France, and held the potential to destabilize German states across the Holy Roman Empire. German rulers felt so threatened in fact that a military campaign was undertaken in 1792 to quell the unrest at its source. But the joint Austro-Prussian force that marched into France stopped short of taking Paris and reestablishing the Bourbon monarchy. Instead, internal dissension and uncertainty about the ultimate aims of the war, together with stiff French resistance, finally convinced them to retreat to the safety of their own borders. The rather ragtag French forces then took the offensive, and within a few months they had taken possession of the left bank of the Rhine, France's "natural border" according to many partisans of the revolution. In the period that followed the French made efforts to compensate the losses of at least the major German princes with offsetting territorial gains taken from the church or the lesser nobility. More of this will be discussed later.

The revolution now seemed a juggernaut destined to sweep away older forms of government and culture wherever it spread. The German princes' inability to unite to fight back resulted in Germany's experiencing years of struggle culminating in political subjugation, almost constant warfare, and life under the dictates of Napoleon. The Hesse-Darmstadt troops were ordered to withdraw from their landgrave's lands on the left bank rather than confront the triumphant French armies.

A set of quotes by Mann and Durant help summarize German life in 1800. Hessians presented no exception to these broader trends.

> In Germany the change [during the Revolutionary period] was one of attitudes far more than of institutions. The economic life of the country at the end of the century does not seem very different from what it had been at the beginning. Cities were small and had not expanded for centuries, if they had not actually shrunk in size. The vast majority of the population continued to earn its living by agriculture and town and country continued to be closely linked. Traffic continued to be slow and small in volume, roads were few and forests large. Part of the aristocracy and some merchants in Hamburg or Frankfurt were rich; bourgeois and officials lived in respectable modesty; the peasants produced almost everything needed for life. Industry as the word came to be understood was in its infancy. [1]

> The Germans of 1800 were a class-conscious people, accepting class division as a system of social order and economic organization; and rare was the man who acquired a noble title except by birth. "In Germany," noted Mme. De Staël, "everybody keeps his rank, his place in society, as if it were his established post." This was less so along the Rhine and among university graduates, but in general the Germans were a more patient people than the French. Not till 1848 did they reach their 1789...Commerce was hindered by

guild regulations, high taxes, and the geographical diversity of measures, weights, coinages, and laws.²

For his part, William IX of Hesse-Kassel directed his energies in this period to securing personal advancement within the Holy Roman Empire. He craved the title of elector, one of the handful of German rulers empowered to vote in the elections for new emperors. Combined with frugal ruling practices, his investment income generated in Frankfurt and England (based on the subsidy moneys earned historically by pawning Hessian troops out as mercenaries) gave him the financial security to loan money to the emperor and so buy favor. He also provided troops for the imperial campaigns against France, for he was a confirmed Francophobe. In 1803 his efforts finally paid off as the emperor extended to him the coveted title. Henceforth, despite the eclipse of the empire just three years later, Hesse-Kassel became known as Electoral Hesse. Kassel in this period remained as subject to the absolute rule of its prince as it had been for centuries. All manner of common social and economic practices were subject to regulation: to discourage regular consumption, coffee still could not be sold in quantities under a pound per person, and tobacco smoking on the streets and in front of houses was forbidden.³

Although the military actions that brought most of central Germany under Napoleon's direct control are beyond the scope of this chapter, the period following Prussian defeat in 1806 in the battles of Jena and Auerstädt saw the French occupy a number of smaller German states. The latter included Hesse-Kassel, which was absorbed into the new Kingdom of Westphalia. Hesse-Darmstadt and Hesse-Nassau in contrast remained nominally independent but politically dominated by Napoleon. They joined a so-called Confederation of the Rhine created by smaller, mainly south German states who resigned from the Holy Roman Empire as the price of joining the French alliance. We will consider the history of the Kingdom and the Confederation in turn.

THE KINGDOM OF WESTPHALIA AND HESSE-KASSEL

Electoral Hesse numbered some 500,000 citizens spread out across over 570 square miles. Its lands included the newly-awarded districts of Fritzlar, Naumburg, Amöneburg, and Neustadt, which had been taken by the French from the archbishop of Mainz and ceded to Kassel in compensation for other territories stripped from her in the Rheinland. The town of Gelnhausen also made its way into Kassel's holdings at this time. Perhaps his strong pride and hatred of the French caused William to fail to come to terms with Napoleon in a treaty of alliance. Instead, he cast his lot with his traditional ally, Prussia. After Prussia's defeat in 1806 Hesse-Kassel was promptly invaded and occupied by French forces late in October. The Hessian army was disarmed, and the elector fled for safety to Prague. His carefully hidden cache of forty-two chests containing the state silver service was soon discovered and seized by the French from his hunting castle at Sababurg. The *Hoffaktor* Rothschild was able to do his old master yet another great service, however, when he saved 600,000 English pounds from the French by handing it over for safekeeping to his son, Nathan, in London.

In 1807 Napoleon created a puppet state incorporating the lands of Electoral Hesse along with the western possessions of Prussia, Brunswick, some Hannoverian lands (including much of the Harz), and scattered other holdings. This "Kingdom of Westphalia" was to be ruled by Jerome Bonaparte, Napoleon's younger, more carefree and dissolute brother. He was a notorious womanizer and spendthrift whose earlier military career at sea had been designed by Napoleon to curb the opportunity for dissolute living, but to little avail. The twenty-three-year-old king assumed power on December 7, 1807, having chosen Kassel as his capital. Jerome and his consort arrived December 10 to take up residence in the beautiful, snow-bedecked palace and grounds of Wilhelmshöhe, immediately renamed *Napoleonshöhe*.

Hesse-Kassel lands were divided into two administrative districts, the departments of the Werra (upper Hesse, Ziegenhain, Hersfeld, Eschwege, and Schmalkalden) and the Fulda (lower Hesse with Corvey, Paderborn, Reckenberg, Rietberg, and Münden). The old Katzenelnbogen, Fulda, and Hanau districts were lopped off and assigned to other administrative areas similarly reorganized and dominated by France. Senior officials called prefects were set up to rule the Hessian areas from seats in Marburg and Kassel.

Restaurants and coffee houses in the French style began to sprout in Kassel and other places where numbers of the new ruling caste settled. Kassel also saw the introduction of itinerant musicians who roamed the streets morning and night playing organs, zithers, violins and woodsmen's horns. Week after week costly feasts, balls, and similar celebrations took place in Kassel at the king's behest. In 1809 carnival came to Kassel for the first time; this first celebration featured the butchers leading a decorated ox through the streets and later donating it to the poor.

Modern French governmental forms now were introduced, fostering fundamental change in German social and political institutions and bringing them out of the torpor from which they had suffered since the Middle Ages. These included: destroying the ancient caste system whereby the hereditary nobility had ruled with an iron hand; centralizing and modernizing the justice system by abolishing the crazy-quilt pattern of local jurisdictions that existed in Hesse; ending (on paper) the tithe and service payments and duties peasants had owed their lords from time immemorial; and breaking up the guilds and monopolies in industry and trade that had choked off economic progress. Even Francophobic observers have acknowledged the importance of the Napoleonic reform program to the emergence of German states as more modern political entities.

Unfortunately, these useful reforms came at a high price. French occupation brought about taxation that produced a torrent of revenue to support Jerome's lavish and wasteful court life as well as the costs of the Emperor's wars. Initially, most of the conquered lands were basically quiet; they were accustomed to rule from above and were not yet chafing under the weight of foreign taxation that simply replaced the existing feudal burdens borne by the townsmen and peasants. Some Hessians, however, true to their warlike roots, nurtured a cordial hatred of the French invaders and laid plans for an uprising. As early as December 1806 unrest was felt in Hersfeld, Sontra, Eschwege, Vacha and other areas centered on the Werra River. The French brutally suppressed revolt by capturing and executing the fomenters, but the spirit of rebellion merely went underground.

When the elector allied himself with a resurgent Austria and organized a Hessian legion to fight the French in 1809, two more local uprisings began to take form. In lower Hesse a revolt flared in April under the leadership of a Col. Dörnberg, who was able to scrape together 5,000 willing but mostly untrained men. In upper Hesse starting in June, retired soldiers and other military men cashiered by the French fanned a rebellion centered on Marburg. They were helped by some local professors still loyal to the old regime. Some of the ex-soldiers were recruited in the taverns by plying them with liberal rations of beer and brandy. Others joined out of fear of the loss of pensions granted by the old government. Recalcitrant local farmers whose support could not be garnered with words were brought into line with beatings, barn burnings and similar coercive measures. In both cases the French snuffed out the revolts with relative ease, rounding up and executing the ringleaders by firing squad.[4]

Over time the economic vitality of Hesse was ground down. Napoleon constantly upbraided his brother for not siphoning off and providing more money for his wars, but despite Jerome's best efforts, the kingdom immediately began to run up huge debts and could never wring out enough support from its hapless population.

Radical public policy reforms were carried out by the new regime in a harsh and cavalier manner, with little regard for the feelings and needs of Hessians for whom many of the previous standards and practices represented comfortable and time-honored traditions. The officials who implemented the reform program tended to be foreigners or local appointees who were seen by the populace as opportunists and turncoats. "They [the French officials] speak kindly, considerately, condescendingly to the poor Westphalians, explaining everything in the lucid French manner as a master might expound to a class of stupid and backward boys, now calling attention to a grace of phrase, now to its inner logical coherence, now to its bearing on life. The official letters and documents of this time all have the air of being written by men who regarded themselves as missionaries of civilization, and who wish to impart the mysteries of their creed."[5]

The reforms saw the abolition of serfdom and the creation of a form of constitutional government derived from the French revolution. The existing rights of landlords were not simply abrogated, however. A decree in January 1808 set this process in motion, with later decrees setting commutation fees variously at sixteen-, twenty- or twenty-five-times the annual value of the old feudal dues. In August 1809 a similar commutation system was established for tithes owed to the churches. It appears that relatively few of the dependent farmers took advantage of this option; ignorance or distrust of the new decrees, the comfortable feeling of relying on existing economic relationships and centuries-old traditional forms, and especially the lack of available cash and rural credit all played a role. The laws remained stacked in favor of the landlords. In addition, state-owned properties on which Jerome's government depended for revenue were not eligible for redemption from feudal duties. Marriage dues paid to the nobility, mandatory domestic service in the masters' houses, and the lords' control of the education and career opportunities of the peasantry were ended, however. This was not true of certain community services owed to the government, including the villagers' support of hunts for the purpose of destroying dangerous animals like wolves.

Monopoly hunting rights of the nobility were ended under the reform program, and uniform systems of weights and measures were introduced. Anyone now could pursue a career in any trade by payment of a small licensing fee; this was another major blow to the already waning power of the guilds. Birth, death and marriage record keeping became centralized. A new monetary system was introduced. Half the lands of the former nobility were given out as royal fiefdoms.

Religious freedom was guaranteed by law, and the passage in early 1808 of a separate law for Jews extended comparable freedom to them as well. With the end of the systematic discrimination they had faced under the old rulers the Westphalian Jews now became some of the most loyal financial and military supporters of the new regime; the Jews of Kassel alone provided 1.8 million francs to the government.

Candidates to join the clergy now had to be approved by the king, and one of the new requirements was that the clerics must pray for him regularly, read certain royal decrees to their congregations, and celebrate the birthdays and battlefield victories of Jerome and Napoleon. They also were told to preach obedience to the throne. Church attendance fell off, and illegitimate births were on the rise. Originally, the government simply taxed the churches a set percentage of the revenue of all their lands, but wholesale confiscation of nunneries and other properties began as early as May 1809. The nuns thus cast out were provided for; otherwise, however, the Westphalian government was extremely reluctant even to pay local ministers the rather low wages they had been accustomed to—when it paid them at all. The pastors also had to vie for the first time with secular officials such as local mayors for authority among the parishioners. Interestingly enough, however, in Hessian Westphalia, it was usually only members of the Reformed faith that were accepted as candidates for state offices.[6]

The *Code Napoleon* provided for equality before the law, especially in bearing the burden of taxation. Nobles were allowed to keep their titles, but without any of their old rights attached to their now merely honorific offices. Judicial reforms were among the most dramatic of the changes. Public trials, judgments by jury only, and a bar on appeals of criminal courts' decisions were new to the German system. Much arbitrariness and ignorance in the trial system came to an end through the demise of noble-dominated courts. Most German jurists apparently took to the new system like ducks to water. Litigation often was cut from a years-long to a months-long process. Lawyers now were made to present cases orally, rather than subjecting judges to piles of documents to be waded through. This alone speeded up the process.

By early 1810 the French also had presided over the vaccination against smallpox of 30,000 Westphalians who otherwise likely would have balked at the new procedure—if it had been offered to them at all. Anyone seeking entrance into universities, public schools, and some workplaces was required to be vaccinated. Large numbers of men received the vaccine as military inductees.

On the negative side, the new laws brought draconian penalties for desertion from the army that were unlike anything previously known in Hesse. Despite the landgraves' threats of punishment for harboring them, deserters historically had found haven among the common people who were sympathetic to their plight, but now ruinous fines and prison terms could be meted out even to fathers who helped their fleeing sons. In April 1813, near the end of Jerome's rule, the laws were even changed to implement the death penalty for those convicted of such actions.[7]

An army of 25,000 had to be raised and equipped at the expense of the Westphalian population to serve in wars that secured the liberties and benefits of rule by their French overlords. German officers were given the choice of being arrested or switching to French service. On two occasions, in 1807-08 and 1812-13 battle losses forced the entire Westphalian army to be fully re-equipped with everything from weapons and uniforms to horses and artillery. Universal conscription was guaranteed as a "fundamental law" of the realm. Over the six-year life of the kingdom, some 600,000 draft-eligible men were identified out of a total population of only 2,000,000. Of those actually drafted, 38,000 eventually were killed or lost abroad. Still, by 1813 upwards of 29,000 men were being maintained in arms. In that year alone the cost of maintaining the French army in Westphalia was an astounding 50,000,000 francs, mostly reckoned in the form of requisition of food and other support from local communities.

The army had been modernized along French lines, but with the German officers and language broadly remaining in place. Pay was raised over that paid in German armies, flogging was outlawed, beatings of common soldiers for even minor infractions— a common occurrence in many of the German forces—were barred. Officers now could come from any of the social strata. Thanks to these reforms, many German troops and officers served ably and loyally for Jerome throughout his rule. Catholics, Protestants, and Jews from across the kingdom volunteered to serve in the army at all levels. This must have created substantial problems for many when assertions of disloyalty were made against them after the final defeat of Napoleon. This is demonstrated by the later experiences of Julius Friedrich von Hille, a young ensign who served with the Brunswick forces in the American Revolution. At first imprisoned at Metz, von Hille later joined the army of Westphalia, serving extensively in Spain and Germany. He rose from captain to colonel in this period. An unnamed Brunswick source indicates that, "Von Hille had become such a good Frenchman during his Westphalian service that he was later ashamed to return to his hometown..." The Westphalian forces served with distinction across the continent, losing 2,000 men while fighting in Germany and 7,200 (out of 8,000!) in the campaign in Spain. The Russian campaign cost 14,000 out of a contingent of 16,000.[8]

Beyond the loss of so many of their sons, Hessians grew increasingly weary of the practical and financial burdens of French rule. All other goals were subordinated to Napoleon's need for cash, men and material for the unceasing war effort. Taxes were raised time and again, a basic land tax being imposed on all citizens. The hearth tax of four francs per house was raised in 1809 to 5.75 francs. Even a landless laborer owed eight francs and thirty *centimes*, and a poor family of four owed a full thirty francs and sixty *centimes*. A moveable property tax was imposed, and indirect taxes on stamps, food and salt were levied. A bewildering array of duties was charged on almost all commodities, with stifling effects on commerce. Every local area had its own pernicious and rather corrupt system of fees, from which the rich were mostly exempt, notwithstanding French promises to the contrary.

The land tax escalated from five to twenty percent over the years from 1809-1812. By 1813 it was consuming up to twenty-five percent of total income, so that peasants were refusing to plant crops to avoid the huge tax burden. In 1812 a graduated personal income tax also was imposed on males over age sixteen. Confiscation of property by state authorities was especially heavy in 1812-13. Draft dodging and desertion produced revenue from fines on heads of families forced to pay for the actions of their sons.[9]

The financial burdens seem to have sapped many Hessians' willingness to work, according to one visiting dignitary:

> A Dutch observer, General Dedem de Gelder, remarked that in Hesse nobody worked. The great men were idlers living on pensions, the people privileged beggars. There was no instruction, no art, no trade, and the primary necessities of life, not to speak of the luxuries, were imported from abroad...it was symptomatic of the whole area [of Westphalia] that no less than one-eighth of its total revenue was paid away in small pensions to persons who regarded a pension as a dispensation from activity.[10]

Material need continued to grow year by year. The French introduced the so-called Continental System, a blockade intended to halt all British trade with the continent. The British imposed their own very effective counter-blockade, and these measures created a terrible burden on most parts of Germany. Among the exceptions were some of the North Sea ports, which did a brisk trade in smuggling. Trade and industry in many areas began to collapse.

French occupation forces often hauled away whatever they could steal, and imposed on the people to provide food and shelter. The emperor had promised only 12,500 French infantry and 1,500 cavalry would be quartered in the kingdom at its citizens' expense, but by late 1811 the number had been increased to 25,000 infantry and 10,000 horsemen. Rents fell in this period, and property values collapsed to the point that many owners were forced to hand over the keys of their property to the town officials because they could not raise the tax money owed on them. Once-successful artisans went out of business for lack of paying customers. The land reserves of the state were systematically sold off to provide for the insatiable demands of war capital and Jerome's high living at court.

Jerome warned his brother in late 1811 that the tax burden and ruin of all the classes would lead one day to a mass uprising against French rule. Eighteen months later he reported that he simply could not collect the contributions demanded by Napoleon because people were fleeing their homes, many even committing suicide, to escape the burdens of the times. By this point the common people were living with feelings referred to by one author as "smothered indignation" against their foreign oppressors. Jerome's own wife lived in fear of imminent assassination of the king by his ill-tempered subjects. By December 1811 Jerome had ordered three saddled horses kept at the ready every night for himself, and six others ready for use by his wife's carriage in the event a quick getaway was required.[11]

In 1812 the French laid plans for a suitable memorial in Kassel to celebrate the achievements of Napoleon. It was to include a large bronze statue of the emperor in the King's or Napoleon's Square. Times were so tough by this time that only a marble copy of the intended bronze could be procured. A measure of the contempt in which the French were held at this point is found in a street rhyme sung by the youth on the streets:

> In Kassel on the *Zaitenstock*
> Missing shirt and missing coat
> Missing shoes and missing pants
> Stands the emperor of France.

When a Russian Cossack relief force came to Kassel the following year, the statue was subjected to further indignities: its nose and right forearm were broken off and carried away.[12]

Perhaps the worst aspect of an otherwise reasonably efficient and modernized French bureaucracy was the state police. This was as hated by the Germans as it was foreign to their culture. Private letters were opened and read by censors, and over time no one trusted the mails anymore. Anyone of prominence in the kingdom was monitored by regular police surveillance. Police were empowered to seize any written work that they believed was opposed to the social order. This activity alone did much to embitter the population against French rule.[13]

The large-scale impressing of men for military service in Spain and Russia obviously had a negative impact on the pool of available rural labor, and drove down birth rates during the period. It seems that the continent-wide blockade on trade, the social dislocations of the sudden changes under the new laws, and the impact of confiscations by the occupation troops, all served to generate a large number of people living as vagabonds and lay-abouts. French policies exacerbated this trend by abolishing local borders and setting aside immigration restrictions. The local parishes who held responsibility for poor relief were in many cases overwhelmed even though strict laws sought to penalize begging by the able-bodied.[14]

A DIFFERENT PATH: DARMSTADT, NASSAU AND THE CONFEDERATION OF THE RHINE

The ruling lines of Nassau (Usingen and Weilburg) lost significant properties on the left bank of the Rhine to the French when their lands were occupied. These lost lands were centered in Saarland and the Palatinate, and included over 75,000 inhabitants and annual income of 447,000 florins. In return, they received compensating properties east of the Rhine previously controlled by the bishoprics of Mainz and Trier. The Rheingau district and the lower Main lands (*Untermainlande*) were taken from Mainz, the Montabaur and Limburg areas from Trier. From the bishop elector of Köln (Cologne) they obtained Deutz, Linz, Königswinter, and other properties. The landgrave in Darmstadt had to surrender his portion of the lower County of Katzenelnbogen to his Nassau cousins, and other bits and pieces of lands from dispossessed lesser nobles also were folded into this aggrandizement. With 129,000 new souls and 905,000 florins in annual income, this increase in land was quite a boon, and more than a fair trade for the lands lost.

On July 16-17, 1806 Nassau-Usingen and -Weilburg each joined the Confederation of the Rhine, a coalition of nominally independent German states dominated from the first by Napoleonic France. This was the emperor's recreation of the Holy Roman Empire in his own image. The Nassauers received even more new lands in the bargain;[15] they clearly owed Napoleon a great deal. On August 30 the two principalities were united as a single Duchy of Nassau under the Weilburg line. The citizens of Nassau would soon begin to pay a high price for Napoleon's largesse, however. The troops they sent to the French armies experienced terrible losses, especially in Spain.[16]

Golo Mann has captured the effect and importance of the massive change in German politics and government brought about by Napoleon.

> The ecclesiastical states, the electorates, the prince-bishoprics and the imperial abbeys and monasteries were secularized. The imperial cities disappeared, and with them—after a new war and a new defeat of Austria in 1806—a Milky Way of imperial princes, counts and knights. The operation was called "mediatization" ...The victims of mediatization were allowed, as privileged subjects, to remain in their castles, where many of their descendants still live today. The victims of "secularization" were made to leave their monasteries, which either went to ruin or became private property. Churches were closed and looted, works of art were sold at give-away prices or gathered together in local museums. The spirit of the age was irreligious and anti-clerical; often the number of monks expelled from the monasteries was pathetically small...The strange clearance sale, formally an internal German affair, was really controlled from Paris. The result was the German states as we have come to know them,

and as with a few changes they still exist today: Bavaria, Württemberg, Baden and Hesse.[17]

Hesse-Darmstadt experienced a similar fate due to its weakness in the face of Napoleon's military and diplomatic might. In 1795-96 the landgraviate had been involved in a war that left the capital of Darmstadt itself with 40,000 guilders in war-related debts. It was a difficult period for the people. In 1799, however, Landgrave Ludwig X signed a treaty of neutrality with France, saving his people from the wars that broke out thereafter between France, England and the Holy Roman Empire.

The landgrave saw significant parts of his land stripped away in the diplomatic dealings of late 1802; specifically, Hanuau-Lichtenberg and the Darmstadt holdings in the lower County of Katzenelnbogen and Eppstein were lost. With them went 45,000 people and annual income of 390,000 florins. However, compensating properties provided to Ludwig demonstrated that Napoleon intended to aggrandize Darmstadt significantly as part of French plans for unifying and rationalizing the lesser German states. An additional 124,5000 citizens and 753,000 florins in annual income were reassigned to Darmstadt's control.

Although this new Hessian state was a creation of France, its expanded population seems to have accepted their status as part of an enlarged political entity, and the new extent of Darmstadt's lands remained a fait accompli that stood even after Napoleon's defeat. In the capital a big feast was held December 8, 1802 in the hospital for invalid soldiers (*Invalidenhaus*) in which the town fathers and officials celebrated the expansion of Darmstadt's holdings. At the same time a feast of meat, wine, rice, coffee, cakes, sugar and bread was put on for the children of the orphan's home. At this time Darmstadt had a civilian population of about 9,800 people. In the ensuing years substantial growth was seen in the number of government officials in the capital.

New properties added to the upper county of Hesse included the districts Gernsheim, Heppenheim, Lorsch, Steinheim, Alzenau, and other possessions of Mainz. From the Palatinate came the districts of Lindenfels, Umstadt, and some smaller properties. The bishopric of Worms gave up its holdings on the east bank of the Rhine, including the abbey of Seligenstadt and the Wimpfen priory. In upper Hesse the Marienschloß abbey and the imperial town of Friedberg were obtained, along with the Duchy of Westphalia. The new possessions formed a third administrative district with headquarters in Arnberg, joining the older provinces of upper Hesse (headquarters in Gießen) and Starkenburg (administered from Darmstadt).

Despite these favorable acquisitions Ludwig held back from a formal alliance with France when it was offered. Only when 20,000 French troops occupied his lands in January 1806 was Ludwig forced to come to terms. Almost every house in the town of Darmstadt had to take in French occupation troops. An artillery unit of 400 men and almost as many horses was quartered in the homes of the people of nearby Eberstadt, and later Arheilgen; the population of the two areas at this time was only about 1,300. The sixty-three homes in Wixhausen were required to put up fifty men. Although official relations were cordial at higher levels, there often was trouble between the French and Hessian soldiers.

In July 1806 the landgrave joined the French-allied Confederation of the Rhine, and like his Nassau cousins he gained some immediate benefits. French occupation of the landgraviate soon came to an end. Ludwig was recognized as a grand duke, his lands henceforth dubbed the Grand Duchy of Hesse. His lands were increased again when his recalcitrant and anti-Napoleonic cousin the landgrave in Hesse-Homburg was driven from power: the counties of Breuberg and Erbach and the landgraviate of Homburg fell to Darmstadt. More lands in upper Hesse were added, including the areas around Friedberg, Staden, Ilbenstadt, and the Wetterau properties of the Counts von Solms (Braunfels, Solms-Lich, Laubach, and Rödelheim). Additional lands in the Vogelsberg and the county of Wittgenstein also came into Ludwig's possession. In 1810, he received another 25,000 souls living in lands held by Fulda and Hanau. Napoleon withheld only the true prize, control of Hesse-Kassel, which he awarded to his brother Jerome for incorporation in the new Kingdom of Westphalia.

French-driven administrative and government reforms were pushed through beginning in the fall of 1806 with the formal ending of the role of the estates in Darmstadt governance. These were historically made up of some thirty local nobles, three clerics and twenty-three townsmen who advised and helped guide the actions of the landgraves. The tax exemptions enjoyed by the lesser nobility also were ended, dealing them an economic death-blow. A consumption tax of a half percent was enacted to redress the difference between the state's annual income of 500,000 guilders and the state debts, which stood at 2.5 million guilders.

Despite loss of their political prerogatives, the estates retained elements of the special rights they had held for centuries. Among these were privileged treatment in separate courts of law, the right to retain their manor holdings, and the ability to maintain local police forces, hunting and fishing monopoly rights, and control over local religious matters. Napoleon's defeat in 1815 of course did nothing to curtail these ancient rights.

As in Nassau, Darmstadters were required to surrender their sons in droves for French military service. This support was one of the prices paid by the landgrave when he joined the Confederation. The first units moved out in October 1806 to fight with the French against traditional Hessian allies in Prussia. They supported similar campaigns against Spain (1808), Austria (1809), and Russia (1812). In the Russian campaign only about one in ten of the 5,000 Darmstadt troops who marched east ever returned. Only in November 1813 did this military support come to an end after Napoleon was defeated at Leipzig by the coalition of European powers. Darmstadters formed five battalions among the French forces who fought that day. Ultimately, of 121 officers and 5,172 soldiers who were sent off to fight Napoleon's wars, only forty-five officers and 359 soldiers ever returned. The losses across the land in even the smaller villages must have been keenly felt. Groß-Bieberau, a village of about 900 souls, lost twenty-four of her men in the wars. She also had to borrow money to pay the government's war-related taxes, and was continuing to pay interest on this debt as late as 1845.

Grand Duke Ludwig, who had become an ardent ally of Napoleon over the years, stated in 1814 that, "Napoleon is my friend, I owe him my thanks, and I will be indebted to him as long as I live."[18] He was one of the last of the German princes to turn on the emperor and formally join the victorious allies.

The population increase and the influence of French governing ideas caused some significant changes in the principality, despite the grand duke's unassailable position as absolute ruler. Up through 1810 the number of Darmstadt city school teachers was doubled from three to six. An inheritance bequeathed to the town by its dying pastor in the same year made possible the outfitting of a hospital near the Bessung gate as a school for girls. Records indicate that the three teachers for girls had charge of over 500 pupils in three different classes arranged by age. This followed on the heels of the creation in 1804 of a private school for Catholic pupils, reflecting the changes brought about by the acquisition of so many Catholic citizens in the expansion of the state by

Napoleon. The Jewish population also experienced better times under French government influence. Even the strong anti-Semitism that reemerged in southern German states in the immediate post-Napoleonic period, reflected in organized rioting in August 1819, could not set back the Jews' attainment of constitutional rights comparable to those enjoyed by other citizens.[19]

THE END OF THE NAPOLEONIC PERIOD: ELECTORAL HESSE (KASSEL)

A Cossack relief column came to Kassel October 1, 1813 as allied armies began to invade the Kingdom of Westphalia with the loosening of the French grip on power. The town was only lightly defended, and Jerome beat a hasty escape to Coblenz. The Russians were received with great jubilation, and they returned the hearty welcome by jubilantly hoisting up local children for rides on their little steppe ponies. They were remembered as having a tremendous taste for spirits that could only be satisfied with a special drink made of water, strong alcohol and pepper. The Russian commander declared the kingdom ended, but he spoke too soon; a French column was on the move and the Russians felt compelled to withdraw once more. The populace was thrown into confusion and fear of impending reprisals.

For four quiet and terrifying days nothing happened, until the call came that French troops were approaching. The French tossed many citizens of the capital into prison in the castle, including senior town officials set up to rule in the brief Russian occupation period. A few days later Jerome himself returned, but soon proved he was only after the booty denied him in his earlier hasty departure. He stripped museums and castles of all sorts of treasures, setting the tone for wholesale plundering by his fellow Frenchmen. Day and night wagon loads of booty creaked out of town bound for France. The price of freight by boat from Kassel to Frankfurt temporarily tripled. Eight days after the allied victory over Napoleon at Leipzig, the joyous news filtered back to Kassel.

Veit Valentin has given us a good description of life in Germany in the aftermath of Napoleon's defeat.

> When the German warriors of liberation came home they found poverty sitting at the hearth. Epidemics and acute famine were racking the country. Foreign oppression now took full effect for the first time. Industries that had sprung up in Germany under the Continental system quickly collapsed for lack of raw materials and also because English goods that had been piling up for want of markets flooded the country...Hard work awaited everybody. Anyone who had to struggle for the sheer necessities of life as the German of that time did might well lose the enthusiasm and drive of patriotic exaltation...[20]

"Hessians, I call you once again by your own name," said a printed flyer sent by the elector from the battlefield at Leipzig late in 1813. His remarks were read aloud from the street corners of the capital. By now in his seventies, the elector returned to Kassel in triumph in 1814, roundly lauded by the citizenry of his capital. They drew his carriage through the town with their own hands and covered the streets before him with flowers. Everyone rejoiced at the departure of the hated French overlords. "I've never witnessed a more moving and touching scene as that of the entrance of the elector," said Wilhelm, one of the famous Brothers Grimm. Germany was not yet fully freed of the French yoke, however, and Kassel's sons turned out in large numbers to be armed and mobilized at the elector's call. The campaign that finally brought down Napoleon ended too quickly for the Hessian forces to take much part.

Electoral Hesse joined the German Confederation formed in 1815 as a grand defensive alliance among most of the German states that earlier had formed the Holy Roman Empire. Elector William was unprepared to accept any of the changes wrought in Hessian society by the sometimes corrupt and profligate, but thoroughly liberalizing experience of seven years of French rule. He was determined to push back the hands of the clock to 1806. All laws of the Westphalian regime were declared void; property transactions were reversed, often without compensation to the Westphalian purchasers; state officials, too numerous now with the shrinking of Hesse-Kassel to its historical borders, were demoted wholesale; even returning army officers who had served ably as colonels in the Westphalian army were reduced to the ranks of lieutenant and captain.

Unrest began to replace the rejoicing at the elector's return. In 1816 William sought to have the reconstituted diet of the estates enact a constitution reconfirming his absolute rule and rejecting more modern governing notions—such as separating his personal finances from those of the state. They balked at his demands, and so he never again convened them for advice. A patriarchal, rather enlightened governing stance towards his subjects ensued, but always with the absolutist principle firmly understood. Kasselers soon began to wish for his departure as heartily as they had welcomed him home two years before. His nickname across the land became "*Siebenschläfer*" or "lazy bones."

Large-scale crop failure in 1816 brought hunger to the door of the economically prostrate middle class. It was difficult to get enough foodstuffs brought to the towns for sale to meet their ongoing needs. Unemployment was high, productivity low. Grain prices rose quickly; by June 1817 a *Viertel* of wheat (about eight liters) sold for over fifteen *Taler*, the same amount of rye over eight *Taler*. Typical prices for these products were five *Taler* for wheat and four for rye. The elector responded to the wide-ranging complaints about the economy from his officials by advancing 2,000 *Taler* for the purchase of grain and another 300 to expand a soup kitchen for the needy. In the Hersfeld and Schmalkald districts the poverty was the worst. These areas had suffered greatly under the French occupation, and the adverse economic conditions and collapse of trade caused people to mostly give up making cloth for trade goods. This brought about the collapse of the major local industry.

Every effort was taken to improve agricultural and industrial productivity, including the purchase of cloth making machinery that brought more modern weaving methods to Hersfeld. Efforts also were made to expand potato production and introduce the production of corn, known in Germany as "Turkish wheat." By 1825 agricultural prices had collapsed as production rose, causing further hardship for the farming classes. In that year the same *Viertel* of wheat cost only a little over three *Taler*, while a comparable measure of rye cost a bit over a *Taler*. The government made substantial purchases to put in storage to try to shore up the prices. In December 1816 the two major Hessian powers gave up their joint control and administration of numerous properties that had been held in common since the death of Philip the Magnanimous in 1567.

A grand new building project was begun to create a palace the elector considered worthy of his high status. But only a few months into its creation the old man died, and progress on the project ended with him. A single story alone had been built, standing for years as a sad reminder of the huge sums he had squandered in so short a time.[21]

At this point the overthrow of the French legal structures was complete, yet the basic concepts of rights and freedoms that were left behind eventually would have significant effects on the progress of social and economic reform. The verdict of history on the period of French occupation in Hesse-Kassel has remained mixed: On the positive side, government was mostly honest and efficient, at least until the waning months of the regime; equality of all citizens before the law was introduced; religious freedom, even extended to Jews, was made the law of the land; people were freer to pursue whatever occupations that suited them; much of the feudal system of tithes, dues and mandatory services was swept away temporarily. On the negative side, crushing taxation combined with stifled trade to destroy economic growth and people experienced real need and hardship; inflation was high; individual initiative and the Hessian work ethic were greatly reduced; thousands of innocent draftees had died in Napoleon's constant war effort; and people had been subjected to life in a French police state for the duration of Jerome's brief rule.[22]

THE GRAND DUCHY OF HESSE (DARMSTADT)

In the Congress of Vienna's deliberations in 1815 it was decided to strip Grand Duke Ludwig of Darmstadt of some of his new holdings, specifically the Duchy of Westphalia, the County Wittgenstein, and Hesse-Homburg; the latter was returned to its previous owners along with the district of Meisenheim by way of compensation. However, Darmstadt again turned up a winner as it received numerous properties on the left of the Rhine, including Mainz, the Alzey circuit, and the lands around Worms, Pfeddersheim, Bingen and Oppenheim; these formed a new province called Rheinhessen. Some properties in upper Hesse were given to Electoral Hesse (Kassel) in exchange for the Isenburg lands. In addition to Rheinhessen, Darmstadt now controlled the two provinces of Starkenburg and Upper Hesse, with a total population of 627,000 inhabitants. In 1815 Darmstadt also joined the German Confederation. In the same year, the capital of Darmstadt numbered over 15,000 citizens, a major increase in just fifteen years. Ludwig X now held the title of "Ludwig I, Grand Duke of Hesse and on the Rhine."

LATENT NAPOLEONIC INFLUENCES AND FUTURE PROSPECTS FOR HESSE

For good or ill, Napoleon's reshaping of dozens of tiny states into larger entities also remained a legacy he bequeathed to Germany, a legacy that proved especially beneficial to Darmstadt and Nassau. Most of the positive French influences found easier root in the countries that formed the Confederation of the Rhine, since they were implemented by nominally sovereign German governments, albeit with prodding from Paris. Even in the Kassel lands, however, the vestiges of French governing ideas were impossible to banish from the memories of those who had experienced them. It seems likely the seed of the idea that common people had some recourse in the face of an inept or evil prince originated in the liberal governmental reforms of the French. This seed would bear fruit in the form of rebellion in Kassel in less than a generation. Finally, in the areas of the Rhineland seized in the 1790s, France had the chance to work almost twenty years to imbue her ideals of government and social order. These lands proved fertile ground for the reforms, and remained a modern and liberal breeding ground for progressive governmental forms in the succeeding century.[23]

NOTES TO CHAPTER 13

[1] Golo Mann, *The History of Germany Since 1789*, Praeger, New York, 1968, p. 19.
[2] Will Durant, *The Story of Civilization*, Vol. XI, *The Age of Napoleon*, Simon and Schuster, New York, 1975, p. 600.
[3] Peter K. Taylor, *Indentured to Liberty: Peasant Life and the Hessian Military State, 1688-1815*, Cornell University Press, New York, 1994, p. 47; Karl Heidelbach, *Kassel, ein Jahrtausend hessischer Geschichte*, Bärenreiter Verlag, Kassel, 1957, p. 211.
[4] Taylor, p. 229; Karl E. Demandt, *Geschichte des Landes Hessen*, Bärenreiter-Verlag, Kassel, 1972, pp. 544-47; Heidelbach, pp. 211-14.
[5] Mann, p. 23; Herbert A.L. Fisher, *Studies in Napoleonic Statesmanship – Germany*, Haskell House Publishers, New York, 1968, p. 256.
[6] Fisher, pp. 257-59, 264-67; The Durants have hazarded some estimates of the value of some of the currencies in 1789 in comparison to United States currencies expressed in 1970 dollars. They estimated the *franc* and the *Mark* at $1.25, the *Thaler* at $5.25, and the *Gulden* at $5.00, in the same period. See Durant, p. x.
[7] Fisher, pp., 259-60, 263-64, 274.
[8] Owen Connelly, *Napoleon's Satellite Kingdoms*, Free Press, NY, 1965, pp. 183-85, 195-96, 206; The quote about von Hille comes from the introduction to his memoirs of the campaign in America by Helga Doblin, *The American Revolution, Garrison Life in French Canada and New York*, Greenwood Press, Westport, CT, 1993, p. XX; Fisher, pp. 274, 303-05. The Westphalian troop losses quoted for Spain and Russia are taken from Will and Ariel Durant, *The Age of Napoleon*, Simon and Schuster, New York, 1975, p.592; Fisher, pp. 303-04.
[9] Connelly, pp. 207-209; Fisher, pp. 288, 308.
[10] Fisher, p. 289.
[11] Fisher, p. 307.
[12] Heidelbach, p. 221
[13] Veit Valentin, *The German People*, Alfred A. Knopf, New York, 1952, p. 330-34; Fisher, pp. 274-75.
[14] Ernst Buchholz, *Ländliche Bevölkerung an der Schwelle des Industriezeitalters*, G. Fischer, Stuttgart, 1966, pp. 5, 10-11; Hans Lerch, *Hessische Agrargeschichte des 17. Und 18. Jahrhunderts*, Hans Ott-Verlag, Hersfeld, 1926, pp. 149-50.
[15] The new lands included the counties Holzappel, Diez, Neuwied, and part of Solms; the manors of Reifenberg and Kransberg, and the holdings of locally dispossessed imperial knights. This brought another 83,000 souls under the control of Nassau for a total population of 270,000.
[16] Demandt, pp. 534-36.
[17] Mann, p. 26.
[18] Manfred Knodt, *Die Regenten von Hessen-Darmstadt*, Verlag H.L. Schlapp, Darmstadt, 1976, pp. 76, 81-82.
[19] Demandt, pp. 561-65; Hajo Holborn, *A History of Modern Germany, 1648-1840*, Alfred Knopf, New York, 1959, pp. 367, 442; Knodt, p. 84; Mann, p. 26; Friedrich Battenberg, *Darmstadts Geschichte*, Eduard Roether Verlag, Darmstadt, 1980, pp. 289-302; *1200 Jahre Groß-Bieberau: Beiträge zu seiner Geschichte*, Magistrat der Stadt Groß-Bieberau, 1987, pp. 86, 260.
[20] Valentin, pp. 383-85.
[21] Mann, p.51; Heidelbach, pp. 223-28; Lerch, pp. 152-54.
[22] Heidelbach, p. 222.
[23] Charles Breunig, *The Age of Revolution and Reaction 1789-1850*, Norton & Co., New York, 1970, p. 94; Holborn, pp. 386-89.

Chapter 14

NINETEENTH CENTURY HESSE IN THE GERMAN CONTEXT: SOCIAL AND POLITICAL HISTORY

Golo Mann has provided a useful overview of German life at the end of the Napoleonic wars:

> The main occupation of the German nation was what it had been a thousand years earlier—agriculture. Three-quarters of the population lived on the land and most townspeople got their livelihood from it. Towns were small and their way of life differed little from that of the country. Agricultural products were Germany's most important export, followed by craftsmen's products. There was no industry in the modern sense; manufacture was a matter of handicraft and home work. In town and country life was patriarchal. At table the farmer presided over the farm hands, the master over the journeymen; prayers were said at meals and only the senior farmhand or journeyman was allowed to speak without being addressed.
>
> Class divisions were as uncomplicated as economic life. There was the "nobility", the "middle class" and the "people". Nobles were landowners and held privileged positions in the army or the civil service. The middle class was composed of members of the academic and liberal professions, middle-rank civil servants, merchants, successful promoters of home industries and townsmen who had bought land. The rest was "the people"—peasants, artisans and tradesmen, soldiers and journeymen, who began—but only in the forties—to be called "proletarians". At the top were the princes: those who still ruled and those who had been "mediatized" and had ceased to rule at the beginning of the century, but who still had certain rights and enjoyed special status in their former territories.[1]

It was a time of quiet but growing social dissatisfaction, for the period of French domination had left everyone feeling that change had not brought them the social, economic and governmental benefits they desired. Hessian rulers had joined other small states in granting constitutions to their subjects when they returned after the wars, but their subsequent actions often violated the spirit and the letter of these documents. The princes and their noble hangers-on longed for the time before their people had come to know the benefits of French-style rights and freedoms. The middle classes wanted more liberties on the French model, including freedom from the shackles of guild- and government-controlled production and policies that stifled entrepreneurship. Liberals wanted a free press, jury trials, and clear lines drawn between the finances of the state and those of the prince. The "people" simply sought personal and economic security: the right to make a decent living even in trying times. They sought to obtain it from governments whose first instinct was to protect their own autocratic privileges. In most cases government policy was good at maintaining control of all facets of life, but mostly lacking when it came to providing tools to promote the general welfare in the face of crop failure, disease, population pressure and foreign competition.

With fairly minor changes, the Congress of Vienna had upheld Napoleon's remaking of the map of Germany. His consolidation of ecclesiastical and secular lands was largely allowed to stand. For the two generations that followed, the Austrian-dominated Germanic Confederation system succeeded in heading off major conflicts among the larger states of Europe. Prussia and Austria increasingly vied with each other for influence and control in Germany, but until 1866 their battles were fought mostly in the diplomatic, not the military sphere. The smaller states like Hesse oscillated back and forth in their allegiances between the two great powers, seeking to maintain as much independence as possible. And peace was bought at a steep price: the stifling of individual freedoms in most areas of life. For the masses who suffered most in the wars, this was probably a good bargain, albeit not a fair one.

A number of German student associations (*Burschenschaften*) grew up from 1815-19 at universities like Gießen and Marburg. Their collective agenda was somewhat confusing but clearly militant, generally opposed to the autocratic approach of their governments as well as any vestiges of earlier, French-imposed policies. They sought thoroughly Germanic governmental forms (by their own unclear definitions), and a unified fatherland that would transcend the existing petty princedoms. They also preached anti-Semitism, for Jewish culture was considered non-German and anti-Christian. As harmless and ineffectual as the *Burschenschaften* were, the tenor of the times was solidly anti-reform. The German princes were easily threatened by any program that promoted change, and they were egged on in their anti-reform policies by Austrian diplomacy. After a deranged student stabbed to death a minor playwright who had insulted the *Burschenschaften*, the Austrian-dominated Confederation approved the Karlsbad Decrees of 1819. These pro-autocratic measures provided a renewed basis for press censorship, dismissal of professors who appeared to encourage student dissent, and banning of the student groups. Other measures generally promoted absolute power in the hands of the princes and limits on those who sought to act in political opposition. The spirit of reform was driven underground and substantially set back.[2]

The decrees were unable to completely block the cause of reform, however, since the generally liberal constitutions remained in effect. The Hesse-Nassau constitution, as an example, was approved as early as 1814, as the duke sought to stitch together disparate lands that had fallen under his control; these had various levels of experience with more liberal rule. For decades a political tug-of-war ensued as the relatively liberal oppositions in the state diets sought to cement and expand the rights embodied in the constitutions even as the princes and their prime ministers tried to circumscribe them.[3]

> None of these constitutions was democratic. All of them emphasized the prerogatives of the crown; they accorded overwhelming influence to feudal and ecclesiastical forces. In spite of the old idea of the estates and the new idea of liberalism these constitutions functioned primarily by official sanction. But all this did not alter the fact that they did exist. They made some slight degree of outspokenness and criticism possible, kept attentiveness toward public affairs astir, and spread some information about political problems...Constitutionalism connected southern and central Germany in some fashion or other with the west—that is, with the modern concept of the state that had grown out of the French Revolution...[4]

In the economic realm the first half of the century was by no means a period of prosperity. Population increased faster than the agricultural productivity needed to support it. Crops failed with alarming frequency. Linen making, the great engine of commerce that for centuries had given many Hessian farmers at least a meager wage to augment the small output of their marginal lands, was being crushed under the weight of foreign manufacturing. Hessian producers were unable to compete with the output of machine-based factory imports from England as well as elsewhere in Germany. Surplus labor drove down wages. In some areas, such as Hesse-Kassel, the guilds enjoyed something of a new lease on life as they embodied the entrenched interests of the past with whom the princes knew how to deal. In most cases, their respite was brief, however.[5]

Repressed political dissent and economic hardship created an environment of unrest that existed just below the surface of society, and required little goading to bring out in the form of rebellion. Such a goad appeared in mid-1830 when the French revolted in an effort to depose the Bourbon king. Saxony, Brunswick, and Hesse all experienced sympathetic uprisings, in some cases chasing their corrupt princes from power in favor of more acceptable brothers or sons of the ruling lines. More on this period in the various areas of Hesse will be treated below. Despite some promising signs that reform might be possible, reaction set in once again under Austrian leadership, and sometimes violent means were used to crush out dissent.

In the 1820s Prussia began to establish a customs union (*Zollverein*) with member states from central and southern Germany. Hesse-Darmstadt was the first to join in 1828. Some rival trade blocs were set up out of a justifiable concern that Prussian influence was too dominant in the region, but over time most of the smaller states had to join to avoid the high tariffs imposed on non-members. Members enjoyed a share of the tariff revenues proportional to their population size, as well as lower tariffs on their own goods. The *Verein* served to knit the economies of the smaller states together with that of Prussia in anticipation of the political unity that was to follow.[6]

Another development with economic and political undertones was the movement to establish railroads across Germany.

> The construction of railroads...promoted traffic and trade. Railroads once and for all tore the small German states away from their self-satisfied pastoral tranquillity; they were no respecters of artificial boundaries or dynastic or bureaucratic considerations, and they produced unprecedented psychological changes. Goods and soldiers were shifted hither and thither. Capital circulated freely, accumulated, and brought in good returns.[7]

Of course, most of this rail building activity only picked up speed after 1845, its positive economic effects more evident in the 1860s and '70s than the 1850s. From 1845-55 the number of miles of rails increased from 1,250 to 5,000. More on the rail building trends in various parts of Hesse is discussed in the following sections.

Even as the railroad industry was beginning to develop and lay the basis for future economic growth, the German economy still was largely stagnating. It seems the standard of living improved little or not at all from 1800-45. Population increased from twenty-five million to over thirty-four million in this period, and it outstripped the countryside's ability to generate enough food. Prices were high and wages low, and governments had no effective responses to boost productivity. The results of agricultural reforms that increasingly freed peasants from their feudal burdens were disappointing, particularly in poorer areas like Hesse. Peasants found little or no improvement in their economic lot. Too little rural credit made it impossible for many to quickly or comfortably buy their way out of the feudal ties that governed their lives even when reforms made this legally possible. Many turned to internal or external migration (to America or Russia) to attempt to escape their difficult lives at home.

A true economic crisis arose in the period 1846-47. A Europe-wide potato blight in 1845 was followed in 1846 by ruinous weather conditions for potatoes and grain crops alike. Staple food prices soared 50%, creating particularly dire straits for the urban poor who faced great shortages of grain in town markets. Flight to the towns was immense, but many who found only greater unemployment and further hardship in the urban areas had to turn to emigration overseas to try and find a better life.

Another political crisis broke out in 1848 in a wave of revolutions that again swept France and many of the German states. It was born not of the economic crises of the lower classes, but the unfulfilled political expectations of the intelligentsia and upper middle class. Some localized peasant revolts did break out: castles were sacked, restricted forests set upon for wood and game, and manor records of peasant debts and duties were seized and burned. Still, these were mainly local disturbances without national political significance. Riots in some towns were carried out by impoverished journeymen and guildmasters under severe economic pressure. Some attacks were made on factories as these were perceived as the source of the skilled handicraftsmen's misfortune. These desperate acts were reactions to a lack of job opportunities and economic security rather than overriding political goals. But as in 1830, the forces of reaction mustered their resources and under Prussian leadership troops were used to snuff out the national Diet in Frankfurt in which revolutionaries from across Germany were seated. The leaders were arrested or forced into exile.[8]

In the 1850s economic expansion began to take hold, but still the increase in productivity on the land and in the towns was inadequate to support the growing population. The decade saw almost one million Germans migrate to other lands, mostly to the United States. But railroad expansion, machine-based factory growth, and better land management techniques such as the use of chemical fertilizers year by year was laying the basis for true national prosperity in the decades to come. In the twenty years after 1850 high prices for agricultural products created strong incentives to expand output. The three-field system of planting was phased out, fertilizer use phased in. New scientific techniques and modern business management practices combined to expand yields exponentially. Wheat yields increased 50% from 1815 to 1878; rye, barley and oats yields doubled. Further large increases in yields occurred in the years prior to 1900. Much of this production had to be diverted to animal feed to support the demand for meat, however, and Germany became a huge net importer of food grains from America. This cheap foreign grain in turn made the more expensive German product much less competitive.[9]

We conclude this section with quotes from Golo Mann and Veit Valentin that nicely sum up the changing socio-economic trends in Germany as it approached the twentieth century.

> There had been factory workers since the destruction of the old village community by the legislation of the early nineteenth century. The landless, and precisely the ablest and most enterprising among them, were attracted into the towns. The more were needed the more followed; advances in medical science and hygiene implied that the new generations would be more numerous than

the old. The increase in the size of the population was followed by industrial expansion which in turn was followed by a further increase in the size of the population...It was not the rural population that increased but the town-dwellers. This was the age of industry...There was a mining industry, a machine industry, a textile industry, a chemical industry, and finally, starting in the eighties, an electrical industry which later achieved the greatest concentrations of capital.[10]

Germany became a wealthy country...There was an increasing tendency to accumulate savings. Even a person of moderate means could hope to acquire capital by his own efficiency and industry. It would have been absurd to speak of the miseries of the working class. Several groups now formed within this class. The skilled worker of the upper stratum, whose wages gradually increased until he was earning a good salary, became more and more bourgeois. He acquired a house and garden, arranged a comfortable life for himself, and spent money on the education of his children. He developed self-confidence and a sense of security that recalled the craftsmen of former days.

...Gainful occupations became commonplace among women. Anyone who was clever and ambitious could make his way quickly. Capitalism was on the look-out for ability and offered unusual opportunities to unusual talent. But even those who were merely industrious and capable soon arrived at a substantial bourgeois way of living, for no employee was let go except when it became stringently necessary to reduce running expenses.

Classes were being reshuffled again in Germany. The new aristocracy was a blend of the feudal class and the upper bourgeoisie. The patricians of title—university professors, judges, high officials—had largely the same interests as the new aristocracy. The middle class became stronger and tried to defend its interests by forming associations for this purpose. All skilled workers were organized into trade unions.[11]

ELECTORAL HESSE (KASSEL)

Emil Ludwig Grimm wrote after the Napoleonic wars that, "The princes, who had been forced to live away from their lands for years, returned unimproved. After the people had expended blood to win back their thrones and lands, the princes treated them without love, but only with ingratitude and hardness. Most princes have only haughtiness, pride, and gold in their hearts."[12] This description aptly fits the returning elector of Hesse-Kassel. A sign of his rejection of all that was new or modern in governing was his re-imposition on his troops of the pig tail, an eighteenth century form of decoration not seen since before the French occupation.

Kassel had to deal with significant territorial changes as a result of the decisions of the Congress of Vienna. To Prussia (and soon thereafter Nassau) went the lower county of Katzenelnbogen. To Hannover went Plesse, Göllingen, Neuengleichen, Uchte, Freudenburg, and Auburg. Sachsen-Weimar gained at Kassel's expense Frauensee, Völkershausen, Vacha, Lengsfeld, a portion of the bailiwick of Kreuzberg, and the district of Friedewald. In return Kassel received the largest part of the former principality of Fulda. Other lands around Büdingen were obtained from Darmstadt in exchange for giving up shared rights to the Babenhausen properties. The town of Salmünster came with the latter exchange. The Prussians also gave up the town of Volkmarsen, whose possession was long a desire of the Hessian ruling line. Also of note was the continued existence of the Rotenburger Quart ruled by a cousin line; the Rotenburgs obtained the duchy of Ratibor and the abbey of Corvey in the settlement of Vienna, and when the line died out in 1834 these properties at last fell to Kassel. Factoring in all the changes, by 1816 Electoral Hesse counted over 567,000 in its population.

Kassel now joined the Germanic Confederation of 1815, dominated by the policies of Austria and to a lesser extent of Prussia. Kassel also began to give up its centuries-long adherence to alliance with Prussia, preferring for reasons we will explore later to develop closer ties to Austria. The elector had promised a new constitution upon returning to power amid the jubilation of his people in 1815; now, he reneged on the commitment because he could not come to agreement on some basic issues with the Hessian diet. These included demands to separate tax and other state revenues from his personal finances, and assignment of taxation rights to the diet. There also was some local pressure on the elector to refuse a new constitution. This came from nobles who foresaw themselves having to pay taxes for the first time under the new constitution. Coupled with hard economic times, this led to widespread unrest and complaints across the land about his hard-heartedness. Typical was a missive from the Diemel area complaining in 1816 that, "The French times were bad, but these are worse." Kassel was unique among most of the German states in retaining age-old restrictions on industrial freedom and maintaining guild-based production until mid-century, by which time almost everyone else had long since adopted more modern approaches.[13]

In 1821 the Kassel lands were reorganized along more modern, Prussian lines. The various regions were apportioned among four main districts in lower and upper Hesse, Fulda and Hanau. Each area was further divided into local bodies known as circuits (*Kreise*). By 1827 the circuits collectively included over 91,000 houses and 614,533 people.

Religious life in Electoral Hesse was also reorganized when in 1818 the Protestant leadership came together to forge a united administration of their faiths along the lines pioneered in a previous union in Hanau. Administrative centers of the faith were set up in Marburg, Kassel and Hanau. Catholic religious administration was reassigned in 1827 to the newly-recreated bishopric of Fulda.

School reforms too occurred in this era, in which seven towns boasted a higher school providing a classic education (*Gymnasium*): Schlüchtern, Marburg, Rinteln, Hersfeld, Hanau, Fulda and Kassel; practical, work-oriented schools at the same level (*Realgymnasien* and town schools) were operating in the latter three towns. The *Gymnasium* schools in 1840 had about 1,000 students and over seventy-five teachers. Marburg University was then Germany's smallest with just 270 students and fifty-two teachers.

Contention between the elector and his people grew more bitter, in large measure because of the terrible perception created by his love life. He openly maintained a mistress, the later Countess of Reichenbach, who meddled in affairs of state. The wife of the elector, a Prussian princess, was so wounded by his affair that she left the electorate in 1826, taking her children with her to Prussian-controlled Bonn. This helped turn the elector further away from Berlin and toward Austria, a relationship cultivated by the Austrians when they accorded the elector's mistress full recognition as his lawful consort. Kassel also joined the Frankfurt-based Central German Union, an unsuccessful competitor to the dominant, Prussian-backed customs union, the *Zollverein*. Kassel lands suffered in the competition, but the elector refused to relent and join the Prussian *Verein*. Only the unrest unleashed in Kassel and the Hanau area by the Paris revolution of 1830 drove him to change his views.

The 1830 revolution caught the elector off guard, and forced him at first to accept a new, more liberal constitution (January 1831). The new constitution accorded important new rights to the parliament in taxation, moving new legislation forward, and making management of the income of the state separate from the electors' own coffers. The constitution was renowned as perhaps the best adopted by any of the smaller German states in this era. Agreement was reached to split the income from ground rents 50/50 between the state and the elector's household funds. But the elector's continued opposition to the constitution, coupled with the return to Kassel of his absent mistress, caused public unrest to break out in Kassel. The countess felt she had to leave town, and headed off to Hanau. The elector followed, never again to return to his capital. Although safer than the capital for the elector, Hanau now also came into its own as a center for liberal political authors.[14]

In September 1831 the elector raised his son, the crown prince, to the status of co-regent, and gave him effective control of the government. By year's end Hesse joined the *Zollverein*, and was even tolerating demonstrations and similar activity by the liberal movement. But this did not mark a change of heart. In mid-1832 the crown prince called to office a reactionary minister named Daniel von Hassenpflug. His political enemies called him *Hessen-Fluch*, or Curse of Hesse, and he clearly was a man of action. Initially, his legislative reforms sought to end vestigial policies from the Middle Ages that still governed the administration of towns. He wanted to better integrate them in the modern Hessian body politic. Other laws set aside feudal burdens on real property, created a rural credit bank, and expanded rights for Jews. He overrode the prerogatives of the diet in issuing these new laws, however, embittering an already bad relationship. The post-1830 atmosphere of renewed reaction was used by the elector and his minister to the full as they sought to ignore and override as many of the liberal provisions of the constitution as possible. Hesse joined Prussia, Bavaria, and other states in instituting a wide persecution of liberal elements. Many were arrested and given substantial jail sentences.

The tragedy for Electoral Hesse deepened in November 1847 when the crown prince succeeded his father as elector. He immediately demanded a new oath of loyalty to himself by the army, where previous oaths had been sworn to protect the constitution. He also publicly belittled and criticized his mother when she objected to his amorous relationship with an untitled woman who was separated from her husband. This further embittered his subjects, who held the old electress in high regard.

At this time Electoral Hesse counted 102,496 houses and 759,816 inhabitants in its nine major districts, a population increase of about 184,000 (32%) since 1819. This fast growth rate slowed to almost nothing by 1837, and population was actually on the decline by 1850. By 1858 only 726,000 citizens remained, including 10,000 Jews. The decline reflected the inability of the stagnating economy to keep up with the demands of the people. Crop failures were still common through mid-century, and the burgeoning railroads had not yet made themselves felt by boosting economic growth.

When the diet voted to invest six million *Taler* in rail projects in 1844, Hesse for the first time joined the ranks of other German states in incurring annual debt. Over a three-year period the building program saw rail lines completed from Kassel to Bebra and on to Eisenach and Leipzig. By 1849 the line reached Warburg, and in 1853 it linked into Westphalia. Connections also were made (1850-52) to the Main-Weser line that ran Kassel-Marburg-Gießen-Frankfurt. Hesse still had no industry to speak of, and its agricultural economy remained at a low level of productivity due to poor lands and the historical partitioning through inheritance that left most farms too small to be productive. The linen industry that so long dominated economic life throughout Hesse was in crisis as well, brought on by competition from foreign, machine-based manufacturing. By 1871 the small-scale weavers were completely wiped out by the machines. Many chose to emigrate overseas to escape their impoverished conditions, accounting for some of the population decline. More on this will be discussed in Chapter 17.[15]

The February 1848 revolution in Paris struck Hesse like a thunderbolt, precipitating much unrest against the new elector. In Hanau open revolt broke out, and spread to most other Hessian towns. Many sent representatives to Kassel in March to further their collective revolutionary aims. Soon the Kassel government was in collapse in the face of organized opposition from a wide swath of social elements including peasants, artisans, workers, and liberal political leaders. The elector was forced to declare freedom of the press, religion, and conscience, grant amnesty to those in revolt, and pledge only to appoint government ministers who held public trust. To prevent further violence from troops who had attacked demonstrators, he had to order his Guard to leave Kassel. The following months saw his grip on power erode further. A law was passed in December to appoint new leadership for the central government, the state manors, the police, and even the circuits and districts across the land.

But with the collapse of the revolutionary parliament in Frankfurt in early 1849 the hints of a counter-reaction were in the air. The elector now shifted his political support to Prussia, which was beginning to mount a counter-revolutionary campaign across Germany. By February 1850 he was back in the driver's seat, and the hated Hassenpflug was called back in as his chief minister. The liberal diet was dismissed and a new, more conservative body called upon by Hassenpflug to approve all existing taxes without a review of the budget. They too refused, and also were dismissed. A new tax decree was issued by government fiat. Now, however, state judges and other officials who had sworn an oath to the constitution refused to enforce government policy.[16]

The return to a confrontational, reactionary bent caused all the government's pre-revolutionary conflicts with its people to reemerge. The country simply refused to pay taxes, an unprecedented level of confrontation for Hessians. Martial law was declared, further exacerbating the conflict. This was soon rescinded and the general who declared it replaced, but this did nothing to quell the unrest. The elector's appeals to the Diet of the Germanic Confederation caused it to issue a strong statement of support for him on September 21. Next, in another unprecedented move, 241 of 277 members of the officer corps resigned their commissions en masse on October 9, 1850. The elector evacuated the town and set up shop in Hanau, but help from the Confederation was soon on the way. On November 1 Bavarian forces invaded, and despite an abortive Prussian invasion from the north that sought to block this intervention, by mid-December Bavarian troops were in possession of Kassel. They occupied most major towns across the land, extracting high costs of maintenance for their forces from the people.

Despite strong opposition from liberal elements, the 1831 constitution now was thrown out, and the Hessian diet was forced to accept a new one drafted by the Diet of the Germanic Confederation. Only in March 1852 was the occupation ended. The new constitution that greeted the elector on his return in April eliminated all the people's constitutional gains of 1848-49, particularly the enhanced rights of the Hessian diet and freedom of the press. The much-hated Herr Hassenpflug came back as well. The elector still resented the new document for not according him the full measure of autocratic control he desired, while the people equally despised it for abrogating their earlier rights. Opposition to his policies and the elector himself continued to percolate, with much frustration all around. In 1862, under pressure from Prussia, the confederation reinstated the 1831 constitution in an effort to bring some peace to the land. The elector was compelled to dismiss his government and Hassenpflug and appoint someone more acceptable to the opposition.[17]

But by this time the populace and its leading elements in the Hessian diet were so embittered with the elector that a political solution was no longer possible. The diet apparently was anxious to see German unification take place under Prussian leadership that would embrace electoral Hesse; the landgrave was completely opposed to this, fearing that Prussia would act to take away his land. This brought him back into alliance with anti-Prussian Austria. His opposition was made felt in disruptive actions within the Prussian *Zollverein*, of which Kassel remained a member when the league was renewed in 1865. The diet did everything possible to frustrate the turn toward Austria. When in 1866 events led to the Austro-Prussian war, the elector sided with Austria, while the diet refused his efforts to mobilize and voted instead to back Prussia. The stage was set for catastrophe.

In June 1866 the mobilization of Hessian troops went forward at the elector's behest. Within three days the Prussians had occupied Kassel and spirited the elector off to prison in Stettin. The Hessians clearly were glad to be rid of him. His own troops refused to lift a finger to save him. On August 20 they surrendered voluntarily to the main Prussian army. In September the elector concluded an agreement with Berlin that guaranteed him an income as he released his subjects from their oath of loyalty to him. He was turned loose and traveled first to Hanau and then Prague, where he took up residence on the Horschowitz manor lands. When he began to raise public complaints against Prussia in 1868, the Prussian king confiscated the Hessian treasury. All hopes of a return to the throne were dashed with the proclamation of the German empire in 1871. In 1873 the elector concluded an agreement with Prussia to recognize the annexation of his lands in exchange for a pension and rights to several castles in Hanau and Fulda. He died in 1875.[18]

Hessians were relieved to have the elector removed, but loud in protesting the peremptory way in which their state lands were simply absorbed by Prussia by decree in July 1867. The Prussians moderated their stance to the extent that they entered into talks with social and political leaders in the Hessian provinces. Administrative concessions were made to mollify the opposition. Provincial diets were set up with at least limited power to manage affairs in agriculture, road building, and administering hospitals and asylums. Prussian state support was made available annually to support these provincial governing bodies.[19]

THE GRAND DUCHY OF HESSE (DARMSTADT)

After the Napoleonic wars the Grand Duchy joined the Germanic Confederation as one of several middling German states without much influence compared to the dominant Prussian and Austrian delegates. The major fortress in Germany, Mainz, now fell to Darmstadt's control, although a joint Austro-Prussian garrison did most of the work of manning this key post. At this time a universal draft was in existence in Darmstadt lands for all men beginning at age twenty. The period of service was six years.

These early years were a time of some upheaval in Hesse-Darmstadt. Leading elements in society were pushing to have the diet fully reinstated. Many wanted to forge a new constitution mirroring the liberal trends of the post-Napoleonic time. Most people, however, were more concerned with keeping body and soul together in the hard times of harvest failure in 1816-17. Some of this unrest quieted down once the grand duke agreed to a new constitution in December 1820. The document established Hesse as a constitutional monarchy inheritable through the male line of the grand duke. A two-house legislature was provided for with one chamber composed of members of the estates, the other of fifty members elected indirectly by secret ballot. The latter included only delegates with at least 1,000 guilders of property or those who paid 100 florins or more in taxes. This restricted the number of potential candidates to barely 1,000 men in the duchy. Justice and administration in the government had been made separate departments by a reform measure of 1817. There were also differences in how the new Rheinhessen area, on the west bank of the Rhine, was administered. Its twenty-year history of French control made it generally more modern and liberal than the rest of the duchy. In particular, some of the old forms and policies of town government dating from the Middle Ages had long since been removed and were not to be reinstated.[20]

A survey of 1824 noted that the population of the provinces of the grand duchy included 235,274 in Starkenburg, 257,914 in upper Hesse, and 178,591 in Rheinhessen. Aside from a few Waldensians and French, all were Germans. 397,569 were Lutherans, 84,208 Reformed Church, 20,600 Jews and 167,582 Catholics. There were also 1,277 Mennonites. The population lived in sixty-six towns, 2,225 villages, mills, hamlets, etc., and there was a total of 98,994 houses. The major towns were Mainz, with 26,350 people, and Darmstadt, with 20,282. The army included 8,863 men, of which 7,303 were in the infantry, 925 cavalry, and 635 in the artillery. Most were not in regular service, presumably allowed to remain at home to work their fields and trades so as to reduce their maintenance costs. There was also a police force of sixty mounted and 110 other officers. The annual state income in 1824 was 6,074,396 guilders, while expenses amounted to 5,816,982 guilders. The debt load stood at an astounding 13,433,625 guilders.[21]

This debt situation constituted a continuing problem. It was of critical importance that taxes be raised to address this problem, but the economic times were so bad that this was a very difficult step to take. Soldiers had to be posted to guard against uprisings. The grand duke even gave a third of his manors and properties over to the state for sale in 1820 to make it possible to liquidate some of the crushing national debts. In 1828 the debt was still over fourteen million guilders, while annual income of the state from taxes and manor dues was just six million. The duke also gave valuable grants of other properties to the state, including museums of treasures and library collections amassed by him and his ancestors.

More school reforms in the grand duchy were carried out in this era. There were state *Gymnasium* schools in Darmstadt, Gießen, Mainz, Büdingen and Bensheim, and a Latin prep school in Friedberg. The University of Gießen was enjoying more prosperous times from its income sources, allowing it to employ thirty professors for its 360 students. Catholic grade schools were reorganized in Papal bulls of 1821 and 1827 at which point the bishopric of Mainz was granted authority in the grand duchy. Seminars for the instruction of school teachers were created in 1817 in Friedberg and Bensheim, thus creating a pool of publicly-trained teachers to replace those historically trained by the church. Other public school reforms were carried out in 1832.[22]

Political reforms were blocked and even set back by the reactionary Karlsbad Decrees forced through the Germanic Confederation Diet by Austria. These responded to revolutionary tendencies that threatened to disrupt the social order across Germany; such disruption was most antithetical to Austrian interests. In upper Hesse these tendencies were reflected in unrest among farmers who were experiencing especially hard times with the collapse of the linen weaving trade and a generally depressed situation for agriculture. An uprising here in 1830 reflected the revolutionary spirit of the times. Even military action to repress the revolt could not stamp out the movement for change. Student groups in universities (*Burschenschaften*) were active in Gießen and elsewhere across Germany in militating for change as well. The backlash of arrests and banning of such groups that occurred with the Karlsbad Decrees drove these groups underground, and some of their leaders and other members emigrated to America to avoid arrest. Many Hessians in the grand duchy longed—as did many of their fellows across Hesse and other German lands—for a larger, more unified and freer German state.

The grand duchy was made a member of the Prussian *Zollverein* January 1, 1828, a step with major social and economic consequences, for it altered trading ties and had significant economic impact across the land. Although initially opposed by the parliament when the grand duke's government joined, after the first year it was admitted that at least parts of the duchy had experienced significant gains. The state treasury also gained some 400,00 florins in the first fifteen months. Agreements in 1843 with Frankfurt and Baden also saw the creation of a state-owned railway system by 1846. The line linking the Main and Neckar rivers ran initially from Frankfurt to Heidelberg. A Mainz-Worms stretch was added by 1855, and a Bingen-Mainz-Aschaffenburg line was operating by 1859. These were followed by a Darmstadt-Worms line in 1869 and an Odenwald line from Darmstadt to Erbach and Eberbach on the Neckar.[23]

Reform efforts went forward in the spiritual as well as political arena in this period. In Rheinhessen in 1822 a merger of the Reformed and Lutheran faiths was accomplished, and this served as a model for developments in some communities in the Starkenburg and Upper Hesse provinces (including Darmstadt) as well. In the 1840s a Lutheran reaction came about that witnessed a separate Lutheran Conference being established in 1851. State relations with the Catholic church were strained over government rights to a role in the appointment of bishops. A peace offering by Grand Duke Ludwig I came in 1827 when he donated the site and helped finance the building of the first Catholic church in the city of Darmstadt, the Church of St. Ludwig (St. Louis). The relationship with Catholics improved greatly after 1850 when a particularly effective bishop was appointed, Wilhelm Emmanuel Freiherr von Ketteler, who was politically astute and worked well with the ducal government.[24]

Grand Duke Ludwig I died in 1830, and was succeeded by Ludwig II. He was not as loved by his people as his father, and as noted above the 1830 revolutions caused unrest here. He reacted by appointing a reactionary minister and suppressing dissent. Hesse was seen by many as a particularly impoverished and politically reactionary state. Numerous critics of the government were driven to emigrate to escape arrest.

The poverty that existed in the duchy, especially in the 1840s and 1850s, created terrible and even unbearable conditions for thousands across the land. This was particularly true in historically impoverished areas. The villages of the Vogelsberg region saw massive emigration to Britain and America, with droves of young girls scarcely out of school taking to the road. Many such girls from villages west of Butzbach were caught up in the white slave trade in which bordellos in England and America contracted for new girls. The poor from upper Hesse were known to form whole street bands in Paris, itinerant wanderers making their living by any means possible. The government was simply overwhelmed by the prospect of enacting policies to address the social and economic problems that led to poverty-driven emigration. Many of the poor stayed in Hesse as well, wandering gypsy-like in an effort to beg, borrow or steal the means of existence.

These years also saw continuing disappointment for political reformers who sought electoral and jurisprudential reforms, enhanced civil rights, the end of censorship, and other changes frustrated by both the grand duke's government and the oppressive hand of Austria continually at work in the Germanic Confederation. The movement toward reform could not be blocked forever, however.

The revolutionary year 1848 broke out in Hesse, forcing the hand of the grand duke in granting some basic reforms. Heinrich von Gagern, a distinguished liberal leader of the opposition that now held the majority in parliament, was appointed prime minister. He issued an edict in March granting at long last many of the changes that had been demanded for decades: freedom of the press, the right to association, freedom of belief, the right to petition government, direct election rights, administration of military oaths to uphold the constitution, the right to bear arms, elimination of many police abuses, jury trials, and others. In the same month the old duke was forced to appoint his son as co-regent in an effort to still the personal opposition he had created. In June he died at age 71, and Ludwig III was proclaimed duke. Unlike his hated father, the new grand duke was a political and military non-entity, leaving such affairs of government to his minister.

In August a law eliminated the remaining legal and economic privileges of the nobility; resentment against these ancient privileges had been made manifest in the March riots and plundering of the von Riedesel castles at Eisenbach and Lauterbach. Among the most politically radicalized areas were Mainz, Gießen and Worms.[25] Life in the duchy over the next two decades has been aptly captured by Golo Mann in a discussion of the southern German states as a whole:

> They were regions where in the last decades life had been comfortable, where taxes were low, where there was none of the burden of an ever-ready army, where citizens were protected by the law, where monarchs were easy-going and capitals artistic, and where, compared with the north, there was as yet little industry.[26]

In foreign policy, the duchy remained inimical to Prussian interests in middle Germany, adhering to the Austrian side in any disputes. This was true in the Austro-Prussian war in 1866, in which Hesse backed the losing side and had to pay three million guilders and surrender her newly-acquired lands in Hesse-Homburg to Prussia. Also given up to Berlin's control were the circuits (*Kreise*) Biedenkopf and Vöhl and part of that of Gießen. In return, certain of the Prussian-annexed lands in Nassau and Electoral Hesse were now assigned to Darmstadt's control. Bad Nauheim was notable among these additions. The grand duke also had to sign on as a member of the new North German Confederation based on the fact that upper Hesse, the portion north of the Main River, was made a member by fiat under the peace agreement between Prussia and Austria. In April 1867 he also had to accept a closer political and military alliance with Berlin; a division of Hessian troops now was organized as an integral part of the Prussian army. Mainz was cleared of Austrian troops and Prussia alone controlled this key fortress.

With the creation in 1871 of the German empire, and despite the opposition of the grand duke, popular opinion favored national union and the grand duchy was forced to join. It enjoyed no special privileges on independent action as had been accorded to the more influential states of Bavaria and Württemberg. With this step any meaningful independence of Hesse-Darmstadt as a separate state effectively came to an end.[27]

THE DUCHY OF HESSE-NASSAU

In the process of sorting out the fallout from the Napoleonic period, Prussia and Nassau entered into successful negotiations toward a treaty of exchange of various territories (1815). Nassau surrendered the circuits of Neuwied, Altenkirchen, Wetzlar and portions of territory around Koblenz that lay east of the Rhine. In return, Nassau was ceded the Nassau-Dillenburg lands that Prussia had obtained previously in other exchanges. In 1816 Nassau also obtained the lower county of Katzenelnbogen that Prussia had obtained from Electoral Hesse. Her lands now contained some 286,206 inhabitants, of whom 82,360 were Lutherans, 78,805 Calvinists, and 125,041 Catholics. Nassau now joined the Germanic Confederation created in 1815, but politically it remained among its least significant members.[28]

The duchy issued some enlightened legislation when it first came into being under Napoleon. In 1803 a law brought general religious tolerance and equal recognition of all faiths. In 1808 serfdom was formally abolished and in 1810 the citizenry gained the right to move and settle freely within the ducal lands. An ordinance of 1815 reorganized the crazy-quilt structure of administrative districts that had grown up in the tiny land. Twenty-eight administrative districts were set up under a uniform code of justice and administration. Nassau was among the first of the German states to implement relaxed rules on industrial production in 1819. A major school reform edict also was forthcoming in 1817 that imposed mandatory school attendance, created schools in which students of all faiths attended together for the first time, and reformed the course of instruction. Existing schools of higher instruction were closed and replaced with four institutions in Dillenburg, Hadamar, Idstein and Wiesbaden. A single state *Gymnasium* for instruction in the classics was created at Weilburg. Eleven *Realschulen* now taught basic education and emphasized preparation of students for service in real-world jobs.[29]

A general synod produced a union of the Protestant faiths in Nassau by an agreement signed in April 1818. Papal bulls of 1821 and 1827 reorganized Catholic reporting structures to bring Nassau Catholics under the jurisdiction of the bishop of Limburg.

A political setback occurred with the ducal legislative package of 1814, which seemed to embody the autocratic forms of the eighteenth century rather than the parliamentary trends of the nineteenth. The rising middle classes and their leaders now took up the cudgel to voice opposition to the duke's legislative reforms; a petition coming from the Dillenburg, Herborn and Haiger areas led the charge. It demanded the end of military conscription and taxes for support of the army, forced labor for road repairs, the public salt monopoly, and inheritance taxes that were a holdover from the Middle Ages. It also requested the courts be made independent and that the state manors be placed under jurisdiction of the diet rather than administered as part of the duke's personal household. The demands came to naught. In early 1830 a process of forced consolidation of fields was put in motion, a progressive step to modernize agriculture and promote productivity. In the coming decades 187 farm communities were fully consolidated, another sixty partially so. This created further uproar and hard feelings towards the government as change came hard and painfully to tradition-minded communities. Opposition to the duke continued to grow.

The economic situation stagnated in these times as the duchy simply had too few resources from which to derive income and build a prosperous state. There was wine production in the Rhine areas, and healthful mineral waters and baths in Wiesbaden, Schlangenbad, Schwalbach, Ems, Soden and Weilbach, but little else in the way of organized industry outside farming. The mineral waters generated annual sales from over two million pots of water sold, as well as income from tourists visiting the baths, but the revenue was never enough. As a result, Nassau became known for generating a large number of wandering tradesmen who often used their supposed trades as a mere smokescreen to disguise regular begging. They plied their trades as far away as Holland, France and England, wandering in bands of itinerant singers, jugglers, dancers, acrobats, and prostitutes. Some emigrated as far as California, where they were known as hurdy-gurdies. Only energetic efforts by the Hessian and Nassau governments reduced the numbers of these bands by the middle part of the century.[30]

The needy suffered greatly in these times across much of Nassau, with poverty especially acute in the Westerwald and Taunus Mountains areas. Major efforts were mounted to boost agricultural productivity in these areas, but without success. Nassau joined the Prussian *Zollverein* customs union in 1836, but the broad prosperity the union brought to many members continued to elude Nassau. The railroad era saw lines built in 1839-40 from Frankfurt to Wiesbaden, by 1856 from Wiesbaden to Rüdesheim and on to Oberlahnstein in 1862, and in the same year from Köln to Gießen by way of Siegen and Dillenburg. Unfortunately, the poorest areas of the duchy in the Taunus and Westerwald were not contiguous to the new rail lines and enjoyed no boost in prosperity as a result of this new economic activity. A more positive impact came from the development of rural self-help associations pioneered in 1849 by a small town Rhineland mayor named Friedrich Wilhelm Raiffeisen. The Raiffeisen cooperatives evolved by 1862 into rural lending banks that did much to support the credit needs of small farmers and alleviate the crushing burden of debt that plagued them.[31]

By 1845 Nassau had 417,708 inhabitants forming over 100,000 family units in 64,135 houses. The 216,725 children included 111,281 boys and 105,444 girls. Some 220,319 were Protestants, 190,476 Catholics, and 6,779 were Jews. The occupational statistics were as follows: 44,146 farmers, 2,056 vintners, 18,517 laborers, and 8,000 involved in mining and metals work. The latter were employed in thirty-eight mechanical hammer works, eighteen iron foundries, and ninety-eight factories and manufacturing works of various kinds. The trades included 2,977 inn-keepers, 2,586 shoemakers, 2,057 small shop keepers, 1,845 linen and damask weavers, 1,835 tailors, 1,835 horse drivers and coachmen, 1,478 cabinet makers, 1,173 blacksmiths, 1,119 merchants, 1,065 bakers, 887 brandy distillers, and 762 cartwrights.

In the latter 1840s the overwhelming poverty in Nassau among small tradesmen and farmers alike caused these groups to militate for economic and social change, although their demands tended to take a back seat in public discourse to the political concerns of the better-educated and well-connected town dwellers. The revolutions of 1848 that broke out in various lands in Germany and abroad touched off a revolutionary spark in Wiesbaden as well. Demands were lodged with the duke for right of the people to bear arms, army loyalty oaths to uphold the constitution, press freedom, conversion of the manors to state control and ownership, and ending of tithes. Another demand was for a popularly-elected, single-house parliament. The revolutionary spirit seized many economically disadvantaged journeymen and masters of the trade guilds, who were rapidly being displaced by the newer industrial forms and techniques. Displaced boatmen on the Rhine attacked steamships, while wagon drivers in the Taunus attacked the local railroad facilities. As the revolt in Wiesbaden continued to spin out of control, the duke called in Prussian and Austrian troops from the garrison in the federal fortress at Mainz. Still, within a year a number of legislative reforms were promulgated, including the enhanced right to local self-administration, and abolishment of tithes. Special legal privileges were repealed, and justice and administration within the government were separated into different departments. Trial by jury also was introduced in July 1849.

The collapse of the self-appointed national diet in Frankfurt saw the reversal of some of the revolutionary gains as previous policies were reintroduced. The duke now led Nassau into closer political alignment with reactionary Prussia. An attempt to put forward a liberal constitution addressing many revolutionary demands (October 1849) was quashed in this time of political reaction. The new constitution finally adopted in 1854 reversed many gains made in the 1848 period, although the self-administration of local communities under elected *Bürgermeister*, councilors, and other officials was allowed to stand. Press freedoms were constrained, as were the rights to assemble and to form associations for political purposes.

KASSEL AND NASSAU LANDS MERGED TO FORM HESSE-NASSAU

Like his counterpart in Kassel, Nassau's duke fell victim to the settlement of the Austro-Prussian war of 1866, in which Berlin simply declared Nassau lands annexed to Prussia. The new Prussian province was called Hesse-Nassau, and merged the former lands of Electoral Hesse with those of Nassau. A torrent of Prussian laws and regulations flooded into the new province in the first year. The population grew restive under the weight of the changes being imposed. In 1867 local administrative headquarters were set up centered in Kassel and Wiesbaden, and similar Prussian concessions to local control were established here as in the Kassel lands (see above). Wiesbaden administered the former Nassau lands, plus Frankfurt and some former Darmstadt lands (not including Vöhl, which was under Kassel). Kassel's control extended into all of her former territories outside Schaumburg and Schmalkalden. Kassel remained the capital of the united province, with the ranking Prussian official, the *Oberpräsident*, in residence. Over time the successful political integration with Prussia reached a stage at which the emperor himself was most comfortable visiting his new province, and did so regularly. Wilhelm I particularly enjoyed the spa at Bad Ems. Wilhelmshöhe in Kassel was another of his favorites, and it served as the imperial summer residence of Emperor Wilhelm II from 1891-1918.

The new province boasted some magnificent forests and spas in the former Nassau, as well as renowned wineries on the Rhine. In 1871 there were 1,400,494 people resident in Hesse-Nassau, of which 987,596 were Protestant, 372,193 Catholic, 3,899 other Christians, 36,400 Jews, and 306 believers in other faiths. The population included 40,263 illiterates and 17,599 who had not attended formal schooling.[32]

Economically, enhanced growth seems to have occurred with the continued expansion of industrialization in Germany. Frankfurt served as a major rail hub for the whole region. By the 1880s the railheads at last had reached into the more impoverished areas of Hesse, such as the Westerwald. Travel now was possible to jobs in industrializing areas, relieving the grinding unemployment and poverty to a large degree. Such an industrial area developed along the lower Main and Rhine rivers. Large, multi-industry industrial regions grew up based around the products of Aschaffenburg (textiles and wood production), Hanau (precious metal working), Offenbach (leather goods), Frankfurt, Höchst, Rüsselsheim (chemical products such as dyes, and later automobiles), Mainz and Wiesbaden. Frankfurt was also a financial center for currency trading, which grew in importance through the final decades of the century.

Energy sources and their means of generation evolved greatly over the course of the century, and never faster than during the Prussian period of rule. Coal, water and oil were the primary sources early on, although gas lighting began in the middle part of the century as it was installed in Kassel in 1847, Wiesbaden 1847-48, and Hanau and Offenbach in 1848. It reached rural areas later in the century, and it was not until the first decade of the twentieth century that electricity broadly penetrated rural areas. Both major and mid-sized cities created electricity works in the 1880s and 1890s.

The old records and state documents of Electoral Hesse were gathered in a state archives in Marburg, and included documentation from Schaumburg, Fulda, Hanau, and later Waldeck. In 1887-91 a thorough redesign and rebuilding of Marburg University was carried out by the Hessian Karl Schäfer, an architect who propounded the German-Christian Gothic style of building. The student body in 1866 was just 257, but by 1914 the number had risen to 2,032, including 165 women. Gießen's university student body then numbered 1,506 (with 105 women).

Overall population trends in the latter nineteenth century also showed strong growth. In the Kassel administrative region the growth from 1885-1905 was 19.3%, while the heavily-industrialized Rhine/Main area boosted the Wiesbaden district population by a whopping 40.8%. From 1871-1905 the province as a whole saw its population grow from 1,400,494 to 2,070,052. The population lived in 104 towns and cities and 2,212 rural communities. Kassel at last came to be a great city in this era, growing from a population of 23,000 in 1810 to 38,930 in 1861. By the end of the century it was continuing to absorb the smaller communities that existed around it.[33]

> Vast suburbs grew up around the old town centers, with uniform, dismal rows streets, named after the battles of the Franco-German wars but lived in by people who cared little about the glory of the fatherland...Around 1830 four-fifths of the German population lived on the land and earned their living in agriculture; in 1860 the number had fallen to three-fifths, in 1882 to two-fifths and in 1895 it was barely one-fifth.[34]

In the chapters which follow we will focus more specifically on the history of life in rural Hesse in the course of the nineteenth century, the social effects of the Industrial Revolution, and a final look at life in the towns.

NOTES TO CHAPTER 14

[1] Golo Mann, *The History of Germany Since 1789*, Praeger, New York, 1968, p. 51.
[2] Mann, pp. 57-59; Hajo Holborn, *A History of Modern Germany, 1648-1840*, Alfred Knopf, New York, 1959, pp. 462-67.

[3] Holborn, *1648-1840*, p. 469.
[4] Veit Valentin, *The German People*, Alfred Knopf, New York, 1952, p. 382.
[5] Valentin, p. 379, Charles Breunig, *The Age of Revolution and Reaction 1789-1850*, Norton & Co., New York, 1970, pp. 223-24.
[6] Holborn, *1648-1840*, p. 461.
[7] Valentin, p. 440.
[8] Hajo Holborn, *A History of Modern Germany, 1840-1945*, Alfred Knopf, New York, 1969, pp. 4-8, 14-18, 58-59.
[9] Holborn, *1840-1945*, pp. 12-23, 370-71.
[10] Mann, pp. 200-01.
[11] Valentin, pp. 533-34.
[12] As quoted in Karl E. Demandt, *Geschichte des Landes Hessen*, Bärenreiter-Verlag, Kassel, 1972, p. 548, translation from the original by Dan Heinemeier.
[13] Demandt, pp. 548-49; Holborn, *1840-1945*, p. 5.
[14] Demandt, pp. 551-52; Valentin, p. 390.
[15] Demandt, pp. 555-556; Holborn, *1840-1945*, p. 386; Ernest F. Henderson, *A Short History of Germany, Volume II, 1648 to 1914*, MacMillan Company, New York, 1919, p. 373; Mann, p. 65.
[16] Demandt, pp. 553-54; Holborn, *1840-1945*, p. 24; Mann, pp. 92-93.
[17] Demandt, p. 558-59; Holborn, *1840-1945*, pp. 96, 113; Valentin, p.436.
[18] Demandt, pp. 560-63.
[19] Holborn, *1840-1945*, p. 203.
[20] Demandt, pp. 565-66.
[21] Manfred Knodt, *Die Regenten von Hessen-Darmstadt*, Verlag H.L. Schlapp, Darmstadt, 1976, p. 90.
[22] Demandt, p. 566, 571; Knodt, pp. 85, 97.
[23] Demandt, pp. 568, 579.
[24] Demandt, pp. 571-72; Knodt, p. 86.
[25] Demandt, p. 573-74.
[26] Mann, p. 186.
[27] Demandt, pp. 575-77; Holborn, *1840-1945*, p. 223, Mann, p. 177; Valentin, p. 480.
[28] Demandt, p. 537.
[29] Demandt, p. 538; Holborn, *1840-1945*, p. 5.
[30] Demandt, p. 539-40.
[31] Demandt, pp. 540-41; Holborn, *1840-1945*, p. 116.
[32] Demandt, pp. 542-43, 577-78, 584; Holborn, *1840-1945*, pp. 59, 203.
[33] Demandt, pp. 580-87.
[34] Mann, pp. 200-01, commenting on German city populations as a whole in this period.

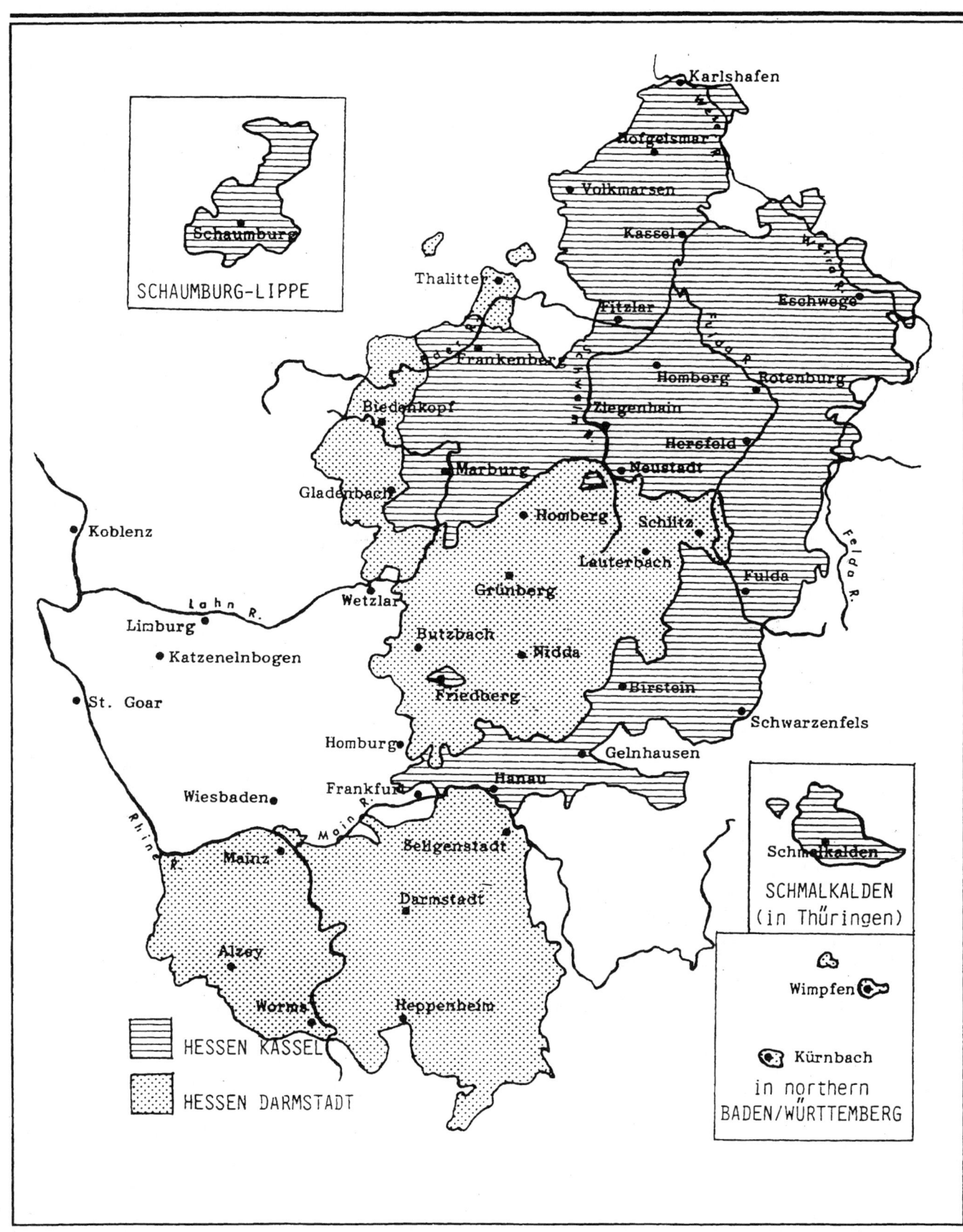

Map 9 This map of Hesse-Darmstadt and Hesse-Kassel shows the boundaries as they were just prior to the Prussian-driven reapportionment of 1867. This and the following map are by Larry O. Jensen, reprinted courtesy of the German Genealogical Digest.

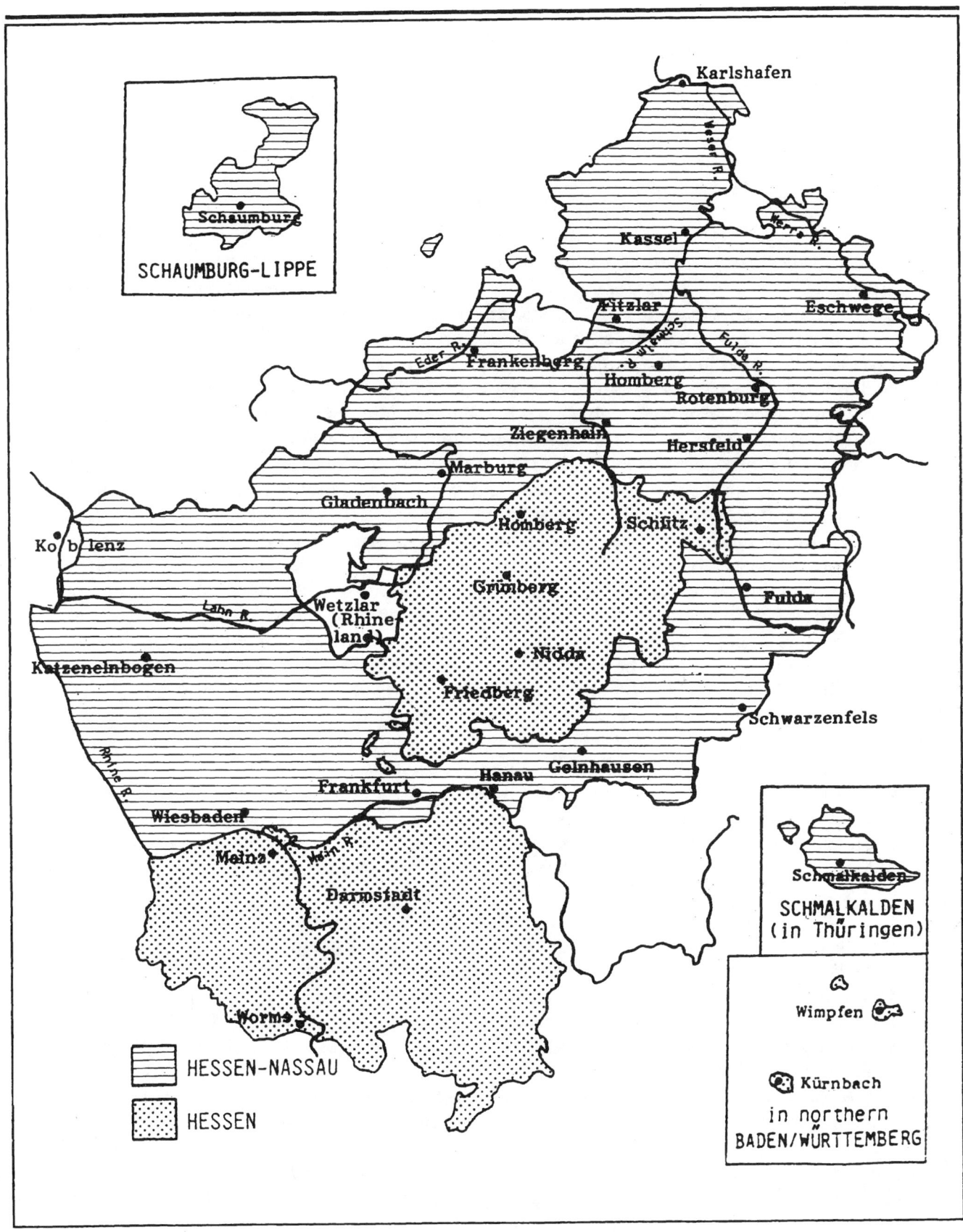

Map 10 Reflects the creation of Hesse-Nassau in its final, pre-empire form. Hesse-Nassau and Electoral Hesse (Kassel) lands were merged to form this Prussian province. The Grand Duchy (Darmstadt) now became known simply as Hesse.

Chapter 15

Life on the Land in Nineteenth Century Hesse

The new century brought a host of changes to rural life in Hesse, some positive and many others both frightening and destructive of comfortable patterns of life that had existed for centuries. Most dramatic and problematic was the collapse of the linen trade, particularly in flax goods, that had been a mainstay of Hessian life for hundreds of years. As people lost their ability to make money in linen making, surplus labor on the land caused wages to fall and remain low for much of the century. Agricultural and staple food prices remained high, however. The introduction of land reform legislation saw the farmers freed of many of their feudal ties to their overlords; at last they could begin to take full possession of their ancestral lands. Yet this became a Faustian bargain; the resulting debt burdens eventually crushed many a Hessian farm family. Poverty or emigration often became their lot. For the better-off farmers land reforms allowed them to acquire land from their impoverished neighbors. By the 1870s improved, chemical-based fertilization caused farm yields to rise greatly. Finally, railroad building and the industrialization that attended it brought the creation of thousands of factory jobs, and the rail-based mobility that allowed people to work in other regions of the country. In the latter part of the century many commuted home to Hesse periodically by rail to be with family and friends left behind in their old *Heimat.*

The individual village economies tended to assume one of two forms based on the amount of productive arable land available to them: in the rich soil regions of the Wetterau and the river plains agriculture predominated, while in the hilly and mountainous areas like the Spessart, Rhön, Vogelsberg, and the Fulda/Werra hills a concentration of handicrafts and small trades formed a large part of the local economy. In most of Hesse, linen weaving was the most important single trade as the nineteenth century opened. Despite regulations that sought to protect city-dwelling weavers in the guilds from low-cost rural competition, the guilds never succeeded in reining in rural sources of linen goods.[1]

After 1814 the end of the Napoleonic wars brought about an expansion of the international textile market, but the long period in which England had been cut off from European trade had spurred her to develop a domestic linen industry centered in Scotland. Highly advanced for its time, this machine-based industry churned out huge supplies of cloth for the American and other overseas markets. Hessian exports were overwhelmed in a tidal wave of English goods. This occurred at the same time as an agrarian crisis in 1816-18, magnifying its effects. An economic slump in the US in 1837 only worsened the situation, as did revolutions that interrupted trade in Latin America. The industry started a steep downward slide ending in collapse by the 1840s.[2]

For villagers without land, shut out from acquiring it by the existing inheritance practices but still burdened by feudal duties of various kinds, few options were available. The guild ordinances designed to protect town-based trades from rural competition remained in force; this plus stiff rural competition reduced the under classes' options for entering money-earning trades. Still, many turned to various forms of handcrafts, and the market became all the more glutted with small-scale tradesmen. This further depressed incomes. Things were especially tough for cobblers and tailors, as everyone took to mending their own clothes to cut costs. These trades fared somewhat better in the larger villages, however. Wages for day laborers fell off; from 1843-47 their standard daily wages fell from about 7.5 to 5.5 silver *Groschen*. Hunger and hardship became the general lot of large numbers of people after the collapse of textiles. One set of trades that held up surprisingly well in the general hard times were those in construction. Skilled masons, carpenters, roofers, and joiners were in demand in many areas because of the need for new farm buildings as stall feeding of animals increased.[3]

COLLAPSE OF THE TEXTILE TRADE: HARDSHIP AND EMIGRATION

The ancient differentiation of farm labor, in which men worked outside in the fields with the plow while women worked in the house and managed the smaller animals in the stalls became much more blended in this period. Both sexes were heavily engaged in whatever household production processes had to be pursued to generate income. With regard to home-made textiles, this was true across wide sections of Electoral Hesse, Nassau, and Hesse-Darmstadt.

> On winter evenings neighbors came together in a single house to conserve lighting. An oil lamp was fastened on a beam, reaching down as far as the table. Near this meager source of light the men sat, one reading to the group or telling tales, the women spinning, mending or knitting...In some villages around Breidenbach the custom existed of little wool spinning clubs of older women. They would come together on winter afternoons or evenings with their spinning wheels to spin all the wool of their hostess through their common labor. Once they had finished the work, they would celebrate together with coffee and cake. Then the next woman would invite them to come to her house, and this would continue until all the wool was spun.[4]

Clearly the social as well as economic benefits of spinning and weaving were deeply ingrained in village life. The loss of the linen trade and the demise of related activities carried out in the home marked a huge change in the lives of the Hessians. In only a few decades the trade had stagnated and then collapsed. Plenty of linen-making for personal consumption must have continued through the nineteenth century, but no longer could large amounts of home-spun yarn and cloth be produced profitably for sale in the market. Two accounts from widely separated time periods reflect knitting habits in the Hessian hinterlands:

> (1781) Everyone here knits woolen socks with astonishing speed. Men and women, old and young busy themselves with it whether at home or wandering the countryside. [The resulting products were carried by sock traders to markets in Cleve, Berg, Cologne, and other places.]

> (1904) The industry of wives in the hinterlands is proverbial. When riding on hay or wood wagons or walking the fields, they have their sock knitting in their hands; even women who carry baskets on their heads can be seen with knitting needles working assiduously. Men also knit, when their work outside slacks off and in winter when they return from their outdoor chores. Knitting is a most remarkable after-work pastime for these folk...[5] [By this time the bulk

trade in these wares in western German markets must have long since come to an end.]

The Hersfeld circuit (*Kreis*), located in east-central Hesse near the Thuringian border, was among the most impoverished in the country. In 1828 hunger stalked this region as it had done many times before. Especially dire was the state of affairs in the generally poorest villages such as those in the districts of Friedewald and Schenklengsfeld. Things were so bad that the state finance minister investigated and issued a report on the appalling conditions. Families lived in squalor in pitiful huts with little more in the way of possessions than the straw on which they slept. The whole 1827 potato crop had been consumed locally by early 1828, and by August scarcely a crust of bread was available. Many resorted to combing the woods for berries to put something in their empty stomachs. With the collapse of the linen trade the main employment for the districts had disappeared, and people had too few tools and animals to farm their lands. A similar study was made in 1827 of the conditions for linen production in the Homberg Circuit, with similar alarming findings based on the collapse in textiles.

Although it acknowledged the problem, the government could not decide on effective means of reducing the poverty. It tried directing local communities to buy flax and provide it to the neediest so they could make cloth and sell it to get by. This failed to take into account the fact that no one wanted to buy home-spun any more, and the communities were too poor to buy the materials anyway. Without meaningful land reform to pare back the crushing burden of feudal tithes and dues, the Hersfelders were in no position to overcome these circumstances.[6]

The Melsungen district south of Kassel was perhaps the heart of linen manufacture in lower Hesse. The district had 317 working looms prior to the Napoleonic wars, and just 216 by 1818. The wealthier landowners who produced linen goods exclusively for their own consumption were mostly unaffected by the ongoing collapse. The trade was so ingrained in this area that in 1831 there were still over 1,000 weavers plying their looms for local consumption across the district. Another observer in the 1840s noted that the loom, not the plow, still was predominant in the local economy of mountainous Melsungen. Wages were extremely low; two adults and several children could labor together for a week producing a piece of cloth that would only bring in eight or ten *Groschen*. The lower classes were so heavily hit by the collapse that the state had to step in to provide alternate means of support, as in 1831 when a state road building project in the Lichtenau and Kassel districts employed about 200 unemployed weavers. In many villages free firewood was provided to the needy.

Further blows came in the 1840s as agricultural reforms partitioned out common lands among enfranchised villagers, sometimes foreclosing existing arrangements where lower class members of the community had been able to keep and pasture at least a minimum number of animals among the community herds and folds. In the 1845-47 period wholesale crop failures drove up food prices and made a bad situation completely untenable. No amount of state-provided assistance could reduce the economic pressure that finally pushed people to outright emigration or seasonal or weekly travel to job opportunities outside the local area.[7] More on this development using the village of Körle as a case in point will be discussed below.

Emigration was the predominant reaction of the under-class villagers[8] to economic pressures through mid-century. Even in the nineteenth century it remained unthinkable that hired farm hands could ever rise to the status of enfranchised

***Figures* 15-1/15-2** Hessian bride in traditional dress from the Schwalm, a highly traditional area celebrated for its adherence to conservative customs and dress. The spinning wheel for generations was among the household goods brought to a marriage by any prosperous and well-bred new wife. Spinning wheel photo is reprinted courtesy of the Open Air Museum, Neu Anspach, Germany.

landholders with rights to the village commons. In mid-century a hired man earned about twenty-four *Taler* a year, a girl only about ten *Taler*. To these wages would be added in-kind products such as a length of homespun cloth, a few pounds of wool, and some raw flax. The girls might also be given some clothing each year, the men a little drinking money. If all these items were added up, an annual wage for a man might amount to about thirty *Taler* or less; girls could hope for only twelve or thirteen *Taler*. Hirelings were prohibited from marrying and were considered part of the household of their employers. They were the lowest social class in the village environment. It is easy to see why the more enterprising among them opted to leave for better wages or a new life abroad.

After mid-century industrial development in Germany created many more job opportunities and emigration to other parts of the country—rather than overseas—became much more common. This could be seasonal, weekly or daily commuting. By the 1850s the industrial centers of Westphalia and the Rhineland were the prime focus of this movement. It provided access to well-paid jobs without requiring the complete severing of ties to the homeland. Daily wages were several times higher in the industrial centers than those paid in rural Hesse, and industry was clamoring for workers.

Once this commuting pattern was established it was difficult to get the harder-working laborers to start commuting the shorter distances to factories in Kassel or Melsungen even when these opened in the 1860s. In 1883 a report indicated that the impoverished population of Hesse was largely forced to commute to better-off regions in order to find work. The poor of upper and lower Hesse mostly worked in industrial Westphalia, while those in the Fulda, Schlüchtern, Gelnhausen and Hünfeld regions worked in the rich agricultural areas along the Nidda, Main and Rhine rivers. Near the Hessian towns rural people often traveled to town to work as masons and stone cutters, but were largely out of work in the winter months in which linen weaving previously had helped take up their slack time.[9]

THE *BAUERNBEFREIUNG* OR FREEING OF THE FARMERS

The highly traditional and conservative outlook among peasant classes everywhere was certainly well represented in Hesse. An inherent distrust of change promoted negative attitudes towards partitioning of the old common lands into personal holdings, even where this might provide more viable and better-laid-out land configurations. Still, the events of 1830 and 1848 demonstrated that many farmers resented their lack of freedom and were willing to militate for change.

The government clearly was not ignorant of the need for change. Rising populations in all areas meant that the land had to be made more productive or continuing crises would result. In the 1780-1800 period efforts were made to encourage the growing of improved clover for fodder and lands planted in these crops were freed from some feudal duties. Prior to 1800 an "improved" three-field system had been introduced in many areas. The entire arable was divided into three large field segments. In annual succession the first area was planted with winter crops (rye and wheat), the second with summer crops (oats and barley), and the third with potatoes and beets for fodder, or with flax, rape, and clover. In fairly productive regions such as the Fritzlar area the combination of using fields previously allowed to go fallow under the old system and the planting of more animal fodder produced a sizable increase in herds of livestock. In the early nineteenth century some initial efforts were made to get villagers to divide up and privatize fields held in common, but this had little practical effect because it was too limited in scope. These early reforms were insufficient to address the population crisis and demand for food on the land.[10]

As early as the eighteenth century calls had gone out from various land reform and improvement commissions for the abolition of tithes and restrictions on free commerce, an end to compulsory peasant services, and transferring title to the land directly to the peasantry. Some of these freedoms had been enacted in the French occupation period. Without state-supported rural credit, however, less than one percent of the land was ever freed by these means. In some areas burdens on the peasants actually were increased in the late eighteenth and early nineteenth century.

Only in 1832 did the Hessian government act to begin to free the farming population from many of its feudal burdens. On June 23 the basis for the "second" freeing of the farmers was enacted. A twenty-fold payment based on the average annual value of taxes and services was the method employed. A rural credit bank was created at the same time to help with loans. A typical loan carried five percent interest and was guaranteed by a mortgage on the land itself. Payments were due in six-month increments. As with modern mortgages the loan payment amount was fixed, and the more payments one made the more principal was retired with each payment.

An example of how the payments were apportioned in a specific village may be seen in the 1828 cadaster records of the village of Wehrshausen, near Schenklengsfeld. The community owed collectively the sum of 2,100 *Taler* to the following landlords:

[11]*Taler*	Landlord
800	*Gymnasium* (grammar school) in Hersfeld (ground-rents)
739	Sovereign Authority (*Herrschaft*) (for service money)
32	Electoral Hesse (ground rents)
11	Lords von Trümbach (ground rents)
120	General von Helmschwert's widow (ground rents)
16	Castle house holder in Schenklengsfeld
381	[Cost of commutation of the tithes]

Taxes and duties owed to landlords among the lesser nobility were often significantly higher than those owed in villages where the landgrave himself was the lord. Sometimes the difference was considerable, as in Kirchberg, just north of Fritzlar, where the subjects owed from nine to fourteen measures of grain in duties compared to only two to four on the landgrave's lands.[12]

Despite this beginning, the government in Electoral Hesse did little to override local objections to the partition of commons, the increase in stall feeding of animals, and other reforms. Worse, there were many burdensome feudal ties which were not even addressed in the 1832 statute, including various forms of landholding arrangements such as *Meier* letter holdings, hereditary leases (*Erbpacht*), and others. These at last were addressed when in August 1848 a new pronouncement was made. The government made the 1848 concessions under the pressure of rural petitions, as well as in response to obvious poverty and overcrowding on the land. The farmer now had the opportunity to obtain complete title to his real property and animals. But as in 1832, too much room was left for exceptions that could derail the process. In many areas only a portion of the common lands were partitioned among the enfranchised farmers, while others were left under the old system as a hedge against unforeseen problems with the new arrangements.[13]

It remained for Prussian-driven laws of 1867 and 1876, which were more energetically followed up, to provide the final legal basis for ending the old feudal arrangements and forcing the partitioning of common lands among individual owners. The 1876 act decreed that an eighteen-fold payment would suffice to end the old ground taxes and other duties. Many of these payments were still being made in 1918 when they were summarily ended. Thus the *Bauernbefreiung* was a century-long process that affected Hessian farmers in varying ways and at different times. Based on his study of the Hersfeld district, Hans Lerch has written the following commentary.

> The Hessian farmer was freed, but he was in no position to celebrate. Mortgage woes and the annual interest costs gobbled up the profit of his hard labor. Harvest failure and other unlucky blows were never out of the question, so the farmer was soon forced to take on new debts. The rural credit bank only made loans towards the first mortgage on the farm, so resort was made to the local Jewish money lender...The hardest labors of men, women and children together were insufficient: the debt burden on their possessions was too great. In his anxious position the farmer often gave himself up to drink, which set farming back even further, until one day the peasant premises came under the auctioneer's hammer. As a beggar the farmer left the land of his fathers, which he had labored his whole life to work and maintain. In the last century, crushing debt, heavy drinking, and the unscrupulousness of money lenders led to much destruction of rural landholding in Hesse. An improvement in the situation only came in the second half of the nineteenth century through the founding of the Raiffeisen self-help associations, which extended credit to farmers at affordable interest rates and thus brought to an end the abuses that destroyed their estates.[14]

These problems were widespread among the low income farmers, as shown in a quote referring to broader areas of the Electorate:

> And then the last cow was taken from the farm...The *Bauernbefreiung*, the loosening of the community regulation of field use, and the partitioning of common lands gave farmers in the last century the possibility of economic freedom. But they were scarcely ready for it. After centuries-long dependence and economic guardianship [under their lords] their entrepreneurial ability and technical skills were stunted; beyond this, they were without investment capital. Many fell into severe distress, and high-handed profiteers had a field day. The usury in money and land, animals and tools reached unbelievable levels and finally brought many farmers to penury. With the increasing pace of industrialization and the introduction of freedom to take up any occupation one might choose, workers, hand craftsmen and small producers found themselves in similar straits. Through the founding of associations by Raiffeisen, Schulze-Delitsch and Haas the population was shown the way to helping themselves...
>
> With a few loaned *Taler* the disaster began. Then the crops in the field and the animal in the stall were mortgaged. The end of this fateful development was the impoverishment and ejection of the farm family from their home.[15]

This indicates the importance of the Raiffeisen associations or cooperatives which began to make it possible for farmers to obtain low-interest loans and avoid the perils of the money-lenders. As the century wore on, these associations grew in numbers across the land, protecting more and more farmers from bankruptcy when inheritance arrangements had to be made or the need arose to expand buildings on the farm property. A similar approach for Hesse-Darmstadt was created by Wilhelm Haas in 1873.[16]

The better-off farmers, such as those with ten hectares or more of land, were able to profit greatly from the land reform efforts, in stark contrast to their poorer neighbors. They had the wherewithal to afford the related costs as the rationalization of the field holdings, abolition of common lands, and ending of the required three-field planting techniques allowed them to shift to intensive agricultural practices using artificial fertilizer. Not surprisingly, there was a significant tendency toward larger and larger operations being created as the smaller landholders were forced to sell off their marginal properties and rely full-time on wage jobs. Operations of thirty to fifty acres in size were increasingly common, as were those in the ten to twenty acre range. Only those farms below ten acres in size experienced significant losses in numbers, the smaller ones dropping off to the largest extent. This corresponded with a renewed period of agricultural downturn in the mid-1850s, and also spurred emigration to America by sons who were not in line of inheritance for land but who received a small stipend when brothers came into their inheritance. This was consistent with the government policy of 1857, which favored the consolidation of lands into large and middling farms, and the squeezing out of the smallest, least productive producers.[17]

For the winners in the land consolidation game, the larger holdings and increased use of chemical fertilizers showed fairly immediate benefits in greatly increased yields. The father of chemical fertilization was Justus von Liebig of the University of Gießen. His experiments in the mid-1800s convinced him that crop rotation and the use of animal fertilizer alone would never dramatically improve yields. He demonstrated that plant nourishment was derived from minerals in the soil, and that by artificially enhancing mineral content a substantial increase in harvests was possible. From the 1880s through the end of the century his ideas were intensively put into practice. By 1911 yields of rye and wheat had doubled. The yields of potatoes, which could produce twice the food per acre of grain crops, also showed huge increases. The discovery in the first half of the century that alcoholic beverages could be distilled from the potato further enhanced its popularity as a cash crop. They remained the poor man's best and often only hedge against the disastrous effects of grain crop failure. They also allowed him to maintain larger herds of the pigs that embodied much of his personal wealth. Large increases in the yields of other fodder crops in this period also brought explosive growth in the numbers of horses and cattle that could be raised on the land.

The partitioning of common fields and enclosure of lands fundamentally altered the production and social structure in the villages. This process was often difficult and controversial, and the law dictated that the majority of villagers had to vote in favor before it was carried out. This resulted in relatively few villages in Electoral Hesse implementing the needed reforms until the Prussian takeover after 1866. After the more complete abolition of rights of the landlords in 1848 the movement toward land reform and the rationalization of land parcels began to pick up, particularly where large and middling farmers predominated. Often these farms had already begun to produce to meet market needs, and both international and intra-German competition in farm products forced them to find means of becoming more efficient producers.

Figure 15-3 A sign for a local Raffeisen rural credit cooperative, one of many that played such an important part in freeing farmers from reliance on money lenders who all too often took over farms from those down on their luck.

Figure 15-4 Flax-working tools, including a spinning reel (lt.) and a scutcher, used to separate the fiber from the plant. Courtesy, Open Air Museum, Neu Anspach, Germany.

In the Prussian period the reforms were more energetically applied. Still, the community's agreement was required, and in many villages (even whole districts) in Hesse the reforms were not fully carried out even by the end of the century. These were mostly the villages in which the small producers who were not involved in production for major markets were in the majority. Yet over time the small and middling farmers were forced to integrate themselves into the developing industrial economy. This process had begun in the early part of the century, culminating in the economic crisis for Hessian linen of the 1840s, and continuing through the 1860s. The lack of local job opportunities forced upon many the choice of leaving home and family to take up seasonal labor elsewhere, or commuting long distances to new jobs elsewhere in the region. Emigration also became the chosen option for many. Small farmers who took jobs in the developing wage economy often left their wives, families, and older relatives at home to work their little farms. This allowed them to attain a living wage, and even put some money aside to expand homes or build new animal stalls that otherwise would have been impossible. Some production of crops for local sale also was possible. In the Fritzlar area as an example, the field products of the local villages were hauled all the way to Kassel for sale, while butter, cheese and similar perishables were taken to the nearby town of Gudensberg.[18]

There were difficulties in finding alternative local job opportunities stemming from the industrial policy pursued by the government under the last two electors. In 1816 the government repealed the French-style industrial freedoms that had been introduced by Napoleon. The old restrictions on the ability to take up a trade without the permission of the largely town-based guilds were thus re-imposed. In the villages only certain trades were permitted to non-guild members: farrier, blacksmith, nail maker, wheel maker, carpenter, mason, roofer, cobbler, peasant tailor, linen weaver, potter and tile maker.

The laws also allowed villagers to bar new residents from settling in their communities. Typically a new resident applying to become a full member of the community would be required to make certifications demonstrating that he was capable of owning his own home, working his land with his own plow animals, (or was a master craftsman according to guild rules), or earned at least 100 *Taler* per year (in communities under 1,000 people). For towns with over 3,000 in population, the rule required a 300-*Taler* income. Further, one had to show he could support a family and owned a substantial amount of household possessions unencumbered by debt.

The old settlement rules and guild ordinances in towns also helped protect the interests of the master craftsmen in the urban guilds. They particularly wanted to block factory operations from locating in the areas where they sold their wares, for obvious competitive reasons. The elector shared the concerns of his guild masters; he wanted his capital to be a worthy and attractive electoral residence, not a dirty factory town. He liked the age-old agrarian and small-scale production character of his town and his subjects and saw no reason to change it. His government often rejected petitions from operators to open factories in town based on a variety of excuses; concern about expected air pollution was just one. The elector was especially opposed to outside capital coming in and creating any of the modern *Aktiengesellschaften*, or joint stock companies, which were the best organized and most effective engines of commerce of their day. His opposition caused even local capital to be invested abroad to obtain the higher returns possible in the new enterprises. Some few exceptions to the ban included these entities created locally: the Frankfurt-Hanau Railroad, the Friedrich-Wilhelm-North Line, and some natural gas works. Unlike in other areas of Germany, local railroad building alone did not spark significant new industrial development in Electoral Hesse.

Although Hesse-Kassel was still a geographical crossroads of Germany, and could have provided rail connections along the shortest lines to connect Prussia's eastern and western holdings, political difficulties between Hesse and Prussia conspired to hold off more extensive rail building in this part of Hesse. The elector was opposed to a robust rail building program, along with landholders reluctant to sell rights of way, wagon masters, coach drivers, river freight haulers, and others with a vested interest in holding back progress. Government action finally broke the logjam by empowering authorities to force land owners to cede rights of way in exchange for compensation. By 1844 the first rail line was given the green light to proceed.

In the first few years up to 7,000 people were engaged in various aspects of railroad building in Electoral Hesse. Only a relatively small portion of these were local laborers, since many of the jobs required experienced men only available from abroad. Belgians and Silesians were commonly used for tunnel and bridge building, while the local people—where they were needed at all—were mostly consigned to pick and shovel work on the road beds. Local labor was also hard to obtain during the harvest and planting seasons, when all available hands were needed in the fields. Wages were low, and hours long in railroad work: often twelve hours a day, seven days a week. Social relations between the foreigners and locals were strained. Philandering with Hessian women caused some out-of-wedlock pregnancies, and local people generally cast aspersions on the honesty and morality of the migrants.[19]

With the demise of the Electorate in 1866, the Prussians managed to drive through a much more robust program of industrial development. Markets in the highly developed Prussian provinces were now thrown open as well. Guild laws and monopoly concessions were tossed out in 1867. Industrial concerns now began to flock to Kassel and surrounding areas. A constraint was the lack of basic local raw materials and mineral deposits like coal and iron, but textile factories grew up in Kassel, Melsungen and Hessisch-Lichtenau. They mostly produced sail cloth, heavy linen and cotton fabric, typically for export. More on the industrial period in the Kassel area appears in the following chapter.

Even this new development could not immediately alter the fundamental character of life in Kassel and surrounding districts. It still retained the feel of a residence town surrounded by a predominantly agricultural and village-based economy. Some smaller towns were being influenced by the industrial development, but the economy of the villages across Hesse remained agriculture- and small trade-based through the 1880s.[20]

The Prussian assertion of control was certainly not met with blind acceptance by the local populace. The old elector admittedly had not been a beloved figure, but tradition dictated that his birthday should be celebrated across the countryside. On August 20, 1866 the inhabitants of Wetter (a sizable village north of Marburg) turned out to celebrate the birthday of their prince even though he had been exiled at the hands of the Prussians. Despite Prussian officials having banned celebrations because of the threat of unrest, school children turned out in large numbers to honor the elector anyway, and enjoy their traditional school holiday. At eight in the evening they showed up at the linden tree in the churchyard to sing patriotic songs and salute their prince. The local police captain ordered them to disperse, which they did, but soon they reformed and reappeared at the church to continue their celebrations. Clearly the children's gesture reflected the deep feelings of misgiving of many in the community, as well as its pastor, about the passing of the old government.[21]

As noted in the last chapter, the Grand Duchy of Hesse was cash-strapped because of the huge debt load it had to maintain as a carry-over from earlier periods of hardship. One solution was to sell off some of the state lands held by the grand duke, and this made it possible for communities and individuals to acquire some long-desired properties. In the village of Groß-Bieberau the local manor house was sold in 1803, and the shepherd's house with its accompanying land in 1805. The community as a whole bought the sheep pasture in 1827 for 7,000 guilders. Not all such acquisitions worked out well, however. The community also bought the "Tithe Barn" in 1841. This old structure was no longer in use since the tithes to the prince and other lords had been converted from produce into monetary equivalents. The intent was to rent out the huge barn at a profit, but this turned out to be a bad investment. The lease income from the building never was enough to pay even a quarter of the interest cost on the loan with which the community purchase had been made. The building had to be re-sold at public auction in 1851. After three auction attempts, the highest bid that could be found was only 1,750 guilders towards the original purchase price of 3,525. Such public auctions were a common thing in all periods of history. Departing emigrants in particular sold off all their household goods as they were leaving, often including large amounts of possessions.[22]

A VILLAGE IN THE VORTEX OF CHANGE: KÖRLE IN ELECTORAL HESSE

About 1825 Körle was a fairly small village of 120 households, including seventy owning both a house and productive land, six owning a house but no land, and forty-four who rented their homes and had no land to work. By this time most of the land rents paid in produce had long since been converted to monetary payments, forcing the farmers to sell produce, products or services in the marketplace to obtain the needed cash. The landholders who maintained side jobs as craftsmen or laborers often were unable to produce enough crops to have much available for sale on the open market. Their money had to come from their wage labor. The most common of these types of jobs among farmers with a house and some land was linen weaving, but this class of farmers also produced a woodsman, two tavern/inn keepers, a miller, two tailors, a shepherd, and a musician. Most of the households involved the entire family in the process of earning money through this so-called "second economy." Linen production is an obvious example in which women and even children could be integrally involved in the production process.

For families with even less land, under three hectares, the non-farming occupation of the head of the household was absolutely critical to making a living. In the households in this position, twenty pursued linen weaving. Eight were tailors, six stone masons, five hired hands, four blacksmiths, five musicians, four shepherds, four carpenters, four joiners, four wage laborers, two nail makers, two wagon masters, two shoe makers, and one each of the following: cooper, herder, miller, tavern keep, nurseryman, roofer, shop keeper, and village official. Two widows also made ends meet with spinning and some embroidery work. These families got by without great difficulty in normal times, but their situation typically did not permit them to afford plow animals to help work their lands.

The forty-four renters with neither houses nor lands were completely dependent on working for others or in a trade. Some also rented a small piece of land on which to grow a garden to provide for some of their produce needs. Another typical situation was that they might receive at least partial board as part of their wages working on the farms of others. The same professions as those cited above were pursued in this group, although they also included male hired hands and young women working as hired girls. Other trades included broom-makers and seamstress.[23]

The trend from 1776 to 1825 was for more and more people to take on side jobs to make ends meet, or to work full time as laborers. The number of such workers in the total village population rose from 19% to 28% in the period. Some nineteen new types of jobs were represented in 1825 compared to 1776. The list of jobs also shows that the goods and services produced were primarily for local consumption. Linen weaving for outside markets was the sole exception. Population growth in an environment of scarce land holding opportunities naturally led to increased numbers of under-class peasant laborers in the village.[24]

Körle suffered from the general stagnation of the linen trade, as the production and spinning of flax into linen was an economic mainstay of much of the population. In 1825 there were still thirty-five weavers at work in the village. The under-class *Beisaßen* who depended for their linen work completely on the major putting-out organizations often did not even own their own weaving looms. They were at the mercy of employers who dictated wages and production rates.

Flax processing by hand was an extremely time-consuming task. After 100 days of growth in the field the flax plants were pulled out by the roots. Next the straw had to be made workable by exposing it to the elements or submerging it in slow-moving water until slight fermentation occurred. Once dried out and broken up the straw was pulled over an iron or wooden comb called a *Riffel* in order to separate the fibers. Seeds would be removed from stalks and pressed to make linseed oil, useful for cooking, medicine making and even paint manufacturing. The remaining seed cake might be used as cattle fodder. The remnants of the stalks could be used for weaving sacks, as stable litter for animals, or mixed with clay to form building materials for the walls in half-timbered houses. Most of the processing tasks traditionally were accomplished by rural women while men did other work on the farm, but in many places the men helped with this work as well. Often it was done in common by groups of people who enjoyed socializing as they worked.[25]

In Körle three groups of linen weavers could be distinguished from one another around 1800:

- Villagers with an average of more than five hectares of land who produced and worked flax on their own lands and mostly created cloth for their own use rather than for sale in the market. The cloth was also given to hired hands as part of their annual compensation, saving the farm holder some costs. Not all of the household members were involved in the production.
- Land holders with an average of fewer than three hectares of land who bought the flax yarn from others and created finished cloth for market. They might sell it themselves or through a local distributor who took it to market for them.
- Small producers working for a putting-out organization that provided the materials and controlled their wages and working conditions.[26]

Highly differentiated soil quality originally caused the division of Körle's arable into fields of comparable productive value, and within each of these the *Hufen* farmers received a portion of their assigned land holdings. This occurred at a very early period. The division of the field holdings ensured that everyone shared in both good and bad fields, but an unfortunate result of this practice was constant arguments as farmers had to enter their neighbors' lands in order to get to their own acreage. As stall-rearing of animals generated more dung for fertilizer, heavy dung wagons caused much damage to fields along the paths they traveled. Deep ruts resulted, especially in the wet weather months. The conflict between large and small land holders was especially acute. The extremely splintered arrangement of the parcels made efficient production most difficult, burdening man and beast alike, and creating many hard feelings in the process.

The rationalization of these parcels was a process with social as well as economic consequences. The first vote in 1885 to undertake the rationalization failed to pass. The small landholders likely voted no out of fear that they would lose out in the division to their better-off fellows. Productivity of the fields as a whole was only fair, enough in a normal year to provide for family needs, but not much extra for market sales. The smaller farmers could not see that the rationalization of the fields alone would raise their yields. They feared the loss of familiar acreage that their ancestors had worked for many generations. What if their new acreage was less productive, acre for acre? Despite the efforts of the *Bürgermeister* to invoke the desire of the state authorities to see the reforms carried out, the smallholders refused to budge. Apparently they could already foresee the negative consequences that lay ahead.

The following year (1886) the majority quickly voted in favor of the rationalization. Why the change? Probably a combination of social pressures from the major landholders who controlled village government as well as continued pressure from higher authorities. The process was begun, but would take another eighteen years to complete. A typical case saw one farmer with 127 separate parcels (the largest one comprising just 8,700 square meters) reduce his holdings to a more compact set of twelve parcels located mostly in one area just north of the village. The largest of his holdings was now over five hectares (50,000 square meters). Each hectare cost the farmers seventy-two marks, a large amount for the less-well-off farmers to amass.

Once complete, this process led to the end of the three-field system and provided farmers the chance to plant whatever they wanted to plant whenever they wished to do so. Intensive agriculture on a more modern basis could now be carried out. The large and middling farmers could begin to compete in larger markets and greatly increase their earnings. The lesser farmholders were not so lucky, and many were pressed even harder to look for full time work in industry or a handicraft trade.

Besides the rationalization of the individual holdings, there were great social consequences surrounding the partitioning of village lands that had been held in common by the farmers' ancestors since time immemorial. Common sheep pasturing rights, use of fallow lands, meadows, stubble-fields, and waste areas were all examples of land used by the community as a whole. Except for the woods, which was still held in common, all the rest was converted to private property. The largest farm holders were apportioned the greatest share of the land. The smaller producers often wound up with less land than would have been necessary to compensate them fully for the loss of common-use lands. They lost the ability to pasture and raise animals in some cases due to this partitioning, for they could not grow enough fodder to maintain a cow through the winter. Only pigs, sheep, goats, fowl, and other small livestock could be kept. Farmers with five or more hectares of land fared better. On the plus side, by holding off the reforms as long as they did, the small producers managed to cause them to occur in an era when alternative job opportunities in industry were no longer so difficult to find. Still, the social consequences in terms of unrest and hard feelings were substantial.[27]

A local saying in Körle was, "hast'e was, bist'e was," or, "if you have something, you are something." A related saying in English might be, "the rich get richer, and the poor get poorer." This seems to have been the outcome of the land reforms, and at least in Körle the wealthier farmers obtained not only more land, but generally better arable than their less-well-off neighbors.[28] Yet it is hard to see how any other course would have made sense, for the broader economic trends and pressures obviously dictated the move to larger, more productive operations. The alternative to land reform would have been economic stagnation and hardship for all.

Prior to the development of the railroads, goods from Körle had to be hauled by wagon or by hand for sale in Kassel. The journey was long and strenuous. A great deal of this trade was carried on by women, especially those in the under class. These women continued in many cases to haul fruit and other produce on foot even after the railroads made the trip much easier. The fifty-five *Pfennig* cost of a rail ride to Kassel in 1852 would have been more than they wanted to spend when cash was so dear. As expected and feared by wagon drivers and boatmen, the railroads soon supplanted most other means of freight shipping.[29]

The closest railroad connection to Körle initially was a station in a neighboring village some four miles distant. After 1860 a significant number of villagers were beginning to commute to Kassel to work in the developing industrial works. The hike to and from the train station was long, and in the winter months, especially difficult. The situation only changed with the opening of a small station in Körle in 1892. By now all thoughts of the problems of rail travel in terms of pollution, adverse land use, and general fear of the unknown and untried had long since vanished. The day the station opened marked a major celebration in the village. A large crowd gathered and greeted the first arriving train at 1:00 PM with a resounding, hurrah! The girls at the front of the crowd held bouquets, bottles of wine and written well-wishes to give to the engineer and the conductor. The rest of the railroad staff on board received little flasks of beer. After the train departed the festivities continued with speeches and singing by the local *Sangverein* and children's groups, and plenty of wine and beer for all.

The integration of Körle into the national industrial economy altered local life in specific ways. This was a process begun in the nineteenth century but not completed until after World War I. The influx of cash from factory workers led to larger amounts of bread and meat being purchased and consumed, and the same held true for canned and other factory-produced food products not available locally. More local building and remodeling was done, and this led to expansion in the local building trades.[30]

RURAL SCHOOL DEVELOPMENTS IN THE NINETEENTH CENTURY

In Protestant lands such as Hesse the prince of the land for centuries had been the senior official of the state church. This ultimately helped smooth the way for the implementation of state-run public schools. Still, religious influences remained strong because of the tradition of church-managed schools, the desire to continue to impart moral and religious teachings, and the commitment of church officials to remain engaged and exert control. The twin influences of the French and Industrial Revolutions were probably the chief catalysts of school reform in the course of the century. Ultimately, the reforms caused this to be called the "century of the public schools." The early period of French rule saw the advent of an anti-religious trend in the schools for the first time. The Napoleonic era brought major changes with the Reorganization Edict of 1803 in Darmstadt. The Interior Ministry was given responsibility for schools and churches alike. A government council was given the authority to review the credentials of teachers in schools and churches and to conduct visitation inspections in both institutions.

Thanks to the Congress of Vienna (1815) Hesse-Darmstadt acquired Rheinhessen, whose school structures were completely different thanks to a longer period of French influence.

The French reforms were all re-codified in the General School Ordinance for the Grand Duchy (1827). Schools were to provide a good general education to create useful members of society and good citizens of the state. The ordinance promoted a very liberal stance on school matters, influenced strongly by the French Revolution and the practices in Rheinhessen.

Under the heavy-handed influence of reactionary Austria, much of this liberality was altered by an edict of 1832. This embodied a religious backlash and brought the church back into more direct control of the schools. Article 24 called out the subjects to be taught to the students to provide positive development of "spiritual and corporeal capacities": religion, biblical history, correct reading, writing and attractive penmanship, numbers, teaching in the mother tongue, and singing. Of lesser importance were: geography, history of the fatherland, music, husbandry, natural history, and grammar. Religious instruction was recognized as the foundation for achieving the goals of public school instruction.[31]

Despite Austrian pressure, learning and teaching goals were altered over time in the direction of more modern and liberal forms in Hesse-Darmstadt. Technical and scientific subjects came more to the foreground as religious subjects were less emphasized. Preparation for a productive life as a citizen became more important than the process of simply inculcating religious belief and values. A recess of 1850 specified religious teaching as only one of six subjects to be taught in the schools, without assigning it top priority. The complete restructuring and freeing up of the job situation also helped drive some school reform. In 1777 only 25% of the people in the grand duchy had worked in trade and commercial pursuits. By 1861 the number was up to 41%.

The Frankfurt Parliament of 1848 again promoted the separation of church and school, which was deemed necessary to increase the amount of instruction time devoted to practical, non-religious subjects. It also became increasingly recognized that industrial development depended on a well-built, well-functioning school system that prepared workers to take up modern jobs. But another backlash against liberalism followed the 1848 revolution, with teachers coming in for much criticism for having fostered the revolutionary movement. The teachers' union was abolished and progressive teachers were purged. Many resigned their positions. School policy reassumed a very conservative stance through the 1860s, when some liberalization occurred. In 1872 the National Liberal Party assumed the majority in the second house of the Hesse-Darmstadt parliament, and retained its stance as majority party in the grand duchy until 1918. This paved the way for some liberalization, although this was heavily influenced by the Prussian administration during the German Empire period beginning in the 1870s.[32]

The Hesse-Darmstadt village of Groß-Bieberau provides an interesting example of how these trends played out in local areas. The village pastors oversaw the transition from church to public schools in this era. Up until 1874 no major changes in the school curriculum were evident. In addition to salary, the teachers received rights to work arable land to supplement their meager wages. In 1830 the village included a community of 121 Jews out of a total population of 1,917 people. A Jewish school and synagogue existed there beginning in 1835.

A church-administered visitation report of March 21, 1826 noted the following.

Item: "Have the school children been effectively discouraged from taking part in festive dancing in public? This apparently has not always been the case..."

Item: "Have the parents of the community strived to promote their children's instruction by working with them at home? Unfortunately! only a few of the parents have indicated they have done so."

Positive attributes of the villagers: Hard working, productive, charitable.

Negative traits: Tendency to drink too much brandy, unchaste, living in sin (unmarried), negligence in child rearing.[33]

In the smaller villages surrounding Groß-Bieberau through the early part of century there were two distinct types and quality of instruction in summer and winter schools. The summer schools, understood to encompass a half year including the summer, had many fewer hours of instruction than the winter school, for children needed to be available for work on the farm. Winter school teachers had lower qualifications than their summer school peers, and were paid much smaller wages. They received a room and the right to the "*Wandeltisch*," or moving from house to house daily among the homes of the students and their parents to obtain meals. This often was a rather degrading exercise for them to endure, little better than organized begging. The children had to bring along the wood to burn for the school stove to provide daily heat. Such schools were maintained at the local community's expense to allow the children to be taught closer to home rather than having to trek daily to neighboring villages. A joint school was opened for the villages of Meßbach and Nonrod in 1834, and in this case the teacher mercifully was paid a salary sufficient to prevent his having to put up with the rigors of the *Wandeltisch*.

The winter schools were common elsewhere in Hesse as well. The Nassau villages of Frickhofen, Derndorf, and Wilsenroth formed a common district, with 292 children receiving instruction in 1730. By 1849 the number was almost the same, at 307. A description of the school written in 1833 noted that at the turn of the century only one book had been in use for instruction of the students: a Biblical history book. By 1833 it had been relegated to the school library. In the early days there also were no proper benches for the children to sit on, just some low footstools. They had to balance their writing tablets on their knees so they could write their lessons in chalk upon them. Until 1822 only winter school was held, from St. Martin's Day in November through May 1. Eight hours of classes were held, from seven to eleven in the morning and noon to four in the afternoon. After 1822 year-round school was implemented as an assistant teacher was hired. The village administration building doubled as the local school house at this time. This was a positive move, for school originally had been held in the upper story of the local bakery, and the heat from the ovens often made life miserable for the children. In the town hall building a classroom was installed for two classes of 123 students under the one assistant teacher. In the late 1870s the windows were altered to provide more light in the always-dim teaching areas. Instruction typically was begun and ended with prayer.[34]

In the village of Münchhausen in Nassau the winter school teacher depended on farming to augment his wages, as was common everywhere. In 1851 he petitioned the village (with support from his superintendent) for a barn near the school to help him with his farm labors, and his request was granted with the purchase of a suitable structure for 510 guilders. He now had a threshing floor and a stable for his animals. Here too the teacher originally had to resort to the *Wandeltisch* to supplement his wages. But in 1810 with the opening of summer school the rotational meals were ended as the teacher's wages were increased.[35]

The Prussian-driven school law of 1874 directed school affairs throughout Hesse for the balance of the imperial period. Religion continued to be a part of the curriculum, more with a view to imparting socially-acceptable morality than strong religious belief, however. Religion was now just one of several pillars of instruction, not the predominant one. Mandatory attendance became a reality in this period. By 1884 only a tiny portion (well under 1%) of Hessian children were unschooled. Public schools were open to all children aged six to fourteen. As we have seen, while the century saw the schools ultimately freed from church control, in practical terms church officials maintained direct oversight and control for most of the century.[36]

RELIGIOUS CUSTOMS AND PRACTICES

The Hessian peasant remained staunchly true to his religious beliefs in this era. Prayers at meal times were mandatory, whether one was eating out in the open field or at home with the family. "Come Lord Jesus, be our guest, and let these gifts to us be blessed" was an ever-popular prayer known even today. Another popular prayer was, "Father, we live from your grace, bless our house, bless our bread, move us to give, from what we have, to those in hunger and need."

In church everyone had his family pew, often numbered for identification. In the little church in Niederhörlen, southwest of Biedenkopf in Nassau land, there was a very strict order of seating. The women sat in the nave, the children, youth and men up to age thirty had places in the altar room; after age thirty they could sit in the upper gallery. In the main seating area men sat in assigned seats such that the older men sat closer to the front of the church, nearest the altar. Other men sat behind them, the younger ones being seated furthest back. In the nave the older women sat towards the back, the younger in front. Communion came at the end of the service, so that those unable or unwilling to take it could be blessed and dismissed. A brief statement by the pastor started this part of the service, followed by the words of institution, and the exhortation, "Come then, all is prepared!" First the men would come forward, eldest to youngest, in three groups of four people each. Then the women and girls would come to the altar in their seating order. Only those newly married into the community or outsiders would find difficulty fitting in without assigned places.

Special services often would be held in recognition of those in the community departing for America, especially in Lutheran areas. This helped promote and perpetuate the religious ties of those departing to those remaining behind. Communion would be served, children confirmed in the faith, and departing families would be given a Bible, catechism and prayer book.[37]

Some village communities could not afford a separate church building, so services were held in a multi-purpose structure that might also be used for community meetings, school classes, etc. In Münchhausen such a building was in use through the nineteenth century. In the tiny Taunus mountains village of Finsternthal dances were held in the same building.

Death was considered a more natural part of life than is typically the case today. Every village church had its graveyard, and the church was often the center point of community life. Week after week the whole community would follow the call of the church bells to Sunday services, passing by the graves of their ancestors who previously had answered the same call. The church in a real sense bound the living and the dead within the community. Emigrants leaving for America would come to the local graveyard to bid farewell to beloved relations from whom they were to be separated in yet another sense. In some areas a little bag of earth would be taken from the graveyard as a memento of home that maintained connections to those who had passed away. This might be buried with the emigrant when his time came to die as yet another connection to home.[38]

Gravestones in the middle part of the century might be decorated with bright colors and made of wood, stone or even cast iron. The colors were in accord with decoration of cupboards, tools and chests that were much loved in community life. Dorothea Hosch of Münchhausen (1824-61), wife of Ludwig, had a typical inscription of its time carved on her marker:

> Sleep dear Dorothea, may the earth, which gave me great pleasure but thee less, rest lightly upon thee. Rest ye early glorified, may the pleasure of the grave overtake the burdens of the world. Thy spirit has gone to become a seraph, may it send heavenly comfort down to the sad ones gathered around the steps of thy early grave to take a last farewell from thee.[39]

Especially prone to mortality were newborns. Even by 1875 in an average year almost 25% of German newborns died before reaching their first birthday. Women who died in childbirth often were buried with their dead babies clasped in their arms. A male friend or relation of the family was typically the one who reported deaths in the village to the authorities.

The body of the dead person would be washed and dressed by friends of the family so as to spare this task to the relations of the dead. Usually the clothing consisted of just a long shirt, although Sunday-best or wedding clothes might also be chosen. Some wives even wove their own death-shirts and kept them in their trunks for time of need. The hands of the dead would be folded over their chests, and children would often have little artificial sprays of flowers attached to their hair. Bodies were laid out on a death bed, covered by a white cloth to ward off the flies. As people came to pay their respects the sheet was carefully folded back to reveal the body so that good-byes could be said.

In the Odenwald area death watches were common until around World War I. Men would sit in a nearby room eating and drinking heartily and keeping an eye on the body. Originally this was to ensure the person was really dead and not simply comatose. In the death chamber a tiny light burned to ward off the devil and evil spirits, largely covered up so as not to disturb the rest of the dead.

Other typical Odenwald burial customs included the following. For burial the body was laid in the coffin, sealed up, and it was carried by pall bearers out of the house. Custom dictated the body be removed feet-first through the door, or bad luck was thought to ensue. The coffin was carried to the grave site as long as it was not too far away. Later, a hearse drawn by black horses was commonly used. A strict order of procession was established for those accompanying the body to the graveyard, for if it was deviated from and disorder followed this was considered a bad omen for those left behind. The minister went first, then a boy holding a wooden burial cross. If a choir was to sing, it followed with the choir master. Next would come the hearse and coffin, surrounded by the pall bearers. Behind them would be the family and friends, then the village men, and lastly the women. The Odenwald folk placed great store in a well-attended and festive funeral celebration, so if possible Sunday funerals were held since this allowed more people to attend.[40]

At the grave site the coffin was lowered into the ground, and the pastor preached about the virtues of the deceased. A prayer was said, and three handfuls of earth were thrown into the open grave by the pastor with the words, "You are dust, and to dust you shall return. May the Lord call you forth on the last day." The Lord's Prayer was then recited by all in attendance. Other statements by friends, fellow club members, and others might follow, after which everyone took leave by dropping flowers or a handful of earth into the grave.

Close relations returned to the home of the bereaved family, while others might adjourn to the local tavern. Coffee, cakes and wine were served up, or even more substantial food. A few funerals ended with dancing and other celebrations, sometimes lasting over the next couple of days. Those left behind adjusted to their loss, and mourning periods for widows were established by custom. A year-long mourning period was common in Nassau.

These customs were not dissimilar across most of Hesse. In some places the local school children would turn out in a choir to accompany the graveside service, for which they each received a penny and some cake. In Ederbringhausen the teacher did this with his students until 1900, at which point it was decided that this interfered too much with the daily lessons. Besides, the children were no longer in such need that they were anxious to receive the money and the cake.[41]

As in school matters, so in religious ones the advent of Prussian control in the imperial period brought many changes. In what had been Hesse-Kassel a royal regulation of July 1873 combined the three Lutheran districts of Marburg, Kassel and Hanau into a single one with headquarters in Kassel. Everyone feared absorption into the Old Prussian Union as had happened to Lutherans in Silesia. Much unrest occurred in communities across upper Hesse who were unready to accept Prussian-dictated religious standards along with the many other political and economic changes flowing from Berlin in this period.[42]

BUILDING AND CONSTRUCTION TRENDS

As the century drew to a close it was increasingly common to repair cracks and holes in the old half-timbered (*Fachwerk*) buildings with more modern and durable materials like tile and limestone. Another change was the switch to painting of these houses in place of the older tradition of stippling and drawing designs in the plaster before it dried. By 1900 the old style of building was no longer being used in new construction. More modern framing techniques were introduced. Also changed was roofing material: the old straw roofs used on half-timbered constructions well into the nineteenth century were increasingly being replaced with modern tile or stone. Straw had become increasingly difficult to obtain cheaply and in sufficient amounts. Modern harvesting machinery broke up the straw and rendered it unfit for roofing. Straw was always considered a fire hazard, even in government regulations dating from the sixteenth century. Once fire insurance became available in the early decades of the nineteenth century, straw roofs cost the owners a big premium compared to other materials.[43]

Still another new development in house building and remodeling in this century was seen in the so-called *Einhäuser* or "single houses" (previously discussed on page 129). In mountainous areas like the Odenwald, Westerwald, Taunus and Rhön the inhabitants would find it difficult to afford the building and maintenance of separate structures for housing, animal stalls, barns, etc. Here the single house was developed in which all necessary building structures were enclosed under the same roof. An inside door provided direct passage between the living area and the stalls. Animal keeping was all-important for these farms, since in the era before chemical fertilizers the land was too poor to produce enough food. In most cases only a handful of animals could be maintained.

As chemical fertilizing was used on a broader basis in the latter nineteenth century, it became possible to grow more on the land. Increased incomes made it possible in many cases to expand the old single houses. Stalls could be built off the barn portion of the house without direct connection to the living space. The old stall areas could then be built out to expand the family living quarters. The better-off farmers might even build barns and stalls separate from the old houses so the entire area of the house became living space. Another use for increasing incomes was in the acquisition of agricultural machinery that mechanized many of the tasks on the farm. By 1882 machines were in use in northern Hesse to sew, thresh, and mow, and by 1895 fertilizer-spreaders and choppers came into use. Potato planters followed in 1907.[44]

Wood shortages were again acute at the beginning of the century, and in Nassau's Westerwald the age-old restrictions on wood use in buildings were finally given some teeth through the enacting of steep fines for violators. Wider spaces between outside wall timbers and the use of fewer horizontal beams were some of the measures required. Second stories had to be built with shorter beams that did not stretch from the ground to the roofline as had been done in the past. A fifty-guilder fine seems to have been steep enough to encourage builders to actually stick to the rules from this time forward. Carpenters continued to make furniture as well as building homes in this period. More ornate and attractive furniture styles were being used than had been the case in the preceding century.

It was not just Nassau that had continuing problems with wood supplies. Hesse-Darmstadt also passed regulations by the early nineteenth century mandating that even village wells should be built of stone and iron. Records from north-central Hesse-Kassel in the 1820s show that firewood was at a premium here also, and the amount made available to each family was determined by its socio-economic standing. A wealthy *Vollspänner* farmer with four or more horses received four cords, a middling farmer with less than four horses received three cords, and a *Kötter* or *Beisaß* villager without horses received just two cords. While this may seem inequitable, it must be remembered that wealthier farmers paid proportionately more taxes and duties, probably including forest use taxes, by virtue of their greater ability to pay. Most important in terms of woods use rights was the ability to pasture animals, especially pigs, in the local woods. If the village had no rights to its own woods access, it typically would pay to obtain such usage rights from the landgrave or another lord who held rights to the local forest. The leaves of softwood trees provided some rough fodder for pigs in winter, and would be gathered to use as padding in the stalls in lieu of the more valuable straw. People would pay by the head for their pigs to be able to forage in the woods and to use the leaves in the stalls. The government took an ever more specific and direct interest in local use of the invaluable forest resources in this century.[45]

The rather impoverished little village of Probbach in Nassau presents an interesting example of building projects undertaken on a community basis. The local bakery and poor house required numerous repairs over the course of the century, beginning with roof and plaster work in 1819, and continuing with more plastering and work done on the door in 1826. In 1840 a new oven was installed, and in 1854-55 a large project was undertaken by carpenters, plasterers, joiners and roofers, the total bill amounting to 200 guilders. The community didn't have the money to pay the bills, however, and a court case ensued. The village lost, and was ordered to pay up by June 1 or the mayor would be fined forty-five *Kreutzer*. The poverty of the inhabitants was such that they simply could not come up with the money, and this was apparently typically the case unless government help was extended to the community.[46]

Road building progressed further in this era as new techniques and materials were used. The Nassau government purchased basalt curbstones and had them installed on the roads around Wiesbaden to discourage the annoying practice of driving up on farmers' fields along the roads to escape the terrible ruts and holes in the roads. The curbing helped employment prospects for both the stone quarrymen and laborers on the road gangs. Roads in the nineteenth century were on average four to five meters wide. The foundation of the road beds was set with larger stones laid close together, over which a layer of gravel was poured. A covering layer of pebbles and fine clay completed the job, and this was compacted with a water-filled roller. The regulations specified that animal droppings were to be carefully removed prior to the water-roller being applied. Rolling was done until the surface was hard enough that passing vehicles did not leave ruts on the road surface. By the second half of the century steam rollers began to come into use that were still more effective in compressing the surfacing material.[47]

SOME OTHER FEATURES OF DAILY LIFE IN THE NINETEENTH CENTURY

The pace and quality of life of our Hessian forebears can be glimpsed by focusing on a host of jobs and other features of life on the land in the nineteenth century. The farm wife typically had the daily responsibility of preparing meals, which meant hauling water and preparing the cooking fire each day. Cooking had to be done over open fireplaces until the latter part of the century when wood stoves slowly became more affordable and available. Wood was always at a premium. Butter and cheese would be churned and stores of food taken in and properly stowed away to avoid spoilage. Fruit could be dried for storage, and meats were pickled and smoked. Some fruits could be cooked and mashed for later use, although modern canning in cooking jars only made its way into rural areas in the late 1890s. Root vegetables were stored in pits and cellars, and cabbage could be preserved by slicing and salting. Modern refrigeration remained an almost unheard-of luxury until after World War II.

In 1850 rural people were spending up to 80% of their income on their food needs. Bread was the primary food source providing people with enough bulk to quell their hunger. Fruits and vegetables from the garden and the forest rounded out the diet, along with milk products, eggs, animal fat, and (less often) fish or meat. Fish (often dried or salted) was better known in Catholic areas for eating on fast days, but was seldom seen on the poor man's table in Protestant lands. The same held true for meat. Fresh, salted or smoked meat mostly went into the soup pot that hung constantly over the fire and was simply augmented with water and other ingredients as it was consumed. Bread was always the staple that supplemented the output of the soup. Cooked meat served separate from the soup pot was usually only enjoyed on feast days and holidays.

Community bake houses were erected across the land in an effort to cut down on the use of wood in individual ovens. The village of Nidda (southeast of Gießen in the Wetterau) provides a good example of the rules and regulations under which these facilities worked. On Saturday evenings bell ringing signaled the time when lots were drawn to determine the order of baking for the coming week. The first family had to fire the cold oven on Monday morning and required an extra bundle of kindling for this purpose. The evening before baking a piece of the sourdough left over from the previous batch was mixed with the new dough. Overnight the entire supply would turn to sourdough. Warm water and salt were added the next day and the whole batch laboriously kneaded. Loaves were formed and placed in wicker baskets for baking.

In some areas a baker might settle in larger villages and bake the villagers' bread in his own oven when the community oven was insufficient to meet the collective need. He was paid separately for his services. A similar service might be provided by a butcher who would work for families unwilling or unable to do their own butchering.[48] The advent of the cash economy and commuting to distant work places of course altered these patterns. More store-bought foods were available and could be acquired within or outside the village itself for later consumption.

Besides cooking, clothes washing was another drudgery that remained the bane of the housewife's existence over the centuries. Soft water was very important to creating the soap suds that promoted good washing. Rain water was especially suited to the task. Laundry was pre-soaked, a process that supposedly did half the work in the washing. Good rinsing was also key. Five waters were needed to get the best job done: soaking, caustic solution, boiling, rinsing and blue water. Rinsing had to be done at the village pump or in a nearby stream. Sun bleaching was used extensively to get the whitest wash. Spun wool and linen woven in the winter also were laid out in the sun in the spring to obtain lighter colors. Sun bleaching often was done near the villages where there was access to meadows and water from a pond or stream. The wash had to be sprinkled periodically to promote the process of the sun "swallowing" stains and yellow tinges.[49]

Ample water supplies were also critical to another aspect of village life: community fire fighting. A raging fire in the confined area of a village, fed by straw roofs and wooden timbers, could wipe out a whole community in no time. New equipment and technology became available to help with the firemen's task. Long, narrow ladder houses were built in which to store ladders for fire fighting. These structures were common in the lands of Nassau and Kassel, but only in the Darmstadt territories north of the Main River. Hoses and pumping equipment were introduced in the latter part of the century, and dedicated fire houses began to be built even in rural areas. Once telescoping ladders came into existence the old ladder houses were no longer needed and many were taken down.

In Hesse-Darmstadt south of the Main River, prior to the creation of volunteer fire fighting units the whole community was expected to turn out to fight village fires. Usually this meant any man who was married—and thus was considered a fully enfranchised member of the community—had to show up to help in the emergency. In 1840 the village of Groß-Bieberau maintained the following gear to fight fires: a fire engine, a hand-held extinguisher, two fire hooks, two fire ladders, a syringe, and 103 fire buckets. In 1859 a new fire regulation made every male citizen from eighteen to fifty-five a member of the local fire brigade. [50]

Hesse-Darmstadt also provides examples of community water works projects in this era. After 1850 the agricultural cooperatives in the grand duchy developed projects to promote drainage in valley areas and irrigation where it was needed. Systems of drainage ditches and water weirs were built to control the water flow and direct it where it was needed. A goal of these efforts was to expand hay production so it could be cut twice per year, increasing the amount of fodder available and promoting more intensive raising of animals during the winter months. A couple of such systems were built and the plans and methods advertised widely so other communities could replicate them. The systems were complex in that water had to be shared equitably among land owners and even millers who depended on the water flow to turn their mills.[51]

Intensive animal rearing was promoted later in the century by these and other means, but throughout the century and before there were outbreaks of disease that threatened to wipe out whole farms. The history of Groß-Bieberau in the eastern portion of Hesse-Darmstadt provides insight into the problems of animal diseases. In 1810 the dreaded "mouth pest" (hoof and mouth) broke out in the nearby village of Rodau. The government issued an order recognizing that the pest had broken out, and that animals so stricken had a buildup of slime in their mouths, were listless, depressed, and hot; they developed blisters on their tongues and mouths. A recommended treatment was as follows:

> Take a pint of vinegar, two spoonfuls of honey, and an ounce of cooking salt, mix these together, and rub this in the animal's mouth four or five times a day using a wooden stick wrapped in linen. After the outbreak of pustules cease this treatment and instead treat the blisters with fresh cream and egg whites until the skin heals. During its illness the cow should have no raw food but only cooked matter and water. The cow should also be curried often and wrapped in wool cloth.

The pest also struck in the grand duchy lands in 1869, 1896, and several times in the years after 1900. Another animal disease of the 1830s was called the "lung pestilence." Three animals were stricken in Groß-Bieberau in 1836. The local veterinarian consulted with his governmental higher-ups, and ruled that the sick animals should be isolated from others and those that died should be buried a full six feet deep. Sick animals should be given fresh air and food and a medicine made of salt, juniper berries, and horseradish. Frequent rubbing of the animal with straw also was said to help with the healing. In addition, a ten-*Taler* fine was prescribed for anyone concealing the outbreak of disease or employing a folk healer to treat it. In this case the initial group of three stricken cows all died, but others in the village remained healthy. Unfortunately another outbreak in early 1837 was not so easily overcome. Local farmers were forbidden to sell or take their animals to market. Within a few weeks three cows and a horse grew sick with the lung disease and were ordered destroyed. This was a terrible loss for the owner, and the community chest was directed to provide recompense. Another eight cows fell ill within a few weeks. By June sixteen cows had to be destroyed. Not until December 1838 was the outbreak declared over.[52]

Intensive animal husbandry and stall feeding and raising led to the ability to store up larger amounts of dung for fertilizer. This was of critical importance to raising yields in the decades prior to the introduction of chemical fertilizers. After about 1830 organized efforts were made by agricultural associations to try to promote the development of dung heaps to collect fertilizer. Training was given to bricklayers and plasterers, and small design models were given to local village officials. Within thirty years over 1,000 dung heaps had been constructed in 400 villages. The specific sizes of ditches needed to store the dung for various numbers of cattle were determined. Four head needed a ditch 4x4 meters, while fifteen head would need a 12x5.5 meter ditch. These ditches would store the resulting dung for up to twelve weeks.

Privies for human waste also underwent change in the course of the century. Village schools were among the first institutions on the land to have out houses. It became official policy to encourage people to build them to promote health and sanitation. Small huts of half-timbered or simple board-work construction sprouted up across the land, often placed near the dung pits. Many sported the characteristic heart shape carved out of their doors.[53]

A fixture on the village scene was the cartwright, who fabricated wooden wheels for carriages and made various farm implements such as plows. One could discern a cartwright's shop at some distance based on the amount of cut and split wood that was laid out for drying. Elm and oak were favored for the production of spokes, wheels, hubs, axles, etc. Beech was preferred for sleigh runners, stools, and wheel crowns. White beech was good for tool handles.

The blacksmith's operation also was well represented in rural areas. Tool fabrication and repairs and the shoeing of animals were much in demand in the farming community. Nails, hooks, horseshoes, iron bands and chains were all the products of his trade, and the smith earned a good living by most local standards. The basic tools were the hammer, anvil and pliers, and of course a forge and bellows to fire the metal. A water bucket was always handy to cool off the worked metal. The work was hard and dirty. A related trade was that of the tinsmith, who produced household goods like pots, kettles, buckets, cans, baking tins, graters, etc. His work was composed of hammering and rolling thin metal sheets of copper, silver, brass, lead and zinc.[54]

A less technical but equally widespread trade was that of the nightwatchman. His cottage, like that of the shepherd, was typically community property provided to him while he held the position. Many villages combined these two jobs based on the similarity of the work. Often the watchman/shepherd was not even considered a full citizen with community rights. With a pike, a lantern and a horn the nightwatchman would wander the streets at night, calling the times out and giving a reassuring feeling of security to the populace.[55]

STYLES OF DRESS: *TRACHTEN* IN THE ODENWALD AND BEYOND [56]

In nineteenth century Hesse there were twenty-seven different territories with distinctive styles of folk dress, one of the richest areas of its kind in all of Germany. The Odenwald was one of these regions. With the repeal of state-mandated clothing ordinances around 1800 a host of changes in form came about. This was especially true of colors. After mid-century many changes in style and habit reflected the blending of historical rural styles with emerging modern tastes.

Styles common about 1840 are described in the writings of a local pastor from the area around Kleestadt, which is east of Darmstadt near Groß-Umstadt. He described the village as having the appearance of a Medieval fortress, and the people as being very conservative in manner and clothing. The men wore knee-length pants made of deerskin, with white wool knee socks and shoes with big silver buckles. Sunday best consisted of an overcoat that reached down below the knees, with broad cuffs and big buttons made of woven mohair. The coat was always of dark brown or black cloth that was so durable that it stood up to almost a lifetime of wear. Under this a dress coat was worn, which was fully lined with white wool. A jersey covered the upper body down to the waist. A shirt similar to that worn by the women also was worn. The men's hats were of various styles depending on the activity they were pursuing. There were felt caps with gold piping on the edges and a gold tassel on top. For work wear they often wore a stocking cap with a tassel on top that hung over one ear.

"Sunday best" hats were of black felt with wide brims fastened to the peak in the style of three-cornered hats. These so-called *"Dreimaster"* hats were worn with one of the points facing forward during most festive occasions. For particularly happy events like family weddings and baptisms one of the broad sides was worn facing forward. In the course of the century a style developed of wearing the hat brim attached to the peak of the hat only in the back, lending it a shovel-shaped appearance that came to be known derogatorily as a "Farmer's Shovel." (*Bauernschippe*). By 1900 more modern styles had begun to take over, and most began to use a round, double peaked, fairly flat hat of felt with a brim about four inches in width.

Women's "Sunday best" clothes consisted of a bodice with elbow-length sleeves. The lower arms were covered with so-called mittens (*Stauchen*) that ended in a v-shaped point that lay on top of the hand. The hands were wrapped in a muff of brown fur with black rings. The skirts were made of dark cloth, laid in many folds from top to bottom. On their heads they wore bonnets made of stiff linen cloth, tied under the chin. A special bonnet of white lace was worn just for communion services. On other Sundays the standard white bonnet was worn, while everyday wear might include bonnets of various colors.

This description (from the northern Odenwald) indicates that men's folk-style clothing varied little over wide parts of Hesse. The description above tracks very closely in fact with a description of styles in the 1820-30 period as they appeared in Egelsbach, northwest of Darmstadt, and in 1844 in Arheilgen, a village suburb of the town. For everyday wear linen leggings were worn over the long wool stockings to keep them clean. The influence of the French Revolution on clothing styles was seen in the eventual disappearance of knee pants in favor of long trousers by about 1850. Even these were protected in field work by wearing linen leggings over them. Long pants were typically white and blue in color, made of linen, woolen or a blend of material. Like the knee pants, they were closed at the top with a buttoned flap, and later had a more modern, slit-style fly. Slits at the bottom of the legs fastened with buttons were also common, and this facilitated wearing the pants over boots or shoes. Suspenders also were typical among those who wore long pants. These could be decorated with attractive needle work.

Women's clothes in contrast differed more markedly in style over various parts of Hesse. As the century began, blue remained the most popular color. Many subtle style alterations might be worn depending on the type of church service, festival, or even

Figures 15-5/15-6 Hessian *Volkstrachten*, or traditional garb, with a key to various styles common to specific areas. The cover photo on this book shoes a Hessian family group in which the man and his sons are wearing more modern head gear, as described in the chapter.

Figures 15-7/15-8 More traditional outfits, and a grouping posed around a classic bride's chest.

325

Figures 15-9/15-10 More *Trachten* reflecting the clothing styles described in this Chapter.

work at home in which the woman expected to participate. The main item of day-to-day clothing that might be changed depending on the task at hand was the apron. Some women had three or four different aprons to be worn based on the work to be done, some made of linen of various grades or perhaps sewn from burlap or other castoff materials if the intended use was for stall cleaning or similar dirty jobs.

The fabrics used in women's dress varied by region. Originally linen predominated outside the areas in which sheep folding was most common. Later, wool came into wider use in all areas. Towards the latter part of the century cotton came to be used as well.

In the villages around Waldmichelbach, far to the south in Hesse-Darmstadt, a description of everyday women's wear survives from the 1890s. Blue material predominated, sometimes with white or green designs on it, and embroidered wool caps were worn, black in color with blue edges. Instead of silk scarves worn only on Sundays, scarves of woolen fabric were the norm. These were light blue with blue and green flowers. For dances colorful skirts were worn, usually in blue and black. Beneath these were worn underskirts of calico and wool. Shirts had long arms with embroidery decorations all over. Springing from common roots in age-old styles of dress, women's *Trachten* costumes developed many different regional variations in the course of the nineteenth century, depending on the level of adoption of more modern dressing styles seen in the towns.

THE HISTORY OF THE HESSIAN JEWS

The Jewish people of Hesse continued to face much discrimination despite the emancipation trends of the Enlightenment, the Napoleonic period and the liberal revolutions of 1830 and 1848. Discrimination came in ways subtle and overt. In the Grand Duchy of Hesse full citizenship rights were never extended to the Jews during the period leading up to the founding of the German Reich. Here the government required in state regulations of 1821 and 1822 that separate vital records of the Jewish population be kept as a basis for assessing the many special charges typically laid upon Jews for protection money, new year's money, school money, etc. In rural areas many Jewish communities remained basically impoverished in the early part of the century, finding it impossible to pay special taxes imposed on them. In 1829 a regulation recognized the Jewish faith as a valid religious expression to the extent that state authorities were to accord it similar protections to those accorded the Christian denominations. Town and village mayors were ordered to report on the condition of their Jewish communities, indicating their local legal status and rights to participate in local government.[57]

In 1823 the mandatory attendance of Jewish children in public (Christian) schools was ordered in Hesse-Darmstadt. By 1828 this was amended to allow schooling in Jewish-run schools, as it was recognized that it was impractical to require attendance in public schools and assess Jews the associated fees.

The economic situation changed slowly for the Hebrew community in Groß-Bieberau, with a handful of Jews finally achieving a more prosperous lifestyle. They lived mostly from small retail trading, especially in domestic animals and produce. In 1873 a synagogue was built, and in 1876 a ritual bath house was added. In 1889 a Jewish cemetery was purchased; up until then community members had been buried in the Jewish graveyard in Dieburg. Still, a large group of the Jews remained impoverished and living in difficult circumstances on the land. The pace of emigration to the US picked up in the 1850s and '60s. Many youths in particular left at this time.

Most of the nineteenth century was a time of steady improvement in the integration of Jews in public life and citizenship in the state. But in the 1880-1900 period a renewed spirit of anti-Semitism broke out, with rural bigots declaring that people should trade in Christian-only animal markets. In these later years growing prejudice and intolerance born of jealousy of the few Jews who had reached social respectability (doctors, merchants, jurists, etc.) became evident.[58]

In Hesse-Kassel many similar trends are apparent. The ideas of the French Revolution had increased official tolerance to some degree. An act of 1816 granted Jews at least nominal equality with other citizens of the realm. For their enhanced status the Jewish community were expected to pay the elector 75,000 *Taler* a year in protection money, just as their forebears had paid the German princes from time out of mind. In the village of Nentershausen (northeastern Hesse, near Sontra) in 1850 there were 237 Jews, totaling 15% of the population. This was a very high proportion by the standard of most villages. Most were small traders specializing in groceries, tobacco, ironware products, and animal trading. From 1850 through the 1860s extremely difficult economic conditions forced many to migrate to America, as was occurring in Hesse-Darmstadt. From this time until after the turn of the century the Nentershausen Jewish population dropped by 59%.[59]

As the century wore on more and more villages saw the building of synagogues, although Jews still lived in small and isolated communities in many areas. Jewish law directed that one must go to worship on foot because it was forbidden to use any traveling conveyance. So it could be quite arduous depending on the weather to travel to the nearest house of worship. The law said that anywhere that ten Jewish men resided could be considered a community for purposes of erecting a synagogue, and so many were founded openly or in secret to eliminate the inconvenience of traveling long distances. The synagogue was a collecting point for people to come and learn about their faith, a place first and foremost for instruction. It was the social center post for the faith community, and weighty matters were debated fervently and loudly within its doors.

This propensity for loud discourse brought about some changes in regulations for the Nentershausen worship community to try to create a quieter environment for worship. Children under six were forbidden from being brought into the worship, since they were incapable of understanding the teachings. Children over six could attend only with the monitoring of their parents, who were directed to make sure their offspring stayed in their proper places and did not disturb. As soon as the service began the doors were to be closed and complete quiet and order were to ensue. Without a pressing cause, no one was to attempt to leave the service before it ended. All conversation during the service was also prohibited.[60]

CONCLUSION

Our earlier overview of the village of Körle exhibited trends that were happening across rural Hesse during the century. Small farmers were being driven off their lands as larger, more efficient operations made it uneconomical for them to sell their produce on the market. At the same time factory operations eliminated the market for small-scale, village-based manufactures. The factories needed workers and paid relatively high wages, which drew many of the displaced farmers to the towns. This influx of labor then created a huge demand for affordable rental housing in urban areas, triggering a construction boom that provided further employment opportunities for outlying villagers during the six months of the year when the weather permitted uninterrupted building. The nationwide rail network that girded Germany in the second half of the century completed the social and economic transformation as workers could commute long distances to take advantage of job opportunities wherever they arose.[61]

NOTES TO CHAPTER 15

[1] Kurt Wagner, *Leben auf dem Lande im Wandel des Industrialisierung: Das Dorf war früher auch keine heile Welt*, Insel Verlag, Frankfurt am main, 1986, pp. 59-60.

[2] Wagner, pp. 60-61;Brigitta Vits, *Die Wirtschafts- und Sozialstruktur ländlicher Siedlungen in Nordhessen vom 16. Bis zum 19. Jahrhundert*, Selbstverlag der Marburger Geographischen Gesellschaft, Marburg, 1993, p. 129. The Vits study looks in depth at villages in three portions of north-central Hesse-Kassel: 1) an area partially encompassing the districts of Volkmarsen, Zierenberg, and Wolfhagen; 2) a larger area centered mainly on the Fritzlar and Gudensberg districts; and 3) a section mostly located within the Homberg District.

[3] Vits, p. 128, 189.

[4] Text taken from the *Breidenbacher Ortschronik*, as quoted in displays at the *Freilichtmuseum Hessenpark*, Neu-Anspach, Germany. Original material provided in German courtesy of Shirley Riemer, Sacramento German Genealogical Society. Breidenbach is located in Nassau in the so-called hinterlands of northwestern Hesse.

[5] Text taken from displays at the *Freilichtmuseum Hessenpark*, Neu-Anspach, Germany. Original German-language material provided by Shirley Riemer. The 1904 excerpt is from a quote by M.J. Flach.

[6] Hans Lerch, *Hessische Agrargeschichte des 17. Und 18. Jahrhunderts*, Hans Ott-Verlag, Hersfeld, 1926, p.155; Vits, p. 128.

[7] Wagner pp. 61-65; Vits, p. 128.

[8] Here we mean wage laborers, hired hands, and others who held no rights to the village commons and otherwise were not considered fully-enfranchised "neighbors" by other village residents.

[9] Wagner, pp. 66-71; Vits, pp. 44, 101.

[10] Vits, pp. 53-54, 122-23.

[11] Lerch, pp. 157-58.

[12] Vits, p. 127.

[13] Vits, pp. 57, 124, 131-32.

[14] Lerch, pp. 158-59.

[15] This text was again taken from displays at the *Freilichtmuseum Hessenpark*, kindly provided to the author by Shirley Riemer. The text accompanied an illustration of a last cow being led from its stall as the farm family bid it goodbye.

[16] Peter Janisch, *Die Hessische Landwirtschaft im Wandel der Zeiten*, Freilichtmuseum Hessenpark, Neu-Anspach, 1996, p. 53.

[17] Vits, pp. 134-35, 217. The author cites a major study undertaken by Electoral Hesse in 1857 comparing trends in sixty-two large farmer communities and fifty-seven smaller farming villages.

[18] Wagner pp. 73-80; Lerch, p. 156; Janisch, pp. 57-59, 63; Vits. pp. 125-27.

[19] Wagner, pp. 101-10.

[20] Wagner, pp. 101-10.

[21] Karl Wenckebach, *Zur Geschichte der Stadt, des Stiftes und der Kirche zu Wetter*, Selbstverlag der Evangelischen Kirchengemeinde Wetter, 1966, pp. 212-13.

[22] *1200 Jahre Groß-Bieberau: Beiträge zu seiner Geschichte*, Magistrat der Stadt Groß-Bieberau, 1987, p. 245.
[23] Wagner, pp. 55-58.
[24] Wagner, pp. 55-58.
[25] Guide to the Open Air Museum Hessenpark, Neu-Anspach, 1998, p. 140; *Guide to Region Lahn-Dill-Ohm*, Open Air Museum Hessenpark, Neu-Anspach, 1989, p. 84.
[26] Wagner, pp. 60-61.
[27] Wagner, pp. 81-96.
[28] Wagner, pp. 96-97.
[29] Wagner, pp. 101-10.
[30] Wagner, pp. 111-17.
[31] *1200 Jahre Groß-Bieberau*, pp. 152-53.
[32] *1200 Jahre Groß-Bieberau*, pp. 153, 155-57, 171.
[33] *1200 Jahre Groß-Bieberau*, pp. 158-60, 164.
[34] Bettina Schümmer, *Mit Seiner Hülf von Oben, Religiöses Leben auf dem Lande*, Freilichtmuseum Hessenpark, Neu-Anspach, 1999, pp. 14, 22-23; Guide to the Open Air Museum Hessenpark, pp. 48-51.
[35] Guide to the Open Air Museum Hessenpark, p. 31.
[36] *1200 Jahre Groß-Bieberau*, pp. 179-80.
[37] Schümmer, pp. 24-25; Peter Assion, *Von Hessen in die Neue Welt*, Insel Verlag, Frankfurt am Main, 1987, p. 191.
[38] Assion, pp. 190-91.
[39] *Guide to Region Lahn-Dill-Ohm*, pp. 52-53.
[40] Schümmer, pp. 30-40, 44-45.
[41] Schümmer, pp. 40-42.
[42] Wenckebach, p. 214.
[43] Bernd Blumenthal, *Aus Holz und Lehm Gebaut...eine kurze Einführung in das ländliche Haus in Hessen*, Freilichtmuseum Hessenpark, Neu-Anspach, 1995, pp. 5, 11, 15, 17, 29.
[44] Blumenthal, pp. 25-26; Vits, n. 2, p. 217.
[45] *Guide to Region Lahn-Dill-Ohm*, pp. 19, 21, 42; Vits, p. 51 and footnote 4.
[46] *Guide to Region Lahn-Dill-Ohm*, pp. 54-55.
[47] *Guide to Region Lahn-Dill-Ohm*, pp. 16-17.
[48] Guide to the Open Air Museum Hessenpark, pp. 138, 142; Schümmer, pp. 5-6.
[49] *Guide to Region Lahn-Dill-Ohm*, p. 31.
[50] *Guide to Region Lahn-Dill-Ohm*, p. 57; *1200 Jahre Groß-Bieberau*, pp. 250, 254.
[51] *Guide to Region Lahn-Dill-Ohm*, p. 63.
[52] *1200 Jahre Groß-Bieberau*, pp. 258-60.
[53] *Guide to Region Lahn-Dill-Ohm*, p. 90.
[54] Guide to the Open Air Museum Hessenpark, pp. 81, 130.
[55] *Guide to Region Lahn-Dill-Ohm*, p. 67.
[56] Gerd J. Grein, *Odenwälder Trachten*, part of the Collection of Popular Folklore of Hesse, Museum in the Old Rathaus, Otzberg-Lengfeld, 1980, pp. 6-9, 11-16, 18-19, 28, 29, 32-34.
[57] *1200 Jahre Groß-Bieberau*, pp. 275-78.
[58] *1200 Jahre Groß-Bieberau*, pp. 280-84.
[59] Schümmer, pp. 58-59.
[60] Schümmer, pp. 59, 62-63.
[61] Janisch, p. 55.

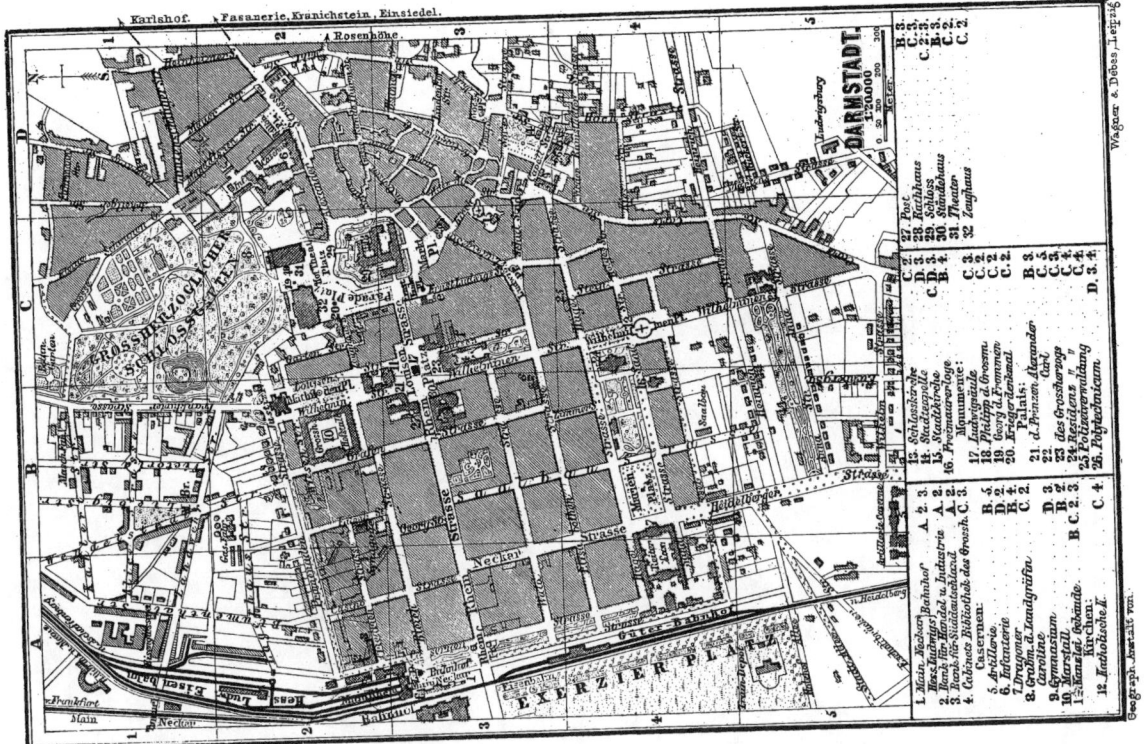

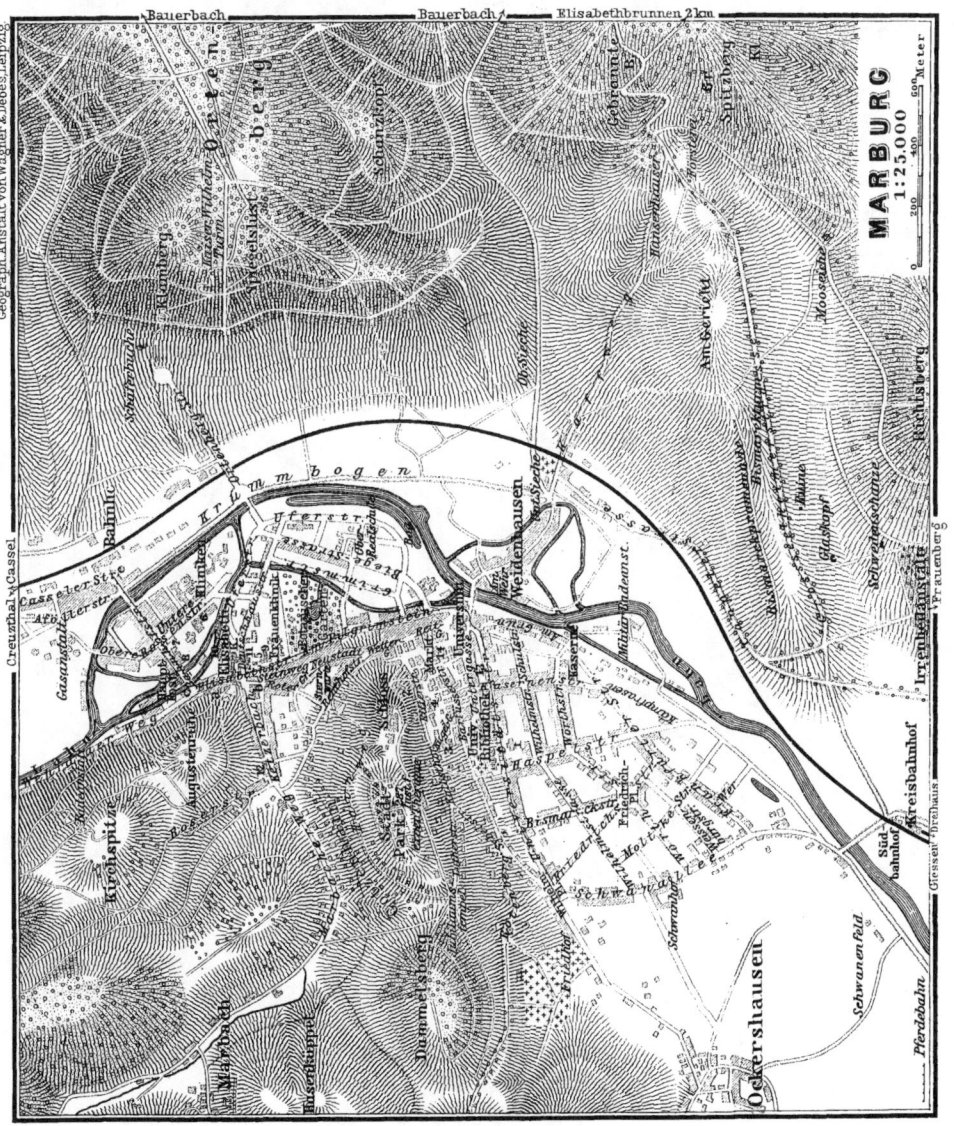

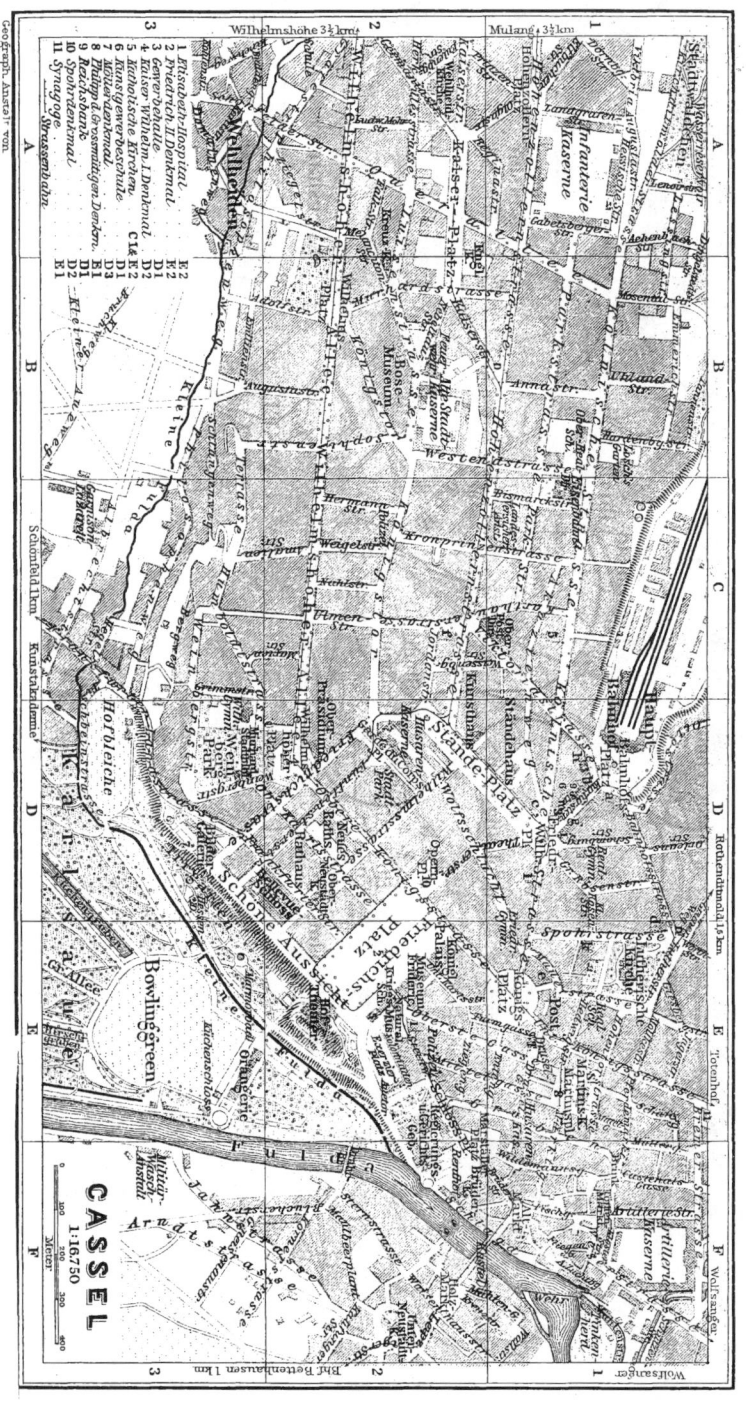
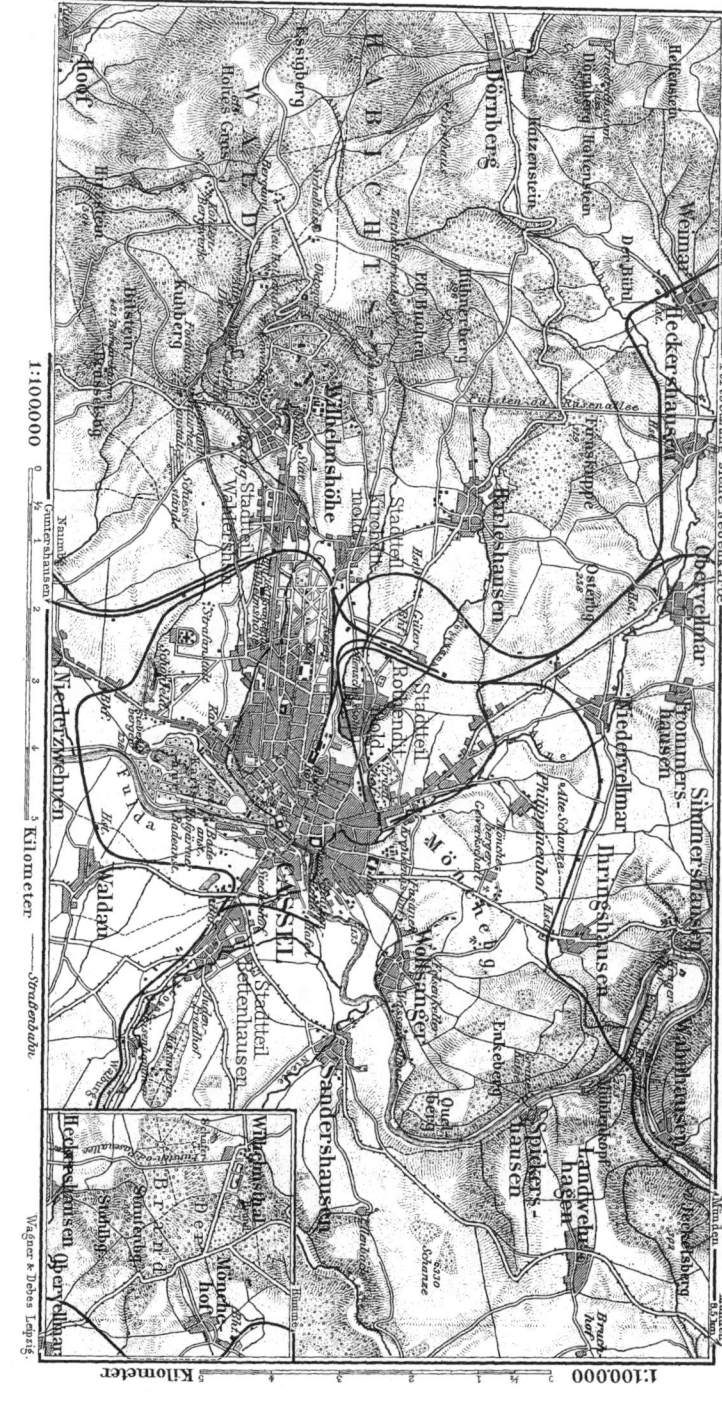

Chapter 16

Industrialization and the Towns: 1800-1900

The nineteenth century was a time of tumultuous political, economic and social change across Germany, throughout Europe, and certainly within the lands of Hesse. The preconditions for later industrial expansion had been coming together since the previous century, in which Huguenot and other Protestant religious refugees with helpful business skills, technical expertise, and entrepreneurial spirit were invited to settle in Kassel and other areas. With the aid of trade privileges and tax relief they established trading companies and "manufactories" (*Manufakturen*) of various kinds; typical of the wares produced by these concerns were textiles, tobacco, china, faience and porcelain. These were among the lineal antecedents of some nineteenth century industrial concerns built along modern lines. The manufactories tended to focus on high-end or mass-produced consumer goods for the wealthy classes or the army. They also served as proving grounds for technical innovations. But their role here was limited because those who sponsored and funded them expected high returns from the investment, sapping the capital available for expansion. It did not help that most were located in small lands surrounded by a sea of competing jurisdictions that imposed taxes and tolls on all foreign goods.[1]

Like all of Germany, Hesse still was overwhelmingly agricultural in the early decades of the nineteenth century. Outside the Rhineland, most production remained in the hands of guild-based handicraftsmen. The guilds guarded their monopoly rights as jealously as they had in the Middle Ages, and kept displaced agricultural laborers and other jobless people from entering new trades. Migration from state to state and town to town also was constrained, as we shall see in the next chapter. Significant social and political change was needed to create the pool of mobile workers that would form the basis of the later industrial expansion, change that was just as necessary and dramatic as the freeing of the farmers from serfdom.[2]

The new century saw a constant series of discussions under way within and among the German states aimed at improving the outlook for trade and industrial development. Relatively little came of this, however, because age-old mercantilist attitudes prevented most statesmen from seeing the benefit of freer trade if it meant allowing foreign goods to freely enter one's one trading sphere. A bewildering array of tariffs were maintained by the dozens of principalities, each with its own unique customs policies and toll collectors. River trade was particularly burdened in this way, and smuggling was widespread to try to skirt the tariff rules. The Prussians advocated a joint customs zone whose members would trade freely while penalizing non-member goods with tolls and duties. But like the other small German states, Hessians feared Prussian political domination if they signed on. Lesser efforts sometimes did go forward, such as a mutual agreement (about 1817) to permit free trade in textiles between the Kassel and Darmstadt lands. Darmstadt and Nassau advocated free trade among German states even as they opposed the Prussian customs zone.[3]

In these trade policy discussions Darmstadt's foreign minister eventually realized that free trade was an impossible standard to sell among his colleagues in the small states. He next pushed for a common customs approach with low tariffs that might help generate some revenue and permit reductions in the high property tax imposed by the grand duke. Nassau was disposed to block all progress on a common approach, while Kassel was even less engaged in trying to reach a settlement. The one common view was fear of Prussian dominance. Prussia's aims in this period were mainly to try to knit together enough of the smaller, contiguous states in a bloc that would ease trade and communication with her geographically-isolated districts in far western Germany.[4]

In 1828 Prussia succeeded at last in engaging one Hessian state, Darmstadt, in its proposed customs union (*Zollverein*). This was a shock to the obstructionists in Nassau and foot-draggers in Kassel, who soon would see real economic benefits beginning to flow to their cousins in Darmstadt. Among these were new roads (built at Prussian expense through Hesse-Darmstadt and Thuringia) to reach the markets of Bavaria and other south German states. By 1831 the economic hardship of foregoing trade combined with the political crisis of 1830 to force Kassel into the *Zollverein*. Prussian-set tax levels now were imposed on wine and tobacco products, while Prusso-Hessian trade in these goods went ahead tax-free. Members also agreed to jointly oppose smuggling. By 1834 most of the other north and south German states had joined as well; Nassau followed suit in 1836. More connecting roads were built with Prussian help, and an official exchange rate was established between the north German *Taler* and the guilder used by the southern states. This promoted trade among the members, as did new common approaches to weights and measures and tariff rates on non-member goods.[5]

The Napoleonic period had left the Hessian states in varying degrees of willingness to brook the historical rights of their local guilds and institute freedom to pursue modern trading and industrial production. In Kassel, the returning landgrave simply swept away the recent French laws and kept his guilds in place until his ouster by Prussia in 1866. Even here, however, by the 1840s exceptions were made for large-scale trading firms and factories. In Darmstadt, the grand duke inherited a number of industrial concerns in the Rhineland whose French-dominated organizational forms prevented him from reimposing guilds; but he maintained the guild regime elsewhere, while allowing factories to compete with them. In little Nassau the French rules were reapplied by 1819, allowing factories easy access to licenses under which they could compete with guilds. Hand work, however, remained everywhere constrained by guild rules.[6]

Common tariffs, freer trade, and reduced guild influence were positive changes toward promoting native industries. A still more important step, however, was to develop the means of transportation to move labor and materials cheaply to the factories, and goods to markets. The advent of steam power was key here, and railroading brought a true revolution in transport. In 1839-40 the Frankfurt-Wiesbaden line was opened, known as the "Taunus Railway." Like most of these early efforts, it was a private, not a state undertaking. Attention next was focused on Rhine/Main connections to the industrial Ruhr area to the north. Nassau wanted the line to connect through her impoverished areas in the Westerwald and Taunus, while Prussia favored a route from Wiesbaden along the right bank of the Rhine to Koblenz and Wetzlar. Progress was hindered for some time until a Wiesbaden-Rüdesheim line opened in 1857, expanded to Oberlahnstein by 1862. At the same time a line running through Deutz to Gießen opened. This opened up the key Nassau iron ore fields to rail access. By the 1850s the network was too complex for states to avoid more direct involvement in the planning and building. Electoral Hesse after long negotiations with her neighbors finally got to work on a Kassel-Bebra-Eisenach line (1845-48), and a line from Kassel to

Frankfurt via Gießen (1852). In 1866-68 a line from Kassel to Frankfurt was built through Fulda and Hanau. Darmstadt for its part was also busy in such undertakings, promoting connections between Frankfurt and Aschaffenburg via Hanau (1848-54); connections to Offenbach were in place by 1848. Over time more and more lines were added, tying in the Westerwald, Odenwald, Vogelsberg, Taunus, etc., and promoting economic development of these historically poorer regions.

This was the era of the joint stock companies (*Aktiengesellschaft* or AG) across Europe, corporate entities that brought large amounts of capital to bear on development projects of all kinds. Railroads, factories, trading firms, and building programs all were invested in by the joint stock firms. Their efforts working with major financial institutions like the Darmstadt Bank created the huge regional industrial complexes. [7]

Among the burgeoning industrial complexes and factories that mushroomed into being in Hesse from 1840-70 were metal works and mines, pottery and tile, textiles, tobacco, steam-powered machines of all kinds, chemicals works and energy-related concerns. Iron foundries required local supplies of ore, coal and water power, all of which was abundant in the Lahn/Dill area, and to a lesser extent in the Odenwald, lower Hesse, and Vogelsberg. Historically the landgraves of Hesse-Darmstadt and their Nassau counts sponsored development of these works. Operators took on these concerns as franchises from the local prince, and often multiple borders would be involved and rights would have to be secured from more than one prince. The Nassau mines produced 37,969 tons in 1828, 81,462 in 1850, and over 463,000 by 1865. The Grand Duchy of Hesse produced 30,900 tons in 1857. Like most mine operations over time, there were many cycles of boom and bust, with competition from cheap English ore a frequent problem. The industry really took off in 1870 as it worked to meet the demands of the war with France. About 7% of the Nassau population lived off its involvement in the mining and foundry industries from 1850-65. Most were local workers who farmed on the side, and thus mine operators had to reckon with periodic labor shortages based on the rhythm of agriculture. Wages were therefore comparatively lower than those found elsewhere.[8]

Pottery and ceramics are other important industries for Hesse in this period. In the previous century Fulda, Höchst and Kassel were among the most renowned names in porcelain and faience; the Napoleonic period and other changes in taste and style forced most out of business by 1850. Stoneware by contrast was thriving, especially in the Westerwald area which made jugs for mineral water sold by the local spas and springs. The related industry of clay pipe making was done in workshops but also on consignment in homes. In 1832 the famous Wächtersbach works was founded near a clay deposit in Schlierbach. Other related industries made building materials in the form of tiles and bricks for roofs and wall construction. In the course of the century more machine-based production cut out some of the hand labor processing.

Much has been said of textile production in previous chapters. With the collapse of local industry much of the mechanized production shifted to the larger factory operations that could compete in international markets. It was constantly necessary to invest in new methods and machines to remain competitive. The Rhine/Main industrial area had many of the surviving complexes.

Tobacco as an industry took off in the first half of the century. Earlier a state monopoly sector, private operators increasingly assumed predominance. Cigars were in vogue at this point, and factories sprang up in Gießen, Darmstadt, Kassel, and Frankfurt, but also in towns throughout many other districts of Hesse. Large numbers of workers were needed, making this an important industry. But wages were always kept low to make the product competitive. After a high point in profitability in 1866-71, economic downturns caused cigars to fall from favor compared to cheaper pipe tobacco. Home-based production further cut costs and women and children became more heavily involved in production later in the century. In some districts women workers were in the majority even by the late 1860s. Health problems dogged the industry workforce.

Steam engines were built and installed in Hesse beginning with a coin stamping machine in Darmstadt in 1831. Merck was one of the first private operators, installing a machine there in 1843. The famous machine works of Henschel developed in Kassel, first as a cannon foundry and clock maker, and by the 1860s a locomotive maker.

Gas works were developed in Hesse in this period, with twelve in existence by 1870. The Hessian capital cities (Wiesbaden, Kassel, Darmstadt) were the first to use the new fuel for street lighting and in public buildings. Within twenty years electricity producers were seeking to supplant gas as the lighting fuel of choice in the major towns. After 1900 inroads were being made in rural areas.

The Rhine/Main area became the industrial heartland of chemical manufacturing in Germany. Dyes, medicines and fertilizer were all key products. Hoechst, Bayer and BASF loomed large as producers, known even today. Merck also made medical products at his works in Darmstadt.[9]

These industries produced more than an array of sought after products: they spawned a new social phenomenon, the industrial workforce. Displaced guild workers and masters, women, manual laborers, small farmers, and children all streamed into the towns to join the work force of the factories, leaving behind long-held customs and patterns in family and work life for an often uncertain future. Housing for these hordes was scarce at best and terribly substandard at worst. Long hours, miserable living and working conditions, and lack of connection to family made for desperate conditions for many thousands. Eventually labor unions and political parties would draw on these masses to militate for social and political change.

Housing shortages were addressed in many towns by employers, who built entire blocks of workers' housing. Towns were at first unwilling to take responsibility for housing conditions, viewing the problem as one affecting only migrant workers rather than current citizens of the towns. As industrialization continued and the numbers increased, however, this began to change. Partnerships were formed with private entities to develop better housing.

Housing was just one potential flash-point for sour employee/employer relations. Work was largely unregulated in the sense that the employer was free to set most conditions of labor—including wages—and insist they be followed on pain of dismissal. The state took no role in monitoring employment matters. Workers were expected to be productive and remain aloof from political agitation or other action that would disrupt the order of the enterprise. Job security was unheard of, and no one had written contracts of labor. Only in the 1870s was any sort of reciprocal agreement required to be signed. Until mid-century work schedules were typically eleven to fifteen hours a day. Thereafter the advent of machines allowed shorter hours to be worked, averaging about twelve hours in the 1860s to about ten hours by 1900. The work day included breaks totaling from ninety minutes to two hours.

Wages were set at the whim of the employer, and they tended to fall in real terms through the first half of the century. The crop failures of the 1830s and 1840s were especially hard on these urban wage earners. Study of a typical worker's situation in Schmalkalden around 1850 has revealed that the family diet consisted mostly of bread and "gravy," made of cooked-down beets or chicory mixed with some milk. This was eaten at six in the morning and one in the afternoon. At nine in the morning and four in the afternoon brandy would be taken in place of the gravy. In the evening a simple soup or cooked vegetables would be eaten. Meat was rarely to be had. For those commuting from the suburbs or nearby rural farms some home-grown vegetables might supplement these rations. More potatoes or milk typically would be available in this way. Wages rose slowly from about the 1860s, but even then a worker's wife and children often would have to work in some way to help make ends meet. In 1850 up to 70% of a worker's salary would go for food, another 10% for rent. By the late 1880s a study found food costs were still upwards of 60% of wages, while rent (16%), clothing (11%) and heating and lighting (5%) took up most of the rest. Alcoholism in these dire conditions was rampant.[10]

Women who worked in comparable jobs apparently earned about a third as much as their men in the course of the century, and their hours were just as long. Small wonder they were a welcome addition to the employer's work force. Laws in 1891 and 1906 set their maximum daily hours at eleven and ten, respectively. Keeping up such a schedule on top of work in the home made many women fall ill. Children too worked in various roles in the factories. Prussian regulations of 1839 only became applicable in Hesse-Kassel in 1866, and they provide some insight into the problem of child labor. The regulations banned children under nine from regularly working in factories, metal works or mines. A three-year-long school program had to be provided at a minimum. For children under sixteen a ten-hour workday was the limit. In Hesse children commonly worked in tobacco, textiles, and leather-making concerns, mines, iron works and tile factories. In 1869 a law was passed to limit the regular employment of children under twelve in factories; those aged twelve to fourteen were to be worked no more than six hours daily and should attend school at least three hours per day. Only after the turn of the century were the regulations more regularly enforced.

The first effort at a workers' safety law was only enacted in 1869 when employers were directed to provide all necessary tools to promote workers' safety in the workplace. Inspectors were established to look into working conditions for children and adults. In the Kassel and Wiesbaden districts inspectors were in place by 1875; Darmstadt lands had them by 1879. Workers who were fired had no state assistance to fall back on, only limited help from the church and private relief societies.

Poor working conditions naturally drove workers to organize to militate for their rights. Workers' societies grew up in the wake of the 1848 revolution in Wiesbaden, Höchst, Mainz, Marburg, Kassel and Fulda. Political reaction against them also was quick to emerge; the elector in Kassel banned workers' organizations in 1850, as did the duke of Nassau in 1851. Within ten years a stronger politicization of the workers sprang up: in the industrialized areas of the Main and Rhine the Turner Clubs often formed the basis for labor organizations with political aims. Dissent spread to all the larger towns. By the 1890s the Social Democratic Party was the major national political group representing industrial workers' concerns.[11]

DEVELOPMENTS IN KASSEL

Previous chapters have discussed the political conflicts between the electors and their citizens in the post-Napoleonic period. In December 1831 street demonstrations occurred in Kassel in which people were vocally supportive of the old electress in preference to her son, the crown prince. On the December 7 troops of the elector's guard were called in to drive off the demonstrators, and liberal use was made of clubs and swords. Unrest continued, but the prince finally succeeded in reimposing order.

In 1848 there again was agitation for political change, at first peaceful and somewhat muted, but increasingly vociferous and unruly as crowds gathered on the street. Some talked of overthrowing the government in favor of a republic, but the crowds were peaceful and unarmed. Catcalls against supporters of the regime were about the extent of the agitation. But the elector's guard corps again turned out and attacked the demonstrators with sword blows. Blood flowed, and with it, word was passed on the streets for the citizenry to turn out. In the ensuing riots the town arsenal was plundered of weaponry and the guards' barracks set afire. Only the withdrawal of the guard from town quelled the violence. The elector was now afraid, and called for help to his allies. Kassel received a most unwanted Christmas present: 5,000 Bavarians marched in to occupy their towns and often their very homes.

Industrialization began to make itself seen and felt in the town. At the beginning of the century Karl Henschel obtained the sole state concession to produce cannon, clocks, pumps, fire engines and other cast metal works. The Henschel works in Kassel were small at first, but after they were destroyed in a fire in 1836 a much larger operation was built. The 1840s saw larger and larger machinery being built in the works, and by mid-century Henschel was the biggest locomotive maker in Europe. Kassel was becoming an important crossroads of the new railroad lines that were spreading across Germany. One of the biggest train stations in Europe was built here.

The 1830s saw much clearance of older structures to make way for beautification efforts of various kinds. The old town hall (*Rathaus*) dating from 1404 was among the buildings pulled down (1837). As recently as the 1820s the town square by the hall had been the place to which all transshipped goods were brought for weighing and assessment of tolls. Untold numbers of merchants and others paused here on their travels to the north German ports. Students from Göttingen and other tourists came through here on their way to visit the beautiful Wilhelmshöhe grounds. The patricians in town all lived on or near the square, and market days or holidays saw legions of puppet shows, choirs, and other community traditions taking place. The market square lost much of its importance as a trading place for south German goods after Bavaria joined the *Zollverein* and developed alternate trade routes north. Even local trade stopped relying as much on the old square as new roads were brought into town by piercing the old town walls.

Social interaction in this period operated through small and self-selected groups of the elite who kept their socializing to themselves based on rank and profession. Courtiers, civil servants and leading citizens had their own circles. Public life for the wider citizenry included coffee houses and wine bars, and increasingly from the 1820s the brewers operated popular taverns. Beer was displacing wine as the drink of choice, and outside beer gardens were popular from the 1830s on; beautiful views of the surrounding countryside and music on summer evenings made the *Felsenkeller* the most popular local drinking spot frequented by those visiting Wilhelmshöhe.

A Prussian visitor in 1839 remarked on the beautiful streets, buildings and squares of Kassel, but lamented that it was like a big stone coffin because the streets were so quiet and devoid of people. Those who were to be seen did not look happy. Similar findings come from a report of 1858 by another visitor. Kasselers appeared to be, "solid people, clever enough among themselves; they like their food well enough and their drink better, they don't act rashly, and like to talk about the "good old times" when things were better. They concern themselves more about the weather than politics, and would rather talk about theater than world history...'Live and let live' was a favorite saying. In 1845 a chronicler criticized the Altstadt as a horrid quarter based on its, "tiny, crooked, antiquated houses." By this time many of the older, smaller shops were losing business to nicer, more modern retail establishments in the new town quarters being built west of town. Most had to move there to remain in business.

The rather peaceful existence in Kassel was interrupted by more than revolution, however, as cholera epidemics sometimes broke out and famine struck after the harvest failures of the late 1840s. The poor were driven to pawn even their beds for cash; public calls for donations were made in wealthier quarters to redeem them. In 1866 the victorious Prussian forces occupied Kassel (June 19), arresting the elector within a week. Kassel became a Prussian provincial capital, and its economy enjoyed the upswing experienced across Germany in the founding years of the German empire. Now her central location astride rail-based trade routes promoted much growth.[12]

DEVELOPMENTS IN MARBURG

The Napoleonic period in Marburg saw few buildings erected, but much road building did occur, which later benefited trade in the town. Public works to improve the water situation were not as successful; huge numbers of people depended on open wells as they would do in a small village. Only when an old woman fell in and almost died did the council take any action. They voted to provide two alder wood trunks for well pipes and planks to cover up the open wells. Pumps had to be bought by pooling private funds, and decades later when these needed to be replaced the council turned down the request because the wells were for private use. Water-starved areas sometimes had to pool resources to have new wells dug. This was nothing new in German towns, as the needs for public works always greatly outstripped the availability of public funding.[13]

Trade was set back in the French period as large amounts of taxes and duties were levied and some trades, such as salt, were simply nationalized and run by the state. Innkeepers, barbers, and wagon masters fared better than most. High taxes made smuggling another growth industry, albeit one that operated in the shadows. By the time the French were chased out, the town was staring bankruptcy in the face.

In 1810 the town brewery burned to the ground, and fire also broke out in the shop of the baker Schott on the town square in 1812. Eleven were killed, and the serving girls provided much help hauling heavy leather buckets of water to put out the flames. A collection was taken up for them and ninety-nine guilders thus raised was used to buy them gloves, scarves, earrings, underwear and socks as a tribute.

Population changed little in this period, standing at about 6,500. Many Jews from Hesse-Darmstadt came to the town to settle thanks to the freer policies on resettlement under Napoleon. In 1810 they were required to register their names at the local synagogue. After the French occupation many were tossed out of town again. A small Catholic community also grew up and King Jerome gave them rights to worship in the gallery of St. Elizabeth's Church (see *Figure* 3-2) in 1811. By 1845 the Catholics comprised just forty-five people out of a population of 6,850, but by 1852 their numbers had grown to 300. This suggests the effects of relocation from Catholic villages. In 1814 there were 708 residences in town. When the French were finally driven off people paraded through town with an old stone lion symbolizing the electorate that had been hidden for years from occupation forces. Supposed French collaborators were hauled into the street and forced to kiss the lion under the tail.

After the French left some disorder on the roads and highways had to be dealt with by police action to disperse bands of robbers and gypsies that threatened order. Little serious crime seems to have occurred. From 1835-63 only one murder is recorded. The perpetrator was caught and executed. Public drunkenness and disorder was a bigger problem, and numerous lesser crimes were penalized with fines or jail time.

The revolutionary period of 1830-31 saw some street demonstrations and uproar, with attendant arrests. In December 1833 a group of 200 attacked a reinforced police patrol that had for several nights been assigned to monitor taverns to ensure they shut down at the appointed closing hour of 10:00. Challenged on the town square, the mob rained stones and other projectiles on the guard and then attacked the police station. The police captain was knocked unconscious and dragged into the square. The electoral government thereafter posted a larger police presence in the town to quell unrest. Numerous arrests were made and some were given sentences of up to eight years.

The reaction to the 1848 revolution by contrast was more along the lines of public unrest expressed in catcalls and some broken windows. People demonstrated from 1848 to early 1849, calling on the government to declare Marburg the state university for Nassau as well as Kassel, to bring other educational institutions to town, improve school buildings, and create new professorships. Others called for expanded civil rights, free press and religion, ending censorship, etc. This was the most revolutionary period in Marburg history, with even the working classes becoming radicalized. The police kept records of numerous political groups, including the democratic socialists, the Turners, and others with regional or national roots. The government finally acted to ban all these groups, and even singing societies, in an effort to halt the unrest. The police sought to keep tabs on travelers at inns and by rail. Bavarian forces arrived in Marburg as in other Hessian towns during the final crackdown in December 1854. Some 1,400 infantry and four squadrons of cavalry had to be housed. A state of war was imposed over the next few years, and revolutionary activity subsided.

By mid-century Marburg's economy was suffering as each of its historical sources of revenue was lagging: the university was small and mostly of local significance; the income from transshipped goods was off due to the new railroads; and no sizable garrison of military forces was assigned to the town. Population in 1866 was 7,718; there were 781 houses. Until that year the town gates were still locked up nightly just as in the Middle Ages. Many at this time were building cottages outside town to which they could go on weekends and holidays to escape the noise and bustle. Marburg still had a Middle Ages look about it. In the 1850s it was remembered by one who said that it still looked like it had been paved by shoe shiners. He indicated that the place had made a generally unhappy impression on him, and at that time he had taken a single room and bath for sixteen *Taler* a semester. His landlord was a decent man who had even taken good care of his border once when he had fallen ill. The landlord's life was all about four ideals, once expressed derisively by a Berliner: the typical Marburg landlord was said to desire only a little house, a little garden, a little pig, and a student.

Another former Marburg student compared it to its more famous counterpart in Göttingen (he also had studied there). "Göttingen is cold, fine and proud. Marburg is warm, crude, and trusting. In Göttingen, louts, heather, professors' daughters and sausages thrive, while in Marburg it's youths, May flowers, dear young girls and earthenware goods. A ball in Göttingen is a glove that the ladies cast off at the circus with the greatest of courtly torpor, and the men fetch and return it to them with awe. In Marburg, a ball is a smiling rose that the students present to the local girls. Göttingen has a university; Marburg is a university, for everyone, from the chancellor of the school to the boot blacks all belong to it. Through Marburg's narrow alleys there flows the spirit of Philip the Magnanimous, and the old houses make reverential secular faces, but through Göttingen only English sea air and the winds of Hannoverian nobility blow." The school was always just a state university for Electoral Hesse; when Prussian control was ushered in after 1866 the 257 students included only twenty-two non-Hessians. The fifty-one professors too were mostly of Hessian stock.

In this period the town patricians and about fifty professors almost all lived in the old section of town (*Altstadt*), creating a real shortage of decent housing. Often the professors had to teach classes at home because of the shortage of classrooms. Also at this time some fifty rundown little houses were for sale, their owners needing the cash and some desiring to leave for America. But no buyers were to be found. Students also complained often about the lack of available rooms. The university was still and always Marburg's biggest single industry and economic asset.

At mid-century road work was going on to widen streets; by 1819 the requirement that neighboring areas provide free labor to work on roads around the town had been ended. The town itself assumed the responsibility and cost. Numerous major connecting roads were improved down to 1840 with help from the state, but these served Marburg less than a generation before the railroad curtailed their usefulness. A huge volume of mail required dedicated fast coaches to ply the roads twice daily to Kassel and Frankfurt and back. The first street lighting appeared about 1863. This consisted of iron chains on which oil lamps were hung. Later, gas was used. The necessary funds for improvements had to come from the town's income, which in 1814 was 2,800 marks, derived in substantial part from fees on city properties. By 1866 the income had risen to 15,300 marks, mostly through inflation in property values. Town debt rose substantially in these times as well. Direct taxes on real property fell from 1815-66, while indirect taxes such as income from the town-owned brewery rose. Large sums were obtained from brandy sales. Annual expenses grew from 20,000 to 74,000 marks, increased mainly by wage costs (up 236%) and school administration (over fourteen times the 1815 expense level).

The first train chugged into Marburg along the line to Kassel in 1850, a true harbinger of the industrial age. Early factories in Marburg included a cloth factory with nine spinning machines operational before 1837; this survived until 1863. Other operations included a tobacco plant and a piano manufacturing facility. A pottery works employed ninety people by 1843, selling Marburg ware around the world. The butchers complained in 1813 that two-thirds of their guild members were living in poverty. Even wealthy people only ate meat three times a week. In 1833 Marburg had sixty-seven tailors, seventy-three bakers, over 100 tavern keepers and 154 shoemakers. The bakers were politically influential in setting prices, so bread was always more expensive in Marburg than elsewhere. In the late 1840s the town was greatly over-endowed with tavern owners, with 125 sellers of various kinds of alcoholic beverages. The town was still village-like in its ties to farming and animal keeping; in 1839 Marburgers kept 168 horses, 368 cattle, seventy goats, 500 pigs and 600 sheep.

Food costs also rose to frightening levels following the 1846-47 crop failures, and famine stalked the land. The government had to set up a feeding station in a bakery building, and sold cheap bread to 750 needy families. Poverty promoted disease outbreaks as well. Cholera broke out in 1831 and 1832, as well as a few cases in 1850, while typhus raged in 1829, 1836 and 1861. In normal times the university students could find fairly plain and inexpensive food in this period. Three silver *Groschen* were sufficient to buy a decent lunch, while a hot evening meal at the museum was twenty-five *Pfennige*. This was apparently more than most students could afford on a regular basis. At the best inn in town one could obtain lunch for six *Taler* a month, although diners were expected to buy wine in addition with each meal.

As the century wore on, the colorful and rather outmoded costumes known as *Trachten* (see previous chapter) no longer were fashionable in town. In the 1830s some of the poorer women such as shepherds' wives would still wear traditional blue aprons as were common in villages. The old *Lederhosen* made of sheep or deer skin also were once popular in town, but by now had disappeared. Only occasionally could they still be seen among manual laborers.

By 1852 there were 5,300 Lutherans, 2,360 Calvinists and thirteen unionists (who practiced a blending of both faiths; another thirty-one adherents of various sects were counted. The oft-discussed unification of the two major faiths of Hesse never was implemented; in fact, cleavage between the two faiths only grew in intensity. The old St. Elizabeth's Church, now used by the Lutherans, suffered major flood damage in 1847 and had to be closed until repairs could be completed. It only reopened for services in 1861.

In October 1866 the Prussians raised a black and white flag to the tolling of the clock chime in the Marburg town hall, indicating the advent of their control. It also symbolized the beginning of a period of previously unknown prosperity for Marburg, in which it was transformed into a modern university town. State support brought huge investment in new buildings from 1874-79. The university budget by 1890 was an undreamed-of 570,000 marks; within twenty years it would top 1,000,000. The age-old problem of water supplies also was solved in the latter part of the century. In 1883 a new water source was purchased and piped to the town reservoir. In 1891 even this was overtaken by the demand and new supplies had to be identified.

Other measures of wealth are apparent in this era as well. Meat consumption increased eightfold from 1866 to 1890, even though the population only doubled. The local carpet distributor and exporter converted his business into a true factory employing 200 workers. Another 110 people worked in a metal fabrication factory that had been converted from a tin foundry. The sleepy little state school town of Electoral Hesse had come into its own at last.[14]

DEVELOPMENTS IN DARMSTADT

Early in the century Darmstadt was engaged in a substantial building program concentrated in the Neckar and Elizabeth streets, and a contemporary description talks of the busy activity in a town that was modern through and through, built in haste and very superficial. Elegant homes were developed in the Wilhelmsplatz at this time. Public buildings also increased in number as barracks for soldiers began to reduce the need for quartering in private homes, and state office buildings alleviated some of the problem of civil servants having to work out of their houses. Numerous barracks went up from 1825-30. By this time a more professional job of street lighting was being done, to the tune of 4,138 guilders in annual costs.

In the 1820s the Ludwigsplatz (square) was developed as a new center for trade. Older shopkeepers in the *Altstadt* had to work hard to stay competitive. The weekly and annual markets and fairs began to be less significant to the economy, and by 1827 the five annual day-long fairs were replaced with two fourteen-day market fairs held in May and October. The handicraft trades in town suffered from external competition as manufacturers in Mainz, Frankfurt and other areas sold their products in the town. Local tailors lost much business to itinerant seamstresses who seemed to set up shop on every corner. In 1822 thirty-five of the 156 shoemakers were too poor to pay taxes, as were thirty of 142 tailors.

There were still forty-four different guilds existing in 1823, at which point some sixty different trades could be identified among the local workforce. Some guilds had only a handful of remaining masters. Old, handwork-based trades were being converted to early factory operations in this period as guild protections were relaxed. In 1829 there were two tobacco and wax candle factories, plus one factory each for the following products: carpets, silver goods, shoes, colored paper, coaches, umbrellas, chairs, flower makers, thread, playing cards, and starch. Numerous windmills and other milling works also are cited.

The already heavily-taxed residents were required to accept another financial duty known as the *Oktroi*, a city consumption tax. A regulation of 1832 and subsequent versions required payments on purchases of wood, grain and produce, wine and brandy, domestic and game animals, and bread. Animals were to be herded into town only via the Bessungen Gate in order to reduce the mess on the streets.

In 1835 the first railroad company was formed in the grand duchy, but building did not begin in earnest for a few years. From 1843-46 the line was completed linking Darmstadt with Frankfurt and Heidelberg. A local Frankfurt-to-Offenbach line opened in 1848, and by 1852 was expanded into upper Hesse, Kassel and on to other middle German states. In September 1837 an industrial exposition was held in town under patronage of the grand duke. An array of products was displayed, from textile, leather and fur goods to carpets, and even expensive new dyes and chemicals produced by the Merck works. There were the works of silversmiths and jewelers, colored paper makers, playing card makers, printers, and heavy machinery such as hydraulic presses, steam engines, pumps, mill works, and a grating machine for beets. Over the next ten years more and more steam-powered industries built factories in the town.

Population likewise grew in this era. The 23,587 Darmstadters in 1837 grew to over 26,000 in ten years. By now there were over seventy factories and 904 handwork-based operations. From 1828 to 1846 the number of houses increased from 1,290 to 1,376. As elsewhere in Hesse the years 1846-47 brought misery with successive failed harvests. Despite price controls, a five-pound loaf of bread almost tripled in price to thirty-three *Kreuzer* from 1845-47. A public soup kitchen and warming room had to be opened in an old school building to help the destitute, and some private relief societies opened similar feeding facilities. This was a time of great emigration to America to escape the hardships, with handicraft tradesmen, cabinet makers and shoemakers widely represented in the exodus. Still, the numbers from Darmstadt were dwarfed by those from poorer rural areas.

News of the Paris revolution of 1848 broke in Darmstadt in late February, creating quite a stir. Unrest on the streets followed, as did the mobilization of the grand duke's guard. Agitation ensued among those demanding press freedom, judicial reforms, etc. Unrest continued to grow, and here too the authorities finally initiated a broad crackdown. Parties, placards, flags and incendiary songs all were banned. Rioters were arrested and tried, and many thrown into prison. Many others fled overseas. A reporter of the *Wetterauer Volksblatt* newspaper, clearly no friend of the regime, described Darmstadt as a boring residence town, an artificial, paltry, well-policed creation, lacking in trade routes, traffic and factories, and built through monstrously-high taxation for the exclusive benefit of the grand duke's police state and an army of officials "big enough to rule the world." In 1850 over 32% of populace were bureaucrats.

In 1853 the town coffers collected over 525,000 guilders in income, great sums being collected via the *Oktroi* tax and fees for use of the local woods. The expenses were over 415,000 guilders. Huge amounts went to salary costs for officials and city workers, from tax officials to builders, pig-herders, watchmen, lamp lighters, etc.

Most factory operations in this period were small and mid-sized firms. Furniture, liqueur, hats, engravings and maps, mirrors, and carved ivory products were all made in the town. Much handwork remained in this production. Only in metalworking was production becoming concentrated in fewer and fewer hands. As rail lines were forged to connect the grand duchy to industrialized areas elsewhere in Germany, the basis was laid for the economy to take off. By 1862 Darmstadt's annual amount of rail passenger traffic topped 500,000, along with 85,000 tons of shipped goods. In 1853 the important Darmstadt Bank had its beginnings. A telegraph line was installed the same year. Gas works were created and expanded from 1848-55, their output used only for lighting of homes and workplaces: work hours now could be expanded. More modern factories were founded. As in other towns, old buildings began to be torn down to make way for street widening and straightening in the 1860s. The old town walls also fell as these efforts progressed.

Population began to take off as industrial production rose. By 1861 the populace numbered 28,375. Nearby Bessungen had another 3,882. Military uniforms were legion on the streets as the grand duke loved military display, and open-air concerts by military bands were common occurrences. There was an active presence of Turners in town as well. They enthusiastically celebrated opening of their new Turnhall in 1862.

When the crown prince brought home his new English bride in the same year huge masses gathered along the streets to cheer the couple's arrival, including guildsmen, Turners, school children, and people of all classes. This turned out to be the last hurrah for the guilds, whose leadership increasingly were being forced to knuckle under to factories, foreign production and resulting competitive pressures. In 1866 the last of the guild privileges went by the boards with the issuance of a new act providing free rights to practice trade. Over the next two years the shoemakers, blacksmiths, locksmiths, roofers, brewers, carpenters, wagon makers, and cabinet makers all closed down one after another. The bakers, tailors, and butchers were the last to go (1868).

Darmstadt's support for the Austrians in the Austro-Prussian War of 1866 saw a number of wounded Darmstadt troops brought to town in July. A makeshift hospital was set up to treat them in the Turner's hall. At the end of the month a victorious Prussian force entered the town, and the grand duke deserted the residence for Bavaria. For seven weeks foreign troops had to be quartered in the town until a peace was signed and the troops were withdrawn. The grand duke then came home.

The German Reich's foundation in 1871 brought a certain loss of status as a capital, and all trappings of foreign policy and ministry were abolished. But the economic upswing of the founding years brought more than scant compensation. Rail lines to the impoverished Odenwald opened up new resources of manpower for industry. Population in 1871 was 33,799. It topped 41,000 by the end of the decade. After Bessungen was absorbed as part of the town, the numbers grew to nearly 50,000. The 1870s brought a new and much-needed water works for Darmstadt, plus a new palace of justice, a new main synagogue, and a bigger building for the Darmstadt Bank.

Progress for some firms occurred even as crisis was experienced by others in the Darwinian struggle for productivity and efficiency through modernized production processes. The 1880s saw a further consolidation of the gains made by key industries such as metalworking, while the 1890s brought a renewed period of strong economic growth. Housing took off in this period too, as building activity increased housing stock from 2,417 in 1870 to 3,628 in 1890. Social programs were expanded with the opening of an institution for neglected children (1888), a larger city soup kitchen (1890), and a public library (1879). A new city hospital was built in 1890. More street building and paving programs were undertaken, and more modern approaches to keeping the streets clean were adopted. In 1885 a centralized station for electric power opened, and the main train station now was lit with electric lighting.[15]

CONCLUSION

This overview of life in the towns in the industrial era has merely touched on the life and times of the urban populace in Hesse, but has attempted at least to highlight trends under way in this century of tremendous change and ferment for the Hessian people. Those who were able to struggle on and weather the terrible times of famine and want, to find gainful employment despite the many economic downturns, and to shift to modern industrial trades as the old guilds and other handicrafts fell away, would live to see better times late in the century. For many thousands of their fellow countrymen, however, life at home was simply too much of a struggle to bear. Resources were simply too few, and debts too great. For them, emigration seemed the only viable course. We turn now to their story in our final chapter.

NOTES TO CHAPTER 16

[1] Klaus Eiler, *Hessen im Zeitalter der industriellen Revolution*, Insel Verlag, Kassel, 1984, pp. 15-16.
[2] W.O. Henderson, *The Industrialization of Europe 1780-1914*, Harcourt Brace, 1969, pp. 10-12, 22; Eiler, p. 34.
[3] The textile agreement is referenced in Eiler, p. 25; Arnold H. Price, *The Evolution of the Zollverein*, Octagon Books, New York, 1973, pp. 10-11, 28, 59.
[4] Price, pp. 85-89, 126-27.
[5] Price, pp. 201-03, 237-39; Henderson, pp. 70-71; Eiler, pp. 18-19.
[6] Eiler, pp. 34, 39-40.
[7] Eiler, pp. 71-73; Henderson, pp. 28-31.
[8] Eiler, pp. 96-101.
[9] Eiler, pp. 122-209.
[10] Eiler, pp. 241, 243-45, 260-61.
[11] Eiler, pp. 285-86, 298-99, 344-46.
[12] This section was largely based on K. Heidelbach, *Kassel, ein Jahrtausend hessischer Geschichte*, Bärenreiter, 1957, pp. 240-81.
[13] Henderson, p. 66.
[14] This section was based predominantly on W. Kürschner, *Geschichte der Stadt Marburg*, Elwertsche Verlagsbuchhandlung, Marburg, 1934, pp. 201-285.
[15] F. Battenberg, *Darmstadts Geschichte*, Eduard Roether Verlag, Darmstadt, 1980, pp. 308-87, provided the basis for this section.

Chapter 17

Hessian Emigration 1800-1900

Germany as a whole was a massive reservoir of emigrants in the nineteenth century, with huge numbers heading off to America to seek their fortunes. Conditions on the land grew desperate for thousands when the economy turned down due to factors such as the collapse of trade in textiles or prolonged periods of low agricultural yields. In the 1850s a million Germans emigrated, most coming to America. The vast majority were economic refugees, including farmers and workers in handcrafts from areas like the Grand Duchy and the Electorate. In some cases the local jurisdictions scraped together the funds to ship them overseas as a means of reducing the relief rolls. But many Germans who arrived in the ports of New York, Baltimore or New Orleans had enough money saved to provide them with a good start in the New World. Many were attracted to the newly-opened farm lands in the mid-west, and their glowing letters home were passed around villages and even printed in local papers, encouraging other to take ship for America. For those who were handy with the tools of trades other than farming, American industry too welcomed them with open arms.

The mid-1850s were also the period in which industrialization in Germany began to take off, opening up many more job opportunities for those who remained behind. The years 1853-54 saw the greatest annual numbers of Germans leaving the Fatherland; thereafter the numbers remained high but tended to moderate somewhat as employment in urban industry rose. Every five year period from 1870-95 saw an average of 475,000 Germans heading overseas, mostly from rural areas and most headed to America.

The total length of German railroad lines doubled from 1850-60, making it possible to draw more and more workers from labor surplus areas to the industrial centers where they were needed most. Emigration was relieving Germany of untold numbers of hungry and hopeless people whose lot otherwise would have been to swell the relief rolls, the numbers of petty criminals, and/or the ranks of a sullen and sometimes rebellious under class. After 1875 Germany increasingly had a place for all who would and could work in industries that brought unprecedented prosperity and even spawned a growing middle class; Germans for the first time could begin to see themselves as a nation on par with France or England.[1]

EARLY EMIGRATION TO AMERICA

There had been substantial early German immigration to the American colonies, with the first organized colony of thirty-four Germans landing in 1683 to found Germantown, Pennsylvania. Many so-called Palatines from lands that later would be part of Hesse left their ancestral homes in areas along the Rhine and Main rivers to escape the recurring attacks of French forces in the early eighteenth century; thousands escaped to England in 1709, and over 600 of these were sent on to North Carolina. Thousands of others settled in New York. A total of perhaps 250,000 Germans lived in the colonies by 1770, mostly in New York, Pennsylvania, and other mid-Atlantic states. When captured Hessian forces arrived as prisoners in these communities during the American Revolution they often found a welcome reception among these *Landsmänner*. Deserters and indentured farm hands from the Kassel and Hanau forces formed one of the earliest identifiable influxes of Hessian immigrants.[2]

Another significant wave of emigration to America occurred in 1817, following a disastrous harvest season and famine in 1816. From May to August it rained almost incessantly, so that the harvest was all but consumed in rot, lightning and hailstorms, and unseasonable snowfall. Many of the 20,000 Germans who left for America after this terrible time came from the lands of Kassel, Nassau and Darmstadt. Another wave of emigrants left the Westerwald in Nassau and the Vogelsberg in Darmstadt for Brazil in 1824-26, based on the recruitment efforts of agents employed by Brazilian landed interests.[3]

PREPARATIONS TO LEAVE

Lawful emigration was prohibited or at least complicated greatly by financial or other penalties in many of the German states as the nineteenth century opened, and Hesse was no exception. Mercantilist policy had long dictated that states should husband their labor resources along with bullion and other assets that promoted a strong economy. But after the Napoleonic wars emigration policies began to ease as a result of decisions of the Congress of Vienna. Even then however, permits and emigration taxes were required, and the ability to leave was limited if one had owed debts to local creditors. Able-bodied men who owed military service were also constrained from migrating before their service duty was performed. In times of economic distress various means of extending local or even state assistance were found to promote the transportation of emigrants so as to reduce the relief rolls. We will look at some of the notable and unusual means employed by Hessian communities to help impoverished members emigrate later in this chapter.[4]

The first requirement of lawful emigration was to obtain two key documents: a release from the ties of subservience to the prince (*Entlassung aus dem Untertanenverband*); and a passport (*Reisepaß*). The process began with an application submitted to the local *Bürgermeister*; he in turn would have to forward the request to the local circuit office (*Kreisamt*) with information on the applicant, including why the request to leave was being made and whether the applicant still owed military service. Questions from the authorities might have to be answered by the *Bürgermeister* as they considered the request, including whether any creditors had come forward to lay claims based on the newspaper advertisement the emigrant's intentions. Once the release was granted the applicant lost all his rights and ties as a citizen of the Hessian state. He could not subsequently return and demand any benefits accorded citizens.

Some Hessians, perhaps fearing that their application would be rejected, dreading military service, or not wanting to foreclose options to return if their American dream came to naught, simply left without obtaining permission. This was easiest for mobile journeymen in the handicrafts trades whose papers allowed free movement within Germany, even to port towns. Once in port, the emigrants found plenty of willingness by those engaged in the emigration business to waive the need to show papers from distant states; they were primarily interested in selling lodgings, food, sea passage, etc.[5]

By the 1820s a relatively small number of Germans were setting off for America, with only 6-8,000 Germans arriving during the decade. Many others chose Russian or Austrian lands in which to make new homes. The long and perilous sea Atlantic voyage was not to be undertaken lightly. In 1833 Hesse-Darmstadt saw the creation of the

Gießen Emigration Society, which was among the first group of its kind to try to organize German emigration with the purpose of creating a "New Fatherland" made up of freedom-loving German settlers. It leafleted widely in search of souls willing to pull up stakes for a New World life. Many of their recruits were intellectuals whose qualifications for a hard farming life were proven lacking once they arrived in Missouri and southern Illinois. The so-called "Latin Farmers" of the Gießen group were more successful at creating libraries, newspapers, and schools wherever they landed. The emigrants dispersed widely, and never succeeded in developing the larger political entity advocated by their sponsors.

Yet the influence of the letters and articles generated by German-American immigrants was having an impact on their families and friends, encouraging them to follow the same path. In the 1830s, some 125,000 more Germans came to America. Local German aid societies to help the immigrants also were being organized.

Many Hessians found it easier in this period to ship out of Le Havre, Antwerp or Rotterdam than Bremen or Hamburg. The latter cities were closest to northern Hessian lands, but only grew in importance for other Hessian emigrants after they enacted a variety of measures in the 1830s to protect and assist emigrants. A widely-dispersed network of emigration agents employed by shipping interests was set up to funnel emigrants to the locations of their employers' firms. Rotterdam and Le Havre interests were operating out of offices in Mainz; agents from Bremen established such firms in Frankfurt. In the 1830s lower-level offices were created even closer to the areas where emigrants lived: Hanau, Darmstadt, Gießen, Hersfeld, Rudolstadt, and Nordhausen. Bremen agents were also active in Mainz by 1850.[6]

The travel to the ports is described in a letter sent home to Hesse on December 25, 1847 from a pair of emigrant families headed by musicians who wound up settling in Pittsburgh. From the Odenwald town of Fränkisch-Crumbach they traveled overland to Mainz, where they caught a steamboat for Köln. Here they spent the night, catching a train the next morning for Antwerp, which was reached at seven in the evening. The writer was much impressed with the train route that included some twenty-five tunnels through mountains, one of which took a half hour to pass through. The Antwerp stay required them to pay for two days' lodgings and a large quantity of food, and this left them with very little money between them. On June 3 they boarded a London-bound steamship with a 300-person carrying capacity. Upon arrival the next day in London the emigrants stayed three days, with lodging apparently paid for by the emigration association that arranged their travel. On June 7 they boarded a large, three-masted English sailing vessel for the voyage to New York. The ship carried 256 passengers.

All suffered to a greater or lesser degree from seasickness for the first ten days of the two-month voyage, and the writer also complained of the cold encountered on the open sea. One man of their party became so sick on the voyage that upon arrival in New York August 2 he had to be carried from the ship. The families rented lodgings at a German-owned inn so he could recover a bit; due to lack of funds they could not stay long. The next day the author and his family struck out from the town for Philadelphia, which they reached August 3. On the following day a steamboat trip brought them to Baltimore. Here the man sat with the family's belongings to protect them from the rampant theft at the port as his wife set out with a German driver to find a cousin who lived in town. Soon he was located, and the family was well received in the home of this wealthy man. He was retired by this time, living off savings and the rents from fifteen properties. As the family wanted to continue on to St. Louis, the cousin provided them with $70.00 (about 175 German guilders). About twenty guilders was sent by letter to

New York to allow the sick relation to travel to St. Louis as well. The Baltimore contingent then set off for Pittsburgh as the first leg of their journey.

Pittsburgh was reached by train after a ten-day trip, during which two of the writer's young boys became gravely ill. In Pittsburgh a kindly, Hessian-born doctor was located to minister to them, and he spoke of a local man who came originally from a village near the family home in Fränkisch-Crumbach. This man was located, and offered to shelter the family until the children were well; at this time a daughter also fell ill. It took four weeks for all to recover, during which time their host had found work for the head of the family with a local house painter. He supplemented his wages with music jobs as well. But anxious weeks went by with unanswered letters to the relatives who had stayed behind in New York. The letter writer's brother and wife now were too sick to travel. At last they were able to come to Pittsburgh, and the brother musicians even succeeded in procuring jobs in a local orchestra. One section of the letter is very instructive about the conditions for emigrants in this period, and indicates clearly the kind of reports home that tended to fuel further emigration.

> The land is very good for working people, the work is well paid and food is also relatively cheap. A worker can earn from six to ten dollars a week depending on his profession, although a newly-arrived German cannot hope to earn so much because the German handiwork is so far behind the American. You can't believe the swiftness with which the Americans work, and how well they undertake things. Even the tools of every trade are much better made. Some jobs are simply unknown here, because they are either being handled by machines or are tied up with other trades.[7]

In the 1840s some 385,000 Germans arrived in the US. In 1843 a partially-Hessian venture sought to send another organized colony to build a "New Germany" on American soil. Prince Carl of Solms-Braunfels was chosen commissioner general of the twenty-four man Nobles Club (*Adelsverein*), which advertised for German settlers willing to pay about $120 for passage and forty acres in Texas. From late 1844 to 1847 some 7,000 answered the call, and although the *Adelsverein* venture was poorly managed and went bankrupt, a firm German foothold was established around Texas hill country settlements like New Braunfels and Fredericksburg. A tragic instance of state-supported emigration in Hesse was that of the transport in 1846 of 700 impoverished folk from Groß-Zimmern in the Grand Duchy. The authorities saw this as a means of reducing the relief rolls locally, but on arrival in New York most of these hapless people were unable to find work and had to be given relief at local expense. A hue and cry went up in American cities over this affair. Other towns around the country with significant and growing German populations in this era included Louisville, Baltimore, Cincinnati, St. Louis, Milwaukee, and Chicago. This was the period of the harvest failures of 1845, the potato blight, and the greatest crisis for agriculture of the century.[8]

The late 1840s brought more disastrous harvests in Germany and a bumper crop of immigrants to America. Wisconsin was now a popular farm-belt destination. German Jews began to emigrate in sizable numbers, and from 1840-80 the American Jewish population grew from 15,000 to 250,000 people, mostly through arrivals from Germany. In large numbers they swelled the ranks of merchants and traders, large and small, in the American cities. In 1854 a high-point was reached as over 230,000 Germans emigrated to the US, including 20,000 Hessians from all areas. The numbers tapered off thereafter, and dried up entirely with the outbreak of hostilities in 1861. After the Civil

War hiatus, German immigration again picked up, again featuring a large number of impoverished folk from all parts of Hesse. Day laborers and other under class elements from rural areas predominated in this wave. Large numbers headed to the remaining farm lands in the Great Plains states.[9]

Travel costs for a sailing ship passage between decks in the period 1840-60 were about 70-100 guilders per adult; children cost about three-quarters as much. Steamships operated out of Bremen beginning in 1847. The trip by sailing ship to New York could last five to eight weeks; to Texas or New Orleans typically took eight weeks or more. Although more expensive, steam ships cut the travel time by two-thirds. By 1880 steam travel had become much cheaper, and largely eclipsed the use of sailing ships for emigrant travel.[10]

One of the plains states, Iowa, was the destination of choice of a young man from the Odenwald village of Ober-Ostern when he emigrated in early 1882. After some months in the new land he wrote to his mother offering some interesting insight on the differences between the drinking and dating habits of Americans compared to those he left behind.

> I haven't forgotten about you all out there...How are my old drinking buddies, are they still drinking Schnaps? I still haven't had that much to drink here in America, because beer is the drink of choice here. When you work here on the land, you don't have much chance to drink...there aren't any taverns like in Germany and anybody who isn't twenty-one years old isn't allowed to go into taverns yet.
>
> What's going on with Georg the hired hand, and Bangert's hired hand? Don't they want to come here next spring, because it's much better and prettier here than in Germany and there's also a lot of pretty girls. Let the fat ones go, and come on over here where there are better ones.[11]

In 1885 another letter from the same writer to the folks back home indicated that the drinking situation had gone from bad to worse:

> Here in the Iowa they aren't making any more beer or Schnaps; the temperance movement has won the battle, but it'll be back again...I like to have a good bottle of beer, and I can still get it not far from here. But the tavern keepers sell it out of their houses and it's too expensive.[12]

Even single girls could find their prospects much improved by emigrating, for wages for maids and female farm help of all kinds were notoriously low, and their marriage prospects limited. The converse was true in may parts of the developing western states in America. Margaretha Meckel from Bicken moved to Texas in 1845, and promptly met and married a German emigrant in 1846. They settled down to farm, had three children by 1851, and soon were more prosperous than Margaretha's well-off cousins back home. Her letter from New Braunfels in 1851 tried to encourage other girls working as maids back home to come out west to enjoy better wages and marriage prospects:

> All poor people, boys and girls, will have it better here than in Germany. A maid earns five or six dollars a month, a hired man twelve to fifteen. A children's

companion makes three dollars a month, a man working for the government makes twenty-five dollars a month. A day laborer earns six bits a day, a dollar is eight bits. In German money, a dollar is two guilders and thirty *Kreutzer*...

To reinforce the notion that marriage prospects were excellent for emigrating women, it should be noted that in the same letter Margaretha indicates her sister was twice a widow in Texas, but had already married a third man and lived in San Antonio.[13]

America was not the only overseas destination chosen by Hessian emigrants, however. From 1850-80 a number opted to go to New South Wales in Australia. Many factors led to this small wave of emigration: local labor shortages after the discovery of gold; a new, government-promoted immigration assistance program; agents in Germany and Australia who advertised for German immigrants and helped line up employers when they arrived; cheap and available land; and sponsorship programs whereby landholders in New South Wales could sponsor new immigrants. The government expressly permitted non-English vineyard workers and coopers to enter the country at this time, and also encouraged the sponsorship of shepherds and farm hands. About a third of the German immigrants came from the Hessian states. Marriage was a government requirement as part of the immigration process, so many either came in family groups or married soon after arrival.[14]

THE DUCHY OF NASSAU

Because of its dire conditions Nassau was among the German states with the highest per capita emigration rates in the nineteenth century. Laws were altered to permit legal emigration in 1816. Population growth far outstripped the productive capacity of the small land. Population in 1819 was about 305,000; by 1850 it had reached over 417,000. Yet population pressure was just one of many reasons to leave.

> ...not just overpopulation—nor the impulse to seek an uncertain fortune—was the grounds for emigration, but rather the lack of hope that it would ever get any better; the fear that worse was yet to come, and the total lack of faith in the support of the government. A feeling of doubt seized people, the notion that there was no more freedom to be had for the poor, that the working class, the largest portion of the population, no longer worked for themselves, but for the prince, the army and the state.[15]

The resulting tide of emigration led the duke to assume a leading role in the Nobles Club that sought to establish a German colony in Texas. He was also a leading investor in the group up until its financial collapse. In Nassau, as in the Darmstadt lands, entire villages sometimes would emigrate en masse; in 1852 such migrations occurred from the villages of Niederfischbach (lower Lahn) and Sespenrod (Westerwald). In 1840, Nassau opened a consulate in New York in recognition of the need to provide help to immigrants from its territories. From 1847-63 the New York office opened sub-branches in Galveston, New Orleans, San Francisco, St. Louis, Cincinnati, Milwaukee, New Braunfels, and Boston.[16]

A record exists of the reminiscences of a man who grew up in Niederfischbach and was a teenager, son of the village *Bürgermeister*, when the great migration from the village occurred. The little *Dorf* was dirt-poor, without a sizable, community-owned forest, and only a small amount of acreage in meadows and fields. Harvest failures over many years forced the villagers to take on crushing debt loads to keep body and soul together. It was the Nassau government itself that in 1853 suggested the mass migration to America to help the villagers get out from under their debts. To do this the small community forest and other lands would have to be sold and the money divided among the villagers to cover their debts. Without this approach, only two or three local families would have been able to scrape together the fifty guilders passage money to Milwaukee.

Everything had been mortgaged over time to Jewish money-lenders in Laufenselden, even the farm animals. Each time a cow was fattened up and made healthy for milking or calving, it would be whisked away and replaced by a poor, sick substitute that would have to be painstakingly fattened up again. Thus butter was a luxury no one could afford, so rye bread and potatoes usually had to be eaten dry, with only salt to flavor them. Every family received a share of cordwood from the community woods, but most had to sell some or all of it for money just to get by. Wood was the one object that was often stolen locally, for there was virtually nothing else available to steal. There were no jobs to be had, for the nearest metal works and forge operations were fully staffed with poor folk from villages closer to the works.[17]

Once all the local woods, meadows and other community acreage was sold, scarcely 2,000 guilders remained for travel and resettlement money. Seventeen families with male heads of household lived in the village at this time, plus five widows with children and two men referred to as tramps. Six families of twenty-three people in all, including three widows, decide to stay behind in Germany. Their share of the community funds was deposited for them in nearby Mittelfischbach. The emigrant families heading for America numbered about seventy-five people. They were well provided for on the journey to Bremen under the watchful eyes of a state commissioner. In New York, a Nassau consular official likewise saw to their needs as they rested two days before heading on to Buffalo. Here they were met by a deputation of four or five men who got them settled comfortably in an inn for a few days. Similar receptions greeted them in Detroit and Milwaukee, their final destination. The Nassau government paid five dollars a head for their upkeep on arrival in Milwaukee.

We end the story with words of an emigrant writer who described the great migration in 1880, a generation after it occurred:

> And then it was time to take leave, some going off to the left, others right. Many remained behind, and the money grew ever tighter. People couldn't make brooms [as had been done for sale in the old country] for there was no broom straw to be had. It was work, hard work, and work was to be had, thank God. Milwaukee was booming and one railroad after another was being built. The Fischbachers worked hard for two years at the railroad building, often twelve hours a day or more under the overseers…

> In his benevolence the Duke of Nassau paid 500 guilders out of his own pocket to support the emigrants, and those of the Fischbachers who are still around even now remember his generosity with gratitude. The inhabitants of Niederfischbach would never have escaped from their terrible conditions without his support.[18]

ELECTORAL HESSE

The electorate only eased its emigration laws over time to permit its citizens to leave the state legally; on joining the German Confederation in 1815 free emigration to other German lands was permitted, and this obviously allowed people to reach the German ports. In 1831 the constitution was revised to permit free emigration. Just two years later a consulate was opened in New York.

Both economic and political grounds lent impetus to emigration. The repressive and generally backward-looking policies of the landgrave's government created a sense of hopelessness in large numbers of people, and the often dire economic straits affected thousands. North America was the primary target of emigration. By mid-century many intending to emigrate were forming local self-help associations to support themselves in their impending travel. In New York, Hessian immigrants founded their own paper and held monthly folk festivals that were popular among recent arrivals. In Washington a group of Darmstadters established a self-help club that likewise drew many who had emigrated from Kassel lands. A similar Hessian association was created in San Francisco. The largest group of this kind was one in Detroit, however. It founded the National League of Hessians of North America in 1896, and held national meetings for its 3,000 members in Toledo in 1897 and Cincinnati in 1898. It continued to grow until it demise during the First World War.[19]

Emigration from Hesse-Kassel did not amount to large numbers until the 1840s, but population growth finally forced increasing numbers to leave their homeland. From 1819-50 population grew from 576,000 to nearly 760,000. In 1843 emigration suddenly began to take off. Only in the constitution of 1830 were Hessians guaranteed the freedom to emigrate. The Melsungen district was one of the areas that were particularly prone to emigration. From 1852-64 it saw an average .67% of the population emigrate per year, a higher annual average than the rest of northern Hesse. In the period 1872-85 the average annual number had fallen to .32%, largely as a result of the increasing employment opportunities afforded in industry in Kassel and elsewhere in Germany.

In 1833 the German Society of New York published a monograph entitled "Well-Meaning Advice" to Germans expecting to emigrate to the US. This was widely disseminated in Hesse after being published by the elector's government in Marburg on March 25, 1833. It endeavored to guide emigrants on the costs and other requirements to be planned for on the journey. For the initial travel to the ports, on foo or by wagon, departing Germans were told to plan to have 1/4 *Taler* per adult per mile (presumably a German mile, or four English miles), and 1/6 *Taler* per child. This amount included food costs. In traveling through France as far as the port of Le Havre, fifty francs per adult and thirty-five per child was recommended. Passage from Le Havre without food cost from 80-150 francs per adult, half as much for children under ten. Packet ships were noted as being the most expensive, but also the best option in terms of obtaining good treatment on board. Purchasing food would cost forty francs per person, child as well as adult. Passage from Bremen or Hamburg generally included food, and cost some thirty to forty Spanish *Taler* (dollars).

Emigrants were urged to take along the following cloth goods: Wool clothing to last a year; linen goods and underwear according to each one's means, a full trousseau; women's clothes for just the trip plus a few months' stay in the New World, since styles were much different in the US; a good supply of shoes and boots. It was recommended that above all the old and infirm should be provided with changes of undergarments for the sea voyage and kept clean to promote their health. For bedding and pillows, only enough for use on the journey should be taken. It was noted that it was best not to bring beds, wagons, tools, furniture and similar items because this made travel difficult and transport costs were so high as to make it cheaper to buy them in America.

For food during the trip, the following was recommended: 80 pounds of salted beef; 100 pounds of hard bread or ship's biscuit (*Schiffszwieback*); 2 bushels potatoes; 25 pounds of rice; 25 pounds of flour; 1 bushel peas or beans; 20 pounds of sugar; 1 pound of tea; 3-4 pounds of coffee. For the first few days some fresh meat and vegetables might be obtained, if this was affordable, as well as wine and similar drinks. The rations per person should be the same for children and adults, since the authors felt that children ate more than usual while traveling on board ship and other conveyances. It was even recommended that groups of emigrants pool their resources and buy food in bulk to obtain better prices.[20]

In Körle the first emigrants announced their intended departure for North America in 1836. Johann Heinrich Seitz in that year approached his *Bürgermeister* seeking permission to be released from his status as a subject of the landgrave. The *Bürgermeister* in turn applied May 3 on Seitz's behalf to authorities in the Melsungen District. The *Bürgermeister*'s report noted that Seitz was essentially an upstanding member of the community and was not in debt. Upon determining that Seitz had the money to transport himself, his wife and their two children to America, the Melsungen authorities gave their permission on May 24. Their higher-ups in Kassel then gave permission effective May 26. From 1840-50 another eight single men headed for America, and it appears from the records that most émigrés from the Melsungen district in this period were unemployed wage laborers in various trades, as well as a few disinherited farmers. There is evidence that emigration received a boost whenever other locals had already headed overseas, even from neighboring villages. When they reported home of successful prospects, this gave even greater impetus to the tendency to leave.[21]

The Statistical Commission of 1857 that looked into conditions on the land (see Chapter 15) was of the view that many émigrés across Hesse were in fact disinherited farmers' sons. Among the trades, especially large numbers of millers and inn keepers were emigrating, and the same was true of cobblers among the handcraftsmen trades. Lower class farmers, particularly the *Häuslinge* and *Beisaßen* who had no land of their own, were also not surprisingly heavily represented among those leaving the country for good. Jews, unaccompanied women and young people increasingly opted for the trek overseas. Wages through the middle part of the century remained low and largely flat even as prices of foodstuffs continue to rise.[22]

A recent analysis of emigration from the Schwalm River valley in 1840-66 draws on some of the findings of this commission report. The analysis looked at one small town and a dozen villages surrounding the Schwalm where it flows south from Treysa and Ziegenhain, an area renowned for good land and the highly traditional outlook and customs of its people. The town in question, Ziegenhain, suffered over time from too much splitting of inherited farm properties among numerous heirs, to the point that individual parcels were too small to support the three-field agricultural system. This led to much poverty. The villages along the river by contrast were blessed with much more fertile land and had mostly stuck to the letter of the law of primogeniture, in which the land went to a single heir in each generation. They enjoyed above average wealth by Hessian standards, selling produce to Ziegenhain as well as other areas. A third group of people lived in villages in the hilly region surrounding the Schwalm. They had poor soils and had practiced partible inheritance as in Ziegenhain; here too little or nothing could be produced beyond what was needed for local consumption. Not surprisingly,

Ziegenhain and the hill country villages saw much greater numbers of their population emigrate as compared to the wealthier farm villages along the river.

An initial wave of emigration to America from 1830-60 occurred as smallholder farmers and handcraftsmen unable to make ends meet left Ziegenhain and other mostly poor communities to seek their fortunes abroad. They typically left in whole family groups. A later wave of emigration after 1880 was characterized by more emigration of single persons from similar socioeconomic circumstances. In most cases the single persons were manual laborers aged twenty to twenty-five. The married household heads tended to be aged thirty to fifty years. Most people left in the period March-May in any given year, with most emigration being finished before the harvest season and stopping almost completely in the winter.[23]

Many rural areas experienced significant losses in population through mid-century. In Körle the 1850s saw the population drop by a net of twenty-one people, or 3.5% of the total. Across the Melsungen district the losses were even greater: From 1849-71 the total loss was over 10% of the population, with 3,282 emigrants moving away. Complete emigration numbers for 1843-64 from across Electoral Hesse are as follows:

Year	Number	Year	Number
1843	270	1855	3307
1844	766	1856	3875
1845	987	1857	5663
1846	1857	1858	2498
1847	2626	1859	2241
1848*	1030	1860	3282
1849*	484	1861	1966
1850*	484	1862	1927
1851	1991	1863	2167
1852	6044	1864	2880
1853	6121	Total	61,596
1854	9130		

*Numbers incomplete. Data taken from *Beträge zur Statistik des vormaligen Kurfürstentums Hessen*, as cited by Kurt Wagner.

These numbers tended to be greater in percentage terms than those for Germany as a whole from at least 1852: from 1852-61 the average annual emigration rate in Electoral Hesse per thousand people was 6.3; the comparable number for Germany was 5.5.[24]

THE GRAND DUCHY OF HESSE

As in Kassel and Nassau population pressure was unrelenting in most of the nineteenth century. The Grand Duchy had over 643,000 inhabitants in 1819; by the mid-1840s this had risen to over 834,000. In 1820 the constitution was revised to permit free and legal emigration worldwide. Darmstadt established a consulate in new York in 1837, hiring a merchant from Mainz, Anton Bollermann, to fill the role. Although he served in this capacity for many years, Bollermann was not the best choice for the job. He was essentially opposed to emigration, and did less than he might have done to assist his government's immigrants as they sought his help on arrival in the

New World. He was eventually dismissed when Darmstadt appointed new consuls general in Philadelphia and St. Louis in 1856. This also indicates the growing need for consulates in Western cities such as St. Louis, which had become preferred destinations by mid-century. Other towns with consular officials representing the duchy included Baltimore, New Orleans, Galveston, and San Francisco.[25]

From 1816-21 a minor religious movement with adherents known as the "Inspired" (*Inspirierten*) came into being in the Wetterau region of the duchy. Believers joined with comrades in the Palatinate and in Alsace under the "Rules of Devotion" dating from 1716 to form a new denomination with large numbers of adherents in Arnsburg, Engelthal and around Ronneburg. Government pressure forced them to emigrate to America in 1842. These settlers created the now-famous Amana colonies in Iowa.

Most Hessians who chose to leave in this period were economic, not religious refugees. The Gießen Emigration Society encouraged them in efforts to form a German state in North America that would be represent perfection in terms of freedom and equality in politics, religion and economic matters. Its promotion efforts included the 1834 publication, "Invitation and Explanation regarding Mass Emigration from Germany to the Free States of North America." These and similar efforts by others saw 16,500 Darmstadters leave for America in 1841-47 alone. Individual communities sometimes had to provide funds to support the impoverished émigrés; in some cases entire communities sold out and left en masse (1842 Wernings, 1847 Pferdsbach, 1854 Seehof, 1855 Enzheim, 1856 Bleichenbach). Liebig's outstanding work in chemical fertilizers that brought such huge yields to Hessian producers came too late in the century for the vast group of emigrants. Decades would pass before it brought real relief across the land.[26]

Prior to leaving, emigrants from the Grand Duchy in the period 1832-70 were supposed to have their intentions announced in local newspapers for the benefit of creditors. Below is a typical announcement of this kind published in the *Mainzer Zeitung*.

> The Grand Ducal Hessian Justice of the Peace of the District of Pfeddersheim: According to the testimony made by the county clerk of the *Kreis* Worms dated March 23, Philipp Maglatt from Heppenheim an der Wies asked for permission to emigrate, and in accordance with paragraph 4 of the law of May 8, 1832:
>
> Any possible creditors of said Philipp Maglatt, 57-year-old farmer, living in Heppenheim an der Wies, who wishes to leave the Grand Duchy and settle in North America, with his wife Elizabetha Kleinhanß, 52 years old, and his children Georg 20, Jakob 19, Johann 17, Philipp 15, Conrad 10, and Peter 8, are invited to file any objections to their planned emigration within three weeks after the last announcement, according to the above-mentioned law. This announcement will be published three times within three consecutive weeks in a Mainz newspaper. Pfeddersheim, March 30, 1838.[27]

Although such reporting was required by law, in practice as was noted earlier many emigrants left without going through the process. There was also the matter of a departure tax that had to be paid to the local landlords amounting to 10% of the value of the emigrant's estate.

Pfeddersheim was a substantial town in the Rheinhessen portion of the Grand Duchy. This area was a major contributor to the emigration from the Pfalz in the eighteenth century, as we saw above. During the nineteenth century some 50-60,000 people flowed out of the area; most headed to North America, although Brazil, Australia, Eastern Europe and even Algeria were other destinations cited. Some 2,000 people from the Oppenheim area emigrated to eastern Wisconsin in this period, the first being Franz Neukirch of Guntersblum, a forester who arrived in 1839. His letters home found their way into local papers, and caused a ground swell of interest in following his lead among villagers around Oppenheim. Farmers and vine dressers predominated among the emigrating families. Most were not completely impoverished, but found themselves facing the possibility of having inadequate land to accommodate their children in this area of partible inheritance practices, where equal shares were given to all.[28]

The story of the mass migration from Wernings has been documented in brief in an article derived from the 650-year history of Wernings written in 1986. Wernings, once located near the modern village of Wenings, is located in upper Hesse, near Büdingen. In 1840 the village was unable to raise enough crops to support itself, particularly given the crushing debt load it carried, amounting to over 22,500 guilders. Other debts held by individual inhabitants further retarded their economic progress. Bad weather, such as occurred in 1815-18 and in the 1830s created real misery as it reduced yields. Most of the locals had to work in a trade outside farming to make ends meet. In 1824 two local families moved to Brazil, where they obtained a sizable amount of land unburdened by feudal duties. Their positive reports encouraged others to opt to leave as well. Solid plans were laid by 1840. Emigration fever was sweeping the area.

One evening in 1840 a village meeting was called in the local inn, and the schoolteacher, Wilhelm Reifschneider, made a plea for organized emigration to address the poverty of the area. Those who wanted to leave then signed a paper to that effect, and permits were requested from government authorities for the thirteen families so inclined. Beyond those attending the meeting, families from three other local villages soon indicated they wanted to join in as well: these included about half the village of Wippenbach, and twenty families from the villages of Seemengrund and Pferdsbach. The latter village sponsored another mass exodus in 1847.

The next step was to find a buyer for their lands and houses, and on January 29, 1841 a contract was signed with a Gießen real estate agent named Brühl to effect the sale. The Count of Solms-Laubach proved an interested buyer, and a total of 110,000 guilders was raised by selling the total common and private assets. Each *Morgen* of land brought seventy guilders, and twenty-eight houses brought a total of 16,300 guilders. On May 17, 1841 a newspaper announcement was made in accordance with law to advise creditors to submit their bills prior to the emigration. After deductions for individual debts and other charges, the community collectively realized the sum of 55,681 guilders. Not until August 22, 1842 were all legal arrangements in place, and official permission to leave was granted by authorities in Büdingen. The emigrants were discharged from submission to the Grand Duke. Next their travel money had to be shipped by a bank in Frankfurt to Bremen to secure their passage. An initial payment to the Frankfurt bank of just over 142 guilders secured its services in shipping the rest of their funds to Bremen for the passage. The bank had to pack the money in barrels to be shipped; it weighed over 700 pounds, and cost 236 guilders to ship!

In the case of this mass migration the government ordered the district secretary in Büdingen, Herr Schaaf, to ensure all arrangements were made to ensure a safe and comfortable trip. He traveled to Bremen, and found a cooperative Swedish captain willing to take the emigrants in his ship, the *Mimer*. The contract was signed September 23 for 156 passengers at the rate of fifty guilders per person. Among those departing were 118 adults, thirty children under age twelve, and eight babies under age one. The oldest was a man of eighty-nine years. Provisions were ordered to last ninety days. Thirty bottles of sweet milk were ordered in Bremerhaven, as was a quantity of fresh meat and a large volume of *Schnaps*. The emigrants took ten days to reach Bremen by wagon train from their village. Schaaf had them shipped by boat to the ship waiting at harbor. In two days' time he himself came on board to deliver some of their money.

As so often happened in the age of the sailing ships, the *Mimer* lay nine days at anchor waiting for an east wind in order to head for the open sea. The wind shifted on October 8, and Schaaf again appeared with the rest of the money. He then paid the captain and bid the departing families a tearful farewell. He was home by October 29.

On December 2, 1842 the ship pulled into harbor at New Orleans. Steamboat passage up the Mississippi was purchased, but river ice forced everyone to debark at Chester, Illinois, and secure wagons for the final stretch to St. Louis. They arrived in St. Louis December 26, 1842, almost 100 days after leaving Wernings. Their final destination was the towns of Waterloo and Columbia in Illinois. Correspondence with the old homeland continued for almost sixty years. Over this period most of their homes in Wernings had been torn down to provide more arable land for those who remained behind. Communal lands became pasture for the same purpose.[29]

Less than twenty miles from the Werningsers in Waterloo was another settlement that began to expand quickly at this time based on immigrants from the Grand Duchy: Mud Creek Prairie, known later as Darmstadt. The first German settlers, Martin and Michael Funk, arrived here from the Dietzenbach area of Hesse (southeast of Frankfurt) in 1835. In 1837 Michael went home to Hesse in order to marry, and brought back a group of Hessian immigrant families with him upon his return. They arrived by ship in Baltimore, and trekked the rest of the way to the Illinois wilderness by crossing the rough terrain of the Allegheny Mountains. In 1838 more Dietezenbachers arrived, including farmers, a weaver and a cobbler. Several had first settled in Ohio before traveling on to Illinois. Still more arrived direct from Hesse in 1843-47, mostly farmers, manual laborers, weavers, masons, and cobblers. Other villages represented among the emigrants were Dreieichenhain, Götzenhain, Langen, Offenbach, Schaafheim, Umstadt, and Sachsenhausen.

The homes of these settlers were built of wood, and typically a single room sufficed as kitchen, bedroom, living area, work room, etc. Three yokes of oxen were used to pull a plow in this area, although it was considered fertile and easy land to work. Wheat and corn were the primary crops, although flax also was grown and woven into clothing as was common in the old country. Socks and gloves were made of wool, however. Until 1844 church services were held in individual homes, but in that year a church was built. It was 24x20 feet in size, and had no bell. The first parishioner to be laid to rest in the little fenced cemetery that adjoined it was Georg Heberer, who died in 1845. Within ten years the church's ranks had been swelled by parishioners from nearby communities without their own churches, and 140 adult members were recorded by about 1855. It was in that year that Mud Creek Prairie's founder, Issac Rainey, renamed the place Darmstadt, evidently in homage to its many Hessian settlers. In 1857 the old church was converted to a schoolhouse as a larger stone church was constructed.

The high point of the settler's year was the annual Dietzenbach *Kerb* or fair, featuring numerous customs brought over with the emigrants from Hesse. Held in late

October or early November, the fair featured a "*Kerb* tree" cut down in the nearby woods. The tree was decorated and erected in the village. Dancing was held in the local hotels, and local restaurants offered two sittings, the midnight one being free of charge. People from areas all around flocked to join the celebrations, amounting to 1,000 revelers in total.

Wheat and corn could be ground into flour at the local mill of former Dietzenbacher Georg Eckert, built in 1863. The mill employed seven people, and its 200-barrel daily output was shipped to Marissa by wagon and on by rail line to St. Louis for sale. The mill was expanded and continued operation until 1905. From the 1830s to 1905 some 102 male inhabitants from Dietzenbach had made the trip to Darmstadt, many of course accompanied by wives and children. This must have made a significant dent in the local population. Another American community with the same name, Darmstadt, Indiana, also grew up in this era populated with people from the Grand Duchy.[30]

It was just four years after the mass migration of the Wernings villagers that the 34-year-old tailor Peter Hausmann left his village of Heubach in the Odenwald to seek his fortune in North America. Whether by saving hard or selling his household goods before leaving, he apparently had the money to take his wife and four children along, and even buy some clothing for his family members to use on the trip. This included a new hat for son Peter Jr., just four years old. Young Peter recalled the hat blowing off his head during the sea voyage, and watching it disappear into the waves. Peter, Sr. seems to have abandoned his tailoring profession once he arrived near Douglas Illinois, about ten miles northwest of Darmstadt. By 1860 he owned farmland worth $2000 and personal property valued at $425. He sold his farm to his son in 1874 and lived on the farm through his retirement years, dying in 1896.[31]

The sale of one's property must have supported the journey to America of many an otherwise poor emigrant. The day wage laborer Peter Fornoff, who left for America in April 1831 with 1,000 guilders in his pocket, was a good example. His parents had previously died of typhus, and only one sister among his siblings survived to adulthood. When this elder sister decided to marry she and her husband bought out her brother's rights to the Fornoff property in Affhöllerbach for 1,210 guilders, thus supplying him with quite an adequate nest egg for the trip. He and his wife set up house in McConnellsburg, near Harrisburg, Pennsylvania, and had eleven children.[32]

In the market town of Groß-Bieberau the year 1831 marked the first documented instance of emigration to America. The town history notes that its population numbered 1,517 people, a full 621 more than a quarter century before. "The land could no longer nourish such a crowd, and so began the great emigration," the record states. In the next thirty years some eighty families left to find a better life in the New World. By 1882 a full 100 families had left. In addition, beginning in 1855 another 133 people left singly, of whom seventy were under the age of twenty: fifty-three boys and seventeen girls. Seven were sixteen years old, six were fifteen, and three were just fourteen. In fifty years over 600 of the locals departed, and the numbers only flagged after 1880. Groß-Bieberau was also proud of its role as the town from which the great scientist Justus Liebig was descended.[33]

Another Odenwald village near Otzberg, Nieder-Klingen, illustrates the lengths to which local communities sometimes had to go in order to provide for the emigration of their poorer citizens. As in Groß-Bieberau, emigration to North America from this areas began in the 1830s. The local innkeeper was even an agent of one of the emigration businesses that operated mail boats to England and America. In 1851 a family headed by a poor carpenter, Wilhelm Grunewald II, was interested in moving to America, but without passage money their goal could not be realized. The Grunewalds lived in a section of the village called the Matzenberg, where mostly landless folk lived. Even by selling their few belongings it would not be possible to raise the travel costs, for the extended family included eleven persons and Herr Grunewald was the only adult male among them. Although the community was still burdened with debts from the Napoleonic wars and had no cash to spare, it decided to cut down twenty-six acres of its scarce wood holdings and sell the wood to fund the trip. Now there was money for travel, and even new clothes, down to a mourning scarf apparently required by local tradition in any complete man's wardrobe. The Grunewald clan arrived in New York November 12, 1851, settling first in New Jersey. By 1858 they had made their way to Foster township, Madison County, Illinois. In 1993 Nieder-Klingen erected a memorial to mark the funding of the Grunewald's trip in the re-forested area in which the wood was originally cut. The woods had been called "the American" since 1851.[34]

Such stories of kindliness are not uncommon, such as another one originating in the Odenwald village of Erzbach, now part of Reichelsheim. It was here that Georg Gemler and his wife Elizabeth were born, a couple with little means who nonetheless agreed to take in a young orphan girl from their village and act as foster parents. When Georg left for America in 1853 Elizabeth was too poor to continue to care for the girl, who had to be sent to live with another family. A year later Georg sent money for Elizabeth to join him in America, and asked that eleven-year-old Katharina Jünger be permitted to come too. The village council took up the matter, and recognizing that the couple considered the orphan to be like their own child and that Katharina wanted to be with them too, the village elders voted to provide the funds for her passage. By October 1854 the local court in Fürth had ruled in favor of allowing her to go as well, and Elizabeth and her young charge were able to set off for new lives in America.[35]

Reichelsheim had a relatively large number of Jewish residents, numbering 172 souls by about 1830. This was the highest proportion of any community in the Odenwald. The first Jewish emigrants to America from here left in 1853. Some 25% of total emigration from the town was comprised of Jews.[36]

CONCLUSION

The later nineteenth century saw a second great wave of German emigration beginning in the early 1880s until 1891. Hard economic times, unemployment, political repression of workers' movements, and other social dislocations fed this wave, and Hessians were very strongly represented in it. From 1867-1910 over 114,000 Nassauers emigrated, as did 55,000 Darmstadters. Comparable statistics for Hesse-Kassel are not available, but must have mirrored those in the neighboring states. By World War I emigration had all but ended, however. The conditions that previously had driven people to leave the country were now just a memory.[37]

In 1926 Hans Lerch summarized the effects of dramatic changes that had brought better times to Hesse. Those who had weathered the hard times at home emerged from those changes in most cases more prosperous than ever before [emphasis added]:

> Times have changed. If one wanders through the Hessian villages he is greeted with an entirely different view than that of the past. The friendly, often newly-renovated structures present a picture of a certain prosperity. Crop yields have been raised appreciably thanks to modern cultivation and chemical

fertilizers. Only rarely now does one encounter an isolated sheep fold in parts of the Fulda valley. Spinning wheel and loom are gone too. They stand covered in dust in the attic and are perceived by the younger generation as tools of their ancestors that no one knows how to use anymore. The Hessian farmer once again enjoys a good reputation as a hard worker: alcoholism is no longer such a problem. He is closely tied to the land from which he takes his daily bread by dint of hard labor. *Only grudgingly do the farmers ever leave their land, and only in the most dire of circumstances would they contemplate emigration. In the 1880s many who could obtain neither work nor bread in their homeland left for America. Even today many children of Hesse must seek bread and work in other lands, but after a while they return with their earnings, for they love their homeland and will not desert it.*[38]

The vast majority of those leaving the Hessian states in the nineteenth century undoubtedly had the same depth of feeling for their land. Though driven by disastrous times to leave it, they must have harbored a love for Hesse that kept the memory of the loss of village, hearth, and relations forever alive in them.

NOTES TO CHAPTER 17

[1] Hajo Holborn, *A History of Modern Germany, 1840-1945*, Alfred Knopf, New York, 1969, pp. 122-23, 367-68.
[2] Anne Galicich, *The German Americans*, part of *The Peoples of North America*, Chelsea House, New York, 1989, pp. 19-20, 32-33, 36.
[3] Peter Assion, *Von Hessen in die Neue Welt*, Insel Verlag, Frankfurt am Main, 1987, p. 35.
[4] Günter Moltmann, ed., *Germans to America, 300 Years of Immigration 1683-1983*, Institute for Foreign Cultural Relations, Stuttgart, 1982, p. 38.
[5] Assion, pp. 143-44.
[6] Galicich, pp. 46-48, 57; Moltmann, p. 39; Assion, pp. 145-47, 173-74.
[7] Ella Gieg, *Auswanderungen aus dem Odenwaldkreis*, Lutzelbach, 1992, pp. 68-74.
[8] Galicich, pp. 48-60; Moltmann, p. 38; Willi Paul Adams, *The German-Americans, An Ethnic Experience*, American Edition, Max Kade Center, Indiana University, 1993, p. 6; Assion, p. 35.
[9] Galicich, pp. 62-63, 74; Assion, p. 36.
[10] Assion, pp. 148-49, 200-01.
[11] Gieg, p. 87-89.
[12] Gieg, p. 91.
[13] Assion, pp. 296-99.
[14] Barbara DeBernardo, "German Settlement of the South Coast of New South Wales," newsletter of the German Genealogical Society of America (GGSA), adapted from a paper by Geoffrey Burkhardt, Volume VIII, Numbers 1 & 2, Jan/Feb 1999, pp. 10-11.
[15] Wolf-Heino Struck, *Die Auswanderung aus dem Herzogtum Nassau (1806-1866)*, Wiesbaden, 1966, as quoted in Peter Assion, p. 34.
[16] Karl Demandt, *Geschichte des Landes Hessen*, Bärenreiter-Verlag, Kassel, 1972, p. 541; Peter Assion, *Von Hessen in die Neue Welt*, Insel Verlag, Frankfurt am Main, 1987, pp. 32, 47, 77-78.
[17] Assion, pp. 42-43.
[18] Assion, p. 44.
[19] Demandt, p. 556; Assion, pp. 47, 77.
[20] Assion, pp. 93-94.

[21] Kurt Wagner, *Leben auf dem Lande im Wandel des Industrialisierung: Das Dorf war früher auch keine heile Welt*, Insel Verlag, Frankfurt am main, 1986, pp. 66-68.
[22] Brigitta Vits, *Die Wirtschafts- und Sozialstruktur ländlicher Siedlungen in Nordhessen vom 16. Bis zum 19. Jahrhundert*, Selbstverlag der Marburger Geographischen Gesellschaft, Marburg, 1993, pp. 135, 221.
[23] Robert von Friedeburg, "Social Structure and Migration: The Case of the Schwalm Valley, Hesse, Central Germany, 1840-1866," *German Connection*, German Research Association Newsletter, Volume 14, Number 1, January 1991, pp. 3-7.
[24] von Friedeburg, p. 5.
[25] Assion, pp. 77-78.
[26] Demandt, pp. 572-73; Assion, pp. 47, 150.
[27] From "Hessen-Darmstadt and the Pfalz," German Connection Newsletter, German Research Association, San Diego, Volume 14, Number 1, January 1991.
[28] Helmut Schmahl, "Emigration from Rheinhessen in the 19th Century," German Connection Newsletter, German Research Association, San Diego, Volume 20, Number 4, 1997; Gieg, p. 81.
[29] Robert Schaefer, article written for the newsletter of the St. Clair County (IL) Genealogical Society, 1991, Number 4, pp. 195-96.
[30] Marilyn Lane, "Emigrants from Dietzenbach, Hesse-Darmstadt, Germany," in St. Clair County Genealogical Society (IL) Quarterly, Volume 20, No. 4, 1997, pp. 133-37.
[31] Jane Shelley, article written for the *Stalker*, newsletter of the Madison County (IL) Genealogical Society, Vol. 6, Number 1, pp. 35-35.
[32] Gieg, pp. 59-62.
[33] *1200 Jahre Groß-Bieberau: Beiträge zu seiner Geschichte*, Magistrat der Stadt Groß-Bieberau, 1987, p. 91.
[34] Betty Greenwood, article written for the *Stalker*, newsletter of the Madison County (IL) Genealogical Society, Vol. 13, Number 4, 1993, pp. 157-58.
[35] Gieg, pp. 66-67.
[36] Gieg, p. 97.
[37] Assion, pp. 357-58.
[38] Hans Lerch, *Hessische Agrargeschichte des 17. Und 18. Jahrhunderts*, Hans Ott-Verlag, Hersfeld, 1926, p. 160. Emphasis added.

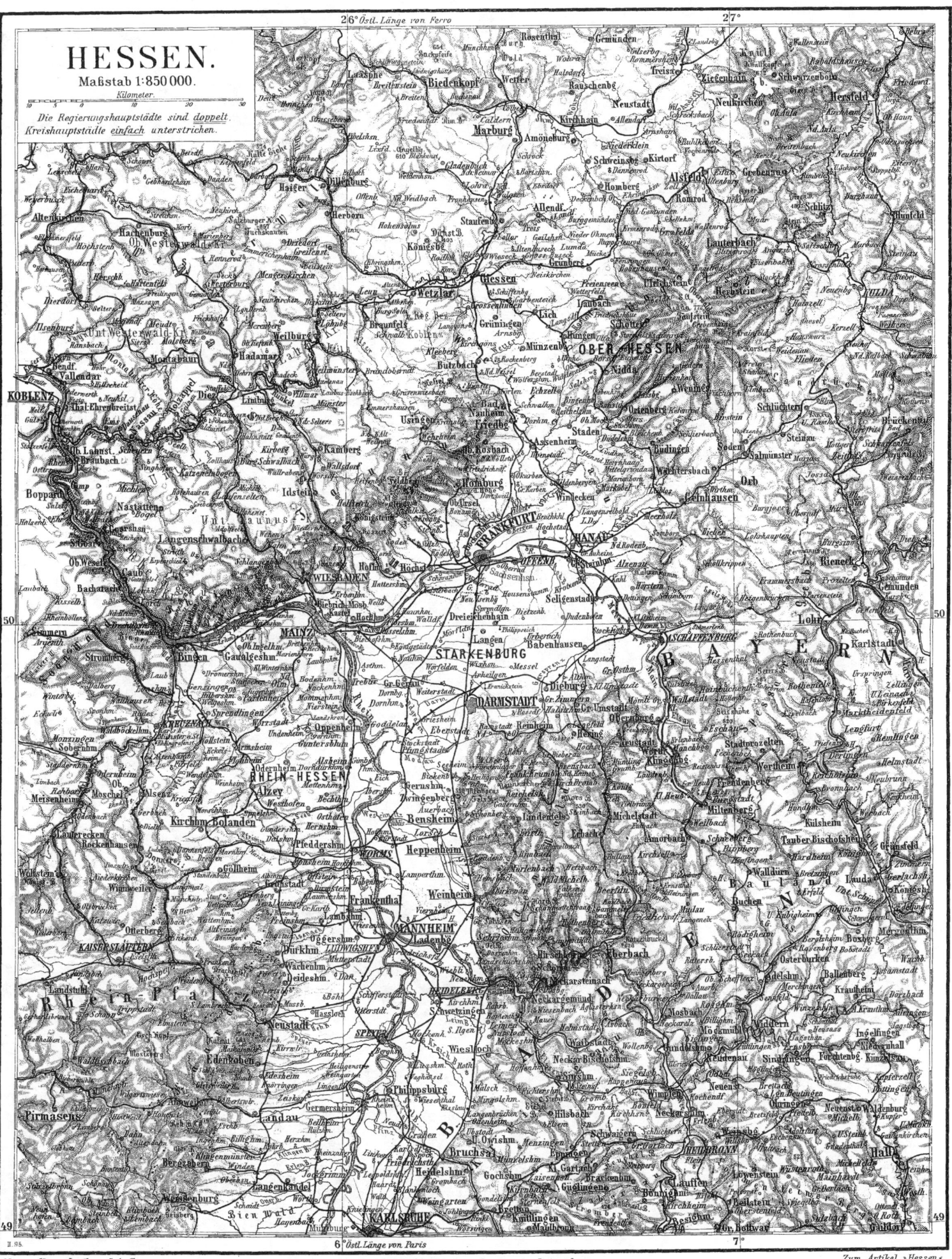

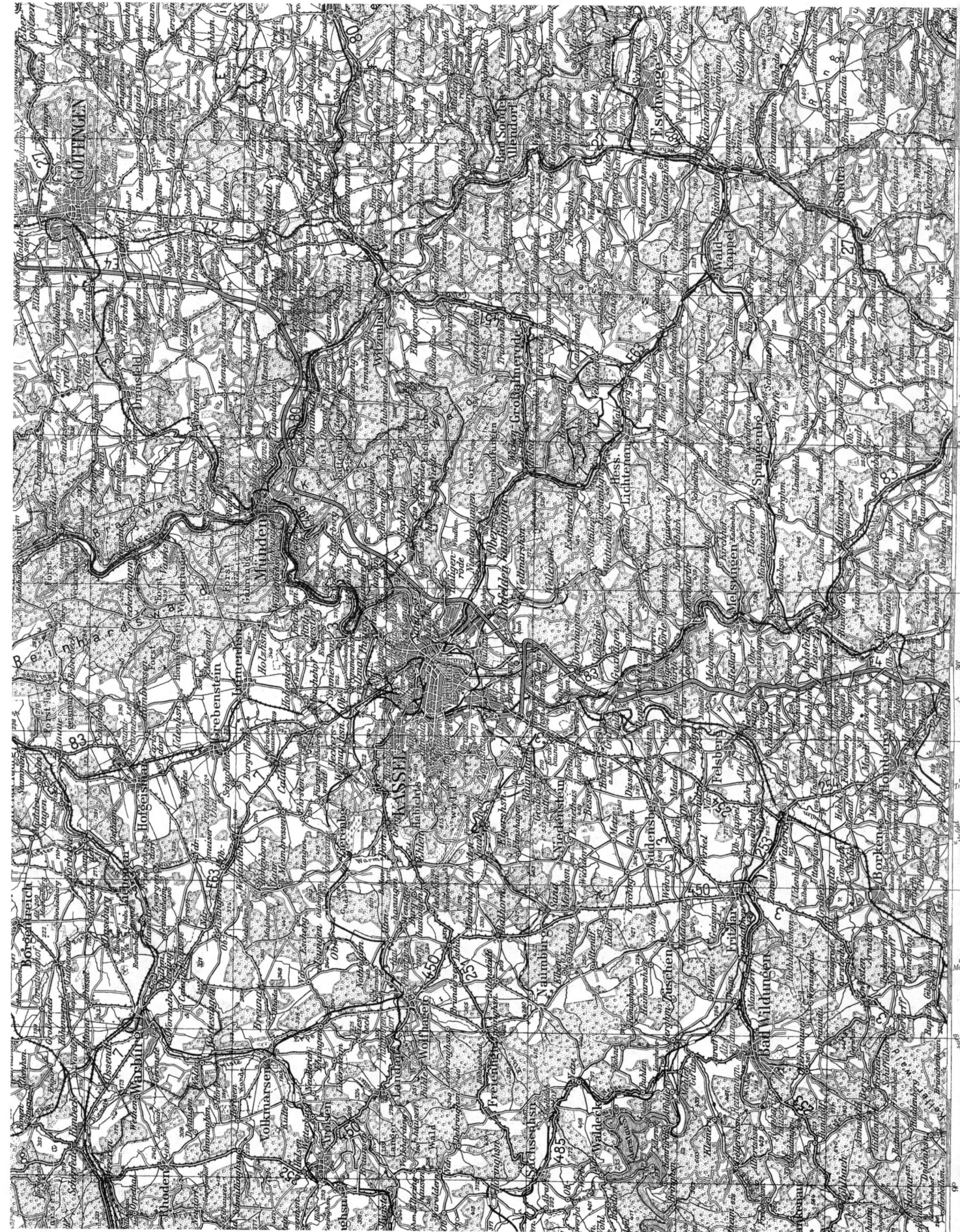

SELECTED BIBLIOGRAPHY

Assion, Peter, *Von Hessen in die Neue Welt*, Insel Verlag, Frankfurt am Main, 1987.

Atwood, Rodney, *The Hessians, Mercenaries from Hessen-Kassel in the American Revolution*, Cambridge University Press, 1980.

Battenberg, F., *Darmstadts Geschichte*, Eduard Roether Verlag, Darmstadt, 1980.

Blumenthal, Bernd, *Aus Holz und Lehm Gebaut...eine kurze Einführung in das ländliche Haus in Hessen*, Freilichtmuseum Hessenpark, Neu-Anspach, 1995.

Burgoyne, Bruce E., *Enemy Views, The American Revolutionary War as Recorded by the Hessian Participants*, Heritage Books, Bowie, MD, 1996.

Coakley, Robert W., and Stetson Conn, *The War of the American Revolution*, Center of Military History, US Army, 1976.

Dannenbauer, Heinrich, *Politik und Wirtschaft in der Altdeutschen Kaiserzeit*, Wissenschaftliche Buchgesellschaft, Darmstadt, Special Reprint, 1966.

Delbrück, Hans, *Medieval Warfare*, History of the Art of War, Vol. III, University of Nebraska Press, Lincoln, 1990.

Demandt, Karl E., *Geschichte des Landes Hessen*, Bärenreiter-Verlag, Kassel, 1972.

Dopsch, Alfons, *The Economic and Social Foundations of European Civilization*, Howard Fertig, New York, 1969 reprint.

Duckett, Eleanor, *Death and Life in the Tenth Century*, University of Michigan Press, Ann Arbor, 1968.

Durant, Will, *The Story of Civilization, Vol. VI, The Reformation*, Simon and Schuster, New York, 1957; *Vol. IX, The Age of Voltaire*, 1965; *Vol. X, Rousseau and Revolution*, 1967; *Vol. XI, The Age of Napoleon*, 1975.

Eiler, K., *Hessen im Zeitalter der industriellen Revolution*, Insel Verlag, Kassel, 1984.

Ernst, Eugen, *Die Hessische Landwirtschaft im Wandel der Zeiten*, Freilichtmuseum Hessenpark, 1996.

Fletcher, Richard, *The Barbarian Conversion, From Paganism to Christianity*, Henry Holt & Co., New York, 1997.

Galicich, Anne, *The German Americans*, part of *The Peoples of North America*, Chelsea House, New York, 1989.

Gieg, Ella, *Auswanderungen aus dem Odenwaldkreis*, Lutzelbach, 1992.

Grein, Gerd J., *Odenwälder Trachten*, part of the Collection of Popular Folklore of Hesse, Museum in the Old Rathaus, Otzberg-Lengfeld, 1980.

Guide to the Open Air Museum Hessenpark, Neu-Anspach, 1998; *Guide to Region Lahn-Dill-Ohm*, Open Air Museum Hessenpark, Neu-Anspach, 1989.

Heer, F., *Charlemagne and his World*, Macmillan Publishing Co., New York, 1975.

Heidelbach, K., *Kassel, ein Jahrtausend hessischer Geschichte*, Bärenreiter, 1957.

Heinemeier, Dan C., *A History of Brunswick*, Heinemeier Publications, Arlington, 1999.

Hessen und die Amerikanische Revolution 1776, Hess. Staatsarchiv, Marburg, 1976.

Holborn, Hajo, *A History of Modern Germany, The Reformation*, (3 Volumes) Alfred Knopf, New York, 1959; *1648-1840*, 1959; *1840-1945*, 1969.

Ingrao, Charles W., *The Hessian Mercenary State, Ideas, institutions and reform under Frederick II, 1760-1785*, Cambridge University Press, 1987.

Janisch, Peter, *Die Hessische Landwirtschaft im Wandel der Zeiten*, Freilichtmuseum Hessenpark, Neu-Anspach, 1996.

Kipping, Ernst, *The Hessian View of America 1776-1783*, Philip Freneau Press, Monmouth Beach, NJ, 1971.

Knodt, M., *Die Regenten von Hessen-Darmstadt*, Verlag H.L. Schlapp, Darmstadt, 1976.

Kürschner, W., *Geschichte der Stadt Marburg*, Elwertsche Verlagsbuchhandlung, Marburg, 1934.

La Baume, Peter, *Romans on the Rhine*, Sammlung Rheinisches Land, Volume 4, Wilhelm Stollfuss Verlag, Bonn.

Lerch, Hans, *Hessische Agrargeschichte des 17. Und 18. Jahrhunderts*, Hans Ott-Verlag, Hersfeld, 1926.

Lortz, Joseph, *Die Reformation in Deutschland*, Vol. I & II, Herder & Co., Freiburg, 1940.

Lowell, Edward, *The Hessians and the other German Auxiliaries of Great Britain in the Revolutionary War*, 1884, reissued by Kennikat Press, Port Washington, NY, 1965.

Mann, Golo, *The History of Germany Since 1789*, Praeger, New York, 1968.

McGarry, D., *Medieval History and Civilization*, MacMillan Publishing, New York, 1976.

Millar, Fergus, *The Roman Empire and its Neighbors*, Delacourt Press, New York, 1967.

Mommsen, Theodor, *The Provinces of the Roman Empire, The European Provinces*, from *The History of Rome*, Volume 5, Book 8, University of Chicago Press, 1968.

Müller, Adolf, *Aus Darmstadts Vergangenheit*, Selbstverlag der Stadt Darmstadt, 1930.

Previte-Orton, C.W., *Shorter Cambridge Medieval History*, Vol. I, Cambridge, 1952.

Robinson, James H., *Readings in European History*, Ginn and Co., Boston, 1906.

Sagarra, Eda, *A Social History of Germany 1648-1914*, Holmes & Meier Publishers, New York, 1977.

Schümmer, Bettina, *Mit Seiner Hülf von Oben, Religiöses Leben auf dem Lande*, Freilichtmuseum Hessenpark, Neu-Anspach, 1999.

Sener, Samuel M., *The Lancaster Barracks, Where the British and Hessian Prisoners were Detained During the Revolution*, Harrisburg Publishing Co. (PA), 1895.

Steinmetz, Rollin C., *Royalists, Pacifists and Prisoners*, Lancaster Co. Hist. Soc., 1976.
Symonds, Craig L., *A Battlefield Atlas of the American Revolution*, Nautical & Aviation Publishing Company, Baltimore, 1986.

Taylor, Peter K., *Indentured to Liberty: Peasant Life and the Hessian Military State, 1688-1815*, Cornell University Press, New York, 1994.

Theibault, John, *German Villages in Crisis: Rural Life in Hesse-Kassel and the Thirty Years' War, 1580-1720*, Humanities Press, Atlantic Highlands, NJ, 1995.

Thompson, James W., *Feudal Germany*, University of Chicago Press, 1928; *History of the Middle Ages 300-1500*, Norton & Co., New York, 1931.

Todd, Malcolm, *Everyday Life of the Barbarians, Goths, Franks and Vandals*, Putnam's Sons, NY, 1972; *The Early Germans*, Blackwell, Cambridge, MA, 1992.

1200 Jahre Groß-Bieberau: Beiträge zu seiner Geschichte, Magistrat der Stadt Groß-Bieberau, 1987.

Vits, Brigitta, *Die Wirtschafts- und Sozialstruktur ländlicher Siedlungen in Nordhessen vom 16. Bis zum 19. Jahrhundert*, Selbstverlag der Marburger Geographischen Gesellschaft, Marburg, 1993.

Von Eelking, Max, *The German Allied Troops in the American War of Independence, 1776-1783*, Heritage Books, Bowie, MD, 1987 (facsimile reprint of 1893 publication by Munsells' Sons, Albany, translated by J. G. Rosengarten).

Wagner, Kurt, *Leben auf dem Lande im Wandel des Industrialisierung: Das Dorf war früher auch keine heile Welt*, Insel Verlag, Frankfurt am main, 1986.

Wand, Norbert, *Die Büraburg bei Fritzlar*, N.G. Elwert Verlag, Marburg, 1974.

Ward, Christopher, *The War of the Revolution*, Macmillan Company, New York, 1952.

Wedgwood, C.V., *The Thirty Years War*, Penguin Books, London, 1957.

Wells, C.M., *The German Policy of Augustus*, Clarendon Press, Oxford, 1972.

Wenckebach, Karl, *Zur Geschichte der Stadt, des Stiftes und der Kirche zu Wetter*, Selbstverlag der Evangelischen Kirchengemeinde Wetter, 1966.

Wolfram, Herwig, *The Roman Empire and its Germanic Peoples*, U. of California Press, Berkeley, 1997.

Wood, I., *Franks and Alamanni in the Merovingian Period*, Boydell, Woodbridge, 1998.

Wright, William J., *Capitalism, the State, and the Lutheran Reformation: Sixteenth-Century Hesse*, Ohio University Press, Athens, 1988.

INDEX

Abterode, 130, 138, 206
Ackermann (farmer), 104
Adelsverein (Noble's Club for emigration promotion) 349, 351
agri decumates, 18, 21, 23
Aktiengesellschaft (business corporation), 307, 335
Alamanni, 16, 22-24, 26-36, 39, 43, 44, 87
alchemy, 78
alcoholism, 94, 109, 111, 112, 125, 148, 159, 161, 254, 260, 304, 337
Alsace, 209, 210, 356
Alsfeld, 137, 144, 160
Amalia Elizabeth (landgravine), 143, 144, 150, 154
America, 217-49, 282, 289, 290, 298, 305, 315, 316, 328, 341, 343, 346-61
Amöneburg, 13, 15, 34, 35, 36, 44, 45, 46, 51, 59, 63, 65, 66, 79, 80, 82, 87, 124, 171, 266
Amtmann (official), 99, 105, 133
Arheilgen, 87, 92, 153, 211, 260, 273
Aschaffenburg, 31, 289, 294, 335
Augustinians, 51
Augustus, 13, 17
Australia, 351, 357
Austria/Austrians, 134, 147, 159, 162, 185, 209, 210, 213, 256, 267, 272, 274, 280, 281, 284, 287, 289-91, 293, 313, 344, 347

Babenberger (German counts), 57, 58, 64
Bad Nauheim, (see Nauheim)
bakers, 78. 85, 93, 105, 116, 145, 148, 151, 188, 198, 199, 252, 254, 259, 260, 292, 315, 319, 320, 339, 341, 344
Baltimore, 346, 348, 349, 356, 358
barley, 8, 67, 68, 106, 121, 130, 197, 282, 302
baths, 77, 78, 85, 94, 112
Bauernbefreiung (freeing of farmers), 302, 304
Bauernschippe (farmers' hat style), 323
Baurmeister (Hessian Major), 232-33
Bavaria/Bavarians, 5, 30, 32, 37, 46, 56, 57, 58, 60, 138, 153, 285, 286, 291, 334, 338, 340, 344
beans, 108, 195
Bede (tax), 81, 86, 90, 92, 105
beer (& mead), 28, 68, 75, 79, 86, 106, 109, 111, 116, 117, 125, 147, 150, 153, 190, 200, 221, 222, 254, 338
beets, 157, 260, 302, 337, 343

Beisaßen/Beisitzer (lower class worker or farmer), 104, 105, 107, 150, 157, 194, 206, 310, 318
Benedictine Monastic Order, 45, 47, 48, 49, 50, 51, 54, 99
Berlichingen, Götz von (robber knight), 95
Bessungen, 87, 92, 93, 260, 262, 344
Biedenkopf, 63, 108, 145, 160, 192, 208, 315
Black Death (see plague)
blacks (in American Revolution), 223, 235, 238, 245
Bleichenbach, 356
Bodo the Peasant, 40-41
Bohemia, 147, 151
Boniface (Saint), 39, 44-48
Bose (Regiment von), 235, 241-44
Boston, 217, 351
Boston Massacre, 217
Boston Tea Party, 217
Boyneburg (incl. counts von), 66, 98, 139
brandy, 125, 147, 158, 200, 221, 254, 292, 337, 341, 343
Brandywine (battle), 232
Braunfels, 170-71, 274
Brazil, 347, 357
brewers/brewing, 78, 105, 116, 190, 200, 254, 338, 339, 341, 344
Brooklyn, 224
Brotherhood of the Star, 66, 82
Büdingen, 357
Buffalo (NY), 352
building styles & practices, 123, 126, 127-28, 129, 181, 203, 317
Bunker Hill (battle), 217
Bürgermeister, 76, 78, 80, 82, 84, 90, 93, 149, 254, 255, 293, 311, 347, 351, 354
burial practices (graves, etc.), 28, 29, 34, 35, 43, 52, 150, 160, 316-17
Burschenschaften (student leagues), 280, 289
butchers, 105, 116, 145, 198, 211, 212, 229, 254, 259, 260, 320, 341, 344

cabbage, 108, 132, 195
cadaster records, 156, 185, 193, 197, 203, 204
Calvinism/Calvinists (Reformed faith), 122-24, 138, 139, 141, 143, 145-49, 155, 158, 159, 161, 187, 251, 252, 262, 288, 289, 291, 342
canabae, 17, 18, 21, 22, 23
Canada, 237
capitalism, 94-96, 105, 112-18, 130

INDEX

Carl, Prince of Solms-Braunfels (Nassau), 349
Catholic(ism), 94, 95, 103, 122, 123, 134, 137, 139, 141, 147, 149, 150, 162, 177, 182, 185, 188, 205, 210, 255, 256, 258, 262, 284, 288, 289, 291-93, 339
cattle, 30, 34, 36, 37, 38, 39, 76, 85, 91, 105, 106, 113, 142, 143, 148, 156, 158, 171-73, 175, 178, 197, 225, 232, 242, 253, 254, 257, 262, 304, 305, 310, 311, 322, 341
cavalry, 135, 138, 145, 151, 153, 155, 162, 182, 252, 253, 258, 271, 340
Celts, 5, 13, 28
Central German Union, 285
charcoal, 172, 198
Charles Martel, 34, 36, 37, 45, 46
Charles the Great, 36, 37, 40, 41, 46-49, 56, 58
Charleston, 232, 242
Chatti, 5, 6, 10-18, 22-24, 26, 32
chemical fertilizer, 305, 318, 322
Cherusci, 12, 13, 14
Chicago, 349
chickens, 107, 109, 156
Christianity/Christians, 32, 33, 35, 37-41, 46-51, 60, 90
Cincinnati, 349, 351, 353
Citeaux, Cistercians, 50, 51, 54, 86, 88, 99
Clinton, Gen Henry, 234, 236-44
clothes washing practices, 320
clothing, 8, 9, 15, 16, 40, 78, 79, 82, 86, 105, 109, 129, 130, 160, 161, 179, 189, 190, 200, 211-12, 238, 244, 247, 248, 255, 299, 302, 316, 320, 322, 323, 327, 342, 353, 358, 359, illustrations: 301, 324-26
Cluny/Cluniacs, 50, 51
Code Napoleon, 269
coinage, 122, 259, 266
Concord (battle), 217
Confederation of the Rhine, 266, 272-74, 276, 277
Congress of Vienna, 280, 283, 347
Conrad of Marburg, 52
Conrad the Elder, 57, 58
Conrad the Younger (German emperor), 58, 59
Conradiner family (Hessian counts), 57, 58, 59, 61
constitutions, 279, 280, 284-88, 290, 293
Continental Congress, 217
Continental System, 270, 275
corn, 358, 359

Cornwallis, Gen., 224, 231-33, 235, 236, 238, 241-44
Cowpens (battle), 241-32
credit (rural/other), 180, 190, 206, 268, 282, 285, 292, 303, 304
crime (see also robbery), 111, 125, 148, 151, 158, 168-69, 186, 197, 203, 253, 340
Croatians, 142-43, 149
crop failure, 178, 186, 188, 191, 276, 280, 285, 300, 304, 305, 336, 339, 341, 343

D'Angelelli (Regiment von), 246
Darmstadt (town of), 74, 87-93, 97, 98, 123, 124, 134, 137, 140, 141, 150-53, 159-62, 207-10, 212, 254, 258-60, 262, 273, 274, 288, 289, 323, 334-36, 342-45, 348, map: 331
Darmstadt Bank, 335, 344
Darmstadt (IL - see also Mud Creek Prairie), 358-59
Denmark/Danes, 123, 134, 140, 149, 155
Detroit (MI), 352, 353
Dieburg, 18, 87, 327
Diepholz, 99
Dietzenbach, 358, 359
Diez, 31, 164, 169-72
Dillenburg, 123, 164, 169-72, 175, 214, 291, 292
Ditfurth (Regiment von), 241
Dominicans (religious order), 81, 82, 87
Domitian, 14, 15, 16, 17, 21
Donauschwaben, 213
Donop (Regiment von), 219, 220, 222, 226, 233, 235, 237, 238, 246, illustrations of reenactors: 239-40
Donop, Col. von, 224, 226, 230, 233, 234
Dorfgrebe (village head), 71, 196
Dorfsteher (village head), 107
Dornberg, 88, 91, 92
Drehhäuschen (punishment device), 186
Dreieich (forest), 87, 88, 97, 150, 174, 210
Dreimaster (farmers' hat style), 323
drunkenness (see alcoholism)
Drusus, 12, 13

East Friesland (Ostfriesland), 101
Eberbach, 88, 289
Eberhard (Conradiner line), 57, 58, 59
Eberstadt, 87, 153, 260, 273
Eder, 6, 13, 17, 22, 45, 164, 199
Edict of Restitution, 139, 140
Einhäus(er) (house style), 129, 318
Elbe, 179

INDEX

Electoral Hesse established, 266, 275
electricity, 336, 345
Elizabeth (Saint), 52, 54, 64, 65, 75, 79, 96, 255
emigration, 298-300, 302, 305, 307, 309, 316, 328, 343, 345, 346, 348, 349, 350, 353, 356, 357, 360
emigration agents, 347-48, 351
emigration statistics (Hesse-Kassel), 355
Ems, 6
enfranchised villagers, 104, 105, 107, 110, 158, 194, 300, 303, 321, 329n.
England/English, 155, 162, 179, 185, 191, 200, 204, 209-11, 214, 217-26, 229-38, 241-48, 257, 258, 262, 275, 290, 298, 335, 341, 344, 346, 359
"enlightened despotism", 180
Enzheim, 356
Ernst Ludwig (Hessian landgrave), 161-62, 207, 258, 259
Ernhaus, 126, 129
Eschwege, 108, 124, 139, 142, 187, 190, 192, 267
"estates," (diet), 66, 70, 71, 180, 185, 186, 206, 209, 274, 276, 280, 284-89, 291, 293
executioners, 84, 85, 87

Fachwerk (building style), 126
factories, 298, 302, 307, 308, 312, 328, 334-37, 341-44
faience ware, 333, 335
Faucitt, Col. William, 217, 235
fire/firefighting, 80, 87, 103, 109, 125, 126, 138, 140, 143-45, 149, 150, 153, 161, 168, 186, 190, 191, 198, 203, 251, 260, 318, 320-21, 338, 339
flax, 8, 105, 106, 141, 190, 199, 200, 298, 300, 302, 310, 358, tools: 306
France/French, 142, 143, 146, 152-59, 161, 162, 168, 172, 177-79, 181, 182, 185, 189, 191, 192, 205, 207, 209-13, 218, 237, 243, 244, 252, 253, 256, 257, 258, 265-84, 288, 292, 334, 335, 339, 340, 346
Franciscans (religious order), 81, 82, 85
franciska (throwing axe), 26, 34, 35
Franconia/Franconians, 37, 56, 57, 58, 59, 60, 61, 62, 68, 70, 112, 213
Frankenberg, 108, 117, 124, 172, 192, 200
Frankfurt, 51, 54, 97, 112, 116, 129, 140, 150, 151, 154, 155, 160, 161, 174, 177, 179, 191, 192, 196, 200, 206, 207, 210, 214, 251, 252, 256, 265, 266, 275, 282, 285, 286, 289, 292-94, 307, 313, 348, 357, 358, 361
Fränkisch-Crumbach, 348, 349

Franks, 16, 23, 26, 29-39, 43-47, 74, 87
Frederick I (Hessian landgrave & Swedish king), 182
Frederick (Hessian landgrave), 185-92, 206, 209
Frederick II (Hessian landgrave), 219, 221, 248, 253, 256-58
Fredericksburg (TX), 349
Friedberg, 13, 15, 17, 18, 51
Friedrich (Hessian landgrave), 133
Friedrich ("Winter King"), 134, 135
Frisia, 44, 45, 51
Fritzlar, 11, 13, 34, 38, 39, 45, 46, 51, 57, 59, 63-66, 96, 108, 130, 140, 157, 266, 302, 303, 307, 329n.
Ft. Mercer (battle), 233-34
Ft. Washington (battle), 225
Fulda, 5, 39, 60, 61, 64, 113, 117, 137, 158, 193, 200, 267, 274, 283, 284, 287, 294, 298, 302, 335, 337, 361
furniture, 200, 344

Gallas (Catholic general), 141, 152
Galicia, 168
Galveston (TX), 351, 356
gas/gas works, 307, 336, 344
George (Hessian landgrave), 139-41, 144, 145, 147, 151-54,
George II (Hessian landgrave), 159-60
George III (English king), 217
German Confederation, 276, 277, 353
German Empire, 313, 344
German (religious) Order, 85, 99
German Society of New York, 353
Germanic Confederation, 280, 284, 286, 287, 289, 290, 291
Germanicus, 13, 14, 16
Germantown (PA), 346
Gerold, 46
Geyso (Catholic general), 153
Gießen, 44, 51, 79, 82, 101, 102, 113, 123, 141, 144, 146-48, 152, 160-62, 280, 286, 288-90, 292, 294, 305, 320, 334, 335, 348, 356, 357, map: 263
Gießen Emigration Society, 348, 356
glass, glass making, 109, 113, 116, 117, 188, 212
goats, 88, 341
Göttingen, 234, 338, 340
Götz (general), 149
Grand Duchy of Hesse established, 273, 277, map: 363
Grandenborn, 139, 142
graves (see burial practices)
Grebe (village head), 107, 158, 203-04,
Gregory II (pope), 45

370

Gregory VII (pope), 62
Gregory the Great, 44, 45
Gronau, 100, 114
Groß-Bieberau, 98, 141, 143, 152, 159, 160-61, 206-08, 214, 274, 309, 313, 314, 321, 327, 359
Gross-Umstadt, 98, 138, 145
Groß-Zimmern, 349
Grubenhaus, 9, 29, 30, 35
Gudensberg, 15, 63, 66
guilds, 76, 80, 82-86, 96, 97, 105, 113-18, 122, 148, 150, 154, 179, 182, 187, 190, 198, 200, 206, 251, 252, 253, 256, 257, 258, 266, 267, 268, 298, 307, 308, 333, 334, 336, 341, 343-45
Guntersblum, 357
Gustav Adolf (Swedish king), 140, 149
gypsies, 340

Haas, Wilhelm (rural credit pioneer) 304-05
Hadrian, 17, 18
Haina, 99, 100, 114, 116, 117
hall (long) house, 9, 29, 35, 126, 129
Hanau, 144, 170, 171, 174-76, 185, 191-92, 284-87, 294, 307, 317, 335
Hanau troops (in American Revolution), 217, 218, 221, 234, 236, 244-46, 250
Hassenplug, Daniel von, 285-87
Hatto of Mainz (archbishop), 57, 58
Haufendörfer, 29, 30
Heister, Gen. Leopold von, 219, 221, 224, 228, 231
Henry the Fowler (Saxon Duke), 58
Henry I (Hessian landgrave), 97
Henry II (German emperor), 60, 61, 74
Henry II (Hessian Landgrave), 65
Henry III (Hessian landgrave), 97
Henry IV (German king), 61, 62
Henschel, Karl (industrialist), 336, 338
Herborn, 63, 96, 126, 169, 170, 291
Hermann the Learned (Hessian landgrave), 76
Hermann (Hessian landgrave), 139, 169
Hermann II (Hessian landgrave), 97
Hermunduri, 10, 14, 22
Hersfeld, 44, 46, 96, 113, 125, 131-32, 137, 140, 144, 156, 187, 195, 197, 200, 267, 276, 278, 284, 300, 303, 304, 348
Heubach, 359
Höchst, 13, 17, 18
Hoffaktor (Jewish financial official), 206, 266
Homberg, 11, 63, 99, 117, 130, 146, 160, 219, 220, 300, 329n.
Homburg, 159, 161

horses, 26, 37, 38, 58, 68, 69, 86, 88, 92, 105-07, 142, 143, 152, 153, 156, 195, 197, 198, 251, 262, 305, 317, 318, 321
Housing, 9
Howe, Gen. Sir William, 224-26, 229-34
Hoya, 99
Hufe (land unit: "hide"), 71, 104, 157, 193
Hufenedikt (land reform decree), 190, 193, 204, 205
Hüfner (wealthy farmer), 104-10
Huguenots, 168, 177, 182, 188, 207, 254
Hungary, 259
Huns, 31
Huyn (Regiment von), 241

Idstein, 164, 165, 168
Illinois, 348, 358-60
immigration (to America), 347-49, 351, 353, 355, 358
Indians (American), 223
inheritance practices:
   Anerbensystem, 192
   Realteilung, 192-93
   Erbpacht, 303
Investiture War, 62, 70
Iowa, 350, 356
Itter, 173

Jäger (Hessian ranger troops), 218, 221, 223-26, 232, 233, 235-38, 241-43, 247
Jerome Bonaparte (king of Westphalia), 266, 267, 269, 270, 271, 274, 275, 277, 339
Jews, 66, 80, 82, 83, 93, 108, 130, 141, 143, 146, 151, 158, 200, 205-07, 211, 258, 260, 262, 268, 270, 275, 277, 280, 285, 288, 292, 293, 304, 314, 327-28, 339, 349, 352, 354, 360

Karl (Hessian landgrave), 154-56, 158, 182, 251, 258
Karlsaue, 182, 184
Karlsbad Decrees (1819), 280, 289
Karlshafen, 182, 188
Kassel (town of), 5, 12, 13, 63-66, 74-81, 83, 93, 96, 97, 99, 102, 107, 117, 115, 117, 122-25, 132-34, 137, 138, 143, 145-50, 154, 158, 159, 182, 185-90, 192-96, 199, 207, 219, 223, 228, 235, 247-49, 251, 252, 255-58, 262, 267, 271, 275, 276, 284-87, 293, 294, 300, 302, 307, 308, 312, 317, 320, 333-41, 343, 353, 354, map: 332

371

INDEX

Katz (Rhine castle), 145, 182, 183-84
Katzenelnbogen, 63, 81, 88, 90, 91, 92, 93, 97, 98, 103, 138, 144, 145, 160, 161, 182, 210, 267, 272, 273, 283, 291
Kerb tree, 359
Kirmes, 110, 197
Knoblauch (Regiment von), 225, 226, 235, 237, 244
Kogelherren (religious order), 77
Kontribution (tax for military), 190, 196-97, 205
Köln (Cologne), 51, 164, 168, 172, 173, 272, 292, 299, 348
Körle, 71, 193-95, 200, 300, 309-12, 354, 355
Kötter/Köter (farmer), 104-08, 110, 157, 318
Kranichstein, 208, 260

Lafayette, 237, 243
Lahn, 5, 31, 34, 35, 44, 46, 54, 57, 58, 63, 79, 81, 88, 96, 97, 164, 168, 170, 335
Lancaster (PA), 229, 230, 235, 244
Landvogt (bailiff), 97
Lederhosen (pants), 342
Le Havre, 348, 353
Leib (Regiment), 219
Leibgut (farm holding), 131, 156
Lentils, 68, 132
Lewis the Child, 57, 58
Lewis the German, 57
Lichtenberg (town/castle), 88, 89, 141, 150, 159, 160
Lichtenberg (Hanau territory), 209-10
Liebig, Justus von, 305, 356, 359
Limburg, 31, 169, 272, 291
limes, 15, 16, 17, 18, 19, 21, 22, 23, 87
Lippe, 191
Liudolfinger family (Saxon counts), 57-59
long house (see hall house)
Lossberg (Regiment von), 225, 226, 229, 235, 237
lottery, 189, 191, 257
Louis the Pious, 56
Louisville (KY), 349
Ludwig (landgrave of Thuringia), 74
Ludwig (landgrave of Hesse-Marburg), 123
Ludwig I (Hessian landgrave), 76, 77, 78, 81, 83, 97
Ludwig II (Hessian landgrave), 78, 97
Ludwig III (Grand Duke), 290
Ludwig V (Hessian landgrave), 123, 137-39, 145, 150, 151, 165
Ludwig VI (Hessian landgrave), 159-62

Ludwig VII (Hessian landgrave), 160
Ludwig VIII (Hessian landgrave), 208-09, 211, 259, 262
Ludwig IX (Hessian landgrave), 209-11, 218, 244, 262
Ludwig X (Hessian landgrave, first Grand Duke), 210, 273, 274, 277, 289
Luther/Lutheranism, 95, 99, 100, 101, 110, 112-14, 118, 122-24, 138, 146, 152, 155, 161, 210, 211, 251, 252, 255, 256, 258, 288, 289, 291, 315, 317, 342

Maden, 11, 96, 157
Main River 5, 12, 13, 14, 15, 16, 17, 18, 21, 24, 30, 31, 34, 57, 60, 87, 162, 165, 168, 169, 174, 175, 272, 286, 289, 290, 294, 302, 320, 321, 334-37, 346, 361
Mainz, 13, 14, 17, 21, 23, 30, 31, 43, 44, 45, 46, 51, 52, 54, 59, 60, 62-66, 74-77, 80-83, 86, 96-98, 101, 112, 113, 117, 140, 141, 150, 153, 155, 164, 168, 169, 172, 173, 175, 176, 221, 266, 272, 273, 277, 287-91, 293-94, 337, 343, 348, 355, 356
Mannfigur (framing technique), 126, 128
Mansfeld (Protestant general), 151
manufactories, 333
Marburg, 39, 44, 51, 52, 54, 63, 64, 65, 74, 79-86, 93, 123, 124, 132, 144, 145, 147, 148, 154, 158, 159, 185, 187, 191, 251-56, 267, 280, 284, 286, 294, 308, 317, 337, 339-42, 345, map: 331
masons/freemasons, 185, 252
Mattiaci, 5
Mattium, 12, 13
Meier (wealthy farmer), 104, 125, 130, 131, 196, 303
Melanchthon (Lutheran theologian), 99, 152
Mellnau, 82
Melsungen, 63, 66, 194, 195, 300, 302, 308, 353-55
mercantilism, 121, 162, 182, 190, 207, 211, 248, 347
metal/metal working, 109, 114, 116, 117, 168-70, 172, 174, 179, 181, 199, 187, 199, 248, 291, 292, 308, 334, 335, 337, 338, 341, 342, 344, 345, 352
militia, 218-19, 231
millet, 8
Milwaukee, 349, 351-52
mines/mining, 28, 96, 97, 154, 179, 214, 248, 335, 337

Minnigerode (Regiment von), 223, 233
Mirbach (Regiment von), 224, 225, 232, 234
Missouri, 348
Mittelfischbach, 352
Moritz (Hessian landgrave), 122-24, 133, 137-39, 146, 148, 149, 174
Mud Creek Prairie (IL), 358
Münden, 75, 76, 149 267
musketeers, 135
Mutzen (hat style), 211

Napoleon, 210, 256, 265-77, 280, 291, 307, 339
Nassau, 103, 123, 155, 164-65, 168-72, 174, 175, 192, 198, 209, 214, 266, 272-74, 277, 278n., 280, 283, 290-93, 299, 314, 315, 317-20, 329n., 333-35, 337, 340, 347, 351, 352, 355, 361, map: 166; map of Hesse-Nassau, 1867: 297
National League of Hessians of North America, 353
Nauheim (Bad), 13, 290, map: 263
Naumburg, 64, 65, 173, 176, 266
New Braunfels (TX), 349-51
New Jersey, 226, 230, 231, 233, 236
New Orleans (LA), 346, 350, 351, 356, 358
New South Wales (Australia), 351, 361
New York, 217, 220, 223-26, 231, 234, 236-38, 241, 243-46, 346, 348-53
Niddagau (district), 18, 21, 22, 141, 58, 77, 160, 210, 302, 320
Nidda River, 31
Nieburg, 99
Niederfischbach, 351, 352
Nieder-Klingen, 359
Nobles' Club (see *Adelsverein*)
Nördlingen, 141, 152
North Carolina (immigration to), 346

oats, 88, 106, 108, 121, 130, 131, 133, 282, 302
Ober-Ostern, 350
Oden/Woden, 10, 15, 44, 48
Odenwald, 44, 87, 91, 97, 129, 141, 159, 162, 169, 210-13, 289, 316-18, 322-23, 335, 344, 348, 350, 359, 360
Oktroi (tax), 343-44
Oppenheim, 357
oppida, 5
orphans, 112, 186-87, 189, 191, 255, 257, 258, 260, 273
Ottonian Line (Nassau counts), 164, 169
ovens, 81, 87, 187, 198, 315, 319, 320
oxen, 40, 143, 152, 197, 201, 204, 358

Palatines/Palatinate (Pfalz), 98, 134, 137, 140, 145, 254, 272, 273, 346, 356, 357
Pastorius, Daniel (German emigrant leader), 214
peas, 67, 68, 75, 132, 195
Peasant's War, 112, 118
Pennsylvania, 226, 229, 230, 232, 235, 346, 359
Pensacola, 236, 241
Pepin, 35, 36, 37, 46
Pferdsbach, 356-57
Philadelphia, 229, 231, 233-36, 244, 348, 356
Philip (landgrave of Hesse Darmstadt), 93, 97-99, 101-03, 108, 111, 113-15, 117, 118, 123, 133, 276, 341
Pietists, 174, 252
pigs, 85, 91, 107, 108, 122, 143, 152, 156, 158, 198, 220, 254, 257, 259, 262, 305, 311, 319, 340, 341, 344
Pirmasens, 209
Pittsburgh (PA), 348, 349
plague, 66, 83, 84, 85, 138-42, 146, 149, 150, 152-54, 160, 177
Platte (Regiment von), 219, 220, 222, 231, 247
plows, 8, 68, 69, 143, 158, 178, 197, 204, 205, 299, 300, 322, 358
porcelain & china, 188, 190, 212, 248, 333, 335
potatoes, 103, 178, 179, 189, 203, 208, 210, 260, 262, 282, 300, 302, 305, 318, 337, 349
potters/pottery, 9, 11, 16, 22, 23, 27, 34, 85, 193, 212, 254, 307, 335, 341
Premonstratensians, 50
Prince Charles (regiment), 238
Prince Frederick (regiment), 244
Prussia/Prussians, 101, 155, 171, 172, 180, 181, 185, 187, 189, 191, 192, 209, 210, 218, 247, 248, 252, 254, 260, 265, 266, 274, 280-87, 289-94, 304, 305, 307, 308, 313, 315, 317, 333, 334, 337-39, 341, 342, 344
"putting-out" (pre-industrial production), 96, 105, 115, 118, 129, 310

quarries/quarrymen, 193

Raiffeisen (rural credit coops), 304, 305, 306
railroads, 282, 282, 285, 292, 293, 298, 307-08, 312, 334, 340
Rall (Hessian col.), 225-26, 228, 232

INDEX

Rall (Regiment von), 218, 225, 226, 230, 235, 246
Ramsey (swedish general), 175
Realteilung (see inheritance)
Reformation, 94, 95, 97, 99, 100, 113, 114, 165, 170, 173
Reichelsheim, 360
Reisepaß (passport), 347
Rheinfels, 92, 97, 138, 144, 145, 155, 181, 182, 183
Rheinhessen, 213, 277, 288, 289, 313, 357
Rhine, 5, 12, 13, 14, 15, 16, 21, 23, 26, 30, 31, 32, 33, 34, 38, 39, 43, 44, 45, 51, 57, 75, 87, 92, 95, 97, 98, 139, 142, 144, 155, 182, 200, 209, 210, 221, 254, 265, 266, 272, 273, 277, 288, 291-94, 334-37, 346
Rhineland, 60, 63, 67, 68, 88, 83, 134, 168, 192, 266, 277, 292, 302, 333, 334
Rhön, 210, 298, 318
Riesengebirge, 12
robbery (see also crime), 141, 154, 156, 158, 161, 191, 210, 349
Röckwäih (womens' complaint), 213
Rödgen, 14
Romans, 5-18, 21-24, 26-36, 43, 44, 46, 49, 60, 68, 69
Rotenburg, 130, 145, 182
Rotenburger *Quart*, 135, 145, 284
Rothaargebirge, 36
Rothschilds (see *Hoffactor*), 191, 206, 266
rum, 221, 229, 236, 242
Rundling (village style), 29
Rupertiner familt (Hessian counts), 57
Rüsselsheim, 88, 102, 137, 150, 160, 161, 211, 260, 294
Russia/Russians, 213, 214, 270, 271, 274, 275, 282, 347
rye, 8, 68, 106, 108, 121, 131, 133, 178, 196, 197, 302, 305, 352

Saalburg, 17, 18, 20
Saarbrücken, 164, 165, 168, 169
Salbücher, 99, 197
Sackdorf (village style), 29
St. Elizabeth Church (Marburg), 53, 64, 81, 85, 255, 339, 342
St. Francis, 85
St. Gall, 62
St. Goar, 124, 144, 145, 182, map: 202
St. Goarshausen, 145, 182, map: 202
St. Louis (MO), 348, 349, 351, 356, 358, 359
St. Martin's Church (Kassel), 77
salt, 28, 31, 270

San Antonio (TX), 351
Sattelhöffe (farm type), 88
Savannah (GA), 236-38, 245
Saxony/Saxons, 35-39, 56, 58, 64, 66
Schaumburg, 97, 99, 144, 191, 293, 294
Schmalkalden/Schmalkald War, 101, 102, 108, 117, 118, 138, 144, 145, 165, 170, 171, 173, 175, 187, 192, 267, 276, 293, 336
Schöffen (town councilmen), 74, 79, 80, 82, 83, 84, 87, 91, 204, 254
schools, 80, 83, 86, 148, 152, 158, 160, 165, 168, 170, 172, 178, 181, 198, 199, 207-08, 210, 251, 253, 258-60, 284, 288-91, 293, 303, 308, 312-17, 322, 327, 337, 340, 341
Schrank (wardrobe), 200
Schultheiß (town mayor), 75, 80, 91, 93, 105, 131, 133, 174,
Schulze-Delitsch (credit pioneer), 304
Schwalm, 5, 143, 354
scramasax, 34, 37, 38
Seven Years War, 172, 181, 185, 186, 251, 252, 254, 256
sheep, 30, 41, 106, 181, 197, 199, 232, 249, 254, 257, 262, 341, 342
shepherds, 107, 309, 322
Sickingen, Franz von (robber knight), 95, 98
Slavery, 30, 32, 36, 37, 40
smoking, 158-59, 161, 266
smuggling, 271, 333, 334, 339
Social Democratic Party, 337
Solms, 165, 168, 170, 176, 196, 274, 278n.
Sontra, 66, 111, 124, 125, 133, 138, 139, 193
Sophie (of Brabant), 64, 65, 75, 80, 96, 97
Spessart, 36, 169, 210, 213, 298
spinning (wheel), 130, 179, 199, 200, 299, 301, 309, 310, 361
starvation, 121, 188, 251, 256, 339, 341, 345, 347
Staunton (VA), 230
steamboat, 358
steamships, 350
steam engines, 336, 343
stoves, 181, 199, 203
street lighting, 336, 341, 342, 344
Sturmi, 46, 47
Swabia/Swabians, 58, 59, 213
Sweden/Swedish, 123, 134, 140-44, 146, 149, 152, 153, 155, 168, 171, 175, 182

Tacitus, 6-12, 15

tailors, 159, 229, 248, 257, 259, 292, 298, 307, 309, 341, 343, 344, 359
Tarleton (English col.), 241-43
Taunus, 5, 6, 12-18, 23, 24, 92, 165, 168, 292, 293, 316, 318, 334, map: 167
taxes, 138, 150, 151, 153, 155, 156, 160, 177, 179, 180, 185, 187-94, 196, 197, 199, 200, 203, 205-07, 214, 253-56, 258, 259, 266, 267, 269, 270, 271, 274, 277, 333, 334, 339, 341, 343, 344
Texas, 349-51
textiles, 129, 130, 179, 188, 190, 248, 283, 294, 298, 299, 300, 308, 333, 335, 337, 343, 345, 346
Thirty Years War, 121, 123, 125, 129, 133, 134, 155, 156, 161, 165, 168, 170, 171, 174, 175, 177, 179, 182, 193, 205, 208, 251, 252
Thor, 28, 44, 45, 48
three-field crop system, 67, 68, 90, 106, 130, 132, 178, 188, 197, 262, 282, 302, 305, 311
three-zone (house style), 126
Thuringia/Thuringians, 30, 32, 45, 52, 56, 57, 63-66, 74-76, 80, 96, 101, 124, 126, 157, 254, 300, 334
Tiberius, 13-14
Tilly (Catholic general), 137-40, 145, 174149, 151
tobacco, 158, 161, 188, 190, 266, 328, 333-37, 341, 343
torture, 94, 111, 139, 148, 151, 186, 191, 210, 262
Tracht/Trachten (see clothing)
trencher, 109
Trenton (NJ), 226, 228, 230-32, 235, 243, 244, map: 227
Treysa, 51, 77, 113, 354
Trier, 31, 43, 44, 45, 52, 98, 164, 165, 171, 272
Trumbach (Regiment von), 235, 236, 241
two-zone (house style), 126, 203

universities, 178, 180, 182, 187, 189, 265, 269, 280, 283, 284, 288, 289, 294

Valley Forge (PA), 234
Varus, 13
Verbesserungspunkte (Reform Points), 123
Verdun, Treaty of, 57
Verlagssystem (see putting-out)
Vespasian, 14
Virginia, 229, 230, 235, 237, 241-44

visitations (clerical inspections), 181
Vogelsberg, 36, 44, 57, 116, 169, 175, 208, 210, 289, 298, 347
Vollbauer (wealthy farmer), 104, 106

Waldeck, counts, etc., 63, 65, 92, 126, 137, 155, 172-74, 294
Waldeck (troops in American Rev.), 217, 225, 226, 229, 236, 241
Wallenstein (Catholic mercenary), 138
Walramian Line (Nassau counts), 164, 165, 168, 169, 171
Wandeltisch (local teacher feeding program), 314-15
Wanfried, 139
Washington, George, 217, 224-26, 228-36, 243
Wazo of Liege (bishop), 63
weavers/weaving, 28, 30, 41, 78, 84, 85, 96, 105, 107, 114, 115, 118, 129, 148, 193, 200, 229, 248, 286, 292, 298-300, 302, 307, 309, 310
Weilburg, 59, 164, 165, 166, 168, 272
Weinkauf (peasant duty), 196
Werra, 122, 137, 138, 140, 142, 144, 154, 157, 198, 267, 298
Wergeld, 33, 34, 35, 33
Werner family (Hessian counts), 62, 74, 96, 164
Wernings, 356-59
Weser, 12, 33, 38, 182, 188, 220, 221, 247, 254
Westerwald, 14, 36, 96, 172, 193, 198, 213, 292, 294
Westphalia, 140, 142, 144, 149, 172, 200, 254, 273, 277, 302
Westphalia (Kingdom of), 266, 268-70, 274-76, 278
Westphalia (Treaty of), 134, 154, 168, 174, 182, 251
Wetter (town), 51, 55, 63-66, 96, 101, 106, 113, 124, 140, 142, 145, 172, 308
Wetter River, 13, 15, 16
Wetterau, 5, 13, 15, 16, 18, 21, 23, 24, 31, 34, 35, 44, 46, 54, 57, 59, 129, 137, 161, 165, 168-70, 170, 174, 175, 197, 210, 214, 253, 298, 320
Wetzlar, 14, 51, 54, 65, 66, 165
wheat, 67, 68, 106, 121, 130, 177, 197, 282, 302, 305, 358, 359
Wiesbaden, 6, 13, 14, 17, 18, 30, 31, 164, 165, 168, 291-94, 319
Wilhelmshöhe, 191, 248, 258, 261, 293, map: 264
William I (Hessian landgrave), 98
William II (Hessian landgrave), 98
William III (Hessian landgrave), 83

375

INDEX

William IV (Hessian landgrave), 133, 150, 154, 158
William V (Hessian landgrave), 139, 140-43, 149
William VI (Hessian landgrave), 150, 154, 158
William VIII (Hessian landgrave), 154, 155, 256
William IX (Hessian landgrave, later Elector), 191-92, 205-06, 217, 223, 252, 253, 257, 258, 266, 276
William the Elder (landgrave of Hesse), 78, 79
Winchester (VA), 230, 235, 244
wine, 78, 79, 83, 84, 86, 87, 91, 109, 117, 125, 147, 148, 150, 151, 161, 162, 254, 255, 292, 293
Wine Road, 87
Wisconsin, 349, 357
Wissenbach (Regiment von), 236
witchcraft, 110-11, 122, 148, 153, 158
Wolfhagen, 126, 172, 192, 219
wolves, 103, 131, 148
Worms, 31, 57, 62, 68, 356
Württemberg, 94, 101, 112

Yorktown (battle), 243-44

Zacharias (pope), 46
Ziegenhain (incl. counts von), 63-66, 77, 97, 102, 138, 267, 354, 355
Zollverein, 281, 285, 287, 289, 292
Zweibrücken, 244

About Heinemeier Publications

Dan Heinemeier is an author, publisher and lecturer based in Arlington, VA. An active genealogist and historian for over 20 years, Dan currently serves as secretary of the German-American Heritage Society of Greater Washington, DC. He is active in numerous other societies devoted to genealogy and German heritage. He also is known in German-American circles for talks based on his books and other topics dealing with the social history of German ancestors.

Publications:

Hunzen in Brunswick (1995)
*A History of Brunswick:
    Life in a German Duchy, Roman Times through 1900*
    (1999)
A Social History of Hesse: Roman Times to 1900 (2002)

[Similar works on other historical German *Länder* are planned.]

Sample Lecture Topics:

* Grand tour of Berlin at the turn of the 20th century
    (slide show presentation)
* *Örtssippenbücher* in German genealogical research
* Social history of our German ancestors (various time periods)
* A glimpse into the life of Hessian soldiers in the Revolution

Contact information:

Heinemeier Publications
4401 N. 33rd Road
Arlington, VA 22207-4423
m-dh@erols.com

Publications Order Form

A Social History of Hesse: Roman Times to 1900

An all-encompassing social history, including the many territorial changes over the centuries, e.g., Hesse-Darmstadt, -Kassel, -Nassau, -Hanau, Waldeck, etc. 380 pp., 8.5"x11", incl. maps and illustrations. **$29.95**
ISBN 0-9671822-1-2

A History of Brunswick: A German Duchy, Roman Times to 1900

A comprehensive social history of the Duchy (*Herzogtum Braunschweig*), emphasizing aspects of interest to genealogists and social historians. 375 pp., 8.5"x11", incl. maps and illustrations. **$23.00**
ISBN 0-9671822-0-4

Hunzen in Brunswick: 800 Years in a Village of Lower Saxony

A village history translated from the German and edited extensively. Offers insight on village life and work, from serving feudal lords to sheltering W.W.II refugees (A.D. 1050-1950).
60 pp., 8.5"x 5.5", incl. maps and illustrations. **$10.00ppd.**

HUNZEN IN BRUNSWICK _____ COPIES @ $10.00 EACH _____

HISTORY OF BRUNSWICK _____ COPIES @$23.00 EACH _____

HISTORY OF HESSE _____ COPIES @$29.95 EACH _____

VA RESIDENTS: PLEASE ADD 5% SALES TAX
($.50 ON $10.00/$1.15 ON $23.00/$1.50 ON $29.95) _____

SHIPPING Hunzen: postpaid; others: $5.00 1st book,
　　　　　　$1.00 each additional book _____

TOTAL ENCLOSED _____
(Checks only, please, made payable to D.C. Heinemeier]

SHIP TO:　　NAME_____

　　　　　　ADDRESS_____

　　　　　　_____

　　　　　　_____

MAIL ORDERS TO: 4401 N. 33RD ROAD, ARLINGTON, VA 22207-4423

Note: I plan books on other historical German states and principalities over time. Let me hear from you about your interests to help in determining future projects.
[EMAIL address: m-dh@erols.com]